— PASSPORT'S —

Bed and Breakfast

— GUIDE TO BRITAIN —

PASSPORT'S
Bed and
Breakfast
GUIDE TO BRITAIN

Elsie Dillard and Susan Causin

PASSPORT BOOKS
a division of *NTC Publishing Group*
Lincolnwood, Illinois USA

This edition first published in 1996 by Passport Books,
a division of NTC Publishing Group, 4255 West Touhy Avenue,
Lincolnwood (Chicago), Illinois 60646-1975 USA.

Published in association with
Which? Ltd., 2 Marylebone Road,
London NW1 4DF
Great Britain

Cover illustration by Paul Saunders

Base mapping © Map Marketing Ltd./
European Map Graphics 1996
Map information © Which? Ltd. 1996

ISBN 0-8442-4870-3
Library of Congress Catalog Card Number: on file

Photoset by Tradespools Ltd, Frome, Somerset
Printed and bound in Great Britain by
Clays Ltd, St Ives plc, Bungay, Suffolk

Contents

ABOUT THE EDITORS

Elsie Dillard and Susan Causin are both British-born, married to Americans and living in Seattle, Washington. From 1976 to 1995, Elsie Dillard ran the Elsie from England Travel Agency, specialising in personalised tours of Britain. Susan Causin worked for the British Tourist Authority in London for 11 years before settling in the USA.

They spend much of the year in Britain, and have undertaken extensive trips to find the best available bed-and-breakfast accommodation. Their researches led to the first edition of *The Good Bed and Breakfast Guide*, published in 1988. This all-new, fifth edition has been completely revised and updated.

Note to B&B proprietors: owing to a recent policy change at Consumers' Association, proprietors are now allowed to advertise the fact that they appear in this guide.

Introduction

Welcome to this completely new edition – the fifth – of *The Good Bed and Breakfast Guide*.

It was with a great deal of pleasure that we travelled the length and breadth of Britain this past year to find the best bed-and-breakfast establishments, and every one in this book has been handpicked to provide the widest choice of independently inspected B&Bs to be found in any published guide. You will find a list of our 20 favourites on page 12.

For this edition there are new full-colour maps to make it easier than ever to locate the selected B&Bs. In England, Scotland and Wales the entries are now arranged according to town or village: first find the 'locality' that you want on the map, then look up the entry under the town name. London entries are still in alphabetical order in the London section, which is now at the beginning of the book in line with the *Guide*'s sister publications, *The Good Food Guide* and *The Which? Hotel Guide*. Two indexes at the back list B&Bs under county, and then in alphabetical order by name of establishment.

Selection of entries

Our criteria for selecting a B&B for the *Guide* include a warm welcome, cleanliness, a friendly atmosphere and, wherever possible, a particularly attractive location or, in some cases, a building that is itself of some historical or architectural interest. Properties may have been excluded for several reasons: possibly negative reports were received from readers, or a B&B failed at inspection; perhaps the owners of an establishment previously featured have retired; or maybe new owners have taken over but too late for our inspection schedule.

Standards vary from one part of Britain to the other, and sometimes a B&B fails to become an entry because one or more of its competitors in the area are that much better. In addition, although we have tried to be as fair and objective as possible in our judgements, some worthy establishments may have been excluded simply because we have not heard about them. This is where you, our readers, come in: your reports and letters are invaluable, as they keep us up to date on new properties or B&Bs worthy to be considered for future editions. We wish to thank all those who have written to us of their B&B experiences over the past two years: this has proved extremely helpful as we researched and wrote this new edition. Report forms are at the back of the book; alternatively, just write a letter or postcard (postage is free in the UK), or email us on: *guidereports@which.co.uk*.

Price information

The prices shown in the entries are based on the information given to us by proprietors, who were asked to quote in autumn 1995 what they believed they would be charging from spring 1996. Tariffs may of course change over the life of this edition, and so it is best that readers verify prices with the B&B when they book, and enquire about additional charges such as single-night supplements, or whether full payment is required upon arrival.

Our ceiling of £30 per head for two people sharing a twin or double room, established two editions ago in 1992, still applies, except in London or where a B&B has something quite exceptional to recommend it. Although other cities and towns are catching up with London in price – most notably Rye, Bath and Edinburgh – bargains (from £12 to £15) are still to be found, especially in coastal resorts and very rural areas. Discounts too are often available for longer stays, and many B&Bs offer significant reductions for children sharing with parents.

In the details at the end of each entry under 'Terms' you will find the rates, as applicable, for a single room, single occupancy of a twin or double room, the price of a twin or double room (i.e. the total that two people would pay for the room), and the price of a family room (this is often approximate because it depends on how many people are sharing). Also included are any price reductions for children, the price of dinner if available, and deposit requirements if applicable. Credit and direct-debit cards, if accepted, are then listed; if no cards are taken, this is also noted.

Meals provided by B&Bs

Many B&Bs offer evening meals, some of which are of an exceptionally high standard; a few in fact feature in the current edition of *The Good Food Guide* (in such cases, we mention this in the details at the end of the entry). But the main focus of *The Good Bed and Breakfast Guide* is on the bed-and-breakfast service provided, not on meals, although we do note whether dinners are available and, if known, the kind of food usually served. When dinner is always included in the price of the room, we say 'rates include dinner' in the details at the bottom of the entry. The great majority of B&Bs do not have an alcohol licence, but most are happy for guests to bring their own wine to dinner. Where this is the case, it is indicated in the entry.

As the public becomes increasingly health-conscious, many more B&Bs are offering alternatives to the traditional fried 'English' breakfast. Home-baked bread, fresh fruit and home-made jams, preserves and yoghurts are appearing on the breakfast menu at more and more places.

Tips for travellers

Most B&Bs welcome children, but some set minimum age restrictions or do not permit them at all. Discrimination against children is not something we endorse, but we do recognise that, since most B&Bs in this guide are also private homes, owners have the right to impose their own conditions just as any home-owner does. Sometimes children are excluded because the house is full of valuable antiques, or because there is no room for them to play, or because some parents look specifically for a property without children for a quiet break. Since it is the aim of this guide to provide the information that its users need to make an informed choice, we either note in the details at the end of each entry 'children welcome' or explain any restrictions. In a very few cases where a B&B does not ban children but does not encourage them either, we have not mentioned children in the end-details at all.

Occasionally proprietors tell us that they accept dogs when in reality dogs are not allowed in the house but are confined to the owner's car or the garden. If this is the case, we say 'no dogs' in the end-details of the entry; if there are restrictions – e.g. owners must bring bedding for dogs – we note that too. In many instances the restrictions are imposed not because proprietors dislike dogs, but because they have their own pets to consider, or they find that other guests are nervous about dogs (or even allergic to them).

The majority of B&Bs now impose at least some restrictions on smoking. Some ban it altogether, others allow it in public rooms only, while others permit smoking in bedrooms only. The restrictions are noted in the end-details, but smokers should also check when booking to see what the current rules of the establishment are.

If a B&B has amenities such as a car park, garden, games room, swimming-pool or tennis court, these are mentioned in the end-of-entry details. If there is no car park, but on-street parking is close by and generally not problematic, we mention that in the main body of the entry.

Tourist boards and B&Bs

We applaud the tourist boards for the work they have done in improving standards of accommodation: this has been to the benefit of millions of visitors. Nevertheless, there may be a less rosy side to these positive achievements. What concerns us now is the pressure that the boards have in recent years placed on small guesthouses continually to 'upgrade' themselves as far as facilities are concerned – pressure which in our opinion has started to have an impact on the very nature of the B&B as a much-loved and valued institution.

Until 1996, hotels, guesthouses and B&Bs in England and Wales have had the option of belonging to two classification and grading schemes run by their respective tourist boards: one scheme based on facilities – such as *en suite* bathrooms, colour TVs and provision of evening meals – and the other on quality. Separate fees had to be paid to belong to each scheme, and although it was possible to belong to the facilities-based scheme alone, establishments could opt out of joining the more expensive quality-based system of assessment.

Understandably, a great many B&Bs and guesthouses chose to join just the facilities-based scheme, for which they were awarded 'crowns' by the tourist boards for number and kind of amenities offered. This situation led to anomalies: it has been quite possible, for example, to find a three-crown guesthouse which in terms of quality is just adequate-to-fair sitting right next door to a superb B&B which, because it has fewer facilities, rates just one crown. (For many people the latter would be the better choice.)

The good news is that, as we went to press, the English and Wales tourist boards were on the verge of combining these assessment schemes, so that in future – assuming the changes go ahead as planned – all participating establishments will be graded both for facilities and for quality. In other words, there can be no 'crowns' without a grade for quality too. Consumers, as a result, should in future have a clearer picture of what is on offer: they will be able to choose, for example, between a 'highly commended one-crown' B&B and an 'approved four-crown' one. The boards' changes will bring England and Wales in line with Scotland, which has operated a combined facility-classification/quality-grading scheme since 1995.

As the tourist boards' planned changes take hold, B&B owners may find themselves under less pressure to add, for example, *en suite* bathrooms to already tiny rooms, or cover every inch of their walls with wallpaper, or install any number of 'mod cons' in bedrooms – in order simply to increase the number of crowns they are awarded. They may instead feel their energies and funds are better focused on the overall quality of their business – and that means maintaining or enhancing the attributes that we outlined above as being at the core of what a B&B is all about: a warm welcome, cleanliness, a happy atmosphere and the intrinsic character of the place.

That said, we also accept that some hotel-style amenities might be entirely appropriate for some B&Bs, and where they exist we describe them in the entries. But do guests really want a telephone or trouser press in their rooms in, say, a farmhouse deep in the countryside, or to be offered dinner in a city-centre B&B with dozens of restaurants and pubs within walking distance? Do they really care whether the walls are covered with paint or wallpaper, providing of course that the establishment is clean and well decorated? We think not, and therefore welcome the boards' efforts to create a better system of assessment.

The benefits of B&B

Bed and breakfast still offers an inexpensive alternative to hotels, and often a much warmer, more memorable experience. After all, most B&Bs are family homes, and guests are usually looked after by the owners themselves. For comparable facilities to those found in hotels, some B&Bs offer a veritable bargain and the variety of places to stay at is of course considerable. Within the pages of this book the reader can find simple bungalows, grand manor houses, working farms, city-centre terraced houses, windmills, oast houses, lighthouses and houses with inspired gardens and magnificent views. At some places visitors can eat at their own table and watch television in the privacy of their rooms; at others they can meet other people around one big dining-room table or while enjoying drinks in front of the sitting-room fire.

For some, a B&B stay is a chance to meet interesting people and make new friends. For others, it is an opportunity to stay in a place of historical or architectural interest, or to find out all about the local area from well-informed hosts. B&Bs are places to take the whole family to – or for a break from the workplace (or indeed the children) and the chance of real peace and quiet.

Wherever you stay, we would like to hear from you (details of where to write are at the back of the book). If you find a wonderful B&B not in this book, let us know about it; if you feel our description of a B&B is not quite right, let us know that too. Your comments and suggestions will be of great help as we research and write future editions of the *Guide*.

Elsie Dillard   *Susan Causin*

The top 20

The list of B&Bs listed below are the Editors' 20 favourites. (The counties listed are those that were correct at the time of going to press; see page 603 for explanation of changes to counties.)

England

Coombe Brook Lodge, Taynton, Oxfordshire
Creed House, Grampound, Cornwall
Hermitage Manor, Canon Pyon, Hereford & Worcester
Horsleygate Hall, Holmsefield, Derbyshire
King John's Lodge, Etchingham, East Sussex
Oak Cottage, Dawlish, Devon
Old Parsonage, West Dean, East Sussex
Pebbles Guest House, Southend-on-Sea, Essex
Romney Bay House, Littlestone-on-Sea, Kent
Scott House, West Malling, Kent
Springfields, Little Thetford, Cambridgeshire
Store Cottage, Buckland Monachorum, Devon
Tilston Lodge, Tilston, Cheshire
Westfield House, Bellingham, Northumberland

Scotland

The Albannach, Lochinver, Highland
Sealladh Sona, Inverness, Highland
Turret Guest House, Edinburgh, Lothian

Wales

Old Rectory, Llanfihangel Glyn Myfyr, Clwyd
Point Farm, Dale, Dyfed

Channel Islands

Tudor Lodge Deer Farm, Forest, Guernsey

London

Alison House Hotel

map 12

82 Ebury Street, SW1W 9QD
TEL: (0171) 730 9529   FAX: (0171) 730 5494

Alison House dates from about 1880 and is run by Gareth Owen, the son of the original owner. It has a welcoming atmosphere and offers fairly basic accommodation. The property is well maintained and three of the bedrooms are on the ground floor. Breakfast only is served. Alison House is within walking distance of Buckingham Palace, Hyde Park and Victoria Station.

OWNER: Gareth Owen   OPEN: all year   ROOMS: 2 single, 3 double, all with wash-basin; 6 twin, 1 with bath/shower, 5 with wash-basin; 1 family, with bath/shower; TV in all bedrooms   TERMS: single/single occupancy £32, twin/double £44, family room £75; babies free; deposit: 1 night's charge or credit card details   CARDS: Access, Visa
DETAILS: children welcome; no dogs; smoking in bedrooms only

Avonmore Hotel

map 12

66 Avonmore Road, W14 8RS
TEL: (0171) 603 4296/3121   FAX: (0171) 603 4035

This pleasant small hotel is located in a quiet residential street conveniently placed for both Olympia and Earls Court. The bedrooms are spotlessly clean and all have a fridge stocked with soft drinks. Breakfast is served in the basement, where there is also a licensed bar. West Kensington Underground is a few minutes' walk away.

OWNER: Margaret McKenzie   OPEN: all year   ROOMS: 1 single, with wash-basin; 2 double, 3 twin, all with bath/shower; 3 family, 2 with bath/shower, 1 with wash-basin; TV in all bedrooms and lounge   TERMS: single £43–£58, single occupancy £58, twin/double £68, family room £68–£78; deposit   CARDS: Access, Amex, Delta, Switch, Visa
DETAILS: children welcome; no dogs; garden

Bickenhall Hotel

map 12

119 Gloucester Place, W1H 3PJ
TEL: (0171) 935 3401   FAX: (0171) 224 0614

The Bickenhall Hotel is part of an elegant Georgian terrace in a very central position within two minutes' walk of Baker Street Station. The *en suite* bedrooms are all individually decorated and colour co-ordinated, and room sizes range from small singles to very spacious family rooms with all possible amenities. Bickenhall is a friendly, informally run hotel with a comfortable reception/guest lounge. Breakfasts are served in the ground-floor dining-room, which leads out on to a pretty patio.

OWNER: Irene Aghabegian OPEN: all year ROOMS: 5 single, 3 with bath/shower, 2 with wash-basin; 4 double, 3 with bath/shower, 1 with wash-basin; 8 twin/triple, 7 with bath/shower, 1 with wash-basin; 3 family, all with bath/shower; TV in all bedrooms and lounge TERMS: single £55, single occupancy £65, twin/double £80, family room £100 CARDS: Access, Amex, Diners, Visa DETAILS: children welcome; small dogs only; garden

Camelot Hotel
map 12

45–47 Norfolk Square, W2 1RX
TEL: (0171) 262 1980/723 9118   FAX: (0171) 402 3412

This mid-nineteenth-century restored terraced house is located in a quietish garden square close to Paddington Station and transport to all parts of London. The management is friendly and the service personal. The hotel is well decorated and furnished in a light modern style, giving it a fresh and airy feel. There is a small, pleasant breakfast room and some seating in the reception area which has TV.

OWNER: David Betteridge OPEN: all year ROOMS: 14 single, 10 with bath/shower, 4 with wash-basin; 12 double, all with bath/shower; 10 twin, all with bath/shower; 1 four-poster, with bath/shower; 7 family, all with bath/shower; TV in all bedrooms and lounge TERMS: single £55, single occupancy £65, twin/double £75, four-poster £100, family room £88–£145; children sharing with parents free CARDS: Access, Delta, Diners, Switch, Visa DETAILS: children welcome; no dogs; no smoking in breakfast room

Collin House
map 12

104 Ebury Street, SW1W 9QD
TEL/FAX: (0171) 730 8031

Dafydd and Beryl Thomas are a helpful couple who take good care of their guests. Collin House is a mid-Victorian terraced property offering fairly basic but good-value central-London accommodation. The bedrooms vary in size, are mostly *en suite*, and three are on the ground floor. Breakfast only is served, but there is a wealth of nearby restaurants and wine bars. Ebury Street is an excellent location for transport and within walking distance of Buckingham Palace. Unsurprisingly, there is no private car park, but the hotel can offer a special rate at a nearby public car park.

OWNERS: Dafydd and Beryl Thomas OPEN: all year exc Christmas ROOMS: 3 single, all with bath/shower; 4 double, 2 with bath/shower, 2 with wash-basin; 4 twin, 2 with bath/shower, 2 with wash-basin; 2 family, both with bath/shower TERMS: single £36–£38, single occupancy £40, twin/double £50–£62, family room £75–£80; deposit: by arrangement CARDS: none DETAILS: children welcome; no dogs; no smoking in breakfast room

Demetriou's Guesthouse map 12

9 Strathmore Gardens, W8 4RZ
TEL/FAX: (0171) 229 6709

Guests continue to endorse the good-value accommodation at this Victorian house tucked away on a quiet residential cul-de-sac within a few minutes' walk of Kensington Gardens and Hyde Park. Notting Hill Gate and Queensway Underground stations are close by and it is also convenient for the bus service to Heathrow Airport. The large bedrooms are simply furnished, with a fresh and bright atmosphere. Two of the *en suite* rooms are on the top floor. The Demetrious are a welcoming couple who do not publicise their business with a sign on the door or in the window, so guests just have to search out Number 9. They have two friendly cats.

OWNERS: Mr and Mrs Demetriou   OPEN: all year exc Christmas and owners' annual holiday (3 weeks)   ROOMS: 1 single, with wash-basin; 3 double, all with bath/shower; 2 twin, both with wash-basin; 2 family; TV in all bedrooms   TERMS: single £30, twin/double £44–£50, family room £88 for 4 people; deposit: 1 night's charge   CARDS: none   DETAILS: no children; no dogs; no smoking in dining-room

Enrico Hotel map 12

79 Warwick Way, SW1V 1QP
TEL: (0171) 834 9538   FAX: (0171) 233 9995

Everything about the Enrico seems to sparkle and shine, so immaculately is it maintained. The bedrooms are simply furnished and modest in size; some have shower cubicles and there are bathrooms and WCs on each floor. Breakfast only is served in the bright basement dining-room and there is a small TV lounge for guests. The hotel is an ideal base for sightseeing and for day trips out of London from Victoria train, bus and coach stations, which are only a few minutes' walk away. This is good-value accommodation.

OWNER: Mr M.G. Desira   OPEN: all year   ROOMS: 4 single, all with wash-basin; 13 double, 5 with shower, 8 with wash-basin; 9 twin, 3 with shower, 6 with wash-basin; TV lounge   TERMS: single £26, single occupancy £30, twin/double £30–£40; deposit: 1 night's charge   CARDS: Access, Delta, Switch, Visa   DETAILS: children welcome; no dogs; no smoking in breakfast room

Harlingford Hotel map 12

61–63 Cartwright Gardens, WC1H 9EL
TEL: (0171) 387 1551   FAX: (0171) 387 4616

The Harlingford Hotel occupies three converted Georgian terraced houses in an attractive leafy crescent in the heart of Bloomsbury.

Guests have access to the crescent gardens, where there are also tennis courts. The hotel has been in the same family for 40 years and is clean, comfortable and well maintained. There is a large ground-floor breakfast room overlooking the gardens, and a lounge with TV. All the bedrooms have *en suite* facilities. The Harlingford is in an excellent location for the British Museum, for public transport and for getting around London. The only parking available is in the nearby NCP car park.

OWNERS: Mr A. Davies and Mr W. Davies OPEN: all year ROOMS: 19 single, 8 double, 5 twin, 12 family; all rooms with bath/shower; TV in all bedrooms and lounge TERMS: single £55, twin/double £68, family room £85; reductions for children sharing with parents in family room; deposit: 1 night's charge CARDS: Access, Amex, Visa DETAILS: children welcome; no dogs; no smoking in dining-room; garden; tennis

Hart House Hotel   map 12

51 Gloucester Place, W1H 3PE
TEL: (0171) 935 2288   FAX: (0171) 935 8561

Hart House Hotel maintains a good standard of comfort and cleanliness and is in an excellent location for shopping and public transport. It is part of a Georgian terrace of family mansions that were once occupied by the French nobility during the French Revolution. The bedrooms have high ceilings and traditional cornicing, and are decorated in light, unobtrusive colours. Breakfast is served in the small mirrored basement dining-room.

OWNER: Andrew Bowden OPEN: all year ROOMS: 6 single, 3 with bath/shower, 3 with wash-basin; 3 double, 2 with bath/shower, 1 with wash-basin; 4 twin, 3 with bath/shower, 1 with wash-basin; 3 family, all with bath/shower; TV in all bedrooms and lounge TERMS: single £45, twin/double £65, family room £92; deposit: 1 night's charge or credit card details CARDS: Access, Amex, Delta, Switch, Visa DETAILS: children welcome; no dogs; no smoking in dining-room

Lincoln House Hotel   map 12

33 Gloucester Place, W1H 3PD
TEL: (0171) 486 7630   FAX: (0171) 486 0166

This Georgian terraced building has recently been refurbished and provides comfortable and well-equipped accommodation. Breakfast is served in the attractive dining-room, and the house is decorated with beautiful silk flower arrangements made by a family friend. Lincoln House stands on busy Gloucester Place and is a few minutes' walk from both Oxford Street and Baker Street.

OWNER: Joseph Shariff OPEN: all year ROOMS: 10 single, 7 with bath/shower, 3 with wash-basin; 6 double, all with bath/shower; 3 twin, 2 with bath/shower, 1 with wash-basin; 3 family, all with bath/shower; TV in all bedrooms TERMS: single £57, single occupancy £65–£69, twin/double £75–£85, family room £89; deposit: by arrangement or credit card details CARDS: Access, Amex, Delta, Diners, Switch, Visa DETAILS: children welcome; no dogs; no smoking in breakfast room during breakfast

Mabledon Court Hotel   map 12

10–11 Mabledon Place, WC1H 9AZ
TEL: (0171) 388 3866   FAX: (0171) 387 5686

This very pleasant small hotel is ideally suited for those wanting to be in the University and British Museum area. It is quietly situated and only a stone's throw from Euston Road, main-line stations and buses. It has a pleasant, friendly atmosphere and the bedrooms are small, bright and cheery with modern furniture. There is a small basement lounge and adjoining attractive breakfast room. The hotel caters mostly for business people and the majority of bedrooms are singles, some of which are on the ground floor. The hotel has a lift. It is under the same ownership as the Harlingford Hotel (see entry).

OWNER: Mr A. Davies OPEN: all year exc Christmas and New Year ROOMS: 21 single, 10 double; all rooms with bath/shower; TV in all bedrooms TERMS: single/single occupancy £55, double £65; deposit   CARDS: Access, Amex, Switch, Visa DETAILS: children welcome; no dogs

Mentone Hotel   map 12

54–55 Cartwright Gardens, WC1H 9EL
TEL: (0171) 387 3927   FAX: (0171) 388 4671

This Georgian terraced town house is in an attractive Bloomsbury crescent. Guests have access to the gardens and tennis courts. The bedrooms are small and basic, and there is a good basement breakfast room. The house has no lounge or lift. Kings Cross, the Underground and buses to most of the tourist attractions and theatres are only a five-minute walk away.

OWNER: Mrs G.J. Tyner OPEN: all year ROOMS: 7 single, 2 with bath/shower, 5 with wash-basin; 14 double, 12 with bath/shower, 2 with wash-basin; 14 twin, 4 family, all with bath/shower; 1 room suitable for wheelchair-users; TV in all bedrooms TERMS: single £35–£48, single occupancy £48, twin/double £59, family room £75; deposit: 1 night's charge or credit card details CARDS: Access, Visa DETAILS: children welcome; no dogs; garden; tennis

---

Bath / shower in the details under each entry means that the rooms have private facilities. The B&B may have other, shared bathroom facilities as well. We say if rooms have wash-basins.

Oxford House Hotel
map 12

92–94 Cambridge Street, SW1V 4QG
TEL: (0171) 834 6467/9681   FAX: (0171) 834 0225

This comfortable Victorian house is in a quiet residential street ten minutes' walk from Victoria Station. The bedrooms are basic, but large, and are decorated with matching wallpapers and curtains. There is a pleasant basement breakfast room and a TV lounge on the first floor. The owners have a cat and keep pet rabbits in the back yard.

OWNER: Yunus Kader OPEN: all year ROOMS: 2 single, 5 double, 4 twin, 6 family; all rooms with wash-basin; TV lounge TERMS: single £30–£32, single occupancy £35, twin/double £40–£42, family room £54–£72; deposit: 1 night's charge or credit card details CARDS: Visa DETAILS: children welcome; dogs in bedrooms only

Parkland Walk Guest House
map 3

12 Hornsey Rise Gardens, N19 3PR
TEL: (0171) 263 3228   FAX: (0171) 831 9489

This large Victorian terraced house is in a pleasant North London suburb, with views across the city from its back garden. It is within walking distance of Highgate Cemetery, and Hampstead Heath is two miles away. Lawrence and Penny Solomons are extremely welcoming people, who go out of their way to make sure their guests are comfortable and are well informed about what to see and do in the area. Most of the bedrooms are in the main house and two are across the road; all are nicely decorated and have books, fresh flowers and TVs. Guests have use of a comfortable TV lounge and breakfast is served in a rather dark dining-room. The Northern Line of the Underground is convenient for travelling into central London.

OWNERS: Lawrence and Penny Solomons OPEN: all year ROOMS: 3 single, 1 with bath/shower; 3 double, all with bath/shower; 1 twin, with bath/shower; 2 family, both with bath/shower; TV in all bedrooms and lounge TERMS: single £23–£32, single occupancy £30–£40, twin/double £42–£55, family room £55–£70; children under 5 free, reductions for older children; deposit CARDS: Amex DETAILS: children welcome; no dogs; no smoking

Parkwood Hotel
map 12

4 Stanhope Place, W2 2HB
TEL: (0171) 402 2241   FAX: (0171) 402 1574

This small, comfortable hotel is in a prime location close to Marble Arch, Oxford Street, Hyde Park and the direct A2 bus to Heathrow Airport. Two of the bright and individually decorated bedrooms are on the ground floor; there is no lift and a lot of stairs to climb to some of the rooms. The hotel is well maintained, and breakfast only is served in the basement breakfast room, which is hung with old posters. On summer days guests can sit at picnic tables on the terrace.

OWNER: Peter Evans   OPEN: all year   ROOMS: 5 single, 1 with bath/shower, 4 with wash-basin; 2 double, both with bath/shower; 7 twin, 6 with bath/shower, 1 with wash-basin, 4 family, 3 with bath/shower, 1 with wash-basin; TV in all bedrooms and lounge   TERMS: single £40–£45, single occupancy £45, twin/double £50–£75, family room £66–£79.50; children free at weekends, £11.50 during the week; deposit: 1 night's charge   CARDS: Access, Switch, Visa   DETAILS: children welcome; no dogs; no smoking in 2 bedrooms

Romany House Hotel
map 12

35 Longmoore Street, SW1V 1JQ
TEL: (0171) 834 5553   FAX: (0171) 834 0495

Romany House is on the corner of a quiet side street only seven minutes' walk from Victoria Station. It is reputed to have been a highwaymen's haunt in former times and may date back as much as 500 years. Today it is a small family-run B&B that is kept spotlessly clean and offers good value for London. The stairs are steep and narrow, the windows latticed and old-fashioned, and some of the furnishings, such as the wall-mounted radios, remain from Romany House's days as a hotel in the 1930s. Good breakfasts are served on attractive china in the basement dining-room. There are three bathrooms for guests' use.

OWNER: Jaffer Jeraj   OPEN: all year   ROOMS: 2 single, 6 double, 2 twin; all rooms with wash-basin; TV in all bedrooms   TERMS: single/single occupancy £25, twin/double £35; children's reductions   CARDS: none   DETAILS: children welcome; no dogs; garden

Swiss House Hotel
map 12

171 Old Brompton Road, SW5 0AN
TEL: (0171) 373 2769   FAX: (0171) 373 4983

Swiss House Hotel has the air of a country-house hotel, with attractive décor and dried-flower displays throughout the house. It stands on the busy Old Brompton Road close to South Kensington and Gloucester Road Underground stations. The bedrooms are comfortable, with three on the ground floor. There is an unusual basement dining-room where a buffet-style Continental breakfast is laid out on a Welsh dresser. There is a £4 supplement for a cooked breakfast. Room service is available from noon till 9pm, with snacks costing from £5.

SWISS HOUSE HOTEL, LONDON

OWNER: Earlsheer Ltd OPEN: all year ROOMS: 4 single, 3 with bath/shower, 1 with wash-basin; 3 double, 3 twin, 5 family, all with bath/shower; TV in all bedrooms and lounge TERMS: single £36–£53, single occupancy £53, twin/double £68, family room £80–£92; children under 3 free; deposit: 1 night's charge or credit card details CARDS: Access, Amex, Delta, Diners, Switch, Visa DETAILS: children welcome; no dogs; no smoking at breakfast; garden

Terstan Hotel ✓

map 12

29–31 Nevern Square, SW5 9PE
TEL: (0171) 835 1900   FAX: (0171) 373 9268

This family-run hotel is in an attractive London square with access to the square's gardens. Terstan is well placed for both the Earls Court and Olympia exhibition halls. It has friendly, helpful staff and continues to provide good value. The bedrooms are pleasantly decorated, and amenities include a modern wood-panelled bar open until 1am, a pool room, a small lounge and breakfast room, and lift access to all floors.

OWNER: Mr S. Tabaka OPEN: all year exc Christmas ROOMS: 22 single, 10 with bath/shower, 12 with wash-basin; 8 double, all with bath/shower; 13 twin, all with bath/shower; 5 family, all with bath/shower; TV in all bedrooms TERMS: single £30–£43,

single occupancy £45, twin/double £53–£57, family room £66–£74; cot for babies £3, reductions for older children sharing with parents CARDS: Access, Amex, Switch, Visa
DETAILS: children welcome; no dogs; no smoking in dining-room; games room

25 Eglington Road

map 3

25 Eglington Road, North Chingford, E4 7AN
TEL: (0181) 529 1140   FAX: (0181) 508 3837

This large semi-detached Edwardian family house stands in an attractive landscaped garden featuring a swimming-pool heated by solar panels, discreetly sheltered by a red-brick wall. It is a spacious house maintained to very high standards, with plenty of hospitality extras provided at no extra expense. Guests will find trays of goodies and nightcap decanters in their rooms and the Clapps are always happy to give guests lifts to and from the station. The bedrooms have recently been redecorated and fitted out with co-ordinated curtains and bed linen, and there is a private bathroom for guests' use. Helen Clapp is a qualified London tour guide and is happy to assist her visitors to plan their days out. She is also a good cook and serves generous and imaginative evening meals by arrangement. Special diets and vegetarian choices can be catered for and guests are invited to bring wine to dinner. The Clapps usually join their guests unless privacy is preferred. North Chingford is north-east of London and 25 minutes by train from the centre.

OWNERS: Helen and Drummond Clapp OPEN: all year exc Christmas ROOMS: 1 double, 1 twin; TV lounge TERMS: single/single occupancy £30; twin/double £60; dinner £15; deposit: 1 night's charge CARDS: none DETAILS: no children under 12; no dogs; no smoking upstairs; garden; swimming-pool

Vicarage Private Hotel

map 12

10 Vicarage Gate, W8 4AG
TEL: (0171) 229 4030

This small private hotel is in an excellent location in the heart of Kensington – just a few minutes' walk from Kensington High Street in an attractive garden square. The Vicarage Hotel is a fine Victorian house with an impressive façade and entrance hall. Each floor has a shower room and WCs, and most bedrooms are good-sized. Hair-dryers and irons are provided on request. The house has a very pleasant atmosphere, and guests have the use of a small sitting-room on the ground floor. A full English breakfast is served in a large dining-room in the basement.

OWNERS: Martin and Eileen Diviney OPEN: all year ROOMS: 8 single, 2 double, 6 twin, 3 family; all rooms with wash-basin; TV in some bedrooms and lounge TERMS: single/single occupancy £36, twin/double £56, family room £68–£76; deposit: 1 night's charge CARDS: none DETAILS: children welcome; no dogs

---

Westminster House Hotel   map 12

96 Ebury Street, SW1W 9QD
TEL/FAX: (0171) 730 4302

Westminster House Hotel is a Regency building situated in the heart of Belgravia, within walking distance of Buckingham Palace and Victoria railway and coach stations. Jane and Glyn Jones are a pleasant couple who are always happy to assist guests with information. Four of the clean and comfortable bedrooms are *en suite* and two are located on the ground floor, as is the cosy dining-room where a full English breakfast is served.

OWNERS: Mr and Mrs D.G. Jones OPEN: all year exc Christmas ROOMS: 2 single, both with wash-basin; 3 double, 1 with bath/shower, 2 with wash-basin; 3 twin, 1 with bath/shower, 2 with wash-basin; 2 family, both with bath/shower; TV in all bedrooms TERMS: single £40, single occupancy £45–£55, twin/double £50–£60, family room £70–£80; deposit: 1 night's charge CARDS: Access, Amex, Delta, Switch, Visa DETAILS: children welcome; no dogs

England

ABINGDON   Oxfordshire   map 2

22 East St Helen Street

22 East St Helen Street, Abingdon OX14 5EB
TEL/FAX: (01235) 533278

This eighteenth-century house stands a storey taller than its neighbours and proudly displays window-boxes on all three floors. Behind the black front door the house is very much its original self, with flagstone floors, old beams, open fireplaces and an interesting staircase up to the comfortable bedrooms. Guests are welcome to sit in the lovely garden on sunny days, and can also enjoy riverside walks or a visit to the thirteenth-century church of St Helen only 200 yards away. Breakfast only is served. On-street parking is limited, but there is a public car park nearby.

OWNERS: Richard and Susie Howard   OPEN: all year   ROOMS: 1 single; 2 double, 1 with bath/shower, 1 with wash-basin; 1 twin, with wash-basin; TV in some bedrooms and lounge   TERMS: single £17–£20, single occupancy £18–£22, twin/double £28–£40; deposit: £10   CARDS: none   DETAILS: children welcome; no dogs; no smoking; garden

ACTON   Suffolk   map 6

Durham Cottage

Melford Road, Acton, nr Sudbury CO10 0BA
TEL: (01787) 370142

This beamed country cottage is close to two of Suffolk's prettiest villages: Long Melford and Lavenham. Vanessa and Hugh Tatum welcome guests to their family home with a hot drink on arrival, and the two friendly dogs, Gus and Charlie, give their own greeting. The good-sized bedrooms have sloping ceilings and are tastefully decorated with attractive wallpapers. TV is available on request. Breakfast only is served in the dining-room-cum-lounge, but the Crown pub almost opposite the cottage serves evening meals and it is only a mile to Long Melford for further options.

OWNERS: Vanessa and Hugh Tatum   OPEN: Easter to Sept   ROOMS: 1 double, 1 twin TERMS: single occupancy £20, twin/double £35; children's reductions; deposit required CARDS: none   DETAILS: children welcome; no dogs; smoking in guests' sitting-room only; car park; garden

B&B rates specified in the details at the end of each entry are given (as applicable) for a single room, for single occupancy of a double room, and then per room in the case of two people sharing a double or twin-bedded room, or for a family room.

AFFPUDDLE   Dorset   map 2

Old Vicarage

Affpuddle, nr Dorchester DT2 7HH
TEL: (01305) 848315
just S of A35 on B3390, 3m E of Puddletown

This mellow-brick, creeper-covered house was rebuilt in 1792 after an extensive fire. It stands in one and a half acres of lawns and mature gardens next to a lovely old church in the Piddle Valley. Although the setting is tranquil, the A35 is only a mile away, making this an excellent location for exploring Hardy country. The house is beautifully furnished and very comfortable; two of the double bedrooms can be made up to be twin beds if desired. Breakfast is served in the dining-room, or on sunny days out on the terrace. Supper is available by arrangement, and only in winter months. Guests may bring their own wine to table as there is no alcohol licence.

OWNERS: Michael and Anthea Hipwell   OPEN: all year exc Christmas and New Year   ROOMS: 3 double, with bath; TV in all bedrooms   TERMS: single occupancy £22.50, double £40; dinner £7–£9; deposit: £10   CARDS: none   DETAILS: no children under 10; no dogs; no smoking; car park; garden

ALDEBURGH   Suffolk   map 6

Brightside

147 Saxmundham Road, Aldeburgh IP15 5PB
TEL: (01728) 454058

Brightside is an immaculate bungalow owned by a delightful retired couple, who have been welcoming guests into their home for five years. The two bedrooms are spacious and well equipped, with TV, radio, hairdryer and trouser press. Wholesome breakfasts featuring locally made sausages and honey are served in the dining-room, which overlooks the landscaped garden. Guests may relax in the conservatory.

OWNER: A.H. Melson   OPEN: Mar to mid-Dec   ROOMS: 2 double/twin, both with bath/shower; TV in all bedrooms   TERMS: single occupancy £20, twin/double £36; deposit: £10   CARDS: none   DETAILS: no children under 12; dogs welcome with own bedding; car park; garden

---

If you are forced to turn up later than planned, please telephone to warn the proprietor.

The end details for each entry state whether dogs are allowed, but it is always best to check when booking.

Wateringfield

Golf Lane, Aldeburgh IP15 5PY
TEL: (01728) 453163

This attractive modern house has been beautifully decorated, and
stands in an acre of landscaped gardens adjacent to a golf course. The
well-appointed, luxurious bedrooms have attractive fabrics and rich
carpets. All overlook either the garden or the golf course. Freshly
prepared breakfasts are served in the parquet-floored dining-room.
Linda Connah is extremely helpful and will provide detailed
directions to the property on booking. Keen walkers will find
numerous footpaths taking them to Snape, or towards the RSPB
reserve on the North Warren.

OWNER: Linda Connah OPEN: Mar to Nov ROOMS: 1 single; 2 double, 1 with shower; 1
twin, with bath/shower; TV in all bedrooms TERMS: single £18, twin/double £38;
deposit: £10 for single room, £30 for twin/double CARDS: none DETAILS: children
welcome; no dogs; no smoking; car park; garden

ALDFIELD   North Yorkshire   map 8

Bay Tree Farm

Aldfield, nr Ripon HG4 3BE
TEL: (01765) 620394
from B6265 turn at sign to Aldfield 3m SW of Ripon

A traditional Yorkshire welcome awaits guests at this 200-year-old
stone-built farmhouse, where the Leemings claim that the kettle is
always on the boil. Most of the farming is based a mile away, but a
few animals can be seen here and the Leemings will happily show
interested guests around the working farm. Tasty home-made meals
are served by arrangement in the licenced dining-room, and
vegetarians can be catered for with advance notice. Accommodation
is in a newly converted seventeenth-century barn, which has its own
sitting-room with a real fire and french windows opening on to the
garden. The beamed bedrooms are tastefully decorated and furnished
to a high standard. Substantial breakfasts are served on an antique
oak table. Fountains Abbey is only half a mile away.

OWNERS: Val and Andrew Leeming OPEN: all year ROOMS: 3 double, 1 twin, 1 four-
poster, 1 family; all rooms with bath/shower; 1 room suitable for wheelchair-users; TV in
all bedrooms TERMS: single occupancy £25, twin/double £38, four-poster £38;
children's reductions according to age; dinner £11; deposit: £30 or £5 for single night
CARDS: Visa DETAILS: children welcome; dogs welcome; smoking area; car park;
garden

If we know a B&B has an alcohol licence, we say so.

Abbotts Way Guest House

Gloucester Road, Almondsbury, nr Bristol BS12 4JB
TEL/FAX: (01454) 613134

This superb, bright house, built in Georgian-style with later
additions, has a simple elegance and provides an impressive standard
of accommodation. It stands in 12 acres of land and has spectacular
views of the two Severn bridges over fields dotted with sheep. The
spacious bedrooms are beautifully furnished and tastefully decorated
with soft, restful colours; all have *en suite* facilities with power
showers. The comfortable TV lounge has an interesting display of
plates and china. Breakfast and dinners (Monday to Thursday,
orders to be placed at breakfast time) are served in the conservatory,
which is positioned to take advantage of the view. Vegetarian options
are available at dinner. Guests are welcome to enjoy the lovely
garden and the patio, and the company of the three friendly dogs. The
swimming-pool and sauna are new additions for 1996.

OWNERS: Pam and Geoff Watkins   OPEN: all year   ROOMS: 2 single, 1 double, 2 twin, 1
family; all rooms with bath/shower; TV lounge   TERMS: single/single occupancy £25,
twin/double £40, family room £40; children under 12 free; dinner £10   CARDS: Access,
Amex, Delta, Diners, Visa   DETAILS: children welcome; dogs welcome; smoking in
lounge only; car park; garden; swimming-pool

Bilton Barns

Alnmouth, nr Alnwick NE66 2TB
TEL: (01665) 830427
1½m W of Alnmouth on minor road to Shilbottle

Bilton Barns stands in lovely countryside with stunning views over
Warkworth Bay. It is part of a 400-acre mixed farm, which guests are
welcome to explore with Brian Jackson if time permits. The spacious
bedrooms have a light pastel décor, Sanderson wallpapers and
duvets, and all have views either of the coast or the countryside. The
house is furnished with solid old-fashioned and antique furniture and
is warm and comfortable. In addition to the lounge a sun room is
available to guests. Breakfast and imaginative home-cooked dinners
are served by arrangement, and vegetarians can be catered for. This
is an ideal spot for walkers and for nature lovers, with plenty of
wildlife to watch. Two self-catering cottages are available.

*Please let us know if you need more report forms and we will send you a
fresh supply.*

OWNER: Dorothy Jackson   OPEN: Easter to mid-Oct   ROOMS: 2 double, 1 twin; all rooms with bath/shower; TV in all bedrooms   TERMS: twin/double £42; dinner £11; deposit required   CARDS: none   DETAILS: children welcome; no dogs; smoking in lounge only; car park; garden

The Grange

Northumberland Street, Alnmouth NE66 2RJ
TEL: (01665) 830401

This 200-year old three-storey stone house was once a granary when Almouth was a busy grain shipping port. Just a few yards from the town centre, the Grange is set in a large landscaped garden overlooking the river Aln and only two minutes' walk from beautiful unspoilt beaches. The house is impeccably maintained, with an attractive drawing-room which has window-seats overlooking the view. The spacious bedrooms are tastefully furnished and two have four-poster beds with *en suite* facilities. Breakfast only is served.

OWNERS: Kathy and Charles Homer   OPEN: Apr to Oct   ROOMS: 1 single, with wash-basin; 3 double, 2 with bath/shower, 1 with wash-basin; 2 four-poster, 1 family, all with bath/shower; TV in all bedrooms   TERMS: single £21, single occupancy £36, twin/double £42, four-poster £46–£48, family room £69; half-price for children 5 to 12 CARDS: none   DETAILS: no children under 5; no dogs; no smoking; car park; garden

ALNWICK   Northumberland   **map 11**

Charlton House

2 Aydon Gardens, South Road, Alnwick NE66 2NT
TEL: (01665) 605185

This stylish Victorian house close to the town centre is decorated with real flair, combining Victorian floral wallpapers, antiques and original fireplaces with modern pine furnishings. The owners live in an extension and the guests have the whole of the house to themselves. All bedrooms have home-made patchwork quilts and satellite TV. The spacious lounge features an old church pew and an open fire. The breakfast menu is extensive and dinners, including vegetarian options, are available by arrangement. Kate Jones is the proud winner of the Cook of the North competition.

OWNERS: Ben and Kate Jones   OPEN: Mar to Nov   ROOMS: 1 single, 3 double, 1 twin; all rooms with bath/shower; TV in all bedrooms and lounge   TERMS: single £18, single occupancy £25, twin/double £36; dinner £10   CARDS: none   DETAILS: no children; no dogs; smoking in lounge only; car park; garden

We asked the proprietors to estimate their 1996 prices in the autumn of 1995, so the rates may have changed since publication.

ALSTONEFIELD   Staffordshire   map 5

Stanshope Hall

Stanshope, nr Ashbourne DE6 2AD
TEL: (01335) 310278   FAX: (01335) 310470
off A515 Ashbourne to Buxton road between Ilam and Alstonefield

This rambling sixteenth-century house in the beautiful surroundings
of the Manifold Valley has been undergoing refurbishment and
redecoration, although original features such as the stone stairs,
flagstone floors and oak beams remain. Local artists have painted
murals in many of the rooms. The large, well-furnished drawing-
room has a moorland scene, and the *en suite* bedrooms have
Egyptian, Moorish and Regency themes. Imaginative evening meals
are served, with vegetarian choices available, and guests can bring
their own wine to dinner, but £2 corkage is charged; packed lunches
can be provided.

OWNERS: Naomi Chambers and Nicholas Lourie   OPEN: all year exc 24 to 26 Dec
ROOMS: 2 double, 1 twin; all rooms with bath/shower; TV in all bedrooms   TERMS: single
occupancy £20–£30, twin/double £40–£60, family room £80; two-thirds reduction for
children sharing with parents; dinner £17; deposit: £10 per person   CARDS: none
DETAILS: children welcome; no dogs; no smoking in bedrooms or dining-room; car park;
garden

ALTON BARNES   Wiltshire   map 2

Newtown House

Alton Barnes, nr Marlborough SN8 4LB
TEL: (01672) 851391
*from Marlborough take A4 west, after 2m turn left at Fyfield, signposted
Lockeridge and Alton Barnes; Mewtown House on right after approx 3m*

This Wiltshire farmhouse dating from the late 1800s stands high up
on the Marlborough Downs overlooking the Vale of Pewsey.
Originally two cottages, the house has been extended and is
surrounded by an attractive garden. Newtown House is principally a
restaurant with three comfortable bedrooms all enjoying lovely
views. The beautifully decorated restaurant is open to non-residents
in the evening from Thursday to Saturday, and has an excellent
reputation locally; packed lunches can be provided. The house is less
than half a mile from the Wansdyke, an ancient Roman barrier, and
the Ridgeway walk runs along one side of the property.

OWNERS: Mr and Mrs Jeremy Shutter   OPEN: all year exc Christmas and Feb   ROOMS: 2
double, 1 with bath/shower; 1 twin   TERMS: single occupancy £30–£35, twin/double
£55–£65; dinner £25; deposit: £10 per room   CARDS: none   DETAILS: no children under
14; no dogs; no smoking in bedrooms or restaurant; car park

ALTRINCHAM   Greater Manchester   map 8

Marron Guest House

15 Manchester Road, Altrincham WA14 4RG
TEL: (0161) 941 5603

This family-run Victorian guesthouse is situated on the main road
just eight miles from Manchester and its airport. The residence is
decorated to a high standard and is well maintained. It has no lounge
for guests, but the large bedrooms have TV and easy chairs.
Breakfast only is served in the dining-room and evening meals are
available at a number of local establishments. This is good-value
accommodation in an area where B&Bs can be hard to find. The
Bartles are a friendly couple and are happy to assist guests in every
way in order to make their stay comfortable.

OWNERS: Mr and Mrs R.W. Bartle OPEN: all year ROOMS: 1 double, 1 twin, 2 family; all
rooms with wash-basin; TV in all bedrooms and lounge TERMS: single £22–£25, single
occupancy £28–£30, twin/double £38–£42, family room £45–£60; deposit: 10%
CARDS: none DETAILS: children welcome; dogs by arrangement only; no smoking in
breakfast room; car park

AMBLESIDE   Cumbria   map 8

Cherry Garth

Old Lake Road, Ambleside LA22 0DH
TEL: (015394) 33128

With a beautiful landscaped garden and a view of the splendours of
Loughrigg Fell, this white-painted Victorian house offers luxury
outdoors as well as inside. Rooms are spacious and comfortably
furnished, with exposed stone walls providing a contrast to modern
décor. Two of the bedrooms have four-poster beds, with co-ordinated
floral designs on bed, walls and curtains in one. Further facilities are
provided by nearby Low Wood Leisure Centre, for which membership
is free to guests of Cherry Garth.

OWNERS: Mo and Roger Knowles OPEN: Feb to Nov ROOMS: 5 double, 3 with bath/
shower, 2 with wash-basin; 1 twin, with bath/shower; 2 four-poster, 2 family; all with
bath/shower; TV in all bedrooms TERMS: single £30–£45, twin/double £44–£58, four-
poster £55–£64, family room £60–£70; deposit: 1 night's charge CARDS: Access, Delta,
Visa DETAILS: children welcome; no dogs; no smoking in bedrooms; car park; garden

*Breakfast at B&Bs tends to mean a cooked breakfast of bacon, eggs and so
on. If you prefer a different style of breakfast, it is best to discuss this when
you make a booking.*

Fern Cottage

6 Waterhead Terrace, Ambleside LA22 0HA
TEL: (015394) 330077

Fern Cottage is a small, comfortable house, with window-boxes full of
flowers in summer, only two minutes' walk from the head of the lake
and the steamer piers. The three bedrooms are comfortable, but they
share one bathroom, and guests are requested not to take showers
early in the morning. There is a small dining area in the lounge
where home-style cooked breakfasts and dinners are served.
Vegetarians can be catered for and guests may bring their own wine
to dinner; packed lunches can also be provided.

OWNER: Mary Brown   OPEN: all year exc Christmas   ROOMS: 2 double, 1 twin; all rooms
with wash-basin; TV lounge   TERMS: single/single occupancy £20, twin/double
£30–£33; dinner £11; deposit: £10 per person   CARDS: none   DETAILS: no children
under 8; dogs by arrangement; no smoking in lounge

Riverside Lodge

Rothay Road, Rothay Bridge, Ambleside LA22 0EH
TEL: (01539) 434208
*approaching Ambleside from the south on A591, take left fork A593
signposted Coniston for 1m*

Riverside Lodge is an extremely attractive early-Georgian creeper-
covered house in an enviable position. It overlooks Rothay Bridge, is
only a short walk from Ambleside, and is surrounded by mature trees
and gardens. Guests are invited to fish on the River Rothay, which
flows through the extensive grounds. Bonnie Prince Charlie is
reputed to have rested here in 1745. Inside is cosy and characterful,
with old beams, tasteful furnishings and décor. The five bedrooms,
one of which is on the ground floor, all have private bathrooms, TV,
telephone and easy chairs. Breakfast only is served in the dining-
room, which overlooks the river, and the relaxing lounge has a slate
fireplace with open fire. Also within the grounds are four luxuriously
appointed self-catering cottages. Keen walkers will note that the
house is at the foot of Loughrigg Fell.

OWNERS: Alan and Gillian Rhone   OPEN: all year exc Christmas and mid-week in winter
ROOMS: 2 double, 1 twin, 1 four-poster, 1 family; all rooms with bath/shower; TV in all
bedrooms   TERMS: twin/double/four-poster/family room £50–£55; deposit: £25
CARDS: Access, Visa   DETAILS: children welcome; dogs welcome; no smoking; car park;
garden

Please let us know if an establishment has changed hands.

*If you intend to spend several days at a B&B, it is worth asking whether
there are reduced rates, particularly if the period is midweek or off-season.*

AMESBURY   Wiltshire
map 2

Ratfyn Barrow House

Ratfyn Road, Amesbury SP4 7DZ
TEL: (01980) 623422
from A303 turn into town centre, turn left at traffic lights, then second road on left

Ratfyn Barrow house was built in 1938 and is situated just off the main road, on the edge of Amesbury. A large bronze-age barrow dominates the garden and Stonehenge is just two miles away. One of the three bedrooms has a large bay window overlooking the lawned garden. Breakfast only is served in the attractive dining-room.

OWNERS: Jean and Larry Bax   OPEN: Apr to end Oct   ROOMS: 1 double, with bath/shower; 2 twin, with wash-basin; TV in all bedrooms   TERMS: single occupancy £15–£18, twin/double £30–£36; deposit: £10   CARDS: none   DETAILS: no children under 5; dogs must have own bedding; no smoking; car park; garden

ANDOVER   Hampshire
map 2

Lotties

23 Winchester Road, Andover SP10 2EQ
TEL: (01264) 323825

This Victorian terraced house lies just off a main road on the edge of Andover. Lottie Waite is a caring, welcoming hostess and keeps an immaculately clean house. The simply furnished, small bedrooms are well decorated. There is a lounge, and breakfast only is served in the dining-room.

OWNERS: Cyril and Lottie Waite   OPEN: all year exc Christmas   ROOMS: 2 single, 1 double, 1 twin, 1 family; all rooms with wash-basin; TV in all bedrooms and lounge   TERMS: single/single occupancy £16, twin/double £32, family room from £40; children's reductions according to age   CARDS: none   DETAILS: children welcome; no dogs; no smoking; car park

ARLINGTON   East Sussex
map 3

Bates Green

Tye Hill, Arlington, nr Polegate BN26 6SH
TEL: (01323) 482039
off A22 / A27, 3m NW of Polegate; from village find lane signposted Arlington Turkeys and Bates Green Farm

Bates Green is an attractive eighteenth-century house in a quiet rural location just outside the tiny village of Arlington. It was originally a gamekeeper's cottage, which was restored and enlarged in 1922 and is part of a 130-acre working farm. Carolyn McCutchan is a keen gardener and her lovely garden is regularly open to the public under the National Gardens Scheme. An ancient woodland renowned for its May bluebells is also on the property, as is a hard tennis court. The three *en suite* bedrooms have pleasant views, and there is both a downstairs and upstairs sitting-room, one with a log fire in winter. Breakfast is served in the attractive dining-room, and light evening meals are also available by arrangement, to which guests can bring their own wine. On arrival, visitors are welcomed with tea and home-made cake. Bates Green is three miles from the South Downs, and only eight miles from Eastbourne and Glyndebourne.

OWNER: Carolyn McCutchan OPEN: all year exc Christmas ROOMS: 1 double, 2 twin; all rooms with bath/shower; TV in all bedrooms TERMS: single occupancy from £30, twin/double £42–£52; dinner £15 CARDS: none DETAILS: no children under 10; no dogs; no smoking; car park; garden; tennis

ARNSIDE Cumbria   map 8

Stonegate

The Promenade, Arnside, nr Carnforth LA5 0AA
TEL: (01524) 761171
from M6 junction 35 take A6 to Milnthorpe, then B5282 to Arnside

David and Jayne Thornhill took over Stonegate in March 1994. This is their first venture in the bed-and-breakfast business, and they are an enthusiastic and friendly couple. The house was built in 1882 and is situated on the promenade with commanding views of the Kent Estuary and the Lakeland hills. The rooms to the front and the dining-room have sea views. The bedrooms have attractive stencilled furniture and share a shower room with WC, plus an additional WC. Evening meals are no longer served, but there is a pub within walking distance.

OWNERS: Jayne and David Thornhill OPEN: all year exc Christmas ROOMS: 1 double, 1 twin, 1 family; all rooms with wash-basin; TV in all bedrooms TERMS: single occupancy £17, twin/double £34, family room from £34; babies free, reductions for children under 12; deposit: £5 per person per night CARDS: none DETAILS: children welcome; no dogs; no smoking; garden

Willowfield

The Promenade, Arnside, nr Carnforth LA5 0AD
TEL: (01524) 761354

This 100-year-old stone house looks out over the Kent Estuary and the hills of the Lake District. The ambience is warm and friendly and the house is clean and comfortable with a mixture of furnishing styles; one bedroom boasts a brass bed. Filling four-course dinners are served in the dining-room; vegetarians can be catered for with advance notice. Owner Ian Kerr has on display several of his own sunset photographs of the view from the house – a view which can be enjoyed for real from the relaxing lounge after a day out in this popular area for walking, bird-watching and exploring the lakes.

OWNERS: Ian and Janet Kerr   OPEN: all year   ROOMS: 2 single, both with wash-basin; 3 double, 2 with bath/shower, 1 with wash-basin; 3 twin, all with bath/shower; 2 family, 1 with bath/shower, 1 with wash-basin; TV in all bedrooms   TERMS: single £19, single occupancy £29, twin/double £38–£42, family room £48–£53; children's reductions; dinner £10; deposit: 50%   CARDS: Access, Visa   DETAILS: children welcome; well-behaved dogs welcome (not on beds); no smoking; car park; garden

ASHBOURNE   Derbyshire   map 5

Collycroft Farm

nr Ashbourne DE6 2GN
TEL: (01335) 342187
just off A515, 2m N of Ashbourne

This whitewashed 250-year old farmhouse is approached up a private lane surrounded by open fields and woodland, and is part of a 25-acre beef and dairy farm. The house has lovely old-fashioned furnishings and is warm and friendly, with a comfortable lounge. There are no wash-basins in the bedrooms, but one has an *en suite* bathroom and the other two have exclusive use of a large bathroom with both bath and shower. Breakfasts are served at times to suit guests and include home-made jams. Prince Charles was a visitor here and was served some of owner Mary Hollingsworth's damson jam. Guests are welcome to explore the farm, which is only a five-minute drive away from Ashbourne, where there are several pubs and restaurants.

OWNER: Mary Hollingsworth   OPEN: all year exc Christmas   ROOMS: 1 double, with bath/shower; 1 twin; 1 family; TV in all bedrooms   TERMS: single occupancy £16–£18, twin/double £36, family room from £32; reductions for children under 10   CARDS: none DETAILS: children welcome; no dogs; no smoking in bedrooms; car park; garden

ASHFORD   Derbyshire   map 9

Corner Cottage

10 Court Lane, Ashford, nr Bakewell DE45 1QG
TEL: (01629) 813985

This pretty stone-built sixteenth-century cottage, with colourful hanging baskets in summer, is in a peaceful spot in an unspoilt village, known locally as Ashford-in-the-Water. There are beams, thick stone walls, creaking floors and low ceilings. Elisabeth Towne has completely redecorated the property herself in pastel colours. Both bedrooms have *en suite* bathrooms; one has a king-sized bed. Breakfast is usually served until 9.30am. Lots of books and information on the area are available to guests. Although evening meals are not served, packed lunches can be requested and the nearby pub does food. There is no private car park, but the adjacent public one is free.

OWNER: Elizabeth Towne OPEN: all year exc Christmas ROOMS: 2 double, both with bath/shower; TV in both bedrooms TERMS: single occupancy £25, double £38; half-price for children; deposit: £10 per night CARDS: none DETAILS: children welcome; dogs welcome

ASHFORD Kent   map 3

River Hall Coach House

Biddenden, nr Ashford TN27 8JE
TEL: (01580) 291565   FAX: (01580) 292137
off A262, 2m from Biddenden

This attractive country house is set in peaceful countryside down a narrow lane. The oldest part of the house dates back to the fifteenth century and was moved from the centre of Biddenden to its present site about a hundred years ago. The lower part of the building served as a market, and the upper part was used as a meeting house, and is now a most attractive and spacious bedroom. Below is the guests' sitting-room. Breakfast is served in either the dining-room or the spacious conservatory, which overlooks the terrace and garden. Evening meals are available by arrangement. The house is only a ten-minute drive from Sissinghurst Gardens, and there are many other National Trust properties nearby.

OWNERS: Sara and Bill Sleigh OPEN: all year exc Christmas ROOMS: 2 twin, both with bath/shower; TV in all bedrooms TERMS: single occupancy £30, twin £50; dinner £16.50 CARDS: none DETAILS: no children under 12; no dogs; no smoking; car park; garden

ASHTON KEYNES Wiltshire   map 2

Two Cove House

Ashton Keynes SN6 6NS
TEL: (01285) 861221
off A419 Cirencester to Swindon road

This sixteenth-century Cotswold manor house with historical associations with the Civil War is set in a pretty garden, in the centre of a village that is part of the Cotswold Water Park. Two Cove House is a comfortable old-fashioned family home. The large beamed drawing-room is in the oldest part of the house, and another small lounge for guests' use has detailed wall maps and lots of brochures to help visitors plan their activities. Barbecues are sometimes held in summer on the patio or in the garden. Dinner is served by arrangement, with the Hartlands often joining their guests.

OWNERS: Peter and Elizabeth Hartland OPEN: all year exc Christmas ROOMS: 1 double, 2 twin; all rooms with bath/shower; TV lounge TERMS: single occupancy £33–£35, twin/double £46–£50; reductions for children sharing with parents; dinner £16.50; deposit: £20 CARDS: none DETAILS: no children under 10 at dinner; small dogs welcome; no smoking during meals; car park; garden

ASHWATER Devon   map 1

Renson Mill

Ashwater, nr Holsworthy EX21 5ER
TEL/FAX: (01409) 211665
8m N of Stowford Cross intersection on A30 between Launceston and Okehampton

This attractively converted grain mill and barn overlooks open countryside, and is just one mile north of the village of Ashwater. The Archers are an interesting and hospitable couple who lived in the Far East before their retirement. Guests are accommodated in a separate wing of the house, and enjoy a large and well-furnished twin-bedded room, bathroom and a small sitting-room with TV, which is sometimes used as a single bedroom. This part of the house has access from the courtyard. Breakfast is served in the farmhouse-style kitchen, where the corn was originally ground when this was a working mill; packed lunches can be provided. Detailed directions to the house are given with the booking confirmation.

OWNERS: Sonia and Geoffrey Archer OPEN: all year exc Christmas and New Year ROOMS: 1 twin, with bath/shower; TV lounge TERMS: rates include dinner; single £30, single occupancy £35, twin £60–£70; free for child in own cot; deposit: £50 for 2 nights or more CARDS: none DETAILS: children by special request only; no dogs; no smoking; car park; garden

AVETON GIFFORD Devon   map 1

Court Barton Farmhouse

Aveton Gifford, nr Kingsbridge TQ7 4LE
TEL/FAX: (01548) 550312
just off A379 Modbury to Kingsbridge road

Dating from the sixteenth century, this charming creeper-covered, stone-built farmhouse sits above the village beside the ancient Norman church. John and Jill Balkwill are the third generation of the family to live in the house, which has a friendly atmosphere and particularly welcomes children. Entry to the farmhouse is by a striking porchway with a heavy front door, which leads into a flagstoned hallway. The oldest part of the house has an interesting spiral staircase. The spacious bedrooms are simply furnished and decorated. A TV, books and magazines can be found in the comfortable lounge, and breakfast only is served in the dining-room. Visitors are welcome to use the swimming-pool and games room. Packed lunches can be provided. Aveton Gifford is convenient for local beaches and only 30 minutes' drive from Dartmoor.

OWNERS: John and Jill Balkwill OPEN: all year exc Christmas ROOMS: 1 single, 2 double, 2 twin, all with bath/shower; 2 family, 1 with bath/shower, 1 with wash-basin; TV in some bedrooms and lounge TERMS: single from £20, single occupancy from £25, twin/double from £36, family room from £45; reductions for children sharing with parents; deposit: 25% CARDS: none DETAILS: children welcome; no dogs; no smoking in breakfast room; car park; garden; swimming-pool

AXMINSTER   Devon   map 2

Millbrook Farm

Chard Road, Axminster EX13 5EG
TEL: (01297) 35351
just off A358

This chocolate-box-pretty, whitewashed and thatched farmhouse dates in part from the tenth century, and is beautifully maintained. It is set in extensive flower-filled gardens with trim lawns and paths, in a rural spot just outside Axminster. The comfortable house is well furnished, with attractive bedrooms. Evening meals using home-made and home-grown produce are available by arrangement in the beamed dining-room, where guests share a communal table. Visitors should bring their own wine as there is no licence; children's helpings, packed lunches and vegetarian choices can be provided on request. The lounge has an inglenook fireplace and beams, and there is a small conservatory. The garden has lots of seats, children's swings and a croquet and badminton set.

OWNERS: J.T. and Sybil Gay OPEN: all year exc Christmas, 2 weeks autumn, 3 weeks winter ROOMS: 2 double; 1 family, with bath/shower; TV in all bedrooms and lounge TERMS: single occupancy £18–£20, double £31–£36; family room from £36; reductions for children under 11 sharing with parents; dinner £10.50; deposit: £10 CARDS: none DETAILS: children welcome; no dogs; no smoking; car park; garden

Many B&Bs offer tea/coffee-making facilities in the bedroom.

If you disagree with any assessment made in this guide, please write and tell us why. Address your letter to The Good Bed and Breakfast Guide, FREEPOST, 2 Marylebone Road, London NW1 1YN.

AYLSHAM   Norfolk   map 6

Old Bank House

3 Norwich Road, Aylsham NR11 6BN
TEL: (01263) 733843

The Old Bank House is an elegant red-brick building dating from
1613. Originally part of it was an inn; later the house became a
private bank. The three traditionally furnished bedrooms are
decorated with Laura Ashley fabrics. The double room has a
Victorian bath and one of the beds in the family room is a half-tester.
Among several interesting features in the house are the pillared hall,
minstrels' gallery and Queen Anne panelling. The cellar provides a
sauna, table-tennis and darts. Guests also have use of a sitting-room
with toys, and a walled garden with pond and swing. Breakfast takes
in a good selection of home-made jams and marmalade. Freshly
prepared home-cooked dinners are available at 7pm, if pre-booked;
children's helpings and vegetarian choices can be requested. Enid
Parry is a super host who has created a warm and friendly ambience
in her interesting home.

OWNER: Enid Parry OPEN: all year exc Christmas ROOMS: 1 double, with bath/shower;
1 twin, with wash-basin; 1 family, with wash-basin; TV in all bedrooms and lounge
TERMS: single occupancy £17–£20, twin/double £34, family room from £34; children
under 2 free, £10 for ages 2 to 14; dinner £9.50; deposit: £10 per room CARDS: none
DETAILS: children welcome; dogs by arrangement; smoking in lounge only; car park;
games room; garden

BABWORTH   Nottinghamshire   map 9

Barns Country Guest House

Morton Farm, Babworth DN22 8HA
TEL: (01777) 706336   FAX: (01777) 709773
on B6420, 1¼m W of East Retford

This beautifully restored eighteenth-century barn, with its original
beams and bricks, is set in a quiet rural area. The well-appointed
bedrooms are colour co-ordinated with warm floral patterns, are
furnished in pine and have *en suite* bathrooms. One with sloping
ceilings is particularly attractive. Breakfasts cooked on the Aga are
served in the large beamed dining-room, and there is a separate TV
lounge. Packed lunches can be provided.

OWNER: Rosalie Brammer OPEN: all year exc Christmas ROOMS: 1 single, 3 double, 1
twin, 1 family; all rooms with bath/shower; TV in all bedrooms TERMS: single £25, single
occupancy £29, twin/double £40–£47, family room £50–£60; deposit: £10 per person
CARDS: Access, Amex, Delta, Visa DETAILS: children welcome; no dogs; smoking in
sitting-room only; car park; garden

Chestnut Farmhouse

The Street, Baconsthorpe, nr Holt NR25 6AB
TEL: (01263) 577614
off A148, 3m SE of Holt

This whitewashed seventeenth-century property is situated in a
quiet village six miles from the North Norfolk coast. Its two spacious
bedrooms have a chintzy décor, *en suite* showers, TV and a sitting
area. Some of the furniture is custom-made by Roger Bacon, who also
sells his work. Margaret's main concern is the food: breakfasts are a
banquet and consist of freshly baked bread, home-made preserves,
fruit, yoghurts, cereals and a large cooked platter. The Strawberry
Parlour and garden, where light lunches and afternoon teas are
served in summer, are also open to the public. Chestnut Farmhouse
has a warm and friendly atmosphere and makes a good base for
exploring the area.

OWNERS: Margaret and Roger Bacon OPEN: all year ROOMS: 1 double, 1 twin; both
rooms with shower; TV in both bedrooms TERMS: twin/double £45–£50 CARDS: none
DETAILS: no children; no dogs; no smoking; car park; garden

Glenander

Lucker Road, Bamburgh NE69 7BS
TEL: (01668) 214336

This warm and welcoming turn-of-the-century house stands to the
west of the village, a short walk from the castle. The house is in good
decorative order, the bedrooms are of a good size, have large *en suite*
bathrooms and are attractively decorated in pink, blue and peach; all
have TVs and hair-dryers. Eileen McDougal is an accommodating
hostess, whose many years of experience in the hotel trade ensure
guests are provided with just about every comfort in an informal
atmosphere. Piping-hot breakfasts are served in the pine-furnished
dining-room, and for evening meals a portfolio of local eating
establishments has been compiled. The spacious lounge is a good spot
to relax in after a busy day on the beach. Although there is no car
park, on-street parking is possible outside the house.

OWNER: Eileen McDougal OPEN: all year exc Christmas ROOMS: 1 double, 2 twin; all
rooms with bath/shower; TV in all bedrooms and lounge TERMS: twin/double £40–£50;
deposit: by arrangement for new guests CARDS: none DETAILS: children welcome;
dogs welcome; no smoking

Green Gates

34 Front Street, Bamburgh NE69 7BJ
TEL: (01668) 214535

This late-Victorian house is only 100 yards from Bamburgh Castle at the bottom of this attractive village. The bedrooms are decorated on a theme of poppies and two have views out to the castle and extending, on clear days, as far as Holy Island. Guests can relax with a selection of books and games in the large lounge, which has an open fire. Breakfasts are served in the dining-room, recently redecorated in blue. Derek Walton's Fire Brigade memorabilia and a small aviation museum can be viewed on request.

OWNER: Mrs E.F. Walton   OPEN: all year exc Christmas and New Year   ROOMS: 1 double, 2 family; all rooms with wash-basin; TV lounge   TERMS: single occupancy £22, double £35, family room £35 plus children's charge; half-price for children sharing with parents; deposit: £20   CARDS: none   DETAILS: children welcome; house-trained dogs welcome; smoking in lounge only; car park; garden

BARDFIELD END GREEN   Essex   **map 3**

Wellcroft

Bardfield End Green, nr Thaxted CM6 3PX
TEL: 01371 830548
from B184 at Thaxted take Bardfield road for ½m, take left turn at triangle, house is on right after ¼m

This enchanting 300-year-old country cottage stands in an acre of traditional gardens with herbaceous borders, surrounded by open farmland. There is just one twin-bedded room, which has its own sitting-room, TV and luxury bathroom. Visitors also have use of an attractively furnished lounge, which has a grandfather clock and an open fireplace. Wellcroft retains its original oak beams, fireplaces and charm. Ruth Gooch-Harris is a charming hostess who takes excellent care of her guests and prepares breakfasts to order on the Aga. Low-fat and special diets can be catered for with advance notice. This is an excellent base from which to explore rural Essex and Suffolk.

OWNER: Ruth Gooch-Harris   OPEN: all year exc Christmas   ROOMS: 1 twin, with bath/shower   TERMS: single occupancy £20, twin £40   CARDS: none   DETAILS: no children; no dogs; no smoking; car park; garden

Use the maps and indexes at the back of the Guide to plan your trip.

If we know of any particular payment stipulations, we mention them in the details at the end of the entry. However, it is always best to check when booking.

BARNARD CASTLE   Co Durham   map 10

Marwood View

98 Galgate, Barnard Castle DL12 8BJ
TEL: (01833) 637493

Behind a line of trees and a well-stocked garden Marwood View combines the convenience of proximity to the main Darlington to Bishop Auckland road with peaceful home comforts. Soft pastel shades in the bedrooms, home-made biscuits by the bed and even a sauna in the converted cellar combine to relax and pamper. For the more energetic a fitness room is also available. Sheila Kilgarriff has made all the curtains and duvet covers herself and the fine embroidery on display is also her work. The Kilgarriffs are equally skilled in the kitchen, where they produce well-presented, good-value evening meals (served at 6.30–7pm). Vegetarians can be catered for and guests are welcome to bring their own wine. The bedrooms all have satellite TV. Marwood View is well placed for touring and exploring the region and for visiting the historic town of Barnard Castle.

OWNERS: John and Sheila Kilgarriff   OPEN: all year   ROOMS: 2 single, 3 double; all rooms with bath/shower; TV in all bedrooms   TERMS: single £18, single occupancy £24, twin/ double £38; dinner £10; deposit: £10   CARDS: none   DETAILS: no children under 10; small dogs by arrangement; no smoking; car park; garden

BASHLEY   Hampshire   map 2

Yew Tree Farm

Bashley Common Road, Bashley, nr New Milton BH25 5SH
TEL: (01425) 611041
on B3058, 1m E of A35 Lyndhurst to Christchurch road

This picturesque thatched New Forest smallholding dates from the early eighteenth century. Its land extends to 12 grazing acres bounded by traditional hedges, and supports cattle, an Arab mare and a flock of hens. There is usually a spare stable, grazing and a sand arena for a visiting horse. Guests can enjoy the delightful cottage garden from the patio area with its chairs and table. The Matthews have lived here for nearly 30 years, and Mrs Matthews has done much of the renovation and decoration herself, to a high standard. She is considerate of guests' needs and provides excellent food. There is no communal sitting-room, but the bedrooms have armchairs; breakfast is served at tables in the bedrooms at any time until 11am. Dinner, by arrangement, is served in the hall or bedrooms. Lots of choice on the à la carte menu includes vegetarian options; guests may bring their own wine as there is no alcohol licence. Yew Tree Farm is in a lovely area of the New Forest, about four miles from the coast.

OWNERS: Mr and Mrs Gordon Matthews OPEN: all year exc owners' holidays ROOMS: 1 double, 1 twin; both rooms with bath/shower; TV in both bedrooms TERMS: single occupancy £35–£40, twin/double £50–£60; dinner from £12.50; deposit: by arrangement CARDS: none DETAILS: no children; no dogs; no smoking; car park; garden

BASSINGTHORPE   Lincolnshire   map 6

Sycamore Farm

Lower Bassingthorpe, nr Grantham NG33 4ED
TEL: (01476) 585274
off A1 / just off B6403, 6m SE of Grantham

This red-brick Victorian farmhouse set in gentle rolling countryside is part of a 450-acre mixed beef, sheep and barley farm, which has been in the family for four generations. The welcome is warm and the Robinsons are dedicated to ensuring their guests are well taken care of. There are three spacious bedrooms with traditional and antique furniture; two have *en suite* bathrooms. The guest lounge is comfortable and contains board games, a piano and TV. Breakfasts are served family-style, and there are several places within an easy drive for other meals (packed lunches can be provided, however). Interested visitors are welcome to explore the farm.

OWNERS: Phil and Sue Robinson OPEN: Mar to end Nov ROOMS: 2 double, 1 with bath/shower, 1 with wash-basin; 1 twin, with bath/shower; TV in all bedrooms TERMS: single occupancy £20, twin/double £36–£40 CARDS: none DETAILS: no children under 10; no dogs; no smoking; car park; garden

BATH   Avon   map 2

Bathurst

11 Walcot Parade, London Street, Bath BA1 5NF
TEL: (01225) 421884

This listed eighteenth-century townhouse is on an elevated terrace by a busy road, adjacent to Hedgemead Park and just a few minutes' level walk from the city centre. Double glazing keeps out most of the traffic noise. The four-poster bedroom has co-ordinated drapes and a wall frieze and is decorated in rich, cosy colours. This and one other room are *en suite*; for the other rooms a trip to the bathroom means going to another floor, and bathrobes are thoughtfully provided for this purpose. The comfortable lounge is equipped with a games table, puzzles and a piano. Guests would be well advised to leave their car here and walk or take the bus into the city centre.

OWNERS: Elizabeth Tovey OPEN: all year exc Christmas ROOMS: 2 single, both with wash-basin; 1 double, with wash-basin; 2 twin, 1 with bath/shower, 1 with wash-basin;

, with bath/shower; TV in all bedrooms TERMS: single £17, single
£22, twin/double £34–£39, four-poster £39; children under 3 free; deposit:
DS: none DETAILS: children welcome; no dogs; no smoking; car park; garden

---

Bloomfield House

146 Bloomfield Road, Bath BA2 2AS
TEL: (01225) 420105   FAX: (01225) 481958

Bridget and Malcolm Cox took over this imposing Grade II listed
property in February 1994. It was built in the 1820s by one of Bath's
leading architects, and is situated on a quiet residential street half a
mile from the city centre. The house has been sympathetically
restored, retaining most of the original features but providing all the
modern comforts. Most of the well-furnished bedrooms are located on
the second floor, and each has a private bathroom. The top floor has a
splendid four-poster bedroom ideal for honeymooners; another
bedroom has an eighteenth-century four-poster bed. There is a large
drawing-room for guests' use, and two self-catering apartments are
also available. Breakfast only is served, but packed lunches can be
provided.

OWNERS: Bridget and Malcolm Cox OPEN: all year ROOMS: 1 single, 2 double, 1 twin, 4
four-poster; all rooms with bath/shower; TV in all bedrooms TERMS: single £35–£40,
single occupancy £45, twin/double £50–£75, four-poster £75–£95; deposit: 50% or
credit card details CARDS: Access, Visa DETAILS: no children; no dogs; no smoking;
garden

Cranleigh

159 Newbridge Hill, Bath BA1 3PX
TEL: (01225) 310197   FAX: (01225) 423143

This impeccably maintained, tastefully refurbished Victorian house
is on a gentle rise about a mile from the city centre. The bedrooms,
two of which are on the ground floor, are beautifully decorated with
rich fabrics made by Chris Webber. All have comfortable beds and the
luxury four-poster bedroom has a peach and green canopy. The
enormous family room has a settee and armchairs. The Webbers are a
friendly, charming couple who work as a team to provide every
comfort for their guests. Breakfast is a banquet, starting with a help-
yourself selection laid out on the antique sideboard, followed by a
choice of seven cooked courses. The large dining-room includes a
comfortable sitting area with TV.

OWNERS: Arthur and Christine Webber OPEN: all year ROOMS: 2 double, 1 twin, 1 four-
poster, 1 family; all rooms with bath/shower; TV in all bedrooms TERMS: single
occupancy £38, twin/double £58, four-poster £75; children's reductions by
arrangement; deposit: £20 CARDS: Access, Visa DETAILS: children by arrangement; no
dogs; no smoking; car park; garden

Greenways

1 Forester Road, Bathwick, Bath BA2 6QF
TEL/FAX: (01225) 310132

Greenways is a pleasant Victorian house on the corner of a quiet
street ten minutes' walk from the city centre. The three attractive
bedrooms are boldly decorated with co-ordinated chintzes and
traditional Victorian furnishings. The guests' lounge is comfortable,
with a large fireplace and many antiques. Breakfasts include
wholefood and traditional options and are served in the pretty dining-
room.

OWNER: Mrs P.A. Goldsmith   OPEN: all year exc Christmas   ROOMS: 2 double, 1 twin; all
rooms with bath/shower; TV in all bedrooms   TERMS: single occupancy £35–£40, twin/
double £40–£50; children under 3 free; deposit: £10   CARDS: none   DETAILS: children
welcome; dogs welcome; car park; garden

Haydon House

9 Bloomfield Park, Bath BA2 2BY
TEL/FAX: (01225) 444919/427351

The approach to this Edwardian house on a quiet residential street is
lined with a display of flowers and hanging baskets. The residence is
beautifully maintained and the bedrooms are exquisitely decorated
with soft, restful colours; all bedrooms have their own bathrooms.
There is a family suite on the top floor. Many fine dried-flower
arrangements are on show, all created by Magdalene Ashman-Marr.
An elegant sitting-room overlooks the flower-bedecked patio. A well-
established garden surrounds the house and guests can sit out here
in fine weather and even take breakfast on the terrace. Magdalene
and her husband have created a guesthouse that is both welcoming
and refined.

OWNERS: Gordon Marr and Magdalene Ashman-Marr   OPEN: all year   ROOMS: 3 double,
1 twin, 1 family; all rooms with bath/shower; TV in all bedrooms   TERMS: single
occupancy £40–£50, twin/double £55–£70, family room £75; deposit: 1 night's charge
or credit card details   CARDS: Access, Amex, Delta, Visa   DETAILS: children by prior
arrangement; no dogs; no smoking; garden

Leighton House

139 Wells Road, Bath BA2 3AL
TEL: (01225) 314769   FAX: (01225) 443079
on A367 Exeter road

This splendid Victorian residence was built in 1873, has fine views
over Bath and the surrounding hills, and is only a ten-minute walk or
a short minibus ride to the city centre. The house has a pleasant,

informal atmosphere and has a comfortable lounge overlooking the garden, and a dining-room where breakfast only is served. Some of the tastefully decorated bedrooms are very large and all have *en suite* facilities; two are on the ground floor.

OWNERS: David and Kathleen Slape   OPEN: all year   ROOMS: 4 double, 3 twin, 1 family; all rooms with bath/shower; TV in all bedrooms   TERMS: single occupancy £42, twin/double £58–£66, family room £80–£90; deposit: £20 per person   CARDS: Access, Delta, Visa   DETAILS: children welcome; no dogs; no smoking in dining-room; car park; garden

Meadowland

36 Bloomfield Park, Bath BA2 2BX
TEL: (01225) 311079   FAX: (01452) 304507

Meadowlands is set in half an acre of secluded gardens in a quiet residential area about one mile out of the city centre. The spacious bedrooms are individually decorated to a high standard and tastefully furnished in a detailed recreation of Georgian style. They are impeccably maintained and equipped with TV, hair-dryer, tea and coffee tray and a trouser press. The large, comfortable drawing-room has a wide selection of books and magazines. Breakfast is served in the charming dining-room, where guests may choose from an imaginative menu. Special diets can be catered for with notice. Evening meals are available at the local pub and the owners are able to recommend a number of personally tried-and-tested restaurants.

OWNER: Catherine Andrew   OPEN: all year exc Christmas   ROOMS: 2 double, 1 twin; all rooms with bath/shower; TV in all bedrooms and lounge   TERMS: single occupancy £40–£45, twin/double £55–£65; deposit required   CARDS: Access, Visa   DETAILS: children welcome; no dogs; no smoking; car park; garden

Somerset House

35 Bathwick Hill, Bath BA2 6LD
TEL: (01225) 466451   FAX: (01225) 317188

Set in a most attractive garden which contains the largest Judas tree in England, this elegant Regency mansion is described by its owners as a restaurant-with-rooms. The Seymours have a passion for food, particularly traditional English cooking, and use home-grown and locally produced ingredients. B&B guests are encouraged to take their evening meals here; there are vegetarian options and an interesting wine list (half a bottle is included in the dinner price). Dinner is served family-style at 7pm (7.30pm on Saturdays; no dinner on Sundays), and Sunday lunch is available. The comfortable bedrooms and two well-furnished lounges retain their original grand proportions.

OWNERS: Malcolm and Jean Seymour   OPEN: all year   ROOMS: 1 single, 4 double, 3 twin, 2 family; all rooms with bath/shower; TV lounge   TERMS: single £20–£31.50, single occupancy £36–£47.50, twin/double £40–£63, family room £58–£88; half-price for children 3 to 10, two-thirds for ages 10 to 13; dinner £22.50; deposit: £20 per person   CARDS: Access, Amex, Visa   DETAILS: children welcome; no dogs in dining-room; no smoking; car park; garden

BATHFORD   Avon   map 2

The Old School House

Church Street, Bathford BA1 7RR
TEL: (01225) 859593   FAX: (01225) 859590
off A4 at junction with A363 to Bradford-on-Avon; after 100 yards turn left in front of Crown pub, then after 200 yards left into Church Street

Built as the village school in 1837, the property became a private house in the early 1970s and has been cleverly converted to provide very pleasant accommodation. The hall still has the school's original bell-pull, and this leads into the old schoolroom, which is now a large sitting/dining-room with wood-burning stove and comfortable armchairs and sofas. Off this is a small conservatory which overlooks the walled garden. Two of the cosily furnished bedrooms are on the ground floor; one is suitable for wheelchair-users. There are some lovely walks through nearby woodland, and Bath, only three miles away, can be reached via a towpath walk along the canal.

OWNERS: Sonia and Rodney Stone   OPEN: all year exc Christmas   ROOMS: 2 double, 2 twin; all rooms with bath/shower; TV in all bedrooms; 1 room suitable for wheelchair-users   TERMS: single occupancy £48–£60, twin/double £65–£70; deposit: £30 or credit card details   CARDS: Access, Visa   DETAILS: no children under 8; no dogs; no smoking; car park; garden

BATTLE   East Sussex   map 3

Kitchenham Farm

Ashburnham, nr Battle TN33 9NP
TEL/FAX: (01424) 892221
on A271 5m SW of Battle

This ivy-clad, welcoming Georgian farmhouse is a comparative youngster alongside the neighbouring listed oast house and other farm buildings. It stands in 820 acres of working farmland, but guests are welcome to walk through meadows and bluebell woods, and coarse fishing is available on the river which runs through the farm. The elegantly furnished house has a relaxed atmosphere and floral and pastel decorations in the bedrooms. The three bedrooms share two bathrooms, and there is an additional ground-floor WC. The sitting-room has a large open fireplace, and evening meals are served by arrangement.

OWNERS: Monty and Amanda Worssam OPEN: all year exc Christmas ROOMS: 1 double with wash-basin; 2 twin, 1 with wash-basin; TV lounge TERMS: single occupancy £20–£25, twin/double £34–£36, family room £40–£50; children under 2 free; dinner £4–£5; deposit: £20 CARDS: none DETAILS: children welcome; no dogs in bedrooms; no smoking; car park; garden

BEDALE   North Yorkshire   map 9

Hyperion House

88 South End, Bedale DL8 2DS
TEL: (01677) 422334

This attractive house is situated at the south end of Bedale, the gateway to the Dales. There are three immaculately clean, comfortable bedrooms; the two doubles now have *en suite* factilities. The well-furnished lounge has TV and video, and guests may be interested in seeing Ron Dean's own video of the local area. The Deans are a warm and friendly couple, and upon arrival guests are greeted with home-baked scones and tea. Breakfast only is served, but packed lunches can be provided on request.

OWNERS: Ron and Sheila Dean OPEN: all year exc Christmas and New Year ROOMS: 2 double, 1 twin; all rooms with bath/shower; TV in all bedrooms and lounge TERMS: single occupancy £25, twin/double £36–£40; children's reductions by arrangement; deposit: £20 CARDS: none DETAILS: no children under 8; no dogs; no smoking; car park; garden

Southfield

96 South End, Bedale DL8 2DS
TEL: (01677) 423510

This 1930s house with a lovely front garden is just five minutes' walk from the centre of Bedale. The house is immaculate, and is decorated in shades of peach. There are no *en suite* rooms, but there are two bathrooms for guests. Mrs Keighley enjoys personal contact with her visitors, tea is offered on arrival and, in the evening, hot chocolate is served in the comfortable lounge at no extra charge. Although no meals other than breakfast are served, packed lunches can be provided for those journeying forth.

OWNERS: Marjorie and Arthur Keighley OPEN: all year exc Christmas ROOMS: 1 single, 1 double, 1 twin, 1 family; all rooms with wash-basin exc single; TV lounge TERMS: single £15, single occupancy £16, twin/double £32; family room price by arrangement; deposit: £5 per person CARDS: none DETAILS: children welcome; no dogs; no smoking; car park; garden

It is always best to check prices, especially for single occupancy, when booking.

Frog Street Farm

Beercrocombe, nr Taunton TA3 6AF
TEL: (01823) 480430
leave A358 at Hatch Inn and follow Station Road, take first left and
continue past turning to Beercrocombe

Frog Street Farm is a large stone farmhouse covered in wistaria, with
many original fifteenth-century features, including beams and
inglenook fireplaces, and Jacobean panelling. It is part of a 130-acre
dairy farm tucked away down a country lane and private track and
takes its curious name from a corruption of the Anglo-Saxon for
'meeting place'. The bedrooms are comfortable and simply decorated.
A large dining-room, two sitting-rooms and a small writing room,
which used to be the cider press, provide plenty of unwinding space
for guests. There are pleasant views from the house and it is
surrounded by a lawned garden with a heated swimming-pool.
Dinner, by arrangement, is prepared using home-grown and local
produce, including salmon from the River Severn, and vegetarian
options are available on request. Places to visit in the area include
Tintinhull House and Muchelney Abbey.

OWNERS: Veronica and Henry Cole OPEN: Mar to Oct ROOMS: 3 double, all with bath/
shower; TV lounge TERMS: single occupancy £30, double £54; dinner £16 CARDS:
none DETAILS: no children under 11; no dogs; no smoking; car park; garden

Whittles Farm

Beercrocombe, nr Taunton TA3 6AH
TEL: (01823) 480301
on A358 turn at sign for Beercrocombe, fork right down Radigan Lane then
1st left after railway bridge

This 200-acre working dairy farm is at the end of a 'no through road'
in the pretty countryside between the Quantock and Blackdown hills.
It is an attractive virginia-creeper-covered sixteenth-century
farmhouse with nineteenth-century additions to the front. Sustaining
breakfasts are served in the large dining-room, at one table and
dinner is eaten in the smaller, cosier dining-room at the rear of the
house, which has an open fire. The farm also produces small
quantities of beef, turkey and lamb which Claire Mitchem uses in her
home-cooked evening meals. The spacious and cosy bedrooms are
prettily decorated and guests also have use of a comfortable sitting-
room. Wesley Lodge, a well-equipped self-catering annexe converted
from a barn, adjoins the farmhouse. Whittles Farm is a mile from the
village of Beercrocombe and seven miles from Taunton.

OWNER: Claire Mitchem OPEN: Feb to Nov ROOMS: 2 double, 1 twin; all rooms with bath/shower; TV in all bedrooms TERMS: single/single occupancy £27, twin/double £44; dinner £13; deposit required CARDS: none DETAILS: no children under 12; no dogs; no smoking in bedrooms; car park

BELLERBY North Yorkshire   map 9

Old Hall

Bellerby DL8 5QP
TEL: (01969) 623028
on A684 from Leyburn to Richmond

This listed sixteenth-century house is in the centre of the village, and has a stream in front. The property is well maintained, clean and comfortable. The large beamed bedrooms are simply furnished; one was originally the priest's hole. Breakfast and evening meals are available, and although Old Hall is unlicensed, guests are welcome to bring their own wine to dinner; packed lunches can be provided.

OWNERS: Richard and Ann Travell OPEN: all year exc end of Dec ROOMS: 1 double, 1 twin; both rooms with wash-basin; 1 family, with bath/shower; TV lounge TERMS: single occupancy £21, twin/double £34, family room from £45; half-price for children sharing with parents; dinner £7–£8.50; deposit: £25 CARDS: none DETAILS: children welcome; no dogs; no smoking in bedrooms; car park; garden

BELLINGHAM Northumberland   map 11

Westfield House

Bellingham, nr Hexham NE48 2DP
TEL/FAX: (01434) 220340
on B6320 opposite fire station in Bellingham

This large Victorian house is approached along a tree-lined drive with lovely views all round. Guests continue to applaud the friendly, relaxing atmosphere and the stylish evening meals made with local and home-grown ingredients. The house is beautifully decorated and new carpets have been laid. Several original features remain, including some interesting fireplaces, and the ground-floor bedroom has an elegant four-poster bed. The sitting-room looks out over the garden, where guests are welcome to relax in fine weather. Dinner is a social occasion, with vegetarian and special diets catered for by arrangement, and guests may bring their own wine. Keen walkers will be glad to find that the Pennine Way passes nearby.

OWNERS: David and June Minchin OPEN: all year ROOMS: 1 double, with wash-basin; 2 twin, 1 with bath/shower, 1 with wash-basin; 1 four-poster, with bath/shower; 1 family, with wash-basin; TV lounge TERMS: twin/double £36–£50, four-poster £50; dinner £13.50; deposit CARDS: Access, Visa DETAILS: well-behaved children welcome; dogs welcome; no smoking; car park; garden

Crit Hall

Cranbrook Road, Benenden TN17 4EU
TEL: (01580) 240609   FAX: (01580) 241743
just off B2086 Benenden to Goudhurst road, 1m W of Benenden on left-hand side

Crit Hall is a Georgian country house set in an acre of attractive gardens with beautiful views over the Weald of Kent. The Bruders are a delightful, hospitable couple who took over the house recently and have done a certain amount of redecoration. The three tasteful bedrooms have unusual soft furnishings and guests have their own comfortable drawing-room, conservatory and elegant dining-room, where dinner can be served by arrangement. Crit Hall is within easy reach of Sissinghurst and Great Dixter gardens, Chartwell, and Hever and Leeds castles.

OWNERS: John and Sue Bruder   OPEN: all year exc 15 Dec to 15 Jan   ROOMS: 1 double, 2 twin; all rooms with bath/shower; TV in all bedrooms   TERMS: single occupancy £30, twin/double £48–£50; dinner £17.50   CARDS: Delta, Switch, Visa   DETAILS: no children under 10; no dogs; no smoking; car park; garden

Cherrypit

Cherry Pit Lane, Beoley, nr Redditch B98 9DH
TEL/FAX: (01527) 62454   FAX: (01527) 62454
on B4101, on N outskirts of Redditch

Set in a secluded six-acre garden, Cherrypit is an attractive red-brick 1930s Tudor-style house covered with wistaria, honeysuckle and roses. The immaculate, spacious rooms are well appointed; one *en suite* bedroom is in an annexe. In winter the well-furnished TV lounge and the separate dining-room, where freshly prepared breakfasts and pre-arranged evening meals are served, have open fires, and there is a small conservatory for guests' use.

OWNER: Anne Elizabeth Howles   OPEN: all year   ROOMS: 2 single, both with wash-basin; 2 twin, 1 with shower, 1 with wash-basin; TV in all bedrooms and lounge   TERMS: single £17–£25, single occupancy £17–£25, twin/double £34–£50; children under 5 free, half-price for ages 5-12; dinner £7–£10   CARDS: none   DETAILS: children welcome; dogs by arrangement; no smoking; car park; garden

---

Entries in the Guide are listed under town or village. There are also two indexes at the back of the book, one listing B&Bs by county, the other by name.

Recommendations for B&Bs for our next edition are very welcome.

BERWICK-UPON-TWEED   Northumberland   map 11

Dervaig Guesthouse

1 North Road, Berwick-upon-Tweed TD15 1PW
TEL: (01289) 307378

Dervaig is a lovely Victorian house set in beautiful gardens in a quiet
part of town in an elevated position. The house is impeccably
maintained, and new curtains and furnishings have recently been
added alongside the antiques which complement the original
features. The large bedrooms have armchairs and fireplaces. The
elegant breakfast room has lace tablecloths and pretty crockery, and
an interesting collection of plates is on display. Dinners are available
on request, including vegetarian options, and guests may bring their
own wine. In addition a list of recommended local eating
establishments has been prepared, thoughtfully including the
walking or driving time to each.

OWNERS: Mick and Betty Noble   OPEN: all year exc Christmas   ROOMS: 2 double, 2 twin,
1 family; all rooms with bath/shower; TV in all bedrooms   TERMS: single occupancy
£20–£25, twin/double £38–£46, family room £45–£50; half-price for children under 10;
deposit: £10   CARDS: none   DETAILS: children welcome; dogs welcome; no smoking in
dining-room; car park; garden

---

3 Scott's Place

3 Scott's Place, Berwick-upon-Tweed TD15 1LQ
TEL: (01289) 305323

Quietly situated, this Georgian town house is just two minutes' walk
from the town centre. Jeannette and Paul Blaaser are a retired
couple who work together to provide good-value hospitality and
accommodation. The large bedrooms are either *en suite* or have
private bathrooms. There is a comfortable, old-fashioned sitting-room
with a piano, which guests are welcome to use. Visitors are treated as
members of the family, and tea with home-baked cakes is offered on
arrival. Evening meals include plenty of fresh vegetables and tasty
home-made soups; vegetarians can be catered for and packed lunches
provided. There is on-street parking close by, as well as a public car
park.

OWNER: Jeanette Blaaser   OPEN: all year   ROOMS: 2 double, 1 twin; all rooms with bath/
shower; TV in all bedrooms   TERMS: single occupancy £20–£25, twin/double £30–£40;
dinner £9.50; deposit: £10   CARDS: none   DETAILS: no children; dogs to be kept in
guest's room or garden; no smoking in dining-room; garden

---

*If there are reduced rates for children, this is mentioned in the details at
the end of the entry. If no reductions are specified, assume you will have to
pay full rates for children.*

BETHERSDEN   Kent   **map 3**

Little Hodgeham

Smarden Road, Bethersden TN26 3HE
TEL: (01233) 850323
*off A28 Ashford to Tenterden road, turn right at Bull pub in Bethersden,
then towards Smarden for 2m*

This idyllic half-timbered Tudor cottage is set in rose gardens and
surrounded by wooded farmland. The house, beautifully furnished
and decorated to a high standard, has a TV lounge, library and
garden room. The three charming bedrooms all have *en suite*
facilities. Meals at Little Hodgeham are like intimate dinner parties,
with a maximum of six guests sitting around the elegantly set dining-
room table. Children eat before the adults. The half-acre garden is
delightful and full of colour, the centrepiece being a pond with
waterfalls and pet ducks. There is also a good-sized swimming-pool.
Breakfast can be served in bedrooms if guests prefer, and bed and
breakfast is not available without dinner.

OWNER: Erica Wallace   OPEN: mid-Mar to end Aug   ROOMS: 1 double, 1 twin, 1 four-
poster; all rooms with bath/shower; TV lounge   TERMS: rates include dinner; single
occupancy £59; twin/double £103, four-poster £103; children's reductions according to
age; deposit: £30   CARDS: none   DETAILS: children welcome; no dogs; no smoking in
dining-room; car park; garden; swimming-pool

BEVERLEY   Humberside   **map 9**

Eastgate Guest House

7 Eastgate, Beverley, Hull HU17 0DR
TEL: (01482) 868464   FAX: (01482) 871899

This long-established guesthouse, located in the city centre, offers
clean and friendly accommodation. The bedrooms are fresh and
bright, with a mixture of old-fashioned and modern furniture; three
are on the ground floor. The guest lounge has its original marble
fireplace as well as books giving helpful information on the area.
Light snacks, such as soups and sandwiches, are available until 9pm,
and guests with heartier appetites will find places for evening meals
within walking distance. There is street parking, or free parking at
the nearby rail station.

OWNERS: Colin and Christine Anderson   OPEN: all year   ROOMS: 6 single, 1 with bath/
shower, 5 with wash-basin; 3 double, all with bath/shower; 3 twin, 1 with bath/shower,
2 with wash-basin; 6 family, 1 with bath/shower, 5 with wash-basin; TV in all bedrooms
and lounge   TERMS: single £17.50–£30, twin/double £30–£44   CARDS: none   DETAILS:
children welcome; dogs by arrangement; smoking in visitor's lounge only

Bickford Grange

Bickford, nr Penkridge ST19 5QJ
TEL: (01785) 840257
from M6 junction 12 take A5 west for 2m, then take right turning to Bickford

This impressive, well-maintained Georgian residence stands in two acres of landscaped gardens. There is an elegantly furnished drawing-room, and a splendid staircase leads to four of the good-sized bedrooms, which share three bathrooms between them. The top-floor accommodation, with its two bedroom suite, is ideal for a family or friends travelling together. Breakfasts, and dinners by arrangement, are available, and packed lunches can be provided. Although there is no licence, guests are welcome to bring their own wine to dinner. There is a heated swimming-pool for guests' use in the summer.

OWNER: Gail Bryant   OPEN: all year exc Christmas   ROOMS: 2 single; 1 double, with bath/shower; 3 twin; 1 family, with bath/shower; TV lounge   TERMS: single/single occupancy £18, twin/double £35–£38, family room £40–£60; children's reductions in family room according to age; dinner £10; deposit: £10   CARDS: none   DETAILS: children welcome; dogs by prior arrangement; smoking in lounge only; car park; garden; swimming-pool

Penpark

Bickington, nr Newton Abbot TQ12 6LH
TEL: (01626) 821314   FAX: (01626) 821101
just off A38 between Ashburton and Bovey Tracey; follow signs for Widecombe-in-the-Moor; Penpark is ½m on right at top of hill

This whitewashed, elegant country house stands in five and a half acres of secluded, mature gardens and woodland with a hard tennis court. The property was designed by Sir Clough Williams-Ellis in 1928, and has wonderful views to Dartmoor and as far as the sea. Well-proportioned and spacious rooms are beautifully furnished and decorated. The double/twin room has a balcony, sofa and armchairs and shares a bathroom with a single room (which is only used when required by the same party staying in the large room). There is also an additional double room, new since the last edition of the *Guide*. Breakfast, and dinner by arrangement, are served in the family dining-room. There is no alcohol licence, but guests may bring their own wine to table; vegetarian dishes and children's helpings can be requested. There is a pub within three minutes' drive serving food.

OWNER: Madeleine Gregson   OPEN: all year exc Christmas   ROOMS: 1 double, 1 double/twin; both rooms with bath/shower; TV in both bedrooms and lounge   TERMS: single occupancy £20–£22.50, twin/double £40–£45; children under 2 free, half-price for ages 2 to 10; dinner £15; deposit CARDS: none DETAILS: children welcome; no dogs; no smoking; car park; garden; tennis

BIDDENDEN Kent map 3

Birchley

Fosten Green Lane, Biddenden TN27 8DZ
TEL/FAX: (01580) 291413
from village green take A262 Sissinghurst road, then after 1m first left opposite Garden Crafts Nursery; Birchley is 1m on left

Birchley is reached up a long drive through park-like grounds. It is a listed, timbered house with lattice windows and has been divided into three sections, which is not obvious from the front. The Randalls live in the oldest part, dating from 1632. The three enormous, bright bedrooms have beams and panelling and have been tastefully furnished; they all have glorious views. Breakfast only is served at a long refectory oak table in the large dining-room with its magnificent carved-oak inglenook fireplace, and there is also a panelled sitting-room with log fire. One of Drummond Randall's hobbies is the miniature railway which runs round the grounds, and he also has a small Christmas tree farm adjoining the property. A large covered, heated swimming-pool is available for guests' use.

OWNERS: Jennifer and Drummond Randall OPEN: mid-Jan to end Nov ROOMS: 3 double; all with bath/shower; TV in all bedrooms TERMS: single occupancy £50–£65, double £55–£70, family room £70–£95; deposit: credit card details CARDS: Access, Visa DETAILS: no children under 12; no dogs; no smoking; car park; garden; swimming-pool

Tudor Cottage

25 High Street, Biddenden TN27 8AL
TEL: (01580) 291913
at junction of A262 and A274

This delightful sixteenth-century black-and-white-timbered cottage with a tile-hung roof, known locally as a 'cat-slide roof', stands in the High Street with its timber-framed houses. It has a friendly atmosphere and is charmingly decorated. The beamed bedrooms have pretty curtains and covers, and the lounge with its inglenook fireplace has a quiet sitting area off it. The house has double glazing, and there are a couple of restaurants opposite; packed lunches can be provided.

OWNER: Susan Morris OPEN: all year exc Christmas ROOMS: 2 double, 1 twin; all rooms with bath/shower; TV in all bedrooms TERMS: single £25, twin/double £35–£39; £10 for children over 10 sharing with parents; deposit: £20 CARDS: none DETAILS: no children under 10; no dogs; car park

BIDEFORD Devon   map 1

Lower Winsford House

Abbotsham Road, Bideford EX39 3QP
TEL: (01237) 475083   FAX: (01237) 425802
just off A39

Lower Winsford House lies on the edge of the village of Abbotsham, in a rural setting half a mile from Bideford and three miles from the beach at Westward Ho. It is a large black-and-white mid-nineteenth-century residence, originally a farmhouse, and is set in large gardens with a pretty courtyard. The comfortable house is attractively decorated, and guests have use of two sitting-rooms, one with TV. Breakfast only is served at one table in the dining-room.

OWNERS: Mr and Mrs J.D. Ogle   OPEN: Apr to Sept   ROOMS: 2 double, 1 with bath/shower, 1 with wash-basin; 1 twin, with wash-basin; TV in some bedrooms and lounge   TERMS: single occupancy £25, twin/double £38–£42; £13 for childen ages 5 to 10   CARDS: none   DETAILS: no children under 5; no dogs; no smoking; car park; garden

BIGGIN HILL Kent   map 3

Oak Mount

18 Aperfield Road, Biggin Hill, nr Westerham TN16 3LU
TEL: (01959) 575443
just off A233 Westerham to Bromley road

Standing in a quiet residential road close to the centre of Biggin Hill with open countryside only one hundred yards away, Oak Mount was built in 1953. The house has a welcoming atmosphere and is very comfortable. One double bedroom is on the ground floor, and the other can also be used as a family room. The attractively furnished sitting-room has a TV and pianola. Breakfast is served in the adjoining sun lounge, which leads into the large secluded garden with a croquet lawn. Guests may bring take-away meals back to the house and there are many restaurants nearby. Bus and train connections to London are excellent.

OWNERS: Keith and Moya Fuller   OPEN: all year exc 20 to 29 Dec   ROOMS: 1 double, 1 double/family, both with bath/shower; TV in both bedrooms and lounge   TERMS: single occupancy £23–£26, double £28–£34, family room £33–£39; children's reductions according to age; deposit: £10   CARDS: none   DETAILS: children welcome; dogs by arrangement; no smoking; car park; garden

If a deposit is required for an advance booking, this is stated in the details at the end of the entry.

If there are any bedrooms with TV, we mention this in the details at the end of the entry.

BISCOMBE   Somerset   **map 2**

Merlands

Biscombe, Churchingford, nr Taunton TA3 7PZ
TEL: (01823) 601606
*from Hemyock take sign to Churchingford, turn left at sign for Biscombe
then first right*

This cottage-style country house is in an isolated and scenic position
in the beautiful Blackdown Hills. The grounds incorporate woodland,
garden, wild-flower meadow and a stream and the lovely walks in the
area might include sightings of deer, badgers, foxes and buzzards.
The Morleys are warm and friendly and Mrs Morley keeps an
impeccable house. The lounge has an inglenook fireplace and door to
the garden, and breakfast only is provided. Solar power provides heat
for the baths and showers and there is spring water to drink.

OWNERS: Mr and Mrs P.W.G. Morley   OPEN: Mar to Oct   ROOMS: 2 double, both with
bath/shower; TV in one bedroom   TERMS: single occupancy £17.50–£22.50, twin/
double £35; half-price for children over 8 sharing with parents; deposit: required for
stays over 2 days   CARDS: none   DETAILS: no children under 8; no dogs; no smoking;
car park; garden

BLACKPOOL   Lancashire   **map 8**

Grosvenor View

7–9 King Edward Avenue, North Shore, Blackpool FY2 9TD
TEL: (01253) 352851

This well-maintained house in Blackpool's quiet North Shore area is
less than a minute's walk to the Promenade. The bedrooms are fresh
and bright with daintily patterned duvets. One of the single rooms is
on the ground floor and has *en suite* facilities. Of the two comfortable
lounges, one is for smokers; otherwise, no smoking is allowed in the
house. Breakfasts and evening meals are served in the bright dining-
room, with vegetarian choices and children's portions available. Dave
and Sheila Jackson are a cheerful couple who are continuing to
upgrade standards: they plan to have TV in all bedrooms sometime in
1996. Lunch-time snacks or packed lunches can be provided, and
because the house is unlicensed, guests are welcome to bring their
own wine to dinner.

OWNERS: Dave and Sheila Jackson   OPEN: all year   ROOMS: 2 single, 1 with bath/
shower, 1 with wash-basin; 7 double, 4 with bath/shower, 3 with wash-basin; 5 'triple',
4 with bath/shower, 1 with wash-basin; 3 family, 2 with bath/shower, 1 with wash-basin;
TV in some bedrooms   TERMS: single/single occupancy £17.50–£21, twin/double
£35–£42, family from £35; children under 2 free, reductions for older children by
arrangement; dinner £5; deposit   CARDS: Access, Amex, Visa   DETAILS: children
welcome; no dogs; smoking in 1 lounge only; car park; garden

La Justholme

14 King George Avenue, North Shore, Blackpool FY2 9SN
TEL/FAX: (01253) 353226

Guests continue to enjoy the lilting Hawaiian music played by Naomi
King, who is originally from an island in the South Pacific. The front
of this Victorian house is bedecked with potted plants and hanging
baskets; guests may sit out here on fine days. Alternatively they may
choose to relax in the spacious lounge with its leaded stained-glass
windows, themselves set in a large bay window. The good-sized
bedrooms with their fitted white wardrobes are clean and bright.
Both breakfast and dinner are served in the licensed dining-room,
which leads to a small bar and conservatory. (Diners may bring their
own wine if they prefer.) Lunches can also be arranged, and packed
lunches provided on request. La Justholme is close to the Promenade
and Blackpool's famous amenities. On-street parking supplements
the small car park.

OWNERS: Naomi and Harry King   OPEN: all year   ROOMS: 6 double, 1 with bath/shower,
5 with wash-basin; 1 twin, with wash-basin; 3 family, 2 with bath/shower, 1 with wash-
basin; TV in all bedrooms and lounge   TERMS: twin/double £32, family room from £39;
dinner £7.50; reductions for children; D,B&B rates also available; deposit   CARDS:
none   DETAILS: children welcome; no dogs; smoking in limited areas only; car park;
garden

Sunray Hotel

42 Knowle Avenue, Blackpool FY2 9TQ
TEL: (01253) 351937   FAX: (01253) 593307

This impeccably maintained family-run guesthouse is just off the
Promenade, and offers nine well-appointed *en suite* bedrooms. There
is a comfortable TV lounge, and a separate dining-room where
breakfasts and evening meals are served. The house is unlicensed,
but guests may bring their own wine to dinner, and vegetarians can
be catered for with prior notice. The proprietors are willing to keep an
eye on children in the evenings if parents wish to eat out.

OWNERS: Jean and John Dodgson   OPEN: all year exc mid-Dec to mid-Jan   ROOMS: 3
single, 2 double, 2 twin, 2 family; all rooms with bath/shower; TV in all bedrooms and
lounge   TERMS: single/single occupancy £25–£28, twin/double £50–£56, family room
from £75; dinner £12   CARDS: Access, Amex, Visa   DETAILS: children welcome; dogs in
bedrooms only; car park; garden

*Any smoking restrictions that we know of are given in the details at the end
of the entry.*

*Many B&Bs, especially if they are unlicensed, allow guests to bring their
own wine to dinner. If this is the case, we say so in the entry.*

BLAGDON Avon   map 2

Aldwick Court Farm

Blagdon, Wrington, nr Bristol BS18 7RF
TEL: (01934) 863308
*just off A38, 10m SW of Bristol, signposted Nempnett Thrubwell and
Butcombe, follow lane for 1¼m*

This large whitewashed period farmhouse is in an idyllic location in a
picturesque valley. The Watts family have farmed their 300 acres for
over 100 years, and Aldwick Court is set in enormous grounds with
trees, flowers and patio; Blagdon Lake, known for its trout fishing
and wildlife, is within walking distance. The house has an inviting,
friendly atmosphere and is very comfortable and well furnished. One
of the three bedrooms has a handsome seventeenth-century four-
poster, and the large, comfortable lounge has a log fire and doors out
to the patio and garden. An adjoining barn houses three self-catering
apartments. Aldwick Court Farm is within easy reach of Bristol,
Bath and Wells. Clay-pigeon shooting takes place on the land.

OWNER: Mrs M.J. Watts OPEN: Apr to end Nov ROOMS: 1 double, 1 twin, 1 four-poster;
all rooms with bath/shower; TV in all bedrooms TERMS: single occupancy from £25,
twin/double from £42, four-poster from £45; deposit CARDS: none DETAILS: no
children under 8; no dogs; no smoking; car park; garden; tennis

BLIDWORTH Nottinghamshire   map 5

Holly Lodge

Ricket Lane, Blidworth, nr Mansfield NG21 0NQ
TEL: (01623) 793853 FAX: (01623) 490977
¼m N of where B6020 crosses A60

This former Victorian hunting lodge stands in its own 15 acres amid
woodlands and peaceful fields where sheep graze. Four of the
bedrooms are on the ground floor in the restored stables, and one twin
with its own sitting area is in the main house. All the rooms are *en
suite* and tastefully furnished in pine and decorated with Laura
Ashley fabrics. Breakfasts only are served in the attractive pink and
green dining-room, which leads to a conservatory overlooking the
garden and woods. A tennis court may be used by guests, and there
are five acres of woodland walks.

OWNERS: Ann and Ken Shipside OPEN: all year ROOMS: 1 single, 2 double, 2 twin; all
rooms with bath/shower; 1 room suitable for wheelchair-users; TV in all bedrooms
TERMS: single/single occupancy £27–£29, twin/double £39–£42 CARDS: Access,
Amex, Visa DETAILS: children welcome; no dogs; no smoking; car park; garden; tennis

BOGNOR REGIS   West Sussex   map 3

2 Norfolk Place

2 Norfolk Place, West Street, Bognor Regis PO21 1XF
TEL: (01243) 865783

This comfortable, attractively furnished town house was built in 1793, and is only 100 yards from the sea and within walking distance of shops and restaurants. Breakfast only is served in the dining-room and there is a pleasant sitting-room with TV. The Downs are close by for those who enjoy walking, and the Chichester Festival Theatre is very popular. Packed lunches can be provided.

OWNERS: Mr and Mrs P.V. Simmonds   OPEN: all year exc Christmas   ROOMS: 2 single, 1 double; all rooms with wash-basin; TV lounge   TERMS: single/single occupancy £15, double £30   CARDS: none   DETAILS: no children under 10; no dogs; no smoking; car park; garden

BOMERE HEATH   Shropshire   map 5

Fitz Manor

Bomere Heath, nr Shrewsbury SY4 3AS
TEL: (01743) 850295
off A528, 5m N of Shrewsbury

This traditional black-and-white timbered manor house dates from around 1450 and has a beautiful interior, as well as a pretty garden that is laid out as it was originally in Tudor times. Rosebeds, herbaceous borders, a croquet lawn and a solar-heated swimming-pool are for guests' enjoyment, and the garden also provides home-grown fruit and vegetables for the kitchen. The oak-panelled sitting-room with its log fire and the large dining-room are furnished with antiques and paintings, and the atmosphere here is relaxed. The three bedrooms have large beds and old-fashioned wash-basins, and one has good views of the Severn Valley and Welsh hills. For children, there is a play-room, and cots and high chairs can be provided. Candlelit dinners can be pre-arranged, and vegetarians are catered for with notice. Fitz Manor is unlicensed, but guests are welcome to bring their own wine to table.

OWNERS: Neil and Dawn Baly   OPEN: all year exc Christmas   ROOMS: 1 single, with wash-basin; 2 twin; TV lounge   TERMS: single £20, single occupancy £25, twin £40–£50; dinner £12.50; deposit   CARDS: none   DETAILS: children welcome; dogs welcome; car park; garden; swimming-pool

If a B&B offers off-street car parking, we note 'car park' in the details at the end of the entry. If we are aware of particular car-parking difficulties, we mention them.

BONSALL   Derbyshire   map 5

Sycamore House

76 High Street, Bonsall, nr Matlock DE4 2AR
TEL: (01629) 823903
*from A5012 1m W of A6 turn at sign for Bonsall, then turn right at end of
village*

This listed eighteenth-century stone-built house stands on the corner
of the road at the top of the village, with views to the hills beyond. The
bright bedrooms are well equipped. Four-course home-style meals (by
arrangement) are served in the dining-room, which has an open fire.
Sycamore House is licensed and drinks can be ordered in the bar at
all reasonable times. Bonsall is only a short distance from the canal
terminus at Cromford and the start of the High Peak Trail.

OWNERS: Ray and Pauline Sanders   OPEN: all year   ROOMS: 2 double, 2 twin, 1 family;
all rooms with bath/shower; TV in all bedrooms and lounge   TERMS: single occupancy
£25–£27, twin/double £42–£44, family room £50–£55; reductions for children sharing
with parents; dinner £11.50; deposit: 10%   CARDS: none   DETAILS: children welcome;
no dogs; smoking in lounge only; car park; garden

BOSHAM   West Sussex   map 3

White Barn

Crede Lane, Bosham PO18 8NX
TEL/FAX: (01243) 573113
*from A259 turn at sign for Bosham, then left after ¾m and left again at
Crede Lane*

White Barn is an interesting-looking modern bungalow on a peaceful
private road. The bedrooms are in completely separate areas and
each is entirely individual in its décor; one is a beamed studio in the
garden. The Trotmans are welcoming, hospitable hosts and the house
has a warm and relaxed atmosphere. The excellent dinners served at
the long refectory table (at 7.15pm) can include vegetarian options if
arranged in advance, and guests can bring their own wine. The
sitting-room has a log fire for winter evenings. The 900-year-old
village church contains the tomb of King Canute's daughter.

OWNERS: Antony and Susan Trotman   OPEN: all year exc Christmas   ROOMS: 1 double;
2 twin; all rooms with bath/shower; TV in some bedrooms and lounge   TERMS: twin/
double £32; dinner £18; deposit: £20 per person   CARDS: Access, Visa   DETAILS: no
children; no dogs; no smoking; car park; garden

---

*Please let us know if you think a B&B should be included in this Guide.
Report forms are at the back of the book – or use your own stationery if you
prefer (no stamps are needed within the UK).*

BOSTON   Lincolnshire   map 6

Fairfield Guesthouse

101 London Road, Boston PE21 7EN
TEL: (01205) 362869

This large Victorian house stands in its own grounds one mile south
of the city centre. Peter and Jean Page are an informal couple who
extend a warm welcome to guests in their well-maintained home.
New carpets have been installed in the lounge, which is busily
decorated with floral wallpaper and ornaments. There is also a small
sitting area in the entrance hall. The nine bedrooms are of a good
size, with firm beds. Breakfasts are substantial, with a help-yourself
buffet for starters followed by a traditional cooked plateful.

OWNERS: Peter and Jean Page   OPEN: all year exc Christmas   ROOMS: 2 single, both
with wash-basin; 4 double, 1 with shower, 3 with wash-basin; 1 twin, with wash-basin;
2 family, 1 with shower, 1 with wash-basin; TV in all bedrooms and lounge   TERMS:
single £17, single occupancy £18–£19.50, twin/double £30–£32, family room £37.50;
half-price for children 3 to 11 sharing with parents   CARDS: none   DETAILS: children
welcome; no dogs in dining-room; car park; garden

BOTALLACK   Cornwall   map 1

Manor Farm

Botallack, St Just TR19 7QG
TEL: (01736) 788525
on B3306, 1m N of St Just

This attractive granite-built seventeenth-century house is part of a
mixed farm and stands on the edge of Botallack with views to the sea
across the fields. It has a well-maintained front garden and the lane
past the farm leads straight to the sea, cliffs and moorlands. The farm
featured as 'Nampara' in the TV series Poldark and as 'Roslyn Farm'
in Penmarric. The house has character and atmosphere, with antique
furniture and pictures and mirrors on every wall. The dining-room
has a beamed ceiling and open fireplace; substantial breakfasts with
plenty of choices are served here. The warm, comfortable bedrooms
are individually decorated.

OWNER: Mrs J. Cargeeg   OPEN: all year exc Christmas   ROOMS: 1 double, 1 twin, 1
four-poster; all rooms with bath/shower; TV in all bedrooms   TERMS: single occupancy
£30, twin/double £40, four-poster £44; children's reductions according to age; deposit:
10%   CARDS: none   DETAILS: children welcome; no dogs; smoking in one room only;
car park; garden

If you intend to spend several days at a B&B, it is worth asking whether
there are reduced rates, particularly if the period is midweek or off-season.

Bourne Eau House

30 South Street, Bourne PE10 9LY
TEL: (01778) 423621

Elegance and interest pervade this lovely Grade II listed house in the
small market town of Bourne. The house was built on the twelfth-
century foundations of an Augustinian hospice and was for a while an
almshouse before becoming a domestic residence. The pretty garden
surrounding the garden is bordered by a stream (the Bourne Eau),
which meanders through the town and is home to swans and geese.
An early-Victorian wrought-iron bridge links the house with a
twelfth-century abbey, where, rumour has it, the ghosts of monks
walk at midnight. Bourne Eau House is beautifully and
harmoniously furnished, with many interesting antique pieces, and is
in immaculate condition. Breakfast and dinner are served in the
Elizabethan dining-room, with its high-backed chairs, beamed ceiling
and enormous fireplace complete with old bread ovens. Wine is
included in the price of dinner. The Bishops often join guests in pre-
dinner drinks in the elegant Georgian drawing-room, and after
dinner during coffee in the music room (guests are welcome to play
the grand piano).

OWNERS: Dr and Mrs G.D. Bishop   OPEN: all year exc Christmas   ROOMS: 1 double, 2
twin, all with bath/shower; TV in all bedrooms   TERMS: single occupancy £35, twin/
double £60; half-price for children under 12; dinner £18   CARDS: none   DETAILS:
children welcome; no dogs; no smoking in bedrooms; car park; games room; garden

Mullions

123 North Road, Bourne PE10 9BU
TEL: (01778) 393978   FAX: (01778) 393990

Mullions stands in secluded gardens on the edge of town. All the
rooms have stone-mullioned windows and most have leaded lights;
the house's oak doors and woodwork are reputed to have come from
Buckminster Hall. The bedrooms are individually decorated, with
antique pine, teak and oak furnishings. All the rooms have *en suite*
showers and hand-basins, and all but one have *en suite* WCs; this
room has sole use of a WC. Guests can relax in the comfortable TV
lounge and enjoy breakfasts, and evening meals if pre-arranged, in
the separate dining-room. Vegetarian and special diets can be catered
for, and children's portions are available. The Mullions is unlicensed,
but guests may bring their own wine to dinner. Polly the Sealyham
terrier and Sam the tail-less black cat are part of the family. For
nature lovers, there is a 400-acre wood close by. Packed lunches can
be provided.

OWNERS: Liz and Jim Essex   OPEN: all year   ROOMS: 2 double, 1 twin, 1 family; all rooms with bath/shower; TV in all bedrooms and lounge   TERMS: single occupancy £23–£27.50, twin/double £36–£45, family room £45–£55; reductions for children over 6 sharing with parents; dinner £12   CARDS: none   DETAILS: no children under 6; no dogs; no smoking; car park; garden

BOURNEMOUTH   Dorset   map 2

Parklands Hotel

4 Rushton Crescent, Bournemouth BH3 7AF
TEL/FAX: (01202) 552529

This small, friendly hotel is conveniently located for the centre of Bournemouth in a quiet street, and has been completely refurbished. The Clarks are a friendly and helpful couple who run it as a family business, with two sons and a daughter-in-law assisting. Off the hall is a comfortable lounge equipped with TV and a compact bar. Beyond lies the dining-room, where breakfast and dinner are served. The pleasant bedrooms are on the ground and first floors. Packed lunches can be provided.

OWNERS: Alan and Sylvia Clark   OPEN: all year   ROOMS: 3 double, 2 with bath/shower, 1 with wash-basin; 4 twin, 2 with bath/shower, 2 with wash-basin; 3 four-poster, all with bath/shower; TV in all bedrooms   TERMS: single/single occupancy £19.25, twin/double £38.50, four-poster £50; reductions for children ages 8 to 15; dinner, £9.50; deposit: £20 per person   CARDS: Access, Visa   DETAILS: no children under 8; no dogs; no smoking in dining-room; car park

Sandhurst

16 Southern Road, Southbourne, Bournemouth BH6 3SR
TEL: (01202) 423748

This cream-and-red painted detached house dates from the early part of the century, and stands in a quiet road very close to the sea. Colourful flowers add a decorative touch to the exterior of the building in summer. There is a comfortable sitting-room with TV, and a dining-room where breakfast and home-cooked dinners are served. Guests may bring their own wine to dinner, as there is no alcohol licence. The bedrooms are neat and snug, vary in size and all have TV. A cliff lift provides easy access to the long sandy beach, and the shopping area is only a two-minute walk.

OWNERS: Jean and Colin du Faur   OPEN: Mar to Oct   ROOMS: 1 single, with wash-basin; 3 double, 2 with bath/shower, 1 with wash-basin; 2 twin, both with bath/shower; 2 family, 1 with bath/shower, 1 with wash-basin; TV in all bedrooms and lounge   TERMS: single £17–£20, single occupancy £25–£30, twin/double £34–£40, family room £51–£60; 75% reduction for children ages 2 to 5, half-price for ages 6 to 8; dinner £6.50; deposit: £15 per person   CARDS: none   DETAILS: children welcome; no dogs; no smoking; car park

Larch House

Station House, Bourton-on-the-Water, nr Cheltenham GL54 2ER
TEL: (01451) 821172
just off A429 Stow-on-the-Wold to Northleach road

Larch House is an immaculately maintained house set in an acre of
pretty gardens, just two minutes' walk from the village. Built from
local stone, the house is stylishly decorated, and the good-sized
bedrooms have matching fabrics and large *en suite* bathrooms. For
those who value privacy, there is a bedroom over the garage. The
comfortable lounge leads to a conservatory which overlooks the
garden and where breakfast only is served. Dorothy and David
Pulham are attentive hosts, happy to outline itineraries and
recommend places for evening meals.

OWNERS: Dorothy and David Pulham   OPEN: all year exc Christmas   ROOMS: 1 double, 1
twin, 1 family; all rooms with bath/shower; TV in all bedrooms and lounge   TERMS: twin/
double £36, family room £45–£50; reductions for children sharing family room; deposit
required   CARDS: none   DETAILS: children welcome; no dogs; no smoking; car park

Windrush Farm

Bourton-on-the-Water, nr Cheltenham GL54 3BY
TEL: (01451) 820419
on A436, 2m W of Bourton-on-the-Water

This Cotswold stone farmhouse with mullioned windows is part of a
working arable farm of 150 acres. The owners are very helpful and
David enjoys chatting with guests and planning trips. The house is
well maintained and a TV lounge for guests' use contains a vast array
of brochures on places to visit in the area. Both bedrooms have rural
views and *en suite* showers, and are decorated with floral chintz
wallpapers, curtains and bedspreads. Excellent cooked breakfasts are
served at one table in the dining-room. The Plough, a seventeenth-
century pub serving good food, can be reached by a 20-minute walk
across the fields.

OWNERS: Jenny and David Burrough   OPEN: Mar to Dec   ROOMS: 1 double, 1 twin; both
rooms with shower; TV lounge   TERMS: single occupancy £25, twin/double £36–£40
CARDS: none   DETAILS: no children; no dogs; no smoking; car park; garden

*If a B&B caters for vegetarians, we note this in the entry. It is always best,
however, to check when booking and make it clear what your requirements
are, especially if you require a special diet.*

Front House Lodge

East Street, Bovey Tracey TQ13 9EL
TEL/FAX: (01626) 832202

This listed house dates from 1540 and is on one of the town's main
streets. It is said that King Charles I was billeted here before a battle.
The Campbells are friendly people and have decorated their home in
a very individual way. Pink and floral chintzes predominate, and the
well-maintained house is full of lace cushions, dolls, china, silk and
dried-flower arrangements. Despite this, there is a sense of
spaciousness and the atmosphere is relaxed. Some of the bedrooms
have wonderful views and two have old baths. There is a large sitting-
room which leads into the bar, and evening meals are served, by
arrangement, in the dining-room. Barbecues sometimes take place in
the pretty garden. Bovey Tracey is a good base for touring Dartmoor
and is not far from Torquay.

OWNERS: Gail and Ian Campbell   OPEN: all year   ROOMS: 3 double, 2 twin, 1 family; all
rooms with bath/shower; TV in all bedrooms   TERMS: single occupancy £25, twin/
double £36–£42, family room £54–£60; dinner £10.50   CARDS: Access, Amex, Visa
DETAILS: children welcome; no dogs; no smoking; car park; garden

---

Storrs Gate House

Longtail Hill, Bowness-on-Windermere LA23 3JD
TEL: (01539) 443272
at junction of A592 and B52874 opposite the marina and lake

Built over 100 years ago of local stone, Storrs Gate House is an
attractive country residence standing in two acres of secluded
gardens. It is well maintained and is just 200 yards from the marina
and lake. Two of the bedrooms have *en suite* bathrooms. Breakfast
only is served, but there are several eating establishments within
walking distance. Coffee can be enjoyed in the bright lounge, which
has a coal fire, TV and video.

OWNERS: Philip and Betty Kilduff   OPEN: Mar to Nov   ROOMS: 3 double, 2 with bath/
shower, 1 with wash-basin; 2 family; TV in all bedrooms and lounge   TERMS: single
occupancy £18, double £30–£40; family room from £40; half-price for children sharing
with parents; deposit: £20   CARDS: none   DETAILS: children welcome; no dogs; car
park; garden

---

*If a deposit is required for an advance booking, this is stated in the details
at the end of the entry.*

BRADFORD-ON-AVON   Wiltshire   **map 2**

Bradford Old Windmill

4 Masons Lane, Bradford-on-Avon BA15 1QN
TEL: (01225) 866842   FAX: (01225) 866648
3m NW of Trowbridge

Standing high above Bradford-on-Avon with wonderful views over
the town, this unusual converted windmill has retained many of its
original features. The bedrooms have been done up with flair and
imagination, one having a water bed and another a round bed, and all
have *en suite* bathrooms cleverly fitted into the curvature of the
house. The large, bright dining-room, with one big table, has french
doors leading out on to a small patio and neatly kept garden with
tables and chairs, and there is a large, comfortable sitting-room.
Vegetarian dinners are served three times a week, by arrangement,
and as there is no alcohol licence, guests are welcome to bring their
own wine.

OWNERS: Priscilla and Peter Roberts   OPEN: all year exc Christmas and New Year
ROOMS: 1 single, with wash-basin; 1 double, 1 twin, 1 family, all with bath/shower; TV in
all bedrooms   TERMS: single £39–£45, single occupancy £45–£55, twin/double
£45–£75, family room £70–£90; £15 per child over 6 sharing with parents in family
room; dinner £18; deposit: 1 night's charge   CARDS: Access, Amex, Visa   DETAILS: no
children under 6; no dogs; no smoking; car park; garden

BRADFORD PEVERELL   Dorset   **map 2**

Dower House

Bradford Peverell, nr Dorchester DT2 9SF
TEL: (01305) 266125
off A37, 3m NW of Dorchester

This lovely old listed house stands in four acres of gardens in the
attractive village of Bradford Peverell. The Eatons are a charming
couple who like to make their guests feel thoroughly comfortable and
relaxed. There is a cosy book-lined sitting-room with a log fire, and
the very pleasant bedrooms have their own bathrooms. Breakfast
only is served, at which home-baked bread and home-produced honey
feature. The Dower House is only eight miles from the sea.

OWNERS: Michael and Kips Eaton   OPEN: Mar to Oct   ROOMS: 1 single, 1 double, 1 twin;
all rooms with bath/shower; TV lounge   TERMS: single £16.50–£18, single occupancy
£21.50–£23, twin/double £33–£36; deposit: required if staying for more than 1 night
CARDS: none   DETAILS: no children under 10; dogs by arrangement; no smoking; car
park; garden

*Any smoking restrictions that we know of are given in the details at the end
of the entry.*

BRAFFERTON   North Yorkshire   map 9

Laurel Farm

Brafferton, nr York YO6 2NZ
TEL/FAX: (01423) 360436
on edge of village reached by minor road off A19 at Easingwold or A1 at Boroughbridge

Laurel Farm is a lovely place on the edge of the village, with an attractive garden and 25 acres of pasture. It has a courtyard, stables and, in the garden, a hard tennis court, croquet lawn and orchards. A listed building dating from around 1760, the house was totally derelict when purchased by Sam and Annie Key, who have lovingly restored it, retaining the charm of a bygone era and furnishing it with antiques and family portraits. They have private fishing rights and plenty of walks on which guests can encounter rare breeds of sheep, ducks and ponies. The Keys both enjoy entertaining and are accomplished cooks, and guests can join them for a candlelit dinner by arrangement. Vegetarian dishes can be provided and the house is licensed. Guests who prefer to eat privately can also be catered for. The family room is a suite of one double and a single with bathroom.

OWNERS: Sam and Annie Key   OPEN: all year   ROOMS: 1 double, 1 twin, 1 family; all rooms with bath/shower; TV in all bedrooms   TERMS: single occupancy £19, twin/double £38, family room £38 plus children's charge; £10 for children under 10; dinner £12; deposit: £10 per person for 3 days or more   CARDS: none   DETAILS: children welcome; dogs welcome in own room; no smoking in public rooms; car park; games room; garden; tennis

BRAMFIELD   Suffolk   map 6

Broad Oak Farm

Bramfield, nr Halesworth IP19 9AB
TEL: (01986) 784232
¾m W of village off A144 at Queen's Head pub

This comfortably solid-looking listed sixteenth-century farmhouse is situated at the end of a private drive about half a mile from the road, surrounded by meadowland and a well-tended garden with a tennis court. The house has many original features, including oak beams and a restored Tudor fireplace. The spacious bedrooms have period furniture and the comfortable guests' lounge has lots of books to please avid browsers. Generous evening meals are served by request and there is also a pub in the village that serves good food. This peaceful retreat is a good base from which to explore this interesting area.

OWNER: Patricia Kemsley   OPEN: all year   ROOMS: 1 double, with bath/shower; 2 twin, 1 with bath/shower, 1 with wash-basin; TV lounge   TERMS: single occupancy £17, twin/

double £32; £10 for children under 12; dinner £9; deposit £10 per person CARDS: none DETAILS: children welcome; dogs welcome; no smoking in public rooms; car park; garden; tennis

BRAMHOPE   West Yorkshire   map 9

The Cottages

Moor Road, Bramhope, nr Leeds LS16 9HH
TEL: (0113) 284 2754
heading out of Leeds on A660, turn left at St Giles' church in Bramhope and go up hill to Moor Road

This delightful property made up of a terrace of eighteenth-century farm cottages stands in a large landscaped garden. It has been tastefully renovated and is well equipped, with quality duvets and pine and oak furniture. The beamed guests' lounge has a stone fireplace, lit on chilly days, and a grandfather clock. Substantial breakfasts are served in the pleasant dining-room on linen tablecloths. Several places in the village serve evening meals. Sue and David Adams extend a warm welcome. Guests are welcome to wander round the orchard and sit in the garden on pleasant days. The Cottages is only three miles from the Leeds/Bradford Airport.

OWNERS: Sue and David Adams   OPEN: all year exc Christmas   ROOMS: 4 double, 1 twin; all rooms with bath/shower; TV in all bedrooms and lounge   TERMS: single occupancy £27, twin/double £42; deposit: £10   DETAILS: no children under 10; no dogs; no smoking; car park; garden

BRAMPTON   Cumbria   map 10

Hullerbank

Talkin, nr Brampton CA8 1LB
TEL: (01697) 746668
from M6 junction 43 take A69 to Brampton; then follow B6413 for 2½m, turn left to Talkin; take Hallbankgate Road and follow signs to Hullerbank

Surrounded by unspoilt countryside, Hullerbank is a charming Georgian farmhouse standing in its own grounds, with a pretty garden, an orchard and 14 acres of pasture. Guests have the use of a cosy sitting-room and of the three individually decorated bedrooms two have *en suite* facilities and the third has a private bathroom. The Stobbarts are a most welcoming couple who offer superb meals that feature home-grown produce, local lamb and trout. Although the house is not licensed, guests are welcome to bring their own wine to dinner. Talkin Tarn Country Park and Hadrian's Wall are nearby, and packed lunches can be provided by arrangement.

HULLERBANK, BRAMPTON

OWNERS: Brian and Sheila Stobbart   OPEN: all year exc Christmas and New Year
ROOMS: 1 double, 2 twin; all rooms with bath/shower; TV lounge   TERMS: single
occupancy £25, twin/double £40; dinner £11 to £13; deposit: £10 per room   CARDS:
Access, Delta, Visa   DETAILS: no children under 12; no dogs; no smoking; car park;
garden

BRAMSHALL   Staffordshire   **map 5**

West Lodge

Bramshall, nr Uttoxeter ST14 5BG
TEL: (01889) 566000
on B5027, 2m from Uttoxeter next door to Butchers Arms

Standards continue to be high at this attractive modern house in two
acres of landscaped gardens, with a summer house for guests' use.
The Udalls greet guests with a cup of tea or coffee on arrival, and are
happy to give advice on local attractions to visit. The good-sized
bedrooms are immaculate, with pretty duvets and modern
furnishings. The ground-floor room has the use of an adjacent
bathroom. Breakfast includes home-made marmalades and honey,
and is served in the sunny dining-room. West Lodge is handy for
Alton Towers and the Derbyshire Dales.

OWNERS: John and Wendy Udall OPEN: all year exc Christmas ROOMS: 1 double, 2 twin; TV in all bedrooms TERMS: single occupancy £20, twin/double £30; £8 for children using folding bed and sharing with parents CARDS: none DETAILS: children welcome; no dogs; car park; garden

BRAN END Essex
map 3

Elmcroft Guest House

Bran End, Stebbing, nr Great Dunmow CM6 3RJ
TEL/FAX: (01371) 856450
from A120 E of Great Dunmow follow signs to Stebbing, continue for 1m beyond church

Five acres of grounds, with a carp pond, a stream, abundant moorhens, ducks, geese, rabbits and squirrels, surround this timber-clad house on the edge of the village. Guests have a separate entrance and the three good-sized bedrooms (all on the ground floor) are spotlessly clean, with richly coloured warm duvets. Excellent fresh breakfasts are served in the lounge/dining-room, where guests will also find a good selection of books and information on the area. Elaine Preou is a down-to-earth, accommodating host. A pub serving evening meals is within walking distance and Stansted Airport is seven miles away.

OWNER: Elaine Preou OPEN: all year ROOMS: 1 single, with wash-basin; 2 twin; TV in all bedrooms and lounge TERMS: single/single occupancy £15–£16, twin £30–£32; children's reductions; dinner £5; deposit: 50% of 1 night's charge CARDS: none DETAILS: children welcome; no dogs; smoking in bedroom only; car park; garden

BRANSCOMBE Devon
map 2

Hole Mill

Branscombe, nr Seaton EX12 3BX
TEL: (01297) 680314
on S coast, 5m E of Sidmouth; in village take lane by Post Office for ¾m over 2 cattle grids and past Hole House

This seventeenth-century building is set in very peaceful, unspoilt countryside and is reached down a narrow and at times steep and twisty lane. A working water-mill until the early part of this century, Hole Mill is mentioned in books written by the historian Tom Lethbridge, who lived in nearby Hole House. The present building incorporates the converted mill and miller's cottage, and offers very comfortable and beautifully furnished accommodation. There are a number of levels, and old beams are just about everywhere. All three bedrooms overlook the garden and stream, and two of them have high brass and iron beds. Rod and Amanda Hart provide a warm welcome, and tea or coffee with home-made cakes are served to guests in the lounge with its inglenook fireplace or, when weather permits, in the garden. The Harts are keen wildlife observers and know all about the animals, birds and hedgerow plants seen in the immediate area. The beaches of Sidmouth and Lyme Regis are within easy reach.

OWNERS: Rod and Amanda Hart OPEN: all year ROOMS: 2 double, 1 with wash-basin; 1 twin, with wash-basin; TV lounge TERMS: single occupancy £20, twin/double £30–£36; children's reductions by arrangement; deposit CARDS: none DETAILS: no children under 6; dogs by arrangement; no smoking; car park; garden

BREDENBURY   Hereford & Worcester   map 5

Grendon Manor

Bredenbury HR7 4TH
TEL: (01885) 482226

Grendor Manor is a listed sixteenth-century house on a 498-acre farm which has corn, cattle, sheep and horses. The glorious views extend as far as the Welsh Black hills. The farmhouse has solid stone walls, sloping floors and an inglenook fireplace with a wood-burning stove. There is also a stone fireplace which has carved panelling depicting Adam and Eve and the serpent, and the sacrifice of Isaac. The three spacious bedrooms have pretty floral wallpapers and are furnished in keeping with the character of the house; they share one large bathroom between them. Huge breakfasts are cooked on the Aga, and there is an interesting old bread oven in the kitchen.

OWNERS: George and Aileen Piggott OPEN: Apr to Oct ROOMS: 2 double; 1 twin; TV lounge TERMS: single occupancy £14, twin/double £28; children's reductions by arrangement CARDS: none DETAILS: children welcome; dogs welcome; car park; garden

BREDWARDINE   Hereford & Worcester   map 5

Bredwardine Hall

Bredwardine, nr Hereford HR3 6DB
TEL: (01981) 500596
from Hereford take A438 Brecon road for 11m, turn left at Staunton on Wye towards B4352 Hay-on-Wye road for 1½m

Bredwardine Hall is an attractive stone Victorian manor house surrounded by large wooded grounds close to the River Wye. The sleepy village with its ancient castle remains and a Norman church is famous for its connection with the Victorian diarist Francis Kilvert, who was Vicar of Bredwardine. The Hall was used by the BBC for the filming of *The Kilvert Diaries*. Entrance is via an impressive reception hall and staircase, and there is a drawing-room with floor-to-ceiling windows that look out over the garden and countryside. The four *en suite* bedrooms are smartly furnished. Pre-arranged dinners

BREDWARDINE HALL, BREDWARDINE

are served in the dining-room, which has a cocktail bar and wine list.
There are opportunities for hill-walking in the area, numerous
castles, and Hay-on-Wye is only seven miles away.

OWNERS: Mr and Mrs Jancey OPEN: Mar to end Oct ROOMS: 2 double, 2 twin; all
rooms with bath/shower; TV in all bedrooms TERMS: single occupancy from £23, twin/
double from £50; dinner £12; deposit CARDS: none DETAILS: no children; no dogs; no
smoking; car park; garden

BRIDGWATER Somerset   map 2

Cokerhurst Farm

87 Wembdon Hill, Bridgwater TA6 7QA
TEL: (01278) 422330
just off A39 in Wembdon, 1½m W of Bridgwater

At the outer edge of Bridgwater, this sixteenth century longhouse
with its old farm buildings escapes the suburbs and gives the feeling
of an entirely rural, away-from-it-all location. Views of the rolling
Quantock Hills open up from here and the farm itself has 100 acres of
wheat, potatoes and 'pick-your-own' soft fruits. The walled garden
was originally used for growing delicate fruits, but guests can now
take advantage of its sheltered warmth and maybe even venture into
the unheated swimming-pool. The three comfortable bedrooms are

reached by a spiral staircase, and the dining-room, where breakfast only is served, has a TV and sitting area, complete with an old beamed ceiling. There is a small lake in the grounds.

OWNERS: Derrick and Diana Chappell OPEN: all year exc Christmas ROOMS: 1 single, 1 double, both with wash-basin; 1 family, with bath/shower; TV in all bedrooms and lounge TERMS: single/single occupancy £17, double £34–£45, family room £34–£45 plus supplement for children; £5 for children under 5, £10 for ages 5 to 10; CARDS: none DETAILS: children welcome; no dogs; no smoking; car park; garden; swimming-pool

BRIDLINGTON   Humberside   map 9

Etherleigh

13 Wellington Road, Bridlington YO15 2BA
TEL: (01262) 673583

This tall Victorian guesthouse is situated in the centre of Bridlington, handy for all the attractions and amenities of the town. George and Margaret Tate are a down-to-earth couple who extend a really warm Yorkshire welcome to their guests. The modestly furnished bedrooms are clean and comfortable, and some have *en suite* facilities. There is also a pleasant guest lounge with red upholstery and curtains. Breakfast and generous home-cooked dinners are served in the dining-room; packed lunches can be provided.

OWNERS: Mr and Mrs G.W. Tate OPEN: all year exc owners' annual holiday ROOMS: 2 single, 1 double, all with wash-basin; 2 twin, 1 with bath/shower, 1 with wash-basin; 3 family, all with bath/shower; TV in all bedrooms and lounge TERMS: single/single occupancy £13, twin/double £26, family room from £32.50; reductions for children sharing with parents; dinner £4; deposit: £10 per person CARDS: none DETAILS: children welcome; dogs by arrangement; smoking in lounge only; car park

Glen Alan

21 Flamborough Road, Bridlington YO15 2HU
TEL: (01262) 674650

Glen Alan is 200 yards from the North Beach, and a few minutes' walk from the town centre. Roy and Judy offer a warm welcome in their friendly guesthouse and provide excellent breakfasts and home-cooked dinners at a modest price. Glen Alan is licensed and packed lunches can be provided. The bedrooms are clean and comfortable, and have modern furnishings, colour co-ordinated fabrics and duvets. There is a guest lounge with TV and a bar.

OWNERS: Roy and Judy Jones OPEN: all year ROOMS: 4 double, 3 with bath/shower, 1 with wash-basin; 1 twin, 4 family, all with bath/shower; TV in some bedrooms and lounge TERMS: single occupancy £16.50–£20.50, twin/double £33–£41, family room from £36; children's reductions according to age; dinner £5.50; deposit: £10 per person CARDS: Access, Amex, Diners, Visa DETAILS: children welcome; no dogs; no smoking in restaurant

The Ryburn

31 Flamborough Road, Bridlington YO15 2JH
TEL: (01262) 674098

This spacious Victorian residence is close to the sea and is within easy walking distance of the town centre. Janet and Bernard Fozzard have refurbished the house to a very high standard, retaining as many original features as possible, including the leaded-light windows, cornices and unique plasterwork. The large, well-appointed bedrooms have Sanderson wallpapers, and colour-matched fabrics. Tasty breakfasts and good home-cooked dinners are available. The house is licensed.

OWNERS: Janet and Bernard Fozzard OPEN: all year ROOMS: 2 single; 4 double, 3 with bath/shower; 4 family, 2 with bath/shower; 1 room suitable for wheelchair-users; TV lounge TERMS: single occupancy £16, double £32–£38; children's reductions by arrangement; dinner £6; small deposit required CARDS: none DETAILS: children welcome; no dogs; smoking in lounge only; car park; garden

The White Rose

123 Cardigan Road, Bridlington YO15 3LP
TEL: (01262) 673245

The White Rose is a pleasant Victorian house standing in a residential area close to the beach, harbour, spa and town centre. Guests have the use of a large lounge with TV. The fresh, bright bedrooms have white furniture and pretty duvets; most have *en suite* facilities. Breakfast and dinner are served in the licensed dining-room, with an early meal at 5.30pm, or a later dinner with more choices available by prior arrangement. Packed lunches can be provided.

OWNER: Christine Young OPEN: all year ROOMS: 2 double, 1 twin, 2 family, all with bath/shower; TV in all bedrooms and lounge TERMS: single occupancy £33, twin/double £38, family room £48–£58; dinner £6 (5.30pm), £10.50 (7 to 9pm); deposit: £15 CARDS: none DETAILS: children welcome; no dogs; no smoking in dining-room or family bedroom; car park; garden

If you disagree with any assessment made in this guide, please write and tell us why. Address your letter to The Good Bed and Breakfast Guide, FREEPOST, 2 Marylebone Road, London NW1 1YN.

BRIGHTLINGSEA   Essex   map 3

Birch House

Church Road, Brightlingsea, CO7 0QT
TEL: (01206) 302877

Set in a large, terraced garden, this handsome red-brick and cream
modern house is in an area popular for sailing, bird-watching, fishing
and water-skiing. The house is airy and bright with spacious,
sparkling-clean rooms. The bedrooms are decorated in various pastel
shades, and the family suite has a large double, an adjoining twin and
an *en suite* shower. Substantial breakfasts include yoghurt and fruit
as well as traditional fare, and are served in the dining-room, which
overlooks the garden. Packed lunches can be provided.

OWNERS: Wendy Bragg   OPEN: all year exc Christmas   ROOMS: 4 single, 2 double, 2
twin, 1 family; all rooms with bath/shower; TV in all bedrooms   TERMS: single/, single
occupancy £22.50–£25, twin/double £38–£40, family room £56–£66   CARDS: none
DETAILS: children in family room only; no dogs; no smoking; car park; garden

BRIGHTON   East Sussex   map 3

Franklins

41 Regency Square, Brighton BN1 2FJ
TEL: (01273) 327016

Franklins is a small terraced house in a narrow street just off stately
Regency Square, convenient for the sea-front and the town centre.
The bedrooms vary in size and are comfortably furnished with small
en suite bathrooms. The attractive sitting-room with TV has
comfortable sofas and is combined with the small breakfast room;
both rooms have their original fireplaces. Evening meals, with
vegetarian options and a licensed bar, are available by arrangement,
and room service is offered between 11am and 11pm.

OWNERS: Sandra Williams and Katrina Cole   OPEN: all year   ROOMS: 1 single, 4 double,
2 twin; all rooms with bath/shower; TV in all bedrooms and lounge   TERMS: single £28,
single occupancy £28–£42, twin/double £36–£48; reductions for children under 10
sharing with parents; dinner £7.50 to £17.50; deposit: 1 night's charge   CARDS: none
DETAILS: children welcome; no dogs

---

*Bath / shower in the details under each entry means that the rooms have
private facilities. The B&B may have other, shared bathroom facilities as
well. We say if rooms have wash-basins.*

*If the establishment does not take credit cards, we say so in the details at
the end of the entry.*

BRILL   Buckinghamshire

map 2

Poletrees Farm

Ludgershall Road, Brill, nr Aylesbury HP18 9TZ
TEL/FAX: (01844) 238276
2m from A41 Aylesbury to Bicester road

This small, listed fifteenth-century brick and stone farmhouse has been beautifully restored, and is set in a pretty garden. Many original features of the farmhouse remain, including the beamed ceilings, an inglenook fireplace and a fifteenth-century window. The large, comfortable bedrooms have an old-fashioned atmosphere, but improvements are ongoing, with the twin now having a wash-basin and toilet, and plans in place for an *en suite* bedroom. Four-course evening meals can be provided, if pre-arranged, but there are two pubs serving food within a mile.

OWNERS: John and Anita Cooper   OPEN: all year   ROOMS: 2 double, 1 twin; all rooms with wash-basin; TV in some bedrooms and lounge   TERMS: single occupancy £20, twin/double £36; babies free, children's reductions according to age; dinner £12; deposit: £20   CARDS: none   DETAILS: children welcome; no dogs; no smoking; car park; garden

BRISTOL   Avon

map 2

Lawns Guest House

91 Hampton Road, Redland, Bristol BS6 6JG
TEL: (01179) 738459

Guests continue to enjoy the warm welcome extended by Mrs Moran in her Georgian residence with Victorian additions. It stands in a large secluded garden, but is only a mile from the city centre. The house is spacious and comfortable, with interesting original features such as the plaster ceilings with decorative cornices and leaded windows. Mrs Moran is president of the local flower club and keeps attractive houseplants as well as looking after the garden, which guests are welcome to use. The bedrooms are fairly large and spotlessly clean. It is advisable to use the excellent local bus service for visiting the city rather than going by car.

OWNERS: John and Nell Moran   OPEN: all year exc Christmas   ROOMS: 1 single, 1 double, both with wash-basin; 3 twin, 1 with bath/shower, 2 with wash-basin; 1 family, with bath/shower; TV in all bedrooms and lounge   TERMS: single £23, single occupancy £28–£32, twin/double £38–£42, family room £55   CARDS: none   DETAILS: children welcome; no dogs; no smoking in dining-room; car park; garden

Most establishments have central heating. When we know this is not the case, we mention this in the entry.

Leasow House

Laverton Meadow, Broadway WR12 7NA
TEL/FAX: (01386) 584526
from B4632 2m SW of Broadway turn at sign for Wormington then take first right

This large, well-kept seventeenth-century Cotswold stone farmhouse is in the heart of the countryside, and it is an informal and relaxing place. The bedrooms are huge and individual: one has an imposing array of beams and a sloping ceiling, another a bare stone wall. One is on the ground floor and designed to accommodate a wheelchair, and one has a whirlpool bath. The drawing-room/library has a well-stocked bookcase and leather sofas and chairs, with a complimentary drinks tray to enhance the country-house atmosphere. Sumptuous breakfasts are served in the attractive dining-room, which looks across the garden to open countryside.

OWNERS: Barbara and Gordon Meekings OPEN: all year ROOMS: 4 double, 1 twin, 2 family; all rooms with bath/shower; 1 room suitable for wheelchair-users; TV in all bedrooms TERMS: single occupancy £38, twin/double £48–£60, family room £48–£60 plus children's charge; £5 for babies, £10 for ages 5 to 10, £15 for older children; deposit: £30 CARDS: Access, Amex, Visa DETAILS: children welcome; dogs welcome; no smoking; car park; garden

Whiteacres

Station Road, Broadway WR12 7DE
TEL: (01386) 852320
on A44 Evesham to Stow-on-the-Wold road

Set back off the road, this turn-of-the-century house is on the edge of Broadway. The house has been decorated with great taste, and the six charming bedrooms are beautifully appointed with soft pastel furnishings. Three of the bedrooms have four-posters, two overlook the garden and one is on the ground floor. An extensive breakfast is served in the dining-room, which has a collection of pretty plates; french doors lead out to the patio and garden. There is also a comfortable guests' lounge.

OWNER: Helen Richardson OPEN: Mar to end Oct ROOMS: 2 double, 1 twin, 3 four-poster; all rooms with bath/shower; TV in all bedrooms TERMS: twin/double £38–£40, four-poster £40–£42 CARDS: none DETAILS: no children; no dogs; smoking in lounge only; car park; garden

If you are forced to turn up later than planned, please telephone to warn the proprietor.

BROBURY   Hereford & Worcester   map 5

Brobury House

Brobury, nr Hereford HR3 6BS
TEL: (01981) 500595   FAX: (01981) 500229
from A438, 8m W of Hereford turn at sign for Bredwardine; house is by Bredwardine Bridge

---

This beautiful country house was built in 1880 and stands in eight acres of formal gardens with spectacular views over the River Wye and magnificent countryside. An American art dealer and his family came on holiday to Hereford in 1970 and ended up staying; the Okarmas' daughter, Leonora Weaver, now manages the business and is always happy to run up a traditional American pancake breakfast. The bedrooms are very spacious and luxuriously furnished, named after the children who used to live here. A gallery situated in the coach house of this elegant estate houses a sizeable display of watercolours dating back to 1820 and over 100,000 antique prints. The drawing-room is a comfortable place in which to relax and there is a separate dining-room. Fishing can be arranged on the River Wye.

OWNERS: Mr and Mrs Okarma   OPEN: all year   ROOMS: 2 single, both with bath/shower; 2 double, both with bath/shower; 2 twin, both with wash-basin; TV in some bedrooms TERMS: single £20, single occupancy £29–£32, twin/double £58–£70; dinner £10 to £12; deposit: 10%   CARDS: Access, Visa   DETAILS: no children under 8; no dogs; no smoking; car park; garden

---

BROCKENHURST   Hampshire   map 2

Caters Cottage

Latchmoor, Brockenhurst SO42 7UP
TEL: (01590) 623225
from Brockenhurst take B3055 towards Bournemouth, go under railway bridge, then 75yds later turn right on to a gravel track

---

Caters Cottage is in the heart of the New Forest and is a pleasant whitewashed building, with lawned gardens to the side of the house and views of undulating moorland and forest. The bedrooms are simply furnished, and breakfast only is served at a long refectory table in a panelled rectangular room, which serves as both dining- and sitting-room. Packed lunches can be provided.

OWNERS: Mr and Mrs Ian Onslow   OPEN: all year exc Christmas   ROOMS: 1 single, 1 double, 1 twin; all rooms with wash-basin; TV in some bedrooms and lounge   TERMS: single £19, single occupancy £25; twin/double £38; reductions for children sharing with parents; deposit: £10   CARDS: none   DETAILS: children welcome; dogs welcome; no smoking in bedrooms; car park; garden

The Cottage Hotel

Sway Road, Brockenhurst SO42 7SH
TEL: (01590) 622296   FAX: (01590) 623014
from A337 in Brockenhurst turn into Brookley Road then left at crossroads

This attractive whitewashed small hotel is about 300 years old and
was originally a forester's cottage. It has been considerably altered to
accommodate up-to-date amenities but still has its oak beams.
Barbara Eisner is a warm and friendly person and the house has a
welcoming atmosphere. One of the attractive bedrooms is on the
ground floor, and others are reached up a steep, narrow staircase.
The cosy beamed lounge/bar has an open fire, and afternoon tea is
served on the garden patio in summer. The Cottage Hotel is licensed
and dinner is served by arrangement only. New Forest ponies wander
through the village, which has a ford.

OWNERS: Terry and Barbara Eisner   OPEN: Feb to Nov   ROOMS: 1 single, 4 double, 2
twin; all rooms with bath/shower; TV in all bedrooms and lounge   TERMS: single £28,
single occupancy £47; twin/double £57–£74; deposit: £20   CARDS: Access, Switch,
Visa   DETAILS: no children under 10; no dogs in dining-room; no smoking in bedrooms
or dining-room; car park; garden

BROOKTHORPE   Gloucestershire   **map 5**

Gilbert's

Gilbert's Lane, Brookthorpe, nr Gloucester GL4 0UH
TEL/FAX: (01452) 812364
just off A4173, 4m S of Gloucester

This beautiful listed Tudor farmhouse is built from local Cotswold
stone and wood from the Severn Valley. Five acres of grounds take in
an organic vegetable garden, sheep, chickens and beehives, providing
fresh ingredients for the kitchen. Breakfasts only are served, but
these are excellent, cooked on the old Aga and served in the kitchen.
Ancient beams and antique furniture, including a grandfather clock
in the hallway, add character; the cosy sitting-room has a wood-
burning stove, games and tourist literature. Four spacious bedrooms
have telephone, TV and *en suite* facilities. Guests may stroll through
the smallholding, which is bordered by a stream. The welcome at
Gilbert's is exemplary, and its location useful for the M5.

OWNER: Jenny Beer   OPEN: all year   ROOMS: 1 single, 2 double, 1 twin; all rooms with
bath/shower; TV in all bedrooms   TERMS: single £23, single occupancy £30–£35, twin/
double £46–£55; children's reductions by arrangement   CARDS: none   DETAILS:
children welcome; no dogs; no smoking; car park; garden

---

*We state at the end of an entry whether children are welcome. If we know of
any restrictions on children, we give them.*

BROSELEY   Shropshire   map 5

Broseley Guest House

The Square, Broseley TF12 5EW
TEL: (01952) 882043
on B4373, 1½m S of Ironbridge

Standing in the centre of the small, quiet town of Broseley, this
friendly guesthouse offers six immaculate, well-appointed bedrooms.
Facilities include remote-control TV in all rooms, radio-alarm and
mini-bar. The comfortable residents' lounge has no TV and makes an
ideal reading room. Geoff Nixey's sense of humour helps to make
everyone feel at home. Excellent breakfasts are served, evening
meals are available if booked in advance, and packed lunches can be
provided. Guests are welcome to bring their own wine to dinner.

OWNERS: Geoff and Laurie Nixey   OPEN: all year exc 23 to 29 Dec   ROOMS: 2 single, 2
double, 1 twin, 1 family; all rooms with bath/shower; TV in all bedrooms   TERMS: single
and single occupancy £25–£29, twin/double £40–£45, family room from £47; children's
reductions according to age; dinner £12   CARDS: Access, Visa   DETAILS: children
welcome; no dogs; no smoking in some bedrooms; garden

BROUGHTON IN FURNESS   Cumbria   map 8

Garner House

Church Street, Broughton in Furness LA20 6HJ
TEL: (01229) 716462
on A595

This stylish cream-coloured Victorian house stands in a secluded
walled garden at the edge of the village. This garden can be enjoyed
from a terrace with seating for guests. All the bedrooms are well
decorated and the spacious lounge features a marble fireplace and a
grandfather clock. The elegant crystal chandelier in the dining-room
comes from Sweden, where Maud Barrett was born, as do many of the
other beautiful objects around the house. Evening meals are not
available, but the village offers several establishments within
walking distance.

OWNER: Maud Barrett   OPEN: all year exc Christmas   ROOMS: 1 double, 1 twin; both
rooms with bath/shower; TV in both bedrooms and lounge   TERMS: single occupancy
£20, twin/double £40; dinner £14; deposit   CARDS: none   DETAILS: no children under 5;
dogs to be kept on lead, no dogs in dining-room; no smoking in bedrooms; garden

---

*Where we know a B&B accepts credit cards, we list them in the details at
the end of an entry. There may be a surcharge if you pay by credit card. It is
always best to check whether the card you want to use is acceptable when
booking.*

GARNER HOUSE, BROUGHTON-IN-FURNESS

BRYHER   Isles of Scilly   map 1

Bank Cottage

Bryher TR23 0PR
TEL/FAX: (01736) 422612

Bank Cottage borders the seashore and has dramatic views of
Bryher's western rocks and the Atlantic. It is a 400-year old beamed
cottage and has light and airy bedrooms, simply and prettily
decorated. The dining-room has a low beamed ceiling, and the lounge
is a bright, comfortable room leading out on to the terrace and garden
filled with colourful flowers. Mr Mace is a diver and collects sea
urchins, selling the shells all over the world. Bryher is the smallest of
the inhabited Isles of Scilly and is under a mile across and less than
two miles from north to south. Weekly bookings only are taken during
the summer months and terms include full English breakfast and a
four-course evening meal; packed lunches can be provided.

OWNERS: Mr and Mrs M.G. Mace   OPEN: Mar to Nov   ROOMS: 1 single, with wash-basin;
1 double, with bath/shower; 3 twin, 2 with bath/shower, 1 with wash-basin; TV in all
bedrooms   TERMS: rates include dinner; single £32, twin/double £70; £2 reduction for
children ages 8 to 12; deposit: 25%   CARDS: none   DETAILS: no children under 8; no
dogs; smoking in some rooms only; garden

Soleil d'Or

Bryher TR23 0PR
TEL: (01720) 422003

This small, modern bungalow offers comfortable, clean accommodation in a relaxed and informal atmosphere. Soleil d'Or is set on the east shore of Bryher just a couple of minutes from the beach. All the bedrooms have wonderful sea views. The lounge has a TV, and meals include local produce whenever possible; packed lunches can be provided. Visitors enjoy seeing seals, puffins and other sea birds, watching the weekly gig races and making trips to the Bishop Rock lighthouse.

OWNER: Angela Street OPEN: Mar to Nov ROOMS: 2 double, 1 twin; all rooms with bath/shower; TV in all bedrooms and lounge TERMS: twin/double £44–£48; reductions for children during early and late seasons; dinner £6; deposit: 33% of total charge CARDS: none DETAILS: children welcome; no dogs; no smoking in dining-room/lounge; garden

---

BUCKLAND MONACHORUM Devon   **map 1**

Store Cottage

The Village, Buckland Monachorum, nr Yelverton PL20 7NA
TEL: (01822) 853117
follow signs to Crapstone and Buckland Monachorum from A386 between Yelverton and Horrabridge

This delightful small cottage is right in the centre of the attractive and unspoilt little village of Buckland Monachorum. Store Cottage is one of a small, three-hundred-year-old terrace of stone buildings by the church, its front patio overlooking the village street. The entrance opens into the cosy sitting-room, with its open fire and low beamed ceiling, which is also where breakfast is served. The two light and airy bedrooms are surprisingly spacious, very well equipped and comfortably furnished. Annabel and John Foulston are friendly, welcoming and very hospitable people. Store Cottage offers excellent value in a wonderful location for exploring Dartmoor, and is close to Plymouth.

OWNERS: Annabel and John Foulston OPEN: all year exc Christmas and New Year
ROOMS: 1 double, 1 twin; both rooms with bath/shower; TV in all bedrooms TERMS: single occupancy £25, twin/double £36 CARDS: none DETAILS: no children under 12; dogs by arrangement; no smoking; car park; garden

---

No stamps are needed if you write to the Guide from within the UK. Report forms are at the end of the book, or use your own stationery if you prefer.

It is always best to book a room in advance, even in winter. B&Bs with few rooms may close at short notice for periods not specified in the details.

Bridge House

Buildwas, nr Telford TF8 7BN
TEL: (01952) 432105
on B4380, 1½m from Ironbridge

Formerly an inn, and converted in 1925 into two houses, Bridge House is a listed seventeenth-century half-timbered property, with views over the River Severn. The comfortable, spacious bedrooms are individually decorated and all have sitting areas; one has an antique brass bed, a Victorian bath and a display of swords, bayonets and knives. The oak-panelled lounge has lots of interesting artefacts, paintings and statuettes on display, and there are old farming implements in the garden. The Meadow Inn pub, a two-minute drive away, serves evening meals.

OWNER: Janet Hedges   OPEN: all year exc Christmas and New Year   ROOMS: 1 double, 1 twin, both with wash-basin; 1 four-poster, 1 family, both with bath/shower; TV lounge   TERMS: single occupancy £26, twin/double £38, four-poster £48, family room £60; children's reductions according to age; deposit: £20   CARDS: none   DETAILS: children welcome; no dogs; no smoking in dining-room; car park; garden

Hill View Farm

Buildwas, nr Ironbridge TF8 7BP
TEL: (01952) 432228
on A4149 between Buildwas and Much Wenlock

This friendly farmhouse is the centre of a small working farm. It provides good-value unpretentious accommodation, is kept immaculately clean and offers hearty breakfasts which may include kippers or fresh fish. The mill pond in the garden is stocked with trout and attracts kingfishers, herons and ducks.

OWNER: Mrs R. Hawkins   OPEN: all year exc Christmas and New Year   ROOMS: 2 double, 1 with bath/shower, 1 with wash-basin; 1 twin, with wash-basin; TV lounge   TERMS: single occupancy £16, twin/double £30; reductions for children under 13; deposit: £10   CARDS: none   DETAILS: children welcome; no dogs; no smoking; car park; garden

B&B rates specified in the details at the end of each entry are given (as applicable) for a single room, for single occupancy of a double room, and then per room in the case of two people sharing a double or twin-bedded room, or for a family room.

Grange Farm

Bulmer, nr York YO6 7BN
TEL: (01653) 618376
on A64 turn at sign to Castle Howard, then left to Bulmer and first left

This family-run dairy farm on the majestic Castle Howard Estate
offers visitors a chance to meet the farm animals during their stay in
the turn-of-the-century red-brick farmhouse. The views extend over
miles of open countryside and woodland and tempt walkers with
many bridleways and footpaths. The house is furnished in a mixture
of modern and traditional styles and the antique sideboard in the
dining-room has been resident for longer than the owners. An
additional WC, with its own fireplace, has been added this year.
Grange Farm is modestly priced and well situated for touring the
North York Moors.

OWNER: Janet Foster   OPEN: Apr to Oct; other times by arrangement   ROOMS: 1 single;
1 double, with wash-basin; 2 twin, 1 with wash-basin; TV in some bedrooms and
lounge   TERMS: single/single occupancy £15, twin/double £30; children under 3 free,
reductions for ages 3 to 14   CARDS: none   DETAILS: children welcome; well-behaved
dogs welcome (not on beds); smoking in guests' lounge only; car park; games room;
garden

Lower Barn

Wandales Lane, Bulmer, nr York YO6 7ES
TEL: (01653) 618575
*leave A64 4m SW of Malton at sign for Bulmer, turn left after village
church*

This tastefully converted 200-year-old stone-built barn is in a remote
location with extensive views of the scenic Rydale countryside. The
ambience is easy-going and the bedrooms are spacious, spotlessly
clean and furnished with antiques. The large lounge has a wood-
burning stove. Isabel Hall is a local lady who loves her business and
welcomes guests with a hot drink and home-made biscuits. Evening
meals must be ordered in advance and everything is home-made with
local produce and meats. Vegetarians can be catered for and guests
are welcome to bring their own wine to dinner.

OWNER: Isabel Hall   OPEN: all year exc Christmas   ROOMS: 2 double, 1 twin; all rooms
with wash-basin; TV lounge   TERMS: single occupancy £14, twin/double £28; £8 for
children; dinner £6   CARDS: none   DETAILS: children welcome; no dogs; no smoking;
car park; garden

*We welcome your feedback about B&Bs you have stayed in. Please make
use of the report forms at the end of the book.*

BURBAGE Wiltshire   map 2

Old Vicarage

Burbage SN8 3AG
TEL: (01672) 810495   FAX: (01672) 810663
take A338 from Salisbury, or A346 from Marlborough to Burbage; from
High Street turn east into Taskers Lane, then third on right (Eastcourt)
and house is on left before church

Built in 1853, this substantial brick-and-flint house was formerly the
rectory to the adjoining church, and stands in two acres of grounds in
the oldest part of the village with its many attractive cottages. The
house has a relaxed feel and is filled with lovely flower arrangements.
Guests have use of the drawing-room and the dining-room, with open
fires and plenty of books and magazines; breakfast only is served. The
well-equipped bedrooms have their original Victorian fireplaces, and
one has an enormous bathroom. TVs can be provided on request.
Shooting and riding are available by arrangement, and Burbage lies
on the edge of Savernake Forest.

OWNERS: Jane Cornelius and Robert Hector   OPEN: all year exc Christmas and New
Year   ROOMS: 1 single, 1 double, 1 twin; all rooms with bath/shower; TV lounge   TERMS:
single £35, single occupancy £40, twin/double £60–£80; deposit: £10 per person or
credit card details   CARDS: Access, Visa   DETAILS: no children; dogs by arrangement;
no smoking; car park; garden

BURCOMBE Wiltshire   map 2

Manor Farm

Burcombe, nr Salisbury SP2 0EJ
TEL: (01722) 742177   FAX: (01722) 744600
just off A30, 6m W of Salisbury

This attractive local stone house was originally a cottage and dates
back to early Edwardian days. It stands in a walled garden on the
edge of the village, in a quiet spot with lovely views of fields and
farms. Inside, it is very comfortable, with a friendly, welcoming
atmosphere. The three bedrooms share a bathroom, and the large
sitting-room has lots of plants and access to the pretty garden. Within
easy reach of Salisbury and Wilton, Manor Farm is an ideal spot for
walking and for those wishing to be in a peaceful place yet with access
to places of interest. Although breakfast only is served, a local pub
does food.

OWNER: Sue Combes   OPEN: Mar to end Nov   ROOMS: 1 single, with wash-basin; 1
double; 1 twin, with wash-basin; TV lounge   TERMS: single £16–£17, single occupancy
£20–£25, twin/double £32–£34; £6 for children under 4 (cot £2 extra), £10 for ages 4 to
10; deposit: £5 per person   CARDS: none   DETAILS: children welcome; no dogs; no
smoking; car park; garden

BURFORD   Oxfordshire   map 2

Chevrons

Swan Lane, Burford OX18 4SH
TEL: (01993) 823416
turn off A40 into Burford then take first right

One of the nicest things about Chevrons is the friendliness of owners
Sheila Roberts and her husband John, who enjoy welcoming guests
into their home – a sash-windowed stone house dating back to the
early sixteenth century. It is tucked away on a quiet side street just
off Burford's attractive High Street and has a small walled garden
with roses. The name springs from the chevroned medieval paintings
in the guests' lounge. The two comfortable bedrooms share a
bathroom. Only breakfast is served but Burford offers a wide range of
eating establishments within easy walking distance.

OWNER: Sheila Roberts   OPEN: all year   ROOMS: 1 double, 1 twin; both rooms with
wash-basin; TV in both rooms   TERMS: single occupancy £24, twin/double £32   CARDS:
none   DETAILS: children welcome; dogs by arrangement; no smoking

BURLEY   Hampshire   map 2

Brandon Thatch

Charles Lane, Bagnum, Burley, nr Ringwood BH24 3DA
TEL: (01425) 474256   FAX: (01425) 478452
*on A31 2m E of Ringwood turn at sign for Burley, take first right then first
left*

Brandon Thatch is truly in the New Forest, reached down a narrow,
wooded lane. It is a beautifully restored seventeenth-century
thatched country house, immaculately furnished and decorated, and
very professionally run. The house stands in peaceful seclusion
surrounded by three acres of glorious gardens and woodland, with a
swimming-pool and golf practice area recently added. The
comfortable lounge has Sky TV, the dining-room overlooks the garden
and there is a small kitchen and fridge stocked with drinks for guests.
Brandon Thatch is popular with honeymoon couples, who are greeted
with champagne in their rooms. Mr Giles is a pilot with Cathay
Pacific and Mrs Giles sometimes travels with her husband, so is not
always available to take bookings. Mr Giles can arrange helicopter
flights for guests.

OWNERS: Mr and Mrs M.J. Giles   OPEN: all year exc Christmas and owners' annual
holiday   ROOMS: 2 double, 1 twin; all rooms with bath/shower; TV in some bedrooms
and lounge   TERMS: single occupancy £38.50–£48; twin/double £48–£60; £10 for
children under 10; deposit: 10%   CARDS: none   DETAILS: children welcome; dogs by
prior arrangement; no smoking; car park; garden

Holmans

Bisterne Close, Burley, nr Ringwood BH24 4AZ
TEL: (01425) 402307
off A31 / A35, 4m SE of Ringwood

This attractive, modern family house is quite substantial, and is surrounded by four acres of gardens on the edge of the village. The two doubles share a bathroom while the twin is *en suite*. Guests have use of a TV lounge, and breakfast only is served at a large mahogany table in the dining-room. There is a stable block in the grounds available for up to four visiting horses, at a cost of £10 per horse per night. The whole area is good for riding and carriage driving, and a beach is not far away. Holmans lies on a quiet road, enjoys open views across the New Forest and is within walking distance of the White Buck Hotel, which has a good local reputation for food.

OWNERS: Mr and Mrs Robin Ford OPEN: all year ROOMS: 2 double, with wash-basin; 1 twin, with bath/shower; TV lounge TERMS: single occupancy £28, twin/double £38–£40; children's reductions by arrangement; deposit: £5 per person CARDS: none DETAILS: children welcome; dogs welcome; no smoking; car park; garden

---

BURNHAM-ON-SEA Somerset **map 2**

Priors Mead

23 Rectory Road, Burnham-on-Sea TA8 2BY
TEL: (01278) 782116
exit M5 at junction 22, follow main road through three roundabouts, then right into Berrow Road and second turning on left

This Edwardian house is set in a large garden with huge willow trees, and is on a quiet tree-lined side street. A relaxed, comfortable atmosphere is provided by the Alexanders, who are a welcoming couple. The large bedrooms are very well equipped, and breakfast only is served at one big table in the dining-room, which also has a baby-grand piano. Guests can use the sofa and armchairs in the hall, and the garden incorporates a croquet lawn and unheated swimming-pool. The town, beach, tennis and golf clubs are all within walking distance.

OWNERS: Peter and Felicity Alexander OPEN: all year exc Christmas ROOMS: 1 double, 1 twin, 1 family; all rooms with bath/shower; TV in all bedrooms TERMS: single occupancy £18–£20, twin/double £30–£32, family room from £41; half-price for children sharing with parents CARDS: none DETAILS: children welcome; no dogs; smoking in 1 public room only; car park; garden; swimming-pool

---

If there are any bedrooms with TV, we mention this in the details at the end of the entry.

BURTON LAZARS Leicestershire   map 5

The Grange

New Road, Burton Lazars, nr Melton Mowbray LE14 2UU
TEL: (01664) 60775   FAX: (01664) 480996
from A606 1m S of Melton Mowbray turn E at Burton Lazars church

Close to the old market town of Melton Mowbray, this large wistaria-
covered country house offers stylish accommodation. It is surrounded
by two acres of attractive gardens, has views over open countryside
and is spacious and elegant inside. The bedrooms (one of which is on
the ground floor) are richly decorated in burgundy, yellow and blue,
and each has its own bathroom and telephone. Antiques sit happily
alongside modern comforts throughout the house, and the sitting-
room, with french windows leading to the terrace and garden,
maintains the traditional feel with an open fire. Pam Holden is a
cordon bleu cook and she prepares fine five-course dinners by
arrangement, with vegetarian options. The Grange is licensed.
Breakfast and light suppers are also available.

OWNERS: Pam Holden   OPEN: all year   ROOMS: 1 single, 1 double, 1 twin, 1 four-poster,
1 family; all rooms with bath/shower; 1 room suitable for wheelchair-users; TV in all
bedrooms   TERMS: single/single occupancy £29.50, twin/double £44.50, four-poster
£44.50, family room £49.50; £5 for children sharing with parents; dinner £13.50   CARDS:
none   DETAILS: children welcome; no dogs; no smoking in bedrooms or dining-room;
car park

BURY ST EDMUNDS Suffolk   map 6

The Glen

84 Eastgate Street, Bury St Edmunds IP33 1YR
TEL: (01284) 755490

This charming seventeenth-century listed building is close to the
town centre. The well-appointed bedrooms are clean and bright, with
traditional furnishings. The family suite, which has its own entrance,
has two bedrooms – one with a double bed, the other with bunks. Pat
and Bill Walker are a friendly, conversational couple who enjoy their
guests' company. There is a separate dining-room and lounge with a
wood stove and lots of tourist information. Sightseeing can begin in
the large garden, which contains the remains of the oldest known
lime kiln in Britain.

OWNERS: Bill and Pat Walker   OPEN: all year   ROOMS: 1 single, 1 double, 2 twin, 1 family;
all rooms with bath/shower; TV in all bedrooms   TERMS: single £17.50, single
occupancy £20, twin/double £38; family room £40; children's reductions according to
age; deposit: 10%   CARDS: none   DETAILS: children welcome; no dogs in public rooms;
no smoking in public rooms; car park; garden

BUSLINGTHORPE   Lincolnshire   map 9

East Farm House

Mill Lane, Buslingthorpe, nr Market Rasen LN3 5AQ
TEL: (01673) 842283
on B1202, 4m S of Market Rasen

Approached up a private lane, this nineteenth-century brick
farmhouse is peacefully situated in a remote spot on a 400-acre
arable farm, complete with a duck pond in the garden. There is plenty
of wildlife about, including squirrels, partridge and a resident
kestrel. The entry-way to the house is made from quarry tiles, and
the beamed sitting-room has stripped pine doors and a Worcester-
sand fireplace. Everything is bright, clean and well maintained.
Substantial breakfasts and, if pre-arranged, home-cooked evening
meals are served in the freshly decorated dining-room with its blue
and yellow dainty wallpaper. For guests wanting to go a little farther
afield for their evening meals, there is a pub about five minutes' drive
away. The two large bedrooms are decorated with Laura Ashley
wallpaper, and one has *en suite* facilities. Packed lunches can be
provided. The farm also has a self-catering holiday cottage.

OWNER: Gill Grant OPEN: all year exc Christmas ROOMS: 1 double, 1 twin, both with
bath/shower; TV in 1 bedroom and lounge TERMS: single occupancy £20, twin/double
£36; half-price for children; deposit CARDS: none DETAILS: children welcome; dogs by
arrangement; no smoking; car park; garden

BUXTON   Derbyshire   map 8

Coningsby

6 Macclesfield Road, Buxton SK17 9AH
TEL/FAX: (01298) 26735

This impressive Victorian house stands in an attractive garden, half
a mile from the town centre. Linda Harry and her charming mother,
Vera Warby, run this elegant guesthouse together, and they extend a
warm welcome to guests. Six spacious bedrooms are beautifully
decorated with smart furnishings, fabrics and satin bedspreads. Two
rooms have Victorian-style fireplaces set with coal-effect gas fires, in
addition to central heating in all six rooms. Original stained-glass
windows and an antique dresser furnish the hallway. Breakfast and
licensed dinners are served in the handsome red dining-room. Linda
cooks the main course, while Vera prepares soups and her speciality
dessert, bread-and-butter pudding. Vegetarian dishes can be
requested, and there is a small wine list.

OWNERS: Dr and Mrs J. Harry OPEN: Feb to Nov ROOMS: 2 double, 1 twin; all rooms
with bath/shower; TV in all bedrooms TERMS: single occupancy £35, twin/double £40;
dinner £14.50; deposit: 10% CARDS: none DETAILS: no children; no dogs; no smoking;
car park; garden

Grosvenor House

1 Broad Walk, Buxton SK17 6JE
TEL/FAX: (01298) 72439

With views across the Pavilion Gardens and the River Wye, this imposing Victorian residence is situated in a conservation area in the heart of Buxton. The bedrooms are all decorated and furnished to a high standard with co-ordinated colour schemes; the more expensive ones are luxurious and boast period furniture. Graham and Anne run their establishment with flair and warmth. Breakfasts and dinners are served, prepared fresh daily from local ingredients; pre-opera dinners can be ordered, and Grosvenor House is licensed. The elegant, tastefully furnished lounge has lots of local information, books and games.

OWNERS: Graham and Anne Fairbairn OPEN: all year ROOMS: 5 double, 1 twin, 2 family; all rooms with bath/shower; TV in all bedrooms TERMS: single occupancy £42.50–£47.50, twin/double £50–£70, family room £70; children's reductions according to age; dinner £14; deposit: minimum £15 CARDS: Access, Visa DETAILS: no children under 8; no dogs; smoking in guests' lounge only; car park; garden

Hawthorn Farm Guest House

Fairfield Road, Buxton SK17 7ED
TEL: (01298) 23230
on A6, N of town centre

This large guesthouse is on the edge of Buxton, ten minutes' walk from the centre, with a regular bus service passing the door. The attractive, whitewashed building is listed and dates from around 1600; it has been in the Smith family for ten generations. There are leaded windows, thick stone walls, old beams and some very low doors. Breakfast only is served at individual tables in the dining-room, which has a carved oak fireplace and grandfather clock. The comfortable guest lounge has an old stone fireplace and a collection of coronation mugs. Seven of the bedrooms are in converted farm buildings adjoining the property, and have electric fires; there are four ground-floor bedrooms. Although it is on the main road, Hawthorn Farm is set back far enough to minimise traffic noise, and guests have use of a large rose-filled garden.

OWNER: David J.S. Smith OPEN: Apr to Oct ROOMS: 4 single, all with wash-basin; 2 double, both with wash-basin; 2 twin, 1 with bath/shower, 1 with wash-basin; 4 family, all with bath/shower; TV lounge TERMS: single £20, twin/double from £40, family room from £45; reductions for children sharing with parents; deposit: £10 CARDS: none DETAILS: children welcome; dogs welcome; no smoking in dining-room; car park; garden

Netherdale

16 Green Lane, Buxton SK17 9DP
TEL: (01298) 23896

Five minutes from the centre of town, this detached Victorian house is situated on a quiet side street. The ten bedrooms are of a good size, with dressing tables and TV; all but the singles are *en suite*, and there are two ground-floor rooms. The house has been redecorated and has new carpets, attractive wallpapers and new curtains made by owner Gwenda Stewart; samples of Gwenda's embroidery are also for sale. A special feature is the licensed four-course dinners served between 6 and 7pm, with children's helpings and vegetarian dishes by arrangement. Home-made desserts such as sticky toffee pudding are followed by coffee served in the comfortable lounge.

OWNERS: John and Gwenda Stewart OPEN: all year exc Christmas and New Year ROOMS: 2 single, both with wash-basin; 6 double, all with bath/shower; 2 family, both with bath/shower; TV in all bedrooms and lounge TERMS: single £21, single occupancy £26, double £42, family room £55; reductions for children sharing with parents; dinner £12 CARDS: none DETAILS: children welcome; no dogs; no smoking; car park; games room; garden

---

BYFORD   Hereford & Worcester   **map 5**

Old Rectory

Byford, nr Hereford HR4 7LD
TEL: (01981) 590218   FAX: (01981) 590499
just off A438, 7m W of Hereford

The Old Rectory dates from 1830 and enjoys rural views and one and a half acres of landscaped gardens. The house is a ten-minute walk from the River Wye, and the Wye Valley Walk passes its gate. All three spacious bedrooms are *en suite* with good views, easy chairs and books. Charles and Audrey Mayson have created a friendly atmosphere and run the house in an informal way. Dinner is served at 7pm by arrangement (bring your own wine) and children's helpings and vegetarian dishes can be requested. Local fishing can be organised, and Hay-on-Wye with its second-hand bookshops is within reach.

OWNERS: Mr and Mrs C. Mayson OPEN: Mar to Nov ROOMS: 2 double, 1 twin; all rooms with bath/shower; TV in all bedrooms TERMS: single occupancy £25, twin/double £33–£40; reductions for children by arrangement; dinner £10–£12.50; deposit: £20 CARDS: none DETAILS: children welcome; no dogs; no smoking; car park; garden

---

Please let us know if you need more report forms and we will send you a fresh supply.

CADNAM Hampshire   map 2

Walnut Cottage

Old Romsey Road, Cadnam, nr Southampton SO4 2NP
TEL: (01703) 812275
at Cadnam roundabout take A31 towards Winchester then turn first right

This 150-year-old simple white brick cottage is on a quiet lane
surrounded by an attractive garden. It is a welcoming family home
furnished with antiques and with a lovely, light sitting-room. The
central hall with its comfortable chairs provides a pleasant
alternative sitting place. Breakfast is served at one large table in the
small dining-room, and one of the three bedrooms is on the ground
floor. There are four old bikes that are lent out free, and a wealth of
information is available on what to do and see in the vicinity. Good
food can be found at the old pub, less than a minute's walk down the
road. Walnut Cottage is just a short distance from the M27 and is
well placed for visiting the New Forest and Southampton.

OWNERS: Charlotte and Eric Osgood OPEN: all year exc Christmas ROOMS: 1 double, 2
twin; all rooms with bath/shower; 1 room suitable for wheelchair-users; TV in all
bedrooms and lounge TERMS: single occupancy £28, twin/double £40–£42; deposit:
£10 CARDS: none DETAILS: no children under 14; no dogs; no smoking in dining-room;
car park; garden

CALDBECK Cumbria   map 10

Swaledale Watch

Whelpo, Caldbeck, Wigton CA7 8HQ
TEL: (01697) 478409
on B5299, ¾m W of Caldbeck

Swaledale Watch is a 300-acre working dairy and sheep farm set
among the peaceful and picturesque rolling fells within the Lake
District National Park. Guests are welcome to explore the farm and
see the animals (including two friendly collie dogs). The house itself
stands opposite a stream and old stone bridge. Inside, it is warm and
comfortable and is decorated in attractive pastels; both the guest
lounge and the dining-room have open fires. All the bedrooms are on
the ground floor, and the owners tell us that all rooms will have *en
suite* facilities by the 1996 season. Breakfasts and optional evening
meals are served, and although Swaledale Watch is unlicensed
guests may bring their own wine to dinner. Alternatively, a pub and
several restaurants are located in the village, which is less than a
mile away. Packed lunches can be provided. The farm is close to the
Cumbrian Way; those touring by car will find it is within striking
distance of Keswick, Penrith, the Solway coast and Hadrian's Wall.

OWNERS: Arnold and Nan Savage OPEN: all year exc Christmas ROOMS: 1 double, 1
twin, 1 four-poster, 1 family; all rooms with bath/shower; TV in all bedrooms and

lounge TERMS: single occupancy £17–£18, twin/double £32–£34, four-poster £34–£36, family from around £40; children's reductions according to age; dinner £9; deposit: £10 CARDS: none DETAILS: children welcome; no dogs; no smoking; car park; garden

---

CAMBRIDGE Cambridgeshire map 6

De Freville House

166 Chesterton Road, Cambridge CB4 1DA
TEL: (01223) 354993 FAX: (01223) 321890

Just a pleasant 15-minute stroll from the town centre, this attractive double-fronted Victorian residence offers tasteful accommodation. It has been fully refurbished while retaining its original character, with bright, spacious bedrooms decorated with pretty wallpapers. The immaculately clean house has many interesting and antique clocks on display, collected by Mr Hunter. The lounge is well furnished and looks out on to a patio and garden. Breakfasts are hearty, combining a help-yourself buffet with cooked dishes, vegetarian options included.

OWNER: Ann Hunter OPEN: all year ROOMS: 1 single, with wash-basin; 5 double, all with bath/shower; 2 twin, 1 with bath/shower, 1 with wash-basin; TV in all bedrooms and lounge TERMS: single £22, single occupancy £30–£35, twin/double £40–£45; deposit: £10 CARDS: none DETAILS: no children under 6; no dogs; no smoking; garden

136 Huntingdon Road

136 Huntingdon Road, Cambridge CB3 0HL
TEL: (01223) 461142 FAX: (01223) 568304

High standards are maintained at this Edwardian house, which stands in a secluded garden within easy walking distance of the colleges and the city centre. The large bedrooms, all on the ground floor, are immaculately clean and have their own bathroom and TV. The furnishings are appropriate to the age of the house and the overall effect is warm and comfortable. Breakfast only is served in the first-floor dining-room. An excellent bus service to the city centre stops nearby.

OWNER: Alice Percival OPEN: all year ROOMS: 1 single, 1 double, 1 twin; all rooms with bath/shower; TV in all bedrooms TERMS: single £34, single occupancy £38, twin/double £54; deposit: £20 CARDS: none DETAILS: no babies; no dogs; no smoking; car park; garden

---

We asked the proprietors to estimate their 1996 prices in the autumn of 1995, so the rates may have changed since publication.

CAMELFORD   Cornwall   map 1

Trethin Manor

Advent, nr Camelford PL32 9QW
TEL: (01840) 213522
off A39, 1½m SE of Camelford, follow signs for Advent church

This delightful old granite manor house is set in peaceful countryside,
just out of Camelford. It is surrounded by several acres of beautifully
kept gardens with trout pool and ducks, and stone outbuildings,
which have been converted into ten self-catering units. The original
house started life as just one room and has been added to over the
centuries. The guests' sitting-room was built in 1650 and bears the
family crest over the attractive stone fireplace. Captain Samuel
Wallace, discoverer of Tahiti, was born at Trethin Manor, and at the
beginning of the century the Siamese royal family lived here. Inside,
it is comfortably furnished and there are four pretty bedrooms. Other
facilities include a launderette; breakfast only is served. The seaside
towns of Tintagel, with its Arthurian legends, and Boscastle are not
far away.

OWNERS: Elizabeth and Donald Brocklehurst   OPEN: Mar to end Oct   ROOMS: 1 single, 3
double; all rooms with bath/shower; TV in some bedrooms and lounge   TERMS: single
£16–£22, single occupancy £24–£33, double £32–£44; deposit: 30% of charge   CARDS:
none   DETAILS: no children; no dogs; no smoking in dining-room or lounge; car park;
games room; garden

CANON PYON   Hereford & Worcester   map 5

Hermitage Manor

Canon Pyon, nr Hereford HR4 8NR
TEL: (01432) 760317
on A4110, 7m NW of Hereford

Hermitage Manor is a winning combination of country-house
elegance and a warm informal atmosphere. It stands in 11 acres of
private grounds, sheltered by an extensive deer park with stunning
views over rural Herefordshire, and is a perfect spot for bird-
watching, walking and exploring the Wye Valley. The baronial-style
hall has a roaring log fire on chilly days, and the leaded windows, oak
panelling, staircase, Tudor ceiling roses and cornices are of particular
interest. The spacious bedrooms all have good-sized bath or shower
rooms. A substantial breakfast cooked to order is served at separate
tables in the elegant dining-room. The water comes from a natural
spring and is gravity-fed to the house. Mrs Hickling is extremely
accommodating and happy to share her knowledge of what to see and
do in the area.

OWNERS: Mrs S.E. Hickling and Mr B.E. Morgan OPEN: Easter to end Nov ROOMS: 5 double, 1 twin; all rooms with bath/shower; TV in all bedrooms TERMS: twin/double £39–£50; deposit CARDS: none DETAILS: no children under 10; no dogs; no smoking; car park; garden

CANTERBURY Kent   map 3

Magnolia House

36 St Dunstans Terrace, Canterbury CT2 8AX
TEL/FAX: (01227) 765121

Standing at the end of a lovely Regency terrace, this late Georgian house has a most attractive walled garden with pergola and summer-house. The property has recently been completely refurbished to a high standard and offers exceptionally comfortable accommodation. Ann and John Davies are very friendly people and are also keen gardeners. The bedrooms are well equipped and the one on the ground floor has a king-sized bed and corner bath. Evening meals are available by arrangement during the winter months and there is a laundry room for guests' use. Magnolia House is only a ten-minute stroll to the city centre.

OWNERS: Ann and John Davies OPEN: all year ROOMS: 1 single, 4 double, 1 twin, 1 four-poster; all rooms with bath/shower; TV in all bedrooms and lounge TERMS: single £36–£45, single occupancy £45, twin/double £55–£60, four-poster £70–£80; dinner £18; deposit CARDS: Access, Amex, Delta, Visa DETAILS: no children under 12; no dogs; no smoking; car park; garden

Oriel Lodge

3 Queens Avenue, Canterbury CT2 8AY
TEL: (01227) 464845
approaching Canterbury on A2 take left turn 400 metres after first roundabout

Oriel Lodge is a large detached Edwardian house built in 1907 in the style of William Morris. It is set in a quiet residential area off the London Road and is within sight of the cathedral, which is about a five-minute walk away. The Rishworths offer a friendly welcome and, being keen gardeners, have a most attractive garden. The furnishings and décor reflect the William Morris influence and there are six well-equipped bedrooms. Breakfast only is served in the large lounge/dining-room, but sample menus from local restaurants are available to help in choosing where to go for an evening meal.

OWNERS: Keith and Anthea Rishworth OPEN: all year ROOMS: 1 single, with wash-basin; 3 double, all with wash-basin; 1 twin, 1 family, both with shower; TV in all bedrooms TERMS: single £20–£26, twin/double £35–£55, family room £51–£73; half-price for children from 6 to 11 sharing with parents; deposit: 25%   CARDS: Access, Visa   DETAILS: no children under 6; no dogs; smoking in lounge area only; car park; garden

Zan Stel Lodge

140 Old Dover Road, Canterbury CT1 3NX
TEL: (01227) 453654

This unusual looking Edwardian house with its beautifully kept garden is next to the Kent County Cricket Ground and only a ten-minute walk to the city centre. At one time the property was a bricklayers' school and the walls surrounding the garden have inset fireplaces of different designs, which were the work of apprentices. The house is comfortable and attractively furnished, and the rooms have their original fireplaces; look for the stained-glass window on the stairs. Breakfast only is served, but there is a wealth of eating establishments in the town. Owners Zandra and Ron Stedman extend a happy welcome to guests.

OWNERS: Zandra and Ron Stedman   OPEN: all year exc Christmas   ROOMS: 1 double, with shower; 1 twin, with wash-basin; 2 family, 1 with shower, 1 with wash-basin; TV in all bedrooms   TERMS: single occupancy £25–£40, twin/double £35–£48, family room £55–£65; children's reductions by arrangement; deposit: 25%   CARDS: none   DETAILS: children welcome; no dogs; no smoking; car park; garden

---

CARLISLE   Cumbria   **map 10**

Avondale

3 St Aidans Road, Carlisle CA1 1LT
TEL: (01228) 23012
just off A69 by St Aidan's church

Avondale is an attractive Edwardian residence situated on a quiet tree-lined road five minutes from the town centre. This is a bright and airy house with an unusual alcove and decorative wooden surround in the sitting-room, which has leaded windows and original covings. The house is furnished in keeping with its character and all bedrooms have fireplaces. Michael and Angela Hayes create a friendly home-from-home atmosphere. Evening meals are available if arranged in advance and vegetarians are catered for, but the owners are keen restaurant-goers themselves and are happy to make local recommendations. On sunny days the well-tended garden is a fine place in which to relax.

OWNERS: Michael and Angela Hayes   OPEN: all year exc Christmas   ROOMS: 1 double, with wash-basin; 2 twin, 1 with bath/shower, 1 with wash-basin; TV in all bedrooms and lounge   TERMS: single occupancy £20–£22, twin/double £34–£38; children's reductions by arrangement; dinner £8.50; deposit: £15   CARDS: none   DETAILS: children welcome; no dogs; no smoking in bedrooms; car park

Blackwell Farm

Blackwell, Carlisle CA2 4SH
TEL: (01228) 24073
*from M6 junction 42 follow sign to Dalston, turn right at Black Lion pub
then left at White Ox pub*

With its cobbled yard outside and traditional beams inside, this 200-year-old dairy farm has a simple traditional look that matches the uncomplicated way it is run. The Westmorlands believe in making guests comfortable and relaxed, while maintaining the feel of a family home. Their two young sons delight in showing guests round the farm and introducing them to the young animals. The bedrooms are modestly furnished and spotlessly clean, and the guests' lounge has a TV. The best way into Carlisle is by bus, but for evening meals plenty of local establishments would suit.

OWNER: Andrea Westmorland   OPEN: all year exc Christmas   ROOMS: 1 twin, 1 family;
TV lounge   TERMS: single/single occupancy £16, twin £30; children's reductions
according to age   CARDS: none   DETAILS: children welcome; dogs welcome; no
smoking upstairs; car park; garden

Courtfield House

169 Warwick Road, Carlisle CA1 1LP
TEL: (01228) 22767

Flower tubs and window boxes provide a colourful welcome to this Victorian red-brick house within walking distance of the town centre. Marjorie Dawes has an eye for décor, as reflected in the very tastefully colour co-ordinated bedrooms, and the lovely dried-flower arrangements throughout the house. Although Courtfield House is on the main road, double glazing keeps traffic noise to a minimum. Home-cooked three-course meals are served between 6 and 7pm; children's portions and vegetarian options are always available, and as the house is unlicensed, guests may bring their own wine to dinner. Packed lunches can be provided.

OWNERS: Eric and Marjorie Dawes   OPEN: all year   ROOMS: 2 double, 1 twin, all with
bath/shower; TV in all bedrooms and lounge   TERMS: single occupancy £20–£25, twin/
double £35; half-price for children under 12; dinner £8   CARDS: none   DETAILS: children
welcome; dogs welcome; car park

Howard House

27 Howard Place, Carlisle CA1 1HR
TEL: (01228) 29159 and 512550   FAX: (01228) 512550

This well-maintained nineteenth-century house in a quiet residential area exudes a pleasant, old-fashioned atmosphere. The lounge has something of a 'parlour ambience', with its piano and marble and tile fireplace, as well as TV and video. In keeping with the house's character, one bedroom has a six-foot four-poster bed. Evening meals can be pre-arranged, and children and vegetarians are catered for. The house is unlicensed, but guests are welcome to bring their own wine to dinner. Lawrence Fisher is a former president of a local genealogical society and, if time permits, is happy to share his knowledge and to arrange tours for 'family historians'. Three affectionate cats live here. Packed lunches can be provided.

OWNER: Sandra Fisher OPEN: all year ROOMS: 2 single, both with wash-basin; 1 double, with bath/shower; 1 twin, with bath/shower; 1 four-poster, with bath/shower; 2 family, both with wash-basin; TV in all bedrooms and lounge TERMS: single £15, single occupancy £25, twin/double £30, four-poster £36, family room from £36; half-price for children under 12; dinner £8; deposit CARDS: Access, Visa DETAILS: children welcome; no dogs; no smoking in dining-room

CARNFORTH   Lancashire   map 8

Thwaite End Farm

Carnforth, Bolton-le-Sands LA5 9TN
TEL: (01524) 732551
on A6 between Carnforth and Bolton-le-Sands

This whitewashed picture-postcard farmhouse, part of a small working beef and sheep farm, dates from the seventeenth century and is within easy reach of the Lake District and the Yorkshire Dales. The beamed bedrooms have solid, old-fashioned furniture. Guests have the use of a sitting-room, TV lounge and furnished patio. Breakfast only is served at separate tables in the dining-room, which has a grandfather clock and the original sandstone fireplace. Geoff and Adelaide Ireland are attentive hosts who go out of their way to please their guests. Several pubs that do evening meals are close by.

OWNER: Mrs A. Ireland OPEN: all year exc Christmas ROOMS: 1 single, with wash-basin; 1 double, with bath/shower; 1 twin, with bath/shower; TV in all bedrooms and lounge TERMS: single £18, twin/double £38 CARDS: none DETAILS: no children; no dogs; smoking in lounge only; car park; garden

If a B&B caters for vegetarians, we note this in the entry. It is always best, however, to check when booking and make it clear what your requirements are, especially if you require a special diet.

Where we know a B&B accepts credit cards, we list them in the details at the end of an entry. There may be a surcharge if you pay by credit card. It is always best to check whether the card you want to use is acceptable when booking.

CASTLE ACRE   Norfolk   map 6

Willow Cottage

Stocks Green, Castle Acre, nr King's Lynn PE32 2AE
TEL: (01760) 755551
just off A1065, 4m N of Swaffham

Situated in the centre of the charming village, Willow Cottage is a
listed Georgian red-brick property next to the medieval church of St
James. Several original features remain, such as old oak beams in the
cosy bedrooms, two of which overlook Stocks Green. There are no TVs
in the bedrooms, but there is one in the tea-shop which is located on
the ground floor, and serves delicious home-made cakes and scones in
season. Some lovely walks can be enjoyed along the River Nar and
nearby Peddar's Way. Also worth exploring are the ancient hill fort
and ruins of the priory founded about 1090 by William the
Conqueror's son-in-law, William de Warenne.

OWNERS: Patricia Johnson and Peter Foster OPEN: all year exc February ROOMS: 2
double, both with wash-basin; 2 twin; TV lounge TERMS: single occupancy £18, double
£30–£35; £5 for children's cot; deposit: £10 per room CARDS: none DETAILS: children
welcome; dogs in bedrooms only; no smoking; garden

CASTLE DONINGTON   Derbyshire   map 5

Weaver's Lodge

65 Station Road, Castle Donington, nr Derby DE74 2NL
TEL: (01332) 812639

This whitewashed cottage was originally the home of the local basket
weaver. Thorough conversion in recent years has adapted it into a
simple, clean and well-designed guesthouse retaining rediscovered
original features such as the bare brick fireplace in the dining-room.
Guests are invited to share the family lounge, which has plenty of
books as well as a TV. The Daleys provide excellent three-course
evening meals by arrangement, with a separate vegetarian menu.
The dining-room is licensed and wine is reasonably priced. Although
Weaver's Lodge is right on the main road, double glazing minimises
the traffic noise. This is a very popular stopover for business
travellers, so book in advance.

OWNERS: Dave and Lynda Daley OPEN: all year ROOMS: 2 single, both with wash-
basin; 1 double, with bath/shower; TV in all bedrooms and lounge TERMS: single £20,
single occupancy £25, double £42; dinner £9.50; deposit: £5 per person per night
CARDS: none DETAILS: no children; no dogs; smoking in lounge only; car park; garden

---

*No stamps are needed if you write to the Guide from within the UK. Report
forms are at the end of the book, or use your own stationery if you prefer.*

Bargate Cottage

Market Place, Castleton, nr Sheffield S30 2WG
TEL: (01433) 620201   FAX: (01433) 621739

This wonderful rickety-rackety old cottage with its thick stone walls,
creaky floors, inglenook fireplace and beamed ceilings has been
restored from an uninhabitable state, and fits modern comforts
around the original features. The cosy bedrooms sport colourful
duvets and curtains and period furniture, and each bed has a resident
rag-doll or teddy bear to welcome guests. The conservatory looks out
on to the terraced garden, its upper reaches thick with colour and
foliage. The Newsomes have lived in the village, part of a
conservation area, for many years and are happy to advise on tours
and walks. Evening meals, with vegetarian options, are served at
6.30pm if arranged in advance, but it is only a few steps from the
front door to the nearest pub.

OWNERS: Derek and Sylvia Newsome   OPEN: all year exc Christmas   ROOMS: 1 double,
1 twin, 2 four-poster; all rooms with bath/shower; TV in all bedrooms and lounge
TERMS: twin/double £41, four-poster £45; half-price for children sharing with parents;
dinner £10; deposit: £20   CARDS: none   DETAILS: children welcome; no dogs; no
smoking; car park; garden

Bessiestown Farm

Catlowdy, Longtown, nr Carlisle CA6 5QP
TEL/FAX: (01228) 577219
*from Longtown take road at Bush Hotel signposted Catlowdy for 6½m;
turn right at B6318 for 1½m*

Part of a working beef and sheep farm, this small, friendly country
house close to the Scottish border is surrounded by moorland and
forests. Beautifully furnished with many items of interest, including
a cheese dish collection and paintings by a local artist, Bessiestown
Farm has five spacious and well-appointed bedrooms, all with either
en suite bathroom or shower. Children are welcome, though the
owners point out that families with children would normally be
accommodated in one of the farm's self-catering cottages. A four-
course evening meal is served at 7pm (not on Sundays), and
vegetarian options are available upon request. Bessiestown is
licensed, and wine is charged by either glass or bottle. A games room
in a separate building is open from May to the end of October and
offers table tennis, pool and darts. The large indoor swimming-pool is
open from mid-May to mid-September.

OWNERS: Jack and Margaret Sisson   OPEN: all year exc Christmas   ROOMS: 2 double, 2
twin, 1 family; all rooms with bath/shower; TV in all bedrooms   TERMS: single

occupancy £27–£29.50, twin/double £40–£45, family room £60; dinner £10.50; deposit: £10 per person per night CARDS: Access, Amex, Switch, Visa DETAILS: children welcome; no dogs; smoking in 1 lounge only; car park; games room; swimming-pool; garden

---

CHAGFORD Devon   map 1

Glendarah House

Lower Street, Chagford TQ13 8BZ
TEL: (01647) 433270   FAX: (01647) 433483

This substantial Victorian house stands on the edge of Chagford in a large garden and has views of the moors from its bay windows. The Bellengers took over Glendarah in 1995, and have created a comfortable, peaceful atmosphere. The house has been decorated in restful colours and there is a small licensed bar, breakfast room and sitting-room. One of the bedrooms is on the ground floor in the Coach House annexe. Chagford is a pretty Dartmoor village and makes a good centre for walking; packed lunches can be provided, and flasks filled with hot drinks.

OWNERS: Julia and Raymond Bellenger OPEN: all year exc 2 weeks Dec and Christmas ROOMS: 3 double, 3 twin; all rooms with bath/shower; TV in all bedrooms TERMS: single occupancy £25–£30, twin/double £45–£55; deposit: £10 per person per night CARDS: Access, Visa DETAILS: no children under 10; dogs welcome in Coach House room (annexe) only; no smoking in bedrooms or breakfast room; car park; garden

---

CHARING Kent   map 3

Barnfield

Charing, Ashford TN27 0BN
TEL/FAX: (01233) 712421
take A20 from Charing roundabout towards Maidstone, then first left down Hook Lane for 2½m

---

This historic fifteenth-century farmhouse is set in very peaceful countryside and is surrounded by buildings that form part of a 50-acre sheep farm. The house has all the beams and inglenook fireplaces that go with a building of this age, and has been in the Pym family since 1936. The bedrooms are simply furnished and share one small bathroom. Guests have use of a large room which is part dining-room and part sitting area, with comfortable chairs and shelves of books. The more formal dining-room is used when there are a number of guests, and evening meals can be arranged with prior notice. There is no alcohol licence, but guests are welcome to bring their own wine to dinner. Outside there is a hard tennis court and a converted barn where functions are sometimes held. Riding can be arranged nearby and this is a lovely area for country walks.

OWNERS: Mr and Mrs Pym   OPEN: all year exc Christmas   ROOMS: 2 single, 2 double, 1 twin, 1 family; all rooms with wash-basin exc 1 single; TV lounge   TERMS: single/single occupancy £20, twin/double £37–£41; family room from £46; reductions for children sharing with parents; dinner £12.50; deposit: £10 per room   CARDS: none   DETAILS: children welcome; dogs by arrangement; no smoking; car park; garden; tennis

CHEADLE   Staffordshire   map 5

Ley Fields Farm

Leek Road, Cheadle, Stoke-on-Trent ST10 2EF
TEL: (01538) 752875
on A522 to Leek, 2m N of Cheadle

Surrounded by its own farmland and a few pet sheep, this listed red-brick Georgian farmhouse is set in beautiful countryside. The comfortable bedrooms are all *en suite*, and an annexe, which has its own lounge, contains a suite for families. The main guest lounge is spacious and has open fires. Breakfast, as well as dinner by arrangement, is available in the dining-room with its antique sideboard and lace tablecloths. There is no alcohol licence, but guests may bring their own wine to dinner. In the words of one visitor, the breakfast is 'excellent', the welcome 'warm' and the rooms 'immaculately clean'. Ley Fields is a good centre from which to explore the Peak District.

OWNERS: Mr and Mrs R.E. Clowes   OPEN: all year exc Christmas and New Year
ROOMS: 1 double, 2 family; all rooms with bath/shower; TV in all bedrooms   TERMS: single occupancy £17–£19, double £32–£34, family room £50–£54; reductions for children sharing with parents; dinner £9–£10   CARDS: none   DETAILS: children welcome; no dogs; no smoking; car park; garden

CHEDDLETON   Staffordshire   map 5

Choir Cottage

Choir House, Ostlers Lane, Cheddleton, nr Leek ST13 7HS
TEL: (01538) 360561
off A520, 3m S of Leek, take Hollow Lane (opposite Red Lion Inn) past church, then left into Ostlers Lane

Set in what was originally the herb garden, Choir Cottage is a stone-built cottage dating back over 300 years, adjacent to the owners' own home. It is immaculate throughout and guests have the use of a comfortable, chintzy lounge with an interesting collection of china. All the rooms are beamed and have pretty wallpaper and elegant furnishings. Both bedrooms have four-poster beds, one king-sized, and one of the rooms can be used for families. Guests are welcome to bring their own wine to dinner, and vegetarian dishes can be arranged; packed lunches can also be provided. This is a convenient location for visiting Alton Towers, the Peak District and the Potteries.

OWNERS: William and Elaine Sutcliffe OPEN: all year exc Christmas and New Year ROOMS: 2 four-poster, both with bath/shower; TV in both bedrooms TERMS: single occupancy £30–£35, four-poster £45–£53; half-price for children over 5; dinner £15; deposit: £30–£50 CARDS: none DETAILS: no children under 5; no dogs; no smoking; car park; garden

CHELMSFORD   Essex   map 3

Aarandale Guest House

9 Roxwell Road, Chelmsford CM1 2LY
TEL: (01245) 251713

This warm and friendly Victorian house is set back from the road on the western side of Chelmsford. It has been modernised and is comfortable and well appointed. The bedrooms, which all overlook the lovely garden, are large, immaculately clean and well furnished, with warm duvets. David and Margaret Chivers are a delightful couple who offer attentive service; David is happy to show guests around the area if desired. Guests visiting the town centre should take advantage of the convenient bus service. The Chivers were formerly in the catering trade and know how to prepare an excellent breakfast.

OWNERS: David and Margaret Chivers OPEN: all year exc Christmas and Easter ROOMS: 4 single, 1 with bath/shower, 3 with wash-basin; 1 double, with wash-basin; TV in all bedrooms TERMS: single £20–£25, single occupancy £25, double £38 CARDS: none DETAILS: no children; no dogs; car park

CHELTENHAM   Gloucestershire   map 5

Hannaford's

20 Evesham Road, Cheltenham GL52 2AB
TEL: (01242) 515181/524190   FAX: (01242) 515181

This lovely, listed Regency house was built in 1853 as part of Joseph Pitt's estate (which includes Pitville Park) and is within walking distance of the town centre and racecourse. The house has retained much of its original character, including some ornate ceilings and marble fireplaces. The bedrooms are well appointed and immaculately kept. Evening meals are available by arrangement, and there is an alcohol licence; packed lunches can be provided.

OWNER: Dorothy Crowley OPEN: all year exc Christmas ROOMS: 2 single, 1 double, 4 twin, 1 family; all rooms with bath/shower; TV in all bedrooms TERMS: single £29–£31, single occupancy £31–£35, twin/double £48–£52, family room £55; reductions for

children sharing with parents; dinner £14; deposit: written confirmation or credit card
details   CARDS: Access, Amex, Visa   DETAILS: children welcome; no dogs; no smoking
in dining-room

Parkview

4 Pittville Crescent, Cheltenham GL52 2QZ
TEL: (01242) 575567

Standards continue to be high at this well-maintained Georgian
residence built in 1826. It is situated on a quiet tree-lined crescent,
just five minutes' walk from the town centre. The house is partly
furnished with items from a Cotswold cottage, which blend in well
with the rest of the pine and period furniture. The spacious bedrooms
are well appointed, and the shared bathroom has a whirlpool bath.
Breakfast only is served in the dining-room, and packed lunches can
be provided.

OWNER: John Sparrey   OPEN: all year   ROOMS: 1 single, 2 twin; TV in all bedrooms
TERMS: single £17.50, single occupancy/twin £35; reductions for babies; deposit: 10%
CARDS: none   DETAILS: children welcome; dogs welcome; no smoking; garden

CHESTER   Cheshire   map 7

Chester Town House

23 King Street, Chester CH1 2AH
TEL/FAX: (01244) 350021

The Chester Town House dates back to the seventeenth century, and
is situated within the city walls in a conservation area of cobbled
streets, 200 yards from most amenities. The cottage-style bedrooms
are bright and clean, and all have *en suite* bathrooms. For those who
value their privacy there is a garden room away from the main house.
Breakfasts are served in the attractive dining-room, which leads into
the conservatory-style lounge overlooking the garden. The pretty
stencilling throughout the house has been done by various family
members. Guests will feel very much at home in the pleasant,
informal atmosphere. Packed lunches can be provided.

OWNER: Mrs V. Bellis   OPEN: all year   ROOMS: 2 single, 2 double, 1 twin; all rooms with
bath/shower; TV in all bedrooms   TERMS: single £25, single occupancy £45, twin/
double £48; deposit: £20   CARDS: Access, Visa   DETAILS: no children; small dogs
welcome; car park; garden

*Entries in the Guide are listed under town or village. There are also two
indexes at the back of the book, one listing B&Bs by county, the other by
name.*

Holly House Guest House

1 Stone Place, Hoole, Chester CH2 3NR
TEL: (01244) 328967

Holly House is an attractive Georgian whitewashed house in a quiet cul-de-sac only a mile from the city centre and has a pretty rose garden. Marilyn Rudham has installed new carpets and redecorated throughout. The bedrooms have pretty pastel furnishings and comfortable beds, and two have *en suite* bathrooms. A window seat on the landing is a pleasant spot to read the books and leaflets provided on what to see and do in the area. Excellent breakfasts are served and packed lunches can be provided. The bus to Chester stops very close to the house and there are several eating places nearby for evening meals.

OWNER: Marilyn Rudham OPEN: all year exc Christmas ROOMS: 1 single, 2 double, all with bath/shower; 1 family, with wash-basin; TV in all bedrooms TERMS: single £17, single occupancy £18, double £30–£32, family room £36; children under 5 free, half-price for older children; deposit: £10 CARDS: none DETAILS: children welcome; no dogs; no smoking in dining-room; car park; garden

Mitchells of Chester

Green Gables House, 28 Hough Green, Chester CH4 8JQ
TEL: (01244) 679004
on A5104 on S side of city

There is an Indian hint to the architecture of this elegant Victorian house close to the town centre. Inside, the spacious bedrooms are plushly decorated in rich colours and pastels, but the overall ambience is unpretentious. Furniture is of the Victorian era, including an old sewing machine and a grandfather clock. The original marble fireplace remains in the dining-room, where delicious breakfasts, including kippers, are served. The guests' lounge has a log fire. Visiting the centre of Chester is best done by public transport or on foot.

OWNERS: Colin and Helen Mitchell OPEN: all year exc Christmas ROOMS: 1 single, 1 double, 1 twin, 1 family; all rooms with bath/shower; TV in all bedrooms and lounge TERMS: single £25, single occupancy £30, twin/double £40, family room £54–£58; children's reductions according to age; deposit CARDS: none DETAILS: children welcome; no dogs; no smoking in bedrooms or dining-room; car park; garden

If there are reduced rates for children, this is mentioned in the details at the end of the entry. If no reductions are specified, assume you will have to pay full rates for children.

Any smoking restrictions that we know of are given in the details at the end of the entry.

Abigail's Guest House

62 Brockwell Lane, Chesterfield S40 4EE
TEL: (01246) 279391

This turn-of-the-century red-brick house stands above the town. The garden slopes downhill and has two ponds and a waterfall, all of which, plus a view of the town, can be admired from the conservatory, where breakfast is served at separate white tables with pink tablecloths. Two of the tastefully decorated and furnished bedrooms are on the ground floor; all are immaculate. Evening meals are served by arrangement, with vegetarian options, or guests can choose the Badger pub nearby. The bus to town stops outside the house and it is wise to use this rather than drive.

OWNERS: Mike and Gail Onza OPEN: all year ROOMS: 2 single, 3 double, 2 twin; all rooms with bath/shower; TV in all bedrooms and lounge TERMS: single £19.50–£22, single occupancy £22, twin/double £38; children under 2 free, half-price for ages 2 to 12; dinner £9.50; deposit required for long stays CARDS: none DETAILS: children welcome; dogs welcome; smoking in lounge only; car park; garden

Sheeplea Cottage Farm

Baslow Road, Eastmoor, nr Chesterfield S42 7DD
TEL: (01246) 566785
on A619, 5m W of Chesterfield

This stone-built farmhouse was once part of the Chatsworth Estate. The house has been upgraded and tastefully decorated throughout, and has a homely ambience with knick-knacks adorning every surface and wall. Sheeplea is part of a 30-acre smallholding which supports Jacob sheep and horses, and also has a formal garden. The bedrooms have comfortable beds with attractive duvets. There is a small cosy lounge, which also serves as the breakfast room, and a local inn for evening meals is within walking distance; packed lunches can be provided. The house is not suitable for children under ten because it has an open staircase.

OWNER: Veronica Norrall OPEN: Mar to Oct ROOMS: 1 double; 1 twin, with wash-basin; TV in all bedrooms and lounge TERMS: single occupancy £20, twin/double £30; deposit: 20% CARDS: none DETAILS: no children under 10; no dogs; no smoking; car park; garden

If we know of any particular payment stipulations, we mention them in the details at the end of the entry. However, it is always best to check when booking.

CHESWICK   Northumberland   map 11

Ladythorne House

Cheswick, nr Berwick-upon-Tweed TD15 2RL
TEL: (01289) 387382
on A1 turn at sign for Cheswick 4m S of Berwick-upon-Tweed

Standing proudly in its beautiful gardens and surrounded by open
countryside, Ladythorne House is a Grade II listed Georgian building
approached via a tree-lined drive. It has all modern comforts but
retains many original features, and is mostly furnished with antiques
in keeping with its character. The front bedrooms have views as far
as Bamburgh Castle, Lindisfarne and the Cheviot Hills. The
atmosphere is friendly and informal, with two TV lounges (one non-
smoking), and TVs are available for bedrooms if required. Breakfast
only is provided, but evening meals are served at a pub one mile
away.

OWNERS: Neville and Valerie Parker, and Mr R.C. Parker   OPEN: all year   ROOMS: 1
single; 1 double, with wash-basin; 2 twin, 1 with wash- basin; 2 family, both with wash-
basin; TV lounge   TERMS: single/single occupancy £14.50, twin/double £29; children
under 2 free, £3 for ages 2 to 4, £7 for ages 5 to 9; deposit: £10   CARDS: none   DETAILS:
children welcome; dogs welcome; smoking in 1 lounge only; car park; garden

CHICHESTER   West Sussex   map 3

Chanterelle

The Lane, Summersdale, Chichester PO19 4PY
TEL: (01243) 527302

Located in Summersdale, a pleasant suburb just north of Chichester,
Chanterelle enjoys a quiet position. A secluded garden, with tables
and chairs in summer, surrounds the attractive, modern house.
Comfortable accommodation and charming owners are plus points
here; the two bedrooms have private bathrooms and are pleasantly
furnished. Guests eat breakfast at one table in the dining-room, and
packed lunches can also be requested. Chanterelle is convenient for
Goodwood racecourse, and sailing.

OWNERS: Mr and Mrs H.B. Gordon   OPEN: all year   ROOMS: 1 double, 1 family; both
rooms with bath/shower; TV in both bedrooms and lounge   TERMS: double £40–£44,
family room £50–£55; half-price for children sharing with parents   CARDS: none
DETAILS: children welcome; no dogs; no smoking; car park; garden

*It is always best to book a room in advance, even in winter. B&Bs with few
rooms may close at short notice for periods not specified in the details.*

Chichester Lodge

Oakwood, Chichester PO18 9AL
TEL: (01243) 786560
take B2178 out of Chichester and 1½m after Salthill Road take second left into Oakwood School drive

Originally the lodge to the big house which is now a boys' school, Chichester Lodge is an attractive single-storey building set in a pretty garden; the Dridges have no connection with the school. The three bedrooms, all with *en suite* facilities, are charmingly decorated, and one has a four-poster bed. Breakfast only is served either in the dining-room or in the breakfast room. Guests can relax in the garden room, the conservatory, or the garden in summer.

OWNER: Jeannette Dridge OPEN: all year ROOMS: 1 single, 2 double, 1 four-poster; all rooms with bath/shower; TV in all bedrooms TERMS: single occupancy £25, double £40–£45, four-poster £45; deposit: £10 CARDS: none DETAILS: no children; no dogs; no smoking; car park; garden

CHIDDINGFOLD Surrey   map 3

Greenaway

Chiddingfold GU8 4TS
TEL: (01428) 682920   FAX: (01428) 605078
just off village green on Dunsfold road

This charming seventeenth-century property is set back from a quiet road, only a few minutes' walk from the picturesque village green. The house is beautifully furnished throughout, with the rooms having low ceilings and beams. The Marshes are a delightful, welcoming couple who enjoy sailing and have an extensive pottery collection. The attractively decorated sitting-room overlooks the garden, and breakfast can be served in either the dining-room or in the kitchen. Chiddingfold is within easy reach of London and Petworth House.

OWNERS: John and Sheila Marsh OPEN: all year ROOMS: 1 single; 1 double, with bath/shower; 1 twin, with wash-basin; TV in all bedrooms TERMS: single £30, single occupancy £40, twin/double £55–£65; children's reductions by arrangement; deposit: 50% CARDS: none DETAILS: children welcome by arrangement; dogs by arrangement; no smoking in bedrooms; car park; garden

Many B&Bs are in remote places, and although in many cases we provide directions, it is always advisable to ask for clear instructions when booking.

If the establishment does not take credit cards, we say so in the details at the end of the entry.

CHIDEOCK   Dorset   **map 2**

Chimneys Guest House

Main Street, Chideock DT6 6JH
TEL/FAX: (01297) 489368

This seventeenth-century thatched guesthouse was converted from
three cottages in 1930. Although the house is on the main road,
double glazing keeps out most of the traffic noise. A cottage-style
front garden is pretty and welcoming, and a more substantial half-
acre at the back has fruit trees and bushes. The interior is quite
spacious although the simply decorated and furnished bedrooms are
small and the bathrooms very compact. The sitting-room has a
traditional beamed ceiling. Evening meals are served in the panelled
dining-room/bar, which is licensed. The village of Chideock lies in a
valley and is only five minutes from the sea; much of the surrounding
coastline is owned by the National Trust.

OWNERS: Brian and Ann Hardy   OPEN: all year exc Christmas, Nov and Jan   ROOMS: 4
double, 3 with bath/shower, 1 with wash-basin; 1 twin, with bath/shower; 1 four-poster,
with bath/shower; TV in some bedrooms   TERMS: single occupancy £19.50–£23.50,
twin/double £35–£41, four-poster £54; reductions for children over 5 sharing with
parents; dinner £17.50 (including wine); deposit: £20   CARDS: none   DETAILS: no
children under 5; no dogs; no smoking; car park

CHIDHAM   West Sussex   **map 3**

Easton House

Chidham Lane, Chidham, nr Chichester PO18 8TF
TEL: (01243) 572514
turn off A259 5m W of Chichester at Chidham Lane, then 1m on left

Easton House has a happy, relaxed family atmosphere, and a good
lived-in feeling. It is an attractive Tudor house located down a
country lane in the pretty little village of Chidham, and only a five-
minute walk from the harbour. The house is a bit on the dark side and
is full of pictures, china, cats and music – guests are welcome to play
on the Bechstein piano, the cello or a double bass. The two bedrooms
are comfortable, if slightly cluttered. There is a pub close by, and a
good choice of eating places in Chichester; packed lunches can be
provided by arrangement.

OWNER: Mary Hartley   OPEN: all year exc Christmas   ROOMS: 1 double, with bath/
shower; 1 twin, with wash-basin; TV lounge   TERMS: single occupancy £30, twin/double
£36–£40; £12 for children under 10   CARDS: none   DETAILS: children welcome; no
dogs; no smoking; car park; garden

Old Rectory

Cot Lane, Chidham, nr Chichester PO18 8TA
TEL/FAX: (01243) 572088
turn S off A259 down Cot Lane at Barleycorn pub, continue for 1m

This spacious country house, set in a lovely garden, is opposite the Saxon church of St Mary. It is reached down a quiet, leafy country lane and has a welcoming, relaxed atmosphere. The large bedrooms have their own bathrooms. The formal drawing-room has TV and a piano, and breakfast only is served in the dining-room. Guests like to sit in the conservatory, which leads out to the garden, beyond which is the swimming-pool and a croquet lawn. The village pub serves food and is within a few minutes' walk. Chidham is on a peninsula, surrounded on three sides by Chichester harbour, and is a wonderful area for bird-watching, sailing and walking.

OWNERS: Peter and Anna Blencowe   OPEN: all year exc Christmas   ROOMS: 1 single, 3 double/twin; all rooms with bath/shower; TV in all bedrooms and lounge   TERMS: single £16–£20, single occupancy £20–£30, twin/double £40–£48; reductions for children according to time of year   CARDS: none   DETAILS: children welcome; dogs by arrangement; no smoking in bedrooms and dining-room; car park; garden; swimming-pool

CHIPPING CAMPDEN   Gloucestershire   **map 5**

Rosary Cottage

High Street, Chipping Campden GL55 6AL
TEL: (01386) 841145

Rosary Cottage started life in the fourteenth century and has the distinction of being the first house in this small town; the High Street was thereafter built around it. The cottage has a cosy ambience and is furnished in keeping with its age. There are oak beams, sloping floors and original doors. The four delightful bedrooms have a chintzy décor and patchwork quilts. One has a four-poster with the drapes and fabric surround made by Rosemary. This is a fascinating house in a useful Cotswold location.

OWNER: Rosemary Spenler   OPEN: all year   ROOMS: 2 double, 1 twin, 1 four-poster; all rooms with bath/shower   TERMS: single occupancy £30, twin/double/four-poster £42
CARDS: none   DETAILS: children welcome; no dogs; no smoking in dining-room

Sparlings

Leysbourne, Chipping Campden GL55 6HL
TEL: (01386) 840505

Sparlings is a seventeenth-century listed building at the north end of the High Street. Tastefully restored, it retains many original features, such as flagstone floors and oak beams. The two bedrooms are well appointed, one having an *en suite* bathroom, the other a private bathroom close by. Breakfast only is served, but there are plenty of eating establishments within walking distance, and packed lunches can be requested. There is no car park belonging to the house, so visitors should ask in advance about arrangements for cars.

OWNERS: Geoffrey E. Douglass and Graeme Black   OPEN: all year   ROOMS: 1 double, 1 twin; both rooms with bath/shower; TV lounge   TERMS: single occupancy £27, twin/double £44–£46; deposit: £25   CARDS: none   DETAILS: no children under 12; no dogs; smoking in lounge only; garden

---

CHIVELSTONE   Devon   map 1

South Allington House

Chivelstone, nr Kingsbridge TQ7 2NB
TEL/FAX: (01548) 511272
3m N of Prawle Point

Directions from the owners are a good idea as South Allington House is very much tucked away in attractive countryside. This imposing country house is part of a working arable farm, and is surrounded by mature trees and well-kept grounds with facilities for bowls, croquet and coarse fishing. There is a friendly atmosphere, and several of the pretty, spacious bedrooms have *en suite* bathrooms, and for those without, there is a good ratio of bedrooms to bathrooms. A sitting area in the entrance hall has a fire, and there is a dining-room where breakfast only is served. In season, the Bakers provide snacks and cream teas, and can also do packed lunches. There is a self-catering flat in the east wing.

OWNERS: Edward and Barbara Baker   OPEN: all year   ROOMS: 1 single, with wash-basin; 4 double, all with bath/shower; 3 twin, 1 with bath/shower, 2 with wash-basin; 2 family, 1 with bath/shower, 1 with wash-basin; TV in some bedrooms and lounge   TERMS: single £18, single occupancy from £25.50, twin/double £34–£48, family room from £40; reductions for children sharing with parents; deposit: 15%   CARDS: none   DETAILS: children welcome; no dogs; no smoking; car park; garden

---

CHOP GATE   North Yorkshire   map 9

Hillend Farm

Chop Gate, nr Stokesley TS9 7JR
TEL: (01439) 798278
just off B1257, 6m S of Stokesley

This seventeenth-century stone farmhouse occupies a very remote location in an elevated position overlooking Bilsdale, within the North Yorkshire Moors Park. The 106-acre farm takes in part of one of the last remaining ancient oak forests, and remains of the jet mining era. Bilsdale is beautiful walking country and there are six footpaths to explore on the land; packed lunches can be provided. The two bedrooms are traditionally decorated in white and pink, one has an *en suite* bathroom, the other has a bathroom close by. Brenda Johnson is a cheery lady who welcomes guests with a cup of tea in the lounge, and serves evening meals at 6.30pm. There is no alcohol licence, so guests may bring their own wine; vegetarian choices and children's helpings can be requested.

OWNERS: Mr and Mrs Johnson OPEN: Mar to Nov ROOMS: 1 double, with wash-basin; 1 family, with bath/shower; TV lounge TERMS: double £33, family room from £37; half-price for children; dinner £10.50; deposit: £10 CARDS: none DETAILS: children welcome; dogs by arrangement; smoking in lounge only; car park; garden

---

CHUDLEIGH   Devon

map 1

Oakfield

Chudleigh, nr Newton Abbot TQ13 0DD
TEL/FAX: (01626) 852194
off A38, 1m NE of Chudleigh

This attractive, cream-painted large country house was built around 1840 and stands in 20 acres of landscaped gardens, orchard and paddocks on the outskirts of Chudleigh. Oakfield has spacious, beautifully furnished and decorated rooms. The three bedrooms are large and tastefully decorated, each with its own character, and with fresh fruit and flowers; one has a half-tester bed. Guests have use of a large, elegant drawing-room, as well as a library and a billiards room. Four-course evening meals, incorporating fresh produce from the kitchen garden, are available by arrangement and are taken with the family; guests may bring their own wine to dinner. Although the house is grand and quite luxurious, the Johnson-Kings are a most welcoming couple and treat their guests like friends. The lovely garden is extensive and includes a small heated swimming-pool, which is in a sheltered position close to the house. There is a loggia where guests can sit and where barbecues are sometimes held on fine evenings. Golf, fishing and riding are all available nearby. Oakfield is well placed for exploring Dartmoor.

OWNERS: Peter and Patricia Johnson-King OPEN: Mar to end Oct ROOMS: 3 double, 1 twin, all with bath/shower; TV in all bedrooms TERMS: single occupancy £40, twin/double £60–£70; dinner £20–£25; deposit: £10 per person CARDS: none DETAILS: no children under 10; no dogs; no smoking; car park; games room, swimming-pool; garden

---

If a B&B offers off-street car parking, we note 'car park' in the details at the end of the entry. If we are aware of particular car-parking difficulties, we mention them.

CHURCH STRETTON   Shropshire   map 5

Brookfields Guest House

Watling Street North, Church Stretton SY6 7AR
TEL: (01624) 722314

Set in half an acre of landscaped gardens amid the Stretton Hills,
Brookfields has good views over the surrounding countryside and is
within easy walking distance of the town centre. The bedrooms all
have *en suite* facilities, modern furniture and amenities such as hair-
dryers and clock radios, as well as TVs. One bedroom is on the ground
floor. Stewart Blower is a trained chef, and breakfasts and evening
meals are served in the sunny dining-room. The guesthouse is
licensed, children's portions are available, and packed lunches can be
provided.

OWNERS: Stewart and Carol Blower, and Audrey Goodall   OPEN: all year   ROOMS: 2
double, 1 twin, all with shower; 1 family, with bath; TV in all bedrooms   TERMS: single
occupancy £27–£35, twin/double £45–£47, family room from £63; children's reductions
according to age; dinner £15.50   DETAILS: children welcome; dogs welcome; no
smoking in bedrooms; car park; garden

CIRENCESTER   Gloucestershire   map 2

26 Victoria Road

26 Victoria Road, Cirencester GL7 1ES
TEL: (01285) 656440

Just five minutes' walk from the town centre, this Victorian house is
immaculately kept and offers good-value accommodation in a friendly
atmosphere. The large dining-room/lounge has a TV for guests' use;
breakfast only is served. There are three large bedrooms, one of
which has *en suite* facilities. Mrs Cremin is a local lady and is happy
to give advice on places to visit in the neighbourhood.

OWNER: Mrs E. Cremin   OPEN: all year exc Christmas   ROOMS: 2 double, 1 with bath/
shower, 1 with wash-basin; 1 twin, with wash-basin; TV lounge   TERMS: single
occupancy £18, twin/double £25–£35; reductions for children sharing with parents;
deposit: 10%   CARDS: none   DETAILS: children welcome; no dogs; car park

Wimborne House

91 Victoria Road, Cirencester GL7 1ES
TEL/FAX: (01285) 653890

This detached Victorian house stands in its own grounds in a
residential road a few minutes' walk from the town centre. Recent
extensive interior redecoration has brought all the rooms up to a
luxurious standard, with colour co-ordinated pastel wallpapers and

matching fabrics; one bedroom has a four-poster. The sitting-room is on the first floor. Breakfast and a good-value dinner, by arrangement and with vegetarian options, are available. Cirencester is home to the Corinium Museum, which houses one of the finest collections of Roman antiquities in Britain.

OWNERS: Dianne and Marshall Clarke OPEN: all year exc Christmas ROOMS: 3 double, 1 twin, 1 four-poster; all rooms with bath/shower; TV in all bedrooms TERMS: single occupancy £20–£25, twin/double £30–£35, four-poster £35–£40; dinner £6; deposit: £5 per person CARDS: none DETAILS: no children under 8; no dogs; no smoking; car park; garden

CLARE Suffolk

map 6

Ship Stores

22 Callis Street, Clare, nr Sudbury CO10 8PX
TEL: (01787) 277834

Ship Stores is a sixteenth-century listed building that encompasses a small village grocer's shop with adjoining tea-rooms. The refurbished bedrooms have exposed beams, pine furniture and floral duvets. One of the bedrooms has a luxury queen-sized bed, Two bedrooms and a lounge are above the shop, one ground-floor room is behind it, and a further two are in a newly converted ground-floor annexe across the

SHIP STORES, CLARE

courtyard. Freshly prepared breakfasts are served in the cottagey dining-room or in the bedrooms. Modestly priced dinners are available by arrangement, vegetarians can be catered for and children's helpings (and packed lunches) provided. There is an alcohol licence, but guests are also welcome to bring their own wine. The property has lots of character and Colin and Debra Bowles are attentive hosts.

OWNER: Debra Bowles   OPEN: all year   ROOMS: 3 double, 1 twin, 1 family; all rooms with bath/shower; 2 rooms suitable for wheelchair-users; TV in all bedrooms and lounge TERMS: single occupancy £20–£25, twin/double £35–£45, family room £40–£55; reductions for children sharing with parents; dinner £7.50; deposit: £10 per room CARDS: none   DETAILS: children welcome; no dogs; smoking in public rooms only; car park

CLEETHORPES   Humberside   map 9

Brentwood Guest House

9 Princes Road, Cleethorpes DN35 8AW
TEL: (01472) 693982

Only five minutes from the sea and town centre, this pleasant black-and-white, turn-of-the-century house with leaded light windows provides functional, clean accommodation. The modestly furnished bedrooms range in size from average to large family rooms. Breakfast and reasonably priced evening meals are served in the dining-room/lounge. Guests are welcome to bring their own wine to dinner, and packed lunches can be provided. Suzanne and Kevin Brown are an amiable couple who extend a home-from-home welcome to their visitors.

OWNERS: Kevin and Suzanne Brown   OPEN: all year   ROOMS: 1 single, 2 double, 3 twin, 3 family; all rooms with wash-basin; TV in all bedrooms   TERMS: single/single occupancy £16, twin/double £24, family room from £30; dinner £5; deposit: £5 per booking   CARDS: none   DETAILS: children welcome; dogs welcome; no smoking in dining-room at meal times; garden

CLEOBURY NORTH   Shropshire   map 5

Charlcotte Farm

Cleobury North, Bridgnorth WV16 6RR
TEL/FAX: (01746) 787238
on B4364, 7m SW of Bridgnorth

This creeper-covered house at the foot of Brown Clee Hill is the charming centre of a working farm. In the past it was linked with the nearby Charlcotte Blast Furnace, the remains of which can still be seen, and the large drawing-room with log fires has a ceiling depicting items manufactured there. Bedrooms are spacious with some old and some new furniture. Wendy Green is a welcoming and friendly hostess. Walking and wildlife-watching are some of the best ways to take in the rural peace of this conservation trust area, and after one and a half miles the local village pubs will offer refreshment and food.

OWNER: Wendy Green OPEN: Mar to Nov ROOMS: 2 double, 1 with bath, 1 with wash-basin; 1 twin, with wash-basin; TV in some bedrooms and lounge TERMS: single/single occupancy £18–£20, twin/double £34–£40 CARDS: none DETAILS: no children; no dogs; no smoking; car park; garden

---

CLEY   Norfolk   map 6

Whalebone House

High Street, Cley, nr Holt NR25 7RN
TEL: (01263) 740336
on A149, 4m NW of Holt

This Grade II listed Georgian property, built of brick and flint, is in the centre of Cley next the Sea, a pretty coastal village. Inside is warm and cosy, and improvements are ongoing. The immaculate bedrooms are of a good size and have old-fashioned furniture, paintings and flowers. An original fireplace and a wrought-iron bed occupy the main double room. There is also a tea-shop on the premises, where breakfasts and lunches are served at smartly dressed tables. Selena makes a feature of local produce, and everything is home-made, including a big selection of cakes and speciality breads. The Cley Marshes Nature Reserve is a mecca for bird-watchers.

OWNER: Stuart and Selena Bragg OPEN: all year exc Christmas ROOMS: 1 single, with wash-basin; 2 double, 1 with bath/shower; 2 twin, 1 with bath/shower; TV in all bedrooms TERMS: single/single occupancy £20–£22, twin/double £32–£48; deposit: £10 per person CARDS: none DETAILS: no children under 10; no dogs; no smoking

---

CLINT GREEN   Norfolk   map 6

Clinton House

Well Hill, Clint Green, Yaxham, nr Dereham NR19 1RX
TEL: (01362) 692079
from Dereham head S on B1135, at Yaxham take sign for Matishall, then turn right at school and continue for 200 metres

---

This large, shuttered 200-year-old building stands behind a lawn with rose-beds, a willow and an old well in this peaceful hamlet. The bedrooms are beautifully decorated and the *en suite* one is in an annexe. The beamed lounge has an inglenook fireplace, which is used on cold days, and the conservatory, where breakfast is served, is

Victorian in style. Guests are welcome to enjoy the grass tennis court and the croquet lawn. Margaret Searle is a thoughtful host who looks after her guests well.

OWNERS: John and Margaret Searle OPEN: all year exc Christmas ROOMS: 2 double, 1 with bath/shower, 1 with wash-basin; 1 twin, with wash-basin; 1 family, with wash-basin; TV in some bedrooms and lounge TERMS: single occupancy £20, twin/double £32, family room £45; babies free, half-price for older children; deposit CARDS: none DETAILS: children welcome; no dogs; no smoking; car park; garden; tennis

---

CLUN   Shropshire   **map 5**

Woodside Old Farmhouse

Clun, nr Craven Arms, SY7 0JB
TEL: (01588) 640695
in village in front of church turn into Vicarage Rd; after 300yds turn right, signposted Woodside; farmhouse is ½m on left

---

Woodside Old Farm stands in a wonderful position with splendid views over the Clun Valley. Its lovely garden with a gentle stream is a pleasant place in which to relax on nice days. The house was built in the seventeenth century as a one-up, one-down labourer's cottage, but was later extended; a six-foot-thick stone wall divides the old part of the building from the 'new'. There is a visitors' sitting-room which leads into a conservatory; breakfast and, if arranged in advance, home-cooked evening meals are served in a separate dining-room. Vegetarian options are available, and packed lunches can be provided. Although Woodside is unlicensed, guests may bring their own wine to dinner. The Walls tell us that dogs are welcome only if kept under control, for 'you will be in sheep country!' Clun is well positioned for exploring Offa's Dyke (five miles away) and the Ironbridge Gorge Museum.

OWNER: R.H. Wall OPEN: March to Oct ROOMS: 1 double, 1 family; both rooms with wash-basin; TV lounge TERMS: single occupancy £16–£18, double £32–£36; half-price for children from 2 to 10; dinner £9; deposit: £10 CARDS: none DETAILS: children welcome; dogs welcome; no smoking; car park; garden

---

CLUNGUNFORD   Shropshire   **map 5**

Keepers Cottage

Clungunford, nr Craven Arms SY7 0PL
TEL: (01588) 660419
off B4367, 4m SW of Craven Arms

This impressive country property was built as recently as 1989, but contains several interesting features taken from an old manor house, such as 400-year old oak beams, quarry-tiled floors and the Aga on which breakfast is prepared. Of special interest are the tall windows with their leaded-glass country scenes. The house is surrounded by beautiful woodland full of animal and bird life. The place is immaculate, and the spacious bedrooms are well appointed, with a chintzy décor and floral wallpapers; one has a jacuzzi bath. There is a large oak-panelled games room for guests' use. A self-catering unit is also available. Clay-pigeon shooting can be arranged, and packed lunches provided.

OWNER: Lynne Colledge   OPEN: all year exc Christmas   ROOMS: 1 double, 2 family; all rooms with bath/shower; TV in all bedrooms   TERMS: single/single occupancy £20, double £40, family room £40; half-price for children under 12   CARDS: none   DETAILS: children welcome; no dogs; smoking in bar/games room only; car park; games room; garden

COLCHESTER   Essex   map 3

Four Sevens Guesthouse

28 Inglis Road, Colchester CO3 3HU
TEL/FAX: (01206) 46093
in town off B1022 Maldon Road

This Victorian residence is on a quiet tree-lined street a few minutes' walk from the town centre. Guests are made very welcome and the atmosphere is informal. The immaculate bedrooms have pine furnishings and attractive blue-and-pink-striped duvets. All have satellite TV, and video recorders can be provided on request, with a huge selection of tapes to choose from in the bright dining-room, where there is also a well-stocked bookcase. Huge breakfasts are served here and dinners are available between 6 and 8pm. Vegetarians can be catered for and guests may bring their own wine. Parking permits are provided.

OWNER: Calypso Demetri   OPEN: all year   ROOMS: 2 double, 1 with bath/shower, 1 with wash-basin; 2 twin, 1 with bath/shower, 1 with wash-basin; 2 family, 1 with bath/shower, 1 with wash-basin; TV in all bedrooms   TERMS: single occupancy £25–£30, twin/double £32–£40, family room £50–£60; children's reductions; dinner £10   CARDS: none   DETAILS: children welcome; no dogs; no smoking in dining-room; garden

14 Roman Road

14 Roman Road, Colchester CO1 1UR
TEL: (01206) 577905

In a quiet square near the centre of town, this Victorian house overlooks the Norman castle and has a Roman wall at the end of the garden. It has two large bedrooms and a comfortable sitting-room, all well-furnished and stocked with information on the area. Filling breakfasts include vegetarian options, and home-made biscuits add a treat to the tea-making facilities.

OWNER: Gill Nicholson   OPEN: all year exc Christmas   ROOMS: 1 double, 1 twin; both rooms with bath/shower; TV in all bedrooms   TERMS: single occupancy £26, twin/double £36–£38   CARDS: none   DETAILS: no children under 12; no dogs; no smoking; car park; garden

Old Manse

15 Roman Road, Colchester CO1 1UR
TEL: (01206) 45154

The Old Manse is a civilised family home with an easy-going atmosphere, in a quiet location close to the town centre. The three tastefully decorated bedrooms are of a good size and have antique furniture and TV; one room is on the ground floor. There is a piano in the comfortable sitting-room. Tea trays with Wendy's home-baked cakes can be provided, and packed lunches requested. Otherwise, breakfast is the only meal served, and is taken at a large, scrubbed pine table. There are several places to eat within walking distance.

OWNERS: Wendy and David Anderson   OPEN: all year exc Christmas   ROOMS: 1 double, 2 twin; all rooms with bath/shower; TV in all bedrooms   TERMS: single occupancy £24–£30, twin/double £36–£42   CARDS: none   DETAILS: no children under 3; no dogs; no smoking; car park

COLLINGHAM   West Yorkshire   map 9

Langston

Langwith Valley Road, Collingham, nr Wetherby LS22 5DW
TEL: (01937) 572476
from A659 turn into Hillcrest and take right-hand fork to bottom of hill

A warm welcome awaits visitors to this modern bungalow built from local stone. It stands in a prize-winning garden and has lovely views of the Wharfe Valley. The three spotless bedrooms are at ground level and two are equipped for disabled guests; the other has an antique high bed. There is a guest lounge and a conservatory overlooking the garden. Mrs Turner is talkative and knowledgeable about the area, and she runs a friendly and informal house. Collingham makes a good touring base and is only 20 minutes' drive from the cities of York, Leeds and Harrogate.

OWNER: Mrs P. Turner   OPEN: all year   ROOMS: 1 double, 1 twin, 1 family; all rooms with bath/shower; 2 rooms suitable for wheelchair-users; TV lounge   TERMS: single occupancy £25, twin/double £40, family room £50; 33% reduction for children under 12; deposit: 50%   CARDS: none   DETAILS: children welcome; dogs welcome; smoking area; garden

The Granary

Church House Farm, Collington, nr Bromyard HR7 4NA
TEL: (01885) 410345
off B4214, 3m N of Bromyard

Guests continue to applaud the Granary, part of a 200-acre farm in a
wonderfully remote location. The house is impeccably maintained,
with all the luxurious bedrooms on the ground floor in a tastefully
converted barn. They are decorated with light floral fabrics and the
attractive beamed ceilings are fully exposed. Breakfasts and candlelit
dinners are served in the elegant dining-room, which has views over
open countryside and also operates as a restaurant in the evening
and for Sunday lunch. Vegetarian meals are available and there is a
short but adequate wine list. The guests' lounge has a well-stocked
bar.

OWNERS: Paul and Margaret Maiden   OPEN: all year   ROOMS: 1 double, 4 twin; all rooms
with bath/shower; 2 rooms suitable for wheelchair-users; TV in all bedrooms   TERMS:
single occupancy £19–£21, twin/double £38–£40; children's reductions by
arrangement; dinner from £10; deposit: £10 per person   CARDS: none   DETAILS:
children by arrangement; no dogs in bedrooms; no smoking in bedrooms; car park;
garden

Old Walls

Combe, Salcombe TQ7 3DN
TEL: (01548) 844440
*in Malborough turn opposite Shell garage, follow signs for Sharpitor
National Trust Gardens for about 1¼m*

This very pretty thatched cottage dates from 1680 and is built of cob.
Deep in the country and only half a mile from the beach, it stands in a
lovely three-quarter-acre garden with a stream running through. Mrs
Sames is a delightful and gregarious lady who runs Old Walls in a
professional way, and Mr Sames is a chef, so guests can be assured of
good home-cooked food. Evening meals are served by candlelight in
the small beamed lounge/dining-room. Bread is freshly made every
morning and fresh fish comes from Salcombe or Plymouth. Although
the cottage is unlicensed, guests are welcome to bring their own wine
or beer. The South Devon Coast Path runs nearby, and there are
footpaths in every direction. Mountain bikes and use of a dinghy can
be arranged, and packed lunches are available.

OWNERS: Barry and Michelle Sames   OPEN: all year exc Christmas   ROOMS: 2 double, 1
twin, 1 family, all with bath/shower; TV in all bedrooms   TERMS: single occupancy

£22.50–£50, twin/double £40–£50, family room £45–£65; children's reductions; dinner £11.50-13.50; deposit: £10 per room per night   CARDS: none   DETAILS: children welcome; no dogs; no smoking in bedrooms; car park; garden

---

COMBE MARTIN   Devon   map 1

Holdstone Farm

Hunters Inn Road, Combe Martin EX34 0PE
TEL: (01271) 883423
off A399, 5m E of Ilfracombe

Reached down a long driveway, Holdstone Farm is a twelfth-century builiding in a secluded position, high up on the downs two miles from Combe Martin. The house is immaculately kept, with only partial central heating, and has low ceilings and a recently discovered inglenook fireplace in the guests' lounge. The two spacious bedrooms are fresh and bright and share a bathroom. There are no drink-making facilities in the bedrooms, but tea and coffee are always available on demand. Evening meals are served by arrangement in the attractive dining-room and Sunday lunch is also available. Vegetarians can be catered for and guests may bring their own wine. The house has a welcoming, friendly and homely atmosphere and is close to cliffs, sandy beaches and the resort of Ilfracombe.

OWNER: Jayne Lerwill   OPEN: all year exc Christmas   ROOMS: 1 double, 1 family; TV lounge   TERMS: single occupancy £16, double £32, family room from £32; dinner £10; deposit: 10%   CARDS: none   DETAILS: children welcome; no dogs; no smoking; car park

---

COMPTON ABBAS   Dorset   map 2

Old Forge

Fanners Yard, Chapel Hill, Compton Abbas, nr Shaftesbury SP7 0NQ
TEL/FAX: (01747) 811881
just off A350, 3m S of Shaftesbury

Tucked away under the downs on the edge of the village of Compton Abbas, this stone house dates from around 1700, and was once part of the blacksmith's forge. Tim and Lucy Kerridge have carefully converted the building and adjoining barn, creating interesting, characterful accommodation. There are lots of ancient beams and sloping ceilings throughout the attractively decorated house, pretty bedrooms, and a cosy breakfast/sitting-room with wood-burning stove, board games and books. There is also a self-catering cottage. A craft shop is now housed in what was the original forge. Tim runs a vintage car restoration business in a converted lorry shed. This is a good area for walking, with National Trust chalk downland nearby, and bicycle hire is available. Shaftesbury is just three miles away. Packed lunches can be provided.

OWNERS: Tim and Lucy Kerridge OPEN: all year exc Christmas ROOMS: 1 single, 1 double, both with wash-basin; 1 twin/family, with shower; TV lounge TERMS: single £25, single occupancy £35, double £40, twin/family room £45–£55; deposit: £20 CARDS: none DETAILS: children welcome; dogs welcome with own basket; no smoking; car park; garden

CONISHOLME Lincolnshire   map 9

Wickham House

Church Lane, Conisholme, nr Louth LN11 7LX
TEL: (01507) 358465

This eighteenth-century cottage beside the village church in a quiet lane has leaded windows, a red-tile roof and roses round the door. Inside, it is tastefully furnished, mostly in pine, and is exceptionally well maintained. The pretty bedrooms, one on the ground floor, overlook the garden or countryside, have attractive duvets and are well-appointed; all have *en suite* facilities (either bath or shower room). Guests will find lots of local information, books, games and magazines in the cosy library, or they can relax in the comfortable sitting-room with its exposed timbers and brickwork. Breakfasts are served in the sunny dining-room at separate tables. Ann and Bill Painter are superb hosts who have created a warm and inviting ambience in their delightful home. This is an ideal base for nature lovers: close by is the Tetney Haven bird reserve, a colony of grey seals can be seen at Donna Nook, and the Marsh offers quiet lanes and footpaths for walking and cycling. Packed lunches can be provided.

OWNERS: Ann and Bill Painter OPEN: all year exc Christmas and New Year ROOMS: 1 double, 2 twin, all with bath/shower; TV in all bedrooms TERMS: twin/double from £37; children's reductions CARDS: none DETAILS: no children under 8; no dogs; no smoking; car park; garden

CONISTON Cumbria   map 8

Arrowfield Country Guest House

Little Arrow, Coniston LA21 8AU
TEL: (01539) 441741
on A593, 1¾m S of Coniston

This white Victorian house nestles safely in its well-maintained garden, while offering wide-ranging views of the surrounding countryside. It is a spacious house with well-appointed rooms. One of the bedrooms has a king-sized bed and the single room is by no means the loser on space. Breakfast is a feast of home-made produce – from the bread to the jam to the eggs. The lounge has an open fire, rich, soft beige furnishings and a bookcase ideal for browsers. Arrowfield provides immediate access to the fells. Menus of local restaurants are provided.

OWNERS: Malcolm and Stephanie Walton OPEN: Feb to Nov ROOMS: 1 single, with wash-basin; 3 double, 2 with bath/shower, 1 with wash-basin; 2 twin, 1 with bath/ shower, 1 with wash-basin; TV in all bedrooms and lounge TERMS: single £18–£21, single occupancy £18–£30, twin/double £32–£45; reductions for children according to age; deposit: £10 per person CARDS: none DETAILS: children welcome; no dogs; no smoking in bedrooms or dining-room; car park; garden

Beech Tree

Yewdale Road, Coniston LA21 8DB
TEL: (01539) 441717

This former vicarage is these days a totally smoke-free and vegetarian guesthouse. Standing at the foot of the Old Man of Coniston, the building dates from 1720, though the east wing was added about a hundred years later. Evening meals, which need to be arranged in advance, are exclusively vegetarian (although the Wattses tell us that about half their guests are non-vegetarian) and cater fully for vegan and special diets. The Beech Tree is licensed and offers a selection of organic wines, or guests may bring their own wine if they so choose. The comfortably furnished rooms are individually decorated, and paintings by the owner's son, James Watts – who is an accomplished artist – are on display. Packed lunches can be provided.

OWNERS: Jean and John Watts OPEN: Feb to Nov, and New Year ROOMS: 3 double, 2 with bath/shower, 1 with wash-basin; 2 twin, 1 with bath/shower, 1 with wash-basin; 1 family, with wash-basin; TV lounge TERMS: twin/double £32–£44 (reductions for single occupancy); reductions for children sharing with parents; dinner £11; deposit: 1 night's charge CARDS: none DETAILS: no children under 6; dogs by arrangement; no smoking; car park; garden

Townson Ground

Coniston, nr Ambleside LA21 8AA
TEL: (01539) 441272
take Hawkshead road from Coniston to head of lake, turn right on road marked 'Brantwood', then first house on left

This well-maintained sixteenth-century house is on the quietest side of Coniston Water, one mile from the village. It stands in a large garden, and there are numerous local walks, as well as access to a private jetty on the lake. A wood-burning stove heats the comfortable lounge, which has a TV. The *en suite* bedrooms are pleasantly decorated in soft pastels with pretty curtains made by Mrs Nelson. Breakfasts only are served in the beamed dining-room, but there are plenty of eating places nearby and packed lunches can be provided. Laundry facilities are available, and there are also three self-catering cottages for rental.

OWNERS: Ken and Barbara Nelson OPEN: all year exc Christmas ROOMS: 1 single, with wash-basin; 1 double, 1 twin, 1 family, all with bath/shower; TV in all bedrooms and lounge TERMS: single from £20, twin/double from £42; family from £49; £7 for children from 3 to 6; half-price for ages 6 to 14 sharing with parents; deposit: £30 per room CARDS: none DETAILS: no children under 3; dogs by arrangement; car park; garden

COPTHORNE   West Sussex   map 3

Linchens

New Domewood, Copthorne, nr Crawley RH10 3HF
TEL/FAX: (01342) 713085
from M3 junction 10 take A264 towards East Grinstead; after 'Airport Parking' on right turn left into private New Domewood road, then first right and, after sharp bend to left, Linchens is first house on right

Linchens is set in a well-planned private estate in three and a half acres of mature and carefully maintained gardens. The house was built about 30 years ago, and the Smyths, who took over the business from Sally's mother in 1993, are in the process of refurbishing the bedrooms. These are bright, good-sized rooms, all with a sitting area. Breakfast is taken at one table in the owner's sitting-room, which overlooks the garden; packed lunches can be arranged. The Smyths have a golden retriever called Murphy.

OWNERS: John and Sally Smyth OPEN: all year exc Christmas ROOMS: 4 single, 2 with bath/shower; 2 double, 1 with bath/shower; 2 twin, 1 with bath/shower; 4 family, 2 with bath/shower; 2 rooms suitable for wheelchair-users; TV in all bedrooms and lounge TERMS: single/single occupancy £30–£35, twin/double £40–£50, family room rates by arrangement; children's reductions by arrangement; deposit: £10 per room CARDS: Access, Visa DETAILS: children welcome; dogs by arrangement; no smoking; car park; garden

CORNFORTH   Co Durham   map 10

Ash House

24 The Green, Cornforth, nr Durham DL17 9JH
TEL: (01740) 654654
adjacent to A1(M), 3 mins from junction 61

This beautifully appointed Victorian house is in a peaceful position facing the green, but only four miles from Durham. The good-value accommodation has a warm ambience and the furniture is mostly Victorian. The spacious bedrooms are pleasantly decorated with floral fabrics. Delia Slack is an excellent host and her husband designs miniatures, some of which are displayed in the house. Breakfast only is served, but there are plenty of establishments nearby for evening meals.

OWNER: Delia Slack OPEN: all year ROOMS: 1 double, 1 twin; both with wash-basin; 1 four-poster/family, with wash-basin; TV in all bedrooms TERMS: single occupancy £22, twin/double £34; family room £48; £10 for children under 10; deposit: £10 CARDS: none DETAILS: children welcome; no dogs; smoking in twin room only; car park; garden

CORSHAM Wiltshire   map 2

Pickwick Lodge Farm

Corsham SN13 0PS
TEL: (01249) 712207   FAX: (01249) 701904
take A4 towards Bath from Corsham, turn right into Guyers Lane, follow lane to end, house on right

Parts of this lovely old Cotswold stone farmhouse, on a 300-acre arable farm, date from the seventeenth century, with the front having been added much later. The old barns, which are set to one side of the house, have been converted into housing, and the newer farm buildings are placed farther away from the house. Steps lead down from the lounge to the attractive dining-room, where breakfasts only are served, and one of the large family/double bedrooms is on the ground floor. Nearby are Stonehenge, Avebury and the quaint villages of Lacock and Castle Combe; Bath is only 15 minutes by car.

OWNER: Gill Stafford OPEN: all year exc Christmas ROOMS: 2 double, 1 twin, 1 family; all rooms with bath/shower; TV in all bedrooms TERMS: single occupancy from £20, twin/double from £34, family room from £40; babies free in own cot, reductions for children sharing with parents; deposit: £20 CARDS: none DETAILS: children welcome; small dogs welcome; no smoking; car park; garden

COVENHAM ST BARTHOLOMEW Lincolnshire   map 9

The Grange

Orange Lane, Covenham, nr Louth LN11 0PD
TEL: (01507) 363678
on A16, 5m N of Louth

Part of an arable and cattle farm, the Grange stands at the end of a lane and alongside a reservoir which has a bird sanctuary and sailing facilities. Antique furniture features in the good-sized bedrooms, and although there are no *en suite* facilities, guests have a bathroom exclusively for their use and an extra WC. Phyl and Jim Shaw are accommodating people who have lived in the house for nearly 50 years. Breakfast is served family-style in the dining-room, which has a grandfather clock and a collection of toby jugs and horse brasses. Guests may choose to relax in the comfortable TV lounge, a sun lounge or a patio area.

OWNER: Phyl Shaw OPEN: all year exc Christmas ROOMS: 1 single, 2 double, 1 family; TV lounge TERMS: single £13.50, single occupancy £18, double £27–£30, prices for family room by request; reductions for children under 12 CARDS: none DETAILS: children welcome; no dogs; smoking in lounge only; car park; garden

COVENTRY   West Midlands   map 5

Abigail Guest House

39 St Patricks Road, Coventry CV1 2LP
TEL: (01203) 221378

This straightforward, good-value B&B is an ideal base for visiting either Coventry or Warwick universities, is close to the railway and bus stations and is only a ten-minute walk from the cathedral and city centre. Roger and Julie are welcoming hosts who are happy to help with sightseeing plans. The house has a well-furnished lounge and a small eating area where tasty breakfasts are served. The bedrooms are fresh and clean and all have sheets as well as warm duvets. Guests share two shower rooms. Visitors arriving by car should be sure when making a reservation to request instructions for navigating the one-way system.

OWNERS: Roger and Julie Griffiths OPEN: all year exc Christmas and New Year ROOMS: 2 single, 1 double, 1 twin, 1 family; all rooms with wash-basin; TV in all bedrooms TERMS: single £16–£18, single occupancy £18–£20, twin/double £30–£32; children under 5 free, half-price for ages 5 to 11 CARDS: none DETAILS: children welcome; no dogs

Crest Guest House

39 Friars Road, Coventry CV1 2LJ
TEL: (01203) 227822   FAX: (01203) 227244

This immaculate city-centre guesthouse is in a quiet location down a cul-de-sac, but only ten minutes' walk from the cathedral and the Transport Museum. The spacious bedrooms have floral duvets with matching curtains, desks and rattan armchairs with cushions that match the duvets. The two single rooms share a bathroom, the twin rooms are *en suite*. Guests enjoy the informal atmosphere created by the owners and aided by their friendly pet whippets, Jim and Paddy. Breakfast only is served in the bright dining-room overlooking the garden. The well-furnished guests' lounge has a TV and log-effect fire.

OWNERS: Alan and Peggy Harvey OPEN: all year exc Christmas ROOMS: 2 single, both with wash-basin; 2 twin, both with bath/shower; TV in all bedrooms and lounge TERMS: single £22, single occupancy £28, twin/double £42; deposit CARDS: none DETAILS: children welcome; dogs by arrangement; car park; garden

---

COWES   Isle of Wight   map 2

Northlands

52 Baring Road, Cowes PO31 8DJ
TEL: (01983) 293764

This large Victorian house is in an elevated position with spectacular views over the Solent. The Kellys are hospitable, welcoming people and the family home has a relaxed atmosphere. Ian comes from the island and is more than happy to share his knowledge of its attractions and sailing facilities with his guests. Both he and Christine enjoy entertaining, and serve good home-cooked dinners in the dining-room overlooking the Solent, at which they join their guests. An attractive wide staircase leads up to the three beautifully furnished bedrooms. This is an excellent place to stay for Cowes week.

OWNERS: Ian and Christine Kelly OPEN: all year exc Christmas ROOMS: 1 double, with wash-basin; 2 twin, 1 with bath/shower, 1 with wash-basin; TV in some bedrooms and lounge TERMS: single occupancy £30–£45; twin/double £50–£70; dinner £18.50; deposit: £50 or 1 night's charge if less CARDS: Access, Visa DETAILS: no children under 12; no dogs; car park; garden

---

COXWOLD   North Yorkshire   map 9

School House

Coxwold, nr York YO6 4AD
TEL: (01347) 868356
6m E of A19, between Thirsk and Easingwold

This seventeenth-century stone cottage was once a coaching-inn and is situated on the edge of Coxwold in a peaceful position. The Richardsons have carefully furnished School House in keeping with the period, and have included a large collection of plates, brass and pictures. The three attractive bedrooms are decorated in pastel colours; all have TV. They share two bathrooms with showers. There is a tea-shop within the property which opens in summer for light snacks and evening meals are served to residents at 7pm (5.30pm high tea on Sundays) in this room throughout the year. Vegetarians can be catered for with notice, and guests may bring their own wine as there is no licence. Coxwold is a good base for walkers. The village was home to Lawrence Sterne, author of *Tristram Shandy*; his house, Shandy Hall, is open to visitors in summer.

OWNERS: John and Jean Richardson   OPEN: all year exc Christmas and New Year
ROOMS: 1 double, 1 twin, 1 family; all rooms with wash-basin; TV in all bedrooms
TERMS: single occupancy from £18, twin/double/family room from £33; children's
reductions by arrangement; dinner £10; deposit   CARDS: none   DETAILS: children
welcome; dogs welcome; no smoking in dining-room; car park; garden

---

CRACKINGTON HAVEN   Cornwall   map 1

Nancemellan

Crackington Haven, nr Bude EX23 0NN
TEL: (01840) 230283
*from A39 at Wainhouse Corner, 7m S of Bude, follow signs W for
Crackington Haven*

This most attractive large house is in a wonderful position at the
entrance to the village and has lovely views. Nancemellan is a
tremendously welcoming place, and the Ruffs are charming hosts
who enjoy looking after their guests. The house is surrounded by nine
acres of beautiful gardens and it is just 500 yards from the beach,
which is reached through the garden. The spacious bedrooms are
stylishly decorated and all have views. The comfortable lounge is
tastefully furnished and breakfast is served in the large family
kitchen. Nancemellan is a perfect place for those who enjoy walking,
beaches or just getting away from it all.

OWNERS: Edward and Lorraine Ruff   OPEN: all year exc Christmas   ROOMS: 2 double, 1
twin; all rooms with bath/shower; TV in all bedrooms   TERMS: single occupancy £20,
twin/double £40–£50; deposit: 1 night's charge   CARDS: none   DETAILS: no children; no
dogs; no smoking; car park; garden

Trevigue Farm

Crackington Haven, nr Bude EX23 0LQ
TEL/FAX: (01840) 230418
*from A39 at Wainhouse Corner, 7m S of Bude, follow signs W for
Crackington Haven; Trevigue is 1½m S on minor road*

This early sixteenth-century farmhouse is built around a cobbled
courtyard, and is only a few hundred yards away from the South West
Coast Path and dramatic cliffs. The farm has been in existence since
before the Norman Conquest and gets a mention in the Domesday
Book. Trevigue Farm is a family-run dairy and beef operation
comprising 500 acres in a remote location. The interior has been
carefully restored; the six *en suite* bedrooms still have beams and
sloping walls, and the sitting-room has relaxing sofas, a log-burning
fire, books and TV. Janet Crocker loves cooking and serves dinner at
7.30pm. There is a wine list. With notice, vegetarians can be catered
for; packed lunches can also be provided.

OWNERS: Mr and Mrs K.A. Crocker   OPEN: Mar to end Oct   ROOMS: 4 double, 2 twin; all rooms with bath/shower; TV in some bedrooms and lounge   TERMS: single occupancy £40, twin/double £52; dinner £15; deposit: £20 per person   CARDS: none   DETAILS: no children under 12; no dogs; no smoking in dining-room or bedrooms; car park; garden

Treworgie Barton

Crackington Haven, nr Bude EX23 0NL
TEL/FAX: (01840) 230233
from A39 at Wainhouse Corner 7m S of Bude, follow signs W for Crackington Haven, take first right and right again

Treworgie Barton is a historic whitewashed building dating from the sixteenth century and set in peaceful countryside. It is reached by a long, narrow private road, about two miles from the beach and the village, and has a very pretty, small walled garden. Pam Mount is a welcoming host and a wonderful cook, which is one reason why her guests keep returning. Breakfast is simple and traditional, but dinner is a four-course extravaganza, with vegetarian options by arrangement; guests are encouraged to bring wine. One of the four pretty bedrooms has a four-poster bed. Behind the house are the farm buildings and an area of lovely walks through the wooded Millook Valley.

OWNER: Pam Mount   OPEN: Apr to Sept (Nov, Feb and Mar advance booking only)
ROOMS: 1 double, 1 twin, 1 four-poster, 1 family; all rooms with bath/shower; TV in all bedrooms   TERMS: single occupancy £20–£25, twin/double £36–£40, four-poster £40, family room £65; dinner £14; deposit: £20   CARDS: none   DETAILS: no children under 10; no dogs; no smoking; car park; garden

CRANBROOK Kent   map 3

Hancocks Farmhouse

Tilsden Lane, Cranbrook TN17 3PH
TEL: (01580) 714645
from Cranbrook take minor road to Tenterden; Tilsden Lane is third on right, then take first farm track on left

The earliest recorded mention of this ancient, timber-framed listed house is in a will of 1520. The building was extended in the sixteenth century, and today is no longer a farm. The Oatens extend a warm welcome and do everything possible to make visitors feel at home. The house is well furnished with period pieces and has lovely old beams; it is clean and well run. One of the three large bedrooms has a handsome, old four-poster bed, one has a small sitting-room, and the one on the ground floor has its own garden entrance. The drawing-room has a large inglenook fireplace with a log fire, and there is a pretty rose-filled garden. Afternoon tea is served, and dinner is by arrangement, usually at 7.30pm. There is no alcohol licence, but guests may bring their own wine. Children's helpings, vegetarian meals and packed lunches can all be provided. Hancocks Farmhouse is in attractive countryside, and is a good base for visiting Sissinghurst Castle Gardens, Bodiam, Leeds and Hever Castles.

OWNER: Bridget Oaten OPEN: all year exc Christmas and occasional closures ROOMS: 1 double, 1 twin, 1 four-poster; all rooms with bath/shower; TV in all bedrooms TERMS: single occupancy £30–£35, twin/double £50–£55, four poster £50–£55; children under 2 free, half-price for ages 2 to 9; dinner £16–£19; deposit: £20 CARDS: none DETAILS: children welcome; dogs by arrangement; no smoking; car park; garden

CRANLEIGH   Surrey   map 3

Bookers Lee

Guildford Road, Alfold, nr Cranleigh GU6 8JS
TEL: (01483) 272442
off A281, 9m S of Guildford, 10m N of Horsham

Bookers Lee is set back from the main road in a beautifully kept large garden. It is an attractive late Georgian house with a relaxed atmosphere, and the Carrs are a most friendly couple. The décor and furnishings are of a very high standard, and breakfasts are particularly good. Guests have the use of a spacious drawing-room, television room and dining-room.

OWNERS: Margaret and Andrew Carr OPEN: all year exc Christmas and New Year ROOMS: 1 single; 1 double, with bath/shower; 1 twin, with wash-basin; TV in some bedrooms TERMS: single £20, single occupancy £25, twin/double £35–£40; £15 for children over 8 CARDS: none DETAILS: no children under 8; dogs in stable only; no smoking; car park; garden

CREWKERNE   Somerset   map 2

Broadview

43 East Street, Crewkerne TA18 7AG
TEL: (01460) 73424
on Yeovil road out of Crewkerne

This unusual bungalow, which dates from 1926, was built by a family returning from the Colonies. It stands high above the main road and is set in an acre of very pretty terraced gardens with interesting shrubs and plants, and a water garden. The entrance to the house is through a sun porch which opens into the dining-room, with its ceiling fans giving it a colonial atmosphere. The lounge is at the back of the house, and the three bedrooms all have TV. Gillian and Robert Swann are a very friendly couple who run the comfortable house very capably. Collections of the owners' china, rugs and pictures cover every wall and surface. Broadview is on the outskirts of Crewkerne and the gardens at Clapton Court are just a few minutes' drive away. Other nearby places of interest include Barrington Court house and garden, and Forde Abbey.

OWNERS: Gillian and Robert Swann   OPEN: all year   ROOMS: 1 double, 2 twin; all rooms with bath/shower; TV in all bedrooms   TERMS: single occupancy £35, twin/double £46–£50; dinner £12; deposit: 1 night's charge   CARDS: Access, Visa (+ 3% charge)   DETAILS: children welcome; dogs by arrangement; no smoking; car park; garden

Dryclose

Newbery Lane, Misterton, Crewkerne TA18 8NE
TEL: (01460) 73161

This lovely old former farmhouse dates from 1550 and was named after the field in which the house was built. It is in a quiet and peaceful location in a two-acre garden with an unheated swimming-pool. Sally Gregory gives her guests a warm welcome and the house is very comfortable with a homely atmosphere. There is a small upstairs sitting-room with TV and another lounge on the ground floor with log fire and TV. Evening meals are available by arrangement and the fruit and vegetables come from the garden. There are National Trust properties close by and lovely walks, including the Liberty Trail, which passes within 200 metres of Dryclose.

OWNERS: John and Sally Gregory   OPEN: all year exc Christmas   ROOMS: 1 single; 2 twin, 1 with bath/shower; TV lounge   TERMS: single £16–£19, twin £32–£42; dinner £12; deposit: £10   CARDS: none   DETAILS: no children under 8; no dogs; no smoking; car park; garden; swimming-pool

CROCKERTON   Wiltshire   map 2

Tanhouse Cottage

Crockerton, Warminster BA12 8AU
TEL: (01985) 214816
on A350, 1m S of Warminster

This seventeenth-century whitewashed building was originally a farmhouse. It stands on the edge of the Longleat Estate, with Longleat House only a couple of miles away. The pretty cottage backs on to a main road, which can be noisy, but the surrounding countryside is quiet and peaceful and there is a small, homely garden, where breakfast is served on sunny mornings. The four bedrooms are small and simple and share one bathroom, with another available downstairs. The cosy oak-beamed sitting-room is shared with the owners. Freshly prepared home-cooked evening meals are served in the pretty dining-room by arrangement.

OWNER: Sheila Dickinson OPEN: all year ROOMS: 1 single, 1 double, 1 twin, 1 family; all rooms with wash-basin; TV lounge TERMS: single £17, twin/double £34, family room £34 plus children's charge; half-price for children; dinner £12.50; deposit required CARDS: none DETAILS: children welcome; dogs welcome; no smoking in bedrooms; car park; garden

CROMER Norfolk   map 6

Beachcomber

17 Macdonald Road, Cromer NR27 9AP
TEL: (01263) 513398

This immaculate Victorian house is in a splendid position 300 yards from the beach and town centre. The bedrooms are attractively decorated in both pastel and rich colours, and most have *en suite* facilities. There is a guest lounge with TV, and a sitting-room with plenty of books. Modestly priced home-cooked evening meals are available, if pre-arranged, and there are several eating establishments within walking distance. Beachcomber is not licensed, but guests may bring their own wine, and packed lunches can be provided. Dusty, the bearded collie, is friendly.

OWNER: Anne Weinle OPEN: all year exc Christmas ROOMS: 1 single, with wash-basin; 5 double, 4 with bath/shower, 1 with wash-basin; 1 family, with bath/shower; TV in all bedrooms and lounge TERMS: single £15–£17, twin/double £30–£34, family room £45; children's reductions by arrangement; dinner £7; deposit CARDS: none DETAILS: children welcome; no dogs; smoking in lounge only; garden

CROOK Cumbria   map 8

Birksey Brow

Crook, nr Kendal LA8 8LQ
TEL: (01539) 443380
from Kendal take B5384 4m W to Crook, pass through village; with Sun Inn on right go ½m up hill past village hall and church

This traditional stone-built, creeper-covered country house stands in its own grounds next to fields and a small stock-rearing farm which the Browns also run. All the bedrooms, one of which is *en suite*, have views of the mountains. The interior has a simple elegance, and in the good-sized bedrooms guests will find fresh fruit and flowers. Honeymooners receive special attention. Afternoon teas are a treat for early arrivals, and excellent breakfasts include home-made jams and marmalades. If booked ahead, traditional home-cooked evening meals are available, with vegetarians catered for. Birksey Brow is unlicensed, but guests may bring their own wine to dinner. Packed lunches can be provided. Holly the sheepdog is very friendly.

OWNERS: Mr and Mrs Robin Brown OPEN: all year exc Christmas ROOMS: 1 double, 1 twin, 1 family; all rooms with bath/shower; TV in all bedrooms and lounge TERMS: single occupancy £35, twin/double £50, family room from £60; dinner £15–£17; children's reductions by arrangement CARDS: none DETAILS: no children under 8; no dogs; smoking in residents' lounge only; car park; garden

CROOKHAM Northumberland   map 11

Coach House

Crookham, nr Cornhill on Tweed TD12 4TD
TEL: (01890) 820293
just off A697, 4m E of Cornhill on Tweed

Several old farm buildings forming a square round a garden courtyard have been imaginatively converted to form the Coach House, with arched windows which lend a slightly church-like appearance. The original coach-house, now a sitting-room, has retained its open-raftered barn-style roof, giving it a tremendous sense of space. Log fires keep it warm on cooler evenings. Bedrooms are warm and large, some with windows facing the courtyard. Most are on the ground floor and four are specifically equipped for wheelchair-users, as are the bathrooms and one roll-in shower with its own plastic wheelchair. Superb four-course dinners are a major feature, many guests returning to enjoy the fine food, and breakfasts are very enticing too. Lynne Anderson is an enthusiastic host who is really in tune with her guests' needs.

OWNER: Lynne Anderson OPEN: Mar to Nov ROOMS: 2 single, 1 with bath/shower; 2 double, both with bath/shower; 5 twin, 4 with bath/shower; 4 rooms suitable for wheelchair-users; TV in some bedrooms TERMS: single/single occupancy £23–£34, twin/double £46–£68; reductions for children under 10; dinner £15.50; deposit: £5 per person per day CARDS: Access, Visa DETAILS: children welcome; no dogs in public rooms; no smoking in dining-room; car park; garden

CROYDE Devon   map 1

Combas Farm

Putsborough, Croyde EX33 1P
TEL: (01271) 890398
signposted on minor road from Croyde to Putsborough

Wistaria and a grape vine ramble over this attractive seventeenth-century whitewashed farmhouse, beautifully situated down a well-maintained track in a quiet valley, with a lovely cottage-style garden and orchard. The Adamses, who have lived here for over 35 years, keep a 140-acre cattle and sheep farm and grow fruit, vegetables and herbs specifically for use in evening meals. The small, pleasant bedrooms are well equipped for families with children. One small 'cabin room' has bunk beds for two children, and all the other rooms now have private facilities. Both the dining-room and sitting-room have open stone fireplaces (one with a bread oven). Dinner is available by arrangement, with vegetarian options, and babysitting can be arranged. Wildlife abounds in this area; Putsborough Sands beach, which stretches for three idyllic miles to Woolacombe, is only a mile away and much of the nearby land and coastline is owned by the National Trust.

OWNERS: John and Gwen Adams OPEN: Mar to Nov ROOMS: 2 double, 1 twin, 2 family (plus children's bedroom); all rooms with bath/shower; TV lounge TERMS: single/single occupancy £16–£19, twin/double £32–£38, family room £32–£38 plus children's charge; children's reductions according to age; dinner £8; deposit: 20% CARDS: none DETAILS: children welcome; no dogs; smoking in lounge only; car park; garden

---

CURRY RIVEL Somerset   map 2

Hillards

High Street, Curry Rivel, nr Langport TA10 0EY
TEL: (01458) 251737
just off A378, 2m SW of Langport

This delightful listed house dating from the end of the sixteenth century retains genuine old-world charm. It has oak panelling, beamed ceilings and huge open fireplaces, and has been furnished in keeping with the period. The bedrooms are beautifully decorated and some are quite large. One lounge is a family TV room and a separate one has comfortable armchairs and a sofa, and when weather permits visitors like to relax in the sheltered courtyard. The original working end of the building has the old cider-making equipment and there are two self-catering units in a converted barn. Plenty of good pubs in neighbouring villages offer evening meals.

OWNERS: Jeannie Wilkins and Mike Carter OPEN: all year ROOMS: 1 single, with wash-basin; 3 double, 2 with bath/shower, 1 with wash-basin; 3 twin, 2 with bath/shower, 1 with wash-basin; TV lounge TERMS: single £20, single occupancy £35–£45, twin/double £36–£55 CARDS: none DETAILS: no children; no dogs; no smoking; car park; garden

---

If you are forced to turn up later than planned, please telephone to warn the proprietor.

B&B rates specified in the details at the end of each entry are given (as applicable) for a single room, for single occupancy of a double room, and then per room in the case of two people sharing a double or twin-bedded room, or for a family room.

Bath / shower in the details under each entry means that the rooms have private facilities. The B&B may have other, shared bathroom facilities as well. We say if rooms have wash-basins.

Lansdowne

Cusop, nr Hay-on-Wye HR3 5RF
TEL: (01497) 820125
*from Hay-on-Wye take narrow country lane signposted Cusop and Cusop
Dingle; after 600 metres turn left, signposted Ancient Church of St Mary;
Lansdowne is on left*

Lansdowne is a small, attractive Victorian house enjoying a peaceful
rural setting, yet only a walk across the fields from Hay-on-Wye. A
conservatory leads out to a pretty garden and patio, where
imaginative breakfasts are served on warm days. The two well-
appointed bedrooms are both *en suite*. Margaret Flack is a charming
and dedicated host, and Robert has a traditional printing press which
he is happy to demonstrate for interested guests. Very early
reservations are recommended for the May/June Literary Festival
and August Jazz Festival.

OWNERS: Margaret and Rob Flack   OPEN: all year   ROOMS: 1 double, 1 twin; both rooms
with bath/shower; TV in both bedrooms and lounge   TERMS: single occupancy
£21–£22, twin/double £32–£35; half-price for children under 10 sharing with parents;
deposit: £10   CARDS: none   DETAILS: children welcome; no dogs; no smoking; car park;
garden

Sliders Farm

Furners Green, Danehill, nr Uckfield TN22 3RT
TEL: (01825) 790258   FAX: (01825) 790125
take A275 S of Danehill for 1m, turn right at Sliders Lane

This listed sixteenth-century farmhouse can be found down a quiet
country lane close to Ashdown Forest. It has all the exposed beams
and inglenook fireplaces one would expect and has been cleverly
converted to provide modern comforts. The *en suite* bedrooms are
spacious and very comfortably furnished; one is on the ground floor,
and there is a large guests' lounge with a billiard table and a log fire
in winter. Extensive grounds include a hard tennis court, heated
outdoor swimming-pool and private trout lakes. There is also a self-
catering cottage. Four-course dinners are available by request at
7pm, and Jean Salmon makes use of home-grown vegetables and soft
fruits – also serving home-made jams for breakfast. Guests should
bring their own wine as there is no licence; children's helpings,
vegetarian choices and packed lunches can be provided.

OWNERS: Jean and David Salmon   OPEN: all year exc Christmas   ROOMS: 2 double, 1
twin, 1 family; all rooms with bath/shower; TV in all bedrooms   TERMS: single
occupancy from £28, twin/double from £38, family room from £57; children's

reductions by arrangement; dinner £14; deposit: £10 per room CARDS: none DETAILS: children welcome; no dogs; smoking in lounge only; car park; garden; swimming-pool; tennis

DARLINGTON   Co Durham   map 10

Woodland House

63 Woodland Road, Darlington DL3 7BQ
TEL: (01325) 461908

Guests continue to enjoy this good-value family-run Victorian house in the centre of the historic town of Darlington. The original stained-glass windows, marble fireplace and tiling survive and the lovely oak staircase is adorned with an attractive display of plates. The bedrooms are clean and comfortable, and guests are welcome to use the kitchen to prepare hot drinks and light snacks.

OWNERS: Philip and Marjorie Hawke   OPEN: all year   ROOMS: 3 single; 1 double; 2 twin, 1 with bath/shower; 2 family; TV in all bedrooms and lounge   TERMS: single £20, single occupancy £24–£28, twin/double £34–£40, family room £42–£48; half-price for children sharing with parents; deposit: £10   CARDS: none   DETAILS: children welcome; dogs welcome; no smoking in some bedrooms and dining-room

DARTMOUTH   Devon   map 1

Broome Court

Broomhill, Dartmouth TQ6 0LD
TEL: (01803) 834275
off B3122, approx 1½m W of Dartmouth

Broome Court stands in an acre of grounds up a quiet lane in the beautiful, undulating Devon countryside. Attractive old, converted farm buildings surround a courtyard filled with flowers and shrubs, with a goldfish pond in the centre. Jan Bird is a very friendly, down-to-earth lady who runs an immaculate house. It has been attractively furnished, mostly in pine, and there are pine floors on the ground level. The rooms are all *en suite*, and the twin and one of the doubles can be used for families (there is a bathroom between). Guests are welcome to sit out in the courtyard and on the sun terrace. A hearty breakfast is served in the old farmhouse kitchen.

OWNERS: Jan Bird and Thomas Boughton   OPEN: all year   ROOMS: 2 double, 1 twin; all rooms with bath/shower; TV in all bedrooms and lounge   TERMS: single occupancy £30, twin/double £50; reductions for children sharing with parents; deposit: £20   CARDS: none   DETAILS: children welcome; dogs by arrangement; no smoking in bedrooms and dining-room; car park; garden

Ford House

44 Victoria Road, Dartmouth TQ6 9DX
TEL/FAX: (01803) 834047

This attractive ivy-covered Regency house is up a steep hill only 500
yards from Dartmouth's historic quay, and close to the town centre.
Ford House has a friendly, lived-in atmosphere. The comfortable
sitting-room has a log fire and a pianola and the three bedrooms are
most attractively decorated, with their own TV, telephone and fridge.
The food is one of the main reasons visitors return here: the evening
menus are most imaginative and all ingredients are purchased fresh
on the day with the accent on locally caught fish and seafood. Guests
eat together at the large mahogany dining table. Henrietta Firth does
the cooking and is keen to discuss menus with guests and willing to
prepare any special favourites. There is no licence but guests can
bring their own wine or have it delivered by a local vintner. Breakfast
is served until noon every day, and fish or devilled kidneys are
available if ordered in advance. Ford House organises special dinner-
party weekends in conjunction with the Carved Angel restaurant.

OWNER: Richard Turner OPEN: Mar to Nov ROOMS: 3 double, 2 twin; all rooms with
bath/shower; TV in all bedrooms TERMS: single occupancy £50, twin/double £65;
dinner £25; deposit: £50 CARDS: Access, Amex, Visa DETAILS: children welcome;
dogs welcome; car park; garden

DAWLISH   Devon   map 1

Oak Cottage

Luscombe Hill, Dawlish EX7 0PX
TEL: (01626) 863120
*from end of M5 at Exeter take A38 then A380 Torquay road, after 2m take
B3192 Teignmouth road, take second left to Dawlish, Oak Cottage is third
house on left after 1½m*

Oak Cottage is a charming and most unusual house on a quiet
country lane well above the resort of Dawlish. A beautiful landscaped
garden complete with croquet lawn, pool and terrace surrounds the
property, which has views over farmland to glimpses of the sea. The
attractive stone building with its mullion windows and Tudor-style
chimneys was built in the mid-nineteenth century as four cottages for
workers on the Luscombe Estate. It was soon converted into a single
house, which was home to Viscount Montgomery's sister, and has
been seen on TV's *Miss Marple* series. Oak Cottage has a series of
stairs and doors, leading to two exceptionally comfortable and
unusual *en suite* guest quarters. There is a lounge with log fire, old
prints and antiques, and a dining-room, where Tony and Liz serve
home-cooked dinners by candlelight. There is no alcohol licence, so

guests should bring their own wine to table. Vegetarians can request
alternative choices. This is a delightful and relaxing place to stay in
lovely countryside, with welcoming hosts.

OWNERS: Tony and Liz Williams OPEN: all year exc Christmas and New Year ROOMS: 1
double, 1 twin; both rooms with bath/shower; TV in both bedrooms and lounge TERMS:
single occupancy £35, twin/double £50; dinner £12; deposit: £10 CARDS: none
DETAILS: children by arrangement; dogs by arrangement; no smoking in bedrooms and
dining-room; car park; garden

Walton Guest House

Plantation Terrace, Dawlish EX7 9DR
TEL/FAX: (01626) 862760
on A379, 10m S of Exeter

This imposing large-windowed Georgian house standing in a small
garden was designed by John Nash and built in 1819. It has been
converted into a friendly family-run guesthouse and is spotlessly
clean and maintained in excellent condition. The six bedrooms are
comfortably furnished and two have four-poster beds. There is a
small sitting-room with a piano, and breakfast only is served at
separate tables in the dining-room. Walton Guest House is in a quiet
road a five-minute walk from the beach and the centre of the pretty
town of Dawlish, where the famous black swans live on the brook
with its series of waterfalls.

OWNERS: John and Doreen Newton OPEN: all year exc Christmas ROOMS: 4 double, 1
twin, 1 four-poster; all rooms with bath/shower; TV in all bedrooms TERMS: single
occupancy £22.50–£25, twin/double £30–£34, four-poster £34–£42; deposit: £15 per
person CARDS: none DETAILS: children welcome; no dogs; no smoking in dining-room;
car park; garden

DEAL Kent   map 3

Beaconhill

Great Mongeham, Deal CT14 0HW
TEL/FAX: (01304) 372809
take M2 / A2, turn left at Whitfield just before Dover

Beaconhill is set in lovely countryside just west of Deal in two acres of
grounds, part of which is a managed nature reserve. The house was
converted from a row of 200-year-old farm cottages and retains some
of its old features, such as narrow staircases and low ceilings. The
Wigginses are a kindly couple and the house has a homely feel to it.
Home-cooked evening meals are available, served with a glass of
wine, and the combined dining-room/lounge has a TV and a wood-
burning stove. A variety of special-interest holidays are available to
guests, including gardening, walking, and painting or sketching in

the fully equipped studio in the grounds. As Beaconhill is difficult to find, guests are recommended to ask for detailed directions when booking.

OWNERS: Angela and Tony Wiggins   OPEN: all year   ROOMS: 3 twin, all with wash-basin; TV lounge   TERMS: single occupancy £18, twin £32; dinner £9.50; deposit   CARDS: none   DETAILS: children welcome; no dogs; smoking in smoking-room only; car park; garden

DEDHAM   Essex   map 3

May's Barn Farm

May's Lane, Dedham, Colchester CO7 6EW
TEL: (01206) 323191
on B1029, 1m from Dedham heading towards Ardleigh turn left into Long Road West, then left again after ¼m

Down a lane away from the road and truly away from it all, this peaceful old farmhouse is settled into the landscape of Dedham Vale in over 300 acres of farmland. The house is traditionally furnished and warmed with an open fire at the first hint of cold. The green and gold lounge is spacious and the bedrooms are of a good size too. The cheerful dining-room is the place for fresh breakfasts and, one mile away, Dedham offers a range of establishments for evening meals.

OWNER: Jean Freeman   OPEN: all year exc Christmas   ROOMS: 1 double, 1 twin; both rooms with bath/shower; TV in both bedrooms and lounge   TERMS: single occupancy £22–£25, twin/double £38–£40; deposit: £10   CARDS: none   DETAILS: no children under 12; no dogs; no smoking in bedrooms; car park; garden

DENT   Cumbria   map 8

Stone Close

Main Street, Dent, nr Sedbergh LA10 5QL
TEL: (01539) 625231

Originally two farm cottages built in the seventeenth century, Stone Close now offers three comfortable, pleasantly furnished first-floor guest bedrooms and, downstairs, a licensed tea-shop that serves excellent lunches and snacks (including many vegetarian options) throughout the day. Much of the original character of the building has been retained: there are flagged floors, exposed beams, two cast-iron ranges and – in the tea-shop – original meat hooks on the ceiling. The guesthouse is totally non-smoking and has not a single TV. It is a popular place for walkers, and early reservations are recommended. Guests may make use of a public car park approximately 50 yards from the property. Packed lunches can be provided, and there are a number of eating establishments in the area that serve evening meals.

OWNERS: Patricia Barber and Graham Hudson   OPEN: all year exc Jan and Feb   ROOMS: 1 single, 1 twin, 1 family; all rooms with wash-basin   TERMS: single/single occupancy £17, twin £30, family room £33–£37; deposit: £10   CARDS: none   DETAILS: children welcome; dogs welcome; no smoking (*The Good Food Guide*)

DETHICK   Derbyshire
map 5

Manor Farmhouse

Dethick, nr Matlock DE4 5GG
TEL: (01629) 534246
from M1 junction 28 take A38 to Alfreton, then A615 signposted Matlock, then after 5m left turn to Dethick

Set in a peaceful hamlet at the gateway to the Peak District, this listed 300-year-old farmhouse was built from the ruins of a thirteenth-century manor. The house has lots of old-world atmosphere, with thick stone walls and low doors. Sir Anthony Babington, who was executed in 1586 for his part in the unsuccessful plot to free Mary Queen of Scots, lived in the house at one time. The good-sized bedrooms are comfortably furnished, and there is a lounge with TV. Breakfast only is served.

OWNERS: Mr and Mrs H. Groom   OPEN: all year exc Christmas   ROOMS: 1 double, with bath/shower; 2 twin, 1 with bath/shower, 1 with wash-basin; TV in some bedrooms and lounge   TERMS: single occupancy £26, twin/double £37; babies free, 66% reduction for children over 8 sharing with parents; deposit: £10 per person   CARDS: none   DETAILS: babies and children over 8 welcome; guide dogs only; no smoking; car park; garden

DEVIZES   Wiltshire
map 2

Rathlin Guest House

Wick Lane, Devizes SN10 5DP
TEL: (01380) 721999

This red-brick Edwardian house is set in an attractive garden, in a quiet residential road about a 15-minute walk to the centre of Devizes. Barbara and Peter Fletcher are a very friendly couple who keep an immaculate property. The three bedrooms are attractively decorated in period style, and the lounge is a small, comfortable room with an open fireplace. Evening meals, by arrangement at 7 to 8pm, are served in the pleasant dining-room; vegetarian dishes can be requested, and guests may bring their own wine as there is no alcohol licence. Packed lunches can also be provided.

OWNERS: Barbara and Peter Fletcher   OPEN: all year exc Christmas   ROOMS: 1 double, 2 twin; all rooms with bath/shower; TV in all bedrooms   TERMS: single occupancy £25, twin/double £40; children's reductions by arrangement; dinner £10; deposit: £10   CARDS: none   DETAILS: children welcome; no dogs; no smoking; car park; garden

DORCHESTER   Dorset   map 2

Westwood House

29 High West Street, Dorchester DT1 1UP
TEL: (01305) 268018   FAX: (01305) 250282

Originally built as a coaching-inn for Lord Ilchester, this listed
Georgian house lies on the main street of Dorchester and has been
decorated to a high standard in keeping with its period. The
comfortable sitting-room leads into a Victorian conservatory, which
takes up almost the whole of the back of the house, and is where
English and Continental breakfasts are served. The individually
decorated bedrooms are luxuriously equipped and some have
whirlpool baths. Although the house is on the main street, double
glazing cuts down the noise from the road. Packed lunches can be
provided and there are plenty of places nearby for evening meals.

OWNERS: Philip and Kate Sevier-Summers   OPEN: all year exc Christmas   ROOMS: 1
single; 4 double, all with bath/shower; 2 twin, 1 with bath/shower, 1 with wash-basin; 1
four-poster, with bath/shower; TV in all bedrooms and lounge   TERMS: single £25–
£29.50, single occupancy £35–£39.50, twin/double £49.50–£54.50, four-poster
£59.50–£65.50, family room £59.50; children's reductions by arrangement; deposit:
credit card details   CARDS: Access, Amex, Visa   DETAILS: children welcome; well-
behaved dogs welcome; no smoking in dining-room

DOVER   Kent   map 3

Linden Guest House

231 Folkestone Road, Dover CT17 9SL
TEL: (01304) 205449

This comfortable Victorian townhouse is on a busy road a five-minute
drive from the centre of town and the ferries. Its owners, who took
over in late 1994, offer a warm welcome and provide a free courtesy
collection from the bus and coach stations and ferry terminals for
guests without their own transport. The house is very clean, windows
are double glazed and there is a pretty lounge for guests to relax in.
The floodlit castle can be seen from the rear of the house and guests
can park in the gated car park. As we went to press, plans were in
place to introduce evening meals by arrangement sometime in 1996.

OWNERS: Jean and Roger Walkden   OPEN: all year   ROOMS: 1 single, 1 double, both
with wash-basin; 3 twin/family, all with bath/shower; TV in all bedrooms and lounge
TERMS: single £14–£18, single occupancy £20–£25, double from £30, twin/family from
£32; babies and young children free, older children £5; deposit: £10   CARDS: Access,
Amex, Delta, Diners, Switch, Visa   DETAILS: children welcome; small, well-behaved
dogs welcome; car park; garden

Tower Guest House

98 Priory Hill, Dover CT17 0AD
TEL: (01304) 208212
from B2011, turn left at roundabout then third on left immediately after main traffic lights; last house on right at top of hill

This low building was a water tower until 1850, and stands in a pretty garden with views of the castle, docks and surrounding hilly countryside. It is a warm and inviting house, and the prettily decorated bedrooms with their chintz curtains and bedspreads are unusually shaped. Breakfast can be provided early for people catching ferries.

OWNERS: Ron and Doreen Wraight   OPEN: all year exc Christmas   ROOMS: 1 double, with bath/shower; 2 twin, 1 with bath/shower, 1 with wash-basin; 2 family, 1 with bath/shower, 1 with wash-basin; TV in all bedrooms   TERMS: single occupancy £18–£25, twin/double £28–£38, family room £40–£50; children's reductions in family room; deposit: £10   CARDS: none   DETAILS: children welcome; no dogs; no smoking; garden

DOWNHAM MARKET   Norfolk   map 6

Dial House

Railway Road, Downham Market PE38 9EB
TEL: (01366) 388358   FAX: (01366) 384844

The Dial House is a Grade II listed Georgian building quietly situated in this small market town. There are three well-appointed, good-sized bedrooms, all with armchairs and one with a marble fireplace. Two have *en suite* facilities and the third has the exclusive use of a bathroom. There are lots of books and information on the area to browse through, and a TV lounge. Excellent breakfasts are served, featuring home-made preserves and home-baked bread. Evening meals are available, if pre-arranged, and all diets catered for. There is no alcohol licence, but guests are welcome to bring their own wine to table. Ann and David Murray are friendly hosts who always greet new arrivals with tea or coffee, and are happy to assist with itineraries.

OWNERS: Ann and David Murray   ROOMS: 3 double, 2 with bath/shower, 1 with wash-basin; TV in all bedrooms and lounge   TERMS: single occupancy £20–£28, double £30–£38; half-price for children 2 to 12 sharing with parents; dinner £12; deposit: £10 per night   CARDS: none   DETAILS: children welcome; no dogs in public rooms; no smoking; car park; garden

Please let us know if you think a B&B should be included in this Guide. Report forms are at the back of the book – or use your own stationery if you prefer (no stamps are needed within the UK).

DOWNTON   Wiltshire   map 2

The Warren

15 High Street, Downton, nr Salisbury SP5 3PG
TEL: (01725) 510263

Parts of this listed building date from the fifteenth century but its
development over the centuries has created a unique character. The
house is spacious, with exposed beams and is furnished with
antiques. The bedrooms are large and well decorated and one has a
500-year-old half-tester bed. All the windows are huge and those at
the back look out over the large walled garden with an expansive
lawn and attractive borders to the church. Breakfast only is served in
the dining-room, which has french windows leading to the garden. An
early fireplace was recently uncovered in the small sitting-room. The
Warren lies in the middle of the pretty village of Downton a mile and
a half from the New Forest.

OWNERS: John and Elizabeth Baxter   OPEN: all year exc Christmas   ROOMS: 2 double,
both with bath/shower; 2 twin, both with wash-basin; 1 four-poster, with bath/shower; 1
family, with wash-basin; TV lounge   TERMS: single occupancy £25–£32, twin/double
£40–£44, four-poster £44; £12.50 for children from 5 to 12; deposit: £15 per room
CARDS: none   DETAILS: no children under 5; dogs by arrangement; no smoking in
breakfast room; car park; garden

DREWSTEIGNTON   Devon   map 1

Ford House

Drewsteignton, nr Exeter EX6 6RD
TEL: (01647) 281243

This substantial whitewashed country house, was originally the
manor house of Drewsteignton. It stands in 15 acres of lovely gardens
and woodland, in a very rural and peaceful location on the northern
edge of Dartmoor. The large bedrooms, with equally large *en suite*
bathrooms, are simply and tastefully decorated. The Victorian
conservatory is particularly lovely in early spring when the mimosa is
in flower, and there is a relaxing sitting-room and games room. The
dining-room, which was originally the winter kitchen, has an old
built-in range with tile surround, and breakfast and dinner are
served here. Michael Page makes and repairs jewellery and guests
are welcome to watch him at work. Ford House is reached down a
series of narrow lanes outside the village, and the owners provide
directions with the booking confirmation.

OWNERS: Michael and Jacqueline Page   OPEN: all year exc Christmas and New Year
ROOMS: 3 double, 2 twin; all rooms with bath/shower; TV lounge   TERMS: single £27,
twin/double £54; dinner £15; deposit: 10%   CARDS: none   DETAILS: no children under
14; no dogs; no smoking; car park; games room; garden

Hunts Tor

Drewsteignton EX6 6QW
TEL: (01647) 281228

Tucked away in the corner of the village square, Hunts Tor is primarily a restaurant serving excellent food, with many of the clientèle coming here to eat and staying the night as well. The front part of the house dates from the nineteenth century and the back part is much older. All the restoration has been sensitively handled and the décor is understated. A recent extension has added an extra couple of sitting-rooms. The main dining-room has separate tables, and the secondary one an old stone fireplace, tiny bar and large corner table. The comfortable bedrooms mostly have old fireplaces, and two have their own sitting-rooms. Residents are given first choice of a table for dinner, which is a no-choice four-course affair with wine included in the price. Guests who require dinner should give 24 hours' notice.

OWNERS: Sue and Chris Harrison OPEN: Feb to Oct ROOMS: 2 double, 2 twin; all rooms with bath/shower; TV in some bedrooms TERMS: single occupancy £30–£40; twin/double £44–£65; dinner £25; deposit: £10 CARDS: none DETAILS: no children under 10; dogs by arrangement; no smoking in dining-room; car park (*The Good Food Guide*)

DULVERTON   Somerset   **map 1**

Town Mills

High Street, Dulverton TA22 9HB
TEL: (01398) 323124

This Georgian mill-house stands in a quiet position in the centre of Dulverton. Town Mills offers very comfortable accommodation with spacious bedrooms, one of which has a log fire; the ground-floor room has its own lounge. A full English breakfast is served in the bedrooms, as there are no public rooms for guests' use. Visitors may make use of a small patio by a stream with seating when the weather permits. Plenty of eating places are within a short drive for evening meals. Dulverton is in Exmoor National Park and is a wonderful base for walking and riding.

OWNERS: Jane and Charles Buckingham OPEN: all year ROOMS: 4 double, 2 with shower, 2 with wash-basin; 1 twin, with wash-basin; TV in all bedrooms TERMS: single occupancy £23–£32; twin/double £33–£42; reductions for children sharing with parents; deposit: 1 night's charge for new guests CARDS: none DETAILS: children welcome; no dogs; no smoking in public areas; car park

---

The end details for each entry state whether dogs are allowed, but it is always best to check when booking.

DUNSTER   Somerset   **map 1**

Dollons House

10 Church Street, Dunster TA24 6SH
TEL: (01643) 821880

This intriguing seventeenth-century listed house is in the centre of
the medieval village of Dunster. It was once the pharmacy and was
renowned for producing marmalade so delicious that it was requested
by the Houses of Parliament. It has elm beams and reed ceilings and
the décor and furnishings are most attractive and show great
individuality. Everything is spotlessly clean and bright, and the
bedrooms are pretty and chintzy, each with its own theme. One is the
tulip room, another the teddy bear room, with a mural of a bear in the
bathroom. The delightful sitting-room on the first floor at the rear has
doors opening out on to a small terrace with countryside views, and
below it is the dining-room, where breakfast only is served. The
Bradshaws are a delightful couple and run a craft shop which takes
up the two front rooms of Dollons. There is no parking at the house, so
guests need to unload their luggage then park in the public car park.

OWNERS: Major and Mrs Humphrey Bradshaw   OPEN: all year exc Christmas   ROOMS: 2
double, 1 twin; all rooms with bath/shower; TV in all bedrooms   TERMS: twin/double
£45–£49; deposit: £10   CARDS: Access, Delta, Visa   DETAILS: no children; no dogs; no
smoking; garden

Spears Cross Hotel

West Street, Dunster, nr Minehead TA24 6SN
TEL/FAX: (01643) 821439

Taken over by new owners at the end of 1994, Spears Cross is a
whitewashed fifteenth-century house. Its entrance is on the main
street of Dunster and is close to the castle, and its side garden has
model houses from different periods and areas set among the plants.
The bedrooms are prettily furnished and have old pine beds, and two
have the original thin wooden walls, which should be avoided by
those who sleep lightly. Another room has beautiful old beams. Both
breakfast and dinner (by arrangement) are served in the most
attractive dining-room, and the beamed lounge is adjacent to the bar
with its open fireplace.

OWNERS: John and Christine Rathbone   OPEN: Feb to Nov   ROOMS: 2 double, 1 twin, 1
family; all rooms with bath/shower; TV in all bedrooms and lounge   TERMS: single
occupancy £20–£32, twin/double £40–£48, family room £40–£48 plus children's
charge; half-price for children; deposit: £20   CARDS: Access, Delta, Switch, Visa
DETAILS: children welcome; dogs welcome; no smoking; car park; garden

DURHAM   Co Durham   map 10

Georgian Town House

10 Crossgate, Durham DH1 4PS
TEL: (0191) 386 8070

Georgian Town House is what is says it is – a listed eighteenth
century terraced house right in town and decorated in a fitting
manner. It has superb views of Durham's top sights, the castle and
the cathedral. The house is spotlessly clean and comfortable, and the
owners offer grilled rather than fried breakfasts which also feature
low-sugar preserves.

OWNERS: Mr and Mrs R.M.D. Weil   OPEN: all year exc Christmas   ROOMS: 3 double, 2
twin, 1 family; all rooms with bath/shower; TV in all bedrooms   TERMS: single
occupancy £35–£40, twin/double £45–£50, family room £50–£55; deposit: £10   CARDS:
none   DETAILS: children welcome; no dogs; no smoking in bedrooms; garden

---

EASINGWOLD   North Yorkshire   map 9

Old Vicarage

Market Place, Easingwold, nr York YO6 3AL
TEL: (01347) 821015
just off A19, 12m NW of York

This eighteenth-century listed house is built of hand-made bricks,
and was used as a vicarage until the beginning of this century.
Surrounding the property are extensive lawns, including a croquet
lawn and a walled rose garden. The spacious bedrooms are
comfortably furnished and have patchwork quilts; all are *en suite* and
have TV and clock radio. There is an elegant drawing-room with a
grand piano, where musical evenings often occur. Breakfast only is
served in the dining-room overlooking the garden. Christine and
John Kirman are an enthusiastic couple who have created a
welcoming ambience in this lovely house. There are several eating
establishments within walking distance, and Easingwold is a
convenient base for exploring York, Thirsk and the Dales.

OWNERS: Christine and John Kirman   OPEN: Feb to end Nov   ROOMS: 1 single, 3 double,
2 twin; all rooms with bath/shower; TV in all bedrooms   TERMS: single £24, single
occupancy £33, twin/double £42–£50; reductions for children sharing with parents;
deposit: £10 per person   CARDS: none   DETAILS: children welcome; no dogs; no
smoking; car park; garden

---

*Entries in the Guide are listed under town or village. There are also two
indexes at the back of the book, one listing B&Bs by county, the other by
name.*

Bodkin Lodge

Torrington Lane, East Barkwith LN3 5RY
TEL: (01673) 858249

The Stamps have had a new house built on their farm (The Grange), and it is from here that they now offer their excellent bed-and-breakfast facilities. Both bedrooms are on the ground floor and are beautifully decorated and furnished. Guests who choose to have an evening meal (which must be arranged in advance) may start with a complimentary sherry in the drawing-room; dinners are a set main course with a choice of starters and deserts. Vegetarian choices, light suppers and special diets can be catered for, and guests are welcome to bring their own wine to dinner as the property is unlicensed. The Stamps are dedicated to the preservation of wildlife, and guests may walk along a nearby nature trail past a lake, wild-flower meadow and four ponds where herons, swans and other water-birds can be spotted. Packed lunches can be provided.

OWNER: Anne Stamp   OPEN: all year exc Christmas, New Year and owner's holidays
ROOMS: 1 double, 1 twin, both with bath/shower; TV in both bedrooms   TERMS: single
occupancy £25–£30, twin/double £40–£50; half-price for children 8 to 12; dinner
£12.50–£14; deposit: £20   CARDS: none   DETAILS: no children under 8; no dogs; no
smoking; car park; garden

Beachy Rise

20 Beachy Head Road, Eastbourne BN20 7QN
TEL: (01323) 639171

Beachy Rise is in the conservation area of Meads Village, not far from the town centre. It is an unassuming semi-detached Victorian house, built in the 1890s, just off a busy road which leads to Beachy Head. The house is surprisingly large inside, with a comfortable sitting-room and a dining-room overlooking the garden, which is its crowning glory. The sheltered south-facing patio has attractive tables and chairs. Most of the bedrooms have original fireplaces and are decorated with pine and antique furniture. Evening meals are available by arrangement in the licensed dining-room. Both the South Downs and the sea are about a ten-minute walk away.

OWNER: Mr R.F. Cooke   OPEN: all year exc Christmas   ROOMS: 4 double, 2 twin, 1
family; all rooms with bath/shower; TV in all bedrooms   TERMS: single occupancy
£25–£34, twin/double £40–£48, family room £40–£48 plus children's charge; children
under 3 free, half-price for ages 3 to 9, 25% reduction for ages 10 to 14; dinner £10;
deposit: £10 per person   CARDS: Access, Visa   DETAILS: children welcome; dogs
welcome; no smoking in dining-room; garden

EAST COWES   Isle of Wight   map 2

Crossways House

Crossways Road, East Cowes PO32 6LJ
TEL/FAX: (01983) 298282

This large Victorian house stands in its own spacious grounds, just off
the main road close to Osborne House. It was formerly part of the
royal estate and built as a residence for Queen Victoria's Admiral
Master of Arms, and later used as a school for the Osborne naval
cadets. The Baldwins are a friendly, hard-working couple, dedicated
to the comfort of their guests. The house incorporates a restaurant
called 'Memories' where lunch and dinner are available, and a tea-
garden is located in the grounds; packed lunches can be provided.

OWNERS: Mike and Hilary Baldwin   OPEN: all year exc Christmas   ROOMS: 2 double,
both with bath/shower; 2 twin, 1 with bath/shower, 1 with wash-basin; 1 family, with
bath/shower; 4 rooms suitable for wheelchair-users; TV in all bedrooms and lounge
TERMS: single occupancy £27.50, twin/double £45, family room £45–£60; children's
reductions according to age; dinner £9   CARDS: Access, Amex, Diners, Visa   DETAILS:
children welcome; no dogs; car park; garden

EAST DEREHAM   Norfolk   map 6

The Elms

3 Shipdham Road, Toftwood, East Dereham NR19 1JJ
TEL: (01362) 692565
on A1075, 1m S of town centre

This attractive red-brick house in central Norfolk has colourful
hanging baskets and landscaped grounds. The well-maintained
house has been fitted with new carpets, and the good-sized bedrooms
decorated with matching fabrics and papers. A bathroom and an
additional WC are shared by the four bedrooms, although the
Lanhams take a maximum of only six guests at any one time, and all
the rooms have a vanity unit. There is a comfortable TV lounge.
Breakfast only is served, but there are several eating establishments
in the town and nearby. Pam and Tony Lanham are a very hospitable
couple who provide reasonably priced accommodation.

OWNER: Pamela Lanham   OPEN: all year exc Christmas   ROOMS: 1 single, 1 double, 1
twin, 1 family; all rooms with wash-basin; TV lounge   TERMS: single £16, single
occupancy £16–£30, twin/double £30, family room from £35; £5 for children under 5,
£10 for ages 5 to 10; deposit: £8–£15   CARDS: none   DETAILS: children welcome; no
dogs; no smoking in bedrooms; car park; garden

---

*If there are any bedrooms with TV, we mention this in the details at the
end of the entry.*

EAST KNOYLE   Wiltshire   map 2

Moors Farmhouse

East Knoyle, nr Salisbury SP3 6BU
TEL: (01747) 830385
just W of East Knoyle on minor road to Gillingham

This charming seventeenth-century farmhouse is in a quiet, isolated
position at the end of a lane on the northern edge of the Blackmore
Vale. The first floor was added after the Napoleonic Wars for the
purpose of storing cheese and the house has had more recent
additions. It is a genuine working dairy farm with a welcoming old-
fashioned farmyard. The accommodation consists of a large, bright
bedroom with adjoining sitting-room and bathroom. Moors Farm is
ideal for country-lovers seeking peace and quiet, yet it is within easy
reach of a variety of places of interest, and just a mile from the village
of East Knoyle.

OWNER: June Reading   OPEN: all year exc Christmas   ROOMS: 1 twin, with bath/shower;
TV lounge   TERMS: single occupancy £25, twin £40; £10 for children   CARDS: none
DETAILS: children welcome; no dogs; car park

EAST LAVANT   West Sussex   map 3

Manor House

Pook Lane, East Lavant, nr Chichester PO18 0AH
TEL: (01243) 781528
½m E of A286

This attractive old brick-built house stands on the edge of the pretty
village of East Lavant in front of Manor Farm. The building has been
split into two, Manor House retaining the major part, and it has a
lovely front garden. The two bedrooms are small, bright and simply
furnished and they share a bathroom. Breakfast is served at one table
in the dining-room, which is also the entrance to the house. The
village pub has a good reputation for its food and is within easy
walking distance. The Hankeys are cheerful, knowledgeable people,
and guests are made to feel part of the family.

OWNER: Lesley Hankey   OPEN: all year   ROOMS: 1 double, 1 twin; TV in 1 bedroom
TERMS: single occupancy £25, twin/double £38–£50; children's reductions for stays
over 1 week; deposit: £5   CARDS: none   DETAILS: children welcome; no dogs; no
smoking; car park; garden

*Breakfast at B&Bs tends to mean a cooked breakfast of bacon, eggs and so
on. If you prefer a different style of breakfast, it is best to discuss this when
you make a booking.*

Coombe Cross House

Coombe Road, East Meon, nr Petersfield GU32 1HQ
TEL: (01730) 823298   FAX: (01730) 823575
off A3 / A272, 5m W of Petersfield; 1¼m S of East Meon village

Coombe Cross is an early Georgian red-brick house on the South
Downs Way with spectacular views in every direction. Ten acres of
paddocks and gardens, where badminton and croquet can be played,
surround the property. It is a very comfortable family home whose
owners are interested in horses; stabling is available for visiting
horses. Inside, it is comfortably furnished, and the bedrooms, one of
which is on the ground floor, all have good views. Guests have use of a
drawing-room and sitting-room, and dinner, by arrangement, is
served in the dining-room. With notice, vegetarians can be catered
for, and guests are welcome to bring their own wine to table as there
is no alcohol licence. Packed lunches can also be requested. The
village of Hambledon, famous for being the home of cricket, is nearby.

OWNERS: Mr and Mrs Bulmer   OPEN: all year exc Christmas and New Year   ROOMS: 1
single; 1 double, with bath/shower; 2 twin, 1 with bath/shower, 1 with wash-basin; TV in
some bedrooms and lounge   TERMS: single £20, single occupancy £30–£40, twin/
double £40–£45; dinner £15; deposit: 50%   CARDS: none   DETAILS: no children exc by
arrangement; no dogs; smoking in downstairs rooms only; car park; garden

Drayton Cottage

East Meon, nr Petersfield GU32 1PW
TEL: (01730) 823472
E of A32 on minor road from West Meon to East Meon

This attractive 200-year-old flint and chalk building was originally
two cottages, and is now arranged so that guests use one end and the
Rocketts live at the other. The two comfortable bedrooms face the
River Meon and there is a small dining-room – off which is a
conservatory – where four-course evening meals can be served by
arrangement. Just a mile away is the picturesque village of East
Meon with its Norman church.

OWNER: Joan Rockett   OPEN: all year   ROOMS: 1 double, 1 twin; both rooms with bath/
shower; TV in both bedrooms and lounge   TERMS: twin/double £36–£40; dinner £12;
deposit: £10   CARDS: none   DETAILS: no children; no dogs; no smoking in bedrooms;
car park; garden

*If a B&B caters for vegetarians, we note this in the entry. It is always best,
however, to check when booking and make it clear what your requirements
are, especially if you require a special diet.*

153

EAST PRAWLE   Devon   **map 1**

Hines Hill

East Prawle, Kingsbridge TQ7 2BZ
TEL: (01548) 511263
from Kingsbridge follow A379 to Frogmore, then signs to East Prawle;
Hines Hill is on the left 200 yards down road towards sea

Hines Hill stands on a 400-foot promontory commanding spectacular
views over Devon's southernmost coastline. Built in 1937, this
attractive house is furnished with an interesting mixture of antique
and oriental furniture acquired from many years of overseas travel.
The three comfortable bedrooms are attractively furnished, and the
sitting-room has marvellous sea views and a good selection of videos,
games and books. David is a retired airline pilot, and Sylvia is a
professional cook who ran a restaurant here during the 1970s. Menus
include mainly French provincial cuisine with a sprinkling of recipes
from other countries where Sylvia has lived; vegetarian choices can
be provided on request. In the evening, guests sit round the one
dining-room table, where the meal is served in a dinner-party
atmosphere. The garden is full of interesting plants, and there is a
tiny beach below the house, as well as the South West Coastal Path.
Packed lunches can be arranged.

OWNERS: David and Sylvia Morris   OPEN: Mar to Oct   ROOMS: 2 double, 1 twin; all
rooms with bath/shower; TV in all bedrooms   TERMS: single occupancy £24–£32.50,
twin/double £38–£52; dinner £15; deposit: £20 per person   CARDS: none   DETAILS: no
children under 12; no dogs; no smoking; car park; garden

EAST WITTON   North Yorkshire   **map 9**

Dale View

38 East Witton, Leyburn DL8 4SH
TEL: (01969) 624113
on A6108, 3m SE of Leyburn

This is a delightful cosy cottage situated at the end of a row at the
head of the village overlooking the green. Terry Dunthorpe has made
a wonderful job of restoring this almost derelict cottage without in
any way detracting from its original character. There are just two
bedrooms, which have attractive stencilled furniture made by Terry
and pretty floral wallpapers. They are well-appointed and include
tea-making facilities and trouser presses. Guests are assured of
personal attention in this charming residence with its home-from-
home ambience. The comfortable guests' lounge has a real fire and a
hand-made grandfather clock. Large freshly prepared breakfasts are
well presented and vegetarians can be catered for. The Blue Lion pub
200 yards away has won a 'Pub of the Year' award.

OWNERS: Mr and Mrs T. Dunthorne OPEN: all year exc Christmas ROOMS: 1 double, 1 twin; both rooms with bath/shower; TV in both bedrooms and lounge TERMS: single occupancy £26–£28, twin/double £38; deposit: 25% CARDS: none DETAILS: no children; no dogs; no smoking in dining-room; car park; garden

---

EBRINGTON Gloucestershire   map 5

Holly House

Ebrington, nr Chipping Campden GL55 6NL
TEL: (01386) 593213
from Chipping Campden take B4035 E towards Shipston on Stour, after garden centre turn left to Ebrington

---

This pale yellow-painted house was built at the turn of the century, and the *en suite* ground-floor bedrooms are in the renovated Wheelwright Shop attached to the property. The interior is fresh and bright, with new pine furniture. Breakfast, prepared by accommodating Candida Hutsby, is taken in the bedrooms. Guests have their own front door, ideal for those who value their privacy. There is a good pub close by. Ebrington is a small village with an ancient church worth visiting, and Chipping Campden is only two miles up the road.

OWNERS: Mr and Mrs Jeffrey Hutsby OPEN: all year exc Christmas ROOMS: 1 double, 1 twin, 1 family; all rooms with bath/shower; TV in all bedrooms TERMS: single occupancy £25, twin/double £34, family room £46; £6 for children sharing with parents; deposit: £10 per night CARDS: none DETAILS: children welcome; no dogs; no smoking; car park; garden

---

ELSING Norfolk   map 6

Bartles Lodge

Church Farm, Church Street, Elsing, nr East Dereham NR20 3EA
TEL: (01362) 637177
off A47, 5m NE of East Dereham

This ranch-style bungalow is in a small courtyard with pond and fountain. Elsing is a quiet village, and Bartles Lodge is set in 12 acres of land that includes a garden and a private lake where coarse fishing can be arranged. The Bartletts have decorated the property with care and have thought of every convenience for the small bedrooms. These are decorated in blue and pink fabrics, and all have *en suite* bathroom, trouser press, hair-dryer and remote-control TV. One room has a four-poster, and the family room consists of two separate bedrooms. Generous breakfasts are served, and guests can relax in a large conservatory.

OWNERS: David and Annie Bartlett OPEN: all year ROOMS: 2 double, 3 twin, 1 four-poster, 1 family; all rooms with bath/shower; TV in all bedrooms TERMS: single occupancy £25–£27, twin/double £44, four-poster £55–£60, family room £50–£55; deposit CARDS: Visa DETAILS: no children under 10; dogs welcome with own bedding; no smoking in dining-room; car park; garden

ELY   Cambridgeshire   map 6

Black Hostelry

Cathedral Close, The College, Ely CB7 4DL
TEL: (01353) 662612   FAX: (01353) 665658

Standing within the walls of Ely Cathedral, this fine medieval building offers a unique and serene experience of the past. It has eleventh-century Norman arches and was once the infirmary of the Benedictine monastery. The rooms are large and comfortable and both can be converted to accommodate up to four people. They look out on a meadow and gardens. Hearty breakfasts include kippers and home-made wholemeal bread.

OWNER: Mrs S. Green   OPEN: all year exc Christmas   ROOMS: 2 double, both with bath/shower; TV in both bedrooms   TERMS: single occupancy £49, double £49; children £10; deposit: £10   CARDS: none   DETAILS: children welcome; dogs welcome; car park

31 Egremont Street

31 Egremont Street, Ely CB6 1AE
TEL: (01353) 663118

Set in lovely walled gardens, this seventeenth-century house with Victorian additions is a ten-minute walk from the town centre and has views of the cathedral. Both well-appointed bedrooms have wicker armchairs; the twin is in the Victorian part of the house. A *chaise-longue* and a collection of clocks are among the antique furnishings that complement the low-beamed ceilings and thick stone walls. Breakfast only is served.

OWNERS: Sheila and Jeremy Friend-Smith   OPEN: all year exc Christmas and owners' annual holiday   ROOMS: 1 double, 1 twin; both rooms with bath/shower; TV in both bedrooms   TERMS: single occupancy £19–£26, twin/double £40–£41; children's reductions by arrangement; deposit: £10   CARDS: none   DETAILS: no children under 12; no dogs; no smoking; car park; garden

It is always best to check prices, especially for single occupancy, when booking.

If you disagree with any assessment made in this guide, please write and tell us why. Address your letter to The Good Bed and Breakfast Guide, FREEPOST, 2 Marylebone Road, London NW1 1YN.

ETCHINGHAM East Sussex   map 3

King John's Lodge

Sheepstreet Lane, Etchingham, nr Ticehurst TN19 7AZ
TEL: (01580) 819232   FAX: (01580) 819127
just off A265, 7m N of Battle

For lovers of history and gardens, this beautiful old house is a must.
It lies down a country lane just outside Etchingham village, and
derives its name from King John II of France's imprisonment here in
the fourteenth century. The oldest part of the house dates from this
period, the remainder being Jacobean and also Edwardian. There are
original leaded lights in stone mullion windows, heavy beams and
stone and inglenook fireplaces. The Cunninghams are responsible for
the house's sympathetic renovation, and Jill for the spectacular
three-acre gardens (open to the public several times a year) which
comprise a secret garden, wild garden with rose walk, white garden
and lily pond. The farm includes sheep and a collection of ostriches.
The Cunninghams lead a relaxed family life and guests are served
breakfast in either the Elizabethan dining-room or on the terrace.
Evening meals are by arrangement; children's helpings and
vegetarian dishes can be provided, and guests may bring their own
wine as there is no alcohol licence. One of the bedrooms, in the oldest
part of the house, has an open loft containing a bed, as well as twin
beds below – ideal for a family. All rooms are beautifully decorated in
period style. Guests can play croquet, use the tennis court and,
weather permitting, use the swimming-pool.

OWNERS: Jill and Richard Cunningham OPEN: all year exc Christmas ROOMS: 2
double, 1 twin, 1 family; all rooms with bath/shower; TV lounge TERMS: single
occupancy £30, twin/double £50, family room from £50; reductions for family groups by
arrangement; dinner £16.50; deposit CARDS: none DETAILS: children welcome; no
dogs; car park; garden; swimming-pool; tennis

EVERTON Nottinghamshire   map 9

Gable Cottage

High Street, Everton, nr Bawtry DN10 5AR
TEL: (01777) 817601
on A631, 3m E of Bawtry

Tucked off the main road in a quiet position, Gable Cottage is a
delightful 200-year-old bow-windowed building in a conservation
village on the Pilgrim Fathers' Trail. Clarence and Jean
Attenborough work as a team to maintain high standards of comfort
and service in their peaceful house. They are a charming couple and
Clarence is a local historian who enjoys sharing his knowledge with
his guests. Separate from the TV room is an attractive reading area.
Jean is a golfer and is well acquainted with the many local courses.

Breakfast only is served, but it is freshly prepared and presented on fine china. Several pubs within walking distance serve evening meals.

OWNERS: Clarence and Jean Attenborough OPEN: all year ROOMS: 2 double, 1 twin; all rooms with bath/shower; TV lounge TERMS: single occupancy £29–£30, twin/double £37.50–£40; deposit: £10 CARDS: none DETAILS: children by prior arrangement; no dogs; no smoking in bedrooms or dining-room; car park

EVESHAM Hereford & Worcester map 5

Brookside

Hampton, Evesham WR11 6ND
TEL: (01386) 443116
just off A44

Brookside is in a peaceful secluded position by the River Isbourne, which is inhabited by kingfishers and ducks. There is a large garden with seating – a lovely place to be on sunny days. The bedrooms are fresh and clean with a bright décor. The single ground-floor room has its own WC and wash-basin, and there are three additional bathrooms exclusively for residents' use. There is a cosy sitting-room and a separate dining-room where evening meals are served. Children's helpings and vegetarian dishes can be requested, and guests are welcome to bring their own wine to table as there is no alcohol licence. The centre of Evesham is less than a mile away and can be reached by a pleasant walk along the river.

OWNERS: Mick and Lynne Mathers OPEN: all year exc Christmas and New Year ROOMS: 2 single, 2 double, 1 twin; all with wash-basin; 1 room suitable for wheelchair-users; TV lounge TERMS: single £16, single occupancy £20, twin/double £28; half-price for children sharing with parents; dinner £7; deposit CARDS: none DETAILS: children welcome; dogs by arrangement; smoking in lounge only; car park; garden

Church House

Greenhill Park Road, Evesham WR11 4NL
TEL: (01368) 40498

This elegant Victorian house, with a pretty front garden, overlooks the town of Evesham. The spacious rooms are tastefully decorated and have *en suite* facilities. The Shaws are a delightful couple who run their home with warmth and humour. They share the work – although Veronica, who speaks fluent French and Spanish, looks after the garden and does most of the cooking. The sitting-room with its blue décor has new curtains, and is a pleasant room to relax in after a busy day. Delicious breakfasts only are served and include brioche and home-made jams; packed lunches can be provided.

OWNERS: Mr and Mrs E.M. Shaw   OPEN: all year exc Christmas and New Year   ROOMS: 1 double, 1 twin, 1 family; all rooms with bath/shower; TV in all bedrooms and lounge   TERMS: single occupancy £26–£35, twin/double £38–£44, family room £50–£60; half-price for children under 12   CARDS: none   DETAILS: children welcome; dogs welcome; no smoking in dining-room; car park; garden

---

EXETER   Devon   **map 1**

The Edwardian

30–32 Heavitree Road, Exeter EX1 2LQ
TEL/FAX: (01392) 76102/54699

The Edwardian provides clean and comfortable accommodation close to the centre of the city and the university. It is on a busy main road and some rooms have views of the cathedral. Rooms have tall windows and some interesting furnishings, including oriental rugs and some rattan chairs; there is an old gramophone player in the guests' lounge. Michael and Kay Rattenbury are constantly on the lookout for Edwardian antiques to help develop the theme. Two bedrooms have four-poster beds. The Rattenburys and their families have been resident in the city for three generations and in the county of Devon longer still, and they are very knowledgeable about every aspect of Devon life and what to see and do.

OWNERS: Michael and Kay Rattenbury   OPEN: all year exc Christmas   ROOMS: 3 single, 1 with bath/shower, 2 with wash-basin; 5 double, all with bath/shower; 3 twin, all with bath/shower; 2 four-poster, both with bath/shower; 1 family, with bath/shower; TV in all bedrooms and lounge   TERMS: single £23–£33, single occupancy £33, twin/double £44, four-poster £48; family room £50   CARDS: Access, Amex, Visa   DETAILS: children welcome; well-behaved dogs welcome; no smoking in dining-room; car park (3 spaces)

Park View

8 Howell Road, Exeter EX4 4LG
TEL: (01392) 71772   FAX: (01392) 53047

Park View is a listed Georgian house standing in a quiet road overlooking Bury Meadow Park and surrounded by trees and shrubs. The accommodation is simple and comfortable, and the bedrooms are on the small side but are well-equipped with telephone, TV and tea- and coffee-making facilities. The pretty breakfast room, decorated in pink and green, overlooks the beautifully maintained small garden. The city centre is a ten-minute walk away.

OWNERS: Phil and Nikki Batho   OPEN: all year exc Christmas   ROOMS: 3 single, all with wash-basin; 7 double, 5 with bath/shower, 2 with wash-basin; 3 twin, 2 with bath/shower, 1 with wash-basin; 2 family, all with bath/shower; TV in all bedrooms and lounge   TERMS: single £20–£28, single occupancy £22–£32, twin/double £35–£43,

family room £48–£54; reductions for children sharing with parents; deposit: £10
CARDS: Access, Amex, Visa DETAILS: children welcome; no dogs; no smoking in dining-
room; car park; games room; garden

Raffles Hotel

11 Blackall Road, Exeter EX4 4HD
TEL: (01392) 70200

Raffles is only a short walk from the centre of town and the cathedral,
but it is in a quiet area. This large semi-detached Victorian town
house retains many of its original features, including the tiles on the
hall floor and the stairway, and is beautifully decorated and
furnished with antiques chosen by Richard Hyde, who restores and
deals in them. Breakfast and home-cooked evening meals are served,
by arrangement, in the small dining-room, which has a particularly
fine dresser displaying china and porcelain plates and pieces. Raffles
is a very comfortable place with attractive bedrooms and a friendly
atmosphere, and guests can relax in the secluded rear garden with its
wistaria-covered arches or in the lounge.

OWNERS: Richard and Susan Hyde OPEN: all year ROOMS: 2 single, 3 double, 1 twin, 1
family; all rooms with bath/shower; TV in all bedrooms TERMS: single £28, single
occupancy £35, twin/double £40, family room £48; half-price for children sharing with
parents; dinner £12 CARDS: Access, Amex, Diners, Visa DETAILS: children welcome;
no dogs in dining-room; car park; garden

FALMOUTH Cornwall   **map 1**

Selwood Cottage

38 Melvill Road, Falmouth TR11 4DQ
TEL: (01326) 314135

Selwood Cottage dates from the 1930s and is tucked away behind a
busy road, with the town and beaches just a few minutes' walk away.
The house has a beautifully kept small garden, which has won the
Britain in Bloom championship for three consecutive years, and is
always admired by guests who return to enjoy the lovely
surroundings. Terry and Alison Trezise offer a friendly and cheerful
welcome and make sure their guests enjoy their stay. All the
bedrooms now have *en suite* showers. There is a small pine-furnished
dining-room where breakfast only is served, and a comfortable
lounge. There are many activities in the area, including water sports,
golf, bowls and fishing.

OWNERS: Alison and Terry Trezise OPEN: Feb to Oct ROOMS: 1 single, 1 double, 1 twin,
1 family; all rooms with shower; TV in all bedrooms and lounge TERMS: single £16–£25,
single occupancy £15–£33, twin/double £30–£36, family room £32–£45; half-price for
children over 5 sharing with parents; deposit: 1 night's charge CARDS: none DETAILS:
no children under 5; no dogs; no smoking in dining-room; car park; garden

FARNINGHAM   Kent   map 3

The Bakery

High Street, Farningham, nr Dartford DA4 0DH
TEL: (01322) 864210
1½m from junction 3 of M25; follow signs for Brands Hatch

The Bakery is a pretty, white-painted seventeenth-century cottage
faced with Kentish weatherboard. It is in the centre of the attractive
village of Farningham, yet conveniently close to the A20 and the M25.
The house has original flagstone floors and the rooms are simply
decorated, with armchairs in the bedrooms. The lovely walled garden,
which is open to the public once a year, borders the local cricket
ground; croquet can be played on the Bakery's lawn. Mrs Lovering
was born in Portugal and speaks four languages as well as English.
She is an artist and has her studio in the grounds. Brands Hatch is
one mile away and Lullingstone Castle and Biggin Hill are also
nearby.

OWNERS: Mr and Mrs Lovering   OPEN: all year exc Christmas   ROOMS: 1 single; 1
double, with wash-basin; 1 twin, with wash-basin; TV lounge   TERMS: single £20–£25,
single occupancy £25, twin/double £40–£45; £15 for children sharing with parents;
deposit: £10 per person   CARDS: none   DETAILS: children welcome; no dogs; no
smoking; car park; garden

FARWAY   Devon   map 2

Keeper's Cottage

Farway, Colyton EX13 6DL
TEL: (01404) 871328
*from Honiton take A375 S; left at B7174, then left to Countryside Park,
after 200yds left again, signposted Farway, to first cottage on right
halfway down steep hill*

Originally a gamekeeper's cottage, this delightful brick-and-flint 150-
year-old house on the edge of the village enjoys a secluded position
overlooking an unspoilt valley. The Ryries are a congenial couple, and
guests are made to feel completely at home here. Flowers in all the
rooms along with comfortable furnishings add to the welcoming
atmosphere. One of the three bedrooms is *en suite* and the other two
share a bathroom. Guests have use of a sitting-room, and breakfast
only is served in an attractive dining-room overlooking the patio and
garden. Keeper's Cottage is five miles away from the sea and is well
sited for visits to a number of National Trust properties.

OWNERS: Mr and Mrs Brian Ryrie   OPEN: all year   ROOMS: 1 single; 1 double; 1 twin, with
bath/shower   TERMS: single £20, single occupancy £39, twin/double £39; deposit:
30%   CARDS: none   DETAILS: no children under 8; no dogs; smoking downstairs only;
car park; garden

Frith Farm House

Otterden, Faversham ME13 0DD
TEL: (01795) 890701   FAX: (01795) 890009
*from A20 after Lenham, turn left to Warren Street, then about 3m
following signs to Eastling village*

Frith Farm House is approached up a gravel driveway and sits high
on the North Downs. Once a farmhouse, this attractive late-Georgian
building is set in six acres of formal gardens with an ornamental pond
and summer-house, and a cherry orchard. The Chesterfields are a
very welcoming couple whose interests include gardening and music,
and a recent addition to the house is the Georgian-style music room.
The comfortable bedrooms are beautifully furnished. Breakfast is
taken in the vine-covered conservatory and dinner in the dining-
room, which has a display of Markham Chesterfield's china collection.
Susan enjoys preparing excellent home-cooked dinners, if arranged in
advance, and packed lunches can be provided. The elegant lounge has
been furnished in keeping with the period of the house and is a
relaxing place for reading. Horse-riding can be arranged. Otterden is
a tiny place between the A2 and A20, and it is advisable to ask for
directions when booking.

OWNERS: Markham and Susan Chesterfield OPEN: all year ROOMS: 1 double, 1 twin, 1
four-poster; all rooms with bath/shower; TV in all bedrooms TERMS: single occupancy
£27.50, twin/double £47, four-poster £52; dinner £17.50; deposit: £10 per person per
night CARDS: none DETAILS: no children under 12; no dogs; no smoking; car park;
garden

The Granary

Plumford Lane, Faversham ME13 0DS
TEL/FAX: (01795) 538416
*from M2 junction 6, take left turn to Faversham, at T-junction turn left,
then first left into Brogdale Road; then take left turn signposted Plumford,
the Granary is a further ½m*

This attractive, beautifully converted stone farm building stands in a
large garden in rural countryside in the midst of hops and apple
orchards. The Brightmans are a most welcoming couple and the
house has a relaxed atmosphere. The house is clean, comfortable and
furnished with taste, with three lovely bedrooms and a large timber
verandah off the lounge. Excellent breakfasts are served in the
farmhouse-style dining-room. The Granary is within easy reach of
Chilham and Leeds Castles, and Canterbury.

OWNER: Annette Brightman OPEN: all year exc Christmas ROOMS: 1 double, 1 twin, 1
family; all rooms with bath/shower; TV in all bedrooms and lounge TERMS: single

occupancy £30, twin/double £39, family room £49; reductions for children sharing with parents; deposit: £10 per room per night CARDS: Delta, Switch, Visa DETAILS: children welcome; no dogs; no smoking; car park; garden

---

FELIXSTOWE   Suffolk   **map 6**

Garfield Lodge

12 Garfield Road, Felixstowe IP11 7PU
TEL: (01394) 274843

The War Ministry built this impressive large brick house for the Air Force Commandant, but it became very run down before Ivan and Liz set to work to transform it into the delightful home and B&B it now is. Several original features remain, including the leaded windows and the fireplace. The bedrooms are tastefully furnished to a high standard and have attractive duvets. The décor in the large lounge is predominantly red and it is a warming spot for relaxing in at the end of the day. Evening meals are served by prior arrangement and guests may bring their own wine. Dinners are not served at Christmas. The house is only two minutes' walk from the beach and four minutes from the town centre. Free transport from the bus or train stations can be arranged.

OWNERS: Ivan and Liz Osborne OPEN: all year ROOMS: 2 single, 1 double, 1 twin, 1 family; all rooms with bath/shower; 1 room suitable for wheelchair-users; TV in all bedrooms TERMS: single/single occupancy £18–£20, twin/double £36–£40, family room £36–£45; reductions for children sharing family room with parents; dinner £10; deposit: £10 CARDS: none DETAILS: children welcome; no dogs; smoking in some rooms only; car park; garden

---

Redbanks

11 Gainsborough Road, Felixstowe IP11 7HT
TEL: (01394) 278080

Redbanks is an immaculate, well-appointed house a few minutes from both the beach and the town centre. The bedrooms are beautifully decorated in a combination of soft pastels and rich floral prints. Excellent breakfasts are served at separate tables in the pleasant dining-room. Sue Port is a friendly host who has a pilot's licence and, for a fee, can arrange flying trips for guests. Five dachshunds live outside the house and form a bustling welcoming committee. The minimum stay is two nights.

OWNERS: Mr and Mrs J. Port OPEN: all year exc Christmas ROOMS: 1 single, 1 double, 1 twin; all rooms with wash-basin; TV in all bedrooms TERMS: single/single occupancy £16, twin/double £32; reductions for children according to age CARDS: none DETAILS: no children; no dogs; no smoking; car park

FENITON   Devon   **map 2**

Colestocks House

Payhembury Road, Feniton, nr Honiton EX14 0JR
TEL: (01404) 850633   FAX: (01404) 850901
2m N of A30 at Payhembury exit, 4m W of Honiton

Colestocks is a delightful thatched sixteenth-century listed house
with later additions. It stands in two acres of immaculate gardens
surrounded by a high cob wall and containing a putting green, golf
nets and croquet lawn. The comfortable sitting-room has a selection
of books and french windows opening out on to the garden, and there
is a licensed lounge bar and dining-room where evening meals are
served. Children's helpings, vegetarian dishes, as well as packed
lunches, can be provided. The *en suite* bedrooms are spacious and one
has a four-poster; two rooms are on the ground floor. Golfers will be
interested to know that 11 golf courses are within a 20-mile radius.
There is also a village riding school, and fishing can be arranged
locally.

OWNER: Gordon Broster   OPEN: Easter to end Oct   ROOMS: 2 single, 4 double, 4 twin, 1
four-poster; all rooms with bath/shower; TV in all bedrooms   TERMS: single £27.50,
single occupancy £37.50, twin/double £55, four-poster £61; dinner £15; deposit: £20
per person   CARDS: Access, Visa   DETAILS: no children under 10; dogs by arrangement;
smoking in bar only; car park; garden

FIFEHEAD MAGDALEN   Dorset   **map 2**

Apple Tree Cottage

Fifehead Magdalen, nr Gillingham SP8 5RT
TEL: (01258) 820689
S of A30 Sherborne to Shaftesbury road

This small, modern house is located just by the church in a quiet
north Dorset hamlet. Guests have a choice of a twin-bedded room
with TV, or a very small double with a lovely view; the two rooms
share a bathroom. Both breakfast and dinner, by arrangement, are
served in the dining-room; packed lunches can be provided. There are
some lovely walks nearby and Bath and Sherborne are within easy
reach.

OWNER: Mrs M. Wootton   OPEN: all year   ROOMS: 1 double, 1 twin; TV lounge   TERMS:
single occupancy £20–£22, twin/double £35–£40; dinner £12–£15; deposit: £5   CARDS:
none   DETAILS: no children; dogs by arrangement; car park; garden

*We state at the end of an entry whether children are welcome. If we know of
any restrictions on children, we give them.*

FIFIELD   Oxfordshire
map 2

South View

Fifield, nr Oxford OX7 6HP
TEL: (01993) 830723
turn off A424 Burford to Stow-on-the-Wold road opposite Merrymouth Inn into Fifield; bungalow is first on right

Jean and Tony Rose continue to offer high standards and a warm welcome in their small stone-built bungalow. It is situated in a quiet spot with lovely views, and a small pretty back garden, with a sitting area in summer. The bedrooms are decorated to a high standard, with tasteful pastel fabrics and wallpaper. Breakfast only is served, but there is a pub within walking distance for evening meals. Fifield is a good base for touring the Cotswolds and is only four and a half miles from Burford.

OWNERS: Jean and Tony Rose OPEN: all year ROOMS: 1 double, 1 twin; both with bath/shower; TV in both bedrooms TERMS: twin/double from £32; children's reductions by arrangement CARDS: none DETAILS: children welcome; no dogs; restricted smoking areas; car park; garden

FILLINGHAM   Lincolnshire
map 9

Church Farm

Fillingham, nr Gainsborough DN21 5BS
TEL: (01427) 668279   FAX: (01427) 668025
off A15 and just off B1398, 9m N of Lincoln

This large farmhouse dating from 1845 stands in an acre of gardens on the edge of the picturesque village of Fillingham. The ambience is warm and guests are treated as friends by owner Christine Ramsay. The three immaculate bedrooms are comfortable, with stripped pine and pretty pink-striped and floral duvets. A separate lounge has TV and open fires. Breakfast, and traditional home-cooked lunches and dinners by arrangement, are served in the bright dining-room. Children's helpings, vegetarian meals and packed lunches can be requested, and visitors should bring their own wine to table as there is no licence. Christine is very knowledgeable about the area and is happy to assist with sightseeing itineraries. Mitzi and Holly, the two long-haired dachshunds, are friendly. John Wycliffe, the first man to translate the Bible into English, was rector of the parish in the fourteenth century.

OWNER: Christine Ramsay OPEN: all year exc Christmas and New Year ROOMS: 2 double, 1 with shower; 1 twin; TV lounge TERMS: single occupancy £20–£25, twin/double £30–£35; children's reductions by arrangement; dinner £11; deposit: £10 CARDS: none DETAILS: children welcome; no dogs; no smoking in bedrooms; car park; garden

FINCHAM   Norfolk
map 6

Rose Cottage

Downham Road, Fincham, nr Downham Market PE33 9HF
TEL: (01366) 347426
on A1122, 4m E of Downham Market

Rose Cottage is a charming red-brick Georgian property standing in
its own grounds, with numerous walks close by. Inside, it is warm
and inviting, and the immaculate bedrooms have attractive
bedspreads. One of the rooms has *en suite* facilities, the other shares
a bathroom which contains a Victorian bath. Croquet can be played in
the garden. Easily located, the cottage is situated on the edge of the
village, just down the road from Downham Market. Angela Vaughan-
Arbuckle speaks fluent German, and also lets a converted stable as
self-catering accommodation. Packed lunches can be provided.

OWNER: Angela Vaughan-Arbuckle   OPEN: all year exc Christmas   ROOMS: 2 twin; 1 with
shower, 1 with wash-basin; TV in both bedrooms   TERMS: single occupancy £18, twin
£30; babies up to 6 months free, children £10; deposit: £10   DETAILS: children welcome;
small dogs welcome; no smoking; car park; garden

FINCHINGFIELD   Essex
map 3

Finchingfield House

Finchingfield CM7 4JS
TEL/FAX: (01371) 810289
at junction of B1053 and B1057

This listed 400-year-old country house stands in two acres of mature,
landscaped gardens overlooking one of the prettiest village greens in
England. It was formerly a residence for the Earls of Caernarvon and
Roslyn. The restoration took over eight years and modern comforts
combine well with old-world charm. There is a magnificent inglenook
fireplace, original panelling in the dining-room, a heavily beamed
drawing-room and a splendid oak staircase. Finchingfield House is
beautifully furnished and offers luxurious accommodation in a
tranquil atmosphere. Owners Lorraine and Brian Patient are a
charming and musically talented couple. Breakfast only is served,
but four pubs within walking distance serve evening meals.

OWNERS: Lorraine and Brian Patient   OPEN: all year   ROOMS: 2 double, 1 twin; all rooms
with bath/shower; TV in some bedrooms and lounge   TERMS: single occupancy
£28–£35, twin/double £40–£48; deposit: £10   CARDS: none   DETAILS: no children; no
dogs; no smoking; car park; garden

*Any smoking restrictions that we know of are given in the details at the end
of the entry.*

FINDON West Sussex   map 3

Findon Tower

Cross Lane, Findon, nr Worthing BN14 0UG
TEL: (01903) 873870
200 yards from junction of Findon bypass (A24) and A280

Findon Tower is an Edwardian house standing in a large secluded
garden with pleasant views. The new housing development next door
is in no way obtrusive and the house is in the village of Findon, which
has one or two good places to eat. Guests have use of a spacious
lounge with TV, a sun lounge and a large snooker room. The three *en
suite* bedrooms are comfortably furnished, and breakfast is served at
one table in the dining-room. The sea and the many amenities of
Worthing are only four miles away.

OWNERS: Thurza and Tony Smith OPEN: all year ROOMS: 2 double, 1 twin; all rooms
with bath/shower; TV lounge TERMS: single occupancy £25–£30, twin/double
£35–£40; £7.50 to £10 for children sharing large double with parents; deposit: £10
CARDS: none DETAILS: children welcome; dogs by arrangement; no smoking; car park;
garden

FLEET Hampshire   map 2

8 Chinnock Close

8 Chinnock Close, Fleet GU13 9SN
TEL: (01252) 613646
4m S of M3 junction 4

Chinnock Close is part of a 25-year-old housing development which
has been laid out with lots of trees and gardens, and is a peaceful spot
on the edge of Fleet. Guests have the use of one end of the house,
which includes a TV lounge with doors leading out to a patio and
small back garden. The bedrooms are very clean and pleasantly
furnished. The Nixes live at the other end of the house, which is
where they make miniatures and figures for dolls' houses, some of
which can be found around the guesthouse. Many people come here
specifically to watch the Nixes at work. This is a popular place for
business people and very convenient for the Farnborough Air Show.
Breakfast only is served but there is a large selection of eating places
close by.

OWNERS: Mr and Mrs R. Nix OPEN: all year ROOMS: 2 single, 1 double, 1 twin; TV
lounge TERMS: single/single occupancy £15, twin/double £30; babies free CARDS:
none DETAILS: well-behaved children welcome; no dogs; no smoking; car park; garden

FORD Wiltshire

map 2

Big Thatch

Ford, nr Chippenham SN14 8RT
TEL/FAX: (01249) 782107
just off A420, 5m W of Chippenham; from Ford village turn left towards Colerne; Big Thatch is immediately on right

This very picturesque thatched cottage built of Cotswold stone dates from the thirteenth century. It is set in the small village of Ford, and although it backs on to the main road, the traffic noise is minimal. Patricia Townson is a delightfully welcoming lady and is happy to tell visitors about the history of the house. The three first-floor bedrooms share a bathroom that is on the ground floor; all the house is immaculately kept and attractively furnished and decorated. The White Hart pub across the road serves food, and the pretty village of Castle Combe is nearby.

OWNER: Patricia Townson   OPEN: all year exc Christmas   ROOMS: 1 single; 1 twin; 1 family, with wash-basin; TV in some bedrooms and lounge   TERMS: single £28, single occupancy £38, twin £45, family room £55; half-price for children; deposit: 25% CARDS: none   DETAILS: children welcome; dogs welcome; no smoking; car park; garden

BIG THATCH, FORD

FORD   Northumberland   **map 11**

The Estate House

Ford, nr Berwick-upon-Tweed TD15 2QG
TEL/FAX: (01890) 820414
on B6353, 3m W of Lowick

John and Maureen Burton took over the Estate House in 1994, since
when they have been busy upgrading and making various
improvements. The house has been freshly decorated throughout and
extra bathroom facilities added. All the spacious bedrooms have easy
chairs and the comfortable drawing-room has a log fire which is lit on
cooler days. Excellent breakfasts, including home-baked bread made
with flour from the local mill, are served in the dining-room, which
overlooks the large, secluded garden. Dinners are served here too
(6.30 to 7.30pm, by arrangement). Vegetarians can be catered for and
guests may bring their own wine. Guests have access to the castle,
which is situated just beyond the garden.

OWNERS: John and Maureen Burton   OPEN: all year   ROOMS: 1 double, with bath/
shower; 2 twin, 1 with bath/shower, 1 with wash-basin; TV in all bedrooms   TERMS:
single occupancy £21, twin/double £36; dinner £12.50; deposit: £10 per person
CARDS: none   DETAILS: children welcome; no dogs; no smoking; car park; garden

FORDHAM   Essex   **map 6**

Kings Vineyard

Fossetts Lane, Fordham, nr Colchester CO6 3NY
TEL: (01206) 240377
off A604, 5m NW of Colchester

Ask for directions when seeking out this hidden-away modern house,
situated on a south-facing slope in unspoilt countryside. Three and a
half acres of land take in a large garden, and grazing for a flock of
rare black St Kilda sheep. There are unobstructed views in all
directions. The bedrooms are attractive, and guests have use of a
comfortable lounge with log fires in winter, and a conservatory where
breakfast is served. Packed lunches can be provided. Mrs Tweed is
very knowledgeable about the area and is happy to give advice on
what to see and do.

OWNER: Inge Tweed   OPEN: all year   ROOMS: 2 double, 1 twin; TV in all bedrooms and
lounge   TERMS: single occupancy £18–£21, twin/double £32–£36; children's reductions
by arrangement; deposit: £10   CARDS: none   DETAILS: children welcome; guide dogs
only; no smoking in bedrooms; car park; garden

*The end details for each entry state whether dogs are allowed, but it is
always best to check when booking.*

FOUR ELMS   Kent

map 3

Knowlands

Five Fields Lane, Four Elms, nr Edenbridge TN8 6NA
TEL/FAX: (01732) 700314
from A25 take B2042, then after junction with B2027 turn left into Five Fields Lane

---

This substantial Victorian property is set in wooded countryside in the Weald of Kent. The extensive well-kept grounds of three and a half acres include a small lake and summer house, and beautiful rose beds. The house is furnished in keeping with its period, and the two comfortable bedrooms have their original fireplaces. Knowlands is convenient for Chartwell, Hever Castle and Penshurst Place. Breakfast and dinner, by arrangement, are served, vegetarian choices are provided and guests may bring their own wine to dinner; packed lunches can also be arranged.

OWNERS: Mr and Mrs J.V. Haviland   OPEN: all year exc Christmas   ROOMS: 2 double, both with wash-basin; TV in both bedrooms   TERMS: single occupancy £35, double £50; dinner £15; deposit: £20   CARDS: none   DETAILS: no children; no dogs; no smoking; car park; garden; tennis

---

FOWEY   Cornwall

map 1

Carneggan House

Lanteglos, nr Fowey PL23 1NW
TEL/FAX: (01726) 870327
4m from Pelynt, on the Polruan road

Carneggan House stands alone in peaceful countryside, midway between Polruan and Polperro, and only a short distance from the sea. A 20-minute walk across National Trust-owned farmland leads to several unspoilt beaches and walks along the coastal path. This former Georgian farmhouse is surrounded by six acres of grounds, including a grass tennis court. The separate guest accommodation includes a restful drawing-room with open fireplace, and a dining-room where home-cooked evening meals are served by prior arrangement. Children are welcome to have earlier supper in the family kitchen. The bedrooms are comfortably equipped, and the largest has particularly lovely views. There is no central heating, but night storage and space heaters provide warmth.

OWNERS: Alan and Sue Shakerley   OPEN: all year exc Christmas   ROOMS: 1 double; 2 twin; all rooms with bath/shower; TV in all bedrooms   TERMS: single occupancy £25–£32, twin/double £40–£54; babies free; half-price for children under 12; dinner £17; deposit: 50%   CARDS: Access, Amex, Visa   DETAILS: children welcome; dogs welcome but not to be left alone in rooms; no smoking in dining-room; car park; garden; tennis

FOXLEY Norfolk map 6

Pol-Na-Chess

Mill Road, Foxley, nr Dereham NR20 4QX
TEL: (01362) 688330
on B1145, 4m W of Reepham

This warm and friendly modern bungalow has a very pretty garden with a patio, fish pond and roses, and is surrounded by unspoilt countryside. All the rooms are on the ground floor and the spacious guests' lounge has a large open fireplace faced with local stone. Breakfast only is served at one table in the pleasant dining-room and a hot-drinks trolley is available on a help-yourself basis at any time. The house's name comes from the owners' favourite part of Scotland.

OWNERS: Richard and Joan Parfitt OPEN: Feb to Nov ROOMS: 1 double, 2 twin; all rooms with wash-basin; TV in one bedroom and lounge TERMS: single occupancy £15, twin/double £30; children £10 CARDS: Diners DETAILS: children welcome; no dogs; car park; garden

FOXTON Leicestershire map 5

Old Manse

37 Swingbridge Street, Foxton, nr Market Harborough LE16 7RH
TEL: (01858) 545456
on A6 take sign for Foxton 1m N of Market Harborough; turn right after church and cross bridge

This seventeenth-century house stands in two acres of park-like gardens with a canal running along the bottom. It is on the edge of a small, quiet village with two pubs which serve food. The well-proportioned bedrooms are tastefully furnished in pastel colours and have plenty of space. The comfortable lounge sports a rich array of foliage and an elegant collection of antique furniture, including a *chaise-longue*. The Pickerings are charming and often invite guests into their private lounge.

OWNER: Rita Pickering OPEN: all year exc Christmas ROOMS: 1 double, with wash-basin; 2 twin, 1 with bath/shower, 1 with wash-basin; TV in all bedrooms and lounge TERMS: single occupancy £20–£23, twin/double £35–£39; half-price for children sharing with parents DETAILS: children welcome; no dogs; no smoking; car park; garden

Many B&Bs are in remote places, and although in many cases we provide directions, it is always advisable to ask for clear instructions when booking.

If you are forced to turn up later than planned, please telephone to warn the proprietor.

FRAMINGHAM EARL   Norfolk   map 6

Oakfield

Yelverton Road, Framingham Earl, nr Norwich NR14 7SD
TEL: (01508) 492605
*travelling SE on A146 3m from Norwich turn right at Gull pub, keep left
then turn left at top of lane*

This attractive modern bungalow has a half-acre garden and four
acres of meadowland. The immaculate ground-floor bedrooms are all
of a good size and have new duvets with pale-coloured covers. The
separate guests' lounge has TV and the dining-room is the place for
excellent and substantial breakfasts which are worth getting up for.

OWNER: Mrs R. Thompson   OPEN: all year exc Christmas   ROOMS: 1 single, with wash-
basin; 1 double, with bath/shower; 1 twin, with wash-basin; TV lounge   TERMS: single
£18–£22, single occupancy £25–£35, twin/double £34–£40; deposit: £10   CARDS:
none   DETAILS: no children under 12; no dogs; no smoking; car park; garden

FRANT   East Sussex   map 3

Henley Farm

Frant, nr Tunbridge Wells TN3 9EP
TEL: (01892) 750242
on B2099, 1½m S of Frant

The entrance to Henley Farm is under a wistaria-covered arch of the
weather-boarded house. Dating from the early 1800s, it was
originally an oast house and it is in a rural setting with a large
attractive garden, a patio for sitting out and a tennis court which Ann
Fleming describes as 'elderly'. This friendly family home has a
welcoming atmosphere and offers four bedrooms all with private
bathrooms. Breakfast only is available.

OWNER: Ann Fleming   OPEN: all year exc Christmas   ROOMS: 2 single, 1 double, 1 twin;
all rooms with bath/shower; TV in all bedrooms   TERMS: single/single occupancy £18;
twin/double £36; babies free, half-price for children under 12; deposit required with
advance bookings   CARDS: none   DETAILS: children welcome; no dogs; no smoking in
bedrooms; car park; garden; tennis

Old Parsonage

Frant, nr Tunbridge Wells TN3 9DX
TEL/FAX: (01892) 750773
*take A267 S from Tunbridge Wells for 2m; in Frant turn left into Church
Lane*

This substantial Georgian house in the pretty twelfth-century village
of Frant was built by the Marquess of Abergavenny for his son, who

was the parish rector between 1820 and 1845, and remained the rectory until acquired by the present owners in 1989. The house is beautifully furnished and has many interesting photos, paintings and prints. The large drawing-room is becoming a museum of local historical photographs and tapestries. Tea and biscuits are offered to guests on arrival in the large conservatory, which is at one end of the terrace and overlooks the secluded walled garden. Breakfast is served in the dining-room, and the comfortable bedrooms are very spacious. There is a restaurant just opposite the Old Parsonage and a couple of nearby pubs serve food. Hever and Chiddingstone castles are within easy reach.

OWNERS: Tony and Mary Dakin   OPEN: all year   ROOMS: 1 twin; 2 four-poster; all rooms with bath/shower; TV in all bedrooms   TERMS: single occupancy from £34, twin/four-poster from £54; half-price for children; deposit: 50%   CARDS: Access, Visa   DETAILS: children welcome; dogs welcome with own bedding; smoking in conservatory only; car park; garden

FREMINGTON   Devon   **map 1**

Muddlebridge House

Fremington, Barnstaple EX31 2NQ
TEL: (01271) 76073
off A39, 3m W of Barnstaple

This substantial Regency country house stands in two acres of grounds containing attractive gardens, an indoor heated swimming-pool, sauna, fully equipped guest laundry and a 'pets corner' complete with pygmy goats, ducks and bunnies. B&B guests share these facilities with those staying in the six self-catering cottages also in the grounds. The B&B accommodation is comprised of three spacious bedrooms with *en suite* shower facilities. Breakfast only is served in the ground-floor sitting/dining-room. Guests are also welcome to use the games room, where they can play snooker, table tennis and darts. Bicycle hire can also be arranged. Evening meals are not provided, but there are a number of pubs and restaurants within easy reach by car.

OWNERS: Graham and Ruth Macdonald   OPEN: Apr to Nov   ROOMS: 1 double, 1 twin, 1 family, all with shower; TV in all bedrooms   TERMS: twin/double £42–£46, family room from £42; children under 2 free, half-price for ages 2 to 14; deposit: 25%   CARDS: none   DETAILS: children welcome; no dogs; no smoking; car park; games room; garden; swimming-pool

Entries in the Guide are listed under town or village. There are also two indexes at the back of the book, one listing B&Bs by county, the other by name.

Most establishments have central heating. When we know this is not the case, we mention this in the entry.

Brookside Forge Hotel

Brookside Road, Freshwater PO40 9ER
TEL: (01983) 754644

Originally the village forge, this substantial brick-built guesthouse is
in a quiet road near the centre of Freshwater. The new owners, Dave
and Jacqui Reynolds, are a friendly couple who take good care of their
guests. The small, well-equipped bedrooms are all *en suite*, and there
is a comfortable lounge with TV. Doors from a small bar lead out to
the patio and pretty terraced back garden,, where there are chairs for
sitting out. Dinner is available, and packed lunches can be provided.
A self-catering bungalow adjacent to the hotel, with two *en suite*
bedrooms, is available for rental. The local swimming-pool is opposite
the house, and some lovely walks on the Downs start here. Visitors
without a car can be collected from the ferry at Yarmouth.

OWNERS: David and Jacqui Reynolds   OPEN: all year   ROOMS: 1 single, 6 double, 3 twin,
2 family; all rooms with bath/shower; TV in all bedrooms and lounge   TERMS: single
£17–£18.50, single occupancy £18.50–£25, twin/double £39; family room from £45;
children's reductions according to age; dinner £8; deposit: £20 per person   CARDS:
Access, Visa   DETAILS: children welcome; dogs welcome; no smoking in dining-room
and some bedrooms; car park; garden

Yarlands Country House

Victoria Road, Freshwater PO49 9PP
TEL: (01983) 752574

This elegant eighteenth-century house, formerly the rectory, stands
in a lovely two-and-a-half-acre secluded garden stretching down to
the River Yar. It is set back from the road, with a wide driveway in
front. The Fairmans are very friendly and work hard at maintaining
both the house and garden. The house has been decorated in restful,
pastel colours and is popular with business people. The large,
comfortable *en suite* bedrooms are all furnished in pine. There is a
lounge with tall french windows leading out to the garden, and a
residents' bar with log fire. Home-cooked dinners, using fresh
produce from the garden, are served in the large dining-room, and
packed lunches can be provided.

OWNERS: John and Pat Fairman   OPEN: Mar to end Oct   ROOMS: 2 double, 2 twin, 2
family; all rooms with bath/shower; 1 room suitable for wheelchair-users; TV in all
bedrooms   TERMS: single occupancy £31–£32, twin/double £52–£54, family room from
£65; half-price for children sharing with parents; dinner £12; deposit: 10%   CARDS:
none   DETAILS: children welcome; small dogs only; no smoking in dining-room or
lounge; car park; garden

FRIETH Buckinghamshire   **map 3**

Little Parmoor Farm

Frieth, nr Henley-on-Thames RG9 6NL
TEL/FAX: (01494) 881600
from Henley-on-Thames take A4155 Marlow road, turn left to Hambleden,
in village take Frieth road, farm on left

This sixteenth-century brick-and-flint farmhouse is surrounded by
attractive gardens and 220 acres of working stock and grain
farmland. There is a relaxed, friendly atmosphere, children are
welcome, and cots and high chairs are provided. The three bedrooms
are individually decorated with delicately patterned, one has an old
brass bed and there is a wealth of oak beams. Log fires warm the
lounge in winter. Evening meals are not available, but the Yew Tree
pub a mile away serves food. This is an ideal spot for nature lovers;
the Thames is less than a couple of miles away.

OWNER: Frances Emmett OPEN: all year ROOMS: 1 single; 1 double, with bath/shower;
1 twin; TV lounge TERMS: single £20, single occupancy £25–£30, twin/double £36–£42;
children's reductions by arrangement; deposit: £15–£20 CARDS: Visa DETAILS:
children welcome; no dogs; no smoking; car park; garden

FRINTON-ON-SEA Essex   **map 3**

Uplands Guesthouse

41 Hadleigh Road, Frinton-on-Sea CO13 9HQ
TEL: (01255) 674889

Uplands is a large, attractive 1920s house in a quiet residential street
just a three-minute walk from the sea and Crescent Gardens. It is
comfortable, well furnished and boasts fine flower displays
throughout. The good-sized bedrooms are decorated in autumnal
colours and the ambience is warm and friendly. The bright dining-
room where breakfasts and dinners (with wine available by the glass
or bottle) are served overlooks the front garden, and there is a large
garden to the rear, approached via the bar and sun room. Transport
from the station can be arranged.

OWNERS: Mrs S.M. Creates and Mr D.E. Fowle OPEN: all year exc Christmas ROOMS: 3
single, all with wash-basin; 2 double, 1 with bath/shower, 1 with wash-basin; 2 twin,
both with bath/shower; TV lounge TERMS: single £21–£26.50, single occupancy
£35–£45, twin/double £42–£52.50; dinner £10–£12; deposit: £10–£15 CARDS: none
DETAILS: no children; no dogs; no smoking in bedrooms or dining-room; car park;
garden

Please let us know if an establishment has changed hands.

FRITH COMMON   Hereford & Worcester   **map 5**

Hunthouse Farm

Frith Common, nr Tenbury Wells WR15 8JY
TEL: (01299) 832277
*6m E of Tenbury Wells; head S from A456 just W of Clows Top or N from
A443 just E of Lindridge*

In a beautiful setting with breathtaking views, this listed sixteenth-
century timbered farmhouse is part of a 180-acre farm. It is
approached up a lane bordered by fields of sheep and horses and busy
with smaller wildlife. This is a 'duck your head' property with low oak
beams and an inglenook fireplace. The three bedrooms are
attractively decorated with matching fabrics. Guests have use of a
separate sitting-room and sumptuous breakfasts are served in the
dining-room, which has one of the best views. The Nag's Head, two
miles away, serves evening meals.

OWNERS: Chris and Jane Keel   OPEN: all year exc Christmas   ROOMS: 2 double, 1 twin;
all rooms with bath/shower; TV lounge   TERMS: single occupancy £22, twin/double £34;
children's reductions; deposit   CARDS: none   DETAILS: no children under 8; no dogs; no
smoking in bedrooms; car park; garden

FRITTENDEN   Kent   **map 3**

Old Rectory

Frittenden, nr Cranbrook TN17 2DG
TEL/FAX: (01580) 825313
between A229 and A274, 8m NW of Tenterden

This brick-built house dates from the nineteenth century and is set in
a wonderful two-and-a-half-acre garden with views of the hills
beyond. It stands in the small and tucked-away village of Frittenden,
and is three miles from Sissinghurst Castle and Gardens. The
bedrooms are spacious and simply furnished, and the Barnetts are a
most welcoming couple. Evening meals are served by arrangement at
one table in the dining-room, and guests also have use of a lounge.
Vegetarians can be catered for with prior notice, and diners may
bring their own wine as there is no alcohol licence. In summer there is
croquet and badminton in the garden.

OWNERS: Alex and Joy Barnett   OPEN: May to Sept   ROOMS: 2 double, 1 with bath/
shower, 1 with wash-basin; 2 twin, 1 with bath/shower, 1 with wash-basin; TV lounge
TERMS: single occupancy £30, twin/double £50; reductions for children depending on
time of year; dinner £10–£12; deposit: 50%   CARDS: none   DETAILS: no children under
12; no dogs; no smoking; car park; garden

Recommendations for B&Bs for our next edition are very welcome.

FYLINGTHORPE   North Yorkshire   **map 9**

Croft Farm

Church Lane, Fylingthorpe, Whitby YO22 4PW
TEL: (01947) 880231
1m E of A171, 4m S of Whitby

Built of red brick and local stone, this eighteenth-century farmhouse
is in a wonderful position on the edge of the village with views over
Robin Hood's Bay, the sea and the moors. Although it was
modernised in the 1970s, the most interesting original features have
been preserved, including an Adam-style fireplace in the lounge, the
open brick fireplace in the dining-room and some of the doors. A new
carpet has been fitted in the lounge. Cooked breakfasts feature fresh
farm eggs and home-made preserves and marmalade, and the village
offers a wide choice for evening meals. A self-contained cottage is
available and horse-riding can be arranged.

OWNERS: Mr and Mrs John Featherstone   OPEN: Easter to mid-Oct   ROOMS: 1 single,
with wash-basin; 1 double, with bath/shower; 1 family, with wash-basin; TV lounge
TERMS: single £16.50–£18.50, single occupancy £17.50–£19.50, twin/double £32–£41;
reductions for children sharing with parents; deposit: £10 per person   CARDS: none
DETAILS: no children under 5; dogs in kennel only; no smoking; car park; garden

GAWSWORTH   Cheshire   **map 8**

Rough Hey Farm

Leek Road, Gawsworth, nr Macclesfield SK11 0JQ
TEL: (01260) 252296
off A523, 3m S of Macclesfield

This friendly seventeenth-century farmhouse with an attractive
garden is in a secluded setting on a 300-acre sheep farm just off the
A523. Two of the rooms were part of an earlier hunting lodge
mentioned in the Domesday Book. Phyllis Worth is an excellent host
who has been making guests feel welcome here since 1984. The
bedrooms are a good size, the double positively large, and all are
tastefully decorated with modern furnishings. Breakfasts only are
served, but a farm track leads conveniently to the local pub, which
serves evening meals.

OWNER: Phyllis Worth   OPEN: all year exc Christmas   ROOMS: 2 single, both with wash-
basin; 1 double, with bath/shower; 1 twin, with wash-basin; TV in all bedrooms and
lounge   TERMS: single £17, single occupancy £25, twin/double £34; 33% reduction for
children sharing with parents   DETAILS: children welcome; no dogs; no smoking; car
park; garden

---

*If a deposit is required for an advance booking, this is stated in the details
at the end of the entry.*

GAYHURST   Buckinghamshire   map 5

Mill Farm

Gayhurst, nr Newport Pagnell MK16 8LT
TEL/FAX: (01908) 611489
take B526 out of Newport Pagnell for 2m, turn left at sign for Haversham; Mill Farm is first on left

A warm family home and the centre of a working farm, Mill Farm is a lovely listed seventeenth-century farmhouse in half an acre of gardens. It has large, pleasantly furnished rooms, some with views over the Ouse Valley. The sitting-room is a comfortable place in which to relax and guests are welcome to sit or wander in the garden. Breakfast only is served in the family dining-room, which has an original bell-pull and fireplace. For sports-minded visitors, there is a hard tennis court and fishing and horse-riding can be arranged locally.

OWNER: Kaye Adams   OPEN: all year   ROOMS: 1 single, with wash-basin; 1 twin, with bath/shower; 1 family, with bath/shower; TV in all bedrooms   TERMS: single/single occupancy £18–£20, twin £35–£40; children's reductions by arrangement; deposit required   CARDS: none   DETAILS: children welcome; dogs welcome; no smoking in some bedrooms; car park; games room; garden; tennis

GLOUCESTER   Gloucestershire   map 5

Lulworth Guest House

12 Midland Road, Gloucester GL1 4UF
TEL/FAX: (01452) 521881

Lulworth is a good-value, straightforward guesthouse in an attractive location close to the park and near the town centre. The fresh and clean bedrooms are modestly furnished and two are on the ground floor (one of these is *en suite*). There is a guests' lounge with TV. Breakfast only is served, but it is no trouble to find somewhere appealing to eat at in town.

OWNER: Mrs M.I. Dickinson   OPEN: all year   ROOMS: 1 single, with bath/shower; 2 double, 1 with bath/shower, 1 with wash-basin; 2 twin, both with bath/shower; 3 family, 2 with bath/shower, 1 with wash-basin; TV in all bedrooms and lounge   TERMS: single £18, single occupancy £16–£18, twin/double £30–£33, family room £40–£42; reductions for children sharing family room with parents; deposit: £10   CARDS: none   DETAILS: children welcome; no dogs in public rooms; no smoking in dining-room; car park

Notley House

93 Hucclecote Road, Hucclecote, Gloucester GL3 3TR
TEL: (01452) 611584   FAX: (01452) 371229

Notley House was established six years ago. Alyn and Jaki George and their family undertook the renovation of this period house, which

178

was at one time a private school. Impeccably maintained, the house has pine furniture and is tastefully decorated. The bedrooms are well appointed; one has a four-poster bed, another an antique brass bed. A second four-poster is in the Coach House, which also has a lounge and kitchen. Breakfast and dinner are served. Guests can bring their own wine to dinner, and packed lunches can be provided. There is a lounge with satellite TV. The owners are pleasant and helpful and are the proud recipients of a 'civic award' for their restoration work.

OWNERS: Alyn and Jaki George OPEN: all year exc Christmas ROOMS: 1 single, 2 double, 2 twin, 2 four-poster, 2 family; all rooms with bath/shower; TV in all bedrooms and lounge TERMS: single £23.50, single occupancy £23.50–£41, twin/double £37.50–£43, four-poster £47; family room from £37.50; babies free; dinner £10; small deposit for new guests CARDS: Access, Delta, Visa DETAILS: children welcome; no dogs; no smoking; car park; garden

GOATHLAND   North Yorkshire   map 9

Glendale House

Goathland, nr Whitby YO22 5AN
TEL: (01947) 896281
2m W of A169 on minor road 5m S of Sleights

Dating from 1860, this house in the centre of this village in the North York moors features as the doctor's house in the TV series *Heartbeat*. Sandra Simmonds is a very welcoming and enthusiastic host who greets guests on chilly days with a hot drink in front of the open fire in the lounge. The bedrooms are immaculate and are decorated with pretty floral wallpapers. The ambience is warm and homely and breakfasts are substantial. There are several eating establishments in the village for evening meals. This is a lovely spot from which to explore the moors and ride the North York Moors Railway.

OWNERS: Keith and Sandra Simmonds OPEN: all year exc Christmas ROOMS: 1 double, 2 family; all rooms with wash-basin; TV lounge TERMS: double £36, family room £36 plus children's charge; half-price for children sharing with parents CARDS: Access, Visa DETAILS: children welcome; no dogs; smoking in guests' lounge only; garden

GOLDEN GREEN   Kent   map 3

Goldhill Mill

Golden Green, nr Tonbridge TN11 0BA
TEL: (01732) 851626   FAX: (01732) 851881
from A26 turn at sign for Golden Green 2m NE of Tonbridge centre; follow road for 1½m

Goldhill Mill was a working water mill for 850 years and is mentioned in the Domesday Book. The present house is part Tudor and part Georgian, with the mill machinery now displayed behind glass in the huge beamed farmhouse kitchen. It is set in 20 acres of grounds with a crayfish farm, orchards, woodlands, paddocks with horses, two

179

acres of formal gardens and a floodlit hard tennis court. The atmosphere is relaxed and the rooms are elegantly furnished and decorated. Two of the three bedrooms have huge jacuzzi baths, one in a bathroom with a *trompe l'oeil* mural; the third bedroom has a four-poster bed, and they are all extremely comfortable and well equipped. There are also two self-catering cottages.

OWNERS: Vernon and Shirley Cole OPEN: Sept to mid-July exc Christmas ROOMS: 3 double, all with bath/shower; TV in all bedrooms TERMS: single occupancy £54.50–£65, double £69.50–£74; £10 for children sharing with parents; deposit: 1 night's charge or credit card details CARDS: Access, Visa DETAILS: children by arrangement; no dogs; no smoking; car park; garden; tennis

GOUDHURST   Kent   map 3

Lamberts

Church Road, Goudhurst, nr Cranbrook TN17 1BH
TEL: (01580) 211496   FAX: (01580) 211707
opposite church on A262

This lovely old house dates from the nineteenth century and is surrounded by rolling countryside. It is surprisingly spacious and with all the old features one would expect, such as uneven floors, low doorways and original woodwork. There are two very attractive, bright bedrooms, one of which overlooks the sizeable and beautifully maintained garden. Breakfast only is served in a room off the kitchen, and there is also a sitting area. Lamberts is located close to Sissinghurst Castle, and there are a couple of pubs within walking distance for evening meals.

OWNER: Jeannette Colin OPEN: all year exc Christmas ROOMS: 1 double, 1 twin; both rooms with bath/shower; TV in both bedrooms TERMS: twin/double £40; half-price for children over 6; deposit: 1 night's charge for new visitors CARDS: none DETAILS: no children under 6; no dogs; no smoking; car park; garden

Mill House

Church Road, Goudhurst TN17 1BN
TEL: (01580) 211703
on A262, 4m NW of Cranbrook

This red-brick, tile-hung sixteenth-century former millhouse stands in two acres of gardens overlooking the cricket ground. The house has a lot of history attached to it: there is an old smugglers' tunnel, and the beamed lounge has old gnarled oak doors and an inglenook fireplace. Breakfast only is served. Mr Russell runs an antique shop in town, and Sissinghurst is only four miles away.

OWNERS: Sally and Brad Russell OPEN: all year exc Christmas ROOMS: 1 double, 1 family, both with shower; TV in both bedrooms and lounge TERMS: single occupancy £40, double/family £40; reductions for children according to age; deposit required CARDS: none DETAILS: children welcome; no dogs; no smoking; car park; garden

GRAMPOUND   Cornwall   map 1

Creed House

Creed, Grampound TR2 4SL
TEL: (01872) 530372
*from Grampound, half-way between Truro and St Austell on A390, take
road signposted Creed; after 1m take T-junction, turn left at church and
house is behind second white gate on left*

This lovely Georgian country house lies down a quiet narrow lane,
about a mile from the village of Grampound. Until the present owners
bought the house 20 years ago it was the rectory to the fourteenth-
century church of St Crida, which is a short distance away. Creed
House stands in a lovely five-acre garden, which is sometimes open to
the public, and includes a walled herbaceous garden and several
ponds. The Croggons are charming people who do everything possible
to ensure their visitors are comfortable. The house has spacious, well-
proportioned rooms and has been furnished with taste and simplicity.
Guests have the use of a sitting-room and all the bedrooms have *en
suite* facilities. Breakfast is served in the farmhouse-style kitchen,
which leads out to a back patio on which guests can relax in summer.
There are plenty of restaurants nearby for evening meals.

OWNERS: Mr and Mrs William Croggon   OPEN: all year exc Christmas and New Year
ROOMS: 2 double, 1 twin; all rooms with bath/shower; TV lounge   TERMS: single
occupancy £25–£30, twin/double £50–£60; deposit: 10%   CARDS: none   DETAILS: no
children under 10; dogs welcome if sleeping in adjacent outside kennels; no smoking;
car park; garden; tennis

GRANGE-OVER-SANDS   Cumbria   map 8

Somerset House

Kents Bank Road, Grange-over-Sands LA11 7EY
TEL: (01539) 532631
from M6 junction 36 take A590 slip road to Grange

Somerset House is a pleasant 100-year-old house situated within a
three-minute walk of the promenade, with views over the Kent
Estuary. There are two lounges for guests, one with TV and one with
a small bar. Four of the good-sized bedrooms have shower cubicles.
Breakfast and dinner are served at separate tables in the dining-
room, and vegetarian choices can be provided. There is only partial
central heating, but all the beds have electric blankets. Parking
permits are available for the nearby car park.

OWNERS: Elizabeth O'Neil and Rose-Marie Wilkinson   OPEN: all year exc Christmas
ROOMS: 2 single, 2 double, all with wash-basin; 4 family, all with shower; 3 rooms
suitable for wheelchair-users; TV in all bedrooms   TERMS: single £16–£18.50, single

181

occupancy £25, double £28–£33, family room £38–£41.50; half-price for children sharing with parents; dinner £7.50; deposit: £10 CARDS: none DETAILS: children welcome; dogs welcome; smoking in bar and bedrooms only

---

Thornfield House

Kents Bank Road, Grange-over-Sands LA11 7DT
TEL: (01539) 532512

Conveniently situated near footpath access to the promenade, this pleasant Victorian house has six immaculate bedrooms, all individually decorated in soft pastels. Some of the rooms have views over Morecambe Bay. The comfortable lounge provides a good place to read or chat. Breakfasts, and dinners if pre-arranged, are served in the dining-room, which also overlooks the bay. The home-style cooked meals include appetising desserts such as queen of puddings and trifle, and vegetarians and those with special dietary needs are well catered for. Guests arriving by train can arrange to be met at the station. Packed lunches are provided on request.

OWNERS: Moray and Margaret Irvine OPEN: all year exc Christmas and New Year
ROOMS: 1 single, 2 double, 2 twin, 1 family; all rooms with wash-basin; TV in all bedrooms TERMS: single/single occupancy £16.50, twin/double £33, family from £49.50; half-price for children from 5 to 10; dinner £7; deposit: £5 per person CARDS: none DETAILS: no children under 5; no dogs; no smoking; car park

---

GRANTLEY   North Yorkshire   **map 9**

Heatherlands

Grantley, Ripon HG4 3PL
TEL: (01765) 620634
1m N of B6265, 5m W of Ripon

This ivy-covered chalet-style bungalow stands in one and a half acres of award-winning gardens. A further 27 acres of grounds support a herd of pedigree Limousin cattle and plenty of wildlife. Guests are treated to good old-fashioned hospitality and a warm ambience prevails. The rooms are of a good size, one on the ground floor and two in the loft conversion. They are furnished with a mixture of pine and wicker and the rest of the house features some dark wood antiques, including a grandfather clock and a dresser with a fine display of china. The comfortable lounge has leaded windows, a piano, lots of interesting knick-knacks and an open fire. Breakfasts only are served, but the village offers a number of eating places within walking distance.

OWNER: Joan Metcalfe OPEN: all year ROOMS: 2 double, 1 twin; all rooms with bath/shower; TV lounge TERMS: single occupancy £21, twin/double £34; children's reductions CARDS: none DETAILS: children welcome; no dogs in lounge or dining-room; no smoking; car park; garden

Rothay Lodge

White Bridge, Grasmere LA22 9RH
TEL: (01539) 435341

Just five minutes' walk from the centre of this beautiful Lakeland
village, Rothay Lodge is a former 'gentleman's residence' dating from
1830. It is set in its own landscaped gardens on the banks of the River
Rothay and has lovely views of the river and surrounding fells. The
comfortable lounge has a conservatory area which overlooks the
gardens. Most of the bedrooms, which are individually decorated, are
en suite, and one (with WC and wash-basin) is on the ground floor.
The guesthouse has drying facilities for walkers. Breakfast only is
served, though the Allans provide a selection of menus for local
restaurants.

OWNERS: Jean and Bill Allan   OPEN: mid-Feb to end Oct   ROOMS: 4 double, 3 with bath/
shower, 1 with wash-basin; 2 twin, 1 with bath/shower, 1 with wash-basin; 1 family,
with bath/shower; TV in all bedrooms   TERMS: single occupancy £20–£25, twin/double
£37–£46, family from £55.50; half-price for children from 8 to 10; deposit: £20 per
person   CARDS: none   DETAILS: no children under 8; no dogs; no smoking; car park;
garden

St Oswald's

Red Bank Road, Grasmere LA22 9PX
TEL/FAX: (015394) 35705

St Oswald's is a handsome Georgian house set in eight acres of
grounds on the edge of the village. All bedrooms overlook the garden,
which becomes wooded hillside inhabited by birds, rabbits, red
squirrels and occasional roe deer. Mr and Mrs Yates are extremely
hospitable and welcome guests into their family home as friends. The
three bedrooms are tastefully furnished, and there is a comfortable
lounge with log fire where substantial breakfasts are served.
Grasmere is a good base from which to explore the Lake District;
boating, swimming, fishing and sailing are available close by.

OWNERS: Mr and Mrs Beverley Yates   OPEN: all year exc Christmas and New Year
ROOMS: 1 single, with wash-basin; 1 double, with bath/shower; 1 twin, with bath/
shower; TV in all bedrooms   TERMS: single £20.50–£21.50, twin/double £46–£53;
deposit: £25   CARDS: none   DETAILS: no children under 11; no dogs; no smoking; car
park; garden

*If you disagree with any assessment made in this guide, please write and
tell us why. Address your letter to The Good Bed and Breakfast Guide,
FREEPOST, 2 Marylebone Road, London NW1 1YN.*

GRAYRIGG   Cumbria

map 8

Punchbowl House

Grayrigg, nr Kendal LA8 9BU
TEL: (01539) 824345
on A685, 5m NE of Kendal

This large Victorian stone-built farmhouse is situated on the Dales
Way walk in the centre of the village. The house has been tastefully
refurbished in keeping with its original character and is beautifully
furnished. The spacious bedrooms are decorated with attractive
wallpapers. Breakfast includes home-made bread and jams, and
evening meals are available if pre-arranged. Guests may bring their
own wine to dinner and vegetarian choices can be provided. The
Johnsons are a charming couple who ensure that their guests are
comfortable; washing and drying facilities are available for walkers,
and packed lunches can be provided. A separate self-catering
property is also available for rental.

OWNERS: Mr and Mrs I. Johnson   OPEN: all year   ROOMS: 2 double, 1 with bath/shower,
1 with wash-basin; 1 twin, with wash-basin; TV in all bedrooms   TERMS: single
occupancy £15.50–£30, twin/double £31–£37; dinner £12.50; deposit: £10   CARDS:
none   DETAILS: no children; no dogs; no smoking; car park

GREAT CHART   Kent

map 3

Worten House

Great Chart, nr Ashford TN23 3BU
TEL: (01233) 622944
*from M20 junction 9 take A20 towards Charing for 1m, then turn left
signposted Godinton, then second turning on right*

Worten House probably dates from the eighteenth century and is a
brick and stone building with a lovely walled garden and pleasant
views over farmland. It is a comfortable family home and guests have
use of a sitting-room with TV. The two large, light bedrooms share a
bathroom with shower attachment, and two toilets. Evening meals
are available with 24 hours' notice and packed lunches can be
provided.

OWNERS: Denise and Charles Wilkinson   OPEN: all year   ROOMS: 2 twin, both with wash-
basin; TV lounge   TERMS: single occupancy £25, twin £40; dinner £15   CARDS: none
DETAILS: children welcome; no dogs; no smoking in bedrooms; car park; garden

*If a B&B caters for vegetarians, we note this in the entry. It is always best,
however, to check when booking and make it clear what your requirements
are, especially if you require a special diet.*

GREAT DUNMOW   Essex
map 3

Homelye Farm

Braintree Road, Great Dunmow CM6 3AW
TEL: (01371) 872127
from A120 1m E of Great Dunmow turn into lane opposite water tower;
farm is at bottom of lane

This is a working arable and cattle farm of 100 acres. Guests'
accommodation is in the converted stables close to the house and
approached through the farmyard, which has plenty of parking space.
The three comfortable, clean, *en suite* rooms all have their own
entrance, fridge and TV. Breakfast is served in the main house.

OWNER: Tracy Pickford   OPEN: all year exc Christmas   ROOMS: 1 single, 1 double, 1
twin; all rooms with bath/shower; TV in all bedrooms   TERMS: single £18.50–£20, single
occupancy £25, twin/double £37–£40; children under 3 free, reductions for ages 3 to
12   CARDS: none   DETAILS: children welcome; no dogs; no smoking; car park; garden

GREAT MALVERN   Hereford & Worcester
map 5

Elm Bank

52 Worcester Road, Great Malvern WR14 4AB
TEL: (01684) 566051
set back from A449 between Great Malvern and Malvern Link stations

This splendid Regency house was built in 1830 and has views of the
hills. Richard and Helen Mobbs have been running it as a B&B for
over 10 years and have created a warm and friendly atmosphere in
their home. Many original features remain, such as ceiling roses,
plasterwork and a lovely curved staircase. The large bedrooms are
tastefully decorated and furnished and the sunny comfortable lounge
has a varied collection of books and local information. On fine days
guests are welcome to enjoy the well-tended garden. Breakfast is
served in the elegant dining-room.

OWNERS: Richard and Helen Mobbs   OPEN: all year   ROOMS: 3 double, all with bath/
shower; 1 twin, with wash-basin; 2 family, both with bath/shower; TV in all bedrooms
TERMS: single occupancy £27–£32, twin/double £38–£46, family room £38–£46 plus
children's charge; children under 2 free, £5–£10 for older children; deposit: £30   CARDS:
Amex   DETAILS: children welcome; dogs by arrangement; smoking in lounge only; car
park; garden

B&B rates specified in the details at the end of each entry are given (as
applicable) for a single room, for single occupancy of a double room, and
then per room in the case of two people sharing a double or twin-bedded
room, or for a family room.

GREAT SNORING   Norfolk   map 6

Red House

Great Snoring, nr Fakenham NR21 0AH
TEL: (01328) 820641
off A148 / B1105, 3m NE of Fakenham

This is an interesting Georgian building in the village of Great
Snoring, less than two miles from the twelfth-century shrine at Little
Walsingham. The house is furnished mostly with antique pieces and
the dining-room table was once owned by Charles Dickens. Excellent
breakfasts are served on fine china; evening meals, cooked on the
Aga, are available if arranged in advance. The one bedroom is
immaculate, with quality linen sheets. A civilised atmosphere
pervades, and early-morning tea is brought to guests. There are lots
of family portraits in the house and Mrs Wells has many interesting
stories to tell about them.

OWNER: Rev Mark Wells   OPEN: all year   ROOMS: 1 double, with bath/shower; TV in
bedroom and lounge   TERMS: double £36; dinner: price by arrangement   CARDS: Visa
DETAILS: no children under 10; small dogs by arrangement; no smoking; car park;
garden

GREAT YARMOUTH   Norfolk   map 6

Senglea Lodge

7 Euston Road, Great Yarmouth NR30 1DX
TEL: (01493) 859632

Situated just minutes from the town centre, this neat, well-
maintained guesthouse offers excellent-value accommodation. Two of
the bedrooms have four-poster beds with lace canopies and attractive
matching curtains made by Julia Formosa. All the bedrooms have
satellite TV. The lounge/dining-room is warm and comfortable.
Modestly priced substantial dinners are available (served at 5.30pm)
and Senglea is licensed. Car parking is available across the street.

OWNERS: Joe and Julia Formosa   OPEN: all year exc Christmas   ROOMS: 4 double, 2
with bath/shower, 2 with wash-basin; 1 twin, with wash-basin; 2 four-poster, 1 with
bath/shower, 1 with wash-basin; TV in all bedrooms   TERMS: single occupancy
£12.50–£14, twin/double £25–£28, four-poster £28; half-price or less for children
according to season; dinner £5   CARDS: none   DETAILS: children welcome; no dogs;
garden

*If a B&B offers off-street car parking, we note 'car park' in the details at the
end of the entry. If we are aware of particular car-parking difficulties, we
mention them.*

GREENHAM   Somerset   map 2

Greenham Hall

Greenham, nr Wellington TA21 0JJ
TEL: (01823) 672603   FAX: (01823) 672307
off A38, 4m W of Wellington

Greenham Hall stands in a large, well-maintained garden complete
with croquet lawn. The rambling house is an impressive Victorian
building built in Gothic-Revival style with a crenellated tower, from
which there are splendid views of the village and countryside. Peter
Ayre was born in Kenya and deals in African antiquarian books;
photographs of African wildlife hang on the walls. There is a vast
hallway, which is the focal point of the house, and the other rooms are
also spacious, with good views. There is a breakfast/sitting-room
where breakfast only is served, although the Ayres can occasionally
provide other meals. Otherwise, food can be found at local pubs and
restaurants. The Ayres are welcoming hosts who enjoy sharing their
house with guests.

OWNERS: Peter and Caro Ayre   OPEN: all year   ROOMS: 2 double, 1 with bath/shower; 2
twin, 1 with bath/shower; 2 family, 1 with wash-basin; TV lounge   TERMS: single
occupancy £22.50–£27.50, twin/double £35, family room from £40; reductions for
children sharing with parents; deposit: 50% for bank hols   CARDS: none   DETAILS:
children welcome; dogs by arrangement; car park; garden

GREENHOW HILL   North Yorkshire   map 9

Mole End

Greenhow, Pateley Bridge, nr Harrogate HG3 5JQ
TEL: (01423) 712565
on B6265, 3m W of Pateley Bridge

This solid modern house was built in 1990 and stands behind a
traditional dry-stone wall with a ranch-style gate. It is set back from
the road, so traffic noise is not a problem, and a panoramic view opens
up to the back. The house is well maintained and decorated to a high
standard, and the beds are comfortable. The *en suite* twin room has a
large bathroom with a power shower, and the best view. Hearty
breakfasts are served in the dining/sitting-room. Evening meals can
be bought in the Miner's pub, two minutes' walk away, or in Pateley
Bridge, where there is a wider choice.

OWNERS: Dennis and Elaine Knowles   OPEN: Apr to Oct   ROOMS: 1 double; 2 twin, 1
with bath/shower; TV in all bedrooms   TERMS: single occupancy £20, twin/double
£32–£36; £5 for children; deposit: 10%   CARDS: none   DETAILS: no children under 12;
dogs by arrangement; smoking in lounge only; car park; garden

The Old Vicarage

Gringley on the Hill, nr Doncaster DN10 4RS
TEL/FAX: (01777) 817248
next to the church in the village, just off A631 between Gainsborough and Bawtry

---

In the centre of an unspoilt village, this is an elegant building set in three acres, with a rock garden, an orchard and a tennis court. A miniature Shetland pony and Henry the labrador wander the gardens, while William the African grey parrot welcomes guests to the house, which is luxuriously furnished with cane, wicker and period furnishings. One of the double rooms has an adjoining room with a single bed and they can be taken together as a family suite. The garden also provides Helena Simmonds with the space to grow her own vegetables for the imaginative dinners she prepares on the Aga. These are served between 7.30 and 8pm and will include vegetarian options if required. The Old Vicarage also has an alcohol licence.

OWNERS: John and Helena Simmonds   OPEN: all year exc Christmas and New Year
ROOMS: 3 double, all with bath/shower; TV lounge   TERMS: single occupancy £30,
double £50; children under 2 free, half-price for ages 2 to 12; dinner £17; deposit: £5
per person   CARDS: Access, Visa   DETAILS: children welcome; dogs by prior
arrangement; smoking in TV lounge only; car park; garden; tennis

---

Church House

Grittleton, nr Chippenham SN14 6AP
TEL/FAX: (01249) 782562
from M4 junction 17 take A429 towards Malmesbury, then first left, continue 3½m to village

---

This elegant Georgian house built of Bath stone stands in 11 acres of gardens and pasture, grazed by a small flock of sheep, and was formerly the rectory. The Moores strive to offer the highest standards while retaining the essential elements of a family country house. Dinner is served in a party atmosphere at the large dining-room table, and Church House is very popular with small groups of friends or families who return again and again, partly for Anna Moore's excellent, unpretentious cooking. Dinner, which includes wine, should be ordered in advance; vegetarian options are available sometimes. The large, simply furnished bedrooms have their own facilities, but not in a separate room – they are screened off in a corner. There is a spacious sitting-room. The heated and covered swimming-pool is right by the house walls and is floodlit at night, and a croquet lawn is available in summer. Church House is located between the village church and the pub, and is close to Badminton House.

OWNERS: Michael and Anna Moore OPEN: all year ROOMS: 1 double, 3 twin; all rooms with bath/shower; TV in all bedrooms TERMS: single occupancy £32.50, twin/double £54.50; half-price for children from 12 to 15 sharing with parents; dinner £15.50; deposit required CARDS: none DETAILS: babies and children over 12 welcome; no dogs; no smoking in dining-room or drawing-room; car park; garden; swimming-pool

GULWORTHY   Devon   map 1

Hele Farm

Gulworthy, nr Tavistock PL19 8PA
TEL: (01822) 833084
from Tavistock take A390 2½m W, then turn right at crossroads and second left

Hele Farm is a 150-acre dairy farm set in peaceful, isolated countryside. The eighteenth-century slate-fronted building stands in a large garden at the end of a dead-end lane and a long gravel track. Simplicity and friendliness are the keynotes, with farmhouse comforts and plenty of space for children, including a play-room. Families with small children can expect a warm welcome from Rosemary Steer. Downstairs there is one large, bright, comfortable room for guests, half of which used to be the old dairy, and it has a big dining table at one end and a sitting area at the other. Hele Farm is clean and cheerful and excellent value for money.

OWNER: Rosemary Steer OPEN: Mar to Nov ROOMS: 2 double, both with bath/shower; TV in 1 bedroom and lounge TERMS: single occupancy £20, double £30–£32; children under 3 free; half-price for children under 10 CARDS: none DETAILS: children welcome; dogs welcome; no smoking; car park; games room; garden

GURNARD   Isle of Wight   map 2

Hillbrow

Tuttons Hill, Gurnard, nr Cowes PO31 8JA
TEL: 01983) 297240

Hillbrow was built in the 1930s as a maternity home, and many people like to return here to see where they were born. The house stands in its own garden and has extensive views over farmland to the Solent. Although rather lacking in character, Hillbrow is very clean and neat and well furnished. Evening meals are available on request, and earlier snacks can be provided; packed lunches can also be supplied. Horse-riding and golf can be arranged, and it is only a 15-minute walk to the centre of Cowes.

OWNERS: Val and Paul Mortlock OPEN: all year exc Christmas ROOMS: 1 single, with wash-basin; 1 double, with bath/shower; 2 twin, 1 with bath/shower, 1 with wash-basin; 1 family, with bath/shower; TV in all bedrooms and lounge TERMS: single £19, single occupancy £24–£28, twin/double £38–£46; family room from £38; children's reductions according to age; dinner £9; deposit: £20 per person CARDS: none DETAILS: children welcome; no dogs; no smoking in dining-room; car park; garden

HALTWHISTLE Northumberland   map 11

Ald White Craig Farm

Haltwhistle NE49 9NW
TEL/FAX: (01434) 320565
follow signs for Hadrian's Wall from E end of Haltwhistle; farm is 1m from the wall

This seventeenth-century croft perches high on the hillside above Haltwhistle and overlooks the South Tyne Valley and the fells beyond. Mrs Laidlow is a delightful host who extends true northern hospitality and knows how to make hearty breakfasts that will fill up her guests, vegetarians included, for the day. The beamed lounge has an open fire and a display of porcelain. The bedrooms are all on the ground floor and have electric blankets for chilly nights. Prize-winning blue-faced sheep and rare Longhorn cattle graze the 14 acres of farmland. The farmhouse has been presented with the Tynedale Customer Choice Award two years running. Self-catering cottages are available.

OWNER: Mrs J.I. Laidlow OPEN: all year ROOMS: 2 double, 1 twin; all rooms with bath/shower; TV in all bedrooms TERMS: single occupancy £24, twin/double £38; deposit: £10 CARDS: none DETAILS: children welcome; no dogs; no smoking; car park; garden

HAMPTON-IN-ARDEN West Midlands   map 5

The Hollies

Kenilworth Road, Hampton-in-Arden, nr Solihull B92 0LW
TEL: (01675) 442681 FAX: (01675) 442941
on A452, 2m S of junction with A45

The Hollies is set back from the dual carriageway on a service road. It is a well-maintained guesthouse with attractive, welcoming floral displays in tubs and baskets outside. Inside, the decorations are mostly in pastel shades and the lounge/dining-room has recently been repainted. The rooms are on the small side, but are kept immaculate and have well-planned storage space. Jim and Tina are a friendly couple who will help guests organise travel to and from the airport and set them up with a good breakfast. The Hollies is conveniently situated for the Birmingham National Exhibition Centre.

OWNERS: Jim and Tina Fitzpatrick   OPEN: all year   ROOMS: 1 single, with wash-basin; 3 double, 2 with bath/shower, 1 with wash-basin; 2 twin, both with bath/shower; 2 family, both with bath/shower; TV in all bedrooms and lounge   TERMS: single £20, single occupancy £25, twin/double £40, family room £45; deposit: £10   DETAILS: children welcome; no dogs; no smoking in 4 bedrooms; car park; garden

---

HAMPTON LUCY   Warwickshire   map 5

Sandbarn Farm

Hampton Lucy, nr Stratford-upon-Avon CV35 8AU
TEL: (01789) 842280
off A439, 4½m NE of Stratford-upon-Avon

Dating from the sixteenth century, this impressive red-brick building stands in ten acres of open countryside and has glorious views towards the Malvern Hills. The spacious rooms have a sense of luxury about them, and the house is furnished with a mixture of the antique and the traditional. The top-floor rooms with their sloping roofs are particularly attractive. Breakfasts include a varied Continental choice. Sandbarn Farm is well-positioned for visits to Stratford-upon-Avon and Warwick.

OWNER: Mrs H.P. Waterworth   OPEN: all year exc Christmas week   ROOMS: 2 single, 3 double, 1 twin, 2 family; all rooms with bath/shower; TV lounge   TERMS: single £25, single occupancy £40, twin/double £50, family from £75; deposit: 25%   CARDS: none
DETAILS: no children under 5; dogs by arrangement; smoking in sitting-room and dining-room only; car park

---

HANLITH   North Yorkshire   map 8

Coachman's Cottage

Hanlith, nr Skipton BD23 4BP
TEL: (01729) 830538
head N from A65 5m W of Skipton at sign for Malham, then turn right in Kirkby Malham opposite Victoria Inn

---

This pretty whitewashed cottage is situated right on the Pennine Way in an unspoilt hamlet with beautiful views. It is 300 years old and restoration work has kept the original oak beams and thick stone walls intact. Guests are welcomed with tea and home-made scones and jams, and will usually find fresh flowers in their bedrooms. Two of these are in the main house, one with a power shower, and the other two are in a barn conversion, which also includes a sitting-room. Furniture is antique and traditional, and the lounge has a log fire. Hearty breakfasts only are served, and for evening meals the Victoria Inn is only 400 yards away downhill. Laundry facilities are available.

COACHMAN'S COTTAGE, HANLITH

OWNERS: Glyn and Monica Jenkins OPEN: all year exc Christmas and New Year
ROOMS: 3 double, 1 twin; all rooms with bath/shower; TV in all bedrooms and lounge
TERMS: single occupancy £19, twin/double £38; children's reductions according to age;
deposit: £10 CARDS: none DETAILS: no children under 7; no dogs; no smoking; car
park; garden

HARBERTON Devon   **map 1**

Ford Farm

Harberton, nr Totnes TQ9 7SJ
TEL: (01803) 863539
off A381, ¾m outside village

This seventeenth-century whitewashed house stands in its own
garden with a stream, in the small village of Harberton. It has a
friendly, homely atmosphere. The three modestly sized but
comfortable bedrooms all have names: Louise's, Flower and
Patchwork (the last has a patchwork quilt). The upstairs sitting-room
has a TV, books and games, tea- and coffee-making facilities, and a
supply of biscuits. Breakfast only is served in the beamed dining-
room, but a number of pubs and restaurants nearby serve evening
meals. Ford Farm is in a peaceful location and is only two miles from
Totnes and seven miles from the sea. Packed lunches can be provided.

OWNER: Sheila Edwards OPEN: all year ROOMS: 1 single, with wash-basin; 1 double, with bath/shower; 1 twin, with wash-basin; TV lounge TERMS: single £22, single occupancy £25–£30, twin/double £40–£42; deposit: £15 per person CARDS: none DETAILS: no children under 12; dogs welcome; smoking in lounge only; car park; garden

HARGRAVE   Cheshire   map 7

Greenlooms Cottage

Martins Lane, Hargrave, nr Chester CH3 7RY
TEL: (01829) 781475
from A41 2m S of Chester turn at sign for Waverton by antiques shop, then right after golf course

A warm welcome is assured at this 150-year-old cottage in a quiet country lane. The ambience is friendly and the cottage is furnished in keeping with its character. The two bedrooms, one of which is on the ground floor, both have *en suite* shower rooms and the upstairs room has a lovely, comfortable high bed. Breakfasts include home-made jams and marmalades, and innovative evening meals are prepared with local vegetables, cooked on the Aga and served *en famille* unless otherwise requested. The owners are a charming couple who have a good sense of humour. Beeston Castle, Bodnant and Little Moreton Hall are all within easy driving distance.

OWNERS: Peter and Deborah Newman OPEN: all year ROOMS: 1 double, 1 twin; all rooms with shower; TV lounge TERMS: single occupancy £20, twin/double £35; dinner £10; deposit: £15 CARDS: none DETAILS: children welcome; dogs welcome; no smoking; car park; garden

HARROGATE   North Yorkshire   map 9

The Alexander

88 Franklin Road, Harrogate HG1 5EN
TEL: (01423) 503348

This lovely Victorian residence looks out on a pretty little front garden with a small pond. Accommodation is of a high standard, with quality décor in harmony with the house's origins. The spacious bedrooms have pink and floral wallpapers and bed linen, and plush headboards, plus attractive dried-flower arrangements and brass candlestick-style lamps adorning the walls. There is a small lounge, and generous breakfasts are served in the separate dining-room. Parking is available on the street.

OWNERS: Richard and Lesley Toole OPEN: all year ROOMS: 2 single, both with wash-basin; 1 double, with bath/shower; 2 family, with bath/shower; TV in all bedrooms and lounge TERMS: single £20, single occupancy £32, double £40, family room £40 plus children's charge; children's reductions; deposit CARDS: none DETAILS: children welcome; no dogs; no smoking

Knabbs Ash

Skipton Road, Felliscliffe, Harrogate HG3 2LT
TEL: (01423) 771040   FAX: (01423) 771515
off A59 6m W of Harrogate, ½m E of Millstone restaurant

Knabbs Ash is a beautifully appointed renovated farmhouse less than a mile from the main road. Although it is no longer a working farm, it has 20 acres of land grazed by sheep and a few hens. The house is immmaculate and the luxurious bedrooms are individually decorated with quality drapes and coronets made by Sheila Smith. She has a flair for décor and has filled the house with colourful dried-flower arrangements. The comfortable sitting-room has an open fire and a stunning view through the patio doors, and there is a separate dining-room where delicious breakfasts are served at separate pine tables. Sheila Smith is a bright, congenial lady who enjoys meeting people and is happy to help guests plan sightseeing trips.

OWNER: Sheila Smith   OPEN: all year exc Christmas   ROOMS: 2 double, 1 twin; all rooms with bath/shower; TV in all bedrooms and lounge   TERMS: single occupancy £25, twin/double £40; deposit   CARDS: none   DETAILS: no children under 10; no dogs; no smoking; car park; garden

Lynton House

42 Studley Road, Harrogate HG1 5JU
TEL: (01423) 504715

Studley Road is a quiet tree-lined avenue, within minutes of the exhibition and conference centre. Joan McLoughlin is friendly and welcoming and runs a sunny establishment. Some lovely pictures are hung throughout the house and a very large fish tank dominates the dining-room, where breakfast only is served. The lounge is well furnished and comfortable and the bedrooms are equipped with toiletries and remote controls for the TVs. Harrogate has a wide choice of places for evening meals.

OWNERS: John and Joan McLoughlin   OPEN: Mar to Nov   ROOMS: 2 single, 1 double, 1 twin, 1 family; all rooms with wash-basin; TV in all bedrooms and lounge   TERMS: single £17–£19, single occupancy £26, twin/double £34–£36, family room £44; children's reductions according to age; deposit required   CARDS: none   DETAILS: no children under 9; no dogs; no smoking

If the establishment does not take credit cards, we say so in the details at the end of the entry.

Most establishments have central heating. When we know this is not the case, we mention this in the entry.

Baker's Chest

Hartburn, nr Morpeth NE61 4JB
TEL: (01670) 772214   FAX: (01670) 772363
on B6343, 7m W of Morpeth

This attractive sandstone cottage is located in the village of
Hartburn, which is well placed for visiting Hadrian's Wall. This is
also an ideal spot for nature-lovers; there are many walks in the area,
and plenty of wildlife including deer and red squirrels. The
immaculate house is comfortably furnished with antiques and
collected ornaments. There is a pleasant TV lounge, and a large
lawned garden with croquet. As well as the two bedrooms in the main
house, guests have the option of staying in one of the two self-catering
cottages. Breakfast only is served.

OWNERS: Richard and Sue Cansdale   OPEN: all year exc Christmas   ROOMS: 1 double,
with wash-basin; 1 twin; TV lounge   TERMS: single occupancy £20–£25, twin/double
£32; £7.50 for children sharing with parents; deposit: £10   CARDS: none   DETAILS:
children welcome; small dogs by arrangement; no smoking; car park; garden

Bolebroke Mill

Edenbridge Road, Hartfield TN7 4JP
TEL/FAX: (01892) 770425
*take A264 from Tunbridge Wells for 6m, then left on B2026 signposted
Hartfield for 1m, then down unmade track on left next to Perryhill Nursery*

This ancient watermill is set in six and a half acres of secluded
woodland, was first recorded in the Domesday Book, and continued as
a working corn-mill until 1948. The machinery and old-world charm
remain, and both the mill and miller's barn have been converted with
great ingenuity, creating most unusual bedrooms and bathrooms
which have exceptional character. Some of the accommodation is
reached by steep staircases, which makes it unsuitable for small
children or the less mobile. The mill stream runs through the large
garden, and there is also a duck pond. Meals are served in an
attractive, beautifully furnished room in the Mill House; packed
lunches can be provided.

OWNER: Christine Cooper   OPEN: all year exc Christmas   ROOMS: 2 double, 1 twin, 2
four-poster; all rooms with bath/shower; TV in all bedrooms   TERMS: single occupancy
£48, twin/double £53, four-poster £70; deposit: 50% or credit card details   CARDS:
Access, Amex, Visa   DETAILS: no children under 7; no dogs; no smoking; car park;
garden

Manifold House

Hulme End, Hartington, nr Buxton SK17 0EZ
TEL: (01298) 84662
on B5054, 2m W of Hartington

This sturdy stone-built house in the centre of the hamlet of Hulme
End has well-developed creepers climbing one exterior wall, and an
attractive white porchway. It is a warm and friendly place with
interesting, well-travelled owners who maintain an informal
atmosphere and keep some equally welcoming pets: George the
border collie, a cat named Jack and a talking cockatiel. The three
large bedrooms are immaculately clean and furnished with antiques.
Evening meals are served, by arrangement, at 7pm, with vegetarian
choices if ordered in advance. Alternatively, guests can eat at the pub
just 200 yards away. A nine-mile walking and cycling trail called the
Manifold Track begins in the hamlet.

OWNERS: Mike and Ann Baber OPEN: all year exc Christmas ROOMS: 1 single; 1
double, with wash-basin; 1 twin; TV in all bedrooms TERMS: single £17, single
occupancy £20, twin/double £34; children's reductions according to age; dinner £8.50
CARDS: none DETAILS: children welcome; no dogs; smoking downstairs only; car park;
garden

Raikes Farm

Hulme End, Hartington, nr Buxton SK17 0HJ
TEL: (01298) 84344
on B5054, half-way between Hartington and Hulme End

This solid stone-built farmhouse covered with well-kept ivy stands in
a walled garden in 12 acres of land surrounded by woods. The thick
walls, exposed beams and uneven floors are in fitting company with
the antique furniture, including a 300-year-old fruitwood settle and a
grandfather clock. The lounge is shared with the family. Breakfast is
served in the cosy dining-room, and dinners, including vegetarian
options, are cooked by arrangement. Guests can wander in the lovely
gardens or range farther afield to Dovedale, the Manifold Valley and
Beresford Dale.

OWNERS: Alan and Valerie Shipley OPEN: all year exc Christmas ROOMS: 2 double, 1
family; all rooms with bath/shower; TV in all bedrooms and lounge TERMS: single
occupancy £22, double £40, family room £40 plus children's charge; half-price for
children; dinner £10; deposit: £10 per person CARDS: none DETAILS: children
welcome; dogs welcome with own bedding; smoking in lounge only; car park; garden

HARTLAND   Devon   map 1

West Titchberry Farm

Hartland, nr Bideford EX39 6AU
TEL: (01237) 441287
from Bideford take A39 Bude road for 10m, ¼m after Clovelly Cross roundabout turn right on to B3248 signposted Hartland, after 1¼m fork right at Lighthouse Cross following Hartland Point / Lighthouse signs for 4½m

This typical Devon longhouse was built around 1760, half a mile from Hartland Point and lighthouse, on the craggy north Devon coast. The Heards are third-generation farmers, and provide simple farmhouse accommodation, a friendly welcome, and excellent value. In addition to the three bedrooms, a large, well-equipped self-catering cottage is also available. The kitchen and dining-room have beamed ceilings and the cosy TV lounge has a wood-burning stove. Unlicensed evening meals (bring your own wine) are available by arrangement at 6.30pm, using meat and vegetables from the farm. Vegetarian dishes can be requested, and children's helpings and packed lunches provided. Visitors may wander around the 150-acre farm and, in springtime, children can feed the lambs. West Titchberry Farm is within easy access of many of the area's beauty spots, including the delightful village of Clovelly, only six miles away.

OWNERS: John and Yvonne Heard   OPEN: all year exc Christmas   ROOMS: 1 double, with wash-basin; 1 twin; 1 family, with wash-basin; TV lounge   TERMS: single occupancy £15, twin/double £27, family room from £27; children's reductions according to age; dinner £7; deposit   CARDS: none   DETAILS: children welcome; no dogs; no smoking in dining-room; car park; games room; garden

HARWICH   Essex   map 3

Reids of Harwich

3 West Street, Harwich CO12 3DA
TEL: (01255) 506796
opposite the high lighthouse

The ground floor of this smart Victorian house is a shop and gallery run by artist-owner Gordon Reid and displaying his watercolours, sketches and hand-painted thimbles. Upstairs it is a modest, clean guesthouse with a large comfortable lounge dominated by the original marble fireplace and decorated in dark colours. The bedrooms are on the second floor. Shampoo, hair-dryers, irons and sewing kits are provided on request, and free parking is available nearby in a public car park. Reids is conveniently located for ferry travellers.

OWNER: Gordon Reid OPEN: Apr to Oct ROOMS: 1 single, 1 double, 1 twin; all rooms with wash-basin; TV in all bedrooms and lounge TERMS: single £16, single occupancy £20, twin/double £32; deposit: 20% CARDS: none DETAILS: no children under 12; no dogs

HASLEMERE   Surrey   map 3

Deerfell

Blackdown Park, Fernden Lane, Haslemere GU27 3LA
TEL/FAX: (01428) 653409
take A286 Haslemere to Midhurst road, turn left into Fernden Lane just after the West Sussex border, then 2½m to entrance gates and first house on left

Deerfell was once the coach house to Blackdown Park, which is still a privately owned house. The stone building is set in a garden, with lovely views across the South Downs towards the Sussex coast. Two of the bedrooms have *en suite* facilities. Breakfast is served in the dining-room or conservatory, and there is a sitting-room for guests' use. Evening meals are available by arrangement and packed lunches can be provided.

OWNERS: Mrs E. and Mr D. Carmichael OPEN: all year exc 15 Dec to 15 Jan ROOMS: 2 twin, 1 family; all rooms with bath/shower; TV in all bedrooms TERMS: single occupancy £22, twin £36, family room £45; reductions for children under 5; dinner £8.50; deposit required for 3 or more nights CARDS: none DETAILS: children welcome; no dogs; no smoking; car park; garden

Quoins

Museum Hill, Haslemere GU27 2JR
TEL: (01428) 658540

This attractive black-and-white Edwardian house is in a quiet residential area close to the centre of Haslemere, yet with lovely views over the surrounding countryside. Quoins stands on the side of a steep hill in a beautiful and colourful garden, and both house and garden are on a series of different levels. The two bedrooms are spacious and comfortable and there is a pretty dining-room where breakfast is served. A conservatory makes a peaceful place in which to relax. The Bells are a charming and hospitable couple and Quoins is an elegant and restful family home. Packed lunches can be provided.

OWNER: Milly Bell OPEN: all year exc Christmas ROOMS: 1 double, 1 twin; both rooms with bath/shower; TV in one bedroom and lounge TERMS: single occupancy £20–£22.50, twin/double £36–£40; £10 for children under 5; deposit: £18–£20 CARDS: none DETAILS: children welcome; no dogs; no smoking; car park; garden

HATFIELD PEVEREL   Essex   map 3

The Wick

Terling Hall Road, Hatfield Peverel, nr Chelmsford CM3 2EZ
TEL: (01245) 380705
just off A12, 3m SW of Witham

This listed sixteenth-century farmhouse enjoys a rural setting and is
surrounded by a large garden with a duck pond and a stream. The
cottage has lots of character, and the relaxing drawing-room has an
inglenook fireplace and books to browse through. The two beamed
bedrooms are comfortably furnished and share a large bathroom. Mrs
Tritton is a friendly, outgoing lady who welcomes arrivals with a hot
drink and can assist with local information. Home-cooked evening
meals are served by arrangement and, with notice, children's
helpings and vegetarian choices can be provided. There is no alcohol
licence, but guests may bring their own wine. Several cats and an
unobtrusive dog also live here.

OWNER: Linda Tritton   OPEN: all year exc Christmas   ROOMS: 2 twin, 1 with wash-basin;
TV lounge   TERMS: single occupancy £20, twin £38; dinner £10   CARDS: none   DETAILS:
no children under 10; no dogs; no smoking upstairs; car park; garden

HAVERIGG   Cumbria   map 8

Dunelm Cottage

Main Street, Haverigg LA18 4EX
TEL: (01229) 770097

Several improvements have been undertaken at Dunelm Cottage,
which started life as two old village properties and was skilfully
converted to a guesthouse in 1990. All the bedrooms now have wash-
basins, and there is a separate dining-room where guests are served
breakfasts (with home-made bread and preserves featuring) and
evening meals. Although the cottage is unlicensed, guests are
welcome to bring their own wine to dinner. The three petite bedrooms
are prettily furnished and have flowered pastel duvets; they share
two bathrooms. Guests may also relax in the sunny lounge with TV.
Dunelm Cottage is within walking distance of the harbour and the
Hodbarrow Nature Reserve. Packed lunches can be provided. Guests
may use the village car park, which is opposite the cottage.

OWNER: Mrs J. Fairless   OPEN: all year   ROOMS: 1 double, 2 twin; all rooms with wash-
basin; TV lounge   TERMS: single occupancy £25, twin/double £43; dinner £12; deposit:
£10   CARDS: none   DETAILS: children by prior arrangement only; dogs by prior
arrangement only; no smoking in bedrooms; garden

199

Brandymires

Muker Road, Hawes DL8 3PR
TEL: (01969) 667482
just to N of Hawes on road signposted to Muker

This ever-popular property is in a peaceful spot just outside the
market town of Hawes. Readers continue to applaud the good food
and tranquil atmosphere found here. Gail Ainley and Ann Macdonald
are superb hosts and adept at making guests feel at home. The
sitting-room is comfortable, with a real fire in the marble fireplace
and lots of books to browse through, and, like the rest of the house, it
remains TV-free. All the bedrooms have their own sitting area too,
and the views from the windows are terrific. Ann's imaginative four-
course meals are served by arrangement at 7pm every day except
Thursday and will include vegetarian choices if notice is given.
Brandymires is licensed. Breakfast includes home-made preserves
and freshly squeezed orange juice.

OWNERS: Gail Ainley and Ann Macdonald   OPEN: Feb to mid-Oct   ROOMS: 1 double, 1
twin, 2 four-poster; all rooms with wash-basin   TERMS: single occupancy £26, twin/
double £36, four-poster £36; dinner £11; deposit: £15   CARDS: none   DETAILS: no
children under 8; dogs by arrangement; no smoking; car park

Tarney Fors Farm House

Tarney Fors, Hawes DL8 3LS
TEL: (01969) 667475
on B6255, 2m SW of Hawes

Tarney Fors takes its name from the small spring rising above the
house, which supplies the property with fresh spring water. This
listed building is a typical Dales longhouse backing on to fell land
with stone walls and sheep grazing. The house is comfortably
furnished in keeping with its character. Breakfast, including home-
made marmalade and freshly baked bread, and dinner are served in
the beamed dining-room with its flagstone floor. Light snacks can be
ordered during the day from the tea-shop on the premises, and a
warm, cosy lounge with exposed stone walls, plenty of books and a TV
is the ideal place in which to relax later on. The views from the house
are exceptional and this is ideal walking country.

OWNERS: Alan and Sue Harpley   OPEN: Mar to Nov   ROOMS: 2 double, both with bath/
shower; 1 twin, with wash-basin; TV lounge   TERMS: single occupancy £40–£45, twin/
double £44–£50; dinner £14; deposit: £25   CARDS: Access, Visa   DETAILS: no children
under 7; no dogs; no smoking; car park; garden

HAWKHURST   Kent

map 3

Conghurst Farm

Hawkhurst TN18 4RW
TEL: (01580) 753331   FAX: (01580) 754579
*from A21 take A268 E; 1½m after Hawkhurst turn right at Shell garage,
continue 1½m down Conghurst Lane, house is on left-hand side*

Conghurst Farm has been in the Piper family for hundreds of years
and family records in the local church go back to AD900. The oldest
part of the house dates from 1599, and the original stone coat-of-arms
is now in the family's sitting-room; the house has been extended over
the years, and the front is Georgian. It is part of a 500-acre working
arable farm set in a large garden with an unheated swimming-pool,
and with beautiful views over the surrounding countryside. A lovely
drawing-room with log fires is available for guests' use, and there is a
smaller room with TV. Rosemary Piper is a charming and efficient
host and provides excellent home-cooked evening meals by
arrangement; packed lunches can also be provided. The three
spacious bedrooms are attractively decorated and have either *en suite*
facilities or private bathrooms. Sissinghurst and Bodiam castles are
nearby.

OWNER: Rosemary Piper   OPEN: Feb to Nov   ROOMS: 1 double, 2 twin; all rooms with
bath/shower; TV in some bedrooms and lounge   TERMS: single occupancy £22, twin/
double £42–£44; dinner £10 to £13   CARDS: none   DETAILS: no children under 12; no
dogs; no smoking; car park; garden; swimming-pool

HAWORTH   West Yorkshire

map 8

Briarmains

South View, Haworth BD22 8EX
TEL: (01535) 642219

Dorothy Willetts warmly welcomes guests to her home, which is just
off the main road in a quiet cul-de-sac. Briarmains was built around
1895 and was neglected until the Willetts undertook the tremendous
task of renovation with loving care. The three good-sized bedrooms
are tastefully decorated with matching quality fabrics, and have
plenty of wardrobe space; one has a brass bed. Trevor is a member of
the Brontë Society Council and is happy to share his knowledge with
guests; he also has over 600 books on the Brontës in the comfortable
guests' lounge. The house is a three-minute stroll from the village
centre and the Brontë Parsonage.

OWNERS: Trevor and Dorothy Willetts   OPEN: all year exc Christmas and New Year
ROOMS: 1 single, with wash-basin; 1 double, with wash-basin; 1 twin, with bath/shower;
TV lounge   TERMS: single £16.50, single occupancy £25, twin/double £32–£34; deposit:
£10   CARDS: none   DETAILS: no children; no dogs; no smoking; car park; garden

Moorfield Guest House

80 West Lane, Haworth BD22 8EN
TEL: (01535) 643689

This detached Victorian house has unrestricted views front and back over Brontë country, and the Brontës' well-trodden path to the waterfall and Top Withens runs right past it. All the bedrooms enjoy the views and have good facilities. The family room is a large double with an adjacent single, plus bathroom. The dining-room opens out on to the terrace and the garden, which overlooks the village cricket field. The lounge has a small bar. Evening meals are served nightly by arrangement and there is always a blackboard special. Breakfasts are large, with home-made marmalade. The conservatory is a treasure trove of tourist information and Brontë books.

OWNERS: Barry and Pat Hargreaves   OPEN: all year exc Christmas and New Year   ROOMS: 1 single, with bath/shower; 3 double, 2 with bath/shower, 1 with wash-basin; 2 twin, both with bath/shower; 1 family, with bath/shower; TV in all bedrooms   TERMS: single £15.50–£17, single occupancy £20–£25, twin/double £32–£38, family room £32–£38 plus children's charge; children's reductions according to age; dinner £6.50–£9.50; deposit: £10 per person   CARDS: Access, Visa   DETAILS: children welcome; no dogs; no smoking in bedrooms or dining-room; car park; garden

---

HAYDON BRIDGE   **Northumberland**   **map 10**

Geeswood House

Whittis Road, Haydon Bridge, nr Hexham NE47 6AQ
TEL: (01434) 684220
off A69, 6m W of Hexham

Dating from the early nineteenth century, this immaculate stone-built house stands in an elevated position surrounded by a beautifully landscaped garden that slopes down to Langley Burn and its waterfall. The comfortable bedrooms are furnished in soft pastels, and although there are no *en suite* bedrooms, two bathrooms are exclusively for guests' use. The lounge has an unusual log fireplace and a handsome galleried staircase. The house has no central heating. Breakfasts are cooked on the Aga, and dinners, which are available by arrangement, include home-made bread and desserts, as well as vegetarian options if booked in advance. Guests are welcome to bring their own wine to dinner as Geeswood House is unlicensed. Packed lunches can be provided.

OWNERS: John and Doreen Easton   OPEN: all year exc Christmas   ROOMS: 1 double, 2 twin; all rooms with wash-basin; TV lounge   TERMS: single occupancy £20, twin/double £34; dinner £10.50; deposit: £10   CARDS: none   DETAILS: no children under 10; no dogs; no smoking; garden

HAYFIELD Derbyshire   map 9

Old Bank House

Hayfield SK12 5EP
TEL: (01663) 747354
just off A624, between Glossop and Chapel-en-le-Frith

This listed Georgian house stands by the River Sett, in the centre of
the picturesque village of Hayfield. There is a comfortable guest
lounge with a Victorian fireplace. Of the three spacious bedrooms, one
has a four-poster made by John Collier, one has an antique brass bed
and two have their original fireplaces. The Colliers are an interesting
couple: Sheila is a blues singer who performs regularly and has made
a CD; John has a Mountain Leadership Certificate and can arrange
walks. Breakfast and dinner (by arrangement) are served at a
scrubbed pine table in the dining-room, which overlooks the walled
garden. As there is no licence, guests are welcome to bring their own
wine to dinner; packed lunches can be provided. The two dogs, Jessie
and Bessie, are friendly.

OWNERS: Sheila and John Johnson   OPEN: all year   ROOMS: 2 double, 1 four-poster, 1
family; all with wash-basin; 1 room suitable for wheelchair-users; TV in all bedrooms
and lounge   TERMS: single occupancy £20, double/four-poster £38; family room from
£47.50; half-price for children sharing with parents; dinner £12   CARDS: none   DETAILS:
children welcome; dogs by prior arrangement; no smoking; garden

---

HAYLING ISLAND Hampshire   map 2

Cockle Warren Cottage

36 Seafront, Hayling Island PO11 9HL
TEL: (01705) 464961   FAX: (01705) 464838
follow A27 from Havant over bridge to Hayling Island, continue to sea-front, turn left and continue 1m

Cockle Warren is a tile-hung cottage, built as a family home in 1979
in traditional farmhouse style. It is set in a large garden on the sea-
front and has a smugglers' tunnel underneath its grounds. It has
been extended to provide pretty *en suite* bedrooms, two with four-
poster beds overlooking the sea, and one in a converted stable block.
The lounge with an open fire has an upright piano and is full of clocks,
plants, horse brasses and family paintings. Breakfast and dinners
are served in the smart conservatory dining-room at the rear of the
house, which overlooks the heated swimming-pool, floodlit at night.

OWNERS: David and Diane Skelton   OPEN: all year   ROOMS: 5 double, 2 four-poster, 1
family; all rooms with bath/shower; 1 room suitable for wheelchair-users; TV in all
bedrooms   TERMS: single occupancy £45–£55, double £52–£84, four-poster £84,
family room £75; £17 for children; dinner £24.50; deposit: credit card details   CARDS:
Access, Amex, Visa   DETAILS: no children under 12; no dogs in public rooms; smoking
in lounge only; car park; garden; swimming-pool

HAZELBURY BRYAN   Dorset   map 2

Droop Farm

Hazlebury Bryan, nr Sturminster Newton DT10 2ED
TEL: (01258) 817244   FAX: (01258) 817806
off A357 / B3143, 4m SW of Sturminster Newton

This picturesque, fifteenth-century thatched farmhouse close to the
village church, enjoys views across the Blackmore Vale to Bulbarrow
with its Iron Age hill fort. Maureen Kirby is a charming, welcoming
host who also has a local reputation for her cooking. Breakfast, lunch
and dinner are served in the beamed dining-room with its inglenook
fireplace and original nineteenth-century bread oven. Visitors can
bring their own wine to table as there is no alcohol licence; children's
helpings, vegetarian meals and packed lunches can be requested. The
house has been beautifully furnished, and the guest accommodation
comprises a twin and a double room, with bathroom, which are let as
one unit to families or friends travelling together, or one of the
bedrooms only is let to a couple. There is also an attractive sitting-
room, and several cats in evidence.

OWNERS: Maureen and Jim Kirby   OPEN: all year   ROOMS: 1 double, with bath/shower; 1
twin; TV in both bedrooms   TERMS: single occupancy £22, twin/double £44; dinner
£14.50   CARDS: none   DETAILS: no children under 12; dogs by arrangement; smoking in
dining-room only; car park; garden

HAZLETON   Gloucestershire   map 5

Windrush House

Hazleton, nr Cheltenham GL54 3
TEL: (01451) 860364
*from A40 midway between Andoversford and Northleach take minor road
signposted Hazleton, then first left and first right*

Windrush House is surrounded by rolling countryside in the unspoilt
hamlet of Hazleton. The house is built from Cotswold stone and
tastefully furnished. Two of the four bedrooms have *en suite* facilities
and the good-sized double on the ground floor has an adjacent WC.
There is a guest lounge with TV, and a music area with a piano which
guests may play. Evening meals are served in the large dining-room.
Sydney Harrison has built up an excellent reputation for her meals,
and there is a small wine list. Packed lunches are available on
request, and riding weekends can be arranged.

OWNER: Sydney M. Harrison   OPEN: all year exc 16 Dec to mid-Jan   ROOMS: 2 double, 1
with bath/shower, 1 with wash-basin; 2 twin, 1 with bath/shower, 1 with wash-basin; TV
lounge   TERMS: single occupancy £20–£25; twin/double £40; dinner £18; deposit: £10
CARDS: none   DETAILS: no children; no dogs; no smoking; car park; garden

HEADCORN   Kent
map 3

Vine Farm

Waterman Quarter, Headcorn, nr Ashford TN27 9JJ
TEL: (01622) 890203   FAX: (01622) 891819
take A274 from Headcorn towards Tenderden, take first right at
crossroads signposted Waterman Quarter, then ¾m

This attractive long, timbered yeoman's farmhouse lies in a very
peaceful setting off a quiet country lane some two miles from
Headcorn. The oldest part of the building, dating from 1560, is now
the guests' sitting-room. The property extends to 50 acres supporting
sheep, and the old barn is about to be converted into further
accommodation. The River Hammer runs along one side, and a lake
which was silted up has been re-stocked with fish and designated as
an area of Special Conservation Interest. Jane Harman is a very keen
gardener and the colourful garden is a lovely spot to enjoy on finer
days, with many birds to be seen. The house has all its original
character, with low-beamed ceilings and an enormous Elizabethan
fireplace in the dining-room, where dinner is served about three
times a week. The house has been very attractively furnished and
decorated, and the spacious bedrooms are comfortable.

OWNER: Jane Harman   OPEN: all year exc Christmas   ROOMS: 2 double, 1 twin; all
rooms with bath/shower; TV in some bedrooms and lounge   TERMS: single occupancy
£25–£28, twin/double £39–£47; dinner £12–£17   CARDS: Access, Visa   DETAILS: no
children under 12; dogs by arrangement; no smoking; car park; garden

HEASLEY MILL   Devon
map 1

Heasley House

Heasley Mill, nr South Molton EX36 3LE
TEL: (01598) 740213
4m N of South Molton

This substantial, listed Georgian property was originally the home of
the captain of the copper mine. It is set in a sleepy little hamlet on the
very edge of Exmoor. The house has a pleasant, friendly and informal
atmosphere, and the Tates are superb hosts. The bedrooms are
simply furnished, and one *en suite* room is on the ground floor. The
dining-room has exposed beams and a large fireplace, and guests sit
at long communal tables. Vegetarian choices are available at dinner,
and packed lunches can be provided. One of the two lounges has TV,
and there is a pretty, terraced garden with pleasant views at the rear
of the property where guests can relax after a day's outing.

OWNERS: Trevor and June Tate   OPEN: all year exc Christmas week and Feb   ROOMS: 3
double, 2 with bath/shower, 1 with wash-basin; 5 twin, 3 with bath/shower, 2 with
wash-basin; TV lounge   TERMS: single occupancy £25, twin/double £51; children under

3 free, half-price for ages 3 to 8 and two-thirds price for ages 8 to 12; dinner £15; deposit: £10 per person CARDS: Access, Delta, Diners, Switch, Visa DETAILS: children welcome; no dogs in dining-room; smoking in TV lounge only; car park; garden

---

HEMSBY   Norfolk   map 6

Old Station House

North Road, Hemsby, nr Great Yarmouth NR29 4EZ
TEL: (01493) 732022
just off B1159, 7m N of Great Yarmouth

Standing well off the road behind a large front garden, this well-maintained turn-of-the-century house is ideally situated for touring the Norfolk Broads and Great Yarmouth area. The immaculate bedrooms are spacious and have pine vanity units. A large TV lounge contains lots of books and overlooks the garden and patio, where guests can sit out on sunny days. Mrs Lake is charming, and the house has a relaxed atmosphere.

OWNERS: Mr and Mrs A. Lake   OPEN: Easter to end Oct   ROOMS: 2 double, 1 family; all rooms with wash-basin; TV lounge   TERMS: single occupancy £20, double £30, family room £40–£45; children's reductions according to age; deposit   DETAILS: children welcome; no dogs; no smoking; car park; garden

---

HENFIELD   West Sussex   map 3

Great Wapses Farm

Albourne Road, Henfield BN5 9BJ
TEL: (01273) 492544
down track half-way between Henfield and Albourne on B2116

Great Wapses Farm stands in peaceful farmland and is reached down a very long and somewhat bumpy track. It is an interesting and very attractive house with intricate brickwork and creepers climbing up the front; the front part dates from the eighteenth century and the back part from considerably earlier. It retains most of its original features and has beams, low ceilings and uneven floors. The Wilkins are a cheerful couple and the house has a relaxed, lived-in atmosphere. This is a splendid place for country lovers and walkers.

OWNERS: Mr and Mrs M. Wilkin   OPEN: all year exc Christmas   ROOMS: 3 double, 1 twin, 1 four-poster; all rooms with bath/shower; TV in all bedrooms   TERMS: single occupancy £23, twin/double £36, four-poster £36; reductions for children sharing with parents; dinner £8 CARDS: Amex   DETAILS: children welcome; well-behaved dogs welcome; car park; garden; tennis

Alftrudis

8 Norman Avenue, Henley-on-Thames RG9 1SG
TEL: (01491) 573099

This large, impressive Victorian house is peacefully situated up a
private tree-lined gravel road, but is only three minutes' walk from
the town centre. The bright, airy rooms are furnished with flair in
keeping with the house's character. Sue Lambert has done all the
decorating, including the elegant stencilling in the bathrooms, and
made the attractive curtains. Breakfast only is served in the dining-
room, which has rather grand antique chairs and overlooks the
garden.

OWNER: Sue Lambert   OPEN: all year   ROOMS: 1 double, with bath/shower; 2 twin, 1
with bath/shower, 1 with wash-basin; TV in all bedrooms   TERMS: single occupancy
£25–£30, twin/double £32–£45; half-price for children sharing with parents; deposit:
£10–£20   CARDS: none   DETAILS: children welcome; no dogs; smoking in bedrooms
only; car park

Lenwade

3 Western Road, Henley-on-Thames RG9 1JL
TEL/FAX: (01491) 573468

This attractive red-brick Victorian house is in a quiet residential
area, just five minutes' walk from the town centre. The house is well
maintained, and has a beautiful stained-glass window in the
entrance way and stripped pine doors. There are four comfortable
bedrooms, decorated with warm colours. Mrs Williams is friendly and
the house has a welcoming, informal atmosphere. Packed lunches can
be provided.

OWNERS: John and Jacquie Williams   OPEN: all year   ROOMS: 1 double, with bath/
shower; 2 twin, 1 with bath/shower, 1 with wash-basin; TV in all bedrooms   TERMS:
single occupancy £25, twin/double £35–£40; free for children under 5 sharing with
parents; deposit: £10 for new guests   CARDS: none   DETAILS: children welcome; dogs
by arrangement; no smoking in dining-room; garden

*It is always best to check prices, especially for single occupancy, when
booking.*

*If there are any bedrooms with TV, we mention this in the details at the
end of the entry.*

HENSTRIDGE   Somerset

map 2

Quiet Corner Farm

Henstridge, nr Wincanton BA8 0RA
TEL: (01963) 363045   FAX: (01963) 343400
at junction of A30 and A357, take A357 S into village, then second left into Vale Street which leads into Oakvale Lane, farm 150 yards on right

Quiet Corner Farm has wonderful views across the Blackmoor Vale and is hidden away on the edge of Henstridge, between Sherborne and Shaftesbury. It is an attractive Victorian house with a collection of older stone farm buildings. There is a pretty garden with table and chairs, cider-apple orchards, and paddocks with sheep and Shetland ponies. Guests have use of a sitting-room with TV, and breakfast only is served in the sun room, reached through the kitchen, or on the terrace in fine weather. The three bedrooms are traditionally furnished; one is *en suite* and the other two share a bathroom. The Thompsons are always happy to provide soup and a sandwich for latecomers or guests not wanting to go out, but there are two excellent restaurants within easy walking distance. Two barns in the grounds have been carefully converted into well-equipped self-catering cottages which are available to rent.

OWNERS: Patricia and Brian Thompson   OPEN: all year exc Christmas Day   ROOMS: 2 double, 1 with bath/shower, 1 with wash-basin; 1 twin, with wash-basin; TV lounge   TERMS: single occupancy £22–£25, twin/double £36–£40; deposit: £10 per room   CARDS: none   DETAILS: children welcome; no dogs; smoking in hall only; car park; garden

HEREFORD   Hereford & Worcester

map 5

Charades

34 Southbank Road, Hereford HR1 2TJ
TEL: (01432) 269444

Charades is a 150-year old house, with a lovely garden, situated in a quiet residential street just a few minutes' walk from the town centre. Mrs Mullen is a charming hostess and the homely house retains several original features, such as the beautiful ceiling-rose in the lounge and the grape-patterned cast-iron staircase. The spacious bedrooms are furnished with flower-patterned curtains and bedspreads, and there is a comfortable lounge for guests' use; the secluded garden, with pleasant views to the Black Mountains, can also be used in summer. Breakfast only is served at separate tables.

OWNER: Mrs B. Mullen   OPEN: all year exc Christmas   ROOMS: 4 double, all with bath/shower; 3 twin, 2 with bath/shower; 1 family; TV in all bedrooms and lounge   TERMS: single/single occupancy £17–£20, twin/double £34–£40, family from £34; children's reductions according to age; deposit: £10   CARDS: none   DETAILS: children welcome; dogs by arrangement; car park; garden

HERMITAGE   Dorset   **map 2**

Almshouse Farm

Hermitage, Holnest, nr Sherborne DT9 6HA
TEL: (01963) 210296
from A352 4m S of Sherborne turn at sign for Hermitage and continue
1¼m along minor road

This solid-looking substantial stone-built house was restored from a
sixteenth-century monastery and stands in a large garden in peaceful
countryside overlooking the Blackmore Vale. The house retains many
original features including oak beams and a magnificent inglenook
fireplace. The Mayos are hard-working farmers – the property is a
traditional 160-acre dairy farm – and guests are welcome to watch
the farming activities. John and Jenny are cheerful, businesslike
people who have been running this B&B for over 20 years. The
accommodation is comfortable and breakfast only is served at
separate tables in the dining-room. Almshouse Farm is between
Sherborne and Dorchester and is ideal for country-lovers looking for
peace and quiet.

OWNERS: John and Jenny Mayo   OPEN: all year exc Christmas   ROOMS: 2 double, 1
twin; all rooms with bath/shower; TV in all bedrooms and lounge   TERMS: single
occupancy £20–£22, twin/double £38–£40; reductions for children sharing with
parents; deposit: £10 per person   CARDS: none   DETAILS: children welcome; no dogs;
no smoking in dining-room; car park; garden

HEXHAM   Northumberland   **map 11**

Middlemarch

Hencotes, Hexham NE46 2EB
TEL: (01434) 605003

This elegant listed Georgian house overlooks the abbey and was itself
used as a chapel until the church was built. It started life as a
thatched stone farmhouse and retains the original flagstone entry
and window shutters. Furnishings are in style with the building,
including some very interesting antiques, and the spacious bedrooms
are decorated in soft spring colours; one has a four-poster bed. The
large, comfortable drawing-room has recently been completely
refurbished and plenty of information on things to do in the area can
be found there. Breakfast only is available, served in the family
kitchen with its warming Aga.

OWNER: Eileen Elliott   OPEN: all year   ROOMS: 1 double, with wash-basin; 2 twin, 1 with
bath/shower, 1 with wash-basin; 1 four-poster, with bath/shower; 1 family, with wash-
basin; TV in all bedrooms   TERMS: single occupancy £25, twin/double £41, four-poster
£49, family room £54; reductions for children from 10 to 12; deposit required   CARDS:
none   DETAILS: no children under 10; small dogs welcome by arrangement; no smoking;
car park

West Close House

Hextol Terrace, Hexham NE46 2AD
TEL: (01434) 603307

This charming detached house, built in 1920, has a lovely large garden with a terrace and a summer house. The spacious bedrooms are tastefully decorated with colour co-ordinated quality fabrics and prints, and have pine and wicker furniture. Breakfast, with the emphasis on wholefoods (although traditional breakfasts are also offered), and light snacks are served in the dining-room/lounge. A drawing-room without TV is also available to guests. French and Spanish are spoken.

OWNER: Patricia Graham-Tomlinson OPEN: all year ROOMS: 2 single, both with wash-basin; 1 double, with bath/shower; 1 family, with wash-basin; TV lounge TERMS: single £17.50, single occupancy £23.50, double £44, family room £35 plus children's charge; reductions for children from 5 to 12; deposit: £10 CARDS: none DETAILS: no children under 5; no dogs; no smoking; car park; garden

---

HIGHAM Suffolk map 6

The Bauble

Higham, nr Colchester CO7 6LA
TEL: (01206) 337254 FAX: (01206) 337263
on B1068, just N of A12 and 7m N of Colchester

Higham is on the Suffolk/Essex border, and this charming period property is in the heart of Constable country. It stands in one and a half acres of beautiful secluded gardens, with three ornamental ponds, a tennis court and heated swimming-pool. The house has a warm, relaxing atmosphere, is exceptionally well maintained and furnished mostly with antiques. The three bedrooms are well appointed, the twins have bathrooms close by, the single has *en suite* facilities; all have TV, hair-dryers, hot-water bottles and bathrobes. In winter a log fire is lit in the comfortable lounge. Nowell and Penny Watkins are delightful hosts who greet guests with a cup of tea on arrival. Imaginative breakfasts are served in the dining-room with its display of Penny's dried- and pressed-flower arrangements.

OWNERS: Nowell and Penny Watkins OPEN: all year ROOMS: 1 single, 2 twin; all rooms with bath/shower; TV in all bedrooms TERMS: single £22–£25, single occupancy £30, twin £40–£45; deposit: £10 per room CARDS: none DETAILS: no children under 12; no dogs; smoking in lounge only; car park; garden; swimming-pool; tennis

---

We state at the end of an entry whether children are welcome. If we know of any restrictions on children, we give them.

HIGH HALDEN   Kent   map 3

Hales Place

High Halden, nr Ashford TN26 3JQ
TEL: (01233) 850219   FAX: (01233) 850716
on A28 in High Halden follow brown tourist signs to Art Studio

This sixteenth-century house is set in a large garden with two duck
ponds overhung by willow trees, one of which has its own jetty and
boat. It is surrounded by peaceful farmland which is home to three
donkeys, sheep and cattle. The Greens are a friendly couple; Ellen,
who comes from Germany, is an experienced vegetarian cook and
Roger is an artist. Roger's work is displayed all over the house and
some of the stables and barns have been converted into art studios
and a gallery. The bedrooms are attractively furnished and there is a
small library and large lounge with an inglenook fireplace. The
evening meals include home-produced free-range and organically
grown food, such as bacon, sausages, pork, eggs, chicken and a very
wide range of vegetables and fruit. Dinners are served by candlelight
in a friendly dinner-party atmosphere, with the Greens often joining
their guests. Hales Place is three miles from the attractive market
town of Tenterden and is well placed for visiting the castles and
gardens of Kent.

OWNERS: Roger and Ellen Green   OPEN: all year exc Christmas   ROOMS: 3 twin, all with
bath/shower; TV lounge   TERMS: single occupancy £21.50–£23.50; twin £43–£47;
babies in cots free; dinner £17.50   CARDS: Access, Visa   DETAILS: children welcome; no
dogs; no smoking; car park; garden

HIGHNAM   Gloucestershire   map 5

Linton Farm

Highnam, nr Gloucester GL2 8DF
TEL: (01452) 306456
*from Gloucester take A40 W for 2m; farm is on A40, 200yds beyond Newent
turnoff*

This traditional 150-year-old red-brick farmhouse is part of an 800-
acre arable farm. There is a pleasant, informal atmosphere in this
comfortable home, which is furnished with antiques and solid old-
fashioned pieces, such as a high mahogany bed in one of the
bedrooms. None of the rooms has a private bath, but there are two
bathrooms shared among them exclusively for guests' use. Breakfast
only is served, however there are a number of pubs nearby and
restaurants in Gloucester. Visitors are welcome to walk round the
farm.

OWNER: Caroline Keene   OPEN: all year   ROOMS: 1 single; 1 double, with wash-basin; 1
family; TV in all bedrooms   TERMS: single/single occupancy £16, double £32, family

room from £42; children under 2 free, £10 for ages 3 to 14; deposit: by arrangement
CARDS: none DETAILS: children welcome; well-behaved dogs welcome; smoking in
bedrooms only; car park; garden

HINTLESHAM   Suffolk   map 6

College Farm

Hintlesham, nr Ipswich IP8 3NT
TEL/FAX: (01473) 652253
*on A1071, 5m W of Ipswich, ¾m beyond Hintlesham village towards
Hadleigh*

This fifteenth-century, pink-washed farmhouse with Tudor
chimneys, in a secluded setting, was once owned by Cardinal Wolsey.
The arable farm comprises 175 acres and is part of a family-run
enterprise of 600 acres. The impeccably maintained house has great
character; there are sloping floors, leaded windows, oak beams and
period furniture. Pay attention when walking about as you often have
to duck your head. The bedrooms are spacious, and there is a TV
lounge, with log fire on cool evenings. Mrs Bryce is from Australia
and has been delighting visitors for over 12 years. Breakfasts are
substantial, including home-made marmalade, local honey and free-
range eggs.

OWNER: Rosemary Bryce OPEN: all year exc last 2 weeks Dec ROOMS: 1 single, with
wash-basin; 1 double, with bath/shower; 1 twin, with wash-basin; 1 family, with wash-
basin; TV lounge TERMS: single £17, single occupancy £22, twin/double £34–£38,
family room prices on request; £10 for children over 8 sharing with parents; deposit: £10
per room CARDS: Diners DETAILS: no children under 8; no dogs; no smoking; car park;
garden

HINTON CHARTERHOUSE   Avon   map 2

Green Lane House

Green Lane, Hinton Charterhouse, nr Bath BA3 6BL
TEL: (01225) 723631
off B3110, 4m S of Bath

This small stone-built house dating from 1725 stands right in the
centre of the conservation village of Hinton Charterhouse, and is well
placed for visiting Bath, Wells, Longleat House and Farleigh Castle.
The property was originally three cottages, and retains two staircases
at each end of the house, with two comfortable, compact bedrooms at
the top of each stairway. Below is a cosy beamed sitting-room and
breakfast room with log-effect gas fires. Although there is no car
park, off-street parking is available.

OWNERS: Christopher and Juliet Davies OPEN: all year ROOMS: 2 double, 1 with bath/
shower, 1 with wash-basin; 2 twin, 1 with bath/shower, 1 with wash-basin; TV lounge

TERMS: single occupancy £24–£37, twin/double £36–£49; children under 3 free, £6–£10 for ages 3 to 12; deposit: £10 per person during high season/weekends CARDS: Access, Amex, Visa DETAILS: children welcome; dogs by arrangement; no smoking in dining-room

---

HITCHAM Suffolk map 6

Hill Farmhouse

Bury Road, Hitcham, nr Ipswich IP7 7PT
TEL: (01449) 740651
from B1115 1½m N of Bildeston turn W by White Horse pub

Hill Farmhouse is approached up a sweeping drive and set in three acres of Suffolk's rolling countryside. It has two ponds inhabited by ducks and goldfish and a friendly dog. The informal rambling house dates from medieval times, with Georgian and Victorian additions. The sitting-room is in the oldest part, which has beams and inglenooks. The bedrooms, one of which is on the ground floor, are comfortable and well furnished and all have country views. The cottage accommodation is ideal for families or groups of friends. Breakfasts – which can include kippers and bloaters – and three-course dinners are taken in the main house. On Tuesdays and Thursdays cheaper, no-frills two-course dinners are served. Guests are welcome to bring their own wine.

OWNERS: Pippa and Andrew McLardy OPEN: Mar to Oct ROOMS: 1 double, 1 twin, 1 family; all rooms with bath/shower; TV in all bedrooms TERMS: twin/double £30–£34, family room from £44.50; children's reductions according to age; dinner £10.50; deposit: 25% DETAILS: children welcome; dogs by prior arrangement; no smoking in 1 bedroom; car park; garden

---

HOLBEACH Lincolnshire map 6

Pipwell Manor

Washway Road, Saracens Head, Holbeach PE12 8AL
TEL: (01406) 423119
off A17, 2m NW of Holbeach

Dating from around 1730, this listed manor house stands in an acre of beautiful gardens in rural surroundings. The house retains many of its original features, and the rooms are luxurious, exquisitely decorated, with antiques much in evidence. One twin room has *en suite* facilities. The sitting-room with its open fire, TV and many books is a comfortable place to relax in. John Honnor is a steam railway enthusiast, and there is plenty of memorabilia about. Breakfasts are served in the attractive dining-room with its pretty china, linens and fresh flowers, and includes free-range eggs from

Pipwell Manor's own hens, fresh fruit and home-made preserves. The Wash shore is an ideal spot for walkers and bird-watchers. OWNER: Lesley Honnor

---

OPEN: all year exc Christmas ROOMS: 1 single, 2 double, 1 twin; all rooms with bath/ shower; TV lounge TERMS: single £20, single occupancy £30, twin/double £36–£38; reductions for children sharing with parents CARDS: none DETAILS: children welcome; no dogs; no smoking; car park; garden

---

HOLFORD Somerset   map 2

Quantock House

Holford, nr Bridgwater TA5 1RY
TEL: (01278) 741439
just off A39, 13m NW of Bridgwater; turn left between garage and pub

---

This seventeenth-century whitewashed house is very pretty with its thatched roof, colourful cottage garden and rural outlook. It stands at the foot of the Quantock Hills in the small village of Holford. The house's attractively furnished interior is decorated with embroidery made by Mrs Laidler, and the beds are covered in patchwork quilts. All three bedrooms have *en suite* facilities, and one is on the ground floor. Guests have use of a comfortable, heavily beamed lounge/ dining-room, which has an inglenook fireplace and doors out on to the garden. Dinner is by arrangement and is at 7pm; children's helpings and vegetarian meals can be provided, and guests may bring their own wine as there is no alcohol licence. Quantock House is wonderfully situated for those interested in walking or horse-riding: there is access to the hills at the end of the lane. Packed lunches can be requested. Three miles away in Nether Stowey is Coleridge's cottage, where the poet lived from 1797 to 1800.

OWNER: Mrs P. Laidler OPEN: all year exc Christmas ROOMS: 1 double, 1 twin, 1 family; all rooms with bath/shower; TV in all bedrooms TERMS: single occupancy £26, twin/ double £38, family room from £38; half-price for children sharing with parents; dinner £11; deposit: £15 CARDS: none DETAILS: children welcome; dogs welcome; no smoking; car park; garden

---

HOLMESFIELD Derbyshire   map 9

Horsleygate Hall

Horsleygate Lane, Holmesfield, nr Chesterfield S18 5WD
TEL: (0114) 289 0333
off A61, midway between Chesterfield and Sheffield

This superb country house was built in 1783 and stands in two acres of beautiful, secluded gardens. There are several areas for sitting out on fine days, and the garden includes two ponds and a stream. The house has been tastefully renovated, incorporating modern comforts

while still retaining the charm and atmosphere of a bygone area.
There is a guest lounge, and the spacious bedrooms are tastefully
decorated in co-ordinating colours. Excellent breakfasts are cooked
on the Aga.

OWNERS: Margaret and Robert Ford   OPEN: all year   ROOMS: 1 double, with bath/
shower; 1 twin, 1 family, both with wash-basin; TV lounge   TERMS: single occupancy
£20–£22.50, twin/double £36–£40, family room £40–£48; £8 for children ages 5 to 10,
£10 for ages 10 to 12; deposit: 10%   CARDS: none   DETAILS: no children under 5; no
dogs; no smoking; car park; garden

HOLMFIRTH   West Yorkshire   map 9

Holme Castle

Holme Village, Holmfirth, nr Huddersfield HD7 1QG
TEL: (01484) 686764   FAX: (01484) 687775
on A6024, 2½m SW of Holmfirth

Holme Castle is in a glorious location at the head of the Holme Valley
in the Peak District National Park. It is a Victorian stone-built folly
which earns its name from its distinctive tower and castellated roof.
It also features an extraordinarily tall landing window. The
bedrooms, named after their individual delightful views, are
generously sized and all have sitting areas. Furniture is traditional
and the parquet-floored lounge has an open fire and oak panelling.
Breakfasts are hearty and include porridge when there is snow on the
ground. Evening meals must be ordered in advance and guests can
chose from a three-course dinner or a simpler supper. Wholefoods,
organic produce and home-grown herbs are widely used. Vegetarians
can be catered for and there is a good selection of wines.

OWNERS: John Sandford and Jill Hayfield   OPEN: all year   ROOMS: 1 single, with wash-
basin; 3 double, 2 with bath/shower, 1 with wash-basin; 2 twin, both with bath/shower;
2 family, 1 with bath/shower, 1 with wash-basin; TV in all bedrooms and lounge   TERMS:
single £30, single occupancy £40–£50, twin/double £50–£65, family room £60–£75; £10
for children sharing with parents; dinner £11.50 or £20.50; deposit: 50% or credit card
details   CARDS: Access, Amex, Delta, Visa   DETAILS: children welcome; no dogs; no
smoking; car park; garden

HOLY ISLAND   Northumberland   map 11

Britannia House

Holy Island, Berwick-upon-Tweed TD15 2RX
TEL: (01289) 389218

This pretty 150-year-old cottage with attractive rooms is on the
village green, close by the ruins of the eleventh-century Benedictine
church and monastery. Remember that Holy Island cannot be
reached from the mainland at high tide, so check the tide tables in

advance. Fires warm the guest lounge on cold evenings and this is a peaceful spot in which to relax. Alternatively, the excellent nearby pubs and eating establishments may tempt. In summer Pauline Patterson runs a tea-room.

OWNERS: Mr R. and Mrs P.A. Patterson OPEN: Mar to Oct ROOMS: 2 double, 1 with bath/shower, 1 with wash-basin; 1 twin with bath/shower; TV lounge TERMS: twin/double £33; reductions for children sharing with parents; deposit: £10 CARDS: none DETAILS: children welcome; no dogs; no smoking in bedrooms

North View

Holy Island, Berwick-upon-Tweed TD15 2SD
TEL: (01289) 389222

Rene Richardson and Alan Robertson fell in love with Holy Island while on holiday and have recently upgraded this house in the centre of the village, retaining an inglenook fireplace and an antique dresser in the dining-room. The bedrooms are fresh and bright, with new beds and *en suite* showers. Breakfast and dinner – a three-course affair which makes the most of local produce and the plentiful supply of fresh fish and shellfish – are served in the licensed dining-room. The owners will advise guests of safe times for crossing the three-mile causeway to Holy Island when they make a reservation and will, if pre-arranged, collect guests from the mainland train or coach stations.

OWNER: Rene Richardson OPEN: all year exc Christmas ROOMS: 2 double, 1 twin; all rooms with bath/shower; TV in all bedrooms TERMS: single occupancy £30, twin/double £45; dinner £12.50; deposit CARDS: none DETAILS: children welcome; dogs in kennels; no smoking; car park; garden

HORLEY Surrey   map 3

Chalet Guest House

77 Massetts Road, Horley RH6 7EB
TEL: (01293) 821666 FAX: (01293) 821619

This small modern guesthouse is on a busy road only five minutes' drive from Gatwick Airport. The rooms are simply decorated and are bright; all except two have minute *en suite* shower rooms. There is a small TV lounge and breakfast only is served. Guests are free to make tea or coffee at any time in the kitchen. The Chalet Guest House offers simple, cheerful accommodation within easy reach of Gatwick.

OWNERS: Daphne and Eric Shortland OPEN: all year exc Christmas ROOMS: 4 single, 2 with shower, 2 with wash-basin; 1 double, 1 twin, 1 family, all with shower; TV in all bedrooms and lounge TERMS: single £24–£32, single occupancy £32, twin/double £42, family room £55; babies free; deposit: £10 or credit card details CARDS: Access, Visa DETAILS: children welcome; no dogs; no smoking; car park; garden

Vulcan Lodge

27 Massetts Road, Horley RH6 7DQ
TEL: (01293) 771522
2m from M3 junction 9

This attractive house stands just off the main road and close to the centre of Horley. Vulcan Lodge is a welcoming place where the accent is on cosiness and comfort. Mrs Pike is a cheerful lady who takes great pride in her home and making her guests happy. The comfortable accommodation is redecorated frequently. Breakfast only is served. Vulcan Lodge is ideally situated for Gatwick Airport, only a few minutes away.

OWNERS: Sandie and Dave Pike OPEN: all year exc Christmas ROOMS: 2 single, 1 with bath/shower, 1 with wash-basin; 1 double, 1 twin, both with bath/shower; TV in all bedrooms TERMS: single £24–£29.50, single occupancy £29.50, twin/double £42; children's reductions by arrangement; deposit: £15 CARDS: Access, Visa DETAILS: children welcome; no dogs; car park; garden

---

HORSEY   Norfolk   **map 6**

Old Chapel

Horsey Corner, Horsey, nr Winterton-on-Sea NR29 4EH
TEL: (01493) 393498
on B1159, ¾m N of Horsey village, 9m NE of Acle

There is little left of the original chapel, situated near the coast on the edge of the Broads, though three months' hard refurbishment work has resulted in a friendly and efficiently run house. Heather Webster and Keith Letchford discovered the Old Chapel when they were looking for a property in the area to buy as a bed and breakfast. There are three good-size bedrooms, all on the ground floor and suitable for wheelchair-users, decorated in soft pastels. Two of the rooms enjoy rural views and are named Sunrise and Sunset. Breakfast, and dinner if pre-arranged, are served in the cosy beamed dining-room and feature local produce. Children's helpings, vegetarian meals and packed lunches can all be requested. A brisk ten-minute walk to the sea and dunes makes this an ideal spot for ramblers and bird-watchers. Well worth a visit is the mill and thousand-year-old thatched church in the village, which is on National Trust land.

OWNER: H.M. Webster OPEN: all year ROOMS: 2 double, 1 with bath/shower, 1 with wash-basin; 1 twin, with wash-basin; all rooms suitable for wheelchair-users; TV in all bedrooms TERMS: single occupancy £22.50–£29.50, twin/double £30–£49; dinner £10; deposit: 20% CARDS: none DETAILS: children welcome; dogs welcome; no smoking; car park; garden

---

If any bedrooms are suitable for wheelchair-users, we mention this in the details at the end of the entry.

217

HUDDERSFIELD   West Yorkshire   map 9

The Mallows

55 Spring Street, Springwood, Huddersfield HD1 4AZ
TEL: (01484) 544684

The Mallows is an elegant listed building on a cobbled street in a
conservation area close to the city centre. The house is impeccably
maintained and the spacious bedrooms are tastefully furnished, with
attractive hand-made curtains. Two bedrooms are in the attic
conversion and have sloping ceilings and skylight windows. The pink
and blue dining-room retains original features: a marble fireplace,
ornate cornicing and a plaster ceiling rose. Breakfast only is served
and packed lunches can be provided.

OWNER: Mrs M.A. Chantry   OPEN: all year exc Christmas and New Year   ROOMS: 1
single, with wash-basin; 1 double, with bath/shower; 4 twin, 2 with bath/shower, 2 with
wash-basin; TV in all bedrooms   TERMS: single £17.50, single occupancy £19.50–
£29.50, twin/double £30–£40   CARDS: none   DETAILS: children welcome; no dogs;
smoking in some bedrooms only; car park

HUNSTANTON   Norfolk   map 6

Sutton House

24 Northgate, Hunstanton PE36 6AP
TEL: (01485) 532552

This large west-facing house in a quiet residential street just 200
yards from the sea is regularly upgraded and is always well
maintained by owners Mike and Pam Emsden. They are a friendly,
helpful couple who treat all their guests as individuals. Three of the
rooms have sea views and all have *en suite* or private bathrooms. The
first-floor sitting-room opens out on to a small balcony which catches
the afternoon sun. Evenings present a choice of full dinner topped off
by home-made ice-cream in the sunny dining-room or light snacks
from the bar. Vegetarians can be catered for with notice and dinner
orders must in any case be placed by noon.

OWNERS: Mike and Pat Emsden   OPEN: all year exc last 2 weeks Nov and last 2 weeks
Jan   ROOMS: 3 double, 3 twin, 2 family; all rooms with bath/shower; TV in all bedrooms
TERMS: single occupancy £30, twin/double £50, family room £60; half-price for children;
dinner £12–£16   CARDS: none   DETAILS: children welcome; dogs welcome; no smoking
in dining-room; car park

---

*Any smoking restrictions that we know of are given in the details at the end
of the entry.*

Use the maps and indexes at the back of the Guide to plan your trip.

The Woolhouse

Grove Lane, Hunton, nr Maidstone ME15 0SE
TEL: (01622) 820778   FAX: (01622) 820645
*from Maidstone take B2010 to Yalding, then turn to Hunton and Grove
Lane is on left*

This attractive, large red-brick seventeenth-century listed barn was
built originally for a wealthy wool merchant to display his goods.
Constructed in the style of a small manor, the house is down a quiet
lane in pleasant farmland in the heart of hop country. It has clematis
around the porch and honeysuckle covering the fences, and is near
the River Beult. The four beamed bedrooms have pretty wallpaper
and old pine furniture. The garden room where breakfast is
sometimes served adds a country feel to the house, and there is a
first-floor drawing-room with TV. Mrs Wetton is a picture framer and
has her studio in a wing of the house. The Woolhouse overlooks a
lake, and there is a tennis court which guests can use.

OWNERS: Gavin and Anne Wetton   OPEN: all year exc Christmas   ROOMS: 2 single, 1
double, 1 twin; all rooms with bath/shower; TV lounge   TERMS: single/single occupancy
£20–£22, twin/double £40–£44   CARDS: none   DETAILS: no children; dogs by
arrangement; car park; garden; tennis

Hammer & Hand

Hutton-le-Hole, nr York YO6 6UA
TEL: (01751) 417300   FAX: (01751) 476732
3m N of A170, between Helmsley and Pickering

This listed Georgian house was built in 1784 as the village beer
house. It stands in a sheltered spot, facing the green and just by the
Ryedale Folk Museum. Plenty of original features remain, such as
stone fireplaces, cruck ceiling beams and panelled doors, and period
furniture fills the rooms. A comfortable sitting-room has a handsome
Georgian fireplace with open log fire. The tastefully decorated
bedrooms have views of either the village green or open moorland.
The dining-room overlooks the front garden. Dinner is served at 7pm;
vegetarian dishes can be requested in advance, and there is a wine
list. Hutton-le-Hole is an attractive place within the North York
Moors National Park, and a good location for reaching York and the
coastal resorts of Whitby and Scarborough.

OWNERS: A. Willis and J.R. Wilkins   OPEN: all year exc Christmas and New Year
ROOMS: 3 double, 1 twin; all rooms with bath/shower; TV in all bedrooms and lounge
TERMS: single occupancy £30; twin/double £38–£44; children's reductions according to
age; dinner £15; deposit: £20 per person   CARDS: none   DETAILS: children welcome;
dogs welcome in guests' bedrooms only; no smoking; car park; garden

Barons Grange

Readers Lane, Iden, nr Rye TN31 7UU
TEL: (01797) 280478
turn W off B2082 in Iden then take first right

Barons Grange is a listed Georgian farmhouse in a quiet location,
part of a 400-acre farm with sheep, orchards and cornfields. It is a
pleasant ten-minute stroll to the village of Iden, and Rye is not far.
An acre of well-tended mature gardens surrounds the house, and
incorporates a hard tennis court, a croquet lawn and a solar-heated
swimming-pool. The Ramuses, who in the past have won Olympic and
Commonwealth medals for sailing and horse eventing, offer a warm
welcome and have created a perfect environment for unwinding. The
bedrooms are pretty and comfortable, and guests have use of a sunny
conservatory on the south-facing side of the house which overlooks
the garden, and where breakfast is frequently served. There is also a
large lounge with inglenook fireplace, and a dining-room with a large
dark table and heavy leather chairs.

OWNERS: James and Joy Ramus   OPEN: all year exc Christmas   ROOMS: 1 double, with
bath/shower; 1 twin, with bath/shower; 1 family; TV in all bedrooms   TERMS: single
occupancy £20–£25, twin/double £35–£50, family room £45–£55; half-price for children
sharing with parents; deposit required when booking in advance   CARDS: none
DETAILS: no children under 7; dogs by arrangement; no smoking in bedrooms; car park;
garden; swimming-pool; tennis

Beechenhill Farm

Ilam, nr Ashbourne DE6 2BD
TEL: (01335) 310274
*near junction of A52 and A523 take minor road to Blore and Ilam, farm is
1m N of Ilam*

This long, low seventeenth-century farmhouse offers tremendous
views which include the picturesque village of Ilam. Guests have
their own entrance, lounge and dining-room, all warm and lovingly
furnished, including stencils and other special decorative effects by
Sue Prince, who is an artist. The bedrooms are spacious and have
pine furniture. Breakfasts are generous and there is something to
suit all tastes, from porridge to yoghurt to a full cooked breakfast.
Children are welcome to help on the farm with feeding and bringing
in the cows. Sheep, cats, dogs and horses extend the animal
population. This peaceful spot is ideal for nature-lovers and walkers.
The farm also has two self-catering cottages, one of which is equipped
for wheelchair-users.

OWNER: Sue Prince OPEN: all year exc Jan ROOMS: 1 double, 1 family; both rooms with bath/shower; TV lounge TERMS: single occupancy £20–£25, double £36; £6 for children under 5, £12 for children 5 to 13; deposit: £10 per person CARDS: none DETAILS: children welcome; no dogs; no smoking; car park; garden

---

IPSWICH Suffolk   map 6

Alpine Villa

29 Constitution Hill, Ipswich IP1 3RL
TEL: (01473) 218899   FAX: (01473) 288155

This typically Victorian house is on a quiet, pleasant road opposite a private wood. Alpine Villa is tastefully decorated, with stripped pine throughout, and is clean and comfortable. Although there is no lounge, all the bedrooms have TV and tea-makers. Home-baked wholemeal bread features at breakfast. Packed lunches can be provided. A frequent bus service to the centre of town operates from the end of the road, and Christchurch Park and Museum are a ten-minute walk away.

OWNERS: Mr and Mrs Mahon OPEN: all year exc Christmas and New Year ROOMS: 2 single, both with wash-basin; 2 twin/double, both with bath/shower; 1 room suitable for wheelchair-users; TV in all bedrooms TERMS: single £17, single occupancy £25, twin/double £30; children's reductions CARDS: none DETAILS: children welcome; dogs welcome; car park

Burlington Lodge

Burlington Road, Ipswich IP1 2HS
TEL: 01473 251868

Peter and Leslie Norton are an accommodating couple who took over this attractive Victorian property towards the end of 1994. It is situated on the corner of a quiet street five minutes' walk from the city centre. The house is well maintained, and the good-sized bedrooms are spotlessly clean with modern furniture, and all with their own shower but no WC. Breakfast only is served, but there are several eating establishments within walking distance. This is a popular venue for business people, as well as tourists.

OWNERS: Mr and Mrs P.W. Norton OPEN: all year ROOMS: 1 double, 4 twin; all rooms with shower TERMS: single occupancy £22, twin/double £35; babies free, reductions for children sharing with parents CARDS: none DETAILS: children welcome; dogs welcome

---

If there are reduced rates for children, this is mentioned in the details at the end of the entry. If no reductions are specified, assume you will have to pay full rates for children.

JACOBSTOWE Devon

map 1

Higher Cadham Farm

Jacobstowe, nr Okehampton EX20 3RB
TEL: (01837) 851647   FAX: (01837) 851410
*from Jacobstowe take A3072 towards Hatherleigh and Bude; just after
church turn right and continue ½m*

Approached down a long lane, the farmhouse is a sixteenth-century
oak-beamed building making up one side of the farmyard. It was
originally a Devon longhouse and has been altered substantially over
the years. The King family, thought to be only the second family to
have owned the farm in all its history, acquired it in 1910, and the
present owners are the third generation to live here. This is a
working beef and sheep farm set in attractive countryside with a
stream at the bottom of the fields. The 'Tarka Trail' country walk
(after the film *Tarka the Otter*) crosses the farm, along with other
marked nature trails which guests are invited to explore. Recent
improvements have extended the number of bedrooms to nine, some
of which are in the renovated cow shed. The dining-room has also
been enlarged and can now accommodate up to 30 for good home-
cooked breakfasts, lunches and evening meals. (Packed lunches can
also be provided.) The house is licensed and drinks are served in the
lounge bar. The prettily furnished bedrooms are well equipped and
one is on the ground floor. Double-bannister rails have been installed
to help those who find climbing the stairs a challenge.

OWNERS: John and Jenny King   OPEN: all year exc Christmas and New Year   ROOMS: 1
single, with wash-basin; 2 double, 1 with bath/shower, 1 with wash-basin; 3 twin, 2 with
bath/shower, 1 with wash-basin; 1 four-poster, with bath/shower; 2 family, 1 with bath/
shower, 1 with wash-basin; 1 room suitable for wheelchair-users; TV lounge   TERMS:
single/single occupancy £16.50–£22.50, twin/double/four-poster £33–£45, family room
£49.50–£67.50; half-price for children under 10, 25% reduction for ages 10 to 15;
dinner £8   CARDS: Access, Delta, Switch, Visa   DETAILS: children welcome, babies by
arrangement; no dogs; smoking in 2 lounges only; car park; games room; garden

KEMPLEY Gloucestershire

map 5

Lower House Farm

Kempley, nr Dymock GL18 2BS
TEL: (01531) 890301
off A449 / B4024 / B4215, 6m NE of Ross-on-Wye

Lower House Farm dates from the sixteenth century, with later
additions, and supports a dairy herd on its 130 acres. The
accommodation is simple yet comfortable, with some antique pieces
and old-fashioned furniture. Evening meals are served by Gill
Bennett, who was formerly in the catering trade; a three-course
dinner could take in lasagne and home-made chocolate fudge cake.

Children's helpings and vegetarian dishes can be requested, and guests may bring their own wine as there is no alcohol licence. The location is superb and is ideal for outdoor-lovers, with 1,300 acres of Forestry Commission routed nature walks, and a lake for coarse fishing. There is an eight-mile Daffodil Walk through the fields and woods around Kempley; packed lunches can be provided. An 18-hole golf course, falconry centre and two family-run vineyards are within a radius of four miles.

OWNERS: Gill and Glyn Bennett OPEN: all year exc Christmas ROOMS: 1 double, 2 twin; all rooms with bath/shower; TV lounge TERMS: single occupancy £18, twin/double £36; children's reductions by arrangement; dinner £10; deposit CARDS: none DETAILS: children welcome; dogs welcome; car park; garden

KENDAL   Cumbria   map 8

Holmfield

41 Kendal Green, Kendal LA9 5PP
TEL/FAX: (01539) 720790

This elegant Edwardian property is set in an acre of grounds, with a swimming-pool and croquet lawn for guests' use. The owners, Eileen and Brian Kettle, are charming and helpful. The three spacious bedrooms are individually decorated with soft colours and matching fabrics; one has a four-poster bed, and they share two bathrooms between them. Breakfast only is served in the well-furnished dining-room, which has an open fire, as does the very comfortable lounge; both rooms overlook the garden. Holmfield is within walking distance of the town centre, where there are several places for evening meals. Brian Kettle is a keen walker and can provide guests with maps and information.

OWNERS: Brian and Eileen Kettle OPEN: all year exc Christmas ROOMS: 1 double, 1 twin, 1 four-poster; TV in all bedrooms and lounge TERMS: twin/double £38–£42, four-poster £40–£44 CARDS: none DETAILS: no children under 12; no dogs; no smoking; car park; garden; swimming-pool

KENILWORTH   Warwickshire   map 5

Ferndale

45 Priory Road, Kenilworth CV8 1LL
TEL: (01926) 53214   FAX: (01926) 58336

Ferndale is a pleasant modernised Victorian house cheerily announcing itself with lots of flower-filled hanging baskets and tubs. All the bedrooms are decorated in Victorian style, with red-rose wallpapers and fabrics. Breakfast only is served in the mock-Tudor dining-room, but there are several places for evening meals close by. Ferndale is licensed and guests may enjoy a drink in the lounge.

OWNER: Joan Wilson   OPEN: all year exc Christmas   ROOMS: 1 single, 2 double, 3 twin, 1 family; all rooms with bath/shower; TV in all bedrooms and lounge   TERMS: single £20, single occupancy £22, twin/double £35, family room £42; children under 4 free; deposit: 25%   CARDS: none   DETAILS: children welcome; dogs welcome; smoking in lounge only; car park

Victoria Lodge Hotel

180 Warwick Road, Kenilworth CV8 1HU
TEL: (01926) 512020   FAX: (01926) 58703

This unusual Victorian house has a first-floor balcony that is bedecked with hanging baskets and climbers and on to which shuttered french windows open from three of the bedrooms. The welcome is warm and friendly and the owners take pride in their well-maintained and sensitively modernised property. The bedrooms are decorated in soft pastel colours and all have a telephone; two are on the ground floor. Victoria Lodge has a licensed bar.

OWNERS: Malcolm and Joyce Chilvers   OPEN: all year exc Christmas   ROOMS: 1 single, 4 double, 2 twin, 1 four-poster; all rooms with bath/shower; TV in all bedrooms   TERMS: single £34, single occupancy £38, twin/double/four-poster £49   CARDS: Access, Amex, Delta, Switch, Visa   DETAILS: children welcome; no dogs; no smoking; car park; garden

KENTISBURY   Devon   **map 1**

Bridwick Farm

Kentisbury, nr Barnstaple EX31 4NN
TEL: (01598) 763416
on A39, 9m NE of Barnstaple and ½m W of Blackmoor Gate crossroads

Built in the 1850s as a 'gentleman's residence', Bridwick Farm is now a 370-acre sheep and beef farm on the edge of Exmoor. Marilyn Purchase is a most friendly lady and guests are made to feel very welcome. Breakfast is served at times to suit individual needs, the washing-machine and dryer can be used, morning papers ordered and babysitting provided. Evening meals are not served, but the dining-room is available for take-away food or picnics. The large bedrooms are spotlessly clean and well furnished, and a comfortable lounge has an open fire on cool evenings. The Purchases have a couple of ponies, and riding can be arranged nearby; guests are welcome to wander around the farm.

OWNER: Marilyn Purchase   OPEN: all year exc Mar and early Apr   ROOMS: 1 double, with bath/shower; 1 twin, with wash-basin; 1 family, with wash-basin; TV in all bedrooms and lounge   TERMS: single occupancy from £16, twin/double £32–£35, family room from £32; children's reductions according to age; deposit: 1 night's charge   CARDS: none   DETAILS: children welcome; no dogs; smoking in lounge only; car park; garden

KERSEY   Suffolk   map 6

Red House Farm

Wickerstreet Green, Kersey, nr Ipswich IP7 6EX
TEL: (01787) 210245
leave A1071 at Boxford and take Kersey road for 1½m

This dignified red-brick house dating from 1850 stands in 250 acres of
arable farmland surrounded by open countryside, with a gravel drive
and mature trees in the garden. The bedrooms are decorated in warm
colours and the dining-room has armchairs and an open fire. The
breakfast room has french windows opening out to the garden. An
extensive menu of traditional evening meals with mouthwatering
deserts is presented on arrival; vegetarian choices can be provided
and all the vegetables are organically grown. A large heated
swimming-pool is available for guests' use.

OWNER: Mrs O.M. Alleston OPEN: all year ROOMS: 1 single, with shower; 1 double, with
wash-basin; 1 twin, with shower; 1 room suitable for wheelchair-users; TV in all
bedrooms TERMS: single £18, single occupancy £20, twin/double £36; dinner £9
DETAILS: no children; dogs welcome; car park; garden; swimming-pool

KESWICK   Cumbria   map 10

Abacourt House

26 Stanger Street, Keswick CA12 5JU
TEL: (01768) 772067

This former private Victorian townhouse in a quiet cul-de-sac was
converted into a guesthouse in 1992, and retains many of the original
features, including cast-iron fireplaces and pitch-pine doors.
Abacourt House now offers comfortable, immaculate accommodation:
all five bedrooms have *en suite* showers and TVs, and the lounge
provides a relaxing place to read or chat. The Newmans are
enthusiastic walkers who are happy to advise like-minded guests.
Breakfast only is served in the pleasant dining-room.

OWNERS: Bill and Sheila Newman OPEN: all year ROOMS: 5 double, all with shower; TV
in all bedrooms TERMS: double £40; deposit: 1 night's charge CARDS: none DETAILS:
no children; no dogs; no smoking; car park

Claremont House

Chestnut Hill, Keswick CA12 4LT
TEL: (01768) 772089
on A591, 1m S of Keswick

Claremont House was built 150 years ago as a lodge for nearby
Fillside Manor. Peacefully situated in three-quarters of an acre of

225

mature gardens and woods, the house provides first-class accommodation. The double glazing keeps residual traffic noise from the A591 to a minimum. The bedrooms, named after local beauty spots, have good views and extra touches, such as lace canopies on the beds and colourful duvet covers. One room has a brass bed. Breakfast includes home-made bread and locally produced bacon. The dinner menu always has vegetarian options, and Claremont House is licensed. The guests' lounge has a pretty window seat and a selection of books on the area. The bus to Keswick stops right outside.

OWNERS: Geoff and Hilda Mackerness OPEN: all year exc Christmas ROOMS: 4 double, 2 twin; all rooms with bath/shower; TV lounge TERMS: single occupancy £32, twin/double £48; children's reductions by arrangement; dinner £16; deposit: £10 CARDS: none DETAILS: children welcome; no dogs; no smoking in bedrooms or dining-room; car park; garden

KETTLEWELL   North Yorkshire   map 8

The Elms

Middle Lane, Kettlewell, nr Skipton BD23 5QX
TEL: (01756) 760224   FAX: (01756) 760380
off B6160, 14m N of Skipton

Standing at the edge of the village in a secluded garden, this attractive stone house was built for a wool merchant in 1872. The three attractive bedrooms, decorated in pale shades of pink, green and dainty floral patterns, have matching fabrics and pine furniture. The comfortable guest lounge has satellite TV and, on chilly days, an open fire. Breakfast only is served family-style in the pleasant dining-room, which has the original covings and a piano. Packed lunches are provided by arrangement; several venues for evening meals are within walking distance. This is a popular area for walkers, and information about walks is available at the Elms. Dogs are not permitted because, the Cuthberts tell us, their three Siamese cats (Garfunkel, Sumo and Simon the Third) would disapprove.

OWNERS: Ian and Jennifer Cuthbert OPEN: all year exc Christmas and New Year ROOMS: 2 double, 1 twin; all rooms with bath/shower; TV in all bedrooms TERMS: single occupancy £27–£29, twin/double £39–£42; deposit: £10 CARDS: none DETAILS: children welcome; no dogs; no smoking; car park; garden

If the establishment does not take credit cards, we say so in the details at the end of the entry.

Bath / shower in the details under each entry means that the rooms have private facilities. The B&B may have other, shared bathroom facilities as well. We say if rooms have wash-basins.

KILMINGTON Devon   map 2

White Hall

Kilmington, nr Axminster EX13 7SB
TEL: (01297) 32067
just off A35

This small Georgian former farmhouse stands in four acres of lovely
grounds and enjoys, from all rooms, views over the Devon
countryside. The house has a peaceful, relaxed feel and a most
charming owner. The two bedrooms share two bathrooms and guests
have use of a sitting-room and quiet library. Breakfast, which is a
substantial meal, features home-made bread and free-range eggs and
is served in the dining-room. Guests can drink the property's own
spring water. Kilmington is in a very convenient location for
exploring the Devon coastline, only six miles away. Food is available
in the fourteenth-century thatched inn nearby.

OWNER: Micheal Keenes OPEN: Mar to Oct ROOMS: 1 double, 1 twin; both rooms with
wash-basin; TV in both bedrooms and lounge TERMS: single occupancy £20, twin/
double £30; reductions for children under 5; deposit: £5 per person CARDS: none
DETAILS: children welcome; no dogs; no smoking; car park; garden

KIMBOLTON Hereford & Worcester   map 5

Lower Bache Farm

Kimbolton, nr Leominster HR6 0ER
TEL: (01568) 750304
*2m NE of Leominster; house signposted at top of hill on A4112 Leysters
Road*

Bache is an old English word meaning 'Valley of the rivulet' – and is
an appropriate name for this seventeenth-century stone farmhouse
nestling in 14 acres of unspoilt Herefordshire countryside. Once
derelict, the house has been lovingly restored, yet retains many
original features such as the wealth of oak beams and flagstone
floors. The dining-room was converted from the stone-built cider-
making annexe, and features the original cider mill. The old granary
houses two delightful suites, each with its own *en suite* shower and
sitting-room, and period pine furniture; it is all enhanced by a fine
display of nineteenth-century maps, prints and original watercolours.
Lower Bache Farm is a fascinating property from which to explore
this lovely area. It has a well-earned reputation for gourmet meals,
featuring some traditional recipes, and whenever possible using
organic meat and produce, with herbs from the garden; packed
lunches can also be provided. Do not be put off by the sign outside,
'unsuitable for vehicles', as this does not apply to access to the
farmhouse.

OWNERS: Rose and Leslie Wiles OPEN: all year ROOMS: 3 double, 1 twin, 1 family; all rooms with bath/shower; 1 room suitable for wheelchair-users; TV in all bedrooms TERMS: single occupancy £59, twin/double £49; dinner £11.50–£17.50; deposit: £10–£25 per person CARDS: none DETAILS: no children under 8; no dogs; smoking in dining-room only; car park; garden

---

KINETON   Warwickshire   map 5

Willowbrook Farmhouse

Lighthorne Road, Kineton, nr Warwick CV35 0JL
TEL: (01926) 640475   FAX: (01926) 641747
exit M40 at junction 12, take B4451 for 3½m into Kineton, turn right signposted Lighthorne and Moreton Morrell; farm is on left after ½m

---

This creeper-covered house is set peacefully on a four and a half acre smallholding. The Howards keep sheep and rare breeds of poultry; free-range eggs appear at the breakfast table. There is a small garden with a pond and a terrace for guests' use. The three well-appointed bedrooms are attractively decorated and have country views. A comfortable sitting-room has a log fire in winter, TV, games and books, and there are a number of antiques and curios, including a glass-bottle and jelly-mould collection. Breakfast only is served in the long dining-room, but menus of local eating establishments are on display. The Heritage Motor Centre at Gaydon is just up the road.

OWNERS: Carolyn and John Howard OPEN: all year exc Christmas ROOMS: 2 double, 1 with bath/shower, 1 with wash-basin; 1 twin, with wash-basin; TV in all bedrooms and lounge TERMS: twin/double £31–£38; reductions for children sharing with parents CARDS: none DETAILS: children welcome; dogs by arrangement; no smoking; car park; garden

---

KINGSAND   Cornwall   map 1

Cliff House

Kingsand, nr Torpoint PL10 1NJ
TEL: (01752) 823110
turn off B3247 to Kingsand 1m S of Millbrook

Cliff House can be found up a very steep and narrow lane right in the centre of Kingsand. It is a listed seventeenth-century building, and far more spacious than its external appearance suggests. The large first-floor drawing-room with open log fire has french windows leading out to a balcony overlooking Plymouth Sound, and the bedrooms are spacious and comfortable. Wholefood evening meals include home-made bread, soups, pâtés, mousses and ice-cream, and vegetarians and people on special diets can be catered for. Light suppers can be provided as an alternative and excellent food is also available in Kingsand. Cliff House is almost next to Mount Edgcumbe Country Park and is a few yards from the South Cornwall Coastal Footpath and the sea.

OWNER: Ann Heasman OPEN: all year ROOMS: 1 double, 2 twin; all rooms with bath/ shower; TV lounge TERMS: single occupancy £25, twin/double £36–£45; babies free, 10% reduction for children; dinner £18; deposit: 25% CARDS: none DETAILS: children welcome; dogs by arrangement; no smoking; car park; garden

KINGSBRIDGE Devon map 1

Galleons Reach

Embankment Road, Kingsbridge TQ7 1JZ
TEL: (01548) 853419

This modern, comfortable bungalow surrounded by an attractive garden overlooks the estuary and is almost on the water's edge. It is on a private service road just ten minutes' walk from the town centre. The house has a warm and friendly atmosphere and the dining-room, where breakfast is served at separate tables, overlooks the water.

OWNER: Mrs S. Bell OPEN: Easter to Oct ROOMS: 2 double, both with wash-basin; TV lounge TERMS: single occupancy £18, double £30; deposit: £6 per person CARDS: none DETAILS: no children under 10; no dogs; no smoking in bedrooms; car park; garden

KINGSEY Buckinghamshire map 2

Foxhill

Kingsey, nr Aylesbury HP17 8LZ
TEL: (01844) 291650
on A4129

This Grade II listed seventeenth-century building fulfils expectations of age and character with creaky floors, sloping ceilings and oak beams. But the large garden with wonderful rural views beyond also boasts a heated swimming-pool available for use during the summer. Indoors there is a huge lounge/breakfast room and a separate sitting area in the hall with plenty of books to dip into. The owners are charming and helpful and the house has a relaxed atmosphere. Although they serve breakfast only, the Hoopers have assembled a guide to local restaurants for guests.

OWNERS: Nicholas and Mary-Joyce Hooper OPEN: Feb to Nov ROOMS: 1 double, with shower; 2 twin, 1 with shower; TV in all bedrooms and lounge CARDS: none TERMS: single occupancy £21–£23, twin/double £38–£42 DETAILS: no children under 5; no dogs; no smoking; car park; garden; swimming-pool

Upper Newton Farmhouse

Kinnersley, nr Hereford HR3 6QB
TEL: (01544) 327727
off A4112

Do ask for directions when seeking out this B&B; there are two
Kinnersleys in Hereford & Worcester, which could make for
confusion. This black-and-white property dates from the eighteenth
century, and is approached up a private lane bordered by fields and
rolling countryside. It stands in a well-tended garden with two
orchards and is part of a 270-acre mixed farm. A welcoming
atmosphere pervades, and the bedrooms are quite luxurious and well
equipped, with Laura Ashley-style décor. Two of the rooms have four-
posters, and antiques, sloping floors, beams and fires in the lounge
and dining-room enhance the delightful ambience. Additional self-
catering accommodation is available in the renovated dairy. Staying
'down on the farm' is also ideal for business people as word-
processing, desk-top publishing and secretarial services are
available. Dinner is not usually served, but the Taylors are prepared
to provide evening meals by prior arrangement. Packed lunches can
be requested.

OWNERS: Pearl and Jon Taylor   OPEN: all year   ROOMS: 1 twin, 2 four-poster; all with
bath/shower; TV in all bedrooms and lounge   TERMS: single occupancy £25, twin £35,
four-poster £40; half-price for children; deposit: £10 per person per night   CARDS:
none   DETAILS: children welcome; no dogs; no smoking; car park; garden

The Courtyard

Fairbank, Kirkby Lonsdale LA6 2AZ
TEL: (01524) 271613

Tucked away in a small courtyard, this elegant Georgian town house
is just a few minutes' walk from the centre of this historic market
town. The rooms are spacious and well furnished, some with antique
pine furniture and original fireplaces. The blue room has a four-
poster bed. Old prints and paintings are displayed throughout the
house. Breakfast is served in the dining-room, with fresh flowers on
the table in season. The stylish drawing-room on the first floor has a
grandfather clock.

OWNER: Gillian Grey   OPEN: all year   ROOMS: 1 single; 2 twin, 1 with bath/shower, 1 with
wash-basin; 1 four-poster, with wash-basin; TV in some bedrooms   TERMS: single
£18–£20, single occupancy £20, twin £40–£45, four-poster £42; deposit: £10   CARDS:
none   DETAILS: no children under 10; no dogs; no smoking; car park; garden

KIRKBY STEPHEN　Cumbria　　　　　　　　　　**map 10**

Fletcher House

Fletcher Hill, Kirkby Stephen CA17 4QQ
TEL: (01768) 371013

This impressive Georgian listed house is situated in the centre of
town. It has been modernised with care and retains many original
features, such as the fireplaces and the entrance-hall archway, which
has been restored to its original splendour. The bedrooms are
tastefully decorated in soft pastels; one room has a half-tester bed,
and one *en suite* bedroom is on the ground floor. Breakfast only is
served in the dining-room, and packed lunches can be provided.
There is a comfortable lounge with TV.

OWNER: Dorothy Bradwell　OPEN: Easter to end Sept　ROOMS: 1 single; 2 double, 1 with
bath/shower, 1 with wash-basin; 2 twin, 1 with bath/shower, 1 with wash-basin; TV
lounge　TERMS: single £17, single occupancy £22, twin/double £34; half-price for
children under 11; deposit: £5　CARDS: none　DETAILS: children welcome; no dogs; no
smoking; car park

KIRKBY THORE　Cumbria　　　　　　　　　　**map 10**

Bridge End Farm

Kirby Thore, Penrith CA10 1UZ
TEL: (01768) 361362
on A66, 8m SE of Penrith

Sitting in the Eden Valley overlooking the Pennine Hills, this
eighteenth-century farmhouse is part of a pedigree Holstein dairy
farm. Inside, the spacious, spotlessly bedrooms have some antique
furniture; the patchwork quilts on the beds are made by Yvonne
Dent, a cheerful, welcoming lady who is interested in crafts and
cooking. Two bedrooms are *en suite* and the third has its own
bathroom; all have their own radio alarms, hair-dryers and TVs. The
guest lounge has a real fire. Home-cooked evening meals are served,
if arranged in advance, and feature lots of fresh vegetables; children's
portions are available. Bridge End Farm is unlicensed, but guests are
welcome to bring their own wine to dinner. Packed lunches can be
provided. Fishing can be arranged, and keen gardeners may wish to
visit Acorn Herb Garden, which is just a few minutes away.

OWNER: Yvonne Dent　OPEN: all year exc Christmas　ROOMS: 2 double, 1 with bath/
shower, 1 with wash-basin; 1 twin, with bath/shower; TV in all bedrooms and lounge
TERMS: single occupancy £20, twin/double £40; half-price for children under 12; dinner
£8.50; deposit: £5　CARDS: none　DETAILS: children welcome; dogs by arrangement; no
smoking; car park; garden

KIRKHARLE   Northumberland   map 11

Shieldhall

Wallington by Kirkharle, Morpeth NE61 4AQ
TEL/FAX: (01830) 540387
on B6342 E of junction with A696

A number of eighteenth-century farm buildings have been combined
with the original 1695 farmhouse to form a delightful, elegant house
based around a courtyard. The bedrooms are on the small side but are
self-contained, and they are on the ground floor. The dining-room has
a beamed ceiling and inglenook fireplace, and is well placed to catch
the sun. Dinner, with vegetarian options available, is served at 7pm
and there is a small bar for guests in the library. Shieldhall overlooks
Wallington Hall, a fine National Trust property with extensive
parkland and attractive gardens.

OWNERS: Stephen and Celia Gay   OPEN: Mar to Oct   ROOMS: 1 single, 3 double, 2 twin,
1 four-poster; all rooms with bath/shower; TV lounge   TERMS: single £20–£30, single
occupancy £30, twin/double £40, four-poster £40; dinner £14; deposit required
CARDS: Access, Switch, Visa   DETAILS: no children under 13; no dogs; smoking in
specified areas only; car park; games room; garden

KIRKWHELPINGTON   Northumberland   map 10

Cornhills Farmhouse

Cornhills, Kirkwhelpington NE19 2RE
TEL: (01830) 540232
turn W off A696 1m N of Kirkwhelpington and continue for 1½m

Cornhills is an impressive stone house at the centre of a large stock-
rearing farm, and guests can experience a taste of 'life on the farm'. It
was built by an ancestor of the present owners in the nineteenth
century and their son James has compiled a comprehensive portfolio
of its history. Plenty of original features remain, including a marble
and tile fireplace in the lounge, a mosaic-tiled hallway and a
Canadian pine staircase. The spacious bedrooms are tastefully
decorated and colour co-ordinated. Breakfast only is served, but good
food can be found at two local pubs. A three-bedroomed self-catering
cottage is also available.

OWNER: Lorna Thornton   OPEN: May to Mar   ROOMS: 1 double; 2 twin, 1 with bath/
shower; TV lounge   TERMS: twin/double £35–£45; children under 2 free, £10 for ages 2
to 12   CARDS: none   DETAILS: children welcome; no dogs; no smoking; car park; garden

---

*If you disagree with any assessment made in this guide, please write and
tell us why. Address your letter to The Good Bed and Breakfast Guide,
FREEPOST, 2 Marylebone Road, London NW1 1YN.*

Balaka

Wetherby Road, Knaresborough HG5 8LQ
TEL: (01423) 864598

Balaka means 'house of content' and the claim is endorsed by
comments in the visitors' book. This lovely detached modern house is
approached via a private lane and stands in a secluded garden. It is
decorated with Laura Ashley fabrics and is beautifully furnished. The
three bedrooms are well appointed and all have garden views. Ron
and Margaret Williams are a charming couple who extend a warm
welcome in their friendly family home.

OWNERS: Ron and Margaret Williams   OPEN: Apr to Oct   ROOMS: 1 single; 1 double,
with bath/shower; 1 twin, with bath/shower; TV in all bedrooms and lounge   TERMS:
single £17.50, single occupancy £25, twin/double £37; children's reductions; deposit:
£10 per person   CARDS: none   DETAILS: children welcome; no dogs; no smoking; car
park; garden

Grove House

14 Boroughbridge Road, Knaresborough HG5 0NG
TEL: (01423) 868857

Set in a large garden with a dovecote, this house is a characterful
conjunction of sixteenth-century and Georgian architecture,
transforming from one era to the other in the length of a staircase. It
has been beautifully restored, retaining beamed ceilings and a
marble fireplace. The bedrooms are pleasantly decorated and the
ground-floor annexe is ideal for families or groups of friends. This is a
friendly and welcoming place and the large lounge with comfortable
leather furniture has a relaxing ambience. Breakfast only is served
but there are plenty of eating places within walking distance in the
town centre. Knaresborough is a good base from which to tour the
Dales.

OWNER: Joan Davy   OPEN: all year exc Christmas   ROOMS: 2 double, both with bath/
shower; 1 twin, with wash-basin; 1 family, with bath/shower; TV in all bedrooms
TERMS: single occupancy £25, twin/double £36, family room £60   CARDS: none
DETAILS: children welcome; no dogs; no smoking; car park; garden

---

*Breakfast at B&Bs tends to mean a cooked breakfast of bacon, eggs and so
on. If you prefer a different style of breakfast, it is best to discuss this when
you make a booking.*

*If you are forced to turn up later than planned, please telephone to warn
the proprietor.*

Bissick Old Mill

Ladock, nr Truro TR2 4PG
TEL: (01726) 882557   FAX: (01726) 884057
on B3275, 7m NE of Truro

Bissick Old Mill is a beautiful stone-built house, which until 25 years ago was a working mill. The building is off the main road in the centre of the village, and has an outside patio with tables and chairs. During the day the Old Mill operates as a tea-room/restaurant, serving meals and delicious home-made cakes and pastries. Elizabeth Henderson is a trained chef and she turns her talents to her guests' advantage in the evening to prepare imaginative French-style dinners using fresh local produce; vegetarian options are always available and the dining-room is licensed. Light suppers are also offered. The three pretty, comfortable bedrooms all have TV, mini-bar and hair-dryer. There is a very comfortable lounge with an open fireplace. A self-catering cottage is available, which is ideal for families.

OWNERS: Keith and Elizabeth Henderson   OPEN: all year exc Christmas and New Year
ROOMS: 2 single, both with wash-basin; 2 double, both with bath/shower; 1 twin, with bath/shower; TV in all bedrooms   TERMS: single £27, single occupancy £35, twin/double £50–£60; dinner £15; deposit: £15 per person   CARDS: Access, Delta, Visa
DETAILS: no children under 10; dogs by prior arrangement; smoking in residents' lounge only; car park; garden

Lodge Down

Lambourn Woodlands, nr Hungerford RG17 7BJ
TEL/FAX: (01672) 540304
from M4 junction 14 follow sign to Wantage for 300 yards, then turn left at sign for Baydon and continue for 4m

This large attractive country house standing in 75 acres of gardens and woodlands was built in the middle of this century, but using much older materials. The huge parquet-floored drawing-room, with its warm, inviting atmosphere, has an open fire, a piano and a fine display of old family photographs. The spacious bedrooms are tastefully and traditionally furnished. The house is full of items of interest, and the remains of a prisoner-of-war camp can be seen alongside the driveway. Lambourn is a major centre for racehorse training and the gallops are visible from the house; John Cook is happy to take interested guests on a tour and, for a modest fee, can arrange a stable visit too. The Cooks are a gracious couple who serve breakfast only, but will point guests in the direction of the best local eating places. The grounds include a tennis court and an outdoor pool.

OWNERS: John and Sally Cook   OPEN: all year exc Christmas   ROOMS: 1 double, 1 twin, 1 family; all rooms with bath/shower; TV lounge   TERMS: single occupancy £20–£25, twin/double £40, family room £50   CARDS: Switch, Visa   DETAILS: children welcome; no dogs; no smoking in bedrooms; car park; garden; swimming-pool; tennis

LANCASTER   Lancashire   map 8

Edenbreck House

Sunnyside Lane, Lancaster LA1 5ED
TEL: (01524) 32464

This large, detached modern house built in the Victorian style is just ten minutes' walk from the town centre, and has a sizeable secluded garden. The house is beautifully decorated with a mixture of contemporary and traditional furnishings. There is a galleried lounge, and each bedroom has its own theme: the Master Bedroom, for example, has a four-poster bed and pink jacuzzi, and the Victorian Room 'is an ideal way to slip back in time'. Breakfast only is served in the attractive dining-room: there is a help-yourself buffet for starters, followed by a cooked choice.

OWNERS: Mr and Mrs Houghton   OPEN: all year exc Christmas   ROOMS: 3 double, 2 twin, 1 four-poster; all rooms with bath/shower; TV in all bedrooms   TERMS: single occupancy £25–£30, twin/double £40, four-poster £50; deposit: £10   CARDS: none DETAILS: children welcome; no dogs in dining-room; no smoking in dining-room; car park; garden

Elsinore House

76 Scotforth Road, Lancaster LA1 4SF
TEL: (01524) 65088
on A6, 3m N of M6 junction 33

This immaculately kept guesthouse is brightened by colourful window boxes in summer. It is a straighforward detached house with high standards. The bedrooms are of a good size and well furnished. Linda Moorhouse is a genealogist and is happy to help guests who are interested in tracing their ancestry. David Moorhouse is a keen painter and several of his works are on show. Lancaster University is nearby.

OWNER: Linda Moorhouse   OPEN: all year   ROOMS: 2 double, both with bath/shower; TV lounge   TERMS: single occupancy/double £30; deposit: £10   CARDS: none   DETAILS: no children under 12; no dogs; no smoking; car park; garden

If a deposit is required for an advance booking, this is stated in the details at the end of the entry.

LANDFORD   Wiltshire   map 2

Landsbrook Farm

Landford Wood, Landford, nr Salisbury SP5 2ES
TEL: (01794) 390220
just N of A36, 6m W of Romsey

Do ask for a map or directions to find this old farmhouse, which
stands just off a busy road on the Wiltshire/Hampshire border. Mrs
O'Brien is a very charming, welcoming lady, who loves gardening and
teaches tennis to children. She is happy to work out itineraries for
guests to visit houses and gardens in the area, Salisbury or the New
Forest. Inside, it is beautifully furnished, and there is a lovely sitting-
room; both breakfast and dinner are served in the dining-room.
Evening meals are by arrangement and can be a light supper or
something more substantial; vegetarian dishes can be requested, and
guests are welcome to bring their own wine as there is no alcohol
licence. A hard tennis court in the attractive garden is available in
the evenings for guests to use, after Mrs O'Brien has finished
coaching.

OWNER: Mrs P. O'Brien   OPEN: all year exc Christmas, Easter and bank hols   ROOMS: 1
single; 1 double, with bath/shower; 1 twin, with bath/shower; TV lounge   TERMS: single
£15, single occupancy £27–£30, twin/double £44–£50; dinner £13–£16; deposit: £10
per person   CARDS: none   DETAILS: no children under 10; no dogs; no smoking; car
park; garden; tennis

LANGLEY MARSH   Somerset   map 2

Deepleigh

Langley Marsh, Wiveliscombe, nr Taunton TA4 2UU
TEL: (01984) 623379
from B3227 at Wiveliscombe follow signs for Langley Marsh

Deepleigh was once a cider house and is a listed whitewashed
building dating from the sixteenth century. It is set in two and a half
acres of landscaped gardens at the foot of the Brendon Hills. The
Clarkes, a capable, friendly couple, took over the house early in 1995
and are in the process of refurbishment. The house has low beamed
ceilings, sloping floors and ancient panelling. The three pretty
bedrooms have lovely views and breakfast and dinner are served in
the sunny dining-room. The Deepleigh Farm Riding Centre, adjacent
to the house, offers riding for both beginners and more experienced
riders. Nearby are a Roman quarry and a Roman road, and plenty of
opportunities for walks through woods and quiet lanes. Deepleigh is
one mile from Wiveliscombe and four from Exmoor.

OWNER: Susan Clarke OPEN: all year ROOMS: 2 double, 1 family; all rooms with shower; TV in all bedrooms TERMS: double £39, family room £49; children's reductions CARDS: none DETAILS: children welcome; no dogs; no smoking; car park; garden

---

LANGTON MATRAVERS Dorset map 2

Maycroft

Old Malthouse Lane, Langton Matravers, nr Swanage BH19 3HH
TEL: (01929) 424305
off B3069 Swanage to Kingston road, turn into Old Malthouse School at top of village, and house is on left past school car park and buildings

---

This substantial Victorian family home is set in a quiet position in a lovely village, with a pleasant garden and good views over the valley to the sea. The house is comfortably furnished and the Bjorkstrands offer a warm welcome and are very helpful. The two bedrooms share a bathroom and WC, and breakfast only is served. Maycroft is well placed for the coastal paths and beaches.

OWNERS: Erik and Janet Bjorkstrand OPEN: Mar to Nov ROOMS: 1 double, 1 twin; both rooms with wash-basin; TV in both bedrooms TERMS: single occupancy £20, twin/double £30–£34; £6 for children over 6 sharing with parents CARDS: none DETAILS: no children under 6; no dogs; no smoking in bedrooms; car park; garden

---

LANGWITH Nottinghamshire map 9

Blue Barn Farm

Langwith, nr Mansfield NG20 9JD
TEL: (01623) 742248
off A616, approx 6m N of Mansfield; write or phone for directions

---

This working farm is approached up a three-quarter-mile private track in the middle of rolling hills on the Welbeck Estate, on the edge of Sherwood Forest. Guests are welcome to explore the 450-acre farm, and to enjoy the garden. The house is homely, but comfortably furnished; the twin room has an *en suite* bathroom. Substantial farm-style breakfasts are served, and there is a separate guest lounge with TV. June Ibbotson is an extremely helpful and accommodating host; a Blue Badge Tourist Guide, she is pleased to offer tours of the area. Packed lunches can be arranged. The farm also offers self-catering accommodation.

OWNER: June M. Ibbotson OPEN: all year exc Christmas ROOMS: 1 double, with wash-basin; 1 twin, with bath/shower; 1 family, with wash-basin; TV in all bedrooms and lounge TERMS: single occupancy £16–£20, twin/double £40; family room from £31; children's reductions according to age; deposit £5 for advance bookings CARDS: none DETAILS: children welcome; no dogs; car park; garden

LANHYDROCK Cornwall   map 1

Treffry Farm

Lanhydrock, nr Bodmin PL30 5AF
TEL/FAX: (01208) 74405
*take B3268 from Bodmin towards Lostwithiel; after 1½m turn right at
mini-roundabout and farm is 300yds down lane on right*

This listed Georgian farmhouse lies in peaceful countryside and was
once the home farm of the Lanhydrock Estate (now owned by the
National Trust). It has a tile-faced front and is part of a 200-acre
dairy farm. The three bedrooms are prettily decorated and all have *en
suite* showers. Features of the house are its extra wide staircase and
the Victorian panelling in the cosy TV lounge, which now has a
restored wooden floor. Breakfast only is served at separate tables in
the dining-room, and packed lunches can be provided on request. The
large, secluded garden has a play area for children. The farm
buildings have now been converted into self-catering units which are
available to rent.

OWNER: Pat Smith OPEN: all year exc Christmas and New Year ROOMS: 2 twin, 1 four-
poster; all rooms with shower; TV in all bedrooms and lounge TERMS: single
occupancy £27.50, twin/four-poster £39; half-price for children over 6 sharing with
parents; deposit: 25% CARDS: none DETAILS: no children under 6; no dogs; no
smoking; car park; garden

LAVENHAM Suffolk   map 6

Meathe House

Hill Green, Lavenham CO10 9LS
TEL: (01787) 247809
just E of A1141, 1m N of Lavenham

This red-brick, red-tiled house is fairly new but built in a traditional
farmhouse style with exposed walls and high ceilings. It sits in an
acre of well-tended gardens with beautiful views of rolling
countryside from all the bedrooms. The guests occupy one side of the
house and the owners live unobtrusively in the other, but are always
available and willing to help. The lounge and dining-room are large,
and a piano and lots of books suggest ways to relax. Exceptionally
high standards are maintained and the bedrooms, individually
decorated in dusty rose, gold and brown, are immaculate; one has a
half-tester bed. Breakfast only is served.

OWNERS: Ken and Margaret Yates OPEN: Easter to Oct ROOMS: 1 single, 1 double, 1
twin; all rooms with wash-basin; TV lounge TERMS: single £20, single occupancy £30,
twin/double £40 CARDS: none DETAILS: no children; no dogs; no smoking; car park;
garden

Weaners Farm

Bears Lane, Lavenham CO10 9RX
TEL: (01787) 247310
off B1071 Sudbury road just S of Lavenham

Weaners Farm is just a mile from the picturesque village of
Lavenham, with its fifteenth-century timbered buildings. The
modern house is on a 20-acre farm which supports pigs and a few
sheep. The three spacious bedrooms are individually decorated, with
floral duvets and matching curtains, comfortable beds and
countryside views, and share two bathrooms between them. One of
the bedrooms has a view of Lavenham Church, floodlit at night.
There is also a spacious TV lounge, and a well-tended garden for
guests' use. Breakfast only is served.

OWNER: Hazel Rhodes OPEN: all year exc Christmas ROOMS: 1 double, 2 twin; TV
lounge TERMS: single occupancy £20, twin/double £35 CARDS: none DETAILS:
children welcome; no dogs; smoking in lounge only; car park; garden

LEAMINGTON SPA Warwickshire   map 5

Charnwood Guesthouse

47 Avenue Road, Leamington Spa CV31 3PF
TEL: (01926) 831074

Charnwood is in a conservation area within walking distance of the
town centre. Lynn and John Booth took over the establishment in
July 1994 and since then have been busy refurbishing. The exterior
has been freshly painted, new carpets have been fitted and one room
converted into a guests' lounge. The bedrooms are being upgraded to
add more *en suite* facilities. The Booths have converted the basement
as their living quarters, leaving the main house solely for the use of
guests. Evening meals are available by arrangement and vegetarians
can be catered for. Snacks are also on offer.

OWNERS: John and Lynn Booth OPEN: all year exc Christmas ROOMS: 1 single, with
wash-basin; 2 double, 1 with bath/shower, 1 with wash-basin; 2 twin, 1 with bath/
shower, 1 with wash-basin; 1 family, with bath/shower; TV in all bedrooms and lounge
TERMS: single £17, single occupancy £17–£27, twin/double £32–£37, family room £48;
children's reductions according to age; dinner £10; deposit: £10 CARDS: Access, Visa
DETAILS: children welcome; dogs by prior arrangement; no smoking in dining-room; car
park

*Many B&Bs are in remote places, and although in many cases we provide
directions, it is always advisable to ask for clear instructions when
booking.*

*Please let us know if you need more report forms and we will send you a
fresh supply.*

LECK   Lancashire map 8

Cobwebs

Leck, Cowan Bridge, nr Kirkby Lonsdale LA6 2HZ
TEL/FAX: (01524) 272141
off A65, 8m E of M6 junction 36

This smart and very well-kept small Victorian country house is set
far enough off the main road to be peaceful but close enough for easy
access by car to the Yorkshire Dales or the Lakes. All the bedrooms
have *en suite* facilities and views of the surrounding countryside.
There are two small sitting-rooms, one with a mixture of soft
furnishings and the other a little more formal. A big attraction here is
the food, served in the 20-seat conservatory dining-room extension.
Yvonne Thompson produces accomplished four-course dinners that
draw people here from near and far, while Paul Kelly provides
cheerful and knowledgeable service; breakfasts too are of a high
standard. Cobwebs is fully licensed, with a large and informative
wine list. Energetic visitors may wish to try the eight-mile circular
walk through 'Brontë country' that starts at nearby Cowan Bridge.
Packed lunches can be arranged.

OWNERS: Paul Kelly and Yvonne Thompson   OPEN: mid-March to end Dec   ROOMS: 3
double, 2 twin; all rooms with bath/shower; TV in all bedrooms   TERMS: single
occupancy £45, twin/double £60; dinner £28; deposit: 10%   CARDS: Access, Visa
DETAILS: no children under 12; no dogs; no smoking in dining-room; car park; games
room; garden (*The Good Food Guide*)

LEEDS   West Yorkshire map 9

118 Grovehall Drive

118 Grovehall Drive, Beeston, Leeds LS11 7ET
TEL: (0113) 270 4445

The Sabines extend a traditional warm welcome to guests staying in
their family home in a suburb three miles south of the centre of
Leeds. The house is spotless and has two bedrooms with sloping
ceilings on the top floor. Rod Sabine has an expert's knowledge of the
area and will gladly assist guests planning days out. The bus service
to the city centre is excellent and the house is within easy reach of the
M1 and M62 motorways. Headingley cricket ground and the Leeds
football ground are nearby.

OWNERS: Rod and Ann Sabine   OPEN: all year exc owners' annual holidays   ROOMS: 1
single, 1 double, 1 twin; TV lounge   TERMS: single/single occupancy £15, twin/double
£25; £10 for children from 10 to 15   CARDS: none   DETAILS: no children under 10; no
dogs; no smoking; garden

LEGBOURNE   Lincolnshire   map 9

Gordon House

Station Road, Legbourne, nr Louth LN11 8LH
TEL: (01507) 607568   FAX: (01507) 609323
on A157, 3m SW of Louth

This turn-of-the-century red-brick country house with bay windows
backs on to the grounds of Legbourne Church and is three miles from
Caldwell Park motor-racing circuit. The attractive bedrooms both
have sloping floors and pine-stripped doors, and one has a Victorian
mahogany suite; they share a private guest bathroom. Mrs Norman is
a cheerful lady who clearly enjoys looking after her guests. The
comfortable TV lounge has a piano, which Tristan, Mrs Norman's
young son, might be persuaded to play. Breakfasts include local
sausages and Lincolnshire plum-bread; evening meals, which must
be pre-arranged, include vegetarian choices and offer children's
portions. The house is unlicensed, but guests may bring their own
wine to dinner. Packed lunches can be provided. The large garden at
the rear with its fish pond has several sitting areas for guests to relax
in.

OWNERS: Keith and Elizabeth Norman   OPEN: all year   ROOMS: 1 double, 1 twin; both
rooms with wash-basin; TV in both bedrooms   TERMS: single occupancy £18.50, twin/
double £33; £10 for children under 10; dinner £8; deposit: 10%   CARDS: none   DETAILS:
children welcome; dogs by prior arrangement; no smoking; car park; garden

LEOMINSTER   Hereford & Worcester   map 5

Copper Hall

South Street, Leominster HR6 8JN
TEL: (01568) 611622

Copper Hall is a charming seventeenth-century house set back from
the main Hereford road in half an acre of beautifully landscaped
gardens. The delightful owners, Pauline Blackburn and Yvonne
Mort, have amassed a collection of plates, bottles and Middle Eastern
copper objects. A Jacobean staircase leads to the spacious, colour co-
ordinated bedrooms. Breakfast is served in the dining-room, which
has potted plants and dried flowers, and large windows giving the
effect of a conservatory. Packed lunches can be provided and there
are numerous places only a few minutes' walk away for evening
meals. Leominster is a good centre for antiques, with a yearly festival
and 20 or more shops in which to browse.

OWNERS: Pauline Blackburn and Yvonne Mort   OPEN: all year exc Christmas   ROOMS: 3
double, 1 family; all rooms with bath/shower; TV in all bedrooms   TERMS: single
occupancy £20, double £35, family room £45   DETAILS: well-behaved children
welcome; small, well-behaved dogs welcome; no smoking; car park; garden

LEVISHAM   North Yorkshire   map 9

Grove House

The Station, Levisham, nr Pickering YO18 7NN
TEL: (01751) 472351
at end of single track road to North Yorkshire Moors Railway; 5m NE of Pickering

Grove House is a handsome old stone house in a superb setting bordered by woods and moorland. The house is adjacent to Levisham Station, which is on the steam North Yorkshire Moors Railway. All is beautifully maintained and the charming bedrooms have Victorian-style furnishings and cream and white curtains made by owner June Carter. Many people come here for the home cooking; dinner is served by arrangement at 7pm, and there is an alcohol licence. This is a property with very gracious hosts and a tranquil atmosphere.

OWNERS: June and Neville Carter   OPEN: Apr to end Oct   ROOMS: 2 double, 1 with bath/shower, 1 with wash-basin; 1 twin, with wash-basin; TV lounge   TERMS: single occupancy £28–£30, twin/double £36–£40; dinner £12; deposit: £10 per person   CARDS: none   DETAILS: no children; no dogs; no smoking; car park; garden

LEWES   East Sussex   map 3

Millers

134 High Street, Lewes BN7 1XS
TEL: (01273) 475631   FAX: (01273) 486226

The millers who ran their business from the front room of this sixteenth-century timber-framed building operated the only known six-sail post mill in the country, and one of the grinding stones can be seen in the walled garden. That room is now the dining-room, with a cosy fire and sitting area, and a table where cooked breakfasts, with vegetarian options, are served. One of the large bedrooms was used as a studio by members of the Bloomsbury Group; it has a magnificent array of exposed beams and, like the other bedroom, a four-poster bed. The house has lots of panelling and natural wood and is decorated to complement its unique character.

OWNERS: Teré and Tony Tammar   OPEN: all year exc 5 Nov, Christmas and New Year   ROOMS: 2 four-poster, both with bath/shower; TV in both bedrooms   TERMS: single occupancy £43, four-poster £48   CARDS: none   DETAILS: no children; no dogs; no smoking; garden

If we know of any particular payment stipulations, we mention them in the details at the end of the entry. However, it is always best to check when booking.

LEYBURN   North Yorkshire   map 9

Secret Garden House

Grove Square, Leyburn DL8 5AE
TEL: (01969) 623589

This Georgian stone house stands in its own large secluded and
sheltered garden, with a summer house which is over 200 years old.
In fine weather there are chairs and tables for sitting out. The house
is filled with antiques and curios, including a display of patchwork,
some of which was made by owner Norma Digges. There is evidence
that part of the house was a theatre in 1800 and that Lord Nelson's
surgeon, Peter Goldsmith, was a past owner. Guests who like to
breakfast late can be served until 9.30am. Evening meals, including
vegetarian choices, are available if pre-arranged, and are served in
the licensed dining-room.

OWNERS: Norma and Dermot Digges   OPEN: Apr to Nov all week, Dec to Mar weekends
only; closed Christmas   ROOMS: 2 double, both with bath/shower; 3 twin, 2 with bath/
shower, 1 with wash-basin; TV in all bedrooms and lounge   TERMS: single occupancy
£19–£24.50, twin/double £38–£49; dinner £22.50; deposit: £10 per person   CARDS:
Access, Visa   DETAILS: no children under 12; dogs welcome; no smoking in dining-
room; car park; garden

LICHFIELD   Staffordshire   map 5

Gaialands

9 Gaiafields Road, Lichfield WS13 7LT
TEL: (01543) 263764

This attractive house built in 1890 stands in a beautiful secluded
garden above the cathedral. Jean White has been running her
immaculate B&B for 22 years. The spacious, bright bedrooms are
tastefully decorated in soft colours and have comfortable beds; one
has an *en suite* bathroom. There is a guest lounge with TV. Breakfast
only is served, but there are several eating establishments within
three minutes' walk, and packed lunches can be provided. This good-
value property is a popular venue with business people and tourists,
so early reservation is necessary.

OWNERS: Mr and Mrs R.W. White   OPEN: all year exc Christmas   ROOMS: 2 single, with
wash-basin; 1 double, 1 twin, both with bath/shower; TV in all bedrooms and lounge
TERMS: single £20, single occupancy £25, twin/double £40; children's reductions by
arrangement; deposit   CARDS: none   DETAILS: children welcome; no dogs; no smoking;
car park; garden

*No stamps are needed if you write to the Guide from within the UK. Report
forms are at the end of the book, or use your own stationery if you prefer.*

LIMPLEY STOKE Avon   map 2

Avonside

Winsley Hill, Limpley Stoke, nr Bath BA3 6EX
TEL: (01225) 722547

True to its name, this eighteenth-century Bath stone house stands on
the banks of the River Avon. It is a comfortable family home in a large
and quiet garden which includes a hard tennis court available to
guests. The house is decorated with some style and furnished with
antiques, and the bedrooms are large. Dinner is served by
arrangement and guests are encouraged to bring their own wine. A
restaurant within five minutes' walk is an alternative dinner venue.

OWNERS: Peter and Ursula Challen OPEN: all year exc Christmas and New Year
ROOMS: 1 double, 1 twin; both rooms with wash-basin TERMS: single occupancy £20,
twin/double £40; babies free; dinner £12 CARDS: none DETAILS: no children under 10,
except babies; no dogs; smoking downstairs only; car park; garden; tennis

LINCOLN Lincolnshire   map 9

Carline Guest House

1–3 Carline Road, Lincoln LN1 1HL
TEL: (01522) 530422

The standards at this smart Edwardian property continue to
improve. The well-appointed rooms have attractive wallpaper and
stripped pine doors, and are all equipped with radio-alarm, hair-
dryer, trouser press, desk and TV. Ten have their own bathroom and
three of these are on the ground floor. An annexe across the road
boasts three beautiful bedrooms and its own sitting-room. Excellent
breakfasts feature delicious speciality sausages and free-range eggs,
and the Pritchards are happy to recommend eating establishments
for lunch and evening meals. The restaurant-style breakfast room
overlooks the small patio. The house is an ideal base from which to
explore the city and only five minutes' walk uphill from the cathedral.
Garage parking is available for a modest charge.

OWNERS: Gillian and John Pritchard OPEN: all year exc Christmas ROOMS: 1 single,
with wash-basin; 7 double, 6 with bath/shower, 1 with wash-basin; 2 twin, both with
bath/shower; 2 family, both with bath/shower; TV in all bedrooms TERMS: single £20,
single occupancy £30, twin/double £32–£38, family room £50; reductions for children
sharing with parents; deposit: £20 DETAILS: children welcome; no dogs; no smoking;
car park; garden

*Many B&Bs, especially if they are unlicensed, allow guests to bring their
own wine to dinner. If this is the case, we say so in the entry.*

Lindum View Guest House

3 Upper Lindum Street, Lincoln LN2 5RN
TEL: (01522) 548894

With the distinction of being the closest guesthouse to the cathedral, this 1873 house is in a conservation area of this historic city. Jacqueline and Bruce Low are an enthusiastic couple who took over the property in 1993 and have been busy upgrading and improving it. The good-sized bedrooms are clean and comfortable, and those on the top floor have cathedral views. There is a cosy sitting-room/reception area, and breakfasts only are served. Lincoln offers plenty of establishments for evening meals.

OWNER: Jacqueline Low OPEN: all year exc Christmas and New Year ROOMS: 2 double, 2 twin; all rooms with bath/shower; TV in all bedrooms TERMS: single occupancy £25, twin/double £38; children's reductions CARDS: none DETAILS: children welcome; no dogs; car park

LINTON Kent   map 3

White Lodge

Loddington Lane, Linton, nr Maidstone ME17 4AG
TEL: (01622) 743129
from M20 junction 8, take B2163 S through Leeds village, turn left after Boughton Monchelsea into Loddington Lane before Linton crossroads

This classic white country house is in a beautiful setting surrounded by lovely gardens and with a small lake at the front. Garden furniture is provided and guests are encouraged to sit out in warm weather. It is unbelievable that this impressive building was once the laundry to Linton Park, the former home of Lord Cornwallis. It is thought that it was built on the site of a monastery, and it has been considerably altered over the years. The house has an informal atmosphere and the bedrooms are all on the first floor, with the exception of the family apartment on the second floor which has its own lounge with TV. Breakfast only is taken in either the breakfast room or the dining-room; packed lunches can be provided.

OWNER: Merrilyn Boorman OPEN: all year ROOMS: 2 single, with wash-basin; 1 double, with bath/shower; 2 twin, both with wash-basin; 1 family apartment, with bath/shower; TV in all bedrooms TERMS: single/single occupancy £20, twin/double £40, family apartment from £65 CARDS: none DETAILS: children welcome; dogs by prior arrangement; smoking in dining-room only after meal; car park; garden

Many B&Bs offer tea / coffee-making facilities in the bedroom.

We welcome your feedback about B&Bs you have stayed in. Please make use of the report forms at the end of the book.

LITTLE LANGFORD   Wiltshire   map 2

Little Langford Farmhouse

Little Langford, nr Salisbury SP3 4NR
TEL: (01722) 790205
leave A36 at Great Wishford and follow parallel road 2m towards Wylye

Little Langford is a Victorian house set in a quiet valley in the
beautiful Wiltshire downs. Only the occasional sound of a passing
train disrupts the peace for a few seconds. Built in 1858 in the Gothic
style, it has its own tower overlooking the large front lawn with
mature trees which extends towards the 650 acres of arable and dairy
farmland tenanted by the Helyers. Families are welcome and guests
can walk round the farm and watch milking or calves being fed. The
three large, attractively furnished bedrooms share two bathrooms,
and one room which has a Victorian brass bed can be combined with a
small neighbouring room to make up a family unit. There is a large,
pleasant lounge, and a dining-room with one big table where
breakfast only is served. Guests also have the use of a games room
with a billiard table.

OWNER: Patricia Helyer   OPEN: all year exc Christmas   ROOMS: 1 double, 2 twin; all
rooms with wash-basin; TV lounge   TERMS: single occupancy £22–£25; twin/double
£37–£39; reductions for children sharing with parents; deposit: 25%   CARDS: none
DETAILS: children welcome; well-behaved dogs welcome; smoking in lounge only; car
park; games room; garden

LITTLESTONE-ON-SEA   Kent   map 3

Romney Bay House

Coast Road, Littlestone-on-Sea, New Romney TN28 8QY
TEL: (01797) 364747   FAX: (01797) 367156

This impressive country house stands in a wind-swept position facing
the sea on an unspoilt stretch of coastline with marvellous views of
the English Channel. It was designed by Sir Clough Williams-Ellis in
the late 1920s for the American actress Hedda Hopper. Later it
became a hotel, and has been sympathetically restored by the present
owners, Helmut and Jennifer Görlich, who are antique dealers,
interior designers and – in Helmut's case – a hairdresser. The house
has been beautifully furnished and decorated, and the comfortable
bedrooms have everything one could need: there is a half-tester in
one, another has a four-poster, and about half have sea views. The
drawing-room has a log fire, and upstairs the little 'look-out' room has
a telescope and books. Dinner is served in the restaurant; afternoon
and cream teas are also available, and are served on the terrace when
it is warm enough, or in the dining-room. The house is licensed. In the

grounds is a tennis court for guests' use, as well as croquet and direct access to the beach. Two golf courses are immediately behind the house. Packed lunches can be provided.

OWNERS: Helmut and Jennifer Görlich   OPEN: all year exc 1 week at Christmas   ROOMS: 1 single, 3 double, 2 twin, 1 four-poster; all rooms with bath/shower; TV in all bedrooms   TERMS: single £35, single occupancy £40–£60, twin/double £55–£75, four-poster £85; dinner £25–£34.50; deposit: £20   CARDS: Access, Diners, Visa   DETAILS: no children; no dogs; smoking in bar and sitting-room only; car park; garden; tennis

LITTLE THETFORD   Cambridgeshire   map 6

Springfields

Ely Road, Little Thetford, nr Ely CB6 3HJ
TEL: (01353) 663637   FAX: (01353) 663130
off A10, 2m S of Ely

Springfields is a modern ranch-style bungalow on the edge of the village with a huge, beautiful garden bordered by mature trees which eliminate any road noise. The ground-floor bedrooms, in a wing adjacent to the main house, are all exquisitely decorated with a touch of luxury: Sanderson wallpapers, lace, rich furnishings and comfortable beds. Breakfast is served family-style in the elegant dining-room on delicate blue-and-white china. An interesting collection of bird-pattern plates and some lovely Victorian cranberry glasses are on display here. Springfields offers high-class accommodation at an affordable price.

OWNERS: Derek and Dawn Bailey   OPEN: all year exc Christmas   ROOMS: 1 double, 2 twin; all rooms with bath/shower; TV in all bedrooms   TERMS: single occupancy £30, twin/double £40; deposit: £10   CARDS: none   DETAILS: no children under 12; no dogs; no smoking; car park; garden

LITTLE WITLEY   Hereford & Worcester   map 5

Ribston House

Bank Road, Little Witley, nr Worcester WR6 6LS
TEL: (01886) 888750   FAX: (01886) 888925
on A443, 7m NW of Worcester

Located in a tranquil spot, with views over the surrounding hills and woods and the ruins of Witley Court, this sixteenth-century property makes for a relaxing retreat. Ribston House has been sympathetically modernised, retaining many period features. The charming owners, Sarah and Richard Wells, provide a warm welcome and are happy to meet trains and coaches, and act as guides to local places of interest. The three well-appointed bedrooms are tastefully decorated; all are *en suite*. There is a comfortable sitting-room with log fire and TV, a garden, and three llamas, Pandora, Perseus and

Sybil, in an adjacent field. Candlelit dinners include wine and are served at 7pm. Everything is home-cooked and freshly prepared; children's helpings and vegetarian meals can be requested. Bookings for dinner, bed and breakfast are preferred.

OWNERS: Sarah and Richard Wells OPEN: all year ROOMS: 1 single, 1 twin, 1 family; all rooms with bath/shower; TV lounge TERMS: rates include dinner; single/single occupancy £35, twin/double £70, family room from £70; half-price for children under 12; deposit: £20 CARDS: none DETAILS: children welcome; no dogs; car park; garden

LIZARD   Cornwall   map 1

Mounts Bay House

Penmenner Road, Lizard TR12 7NP
TEL: (01326) 240221
take B3083 from Helston to Lizard, turn right into Penmenner road after village green, then up drive signposted Mounts Bay House Hotel

Along the length of the Lizard peninsula there is barely a glimpse of the sea, so the view looking out to Kynance Cove and Land's End as one rounds a bend in the driveway comes as something of a surprise. This small Victorian house is set in a one-and-a-half-acre garden, and has some original stained-glass windows. There is a cosy bar, and a dining-room with sea views, where evening meals can be served by arrangement. The accommodation is simple and most rooms have *en suite* showers. Within easy reach are clifftop walks, sandy beaches and fishing harbours.

OWNERS: Grace and Sam Crossley OPEN: all year exc Nov ROOMS: 1 single, 5 double, 1 twin; all rooms with shower; TV lounge TERMS: single £19–£23, single occupancy £24–£28, twin/double £38–£46; dinner £11.50; children's reductions by arrangement; deposit: £6 per person CARDS: Access, Visa DETAILS: children welcome; no dogs in dining-room; car park; garden

LLANWARNE   Hereford & Worcester   map 5

The Lawns

Llanwarne, nr Hereford HR2 8EN
TEL: (01981) 540351
on A466, 8m S of Hereford

This beautiful 300-year-old country house in 25 acres of grass and woodland, surrounded by sheep farming, is a good place for a relaxing stay. Elizabeth and Ralph Howard are a charming couple and guests are invited to join them in their drawing-room in the evening, and use the patio and garden on fine days. The spacious bedrooms with floral fabrics are pleasantly furnished, and the house has several unique features, including a 125-foot well which was discovered during renovation. Imaginative breakfasts include yoghurts, fresh fruit and, on occasion, duck eggs.

OWNERS: Ralph and Elizabeth Howard   OPEN: Jan to mid-Nov   ROOMS: 1 double, with bath/shower; 2 twin, 1 with bath/shower, 1 with wash-basin; TV in all bedrooms and lounge   TERMS: single occupancy £40, twin/double £48; deposit: £10 per room   CARDS: none   DETAILS: no children under 9; no dogs; no smoking; car park; garden

LLANYMYNECH   Shropshire   map 5

Hospitality

Vyrnwy Bank, Llanymynech SY22 6LG
TEL: (01691) 830427
on B4398, ¼m from centre of village

Hospitality is an eighteenth-century building on the edge of the Welsh border, with views over Shropshire farmland. The atmosphere here is homely, old-fashioned, comfortable; all three pleasant bedrooms have TV, and there are two bathrooms and one shower room for guests' use. Carol Fahey trained as a caterer and offers excellent breakfasts, as well as evening meals (including vegetarian choices if ordered). Hospitality is not licensed but guests may bring their own wine to dinner; packed lunches can be provided.

OWNERS: Mr and Mrs B.J. Fahey   OPEN: March to Dec exc Christmas   ROOMS: 1 single, 1 double, 1 twin, 1 family; all rooms with wash-basin; TV in all bedrooms and lounge   TERMS: single/single occupancy £15, twin/double/family room from £30; children's reductions by arrangement; dinner £8   CARDS: none   DETAILS: children welcome; dogs welcome; smoking in sitting-room only; car park; garden

LONG COMPTON   Warwickshire   map 5

Butler's Road Farm

Long Compton, nr Shipston on Stour CV36 5JZ
TEL/FAX: (01608) 684262

A warm welcome awaits visitors to this unpretentious, no-frills farmhouse dating from 1726, where Eileen Whittaker treats her guests as friends. It stands in a 120-acre dairy farm, which guests are invited to explore, making use, if necessary, of one of the 30 pairs of wellington boots of all sizes set aside for the purpose. Several original features remain, including flagstone floors, oak beams, stone walls and an inglenook fireplace. The cosy sitting-room has skittles and puzzles as well as TV. Substantial breakfasts start the day, and evening eating places are within walking distance. The comfortable bedrooms share a large bathroom with a power shower. The interesting village of Long Compton dates back to the fourteenth century.

OWNER: Eileen Whittaker OPEN: all year ROOMS: 1 double, 1 twin; both rooms with bath/shower; TV lounge TERMS: single occupancy £16, twin/double £30; children's reductions according to age CARDS: none DETAILS: children welcome; dogs welcome; no smoking in bedrooms; car park; games room

---

LONG MELFORD Suffolk   map 6

1 Westropps

1 Westropps, Long Melford, nr Sudbury CO10 9HW
TEL/FAX: (01787) 373660

This comfortable modern house situated at the edge of the village is furnished in traditional style. The double bedroom is *en suite* and the others have their own WCs but share a bathroom. There is a separate sitting-room, and a dining-room where freshly grilled breakfasts are served. A new patio area gives a pleasant view of the garden with a fish pond stocked with koi carp. Audrey Fisher was born in nearby Lavenham and is happy to share her knowledge of the area with guests.

OWNER: Audrey Fisher OPEN: all year ROOMS: 1 single, with wash-basin; 1 double, with bath/shower; 1 twin, with wash-basin; TV in all bedrooms and lounge TERMS: single £18, single occupancy £22, twin/double £36; £10 for children under 12, £15 for ages 12 to 15 CARDS: none DETAILS: children welcome; dogs welcome; no smoking; car park; garden

---

LOOE Cornwall   map 1

Marwinthy Guest House

East Cliff, East Looe PL13 1DE
TEL: (01503) 264382
from Fore Street, turn left at Ship Inn signposted coast path; house 140yds up hill just beyond crossroads

---

Marwinthy Guest House stands in the centre of Looe, in a quiet location, up a steep narrow lane with wonderful views over the town, harbour and beach. The Mawbys are a friendly couple who thoroughly enjoy running their guesthouse. The sitting-room is shared with the owners, and has a balcony and telescope for enjoying the view, and all the bedrooms have the marvellous outlook. The dinner menu is quite extensive, with plenty of curry choices – one of the specialities of the house; packed lunches can be provided. Marwinthy is located right on the coastal footpath.

OWNERS: Eddie and Geraldine Mawby OPEN: all year exc Nov ROOMS: 3 double, 2 with bath/shower, 1 with wash-basin; 1 twin, 1 family, both with wash-basin; TV in some bedrooms and lounge TERMS: single occupancy £15–£33, twin/double £30–£36, family room £48; £9 for children sharing with parents; dinner £7 plus wine; deposit: 1 night's charge CARDS: none DETAILS: children welcome; dogs welcome; no smoking in dining-room and WCs; car park

Garendon Lodge

136 Leicester Road, Loughborough LE11 2AQ
TEL: (01509) 211120

This pristine turn-of-the-century house is set back from the main
road up its conifer-lined drive. It has recently been redecorated to a
high standard with new carpets and curtains in soft, restful colours.
The six well-equipped bedrooms all have bathroom, TV and radio
alarm. Breakfast and evening meals are served by arrangement in
the attractive dining-room. Vegetarians can be catered for and guests
are welcome to bring their own wine. Garendon Lodge is only one
mile from the city centre.

OWNER: Pamela Dunham OPEN: all year ROOMS: 2 single, 2 double, 1 twin, 1 family; all
rooms with bath/shower; TV in all bedrooms TERMS: single £22, single occupancy £25,
twin/double £35, family room £42; dinner £6.50 CARDS: Amex DETAILS: children
welcome; no dogs; no smoking; car park; garden

Highbury Guest House

146 Leicester Road, Loughborough LE11 2AQ
TEL: (01509) 230545

A warm welcome awaits guests at this simple, immaculately kept
guesthouse in a central position, but double glazed to minimise traffic
noise. The rooms are all a good size and are comfortably furnished.
The conservatory lounge is spacious and bright, and there is also an
alternative quiet lounge without TV. A leaded stained-glass window
in the hall and the collection of antique plates are worth noting.
Breakfast and evening meals are served by arrangement. There is an
alcohol licence but guests can also bring their own wine.

OWNERS: John and Sadie Cunningham OPEN: all year ROOMS: 2 single, 1 with bath/
shower, 1 with wash-basin; 3 double, all with bath/shower; 3 twin, 1 with bath/shower;
2 family, both with bath/shower; 1 room suitable for wheelchair-users; TV in all
bedrooms and lounge TERMS: single £18–£22, single occupancy £25, twin/double £35,
family room £46; children's reductions according to age; dinner £6 CARDS: none
DETAILS: children welcome; small dogs welcome; car park; garden

*If any bedrooms are suitable for wheelchair-users, we mention this in the
details at the end of the entry.*

*Many B&Bs, especially if they are unlicensed, allow guests to bring their
own wine to dinner. If this is the case, we say so in the entry.*

LOVESOME HILL   North Yorkshire   map 9

Lovesome Hill Farm

Lovesome Hill, Northallerton DL6 2PB
TEL: (01609) 772311
on A167, 4m N of Northallerton

The Pearson family have owned this 165-acre mixed farm since 1940.
The granary has been converted into warm and comfortable
accommodation including two ground-floor bedrooms, a single, and a
double which is suitable for wheelchair-users. The rooms are beamed
and furnished according to their names: 'Oak' and 'Pine', for example.
Guests are greeted upon arrival with a hot drink in the quiet lounge.
Breakfasts are served in the main house and include free-range eggs
and home-made marmalade. Dinners are available by arrangement
and vegetarians can be catered for with advance notice. The owners'
teenage sons enjoy showing visitors around the farm. The garden has
apple trees and slides for children to play on.

OWNERS: Mr and Mrs J.C. Pearson   OPEN: Mar to Nov   ROOMS: 1 single, 1 double, 1
twin, 1 family; all rooms with bath/shower; 1 room suitable for wheelchair-users; TV in
all bedrooms and lounge   TERMS: single £17–£21, single occupancy £20–£25, twin/
double £34–£42, family room £30–£42 plus children's charge; children's reductions
according to age; dinner £9; deposit: 10%   CARDS: none   DETAILS: children welcome;
no dogs; smoking in lounge only; car park; garden

LOWESTOFT   Suffolk   map 6

Coventry House

8 Kirkley Cliff, Lowestoft NR33 0BY
TEL: (01502) 573865

This three-storey Victorian building is opposite the public gardens
and faces the sea. The house has double glazing which eliminates
most of the traffic noise. All the bedrooms are immaculate, and one is
on the ground floor with *en suite* facilities. Evening meals, including
vegetarian dishes on request, are served except on Sunday and
Monday. There is no licence, but guests may bring their own wine to
dinner, and packed lunches can be provided.

OWNER: Gill Alden   OPEN: all year exc Christmas   ROOMS: 2 single, both with wash-
basin; 2 double, 1 with bath/shower, 1 with wash-basin; 1 twin, 1 family, both with bath/
shower; TV in all bedrooms and lounge   TERMS: single £17, single occupancy £20,
twin/double £30–£36, family room from £35; half-price for children under 12; dinner £6;
deposit: 10%   CARDS: none   DETAILS: children welcome; well-behaved dogs welcome;
no smoking in dining-room; car park

Longshore Guest House

7 Wellington Esplanade, Lowestoft NR33 0QQ
TEL: (01502) 565037

This well-maintained Victorian guesthouse faces the sea. Most of the bedrooms have sea views, and are decorated with floral fabrics and duvets; all of the rooms are equipped with hair-dryer, radio, iron and TV. Although the terraced property is located on the promenade, the double glazing eliminates most of the traffic noise. Breakfast only is served in the mock-Tudor dining-room, but there are several restaurants and pubs serving evening meals within walking distance. Frank and Sandra Nolan are an accommodating couple who extend a warm welcome.

OWNERS: Frank and Sandra Nolan   OPEN: all year exc Christmas   ROOMS: 2 single, 2 double, 1 twin; all rooms with bath/shower; TV in all bedrooms   TERMS: single £20–£26, single occupancy £26, twin/double £36–£42; deposit: £20 per person   CARDS: Access, Delta, Visa   DETAILS: children welcome; dogs welcome; car park

LOXLEY   Warwickshire   **map 5**

Loxley Farm

Loxley, nr Warwick CV35 9JN
TEL: (01789) 840265
off A429 / A422, 4m SE of Stratford-upon-Avon

This charming, thatched and half-timbered house of cruck-frame construction uses naturally curved wood to form an arch supporting the end walls. The interior is furnished with antiques and old equestrian drawings, and has polished wooden floors. There is a comfortable snug room, and breakfast only, cooked on the Aga, is served in the traditional dining-room. The two ground-floor *en suite* bedrooms, as well as a sitting-room, are in the barn conversion. A pleasant, secluded garden takes in Shetland ponies and chickens, and croquet and badminton. The village has a Saxon/Norman church and is only four miles from Stratford-upon-Avon.

OWNERS: Mr and Mrs R.P.K. Horton   OPEN: all year exc Christmas   ROOMS: 2 double; both rooms with bath/shower; TV in one bedroom   TERMS: single occupancy £32, double £44; reductions for children according to age; deposit: £15   CARDS: none   DETAILS: children welcome; no dogs in public rooms; car park; garden

B&B rates specified in the details at the end of each entry are given (as applicable) for a single room, for single occupancy of a double room, and then per room in the case of two people sharing a double or twin-bedded room, or for a family room.

Cecil Guest House

Sheet Road, Ludlow SY8 1LR
TEL/FAX: (01584) 872442

This immaculately kept guesthouse is one mile from the town centre.
It is a modern building which conceals a lovely well-developed
garden, which guests can relax in. The bedrooms are fresh and bright,
decorated in low-key light colours, and two are on the ground floor. A
sunny bar/lounge overlooks the garden. Gillian Phillips is an
excellent cook who prepares imaginative evening meals which she
calls 'discerning family dinners'. Vegetarians and those on special
diets can be catered for with advance notice.

OWNERS: Maurice and Gillian Phillips   OPEN: all year exc Christmas   ROOMS: 3 single, all
with wash-basin; 1 double, with bath/shower; 5 twin, 2 with bath/shower, 3 with wash-
basin; 1 family, with wash-basin; TV in all bedrooms   TERMS: single £18, single
occupancy £23, twin/double £36, family room £36 plus children's charge; children's
reductions according to age; dinner £11; deposit   CARDS: Access, Visa   DETAILS:
children welcome; no dogs in public rooms; smoking in bar only; car park; garden

Number Twenty Eight

28 Lower Broad Street, Ludlow SY8 1PQ
TEL/FAX: (01584) 876996

This impeccably maintained, listed half-timbered house is sited close
to the town centre, not far from the Ludford Bridge on the River
Teme. The bedrooms are elegantly furnished in pine and soft pastels.
Two are in a nearby renovated seventeenth-century mews and have
patchwork quilts, their own sitting-room, patio and garden. Meals
are taken in the main house; umbrellas are thoughtfully provided to
guests walking between the two buildings on rainy days. Imaginative
evening meals, including at least one vegetarian option, are served
nightly in the dining-room. Number Twenty Eight is fully licensed,
and pre-dinner drinks and after-dinner coffee or liqueurs can be
enjoyed in the small walled garden, weather permitting. There is no
car park, but street parking is unrestricted.

OWNER: Patricia Elm Ross   OPEN: all year   ROOMS: 2 double, 2 twin; all rooms with
bath/shower; TV in all bedrooms and lounge   TERMS: single occupancy £35–£55, twin/
double £50–£60; dinner £25; deposit: credit card details or written confirmation
CARDS: Access, Amex, Delta, Visa   DETAILS: children welcome; dogs welcome; no
smoking in dining-room; garden

---

*No stamps are needed if you write to the Guide from within the UK. Report
forms are at the end of the book, or use your own stationery if you prefer.*

LUTON   Bedfordshire   map 3

Belzayne Guest House

70 Lalleford Road, Luton LU2 9JH
TEL: (01582) 36591

Andy and Elsie Bell are a delightful couple and staying here is like
visiting friends. They join their guests in the lounge in the evening for
a chat and a cup of tea or coffee. There are no fancy frills here, just
old-fashioned hospitality in a well-maintained modern house in a
residential street. Modestly priced tasty home-cooked dinners, which
may include home-made pies and soups, are available by
arrangement. Belzayne is a five-minute drive from Luton Airport.

OWNERS: Andy and Elsie Bell   OPEN: all year exc Christmas and New Year   ROOMS: 1
single, 2 twin; TV lounge   TERMS: single/single occupancy £18, twin £22; children's
reductions; dinner £8; deposit: £5   CARDS: none   DETAILS: no children under 6; no
dogs; car park; garden

LYDLINCH   Dorset   map 2

Holebrook Farm

Lydlinch, Sturminster Newton DT10 2JB
TEL: (01258) 817348   FAX: (01258) 817747
*from village take lane signposted 'Lydlinch Church and Holebrook only'
for 1½m S*

Just south of the small village of Lydlinch in peaceful countryside,
Holebrook Farm is a pretty farmhouse and converted stables on a
working farm. Guests are welcome to look round the farm and come
and go as they please. All the bedrooms, except one, are in the
converted stables and most have TVs and their own bathrooms.
Guests have use of a sitting-room, and good home-cooked evening
meals are available if arranged in advance; the farm has an alcohol
licence. Other facilities include a small outdoor swimming-pool, a
mini-gym and a games room with pool table, table tennis and darts.
Clay-pigeon shooting can be arranged on the farm, and there are also
self-catering cottages. It is advisable to ask for full directions to the
farm when booking.

OWNER: C.S. Wingate-Saul   OPEN: all year exc Christmas   ROOMS: 2 double, both with
bath/shower; 7 twin, 6 with bath/shower, 1 with wash-basin; 3 rooms suitable for
wheelchair-users; TV in some bedrooms and lounge   TERMS: single occupancy
£26–£46, twin/double £42–£46; dinner £13.50; deposit: 33%   CARDS: none   DETAILS:
children welcome; no dogs; car park; games room; garden; swimming-pool

---

*If the establishment does not take credit cards, we say so in the details at
the end of the entry.*

Rashwood Lodge

Clappentail Lane, Lyme Regis DT7 3LZ
TEL: (01297) 445700

This highly unusual, octagonal white-painted house is set in its own grounds in a peaceful position on the edge of town. Mrs Lake is a cheerful and hospitable host who enjoys welcoming guests to her tastefully furnished home. The two bedrooms have sea views and are charmingly decorated in pale colours. There is a pleasant sitting-room and a breakfast room. Visitors are welcome to use the lovely garden with its sloping lawn and seating.

OWNER: Diana Lake   OPEN: Mar to end Nov   ROOMS: 2 double, both with bath/shower; TV in both bedrooms   TERMS: single occupancy £26, double £36–£44; deposit   CARDS: none   DETAILS: no children under 5; no dogs; no smoking; car park; garden

The Red House

Sidmouth Road, Lyme Regis DT7 3ES
TEL/FAX: (01297) 442055

This large 1920s house stands above Lyme Regis in an extensive garden, adjacent to open countryside. It enjoys spectacular views of the coast and is within walking distance of the town centre and picturesque harbour. It was built for a distinguished mariner and is now kept ship-shape by a retired naval officer and his wife. A balcony runs around the front, with tables and chairs for sitting out on warm days. The three large, comfortable bedrooms have attic-type sloping ceilings, and all have private bathrooms.

OWNERS: Tony and Vicky Norman   OPEN: Mar to Nov   ROOMS: 1 double, 2 twin; all rooms with bath/shower; TV in all bedrooms   TERMS: single occupancy £30–£35, twin/double £36–£48; reductions for children over 8 sharing with parents; deposit: 15% CARDS: none   DETAILS: no children under 8; no dogs; no smoking; car park; garden

Willow Cottage

Ware Lane, Lyme Regis DT7 3EL
TEL: (01297) 443199

Formerly owners of the Red House (see entry, above), a short distance away, the Griffins have recently moved to much smaller premises. Willow Cottage stands on a quiet country lane with lovely sea views. Guests have their own wing of the house, which includes a double *en suite* bedroom, with balcony to take advantage of the view, and a single room which can only be let to a third member of a family or a party, as it shares the shower room and TV with the double. The Griffins are very friendly people, and guests are made to feel very welcome. Breakfast only is served.

OWNERS: Geoffrey and Elizabeth Griffin OPEN: Mar to Nov ROOMS: 1 single; 1 double, with shower; TV in double bedroom TERMS: single £20, double £48 CARDS: none
DETAILS: no children under 8; no dogs; car park; garden

LYMINGTON Hampshire   map 2

Wheatsheaf

25 Gosport Street, Lymington SO41 9BG
TEL: (01590) 679208

Originally a coaching-inn, this attractive listed seventeenth-century building can be found right in the centre of Lymington. One enters the house straight into the sitting-room, an unusual and lovely room with a fireplace on each side, beams, brick pillars and a wooden floor. The house has a warm and friendly atmosphere and is furnished as a family home, with ornaments and antique furniture. Double glazing in the front of the house helps to minimise any noise from the street. Wheatsheaf is an ideal place to explore this delightful old market town, and is convenient for ferries to the Isle of Wight.

OWNERS: Jennifer and Peter Cutmore OPEN: all year exc Christmas ROOMS: 2 double, 2 twin, 2 family; all rooms with bath/shower; TV lounge TERMS: single occupancy £30, twin/double £50, family room terms on application; deposit: 25% CARDS: none
DETAILS: children welcome; dogs by prior arrangement; no smoking; car park

LYNTON Devon   map 1

Fernleigh

15 Park Street, Lynton EX35 6BY
TEL: (01598) 753575

Purpose-built as a guesthouse in 1986, Fernleigh stands on a quiet side street within walking distance of restaurants, pubs, shops and the harbour. The Emersons, who have run the guesthouse since 1992, previously had a bed and breakfast in Blackpool and are happy to provide local information and arrange walks for guests. The house has a comfortable, warm and homely atmosphere, is immaculately clean and has been attractively furnished. The six bedrooms are all *en suite* and well-appointed. Both breakfast and evening meals are served at separate tables in the dining-room, which overlooks the garden. Vegetarians can be catered for, and, as Fernleigh is unlicensed, guests may bring their own wine to dinner. Packed lunches can be provided.

OWNERS: Pat and Terry Emerson OPEN: Mar to Nov ROOMS: 4 double, 2 twin, all with bath/shower; TV in all bedrooms TERMS: single occupancy £18 (low season only), twin/double £30–£36; children's reductions; dinner £8 to £10; deposit: £10 per person CARDS: none DETAILS: no children under 12; small dogs welcome; no smoking; car park; garden

---

MACCLESFIELD Cheshire   map 8

Chadwick House

55 Beech Lane, Macclesfield SK10 2DS
TEL: (01625) 615558

This efficiently run house is a pleasant Victorian property close to the town centre. Nearly all the rooms have *en suite* facilities, and all are colour co-ordinated and have Sky TV. The luxury suite has a four-poster bed with a white lace canopy. The house is licensed, and guests have the use of two lounges, one with a bar and the other with a TV. Dinner is served at 7pm, and vegetarians can be catered for with advance notice. Packed lunches can be arranged.

OWNERS: William and Karen Danson OPEN: all year ROOMS: 5 single, 3 with bath/shower, 2 with wash-basin; 5 double, all with bath/shower; 2 twin, 1 with bath/shower, 1 with wash-basin; 1 four-poster, with bath/shower; TV in all bedrooms and lounge TERMS: single £25–£35, single occupancy £40, twin/double/four-poster £55; children's reductions by arrangement; dinner £9; deposit CARDS: Access, Amex, Diners, Visa DETAILS: children welcome; no dogs; smoking in TV lounge only; car park

---

MACCLESFIELD FOREST Cheshire   map 8

Hardingland Farm

Macclesfield Forest, Macclesfield SK11 0ND
TEL: (01625) 425759
heading out of Macclesfield on A537, turn right opposite millstone 100yds after Setter Dog pub and follow B&B signs

---

Hardingland Farm is a beautifully furnished Georgian house in a remote and peaceful spot with stunning views of the Cheshire plains and the Welsh mountains. The spacious house is tastefully furnished in Georgian style. The bathrooms are large and one bedroom has an antique French bed. The guest lounge is very comfortable. Anne Read is a fully trained caterer and offers three-course gourmet dinners by arrangement, with vegetarian and special diets catered for. Guests may bring their own wine to complement the meal. This is a wonderful place from which to explore the Peak District.

OWNER: Anne Read OPEN: Mar to Nov ROOMS: 1 double, with bath/shower; 2 twin, 1 with bath/shower, 1 with wash-basin; TV lounge TERMS: single occupancy £30–£40, twin/double £36–£44; dinner £13; deposit £20 CARDS: none DETAILS: no children; no dogs; no smoking; car park; garden

MAIDENHEAD   Berkshire   **map 3**

Beehive Manor

Cox Green Lane, Maidenhead SL6 3ET
TEL: (01628) 20890
off M4 at junction 8 / 9, then A404(M) till left turn for Cox Green

This beautiful medieval manor stands in a lovely peaceful garden,
but is only 15 minutes from Heathrow Airport. Many original
features have been retained such as the thick stone walls, oak-
panelled doors and carved stone fireplaces, and the spacious
bedrooms are tastefully decorated in soft colours. The cosy beamed
drawing-room has TV, and there is a separate dining-room where an
extensive cooked breakfast is served at one large table. For evening
meals, a nearby pub is within walking distance, and a selection of
local restaurant menus is available. Beehive Manor is very
convenient for the Thames Valley, including Henley, Ascot and
Windsor.

OWNERS: Bar Barbour and Sue Lemin   OPEN: all year exc Christmas   ROOMS: 2 double,
1 twin; all rooms with bath/shower; TV lounge   TERMS: single occupancy £36, twin/
double £56   DETAILS: no children under 12; no dogs; no smoking; car park; garden

MAIDSTONE   Kent   **map 3**

Willington Court

Willington Street, Maidstone ME15 8JW
TEL: (01622) 738885   FAX: (01622) 631790
*1½m E of Maidstone at junction of A20 Ashford Road and Willington
Street*

Although the appearance of this Grade II listed building is Tudor, it
was in fact built only 100 years ago from old materials. The house
stands on a grassy bank above the Ashford road and is a mile and a
half east of Maidstone town centre. There is a carved oak staircase
and an inglenook fireplace in the dining-room, where breakfast only
is served. One of the three comfortable bedrooms has a four-poster
bed, and there are two lounges for guests to use, one for smokers.
Leeds Castle and Mote Park are nearby.

OWNERS: Mandy and David Waterman   OPEN: all year   ROOMS: 1 double, 1 twin, 1 four-
poster; all with bath/shower; TV in all bedrooms and lounge   TERMS: single occupancy
£25–£33, twin/double £38–£42, four-poster £46; deposit: £10 per person   CARDS:
Access, Amex, Diners, Visa   DETAILS: no children; no dogs; smoking in 1 lounge only;
car park; garden

MALPAS   Cheshire   map 7

Laurel Farm

Chorlton Lane, Malpas SY14 7ES
TEL/FAX: (01948) 860291
*on B5069 1m W of Malpas, turn at sign for Chorlton then turn right
after 1m*

This large red-brick farmhouse stands in nine and a half acres that
include a duck pond with well-established reed beds. It is elegantly
furnished throughout with period furniture and stripped pine. The
oldest part of the house is the entrance hall, which has a Welsh
quarry tile floor. One bedroom is on the ground floor and there is a
sun lounge with TV. Friendly Anthea Few creates a free and easy
atmosphere and is adept at making guests feel welcome. She cooks
breakfast and light snacks on the Aga, and serves dinner by
arrangement for parties of four or more. There is also an excellent
range of pubs and restaurants two miles away in Malpas.

OWNER: Anthea Few   OPEN: all year   ROOMS: 2 double, 1 twin, 1 twin/family; all rooms
with bath/shower; TV in all bedrooms   TERMS: single occupancy £40, twin/double
£50–£55, family room £65–£72; dinner £20; deposit: 25%   CARDS: none   DETAILS: no
children under 12; no dogs; no smoking; car park; garden

MALPAS   Cornwall   map 1

Woodbury

Malpas, nr Truro TR1 1SQ
TEL: (01872) 71466
2m SE of Truro

Woodbury stands just above a narrow dead-end road which follows
the river from Truro. The house has lovely views and is surrounded
by a garden, where guests can relax. The sitting-room leads through
to a large sun-porch/conservatory where breakfast and dinner are
served and which overlooks the river; as the house is not licensed,
guests are welcome to bring their own wine to dinner. The three
small, simply furnished bedrooms all have river views and share a
large bathroom. A billiard table and dartboard are also available for
guests to use. Packed lunches can be provided. There is a pub serving
food in the village, only a few minutes' walk away.

OWNER: Marion Colwill   OPEN: all year exc Christmas   ROOMS: 1 single, 2 double; TV
lounge   TERMS: single £14, single occupancy £18.50, double £33; dinner £9.50; deposit
CARDS: none   DETAILS: children welcome; no dogs; smoking in lounge or conservatory
only; car park; garden

Mellbreak

177 Wells Road, Malvern Wells WR13 5DZ
TEL: (01684) 561287
on A449 road to Great Malvern

Mellbreak is on the main road just beyond the Three Counties
Agricultural showground. It is a detached listed property dating from
1830 and was once the home of the headmaster of Wells House
School. The house is surrounded by a terraced garden, and has fine
views over the Severn and Avon valleys. The interior contains a
varied selection of furniture, paintings and ornaments. The
comfortable bedrooms are attractively decorated and there is a large
guest lounge with TV, books and a log fire in winter. Mrs Cheeseman
prepares evening meals from traditional recipes and there is a
comprehensive cellar of 300 wines from around the world; packed
lunches can be provided.

OWNER: Mrs R.A. Cheeseman OPEN: all year ROOMS: 1 single, 2 double, 1 twin; all
rooms with bath/shower; TV in all bedrooms and lounge TERMS: single £21; twin/
double £42; babies free, children under 8 half-price; dinner £12.50; deposit: 50%
CARDS: none DETAILS: well-behaved children welcome; no dogs; smoking in lounge
only; car park; garden

Old Vicarage

Hanley Road, Malvern Wells WR14 4PH
TEL: (01684) 572585
*from Great Malvern, take A449 Wells road, turn left down B4209 Hanley
road*

The Old Vicarage is an elegant Victorian house situated on the slopes
of the Malvern Hills overlooking the Severn vale. It is in a quiet side
street within walking distance of the Three Counties Agricultural
showground. The house is in excellent decorative order, with stripped
pine doors. The spacious bedrooms are warm and comfortable and
have good-sized bathrooms. There is a large sitting-room with lots of
brooks to browse through. Dinner is available, if pre-arranged, the
house is licensed and packed lunches can be provided.

OWNER: Michael Gorvin OPEN: all year ROOMS: 3 double, 2 twin, 1 family; all rooms
with bath/shower; 1 room suitable for wheelchair-users; TV in all bedrooms TERMS:
single occupancy £28–£32, twin/double £44–£46, family room £52–£56; free for
children under 5, reductions by arrangement for children over 5; dinner £15 CARDS:
none DETAILS: children welcome; no dogs in dining-room or lounge; no smoking in
dining-room; car park; garden

Castle Gayer

Leys Lane, Marazion TR17 0AQ
TEL: (01736) 711548
off A30, 2m E of Penzance

Castle Gayer is a whitewashed Victorian property, formerly a sea
captain's house, standing high up on the edge of a cliff, looking out
over St Michael's Mount and having sea views nearly all the way
around. A quiet lane leads to the village. At the bottom of the garden
is a small listed folly, which resembles the top of a lighthouse. The
two comfortable bedrooms are reached via a narrow staircase off the
dining-room, where breakfast only is served. The lounge has a log
fire, baby-grand piano and views of the Mount. Brian Ivory carries
out his chiropody practice from the house, and John Trewhella has
his psychology practice here.

OWNERS: T.M.J. Trewhella and B.S. Ivory   OPEN: all year exc Christmas and New Year
ROOMS: 2 double; both rooms with bath/shower; TV in both bedrooms   TERMS: single
occupancy £25, double £45; deposit: £20 per person   CARDS: none   DETAILS: no
children; no dogs; no smoking; car park; garden

Merzie Meadows

Hunton Road, Chainhurst, Marden TN12 9SL
TEL: (01622) 820500
*from A229 Maidstone to Hastings road take B2079 to Marden; then first
right Pattendane Lane for 2m; after Chainhurst sign turn right into drive*

This ranch-style stone and weather-boarded bungalow is set in open
countryside in 20 acres of grounds. Mrs Mumford is a charming,
enthusiastic host and the house is beautifully furnished and
decorated. The guest accommodation is on the ground floor, in one
wing of the house, with doors out to the garden and unheated
swimming-pool. Breakfast only is served in the garden room
overlooking the pool. Merzie Meadows is near Leeds and Sissinghurst
castles, and Rye.

OWNERS: Rodney and Pamela Mumford   OPEN: all year exc Christmas   ROOMS: 1
double, 1 family; both rooms with bath/shower; TV in one bedroom and lounge   TERMS:
single occupancy £30, double £36–£40, family room from £51; reductions for children
over 12 in family room; deposit: £5 per person   CARDS: none   DETAILS: no children
under 12; no dogs; no smoking; car park; garden; swimming-pool

MARGARET RODING   Essex   **map 3**

Greys

Ongar Road, Margaret Roding, nr Great Dunmow CM6 1QR
TEL: 0245 231509
by A1060 in village

Greys used to be two 200-year-old beamed farm cottages. It is situated in an acre of gardens in this unspoilt area of Essex, surrounded by its own farmland, which guests are encouraged to look round. Apart from the three bright and clean bedrooms, guests have a choice of the lounge/dining-room with TV or a quiet sitting-room. Geoffrey and Joyce Matthews are retired and work as a team to provide a warm welcome in their home. Breakfast only is served but there are several eating places nearby.

OWNER: Joyce Matthews   OPEN: all year exc Christmas   ROOMS: 2 double, 1 with wash-basin; 1 twin, with wash-basin; TV lounge   TERMS: single occupancy £20, twin/double £37   CARDS: none   DETAILS: no children under 10; no dogs; no smoking; car park; garden

MARHAMCHURCH   Cornwall   **map 1**

Old Rectory

Marhamchurch EX23 0ER
TEL: (01288) 361379

This lovely Georgian house set in its own garden is in the village of Marhamchurch, just a couple of miles from Bude, which can be reached along canal bank paths. The house is attractively furnished and decorated, and guests have use of a large sitting-room. Breakfast and evening meals are available in the dining-room. From Bude itself the coastal path walk provides wonderful views.

OWNER: Mrs J.R. Pengelly   OPEN: all year exc Christmas   ROOMS: 2 double, 1 twin; all rooms with bath/shower; TV in all bedrooms and lounge   TERMS: single occupancy £30, twin/double £56; £18 for children over 5; dinner £12; deposit: 10%   CARDS: none   DETAILS: no children under 5; no dogs; no smoking; car park; garden

It is always best to book a room in advance, even in winter. B&Bs with few rooms may close at short notice for periods not specified in the details.

We asked the proprietors to estimate their 1996 prices in the autumn of 1995, so the rates may have changed since publication.

Most establishments have central heating. When we know this is not the case, we mention this in the entry.

MARNHULL   Dorset   map 2

Old Lamb House

Walton Elm, Marnhull, nr Sturminster Newton DT10 1QG
TEL: (01258) 820491   FAX: (01258) 821464
*on B3092 at Walton Elm crossroads, ½m S of Marnhull and 2½m N of
Sturminster Newton*

Old Lamb House is an attractive stone Georgian house set in quiet
countryside with views across the Blackmoor Vale to Cranborne
Chase. It was once a coaching-inn and is reputed to be 'Rollivers' in
Hardy's *Tess of the d'Urbervilles*. The interior is attractively
decorated and spacious. The two bedrooms have easy chairs and TV
and share a bathroom. Guests can relax in the elegant drawing-room
or in the pretty conservatory and are welcome to use the garden. A
games room and tennis court next door are available at a small
charge. Breakfast can either be taken in the dining-room overlooking
the walled garden or in the bedrooms. There are several pubs in the
vicinity serving food, and Shaftesbury, Sherborne and Blandford
Forum are all within easy driving distance.

OWNER: Mrs J.J. Chilcott   OPEN: all year exc Christmas   ROOMS: 1 double, 1 family; TV
in both bedrooms   TERMS: single occupancy £20, double £34, family room from £34;
children under 3 free, £12 for ages 3 to 10; deposit: 33%   CARDS: none   DETAILS:
children welcome; no dogs; no smoking; car park; garden

MARTOCK   Somerset   map 2

Wychwood

7 Bearley Road, Martock TA12 6PG
TEL: (01935) 825601
off B3165, 6m NW of Yeovil

Mrs Turton more than makes up for this modern house's location in a
suburban development. She is knowledgeable, chatty and does
everything possible to make sure her guests have a pleasant and
interesting time. The three bedrooms have lots of useful items and
are either *en suite* or have private bathrooms. Dinner is by
arrangement at 7pm; vegetarian dishes can be requested and, as
there is no alcohol licence, diners may bring their own wine. The TV
lounge is comfortable and cheerful, and there are videos of the area
featuring interesting gardens and stately homes, such as Montacute
House and Barrington Court.

OWNERS: Norman and Helen Turton   OPEN: all year exc Christmas and New Year
ROOMS: 2 double, 1 twin; all rooms with bath/shower; TV in all bedrooms and lounge
TERMS: single occupancy £24–£28; twin/double £34–£38; dinner £13.50; deposit: £5
per person per night   CARDS: Access, Delta, Visa   DETAILS: no children; no dogs; no
smoking; car park; garden

MATLOCK   Derbyshire   **map 9**

Bradvilla

26 Chesterfield Road, Matlock DL4 3DQ
TEL: (01629) 57147

This well-kept Victorian house offering good-value accommodation
stands in its own grounds five minutes from the town centre – or ten
minutes, walking back up the hill. There are several steps up to the
house, making it essential that those coming to stay are fairly fit. One
of the two double bedrooms has an adjacent bathroom and small
sitting-room. Breakfast only is served. Jean Saunders is friendly and
helpful, and makes guests feel at home.

OWNER: Jean Saunders   OPEN: all year exc Christmas   ROOMS: 2 double, 1 with bath/
shower, 1 with wash-basin; TV in both bedrooms   TERMS: double £30–£33; £8 for
children under 10, £10 for children over 10; deposit required for advanced bookings
CARDS: none   DETAILS: children welcome; no dogs; smoking in conservatory only; car
park; garden

Kensington Villa

84 Dale Road, Matlock DE4 3LU
TEL: (01629) 57627

If one thing makes this Victorian guesthouse special, it is the warm
and friendly couple who own it. They have created a 'home from
home' atmosphere in a town-centre property with bright, fresh and
clean rooms. There are several steps on the approach to the house
which make it unsuitable for infirm people. Generous breakfasts
start the day in the sunny dining-room, which looks out on the small
patio garden in which guests may relax on sunny days.

OWNERS: Bill and Val Gorman   OPEN: all year exc Christmas   ROOMS: 2 double, 1 twin;
all rooms with wash-basin; TV in all bedrooms   TERMS: single occupancy £16–£17;
twin/double £32–£34; children under 3 free, half-price for ages 3 to 11   CARDS: none
DETAILS: children welcome; no dogs; no smoking; car park; garden

Sunnybank

37 Clifton Road, Matlock DE4 3PW
TEL: (01629) 584621

Sunnybank, built as a 'gentleman's residence' in 1883, is situated in a
secluded cul-de-sac in peaceful surroundings with views of Wild Cat
Tor and Cromford Moor. It is full of character and has a most
attractive ceiling rose and coving in the beautiful lounge, where log
fires burn on chilly days. The well-appointed bedrooms are tastefully
furnished and the rooms to the rear have garden views. The house is
warm and welcoming, and excellent breakfasts and dinners,

featuring old-fashioned cooking with mouth-watering puddings such as rhubarb crumble, are available. Tea can be taken in the lovely gardens on pleasant days.

OWNERS: Peter and Daphne West OPEN: all year exc Christmas ROOMS: 1 single, with wash-basin; 2 double, both with bath/shower; 2 twin, 1 with bath/shower, 1 with wash-basin; TV in some bedrooms and lounge TERMS: single £22, single occupancy £26–£29, twin/double £44–£50; dinner £13.50; deposit: £10 per person CARDS: Access, Amex, Visa DETAILS: no children under 10; no dogs; no smoking; garden

MAWNAN SMITH   Cornwall   map 1

Carwinion

Mawnan Smith, nr Falmouth TR11 5JA
TEL: (01326) 250258
from A394 near junction with A39 follow signs for Mabe and then Mawnan Smith; at Mawnan Smith turn left at Red Lion pub, continue for 500yds

Carwinion is a delightful country house lying on the edge of the small village of Mawnan Smith and is in a beautiful part of south Cornwall. The ten-acre garden which surrounds the house is open to the public, and has one of the finest collections of bamboos in the UK, originated by Anthony Rogers's grandfather. The house is an informal, comfortable and lived-in family home and has large rooms. The bedrooms all have *en suite* bathrooms and some enjoy the lovely views. Guests have use of a large drawing-room, and a room leading out to the garden that is warmed with an open fire in winter and where cream teas are served in summer. Evening meals with vegetarian options are served by arrangement in the formal dining-room and guests are welcome to bring their own wine.

OWNER: Anthony Rogers OPEN: all year ROOMS: 1 double, 3 twin; all rooms with bath/shower; 3 rooms suitable for wheelchair-users; TV in all bedrooms and lounge TERMS: single occupancy £25, twin/double £50; babies free, half-price for children; dinner £12.50 CARDS: none DETAILS: children welcome; dogs welcome; car park; games room; garden

MAYFIELD   Staffordshire   map 5

Lichfield House

Bridge View, Mayfield, nr Ashbourne DE6 2HN
TEL/FAX: (01335) 344422
off A52 Ashbourne to Leek road take Mayfield road 1½m from Ashbourne, then 300yds up hill to first house on left

Lichfield House is a beautifully maintained Georgian building in two acres of landscaped gardens in an elevated position with superb views of the River Dove below. Improvements are ongoing, and new carpets have been fitted in the bedrooms and dining-room. The large, well-appointed bedrooms are all decorated in soft pastels. Breakfast only is served in the dining-room, which has antique pine furniture. There is also an elegant lounge with a green and pink décor. The Tissington trail is an interesting walk nearby and the short walk to the village is along the river. Packed lunches can be provided. Self-catering accommodation is also available.

OWNERS: Mr and Mrs K. Mellor OPEN: all year exc Christmas and Boxing Day ROOMS: 1 single, with wash-basin; 1 double, with bath/shower; 1 twin, with wash-basin; 1 family, with bath/shower; TV in all bedrooms and lounge TERMS: single £18–£20, single occupancy £20–£25, twin/double £37–£40, family room from £45; children's reductions according to age; deposit: £10 CARDS: none DETAILS: children welcome; no dogs; no smoking; car park; garden

MELTON MOWBRAY Leicestershire map 5

Quorn Lodge

46 Asfordby Road, Melton Mowbray LE13 0HR
TEL: (01664) 66660 FAX: (01664) 480660

This nineteenth-century hunting lodge has been extensively refurbished and extended in recent years. It is well maintained and comfortable, with spacious rooms, attractively decorated around a theme of peach and pink tones. All bedrooms are furnished to a high standard with facilities which include hair-dryer and direct-dial phone. The staircase to the upstairs rooms is something of a feature with its galleried landing. Three ground-floor rooms are suitable for wheelchair-users. The lounge/bar has real fires and the licensed dining-room operates at breakfast, lunch and dinner, always with vegetarian options. This is a popular destination, especially for business travellers who can take advantage of the fax, photocopying and secretarial services offered.

OWNERS: John and Julie Sturt OPEN: all year ROOMS: 2 single, 8 double, 8 twin, 1 four-poster; all rooms with bath/shower; 3 rooms suitable for wheelchair-users; TV in all bedrooms and lounge TERMS: single £35–£43, single occupancy £45, twin/double £40–£55, four-poster £59; £10 for children sharing with parents; dinner £13; deposit: £15 CARDS: Access, Delta, Switch, Visa DETAILS: children welcome; dogs by arrangement; no smoking in some rooms; car park; garden

Any smoking restrictions that we know of are given in the details at the end of the entry.

Please let us know if you think a B&B should be included in this Guide. Report forms are at the back of the book – or use your own stationery if you prefer (no stamps are needed within the UK).

MENDHAM   Norfolk   map 6

Weston House Farm

Mendham, Harleston IP20 0PB
TEL: (01986) 782206
on A143 Harleston bypass turn at sign for Mendham then follow signs for farm from the village

A private driveway leads through farmland up to this 300-year-old listed farmhouse with Dutch-style gable ends. The remote location makes this an ideal spot for getting away from it all. June Holden has been running this successful establishment for over 15 years and she extends a warm welcome and keeps the bedrooms spotlessly clean. The lounge has a well-stocked bookcase for guests who prefer not to switch on the TV. Fishing is available on the River Waveney two miles away and the Norfolk Broads are within easy driving distance.

OWNER: June Holden   OPEN: all year exc Christmas   ROOMS: 2 twin, 1 family; all rooms with bath/shower; TV lounge   TERMS: single occupancy £18–£21, twin £32–£36, family room £40–£54; half-price for children under 12 in family room; dinner £10; deposit: 20%   CARDS: Amex   DETAILS: children welcome; dogs by arrangement; no smoking; car park; garden

MENDLESHAM GREEN   Suffolk   map 6

Cherry Tree Farm

Mendlesham Green, nr Stowmarket IP14 5RQ
TEL: (01449) 766376
off A140 Needham Market to Norwich road

This restored fifteenth-century timber-framed Suffolk farmhouse is set in an unspoilt hamlet, surrounded by a large garden with an orchard and duck pond. The house is immaculate and prettily decorated. All the bedrooms are now *en suite*; one has a beamed sloping roof and oak furnishings and overlooks the garden. The guest lounge has an inglenook fireplace with a log-fire blazing on chilly days. The dining-room has been restored to its original style and has exposed beams, and meals are served round a refectory table. Food is a feature here, using vegetables from the garden, home-baked bread and free-range eggs. An interesting selection of local wines is also available.

OWNERS: Martin and Diana Ridsdale   OPEN: all year exc Christmas and New Year ROOMS: 3 double; all rooms with bath/shower; TV lounge   TERMS: single occupancy £30–£35, double £42–£50; deposit; dinner £15   CARDS: none   DETAILS: no children; no dogs; smoking in lounge only; car park; garden

MEVAGISSEY Cornwall   map 1

Southcliffe

Polkirt Hill, Mevagissey PL26 6UX
TEL: (01726) 842505
just off B3273, 6m S of St Austell

This friendly guesthouse can be found on the cliff road just outside
the pretty town of Mevagissey. It has lovely sea views and there is a
beach at Portmellon, only a five-minute walk away. The bedrooms
have views of St Austell Bay and the headland at Chapel Point. The
large lounge, the dining-room, where four-course evening meals are
served by arrangement, and the attractive terraced garden also enjoy
sea views. A self-catering flat is in part of the building, with its own
entrance.

OWNERS: Ronald Haskins and David Templeton OPEN: all year exc Christmas ROOMS:
3 double, 1 twin; all rooms with wash-basin; TV in all bedrooms TERMS: single
occupancy £15.50–£21.50, twin/double £31–£33; dinner £11; deposit: £10 per person
CARDS: none DETAILS: no children under 14; no dogs; car park; garden

MEYSEY HAMPTON Gloucestershire   map 2

Old Rectory

Meysey Hampton, nr Cirencester GL7 5JX
TEL/FAX: (01285) 851200
off A417 Cirencester to Lechlade road

Standing in two acres of lovely landscaped gardens in a quiet
Cotswold village is this elegant, listed seventeenth-century rectory.
Owner Caroline Carne extends a warm welcome to her guests and
nothing is too much trouble to ensure their comfort. Freshly prepared
breakfasts only are served in the dining-room/lounge, which has
comfortable chairs and a TV. For evening meals, there is a pub
serving good food within walking distance. Guests are welcome to use
the garden and swimming-pool on summer days.

OWNERS: Mr and Mrs R. Carne OPEN: Feb to Nov ROOMS: 1 double, 1 twin; both
rooms with bath/shower; TV lounge TERMS: single occupancy £28–£30, twin/double
£42–£45, twin/double as family room £55; babies under 2 free (charge for cot £5), older
children's reductions according to age; deposit: £10 CARDS: none DETAILS: children
welcome; no dogs; no smoking; car park; garden; swimming-pool

*Entries in the Guide are listed under town or village. There are also two
indexes at the back of the book, one listing B&Bs by county, the other by
name.*

MILFORD ON SEA   Hampshire   map 2

Seawinds

Westminster Road, Milford on Sea SO41 0WU
TEL: (01590) 644548
off B3058, 1m W of village

This comfortably furnished modern house is a few yards from the
clifftop and beach. The Crunkhorns are a very hospitable couple who
keep their guesthouse immaculately clean. Breakfast is served in the
dining-room, which looks out on the garden. The attractive town and
sailing centre of Lymington is nearby.

OWNERS: Eric and Joy Crunkhorn   OPEN: all year   ROOMS: 1 double, 1 twin; both rooms
with bath/shower; TV in both bedrooms   TERMS: single occupancy £28, twin/double
£40; deposit: 10%   CARDS: none   DETAILS: no children; no dogs; no smoking; car park;
garden

MILLOM   Cumbria   map 8

Buckman Brow House

Thwaites, Millom LA18 5HX
TEL: (01229) 716541
on A595, 2m SW of Broughton-in-Furness

With marvellous views of the Duddon Valley, this former schoolhouse
(and, later, family home) was built in 1845. The bedrooms are
impeccably furnished and decorated; one is on the ground floor and is
suitable for wheelchair-users. The dining-room/lounge is huge, and is
where guests can enjoy breakfast as well as evening meals; both
residents and non-residents are welcome at dinner, so it is always
best to book ahead. Evening meals are six courses and include
vegetarian choices; the house is unlicensed, but guests may bring
their own wine to dinner. Packed lunches can be provided. From the
lounge guests can enjoy watching the many varieties of birds that
come to feed on the terrace.

OWNER: Gwen R. Dunn   OPEN: all year exc Christmas   ROOMS: 2 double, both with
bath/shower; 1 twin; 1 family; 1 room suitable for wheelchair-users; TV in all bedrooms
TERMS: single occupancy £30, twin/double £45, family room £45; children under 3 free,
half-price for ages 3 to 10; dinner £17.50; deposit: 10%   CARDS: none   DETAILS:
children welcome; no dogs; no smoking; car park; garden

*If a B&B caters for vegetarians, we note this in the entry. It is always best,
however, to check when booking and make it clear what your requirements
are, especially if you require a special diet.*

Please let us know if an establishment has changed hands.

MINCHINHAMPTON   Gloucestershire   **map 2**

Hunters Lodge

Dr Brown's Road, Minchinhampton, nr Stroud GL6 9BT
TEL: (01453) 883588   FAX: (01453) 731449
off A419 / A46, 3m SE of Stroud

This beautiful Cotswold-stone house built in the early 1900s stands
in an acre of landscaped gardens, adjoining 600 acres of National
Trust land and a golf course. Hunters Lodge is luxuriously appointed
and the three large bedrooms are decorated in soft pastel colours:
pink, peach and green. One has *en suite* facilities, the others both
have their own bathrooms. The house is warm and inviting and
furnished partly with antiques. The TV sitting-room leads on to a
conservatory and there are two stone fireplaces. Excellent freshly
prepared breakfasts are served at a refectory table overlooking the
garden. Mr and Mrs Helm are welcoming hosts, and Mr Helm is
happy to assist guests with what to see and do in the area.

OWNER: Margaret Helm   OPEN: all year exc Christmas   ROOMS: 1 double, 1 twin, 1
family; all rooms with bath/shower; TV in all bedrooms and lounge   TERMS: single
occupancy £25–£27, twin/double £36–£42, family room £50–£54; deposit: £10
DETAILS: children welcome; no dogs; smoking in lounge only; car park; garden

MINEHEAD   Somerset   **map 1**

Hindon Farm

Minehead TA24 8SH
TEL/FAX: (01643) 705244
*take A39 from Minehead to Porlock, then turn right after 1m signposted
Bratton, over stream and signpost to Hindon Farm at junction*

Hindon Farm dates from the late seventeenth/early eighteenth
century and is tucked away behind the cliffs of the beautiful Somerset
coast in lovely countryside. The attractive and well-kept house has a
very relaxed family atmosphere. The Webbers have farmed here for
three generations and it is an idyllic farm setting with sheep, pigs,
goats, horses, cows and poultry. There is a donkey, riding can be
arranged and there is also stabling for visitors' horses. The three
pretty bedrooms share the guests' bathroom. Breakfast and
occasional evening meals, by arrangement, are served in the dining-
room, which has dark wood flooring and an open fireplace; the lounge
has a TV and games and is shared with the family. Packed lunches
can be provided and self-catering accommodation is also available.

OWNERS: Roger and Penny Webber   OPEN: all year exc Christmas and New Year
ROOMS: 2 double, 1 twin; all with wash-basin; TV lounge   TERMS: single occupancy
£20–£24, twin/double £36–£40; £15 for children under 10; dinner £15; deposit: 25%
CARDS: none   DETAILS: children welcome; dogs welcome; no smoking; car park; games
room; garden; swimming-pool

271

MITCHELDEAN   Gloucestershire   map 5

Gunn Mill House

Lower Spout Lane, Mitcheldean GL17 0EA
TEL: (01594) 827577
from A48 6m SW of Gloucester turn at sign for Mitcheldean, then straight over Y-junction after 2½m up unmade road

This splendid Georgian house stands in a tranquil setting by the old mill – an ancient monument – in five acres of grounds that include a meadow and a stream. David Anderson is in the film industry and he and Caroline have named the bedrooms after famous actors and actresses. The Lansbury, Connery and Chevalier rooms are all elegantly furnished with large, old-fashioned *en suite* bathrooms. Items of interest collected from around the world are displayed around the house. The Andersons are keen cooks and evening meals are a special feature, more like dinner parties, after which guests can curl up in front of a log fire, browsing through the well-stocked bookshelves. Gunn Mill House is licensed and vegetarian meals are available on request. A little extra luxury at breakfast comes in the form of freshly squeezed orange juice and home-made preserves. For the hardy there is an unheated outdoor swimming-pool.

OWNERS: David and Caroline Anderson   OPEN: all year   ROOMS: 2 double, 1 twin; all rooms with bath/shower; TV in all bedrooms   TERMS: single occupancy £24, twin/double £39; £10 for children under 12; dinner £17   CARDS: none   DETAILS: children by arrangement; dogs by arrangement; no smoking; car park; garden; swimming-pool

MOBBERLEY   Cheshire   map 8

Laburnum Cottage

Knutsford Road, Mobberley, nr Knutsford WA16 7PU
TEL/FAX: (01565) 872464
on B5085, 1½m NE of Knutsford

Laburnum Cottage has won no less then six tourism awards, most notably for its beautifully landscaped country garden full of fragrant flowers, in which guests are welcome to wander or even to play croquet. Hanging baskets adorn the entrance and outbuildings of this 1930s country house and even the beds are scented with lavender. The house is luxuriously furnished with each bedroom decorated in co-ordinated fabrics. Home-made jams and an abundance of fresh seasonal fruit grace the table at the generous breakfasts. Guests are treated as visiting friends in the cosy, gentle atmosphere, and there are books to read, porcelain and pictures to look at and a log fire to keep the comfortable lounge warm in winter.

OWNERS: Shirley Foxwell and Malcolm Collinge   OPEN: all year   ROOMS: 2 single, 1 with bath/shower, 1 with wash-basin; 1 double, with bath/shower; 2 twin, both with bath/

shower; TV in all bedrooms and lounge TERMS: single £28–£38, single occupancy £38, twin/double £48; children's reductions by arrangement; deposit: £10 CARDS: none DETAILS: children by arrangement; no dogs; no smoking; car park; garden

MODBURY Devon   map 1

Goutsford

Modbury PL21 9NY
TEL: (01548) 830633
leave A379 2m W of Modbury at sign for Orcheton, take first right into private lane

This attractive old cottage and converted barn is in an isolated and peaceful woodland setting. The Ewens are supremely welcoming and friendly people and go out of their way to ensure their guests have a comfortable stay. The house has its original beams in two of the bedrooms, and the pine and tiled fireplace in the dining-room came from Ted and Maureen's previous house. The large garden, with patio, runs into the woods, where wildlife abounds. The attractive bedrooms have TVs and armchairs, and breakfast only is served. There are many pubs nearby serving food, and Goutsford is in a good area for boating, water sports and walking.

OWNERS: Ted and Maureen Ewen OPEN: all year exc Christmas ROOMS: 1 double, 2 twin; all rooms with bath/shower; TV in all bedrooms TERMS: single occupancy £22, twin/double £34–£36; deposit: £10 CARDS: none DETAILS: no children under 10; no dogs; no smoking; car park; garden

MONKTON COMBE Avon   map 2

Dundas Lock Cottage

Monkton Combe, nr Bath BA2 7BN
TEL: (01225) 723890
just off A36, 5m E of Bath

This rose-and-honeysuckle-covered cottage was built of Bath stone in 1801 for the lockkeeper and his family. Now extended to provide pleasant accommodation, the house has three guest bedrooms that overlook two historic canals – the Somerset Coal and the Kennet & Avon canals. The Wheeldons themselves are great enthusiasts and spent some time restoring the canal through their own garden. Breakfast only is served in the beamed sitting-room.

OWNERS: Tim and Wendy Wheeldon OPEN: all year exc Christmas ROOMS: 1 single, with wash-basin; 1 double, 1 twin; both with bath/shower; TV lounge TERMS: single £20, twin/double £40–£45; deposit: £10–£20 CARDS: none DETAILS: children welcome; no dogs; no smoking; car park; garden

MONKTON FARLEIGH   Wiltshire

map 2

Fern Cottage

Monkton Farleigh, nr Bradford-on-Avon BA15 2QJ
TEL: (01225) 859412   FAX: (01225) 859018
off A363 mid-way between Bath and Bradford-on-Avon

This attractive stone-built listed cottage stands in the main street of the historic conservation village of Monkton Farleigh. The house is surprisingly spacious and has a lovely secluded back garden, a favourite place for guests to sit. The old garage building has a very pretty conservatory to one side of it, which is the guests' sitting-room, and above is a family suite. The other two bedrooms are in the main house and all are extremely comfortable and well equipped. Breakfast is served in the family dining-room. The house is warm and comfortable and the Valentines are a solicitous and welcoming couple. The pub almost opposite the house serves evening meals.

OWNERS: Christopher and Jenny Valentine   OPEN: all year   ROOMS: 3 double, all with bath/shower; TV in all bedrooms   TERMS: single occupancy £25–£30, double £45–£50; children's reductions by arrangement   CARDS: none   DETAILS: children by arrangement; dogs by arrangement; no smoking; car park; garden

MORECAMBE   Lancashire

map 8

Yacht Bay View

359 Marine Road, Promenade, Morecambe LA4 5AQ
TEL: (01524) 414481

This pleasant Victorian house is situated on the promenade. Beryl and Derek Woods have been operating their successful B&B business for the past 25 years. The modestly furnished bedrooms all have TV and six have sea views. Breakfast and home-cooked dinners are available, if pre-arranged, and guests may bring their own wine to dinner. There is also a lounge with an open fire. This is a friendly establishment where guests are well looked after. There is electric storage heating in the public rooms, with individual heaters in the bedrooms.

OWNERS: Beryl and Derek Woods   OPEN: all year exc Christmas   ROOMS: 4 double, 2 twin, 3 family; all rooms with bath/shower; TV in all bedrooms and lounge   TERMS: twin/double £32, family room £40; half-price for children sharing with parents; dinner £5; deposit: £20   CARDS: none   DETAILS: children welcome; small dogs welcome; no smoking in dining-room; garden

---

We asked the proprietors to estimate their 1996 prices in the autumn of 1995, so the rates may have changed since publication.

MORETON Dorset   **map 2**

Vartrees House

Moreton, nr Dorchester DT2 8BE
TEL: (01305) 852704
on B3390, 5m E of Dorchester and ½m S of Moreton station

Vartrees House is a pleasant country house reached down a
rhododendron-lined driveway. Mrs Haggett is a most welcoming lady,
and guests can enjoy the peaceful atmosphere and three-acre garden.
Breakfast only is served in the family dining-room overlooking the
lawns and there is a small sitting-room. Of the simply furnished
bedrooms, the twin with its own shower unit is exceptionally large
and can also be used as a family room. Although dinner is not served,
packed lunches can be made up, and there is a pub within walking
distance serving food.

OWNER: D.M. Haggett   OPEN: all year exc Christmas   ROOMS: 2 double, with wash-
basin; 1 twin, with bath/shower; TV in some bedrooms and lounge   TERMS: single
occupancy £16–£23, twin/double £36–£46, twin as family room £56; deposit   CARDS:
none   DETAILS: no children under 10; no dogs in dining-room; no smoking in bedrooms
or dining-room; car park; garden

MORWENSTOW Cornwall   **map 1**

Old Vicarage

Morwenstow, nr Bude EX23 9SR
TEL: (01288) 331369   FAX: (01288) 356077
*off A39; in Morwenstow follow signs for church, turn right down public
footpath (suitable for car) just before church*

This interesting stone house, built in the 1830s by the eccentric
Victorian poet the Rev R.S. Hawker, stands in a peaceful position on
the coast surrounded by unspoilt National Trust land. The unusual
chimneys, all of which are different, are a feature of the property; one
is a life-sized replica of the Rev Hawker's mother's coffin. A link
footpath from the Coastal Path runs through the attractive grounds,
bringing walkers in a matter of minutes to dramatic sea views. It was
along this path that the Rev Hawker built a small hut out of wood
from shipwrecks where he would write poetry. Many of the
shipwrecked sailors are buried in the churchyard. The tiny village
consists of the vicarage, the church and a tea-shop. The house has an
informal atmosphere, and the Wellbys are welcoming hosts. The
comfortable rooms include a dining-room, where dinner is served by
arrangement, a study with TV and a large selection of books, and a
billiard room. In summer there are tables and chairs in the garden.
Packed lunches can be provided.

OWNERS: Richard and Jill Wellby   OPEN: all year exc Dec   ROOMS: 1 single, 1 double, 1
twin; all rooms with bath/shower   TERMS: single/single occupancy £20, twin/double

£40; half-price for children under 12; dinner £15; deposit: £10 per person CARDS: none DETAILS: children welcome; no dogs; smoking in billiard room and study only; car park; games room; garden

---

MUNDFORD   Norfolk   map 6

Colveston Manor

Mundford, nr Thetford IP26 5HU
TEL: (01842) 878218
from Mundford take A1065 to Swaffham for ½m, signposted on left

---

This chalk-and-red-brick manor is set in extensive grounds with informal gardens inhabited by peacocks, squirrels and rabbits, and is surrounded by arable and livestock farmland. An air of simple elegance pervades: the spacious rooms are beautifully furnished, original fireplaces and a collection of prints are on show, and the antique-furnished lounge has log fires in winter. There is a single room on the ground floor with a bathroom close by, the other three bedrooms are upstairs and share a bathroom except for the four-poster, which is *en suite*. Wendy Allingham is a charming hostess who really enjoys sharing her lovely home with visitors, and is well-known for her cooking – all meals are prepared on the Aga. Guests may bring their own wine to table as there is no licence; vegetarian choices and packed lunches can be requested. Wendy and her husband Edwin join their guests for dinner unless the latter show a desire for privacy.

OWNER: Wendy Allingham OPEN: all year ROOMS: 1 single; 1 double, with wash-basin; 1 twin, with wash-basin; 1 four-poster, with bath/shower; TV in some bedrooms and lounge TERMS: single £18, single occupancy from £25, twin/double from £36, four-poster from £40; dinner £14 CARDS: none DETAILS: no children under 12; dogs by arrangement; no smoking; car park; garden

---

MURSLEY   Buckinghamshire   map 3

Richmond Lodge

Mursley, nr Milton Keynes MK17 0LE
TEL: (01296) 720275
on B4032, 3m E of Winslow

Approached up a tree-lined drive, Richmond Lodge stands in three acres of grounds that include beautiful gardens, paddocks, a grass tennis court that guests may use and an orchard where sheep graze. Christine and Peter Abbey are very welcoming hosts, and treat guests as visiting friends. The three bedrooms are attractively decorated with colour co-ordinated fabrics, and guests have the use of a comfortable lounge. Evening meals, which must be arranged in advance, are served on the patio if weather permits, and breakfasts feature home-made jams. The house is unlicensed, but guests may bring their own wine to dinner. Packed lunches can be provided.

OWNERS: Peter and Christine Abbey   OPEN: all year   ROOMS: 1 double, with wash-basin; 2 twin, 1 with bath/shower, 1 with wash-basin; TV in all bedrooms and lounge   TERMS: single occupancy £28, twin/double £38–£42; children's reductions; dinner £14.50; deposit required   CARDS: none   DETAILS: no children under 7; no dogs; no smoking; car park; garden; tennis

---

NAILSEA   Avon   **map 2**

Highdale Guesthouse

82 Silver Street, Nailsea, nr Bristol BS19 2DS
TEL: (01275) 858004   FAX: (01275) 810175

This detached Victorian house is set in an acre of grounds with an immaculate lawn and colourful borders. Special attention is paid to business guests here: not only are message-taking, photocopying and fax services available, but in addition the guests' lounge is offered as a venue for business meetings during the day and a 24-hour chauffeur service is provided. The spacious colour co-ordinated bedrooms are tastefully furnished. Breakfast is served family-style in the dining-room and features eggs from the owner's chickens. Several pubs and restaurants are nearby for dinner. Nailsea is seven miles from Bristol.

OWNER: Fran Davey   OPEN: all year   ROOMS: 3 double, 1 with bath/shower, 2 with wash-basin; 1 twin, with wash-basin; TV in all bedrooms   TERMS: single occupancy £22.50, twin/double £42; half-price for children under 12   CARDS: none   DETAILS: children welcome; dogs welcome; car park; garden

---

NANTWICH   Cheshire   **map 7**

Stoke Grange Farm

Chester Road, Nantwich CW5 6BT
TEL: (01270) 625525
E of A51, 3m N of Nantwich

This attractive farmhouse, which backs on to the Shropshire Union Canal, has been upgraded recently. It now has an additional bedroom with a balcony that overlooks the canal, the farm's geese and the pony – as well as a sitting-room and conservatory. The bedrooms are large and so are the breakfasts, which can include vegetarian options. Guests are welcome to enjoy the garden, which includes a sailing dinghy converted into a large plant pot. A stroll along the towpath can be combined with an evening meal at the local pub.

OWNER: Georgina West   OPEN: all year   ROOMS: 1 double, with bath/shower; 2 twin, both with bath/shower; 1 family, with wash-basin; TV in all bedrooms and lounge   TERMS: single occupancy £20–£25, twin/double £40; babies free, £10 for children over 5 sharing with parents; deposit: £10 per person   CARDS: none   DETAILS: children welcome; no dogs; car park; games room; garden

Buckle Yeat

Near Sawrey, nr Ambleside LA22 0LF
TEL/FAX: (01539) 436446/436538

This beautifully restored cottage, illustrated in Beatrix Potter's *The Tale of Tom Kitten*, is set in the heart of the Lake District and makes an ideal base for touring. Many original features remain, such as the low oak beams and the flagstone floor in the spacious lounge, where log fires are lit on chilly days. The rooms have been freshly decorated in a chintzy style and have traditional and antique furniture. Front rooms have the best views, but are closer to the road; there is one ground-floor bedroom. Breakfasts include both traditional and vegetarian cooked options, and a tea-shop on the premises serves home-made cakes and light snacks; packed lunches too can be provided. For guests in search of a nearby evening meal there is a pub about 100 yards away in the centre of the village.

OWNERS: Robert James Kirby and Helen Margaret Kirby OPEN: all year ROOMS: 1 single, 4 double, 2 twin, 1 family; all rooms with bath/shower; TV in all bedrooms and lounge TERMS: single £20–£22, single occupancy £30–£35, twin/double £40–£44, family room £50–£60; half-price for children sharing with parents; deposit: £30 per room CARDS: Access, Amex, Delta, Switch, Visa DETAILS: children welcome; no dogs in lounge or dining-room; no smoking in dining-room; car park; garden

High Green Gate

Near Sawrey, nr Ambleside LA22 0LF
TEL: (01539) 436296

High Green is right at the centre of the village, famous for its associations with Beatrix Potter. The converted farmhouse dates from the eighteenth century and stands in its own cottage garden with its magnolia tree and fish pond; guests enjoy sitting out on fine days. Otherwise, a lounge and a TV room offer comfortable places to relax inside. The cottagey bedrooms have the benefit of rich wood furnishings; most have *en suite* facilities and one is on the ground floor. Home-cooked evening meals have lots of fresh vegetables and feature home-made desserts; children's portions, and vegetarian choices with prior notice, are available. Guests may bring their own wine to dinner, since the guesthouse is unlicensed. Packed lunches can be provided.

OWNER: Gillian Fletcher OPEN: Apr to Oct ROOMS: 1 double, with bath/shower; 4 family, 2 with bath/shower, 2 with wash-basin; TV lounge TERMS: single occupancy £22–£25, double £38–£44; family room from about £40; reductions for children; dinner £11; deposit: £5 per person CARDS: none DETAILS: children welcome; dogs welcome; car park; garden

Regency Guest House

Neatishead, nr Norwich NR12 8AD
TEL: (01692) 630233
1m E of A1151 between Wroxham and Stalham

This seventeenth-century house with beamed ceilings is in the centre of Neatishead, a village in the heart of the Broads and not far from the coast with its sandy beaches. The rooms are decorated with quality fabrics and three have new carpets. It is worth trying to book into one with a view of the delightful garden. Large, freshly prepared breakfasts are served at oak tables in the dining-room, which has leather chairs and red velvet curtains, and evening meals are easily found nearby. A sitting-room is available for guests.

OWNERS: Alan and Sue Wrigley   OPEN: all year   ROOMS: 3 double, 2 with bath/shower, 1 with wash-basin; 2 twin, 1 with bath/shower, 1 with wash-basin; 1 family, with bath/shower; TV in all bedrooms   TERMS: single occupancy £20, twin/double £38–£44, family room £50; children's reductions according to age; deposit: £10   CARDS: Diners   DETAILS: children welcome; dogs in bedrooms only; smoking in bedrooms only; car park; garden

Mill House

Badley, nr Needham Market IP6 8RR
TEL: (01449) 720154   FAX: (01449) 720886
from A14 Bury St Edmunds to Ipswich road, take A1120, then turn left on to B1113; house is adjacent to the Roots an' Shoots garden centre

Mill House is a listed sixteenth-century farmhouse set in a pleasant garden in the heart of the Gipping Valley. Avril Hunt is a most accommodating host. There is a very large oak-beamed dining-room/lounge which has an inglenook fireplace. Breakfast, as well as evening meals by arrangement, is served in the dining-room, and guests may bring their own wine to dinner; packed lunches can be provided. The three good-sized bedrooms all have private facilities and one room is on the ground floor.

OWNER: Avril Hunt   OPEN: all year   ROOMS: 1 double, 1 twin, 1 family; all rooms with bath/shower; TV in all bedrooms   TERMS: single occupancy £25, twin/double £35; children under 4 free; £7.50 for ages 5 to 15 sharing with parents; dinner £12.50; deposit: £10   CARDS: none   DETAILS: children welcome; no dogs; no smoking; car park; garden

If there are any bedrooms with TV, we mention this in the details at the end of the entry.

NETHERBURY   Dorset

map 2

Heritage

Netherbury, nr Bridport DT6 5LS
TEL: (01308) 488268
just off A3066 Beaminster to Bridport road

Heritage stands in a quiet and peaceful location on the outskirts of the village of Netherbury. The house was built in the 1940s in Tudor-style and has a lovely garden at the back enclosed by a yew hedge with a patio where guests can sit. The house is run by a charming French lady and is neat and spotlessly clean. The pretty bedrooms share one bathroom between them. A small, comfortable sitting-room with TV leads to the garden, and next door is the dining-room where breakfast and dinner are served. As there is no licence, guests are welcome to bring their own wine to dinner, and packed lunches can be provided on request.

OWNER: M.G. Seymour   OPEN: all year exc Christmas   ROOMS: 1 single, 1 double, 1 twin; TV lounge   TERMS: single/single occupancy £17, twin/double £34; dinner £10; deposit: required if booking in advance   CARDS: none   DETAILS: no children under 7; no dogs; no smoking; car park; garden

NEWLYN EAST   Cornwall

map 1

Degembris Farmhouse

Newlyn East, nr Newquay TR8 5HY
TEL: (01872) 510555   FAX: (01872) 510230
just off A3058 Truro to Newquay road; after Summercourt village take third left signposted Newlyn East, then second lane on left

Degembris is a listed eighteenth-century farmhouse built on the site of an old manor. It is a neat, slate-tile-faced building, part of a 165-acre working arable farm, set in an elevated position with beautiful views over a peaceful wooded valley. The house is bright and cheerful and Kathy Woodley provides a warm welcome. The lounge has TV, books and games, and breakfast and four-course dinners are served in the small dining-room at separate tables; packed lunches can be provided on request. The bedrooms are immaculately clean and freshly decorated, most having lovely views. There is a country trail which can be followed from the farm.

OWNER: Kathy Woodley   OPEN: all year exc Christmas   ROOMS: 1 single, 1 double, both with wash-basin; 1 twin, 2 family, all with bath/shower; TV in all bedrooms and lounge   TERMS: single/single occupancy £18, twin/double £40, family room from £50; half-price for children under 10 sharing with parents; dinner £10; deposit: 25%   CARDS: none   DETAILS: children welcome; no dogs; car park; garden

Trewerry Mill

Trerice, Newlyn East, nr Newquay TR8 5HS
TEL: (01872) 510345
3m S of Newquay

Trewerry Mill stands in a peaceful part of north Cornwall, reached down a series of narrow lanes. Dating from 1639, it is a converted watermill, which was once the corn mill for nearby Trerice country house (owned by the National Trust and open to the public). The mill sits amid five acres of lovely gardens and wild meadow areas rich in wildlife, and it has a sun terrace which overlooks them. The bedrooms are small and clean and the guests' lounge has a large stone fireplace and a view of the mill wheel. Meals, including vegetarian options, are served at separate tables in the licensed dining-room and Cornish cream teas are served in the tea garden.

OWNERS: Rowland and Ethel Grateley OPEN: Easter to Oct ROOMS: 2 single, 3 double, 1 twin; all rooms with wash-basin; TV lounge TERMS: single/single occupancy £15, twin/double £30; half-price for children from 7 to 12; dinner £8; deposit: £10 CARDS: none DETAILS: no children under 7; no dogs; no smoking; car park; garden

NEWMARKET Suffolk   map 6

Derby House

27 Exeter Road, Newmarket CB8 8LL
TEL: (01638) 662887/663969   FAX: (01638) 663969

Derby House was built in 1878 by the famous jockey Fred Archer for his sister. It retains the original pine doors and has an interesting antique umbrella stand. The five bedrooms are comfortable and share the use of two bathrooms and three WCs. Four friendly fox terriers live in the house. It is only a ten-minute walk to the centre of Newmarket.

OWNERS: Roger and Beryl Kay OPEN: all year exc Christmas ROOMS: 1 double, 3 twin, 1 family; all rooms with wash-basin; TV in all bedrooms TERMS: single occupancy £22.50, twin/double £35, family room £55; deposit: 50% of 1 night's charge CARDS: none DETAILS: children welcome; no dogs; no smoking in dining-room; car park

Breakfast at B&Bs tends to mean a cooked breakfast of bacon, eggs and so on. If you prefer a different style of breakfast, it is best to discuss this when you make a booking.

If you disagree with any assessment made in this guide, please write and tell us why. Address your letter to The Good Bed and Breakfast Guide, FREEPOST, 2 Marylebone Road, London NW1 1YN.

Moor Hall

Newney Green, nr Chelmsford CM1 3SE
TEL: (01245) 420814
heading W from Chelmsford on A1060 turn left at Hare and Hounds pub,
first left and left at T-junction, then right 200m after the Duck pub

Medieval and Tudor origins are evident everywhere in this old
farmhouse, which has a wealth of oak beams, panelling and doors,
and several inglenook fireplaces. It stands in open countryside in two
acres of gardens surrounded by 500 acres of arable farmland, and has
an air of tranquility lent by the location and the old-world ambience.
The house is elegantly furnished and the spacious bedrooms are quite
luxurious. Breakfast is served family-style on a refectory table in the
delightful dining-room and the nearby Duck pub is a good spot for
evening meals.

OWNER: Sue Gemmill OPEN: all year exc Christmas ROOMS: 2 family; TV lounge
TERMS: single occupancy £21, family £38–£40 plus children's charge; children under 3
free, £11 for ages 3 to 14 CARDS: none DETAILS: children welcome; no dogs; no
smoking; car park; garden

Great Park Farm

Betty Haunt Lane, Newport PO30 4HR
TEL: (01983) 522945
from Newport take A3054 for 2½m, turn left 500yds after petrol station
into Betty Haunt Lane

Part of a 1,000-acre family-run arable farm, this lovely Georgian
farmhouse offers two double rooms with *en suite* bath or shower and
one twin room with its own bathroom. The farm is set in peaceful
countryside a couple of miles outside Newport and within striking
distance of many of the island's attractions. The panoramic views are
marvellous, and there are lovely country walks nearby. The
Brownriggs provide a warm welcome, and breakfast only is served in
the dining-room; there is also a sitting-room with TV.

OWNER: Sheila A. Brownrigg OPEN: Mar to Oct ROOMS: 2 double, 1 twin, all with bath/
shower; TV lounge TERMS: single occupancy £16.50–£18, twin/double £33–£36; £12
for children over 8; deposit: 10% CARDS: none DETAILS: no children under 8; no dogs;
smoking in lounge only; car park; garden

If we know of any particular payment stipulations, we mention them in the
details at the end of the entry. However, it is always best to check when
booking.

Salween House

7 Watergate Road, Newport PO30 1XN
TEL: (01983) 5234546

This spacious Victorian house has a most attractive back garden and stands in a quiet road only a ten-minute walk to the town centre. Carol Corke is responsible for the décor, and makes lovely quilts as a hobby. Guests have a choice of three attractively furnished bedrooms, all *en suite* or with private bathroom; one has a four-poster bed. There is a comfortable sitting-room, and breakfast only is served in the dining-room, which overlooks the garden. Visitors enjoy this centrally located establishment, which attracts many cyclists and walkers.

OWNER: Carol Corke OPEN: all year exc Christmas ROOMS: 2 twin, 1 four-poster; all rooms with bath/shower; TV in all bedrooms TERMS: single occupancy £21, twin £32–£36, four-poster £40; £5 reduction for children CARDS: none DETAILS: children welcome; no dogs; no smoking; car park; garden

---

NEWQUAY   Cornwall   **map 1**

Michelle Guest House

3 Manewas Way, Newquay TR7 3AH
TEL: (01637) 874521
off A30 at Indian Queens, take A392 to Newquay; at Quintrell Downs roundabout take right-hand turn signposted Newquay (Porth); at Riviera Hotel turn right signposted Lusty Glaze Beach, then 300yds into Manewas Way, third house on left

This modern detached house is in a quiet and pleasant residential area. The Wheelers are a friendly couple, and guests are welcomed with a cup of tea on arrival. Two of the prettily decorated *en suite* bedrooms are on the ground floor, and some have sea views. The comfortable TV lounge opens into the dining-room, where breakfast and dinner are served. The Wheelers sometimes organise theme weekends. Michelle Guest House is just 75 yards from Lusty Glaze Beach, only minutes from Tolcarne and Porth beaches, and is within easy walking distance of Newquay town centre.

OWNERS: Jan and George Wheeler OPEN: Mar to Nov ROOMS: 4 double/twin, 2 family; all rooms with bath/shower; 25% reduction for children over 12 sharing with parents; deposit; 1 room suitable for wheelchair-users; TV in all bedrooms TERMS: single occupancy £18, twin/double £32, family room £56; dinner £8 CARDS: none DETAILS: no children under 12; no dogs; no smoking; car park

---

Many B&Bs are in remote places, and although in many cases we provide directions, it is always advisable to ask for clear instructions when booking.

ENGLAND

NEWTON Suffolk

Mill House

The Green, Newton CO10 0QY
TEL: (01787) 372427
just off A134, 3m E of Sudbury

This red-brick, half-whitewashed house was formerly two cottages but has since been tastefully renovated. It stands in a large, well-tended garden which has a pond and backs on to an 18-hole golf course. The accommodation consists of three comfortable bedrooms, the two upstairs rooms sharing a bathroom and WC, and the ground-floor room having its own wash-basin and WC as well as use of the shower in the indoor swimming-pool. Guests may use the pool at no extra charge; there is also a lounge with TV. Breakfast sometimes includes delicious local sausages, and as Mill House does not offer dinner, one suggestion is to take evening meals at the pub across the green. Brenda White is a very congenial hostess, with two dogs and two cats, and there is a relaxed atmosphere.

OWNER: Brenda White OPEN: all year ROOMS: 2 double, 1 twin; all rooms with bath/shower; TV in all bedrooms TERMS: single occupancy £17.50, twin/double £35; children £12; deposit: £10 CARDS: none DETAILS: children welcome; no dogs; car park; garden; swimming-pool

NORTHAMPTON Northamptonshire

map 5

St Georges Private Hotel

128 St Georges Avenue, Northampton NN2 6JF
TEL: (01604) 792755

Just off the main Northampton-to-Kettering road, this substantial Victorian house is opposite a park and just a mile and a half from the town centre. The good-sized rooms with their floral bedspreads are comfortably furnished, and most have *en suite* facilities; four have their original fireplaces, and two are on the ground floor. The house retains some of its period features, such as the brass and wrought-iron-surround fireplace in the large lounge, and the stained-glass and mosaic tiles at the entrance way. Breakfast only is served in the bright basement dining-room. Packed lunches can be provided.

OWNER: T. Goodwin OPEN: all year exc 25 and 26 Dec ROOMS: 3 single, all with wash-basin; 3 double, 2 twin, 2 family, all with bath/shower; TV in all bedrooms and lounge TERMS: single/single occupancy £25–£27.50, twin/double £37.50–£42.50, family room £45–£60; reductions for children sharing with parents CARDS: Visa DETAILS: children welcome; dogs by arrangement; no smoking in bedrooms; car park; patio

NORTH BOVEY   Devon   map 1

Gate House

North Bovey, nr Moretonhampstead TQ13 8RB
TEL/FAX: (01647) 440479
*on B3212, 1½m W of Moretonhampstead turn at sign for North Bovey, keep
to left of village green*

This is one of several picturesque whitewashed thatched houses in
the unspoilt little village of North Bovey. The Gate House dates from
the fifteenth century and stands next to the village pub, which is an
even earlier building constructed to house the workmen who built the
church. The pretty cottage garden has an unheated swimming-pool,
but the lovely countryside views may be more enticing. Almost every
room has beams and the cosy sitting-room has a massive granite
fireplace and bread oven. Both breakfast and evening meals are
served in the small, attractive dining-room, warmed by the Aga in
winter. The bedrooms are fresh and bright and simply furnished. The
Gate House is a very peaceful and comfortable place, and an ideal
base for exploring Dartmoor.

OWNERS: John and Sheila Williams   OPEN: all year   ROOMS: 3 double, all with bath/
shower; TV in all bedrooms   TERMS: single occupancy £29, double £48   CARDS: none
DETAILS: no children; no dogs in dining-room; no smoking; car park; garden; swimming-
pool

NORTHLEACH   Gloucestershire   map 5

Market House

Market Square, Northleach, nr Cheltenham GL54 3EJ
TEL: (01451) 860557

This converted former covered sheep-fleece market stands in the
centre of a pretty village, opposite the square. In 1950 it became a
single dwelling, but kept several original features, such as the
inglenook fireplaces, flagstone floors and oak beams. Breakfast is
served in the bright dining/sitting-room, where log fires burn in
winter. There are lots of books to read and a good supply of brochures
describing local places of interest. The three charming bedrooms have
exposed stone walls and original fireplaces; one has a private
bathroom. There is a secluded garden full of climbing evergreens,
mature trees and shrubs. Packed lunches can be provided

OWNERS: Theresa and Mike Eastman   OPEN: all year exc Christmas   ROOMS: 2 single,
both with wash-basin; 1 double, with bath/shower; 1 twin, with wash-basin; TV lounge
TERMS: single £18–£19, twin/double £32–£40; deposit: 1 night's charge   CARDS: none
DETAILS: no children under 12; no dogs; no smoking; car park; garden

NORTHLEIGH Devon   map 2

Old Rectory

Northleigh, nr Colyton EX13 6BS
TEL: (01404) 871300
Northleigh is on a minor road between Honiton and Colyton

This pleasant country house built in the 1820s stands in an unspoilt
Devon valley and has lovely views. Rosemary Cohen, a friendly,
welcoming young mother, specialises in interior décor for period
properties and her interest in antiques and *objets d'art* is evident.
The three *en suite* bedrooms have been decorated to a high standard
and have sofas and armchairs. Breakfast and light 'tray suppers' are
served, on request, in the small conservatory or the library, and there
is a second conservatory filled with the scent of mimosa in
springtime. The attractive garden is full of mature shrubs and the
house stands above and a little way out of the village of Northleigh.

OWNER: Rosemary Cohen OPEN: all year ROOMS: 1 single, 1 double, 1 twin; all rooms
with bath/shower; TV in all bedrooms TERMS: single/single occupancy £17.50; twin/
double £35–£39; half-price for children; dinner £4.50–£6; deposit required CARDS:
none DETAILS: children welcome; dogs by arrangement; smoking in conservatory only;
car park; garden

NORTHLEW Devon   map 1

Howards Gorhuish

Northlew, nr Okehampton EX20 3BT
TEL: (01837) 53301
7m NW of Okehampton; ask for detailed instructions when booking

With a pear tree by the door and views across Dartmoor, this
pinkwashed sixteenth-century Devon longhouse stands in several
acres of landscaped gardens and orchards in which the owners grow
much of the produce used in evening meals. There has been a house
on this site since the Domesday Book, which mentions it as forming
part of the Manor of Gorhuish. Paul and Heather Richards have done
a splendid job renovating the property which is simply and
attractively decorated and furnished. On cold days log fires burn in
the beamed sitting-room. Guests have the run of the house, as well as
the games room in a converted outhouse, which is equipped with
table tennis, darts and board games. The comfortable bedrooms are
prettily decorated, the beds covered with patchwork quilts, and are
quite large. The twin room is split-level, with a bed on each of the two
levels. Dinner is available, by arrangement, on four nights of the
week, and plenty of local pubs are worth investigating on other
nights. Vegetarians can be catered for and guests are welcome to

bring their own wine. Two stables and a paddock are available for any guests wishing to bring horses – proof of vaccination is essential.

OWNERS: Paul and Heather Richards   OPEN: all year exc Christmas and New Year
ROOMS: 1 single, 2 double, 1 twin; TV lounge   TERMS: single £15–£18, single occupancy
£20, twin/double £36; dinner £10   CARDS: none   DETAILS: no children under 10; no
dogs; no smoking; car park; games room; garden

NORWICH   Norfolk   map 6

Linden House

557 Earlham Road, Norwich NR4 7HW
TEL: (01603) 451303   FAX: (01603) 251640

This neat and unpretentious detached house with an arched doorway
is conveniently situated for visiting the city centre – the bus stops
right outside. Carol and Don Peters are a friendly couple who have
travelled widely, and they combine high standards with an informal
atmosphere. Home-cooked evening meals are provided by
arrangement and vegetarians can be catered for. Guests are welcome
to bring their own wine. The bedrooms are in an extension away from
the road at the back of the property. Linden House is popular with
both tourists and business travellers, who are offered fax,
photocopying and secretarial services. Laundry facilities are also
available.

OWNERS: Carol and Don Peters   OPEN: all year exc Christmas   ROOMS: 1 double, 1 twin,
1 family; all rooms with bath/shower; TV in all bedrooms   TERMS: single occupancy
£25–£29, twin/double £31–£39, family room £31–£39 plus charge for children; children
under 5 free, reductions for older children according to age; dinner £9; deposit: £10
CARDS: Access, Visa   DETAILS: children welcome; dogs welcome; smoking in bedrooms
only; car park; garden

OAKAMOOR   Staffordshire   map 5

Bank House

Farley Lane, Oakamoor, nr Stoke-on-Trent ST10 3BD
TEL: (01538) 702810
on B5417, 2½m N of Alton Towers

This elegant country house stands in a large garden with woodland.
The house is beautifully furnished with old family pieces, and the
bedrooms, two of which have luxury *en suite* bathrooms – one with a
jacuzzi – are immaculate. Two of the bedrooms have four-poster beds,
and two of the adjacent rooms can be arranged as a family suite.
There is an enormous drawing-room with log fires, and a library. The
dining-room opens on to a terrace and breakfast can be taken outside
in warmer weather. Evening meals are available, if pre-arranged,

using locally grown vegetables and salads, and offering home-baked desserts and ice-cream. The owners often join their guests at dinner, or for drinks beforehand and coffee afterwards. Packed lunches can also be provided by arrangement.

OWNERS: Mr and Mrs J. Egerton Orme OPEN: all year exc Christmas ROOMS: 1 single, 1 double, 2 twin; all rooms with bath/shower; TV in all bedrooms and lounge TERMS: single £38, single occupancy £33–£43, twin/double £50–£70; children's reductions according to age; dinner £16–£30; deposit: £10 per person per night CARDS: Access, Visa DETAILS: children welcome; dogs by prior arrangement; no smoking upstairs and in bedrooms; car park; garden

OAKFORD Devon map 1

Newhouse Farm

Oakford, nr Tiverton EX16 9JE
TEL: (01398) 351347
on B3227, 5m W of Bampton

Reached down a long, rutted track, Newhouse Farm is a traditional working farm complete with cows, sheep and 40 acres of grass and woodland. It is beautifully set on the southern fringes of Exmoor National Park, and guests are welcome to walk round the farm and to use the pretty sheltered garden, which follows the valley down to a trout stream and small pond. The house dates from around 1600 and has lots of original features, such as low ceilings, sturdy oak beams, inglenook fireplace and bread oven. The extended family is friendly and hospitable, and two of the three comfortable bedrooms have recently been redecorated. The tiny guests' kitchen is useful for making drinks and picnic lunches. Anne Boldry is an enthusiastic and excellent cook who bakes her own breads and makes her own jams and marmalade. Evening meals are available by arrangement, and vegetarians are catered for. The farm is unlicensed, but guests are welcome to bring their own wine to dinner.

OWNER: Anne Boldry OPEN: all year exc Christmas ROOMS: 2 double, 1 twin, all with bath/shower; TV in all bedrooms TERMS: single occupancy £20–£22, twin/double £32–£40; dinner £10; deposit: 20% CARDS: none DETAILS: no children under 10; no dogs; car park; garden

If a B&B caters for vegetarians, we note this in the entry. It is always best, however, to check when booking and make it clear what your requirements are, especially if you require a special diet.

Many B&Bs, especially if they are unlicensed, allow guests to bring their own wine to dinner. If this is the case, we say so in the entry.

POLAND MILL, ODIHAM

ODIHAM Hampshire   **map 2**

Poland Mill

Odiham, nr Basingstoke RG29 1JL
TEL: (01256) 702251
*from M3 junction 5 take A287 signposted Guildford, after 1m turn left on
to B3016 signposted Winchfield, turn left at crossroads, follow to end of
lane*

This interesting old house is situated in a quiet position at the end of
a lane and surrounded by fields. It dates mostly from the sixteenth
century, with earlier foundations and later additions, and even gets a
mention in the Domesday Book. Janice Cole is a charming, hospitable
lady who sells antique linen and lace; the interior is decorated and
furnished to a high standard of comfort and elegance. There is a
lovely dining-room where breakfast only is served, and a pleasant
sitting-room. One of the bedrooms has a four-poster; two rooms have
en suite facilities, and the small double and single share a bathroom.
A most attractive garden with mill pond and peacocks surrounds the
house.

OWNERS: Brian and Janice Cole   OPEN: all year   ROOMS: 1 single; 1 double; 1 twin, with
bath/shower; 1 four-poster, with bath/shower; TV in some bedrooms and lounge

TERMS: single £22, single occupancy £25–£27, twin/double £38–£45, four-poster £45; children's reductions by arrangement   CARDS: none   DETAILS: children welcome; no dogs; car park; garden

OLD   Northamptonshire   map 5

Wold Farm

Old, nr Northampton NN6 9RJ
TEL: (01604) 781258
6m SW of Kettering, between A43 and A508

This attractive, wistaria-clad 300-year-old farmhouse is still very much a part of a working sheep and cattle farm. Three of the bedrooms are in the main house, and three are in the restored granary and piggery at the bottom of the garden; one bedroom is on the ground floor. Both buildings have a TV lounge. Breakfasts and pre-arranged dinners are served in the dining-room in the main house; it has oak beams and an old dresser, as well as a wood-burning stove and an enormous fireplace. Wold Farm is unlicensed, but guests are welcome to bring their own wine to dinner. Packed lunches can be provided.

OWNER: Ann Engler   OPEN: all year   ROOMS: 2 single, 3 double, 3 twin; all rooms with bath/shower; TV in 1 bedroom and lounges   TERMS: single/single occupancy £20–£22, twin/double £40–£44; half-price for children under 14; dinner £13.50; deposit: £10   CARDS: none   DETAILS: children welcome; dogs by arrangement; smoking in 1 lounge only; car park; garden

OMBERSLEY   Hereford & Worcester   map 5

Eden Farm

Ombersley, nr Droitwich WR9 0JX
TEL: (01905) 620244
just W of A449, 5m W of Droitwich

This listed seventeenth-century house is part of a 200-acre mixed farm that is also given over to breeding horses. Eden Farm has solid old-fashioned furniture, and the two spacious bedrooms have *en suite* showers. As the house has just two bedrooms, guests are assured of personal service from the Yardleys. Substantial breakfasts are taken in the pleasant dining-room-cum-lounge (packed lunches can be requested). Ombersley, just a mile away, is a distinguished, unspoilt village with several black-and-white-timbered houses.

OWNERS: W.D. and M.A. Yardley   OPEN: all year exc Christmas   ROOMS: 1 twin, 1 family; both rooms with shower; TV lounge   TERMS: single occupancy £20, twin £36, family room from £36; children's reductions according to age; deposit   CARDS: none   DETAILS: children welcome; no dogs; no smoking; car park; garden

OTLEY   Suffolk   map 6

Otley House

Helmingham Road, Otley IP6 9NR
TEL: (01473) 890253   FAX: (01473) 890009
on B1079 at N end of village

This seventeenth-century manor house stands in peaceful, mature grounds with a small lake and plenty of wildlife. Thomas and Colette Hoepli are a Swiss couple who took over the house in 1994 and have been busy upgrading and refurbishing the property to luxurious standards. Many original features remain, including a Grade I listed Queen Anne staircase and a splendid Tudor fireplace, and the furnishings are in keeping with the grandeur of the property. One of the bedrooms has a four-poster bed and there is a suite consisting of bedroom, bathroom and private drawing-room on the ground floor. The public drawing-room is decorated in a light Continental style, while the billiard room has a more traditional air, with comfortable leather chairs. Breakfast and dinners are served in the candlelit dining-room, with a good selection of vintage wines available. Vegetarian dishes can be provided with prior notice. Colette is a trained cook. The tranquil garden has a croquet lawn and a relaxing summer-house. French and German are spoken.

OWNERS: Thomas and Colette Hoepli   OPEN: Mar to Oct   ROOMS: 2 double, 1 twin, 1 four-poster; all rooms with bath/shower; TV in some bedrooms and lounge   TERMS: single occupancy £42–£52, twin/double £58–£72, four-poster £72; dinner £19.50; deposit: £30 single, £50 double   CARDS: none   DETAILS: no children under 12; no dogs; smoking in billiard room only; car park; games room; garden

---

OXFORD   Oxfordshire   map 2

Cornerways

282 Abingdon Road, Oxford OX1 4TA
TEL: (01865) 240135

Cornerways is a small, friendly guesthouse set in a pretty garden with a white fence, and decorated with flower-filled hanging baskets, tubs and window boxes. The house is only a mile from the city centre and there is a frequent bus service. The bedrooms are immaculately clean, and tastefully decorated in pink and green; one room is on the ground floor. Carol Jeakings is a delightful lady who takes pride in her well-run establishment. Breakfast only is served, but there are lots of eating places within easy reach.

OWNERS: Carol and Terry Jeakings   OPEN: all year exc Christmas   ROOMS: 1 single, 1 double, 1 family; all rooms with bath/shower; TV in all bedrooms   TERMS: single £26–£27, single occupancy £30, double £42–£44, family room £55–£60; babies under 2 free, older children's reductions according to age; deposit: £20   CARDS: none   DETAILS: children welcome; no dogs; no smoking in dining-room; car park; garden

Cotswold House

363 Banbury Road, Oxford OX2 7PL
TEL/FAX: (01865) 310558

This impeccably maintained property is situated in a leafy part of
north Oxford, two miles from the city centre. The house is furnished
to a very high standard, and the pleasant entrance hall has oriental
rugs; beautiful flower arrangements abound. There is a small sitting-
room, and a separate dining-room where excellent breakfasts are
served. The good-sized bedrooms all have *en suite* shower rooms. This
is an excellent base for exploring Oxford.

OWNERS: Jim and Anne O'Kane   OPEN: all year exc Christmas   ROOMS: 2 single, 2
double, 1 twin, 2 family; all rooms with bath/shower; TV in all bedrooms   TERMS: single
£37, single occupancy £37–£51, twin/double £54, family room £54–£65; £11 for
children over 5 sharing with parents   CARDS: none   DETAILS: no children under 5; no
dogs; no smoking; car park; garden

The Gables

6 Cumnor Hill, Oxford OX2 9HA
TEL: (01865) 862153   FAX: (01865) 864054

The Gables is an attractive whitewashed building occupying a corner
site on one of the main roads into Oxford, only a couple of miles from
the city centre. All of the recently refurbished bedrooms are prettily
decorated in pastel colours and have *en suite* bathrooms. There is a
small lounge, and breakfast only is served in the dining-room. Guests
are welcome to sit in the garden on fine days.

OWNERS: Sally and Tony Tompkins   OPEN: all year exc Christmas   ROOMS: 2 single, 2
double, 1 twin, all with bath/shower; 1 family, with wash-basin; TV in all bedrooms
TERMS: single £22–£25, single occupancy £30–£35, twin/double £40–£46, family room
£50–£60; children's reductions according to age; deposit: cheque or credit card
details   CARDS: Access, Visa   DETAILS: children welcome; no dogs; smoking in some
rooms only; car park; garden

Norham Guest House

16 Norham Road, Oxford OX2 6SF
TEL: (01865) 515352

This traditional Victorian house is in a conservation area near the
beautiful University parks, and only a 15-minute walk to the town
centre. The house is in excellent decorative order, and all but one
bedroom have *en suite* facilities. Generous breakfasts are served in
the bright dining-room, which overlooks the pretty rose garden.

OWNERS: Rosemary and Peter Welham   OPEN: all year   ROOMS: 2 single, 3 double, all
with bath/shower; 2 twin, 1 with bath/shower, 1 with wash-basin; 1 family, with bath/

shower; TV in all bedrooms TERMS: single £30–£33, single occupancy £40–£42, twin/
double £44–£52, family room £60–£64; deposit: 50% CARDS: none DETAILS: no
children under 5; no dogs; no smoking; car park

PADSTOW   Cornwall   **map 1**

Dower House

Fentonluna Lane, Padstow PL28 8BA
TEL/FAX: (01841) 532317

This attractive, granite-built listed house dates from 1858. It stands
on the edge of Padstow old town in a lovely, quiet position with
excellent views. The *en suite* bedrooms are large, airy and smartly
decorated. There is a comfortable lounge, small licensed bar and red
dining-room with mullion windows. The breakfast menu has lots of
choice, and on Mondays in summer Paul Brocklebank does a
barbecue on the terrace, served inside if wet. The house has a
welcoming, friendly atmosphere, and is a good place to stay for those
looking for quiet and comfortable accommodation within easy reach
of the bustling harbour town.

OWNERS: Paul and Patricia Brocklebank OPEN: Apr to mid-Dec ROOMS: 1 single, 2
double, 2 twin, 1 family; all rooms with bath/shower; TV in all bedrooms and lounge
TERMS: single £30, single occupancy £42, twin/double £40–£65, family room £70–£85;
reductions for children under 13; barbecue dinner £12; deposit: £30 per person
CARDS: Visa DETAILS: children welcome; dogs welcome (not on beds); smoking in bar
room only; car park

Khandalla Guest House

Sarahs Lane, Padstow PL28 8EL
TEL: (01841) 532961

This semi-detached Edwardian house stands in a quiet residential
road above the town of Padstow. The three well-equipped bedrooms
are very comfortable, and one has a balcony and views of the Camel
Estuary. Lisa Hair makes her guests feel at home and serves an
excellent breakfast. The centre of Padstow is only about a seven-
minute walk, with the uphill return journey taking somewhat longer.
There are plenty of eating establishments nearby for evening meals,
and packed lunches can be provided.

OWNER: Lisa Hair OPEN: all year ROOMS: 1 single, 1 double, 1 family; all rooms with
bath/shower; TV in all bedrooms and lounge TERMS: single £16–£20, single occupancy
£30, double £32–£35, family room £45–£50; half-price for children sharing with parents;
deposit: £10 CARDS: none DETAILS: children welcome; dogs welcome; no smoking;
car park; garden

Weir View House

9 Shooters Hill, Pangbourne, nr Reading RG8 7DZ
TEL: (01734) 842120
on A329, 6m NW of Reading

Weir View is situated in a good position overlooking the Thames, with
a main road between it and the river. The spacious, recently
redecorated bedrooms are fresh and bright, all have TV, and those at
the front enjoy views of the weir. Breakfast only is available and is
served in the Spanish-style dining-room. The riverside Swan Inn,
opposite, serves food. Guests can accompany owner Robert King on
his daily trip to feed the swans. Visitors arriving from London on the
fast commuter link may be interested to learn that the railway line
runs just above the house and that the station is only a few minutes'
walk away.

OWNERS: Robert and Eileen King OPEN: all year exc Christmas ROOMS: 2 double, 1
with bath/shower, 1 with wash-basin; 1 twin, with wash-basin; TV in all bedrooms and
lounge TERMS: single occupancy £30–£40, twin/double £40–£50; deposit: £10
CARDS: Access, Visa DETAILS: no children under 7; no dogs; no smoking; car park

Bruce House Farm

Top Wath Road, Pateley Bridge, nr Harrogate HG3 5PG
TEL: (01423) 711813
off B6265, 11m NW of Harrogate

Approached up a quiet lane, Bruce House Farm stands in an elevated
position with wonderful views over Nidderdale. Six acres of land are
inhabited by guinea-fowl, ducks, geese and chickens, from which
fresh eggs arrive in time for breakfast. Mrs Treble is a dedicated host
who has succeeded in creating a home-from-home ambience. Three
large, comfortable bedrooms have easy chairs and TV. Breakfasts,
and evening meals by arrangement, are served in the green and
peach dining-room on a handsome table. Children's helpings,
vegetarian dishes and packed lunches can be provided; guests can
bring their own wine to dinner as there is no licence. Leading off the
dining-room is a conservatory. The farm is a popular place for
walkers; laundry facilities are provided. The interesting rock
formations of Stump Cross Caverns are nearby, as is Fountains
Abbey.

OWNER: Mrs M. Treble OPEN: Apr to end Oct ROOMS: 2 double, 1 twin; all rooms with
bath/shower; TV in all bedrooms TERMS: single occupancy £21, twin/double from £34;
half-price for children; dinner £10; deposit: £5 per person CARDS: none DETAILS:
children welcome; no dogs; no smoking in bedrooms; car park; garden

PELYNT   Cornwall   **map 1**

Trenderway Farm

Pelynt, nr Polperro PL13 2LY
TEL: (01503) 272214
turn S off B3359 1m S of Pelynt

Trenderway Farm is a delightful sixteenth-century building with attractive hill views, tucked away down a quiet country lane. It is part of a 450-acre mixed farm and some of the old stone farm buildings have been converted into additional rooms. These are spacious, with whitewashed stone walls, beams and easy chairs, and one unit can also be self-catering. The house is elegantly and simply decorated and one of the bedrooms is a four-poster. Bathrooms are large and one has an old-fashioned bath with claw feet and a separate shower. The relaxing sitting-room, decorated in pink and grey, has an open fire and leads via a curtained archway to the modern sun porch extension where breakfast only is served. Eating places in the area include a sixteenth-century inn.

OWNERS: Anthony and Lynne Tuckett OPEN: all year exc Christmas and New Year
ROOMS: 2 double, 1 twin, 1 four-poster; all rooms with bath/shower; TV in all bedrooms
TERMS: single occupancy £30, twin/double £60, four-poster £60; deposit: £30 CARDS: none DETAILS: no children; no dogs; no smoking; car park; garden

PENRITH   Cumbria   **map 10**

Barco House

Carleton Road, Penrith CA11 8LR
TEL: (01768) 863176

Just half a mile from the town centre, this well-maintained Victorian house with its pretty front garden sits back from the main road. Delicate pastels characterise the three bedrooms, two of which have their own showers. The Victorian-style dining-room is the venue for breakfasts and – if pre-arranged – four-course evenings meals; the dining-room, which is adjacent to a small bar/lounge, is also open to non-residents. Although Barco House is licensed, guests may bring their own wine to dinner.

OWNER: Christine Stockdale OPEN: all year ROOMS: 1 double, with shower; 1 twin, with wash-basin; 1 family, with bath/shower; TV in all bedrooms TERMS: single occupancy £18–£20, twin/double £38–£40, family room £46; reductions for children according to age; dinner £10 CARDS: none DETAILS: children welcome; well-behaved dogs welcome; no smoking in dining-room; car park; garden

The end details for each entry state whether dogs are allowed, but it is always best to check when booking.

Clare House

20 Broad Street, Penryn, nr Falmouth TR10 8JH
TEL: (01326) 373294

This listed seventeenth-century house is easy to find with its bright
white and blue exterior, window box and hanging baskets. It stands
in the main street of the old town of Penryn, which lies on the
outskirts of Falmouth, and has a pretty, well-maintained back
garden reached through a narrow and colourful conservatory. Jean
and Jack Hewitt are a delightful warm couple and offer their guests
the opportunity to pick a bunch of grapes from the ancient Black
Hamburg vine, a feature of the conservatory. The bedrooms and the
drawing-room, which has plenty of books and magazines, are all large
and comfortable. Breakfast includes home-made bread and
preserves, and cooked choices extend to mackerel and haddock. Tea,
coffee and hot chocolate are freely available in the breakfast room at
all times. Visitors to the area like to explore the beaches and coves
and walk the coastal path.

OWNERS: Jack and Jean Hewitt   OPEN: all year exc Christmas and New Year   ROOMS: 3
twin, all with bath/shower; TV in all bedrooms   TERMS: single occupancy £25, twin
£38–£50; deposit: 20%   CARDS: none   DETAILS: no children under 12; no dogs; no
smoking; car park; garden

Prospect House

1 Church Road, Penryn, nr Falmouth TR10 8DA
TEL/FAX: (01326) 373198

This small listed Regency house built in 1830 stands back from the
main road into Falmouth. To one side it has a small, immaculately
kept walled garden, where guests are welcome to sit. The house has
been tastefully and restfully decorated and furnished as much as
possible in keeping with the period. It has stained-glass windows,
mahogany doors and painted cornices, and the hall and lounge have
their original ceilings. The dining-room, where four-course dinners
are served (vegetarian options with advance notice), has a flagstone
floor, beautifully set communal table and unusual Dutch mid-
nineteenth-century chairs. The bedrooms are very comfortable and
drink-making facilities, together with a small fridge, are provided in
a little cubby-hole in the upstairs hallway. The lounge is a
comfortable room, where drinks and after-dinner coffee are
dispensed.

OWNERS: Cliff Paul and Barry Sheppard   OPEN: all year exc Christmas   ROOMS: 2
double, 1 twin; all rooms with bath/shower   TERMS: single occupancy £30–£35, twin/

double £47–£53; dinner £18; deposit: 25% CARDS: Access, Visa DETAILS: no children under 12; dogs welcome with own bedding; no smoking in dining-room; car park; garden

PENSHURST   Kent   map 3

Swale Cottage

Old Swaylands Lane, Penshurst TN11 8AH
TEL: (01892) 870738
off B2176, ¾m SE of Penshurst Place, turn into Poundsbridge Lane, then first right

This sensitive conversion of a listed eighteenth-century Kentish barn is in a remote location with wonderful views over the hilly woodlands of the Medway Valley and a small lake. It retains its old character, with a dark weatherboarded exterior and latticed windows, and oak beams and an inglenook fireplace inside. Some stable-style doors remain and the cheerful garden has bright floral borders. Cynthia Dakin is an artist and her paintings are displayed throughout the house. All the delightful bedrooms have interesting beds, one a romantic four-poster, and there is an elegant sitting-room with TV. Breakfast is served at an antique refectory table in the dining-room. Swaylands, which became the fictional home of Wendy in J.M. Barrie's *Peter Pan*, is nearby, as is Penshurst Place, the home of the Sidney family since 1552.

OWNER: Cynthia Dakin OPEN: all year ROOMS: 1 double, 1 twin, 1 four-poster; all rooms with bath/shower; TV in all bedrooms and lounge TERMS: single occupancy £34, twin/double £52, four-poster £54; deposit required CARDS: none DETAILS: no children under 10; no dogs; no smoking; car park; garden

PENTEWAN   Cornwall   map 1

Polrudden Farm

Pentewan, nr St Austell PL26 6BJ
TEL: (01726) 842051/843213
off B3273, 3m S of St Austell

Polrudden Farm is a modern bungalow dating from the 1960s located on the site of an earlier building. It stands in a spectacular clifftop position looking out to sea and can be reached down a long driveway up a very steep hill from the neat little village square of Pentewan. The 75-acre sheep and beef farm extends to the shore, and there is a path that leads to a small private beach. A terrace runs in front of the house, with tables and chairs for sitting outside. The accommodation is simple and the welcome warm, and there is a pleasant, relaxing atmosphere; the house is now run by former owner Margaret

Bainbridge's daughter and son-in-law. This is a great place for families with children. Evening meals are available by arrangement and packed lunches can be provided.

OWNERS: Andrew and Johanna Jackson OPEN: all year ROOMS: 1 double, 2 twin; all rooms with bath/shower; TV in all bedrooms and lounge TERMS: single occupancy £18.50, twin/double £33; £5 reduction for children CARDS: none DETAILS: children welcome; dogs by arrangement in stable; no smoking; car park; garden

PENZANCE Cornwall   map 1

Lombard House

16 Regent Terrace, Penzance TR18 4DW
TEL/FAX: (01736) 64897

Rita and Tom Kruge, the new owners of Lombard House, are a friendly young couple who continue to provide good, simple accommodation. Lombard House is a welcoming pink house in a Regency terrace, only one street back from the sea-front road. Although it is very conveniently located for the town centre, the street has no through traffic and is relatively quiet. The bedrooms at the front are quite large and have good views, and some of the ground-floor rooms have their original cornices and fireplaces. The bar/dining-room/TV lounge has doors that lead to the front garden, which is a good place to relax and take in the sea views. Evening meals are available by arrangement and parking facilities are provided while guests visit the Scilly Isles.

OWNERS: Tom and Rita Kruge OPEN: all year ROOMS: 1 single, with wash-basin; 4 double, 1 with bath/shower, 3 with wash-basin;; 4 family, all with bath/shower; TV in all bedrooms and lounge TERMS: single £16, single occupancy £20–£29, twin/double £32–£40, family room £32–£40 plus children's charge; children under 3 free, 25% reduction for ages 3 to 12; dinner £10–£12.50; deposit: 1 night's charge CARDS: Access, Delta, Visa DETAILS: children welcome; dogs by arrangement; no smoking in lounge or dining-room; car park; garden

PERRANPORTH Cornwall   map 1

Morgans of Perranporth

3 Grannys Lane, Perranporth TR6 0HB
TEL: (01872) 573904 FAX: (01872) 572425
on B3285, 4m off A30

Morgans stands above the town of Perranporth, with lovely views from the front patio of the sea and surfing beach. It is a compact modern house standing in a quiet lane and run by a friendly couple who make their guests feel at home. Two of the small bedrooms also have sea views, and there is a combined lounge/dining-room overlooking the beach in which breakfast and dinner are served. Guests are welcome to bring their own wine to dinner and packed lunches can be provided.

OWNERS: Charles and Yvonne Morgan   OPEN: all year exc Christmas and New Year
ROOMS: 1 single, with wash-basin; 2 double, 1 with bath/shower, 1 with wash-basin; 2 twin, 2 family, all with bath/shower; TV in all bedrooms and lounge   TERMS: single £20, single occupancy £30, twin/double £35–£39; reductions for children over 12 sharing with parents; dinner £12.50; deposit   CARDS: none   DETAILS: no children under 12; house-trained dogs welcome; smoking in lounge only; car park; garden

---

PERRANUTHNOE   Cornwall   map 1

Ednovean Farm

Perranuthnoe, nr Penzance TR20 9LZ
TEL: (01736) 711883
from Penzance take A394 Helston road beyond Marazion, turn right at Bertie Wooster's Restaurant, farm drive on left by postbox

---

The Taylors have converted this seventeenth-century granite barn into a comfortable and unusual family home. An open-plan beamed sitting/dining-room occupies the first floor and is where breakfast is served at one table. The house is cosy and informal, with friendly cats and a dog. Three prettily decorated bedrooms are all on the ground floor, two in the main building and one with its own courtyard entrance. A small garden encircles the property, which enjoys lovely views of St Michael's Mount and the whole bay looking across to Penzance and Mousehole. The farmland extends to 22 acres and supports horses, which are trained here and compete in shows. One can walk along the coastal path, or across the fields to the village of Perranuthnoe, where there is a sandy beach and a pub serving food.

OWNER: Christine Taylor   OPEN: all year exc Christmas   ROOMS: 3 double, 2 with bath/shower, 1 with wash-basin; TV in all bedrooms and lounge   TERMS: single occupancy £20–£30, double £40–£50; deposit: £10   CARDS: none   DETAILS: no children under 9; dogs by arrangement; no smoking; car park; garden

---

PETERBOROUGH   Cambridgeshire   map 6

Willow End

313 Eastfield Road, Peterborough PE1 4RA
TEL: (01733) 62907

This immaculate Edwardian house is decorated with real flair thanks to the creative talents of Mrs Rowell. The garden is equally lovely and has a fish pond. The spacious, well-furnished bedrooms are comfortable and there is a separate guests' lounge. Breakfast only is served but the house is conveniently near the city centre, where there is no shortage of venues for evening meals.

OWNERS: Mr and Mrs M. Rowell OPEN: all year ROOMS: 1 double, with wash-basin; 3 twin, 2 with bath/shower, 1 with wash-basin; TV in some bedrooms and lounge TERMS: single occupancy £20–£24, twin/double £30–£34; half-price for children over 6; deposit: £10 CARDS: none DETAILS: no children under 6; no dogs; car park; garden

---

PETER TAVY   Devon   map 1

The Barn

Higher Churchtown Farm, Peter Tavy, nr Tavistock PL19 9NR
TEL: (01822) 810337
1m off A386, 3m NE of Tavistock

This attractive barn conversion offers good-value accommodation. It is set in a large garden with picnic tables, in a very peaceful location on the edge of the village of Peter Tavy – an ideal base for exploring Dartmoor. The two smallish bedrooms are in an annexe, sharing a WC and wash-basin. The shower, for which a small additional charge is made, is in the main house. Although the annexe is not centrally heated, the bedrooms have wall-mounted electric fires. Jane Burden is friendly and is happy to make up the bedrooms as twins/doubles or combined as one family room. Breakfast only is served in the window of the spacious sitting-room with its lovely views over the pretty garden; packed lunches can be provided.

OWNER: Jane Burden OPEN: all year exc Christmas week and owner's holidays
ROOMS: 2 twin/double; TV in both bedrooms TERMS: single occupancy £14, twin/double £28; children's reductions according to age; deposit: £5 per person (peak season only) CARDS: none DETAILS: children welcome; no dogs; no smoking; car park; garden

---

Churchtown

Peter Tavy, nr Tavistock PL19 9NN
TEL: (01822) 810477
1m off A386, 3m NE of Tavistock

This solid, granite-built Victorian house is surrounded by an attractive garden with a croquet lawn. There are wonderful views to the front and of Dartmoor behind. Churchtown is comfortable and welcoming; Major and Mrs Lane used to keep horses in training for three-day events, and now they have miniature long-haired dachshunds that are popular with guests. They also have an old pony for children to ride. The bedrooms are spacious; two singles share a bathroom and a shower room, two doubles each have their own private bathrooms. Peter Tavy is a great place for walking, pony-trekking, golf and fishing. The neighbouring village pub serves food.

OWNERS: Major and Mrs Lane   ROOMS: 2 single; 2 double, both with bath/shower; TV in all bedrooms   TERMS: single/single occupancy £12–£14, double £24–£28; deposit: £10   CARDS: none   DETAILS: no children under 10; no dogs; car park; garden

PICKERING   North Yorkshire   map 9

Bramwood Guest House

19 Hallgarth, Pickering YO18 7AW
TEL: (01751) 474066
off A169 heading out of Pickering centre towards Whitby

This eighteenth-century Grade II listed house is in tune with the nostalgic appeal of historic Pickering. It has florally decorated bedrooms, the top-floor pair with attractive sloping ceilings and original fireplaces. The lounge is large and comfortable, with an open fire. Guests are welcome to relax in the walled garden. Traditional English home-cooked meals are served at 6.30pm and include vegetarian choices if they are requested in advance. Guests can buy the preserves, jams and marmalades made here and included in the breakfasts.

OWNERS: Brian and Ann Lane   OPEN: all year exc Christmas   ROOMS: 4 double, 2 with shower, 2 with wash-basin; 2 twin, both with wash-basin; TV lounge   TERMS: single occupancy £15–£16, twin/double £30–£36; £10 for children over 3 sharing with parents; dinner £9; deposit: £25   CARDS: Access, Visa   DETAILS: no children under 3; no dogs; no smoking; car park; garden

PICKET HILL   Hampshire   map 2

Picket Hill House

Picket Hill, nr Ringwood BH24 3HH
TEL: (01425) 476173   FAX: (01425) 470022
heading W on A31, 1m before Ringwood take exit marked Hightown and Crow and then first driveway on left

This attractive family home stands in a lovely garden with well-kept lawns and shrubs. A seven-foot-high fence surrounds the property, to keep out the deer from the heathland of the New Forest, which can be accessed direct from the grounds. Audrey Pocock gives her guests a warm welcome and is a helpful and friendly lady. Dinners are not offered as a matter of course, but she is happy to cook for guests by arrangement and can include vegetarian options. The accommodation is comfortable with pleasant *en suite* bedrooms and a large lounge which has TV, books and games for guests to use. The Pococks keep horses, as well as a cat and two dogs, and can accommodate guests' horses by arrangement.

OWNERS: Audrey and Norman Pocock   OPEN: all year exc Christmas and New Year   ROOMS: 2 double, 1 twin; all rooms with bath/shower; TV lounge   TERMS: single occupancy £25–£30, twin/double £33–£40; dinner £13.50; deposit: 20% CARDS: none DETAILS: no children under 10; no dogs; smoking in guests' lounge only; car park; garden

---

PLAXTOL   Kent   map 3

Jordans

Sheet Hill, Plaxtol, nr Sevenoaks TN15 0PU
TEL: (01732) 810379
from M25, take A25 to Ightham, then join A227 for 2m, Plaxtol on left

---

Jordans is a fifteenth-century Tudor house with leaded windows, inglenook fireplaces and oak beams. It lies on a quiet country lane surrounded by orchards and woodland. Jo Lindsay is a painter and gardener, and a Blue Badge guide, and the house has a friendly and relaxed atmosphere. The single bedroom adjoins one of the doubles, and together they can be let to families. The comfortable sitting-room with TV is attractively furnished, and guests are welcome to explore the acre of beautifully maintained garden. Breakfast is normally Continental, but a full English breakfast can be served for a supplement.

OWNER: Jo Lindsay ROOMS: 1 single, with bath/shower; 2 double, one with bath/shower; 1 family, with bath/shower; TV in all bedrooms TERMS: single/single occupancy £27, double £50, family room from £75; deposit: 50% CARDS: none DETAILS: no children under 11; no dogs; car park; garden

---

PLYMOUTH   Devon   map 1

Park View

13 Radford Road, West Hoe, Plymouth PL1 3BY
TEL: (01752) 260669

This guesthouse extends a friendly and welcoming atmosphere and offers spotlessly clean accommodation in a central part of Plymouth. Just a short walk from the sea front, citadel and Hoe, it is a Victorian terraced building in a side street overlooking a square with a garden and tennis court. The house is comfortably furnished and the lounge/dining-room, where breakfast only is served, overlooks the square.

OWNER: Beryl Mavin OPEN: all year exc 25 and 26 Dec ROOMS: 2 single, 2 double, 1 twin; all rooms with bath/shower; TV in all bedrooms and lounge TERMS: single/single occupancy £16, twin/double £31; half-price for children under 10 CARDS: none DETAILS: children welcome; dogs welcome

---

If the establishment does not take credit cards, we say so in the details at the end of the entry.

Rosaland Hotel

32 Houndiscombe Road, Mutley, Plymouth PL4 6HQ
TEL: (01752) 664749   FAX: (01752) 256984

This large Victorian terraced house dates from 1888. It is very well maintained and attractively decorated and is in a quiet residential street near the railway station and the university. The bedrooms are quite small with pine furniture and all have telephones and satellite TV. The residents' lounge is furnished in Victorian style with leather armchairs, a large fireplace and a rich red carpet. There is a licensed bar and a relaxed modern dining-room with pine chairs and tables, where breakfast and evening meals are served. The Hoe and Barbican are a 15-minute walk away.

OWNERS: Peter and Heather Shaw OPEN: all year ROOMS: 3 single, all with wash-basin; 2 double, both with bath/shower; 1 twin, with wash-basin; 2 family, both with bath/shower; TV in all bedrooms TERMS: single £17, single occupancy £22, twin/double £30–£35, family room £40–£45; children's reductions; dinner £8; deposit required CARDS: Access, Amex, Diners, Visa DETAILS: children welcome; no dogs; smoking in bedrooms only; car park; garden

PORT ISAAC   Cornwall   map 1

Archer Farm

Trewetha, Port Isaac PL29 3RU
TEL: (01208) 880522
off B3267, 5m N of Wadebridge

Archer Farm is set in peaceful, unspoilt countryside just 15 minutes' walk from the charming fishing village of Port Isaac, and is close to sandy beaches, coves and cliff walks. It has the appearance of a modern house, both from the outside and the inside, but was once an almost derelict rambling farmhouse. Vicki and David Welton carried out the conversion to provide the present comfortable accommodation. The simply furnished bedrooms vary in size, with one room on the ground floor and two having balconies. There is a relaxing lounge/bar, a spacious and bright dining-room, a small TV lounge – and drinks can be taken on one of the outside patios.

OWNERS: Vicki and David Welton OPEN: Apr to end Oct ROOMS: 1 single, with bath/shower; 4 double, 3 with bath/shower, 1 with wash-basin; 1 twin, 1 family, both with bath/shower; TV in all bedrooms and lounge TERMS: single £21, single occupancy £22.50, twin/double £48, family room from £60; babies free, reductions for ages 3 to 10 in family room; dinner £15; deposit: 10% CARDS: none DETAILS: children welcome; dogs by prior arrangement; smoking in bar/lounge and TV lounge only; car park; garden

PORTLAND   Dorset   map 2

Old Higher Lighthouse

Portland Bill, Portland D15 2JT
TEL: (01305) 822300
take Portland Bill road, first right after the lighthouse (road marked 'MOD Navy Private Road')

The Old Higher Lighthouse was built in 1750 and was in use until 1905. It was formerly the home of Dr Marie Stopes, who entertained such famous visitors as George Bernard Shaw, H.G. Wells, Thomas Hardy and Dame Margot Fonteyn. After a long period of decay and neglect the house was bought by the present owners and completely restored. There is a tiny dining-room in the bottom part of the tower, and guests have the choice of two small downstairs sitting-rooms with TV, one of which is non-smoking. The simply furnished bedrooms are on the ground floor, and there is an *en suite* studio above the garage, with sea views on every side. At the top of the tower there is a sun lounge/observatory, and binoculars are provided to give spectacular 360-degree views up to 40 miles in any direction. Outside there is a heated swimming-pool and jacuzzi. The lower lighthouse, at one time owned by Sir Peter Scott, is now home to a bird sanctuary.

OWNERS: Leslie Nickson and Fran Lockyer   OPEN: all year exc Christmas   ROOMS: 2 double, 2 twin; all with wash-basin; 2 family, 1 with bath/shower, 1 with wash-basin; TV in some bedrooms and lounge   TERMS: single occupancy £25–£35, twin/double £40–£50, family room £40–£70; reductions for children sharing with parents; deposit: £5 per person per night   CARDS: none   DETAILS: children welcome; no dogs; smoking in 1 lounge only; car park; garden; swimming-pool

PORTSMOUTH   Hampshire   map 2

Fortitude Cottage

51 Broad Street, Old Portsmouth PO1 2JD
TEL/FAX: (01705) 823748
from M27 junction 12 follow signs through town to Isle of Wight Car Ferry, then follow signs to Cathedral and Old Portsmouth

Fortitude Cottage is a very unusual narrow, terraced house with bow windows and is almost surrounded by water, with views over the harbour to the Isle of Wight. The cottage was built after World War II by Mrs Harbeck's parents and is at the very end of Old Portsmouth; in summer it is a wonderful picture with a profusion of hanging baskets. It is also opposite the quay for the five-minute waterbus ride to HMS Victory and the Mary Rose. Mrs Harbeck has lived in the cottage most of her life and is a most friendly and enthusiastic lady. The bedrooms are tiny, two being *en suite*, and they are prettily decorated, warm and cosy. Breakfast only is served at one end of the owner's sitting-room. (Mrs Harbeck's mother, who lives in a house to the rear of the cottage, also does bed and breakfast and she has two double rooms, both with wonderful views.)

OWNER: Carol A. Harbeck OPEN: all year exc 25 and 26 Dec ROOMS: 1 double, 2 twin; all rooms with bath/shower; TV in all bedrooms TERMS: single occupancy £24–£30, twin/double £42; deposit: £20 CARDS: Visa DETAILS: no children under 12; no dogs; no smoking

POULSHOT Wiltshire   map 2

Middle Green Farm

The Green, Poulshot, nr Devizes SN10 1RT
TEL: (01380) 828413   FAX: (01380) 828826
1m off A361 Devizes to Trowbridge road

This lovely Georgian house stands in a picturesque position on the village green in a peaceful village. The house is surrounded by an attractive garden and has a welcoming atmosphere. The three bedrooms share a bathroom, and there is also a garden annexe which has its own bathroom and small kitchenette. Guests have use of a drawing-room with TV, and breakfast only is served, but evening meals are available in the nearby village inn.

OWNERS: Angela and Derek Bullen OPEN: all year exc Christmas and New Year ROOMS: 2 single; 2 double, both with bath/shower; TV in some bedrooms and lounge TERMS: single £15, single occupancy £25–£30, twin/double £38; children's reductions if sharing with parents CARDS: none DETAILS: children welcome; no dogs; no smoking; car park; garden

PRINCETOWN Devon   map 1

Duchy House

Tavistock Road, Princetown PL20 6QF
TEL: (01822) 890552
off B3357, 7m E of Tavistock

This 100-year-old semi-detached building is almost opposite the prison and right in the heart of central Dartmoor; it is both a guesthouse and licensed café. Although the Trimbles have been running Duchy House only since the mid-1990s, they are very knowledgeable about the area and happy to advise on walking, bird-watching, pony-trekking and golfing. The house is simply furnished, with spacious rooms, and the upstairs guest lounge (which overlooks the moor) has TV, video and lots of games and books. The café serves home-made cakes and scones, as well as lunch and evening meals, and is open most of the day. Children's helpings and vegetarian choices are available. Packed lunches, too, can be provided.

OWNERS: Ernie and Hilary Trimble OPEN: all year ROOMS: 1 single; 1 double, with bath/shower; 1 twin, with wash-basin; TV lounge TERMS: single £15, single occupancy £15–£20, twin/double £30–£38; £5 for children under 16 sharing with parents; dinner £10; deposit: £5 per person CARDS: none DETAILS: children welcome; dogs welcome; no smoking; car park; garden

RAYDON Suffolk map 6

Goodlands Farm

Raydon, nr Ipswich IP7 5LQ
TEL: (01473) 310287
from A12 take B1070 towards Hadleigh, through Holton, and after Raydon village farm is on right

Approached via a long private drive, this eighteenth-century farmhouse is in a peaceful position in open countryside. There is a wooded area for bird-watchers, a hard tennis court, and a games room with table-tennis, darts and games for smaller children. Joan Hassell is a pleasant host, and there are no petty rules, just good old-fashioned hospitality. There is a guest lounge, and a separate dining-room where three-course home-cooked meals are served; guests may bring their own wine to dinner. Visitors may use the garden, and the services of a professional tennis coach can be arranged if required. A self-catering unit is also available.

OWNER: Joan Hassell OPEN: all year ROOMS: 1 single, 1 double, 1 twin, all with wash-basin; 2 family, 1 with bath/shower, 1 with wash-basin; TV in some bedrooms and lounge TERMS: single/single occupancy £16.50, twin/double £30, family room from £68.50; children's reductions; dinner £7 for children, £10 for adults CARDS: none DETAILS: children welcome; no dogs; smoking in lounge only; car park; games room; garden; tennis

READING Berkshire map 2

Chazey House

64 Chazey Road, Caversham Heights, Reading RG4 7DU
TEL: (01734) 477249
off A4074, 1½m N of town centre

This modern red-brick detached family house stands in a large garden in a quiet residential street one and a half miles north of Reading town centre. The spacious bedrooms have a soft pastel décor; all have pine furniture and attractive quilts made by Jean Earle and one has a king-sized bed. The Earles are an interesting couple who have travelled extensively (German is spoken), and enjoy providing excellent-value accommodation. There is a comfortable sitting-room with TV, and guests can sit in the lovely gardens and the new conservatory. Evening meals are no longer served, but there is a good bus service to the town centre. Guests can be picked up and dropped off at the bus or train station if pre-arranged.

OWNERS: Major and Mrs J. Earle OPEN: all year exc Christmas ROOMS: 1 single; 2 double, both with wash-basin; 1 twin; TV in some bedrooms and lounge TERMS: single £18, single occupancy £20, twin/double £34 CARDS: none DETAILS: no children under 12; well-behaved dogs welcome; no smoking; car park; garden

Rainbow Lodge

152 Caversham Road, Reading RG1 8AY
TEL: (01734) 588140   FAX: (01734) 586500

This immaculate hotel-lodge, within half a mile of the town centre, offers eight modestly sized rooms with modern furniture. Breakfast is taken in the hotel restaurant, which also serves dinners. It is licensed and vegetarian meals are always on offer. Snacks and sandwiches are also available on request. The lodge is well maintained and benefits from a recent refurbishment. Bedrooms facing the street are subject to noise, so light sleepers should ask for one of the rear bedrooms.

OWNER: Mr D. Staples OPEN: all year exc Christmas ROOMS: 1 single, 2 double, 5 twin; all rooms with bath/shower; TV in all bedrooms TERMS: single £38, single occupancy £44, twin/double £44; dinner £12 CARDS: Access, Amex, Delta, Diners, Switch, Visa DETAILS: children welcome; no dogs; car park

REDLYNCH   Wiltshire   **map 2**

Templeman's Old Farmhouse

Redlynch, nr Salisbury SP5 2JS
TEL: (01725) 510331
from Salisbury take A338 S for 5m, turn left at Downton traffic lights, first left after sign for Redlynch, first right, fork left and follow to end of lane

If the directions make finding this house sound tricky, the Dabells can arrange to send a map beforehand. This handsome seventeenth-century farmhouse was presented to Lord Nelson's family by a grateful nation. Its quiet hilltop position takes in panoramic views over the New Forest. Ten acres of garden complete with croquet lawn, hard tennis-court and paddocks with sheep surround the property. June and Peter Dabell have created a friendly, family atmosphere; visitors have use of an elegant drawing-room, and breakfast only is served in the dining-room. All three bedrooms are spacious, and the twin has the best views looking towards the New Forest.

OWNERS: June and Peter Dabell OPEN: Apr to Oct ROOMS: 1 single, 1 double, 1 twin; all rooms with wash-basin; TV lounge TERMS: single £17–£19, single occupancy £25,

twin/double £34–£38; £12 for children under 12; deposit: by arrangement CARDS:
none DETAILS: children welcome; no dogs; smoking in drawing-room only; car park;
garden; tennis

RICHMOND   North Yorkshire   map 9

Old Brewery

29 The Green, Richmond DL10 4RG
TEL: (01748) 822460   FAX: (01748) 825561

This former inn occupies a prime position overlooking a green, in a
secluded corner of this historic town. The Old Brewery has been
decorated in Victorian style and furnished with antiques, yet offers
all modern comforts. It is full of interesting nooks and crannies, with
thick stone walls. One bedroom has a hand-made four-poster with a
Yorkshire rose, and there is one ground-floor bedroom; all rooms but
one have *en suite* facilities – although this room does have its own
bathroom. There is a comfortable lounge, and a sheltered patio area
in the garden for residents' use. Three-course evening meals are
served if arranged in advance; vegetarians can be catered for and
guests should bring their own wine to table as there is no licence. A
tea-shop on the premises opens during the season for home-made
light snacks. Packed lunches can also be requested. Although there is
no private car park, visitors can park around the green.

OWNER: Mrs Y.F. Mears   OPEN: all year exc Christmas and New Year   ROOMS: 3 double,
1 twin, 1 four-poster; all rooms with bath/shower; TV in all bedrooms and lounge
TERMS: single occupancy £29.50, twin/double £38, four-poster £38; dinner £12   CARDS:
none   DETAILS: no children; no dogs; garden

West End Guesthouse

45 Reeth Road, Richmond DL10 4EX
TEL: (01748) 824783

This charming and unusual Victorian property is on the outskirts of
Richmond, well set back from the main road in half an acre of
secluded gardens with a monkey-puzzle tree. The house is in
excellent decorative order and is immaculately maintained. The
bedrooms, decorated in pastels, have pine furniture and fitted
wardrobes. There is one ground-floor room. The comfortable lounge
has a piano and is warmed by a gas fire. The charming owners have
provided everything possible to ensure their guests' comfort. Tasty
three-course dinners are served at 7pm and there is an alcohol
licence. The house is very near the river and open countryside. Four
self-catering cottages are available in the grounds.

OWNERS: Trevor and Kath Teeley   OPEN: all year exc Christmas and New Year   ROOMS:
1 single, 3 double, 1 twin, 1 family; all rooms with bath/shower; TV in all bedrooms

TERMS: single £19.50, single occupancy £27.50, twin/double £39, family room £49; dinner £12; deposit: £10 CARDS: none DETAILS: children welcome; dogs welcome; smoking in lounge only; car park; garden

RICHMOND Surrey   map 3

Riverside Hotel

23 Petersham Road, Richmond TW10 6UH
TEL/FAX: (0181) 940 1339
on A307, Kingston-upon-Thames to Richmond road

This popular Victorian hotel is superbly located on the Thames, with views of the river and the picturesque town of Richmond. The well-appointed bedrooms are furnished in keeping with the character of the house, and have *en suite* facilities. There is an original marble fireplace in the dining-room where a substantial breakfast is served. There are some lovely river walks from the hotel and the town centre is just a few minutes away. Parking may be a problem as the hotel's car park holds only four cars.

OWNERS: Mr and Mrs Monti OPEN: all year ROOMS: 4 single, 7 double, 3 twin, 1 four-poster, 1 family; all rooms with bath/shower; TV in all bedrooms and lounge TERMS: single £45, single occupancy £50, twin/double £60–£65, four-poster £70, family room £70–£75; children under 5 free CARDS: Access, Amex, Visa DETAILS: children welcome; dogs by prior arrangement; car park

RINGMORE Devon   map 1

Ayrmer House

Ringmore, nr Kingsbridge TQ7 4HL
TEL: (01548) 810391
from A379 2m E of Modbury take B3392 towards Bigbury-on-Sea then follow signs to Ringmore from St Ann's Chapel

Although this 1960s house is nothing special to look at, the large modern windows and balcony make the most of its wonderful position above a pretty village with views down the valley to the sea. Inside it is very bright and light and the bedrooms are spacious and comfortably furnished; three of them lead out on to the wide balcony. There is also a suite with a twin-bedded room, a double room and a bathroom. The relaxing lounge has a dining area at one end, and opens out on to a terrace, which is a pleasant spot on fine days. Evening meals are available by arrangement and vegetarians can be catered for. A track leads down to the relatively unspoilt beach.

OWNER: Isabella Dodds OPEN: all year exc Christmas ROOMS: 2 double, 1 with bath/shower, 1 with wash-basin; 1 twin; 1 family, with bath/shower; TV in all bedrooms and lounge TERMS: single occupancy £24, twin/double £34–£40, family room £36 plus children's charge; half-price for children over 10 sharing with parents; dinner £10; deposit: 20% CARDS: none DETAILS: no children under 10; no dogs; no smoking; car park; garden

RINGWOOD Hampshire   map 2

Little Forest Lodge

Poulner Hill, Ringwood BH24 3HS
TEL: (01425) 478848
just off A31 Ringwood to Cadnam road

Little Forest Lodge is a large country house set in three acres of landscaped gardens in the New Forest. Eric and Jane Martin are a welcoming couple and they have furnished their house to a high standard of comfort. Breakfast only is served in the oak-panelled dining-room overlooking the garden, and packed lunches can be provided. Drinks can be enjoyed in the bar, and a log fire burns on cooler evenings in the elegant lounge. The well-equipped bedrooms are attractively furnished and decorated. Little Forest Lodge is a convenient location for the New Forest and for visiting Salisbury, Bournemouth and Winchester.

OWNERS: Eric and Jane Martin OPEN: all year exc Christmas ROOMS: 2 double, 1 twin, 2 family; all rooms with bath/shower; TV in all bedrooms TERMS: single occupancy £29–£39, twin/double £39–£61, family room £55–£69; children's reductions by arrangement; deposit: credit card details CARDS: Access, Visa DETAILS: children welcome; dogs by arrangement; no smoking in bedrooms or dining-room; car park; garden

Moortown Lodge

244 Christchurch Road, Ringwood BH24 3AS
TEL: (01425) 471404   FAX: (01425) 476052
on B3347, 1½m S of Ringwood

This Georgian house is on the edge of the New Forest and was formerly a fishing lodge on the Moortown Estate, which was once owned by William Gladstone. The small, prettily decorated bedrooms are all *en suite*, one having a four-poster bed, and there is a lounge and bar. The owners run a restaurant which is also open to non-residents, and Jilly Burrows-Jones enjoys preparing freshly cooked food from locally produced ingredients. There is fishing on the River Avon, and the area offers good walks, golf and horse-riding.

OWNERS: Jilly and Bob Burrows-Jones OPEN: all year exc 24 Dec to mid-Jan ROOMS: 1 single, 2 double, 2 twin, 1 four-poster, 1 family; all rooms with bath/shower; TV in all bedrooms TERMS: single £29, single occupancy £38, twin/double £56, four-poster/family room £62; dinner £15; deposit: credit card details CARDS: Access, Amex, Visa DETAILS: children welcome; no dogs; no smoking in dining-room and some bedrooms; car park

ROADWATER   Somerset   map 1

Wood Advent Farm

Roadwater, Watchet TA23 0RR
TEL/FAX: (01984) 640920
from A39 in Washford turn at sign to Roadwater, follow sign to farm from village

This spacious listed farmhouse dates from 1804 and is part of a large working farm. It stands at the foot of the Brendon Hills within Exmoor National Park. The house has a friendly and relaxing atmosphere and John and Diana Brewer are welcoming hosts. The individually decorated bedrooms have pleasant views of the grounds and the large sitting-room has a log fire. Dinner (vegetarian options by arrangement) is served at separate tables in the licensed dining-room, and meals include fresh produce from the farm. Sunday lunch is offered too. The large garden includes a small heated swimming-pool and an imperfect grass tennis court. Horse riding and clay-pigeon shooting can be arranged and marked footpaths run across the farm. The main coastal road and Blue Anchor Bay are two miles away.

OWNERS: John and Diana Brewer   OPEN: all year   ROOMS: 3 double, 2 twin; all rooms with bath/shower; TV lounge   TERMS: single occupancy £30, twin/double £39; dinner £12   CARDS: none   DETAILS: children welcome; dogs welcome; smoking in 1 lounge only; car park; garden; swimming-pool; tennis

ROBIN HOOD'S BAY   North Yorkshire   map 9

Devon House

Station Road, Robin Hood's Bay YO22 4RL
TEL: (01947) 880197
5m S of Whitby at end of B1447

High standards continue to be maintained at this modest, but immaculate, Victorian house in the town centre. It is in excellent decorative order, with new carpets and new drapes, and one bedroom has plush pink and white tent-style drapes decorating the ceiling. Lace and dried-flower arrangements made by Daphne Duncalfe's mother adorn the house. There are two bathrooms exclusively for guests' use. Devon House is easily located in the summer, when the entrance is ablaze with colour from hanging baskets and potted plants. Breakfast only is served. There is a public car park opposite.

OWNER: Daphne Duncalfe   OPEN: all year exc Christmas   ROOMS: 1 double, 2 family; all rooms with wash-basin; TV in all bedrooms   TERMS: double £30, family room £37.50–£67.50; half-price for children sharing with parents; deposit: £10   CARDS: none
DETAILS: children welcome; no dogs; no smoking; garden

ROCKBOURNE Hampshire

map 2

Shearings

Rockbourne, Fordingbridge SP6 3NA
TEL: (01725) 518256   FAX: (01725) 518255
take turning to Rockbourne off A354 1m S of Coombe Bissett

This picture-book sixteenth-century listed thatched cottage with
uneven floors, oak beams and inglenook fireplaces is set in a lovely,
well-maintained garden of lawns and shrubs. Shearings faces a
stream in the pretty village of Rockbourne with its thirteenth-
century church, Roman villa and delightful old pub. Guests are
treated as friends and there is a small sitting-room with TV, books
and brochures. The bedrooms are comfortable and well equipped.
Guests can play croquet on the lawn in the summer, and a summer
house and a sunny patio can also be found in the garden. Shearings
makes a delightful base for visiting the New Forest, the Solent, and
for golf, riding and fishing.

OWNER: Colin Watts OPEN: mid-Feb to mid-Dec ROOMS: 1 single, 1 double, 1 twin; all
rooms with bath/shower; TV lounge TERMS: single £23, single occupancy £30, twin/
double £46–£50 CARDS: none DETAILS: no children under 12; no dogs; no smoking
upstairs and in bedrooms; car park; garden

SHEARINGS, ROCKBOURNE

RODBOURNE   Wiltshire   map 2

Angrove Farm

Rodbourne, nr Malmesbury SN16 0ET
TEL: (01666) 822982
from Malmesbury take A429 Chippenham road for 1m, turn left into
Grange Lane, after 2m turn left into Angrove Lane

This modernised stone farmhouse stands in a large garden in
peaceful countryside, the house being set apart from the farm
buildings which serve the 200 acres of beef and arable farmland. Mrs
Parfitt is a delightful and welcoming lady who does everything
possible to please her guests. The house is comfortable, clean and well
decorated, and the large dining-room has separate tables where
breakfast only is served. The River Avon and Angrove Wood border
the property, and trout and coarse fishing are available, as well as
plenty of walks.

OWNERS: Ronald and Cynthia Parfitt   OPEN: Feb to end Nov   ROOMS: 2 double, 1 twin,
all with bath/shower; TV lounge   TERMS: single occupancy £20, twin/double £32–£36;
deposit: £5 per person per night   CARDS: none   DETAILS: children by arrangement; no
dogs; no smoking; car park; garden

ROGATE   West Sussex   map 3

Cumbers House

Rogate, nr Petersfield GU31 5EJ
TEL: (01730) 821401
on A272, 4m W of Midhurst

Down a quiet rhododendron-lined driveway off the main Midhurst-
Petersfield road, Cumbers House stands in the comfortable
surroundings of its own three and a half acres of woodland garden. It
dates from the 1930s and is a large family house furnished with
antiques. The atmosphere is warm and relaxed, and open fires burn
in both the drawing-room and dining-room. Mrs Aslett offers home-
baked bread and home-produced eggs and honey at breakfast.

OWNERS: Major and Mrs Jon Aslett   OPEN: all year exc Christmas and Jan   ROOMS: 1
single, with wash-basin; 2 twin, 1 with bath/shower, 1 with wash-basin; TV lounge
TERMS: single £20, twin £40–£44; deposit   CARDS: none   DETAILS: no children; no dogs;
no smoking; car park; garden

Breakfast at B&Bs tends to mean a cooked breakfast of bacon, eggs and so
on. If you prefer a different style of breakfast, it is best to discuss this when
you make a booking.

Mizzards Farm

Rogate GU31 5HS
TEL: (01730) 821656   FAX: (01730) 821655
from A272 at Rogate turn S at crossroads, then right after crossing river

A welcoming glow emanates from the mellow-brick and stone exterior
of this seventeenth-century farm at the edge of a delightful village.
Mizzards is set in 13 acres of pleasant gardens and fields bordering
the River Rother. The house has ancient flagstone floors and a
beautiful wooden staircase leading to a galleried landing. The vaulted
dining-room with a stone fireplace, lovely old furniture and
interesting pictures lends a sense of grandeur to traditional
breakfasts (which may include kippers and kedgeree). The elegant
drawing-room has a grand piano. The largest bedroom has a four-
poster bed on a raised hexagonal platform and an *en suite* ornate
marble bathroom full of mirrors. Extra accommodation is available in
an adjoining cottage, and guests have use of a covered swimming-pool
(open from May to the end of September). The gardens include a
lovely woodland area, ducks on the lake, deer and badgers. The
owners are happy to guide guests to the best local establishments for
evening meals.

OWNERS: Mr and Mrs J.C. Francis   OPEN: all year exc Christmas   ROOMS: 1 double, 1
twin, 1 four-poster; all rooms with bath/shower; TV in all bedrooms   TERMS: single
occupancy £30–£36, twin/double £50, four-poster £56; deposit required for long stays
CARDS: none   DETAILS: no children under 8; no dogs; no smoking; car park; garden;
swimming-pool

ROSS-ON-WYE   Hereford & Worcester   **map 5**

Edde Cross House

Edde Cross Street, Ross-on-Wye HR9 7BZ
TEL: (01989) 565088

This elegantly restored Georgian townhouse overlooks a horseshoe
bend of the River Wye, and is only a few minutes' walk from the
centre of town. The house was once the home of Sybil Hathaway, the
Dame of Sark. The rooms are beautifully furnished in old pine and
tastefully decorated; the comfortable lounge has books and
magazines. Breakfasts only are served, and include both traditional
fare and substantial cooked vegetarian options. There is a helpful list
of nearby restaurants and pubs that offer evening meals. On pleasant
days guests are welcome to use the garden.

OWNER: Renate Van Gelderen   OPEN: Feb to Nov   ROOMS: 2 double, 1 twin; all rooms
with bath/shower; TV in all bedrooms   TERMS: single occupancy £25–£30, twin/double
£42–£46; deposit: £20   CARDS: none   DETAILS: no children under 10; no dogs; no
smoking; car park; garden

ROWLAND   Derbyshire

map 8

Holly Cottage

Rowland, nr Bakewell DE45 1NR
TEL: (01629) 640624
from B6001 at Hassop turn at sign for Rowland, then take first right

Holly Cottage is in ideal walking territory, situated at the end of an attractive hamlet on a dead-end road leading directly to the hills of the Peak District. It is also well placed for visiting the stately homes of Chatsworth House, Haddon Hall and Hardwick Hall. The stone-built cottage dates from the eighteenth century and is set among landscaped gardens with a patio of old stone. Mary Everard is a friendly hostess who was once English Ladies' Golf Champion and can give interested guests extensive information on several nearby golf courses. The lounge is large and comfortable and an open fire burns in the hall on chilly days. The bedrooms are spotlessly clean and have comfortable beds.

OWNER: Mary Everard   OPEN: Jan to Oct   ROOMS: 2 twin, 1 with wash-basin; TV lounge   TERMS: single occupancy £23, twin £37–£38; children's reductions by arrangement; dinner £11; deposit: £10   CARDS: none   DETAILS: children welcome; no dogs; no smoking; car park; garden

RUDGEWAY   Avon

map 2

Friezecroft

Rudgeway, nr Bristol BS12 2SF
TEL/FAX: (01454) 412276
off A38, 2m N of M4/M5 junction

This warm and welcoming seventeenth-century cottage approached by a private lane is in a rural setting not far from the Severn Estuary, and yet is very convenient for the M4 and M5 motorways. Melodie Morris is a charming host who makes her guests feel at ease and spoils them – for example, by providing breakfast to order rather than limiting the choices. She and her husband are very familiar with the area and are always happy to help guests plan their days. The house is brimming with old-world charm and has thick stone walls, beams and an inglenook fireplace. The bedrooms are well appointed with Laura Ashley décor.

OWNER: Melodie Morris   OPEN: all year exc Christmas   ROOMS: 2 single, 1 double, 1 twin, 1 family; all rooms with bath/shower; TV in some bedrooms and lounge   TERMS: single £22.50, single occupancy £25, twin/double £50; family room from £75   CARDS: none   DETAILS: children welcome; no dogs; no smoking in bedrooms; car park; garden

RYARSH   Kent

map 3

Heavers

Chapel Street, Ryarsh, nr West Malling ME19 5JU
TEL/FAX: (01732) 842074
*from M20 junction 4 take A228 to Leybourne, then right on A20 towards
Wrotham Heath and turn right to cross motorway*

At the top of a hill, up a narrow dead-end lane from a tiny village,
Heavers is a traditional smallholding, with sheep, geese, chickens
and bees. This seventeenth-century house with a clematis-covered
porch is comfortable and compact, with small rooms and low ceilings.
Guests are treated as members of the family and invited to make
themselves at home. Evening meals using home-grown produce are
served by arrangement and vegetarians can be catered for. Honey
from the owners' bees is for sale.

OWNERS: James and Jean Edwards   OPEN: all year exc Christmas and New Year
ROOMS: 1 double, 2 twin; all rooms with wash-basin; TV lounge   TERMS: single
occupancy £20–£22, twin/double £34–£38; half-price for children under 10; dinner £13;
deposit: 33%   CARDS: none   DETAILS: children welcome; dogs by arrangement; no
smoking; car park; garden

RYE   East Sussex

map 3

Green Hedges

Hillyfields, Rye Hill, Rye TN31 7NH
TEL: (01797) 222185

Green Hedges is an attractive Edwardian house in a very quiet
residential street a little above the centre of the town. It stands in
extensive and lovely gardens with an outdoor heated swimming-pool.
The house is tastefully furnished and has a warm and welcoming
atmosphere. Both the sitting-room and dining-room have lovely views
across the garden to Rye, which is just a short stroll away. The
bedrooms are comfortable and well appointed. Breakfast includes
home-made preserves, fruit from the garden, vegetarian alternatives
and organic produce.

OWNER: Sheila Luck   OPEN: all year exc Christmas   ROOMS: 2 double, 1 twin; all rooms
with bath/shower; TV in all bedrooms   TERMS: single occupancy £40, twin/double
£50–£57; deposit: £5 per person per night   CARDS: Access, Visa   DETAILS: no children
under 12; no dogs; no smoking; car park; garden; swimming-pool

*Any smoking restrictions that we know of are given in the details at the end
of the entry.*

Half House

Military Road, Rye TN31 7NY
TEL: (01797) 223404

Half House is set back a little off the road with a very colourful front garden, and offers comfortable accommodation within a ten-minute walk of the centre of Rye. It was built at the turn of the century and has bright and attractively decorated bedrooms. Breakfast only is served in the pretty breakfast room, but there are plenty of eating places nearby for evening meals. Bicycles can be provided for guests' use.

OWNERS: Norman and Agnes Bennett OPEN: all year ROOMS: 3 double, all with wash-basin; 2 twin, 1 with bath/shower, 1 with wash-basin; 1 family, with wash-basin; TV in all bedrooms TERMS: single occupancy £20–£25, twin/double £30–£40, family room £30–£40; half-price for children sharing with parents; deposit: £15 CARDS: Access, Visa DETAILS: children welcome; no dogs; no smoking in dining-room and some bedrooms; garden

Jeake's House

Mermaid Street, Rye TN31 7ET
TEL: (01797) 222828   FAX: (01797) 222623

Jeake's House can be found in one of Britain's most famous streets, right in the centre of the lovely town of Rye. This listed building was originally used as a storehouse, and was built in 1689 by Samuel Jeake, a wool merchant. It was later used as a Baptist school, and in 1924 became the home of the American author Conrad Aiken, whose visitors included writers and artists such as T.S. Eliot, E.F. Benson, Edward Burra, Paul Nash and Malcolm Lowry. Jenny Hadfield is an extremely friendly hostess who runs a superb establishment. She is responsible for all the décor and furnishings, which are in keeping with the period of the house; original features such as oak beams and wood panelling are also much in evidence. The beautifully appointed bedrooms overlook the rooftops of the town or face south across the marsh to the sea. Breakfast is served in the eighteenth-century dining-room, which was once used as a Quaker meeting place, and there is a licensed bar. As the approach to Jeake's House is up a steep cobbled street, and there are steep stairs in the house, it is not suitable for disabled or elderly people. Car parking is at the bottom of the street.

OWNER: Mrs J.P. Hadfield OPEN: all year ROOMS: 1 single, with wash-basin; 6 double, 5 with bath/shower, 1 with wash-basin; 1 twin, 2 four-poster, 2 family, all with bath/shower; TV in all bedrooms TERMS: single £22.50, single occupancy £35–£53, twin/double £41–£59, four-poster £82, family room £73–£106; babies free, half-price for children sharing with parents; deposit: £25 CARDS: Access, Visa DETAILS: children welcome; no dogs in dining-room; no smoking in dining-room

Little Orchard House

West Street, Rye TN31 7ES
TEL: (01797) 223831

Dating from the 1700s, Little Orchard House is set in a large,
secluded walled garden right in the town centre. Previous owners of
Little Orchard have included those prominent in local politics, and
Lloyd George stayed here. The house has a warm and pleasant
atmosphere and fine Georgian panelling, period furnishings, oil
paintings and prints. It is clean and comfortable and each bedroom
has its own sitting area with TV. There is a sitting-room with open
fireplace, a small library/games room, and a dining-room where
breakfast only is served. An eighteenth-century smuggler's
watchtower stands in the garden, where self-catering accommodation
is also available. Guests can unload their luggage at the house and
then park in one of the public car parks close by.

OWNER: Sara Brinkhurst OPEN: all year ROOMS: 1 double; 1 twin; 1 four-poster; all
rooms with bath/shower; TV in all bedrooms TERMS: single occupancy £40–£60, twin/
double £60–£80, four-poster £70–£84; deposit: cheque or credit card details CARDS:
Access, Delta, Visa DETAILS: no children under 12; no dogs; smoking in public rooms
only; car park; garden

Old Vicarage

66 Church Square, Rye TN31 7HF
TEL: (01797) 222119 FAX: (01797) 227466

This 400-year old pink-washed residence was a vicarage until 1889.
Among its famous owners were the seventeenth-century dramatist
John Fletcher and Henry James, who wrote *The Spoils of Poynton*
while living here. The Old Vicarage is a highly attractive listed
building in a delightful cobbled setting by the ancient church of St
Mary's. The beamed sitting-room and the dining-room, with its log
fire in winter, overlook the pretty walled garden. Six small, well-
appointed bedrooms with Laura Ashley designs have views mostly
over the rooftops and across the churchyard to the distant sea. One of
the most popular rooms is on the second floor with a small sitting
area and exposed beams. Two rooms have four-posters and one a
coronet bed. Breakfast only is served and includes freshly ground
coffee and home-baked scones. The price includes a complimentary
newspaper and sherry. There are numerous restaurants, pubs and
cafés in the town.

OWNERS: Julia and Paul Masters OPEN: all year exc Christmas ROOMS: 2 double, 1
twin, 2 four-poster, 1 family; all rooms with bath/shower exc 1 double, with wash-basin;
TV in all bedrooms TERMS: single occupancy £35–£50, twin/double £40–£58, four-
poster £59, family room £66; deposit: 50% CARDS: none DETAILS: no children under 8;
no dogs; no smoking in bedrooms and dining-room; car park

Playden Cottage

Military Road, Rye TN31 7NY
TEL: (01797) 222234

Contrary to what its name may evoke, this is a large, attractive whitewashed house built into the side of the cliff in the Playden district of Rye, overlooking the River Rother and Romney Marsh. It has a spectacular and colourful garden, which is irrigated by a 'water catchment' system from springs in the cliff behind the house, and is looked after by Sheelagh Fox, who is a keen gardener. Playden is a Domesday village, and Playden Cottage is reputed to be the house called *Grebe* in E.F. Benson's *Mapp and Lucia* novels. It is a relaxing, friendly house in a peaceful spot away from the crowds of Rye. The long sitting-room has TV, books and games for guests' use, and the writing-room leads to a small patio in a quiet part of the garden. Two of the spacious *en suite* bedrooms have garden views, and the third has a peaceful woodland outlook. Breakfast only is served in the dining-room and there are plenty of places for evening meals in Rye, which is less than a mile away.

OWNER: Sheelagh Fox   OPEN: all year   ROOMS: 1 double, 2 twin; all rooms with shower; TV lounge   TERMS: single occupancy £37.50–£45, twin/double £50–£60; reductions for children over 12 sharing with parents; dinner £10   CARDS: Access, Visa   DETAILS: no children under 12; no dogs; no smoking in dining-room; car park; garden

---

RYTON   Shropshire   map 5

The Old House

Ryton, Dorrington, nr Shrewsbury SY5 7LY
TEL: (01743) 718585
leave A49 5m S of Shrewsbury at Dorrington then follow signs for Ryton, turn right at end of village, then left 50yds before the Fox pub

This whitewashed Tudor manor house has retained much of its original oak frame, beams and panelling. It is surrounded by two acres of well-kept gardens with a croquet lawn and has views to the rolling hills of south Shropshire. The house is immaculately maintained and the three lovely bedrooms are furnished with antiques. Susan Paget-Brown is a professional dried-flower arranger and many of her creations decorate the house. The comfortable lounge is a sociable place in which to relax, and the Fox pub nearby is convenient for evening meals.

OWNERS: James and Susan Paget-Brown   OPEN: all year   ROOMS: 3 double, all with bath/shower; TV lounge   TERMS: double £36; deposit   CARDS: none   DETAILS: children welcome; no dogs; no smoking; car park; garden

Coastguards

St Agnes TR22 0PL
TEL: (01720) 422373   FAX: (01720) 423326

This disused coastguard station is attached to a row of cottages, and
the accommodation is in two of the three cottages which were built
back to front (the fault of the architect). Coastguards has the
distinction of being the most southerly guesthouse in Britain, and is a
friendly family home, with guests and family sharing the facilities. It
stands on one of the highest points of the island of St Agnes and has
good sea views overlooking Bishop Rock Lighthouse. The comfortable
sitting-room has books, games and jigsaws, and evening meals are
available by arrangement. There is a garden for guests' use. St Agnes
is a beautiful island inhabited by a tightly knit community that
welcomes visitors who come to relax and enjoy the peace and quiet,
the mild climate and the wealth of flora and fauna. The islands
attract bird-watchers, particularly during the autumn migration.
The terms here are for dinner, bed and breakfast.

OWNERS: Danny and Wendy Hick   OPEN: all year exc Christmas & New Year   ROOMS: 2
double, 1 with bath/shower; 1 twin   TERMS: rates include dinner; single occupancy £26,
twin/double £52; children's reductions according to age; deposit: 25%   CARDS: none
DETAILS: children welcome; dogs by arrangement; no smoking; garden

---

Covean Cottage

St Agnes TR22 0PL
TEL: (01720) 422620

Although a walk round St Agnes need only take a morning (the island
is less than a mile long and half a mile wide), there are rocky coves,
beaches, footpaths and views that are best explored at leisure. This
small stone guesthouse is a short walk from the sea, and doubles as a
tea-room in season. The Sewells are a friendly couple who offer
accommodation in both the main house and Little Cottage, in the
grounds, for those requiring more privacy. Although there is no
central heating, heaters can be provided for bedrooms if needed.
Lunch and dinner (7pm) are served; vegetarian choices and packed
lunches can be requested, and guests may bring their own wine as
there is no alcohol licence.

OWNERS: Mr and Mrs P. Sewell   OPEN: Jan to end Oct   ROOMS: 3 double, 2 with bath/
shower, 1 with wash-basin; 2 twin, 1 with bath/shower, 1 with wash-basin; TV in some
bedrooms and lounge   TERMS: single occupancy £30, twin/double £57–£60; dinner
£11.50; deposit: £30 per person   CARDS: none   DETAILS: no children under 9; no dogs
in dining-room or lounge; no smoking in dining-room or lounge

ST ALBANS Hertfordshire

map 3

Care Inns

29 Alma Road, St Albans AL1 3AT
TEL: (01727) 867310

This friendly semi-detached Victorian house is only three minutes from the station and seven from the town centre. The house is well maintained and all bedrooms have a small fridge. Karin Arscott is a well-travelled lady who enjoys people and languages, and herself speaks French, Spanish, Italian and German. Breakfast only is available, but a good selection of restaurants and pubs can be found a couple of minutes' walk away.

OWNER: Karin Arscott OPEN: all year ROOMS: 1 single, 1 double/family, 1 twin; all rooms with bath/shower; TV in all bedrooms TERMS: single/single occupancy £25, twin/double £39, family room £45; half-price for children under 12 CARDS: none DETAILS: children welcome; dogs by arrangement; no smoking in breakfast room; car park

ST AUSTELL Cornwall

map 1

Poltarrow Farm

St Mewan, nr St Austell PL26 7DR
TEL: (01726) 67111
off A390 St Austell to Truro road, turn right 1m after St Austell, then ¼m

This whitewashed, wistaria-clad stone farmhouse is set amid fields, just out of the small village of St Mewan in an away-from-it-all spot. The house is surrounded by spacious grounds and a farmyard, and the 45 acres support cows, sheep, geese and ducks. Poltarrow has a welcoming, relaxed atmosphere and is a wonderful place for children. The comfortable accommodation comprises a pleasant sitting-room, and a dining-room where breakfast and dinner are served. Nearby there are old tin mines to visit and coastal paths to enjoy, and the old ports of Mevagissey, Fowey and St Mawes are all within easy reach. Self-catering accommodation is also available.

OWNER: Judith Nancarrow OPEN: all year exc Christmas and New Year ROOMS: 3 double, 1 twin, 1 family; all rooms with bath/shower; TV in all bedrooms and lounge TERMS: single occupancy £22, twin/double £40, family room £60; dinner £10 CARDS: Access, Visa DETAILS: children welcome; no dogs; no smoking in bedrooms; car park; games room; garden

---

If you are forced to turn up later than planned, please telephone to warn the proprietor.

ST BRIAVELS   Gloucestershire

map 5

Cinderhill House

St Briavels, Gloucester GL15 6RH
TEL: (01594) 530393   FAX: (01594) 530098
take A46 from Chepstow towards Monmouth, go over Bigsweir Bridge,
follow sign for St Briavels and then turn left

Cinderhill House is in an idyllic situation below St Briavels Castle, with breathtaking views over magnificent countryside and the River Wye. The house is full of character, with parts dating from the fourteenth century, and has exposed beams, inglenook fireplaces, flagstone floors and an old bread oven. It has been lovingly restored and is tastefully decorated and furnished in keeping with its character. There is a comfortable beamed sitting-room with TV, and a games room. All the bedrooms are well appointed and there are also three self-catering cottages. Gillie Peacock makes her guests feel relaxed and takes pride in her well-balanced meals; all diets can be catered for. Cinderhill is licensed and there is an extensive wine list; packed lunches can be provided.

OWNER: Gillie Peacock   OPEN: all year exc Christmas   ROOMS: 1 double, 2 twin, 2 four-poster, 1 family; all rooms with bath/shower; 1 room suitable for wheelchair-users; TV in some bedrooms and lounge   TERMS: single occupancy £30, twin/double £50, four-poster £64, family room £60; children's reductions by arrangement; dinner £18; deposit required   CARDS: none   DETAILS: children welcome; no dogs; no smoking in bedrooms or dining-room; car park; games room

ST HILARY   Cornwall

map 1

Ennys

St Hilary, nr Marazion TR20 9BZ
TEL/FAX: (01736) 740262
signposted on B3280, 2m E of Marazion

Approached down a long tree-lined drive and surrounded by its 50-acre farm, Ennys is an elegant creeper-clad stone manor house dating from the seventeenth century. It is set in peaceful wooded countryside close to the River Hayle and there are many pleasant walks and picnic sites along the river banks. Relaxing and satisfying dinners are served by candlelight at separate tables and include locally caught fish, herbs and organic vegetables from the garden, and home-baked bread. Children's portions at a reduced price are available. On warm days breakfast can be served on the patio which overlooks the walled garden. Three spacious, attractively decorated and comfortable bedrooms, two of which have four-poster beds, are in the main house, and a converted barn contains two family suites. The rooms have patchwork quilts, paintings and prints. The cosy sitting-room with its log fire is a good place to gather before dinner on colder evenings. The grounds include a grass tennis court and a heated swimming-pool.

OWNERS: Sue and John White OPEN: all year ROOMS: 1 twin, 2 four-poster, 2 family; all rooms with bath/shower; TV in all bedrooms TERMS: single occupancy £30–£35, twin £40–£55, four-poster £55, family room £55–£90; dinner £17.50; deposit: £25 per person CARDS: Access, Visa DETAILS: children welcome; no dogs; smoking in sitting-room only; car park; games room; garden; swimming-pool; tennis

ST IVES   Cornwall

map 1

The Count House

Trenwith Square, St Ives TR26 1DJ
TEL: (01736) 795369

The Count House stands in a quiet square with wonderful views of the town, harbour and bay. It is an old granite house which gets its name from the days when tin miners' wages were counted here. The Cannings are warm and helpful people who make sure their guests enjoy their stay, and Ken, a decorator by trade, has produced some imaginative paint details throughout the house. An outside patio has tables and chairs, and the indoor sitting area has beams and a log fire plus plenty of books. Good-value evening meals are served in the dining-room, the bar stocks a number of wines and Cornish cream teas are also available.

OWNERS: Kenneth and Cheryl Canning OPEN: all year ROOMS: 2 single, 5 double, 1 twin, 1 four-poster; all rooms with bath/shower; TV in some bedrooms and lounge TERMS: single £26, single occupancy £30, twin/double £40, four-poster £44; dinner £9.50; deposit CARDS: none DETAILS: no children; no dogs; no smoking; car park; garden

Sunrise Guest House

22 The Warren, St Ives TR26 2EA
TEL: (01736) 795407

This terraced guesthouse can be found in one of the oldest, narrowest streets in St Ives, just by the rail and bus station, and close to the sea and harbour. Sunrise is now run by Mrs Mason's daughter, who has added an extra *en suite* room, and offers good-value accommodation arranged on different levels. The snug TV lounge and attractive breakfast room are on the lower level, with a flight of steep, narrow stairs leading up to the small bedrooms. At the rear of the property are more stairs leading up to the top bedrooms, which have wonderful sea views and two small patio areas for sitting out. This top floor has access to the street above and is opposite the bus station. Although the house is unlicensed, guests are welcome to bring their own wine to dinner, and packed lunches can be provided.

OWNERS: Mr and Mrs Mason, and Mrs Adams OPEN: all year exc during owners' holiday ROOMS: 1 single; 5 double, 4 with bath/shower, 1 with wash-basin; 2 twin, 1 with bath/shower, 1 with wash-basin; 1 family; TV in all bedrooms and lounge TERMS: single £17, single occupancy £20, twin/double £32–£40, family room £40–£50; half-price for children sharing with parents; deposit: £20 per person CARDS: none DETAILS: children welcome; dogs welcome; no smoking in dining-room; car park; garden

ST LAWRENCE   Isle of Wight   map 2

Lisle Combe

Undercliff Drive, St Lawrence, Ventnor PO38 1UW
TEL: (01983) 852582
off A3055 W of Ventnor next to Rare Breeds Park

Formerly the home of the poet and author Alfred Noyes, this Elizabethan-style farmhouse has become a guesthouse under the ownership of his son. The house has wonderful views overlooking the English Channel and is surrounded by large, attractive grounds which feature the Rare Breeds and Waterfowl Park, to which guests have free entry. The entire area is listed as an Area of Outstanding Natural Beauty. Mrs Noyes is most welcoming and has endless energy and enthusiasm. The rooms are spacious and furnished with antiques, and guests have use of a TV room. The twin bedroom converts easily into a family room and this is a wonderful place for children, with lots of interesting things to see in the 36 acres belonging to the property, and beaches and coves nearby.

OWNERS: Hugh and Judy Noyes OPEN: all year exc Christmas ROOMS: 1 single, 1 double, 1 twin; all rooms with wash-basin; TV lounge TERMS: single £16.50–£18, twin/double £33–£36; childrens reductions in low season; deposit required CARDS: none DETAILS: children welcome; no dogs; no smoking in bedrooms; car park; garden

Little Orchard

Undercliff Drive, St Lawrence, Ventnor PO38 1YA
TEL: (01983) 731106
on A3055, 3m W of Ventnor

Little Orchard is a stone building dating from around 1750 with a friendly, welcoming atmosphere. It is a comfortable house and has been tastefully furnished and decorated. One of the bedrooms has just a curtain separating the room from the *en suite* bathroom. Guests are welcome to share the family sitting-room and the attractive, hilly garden. The house is not suitable for those without a car, as the main road outside is dangerous for pedestrians. The Rare Breeds and Waterfowl Park is nearby as are beaches, a golf course and botanic gardens.

OWNERS: Paul and Heather Nolan OPEN: all year ROOMS: 3 double, all with bath/shower; TV in all bedrooms and lounge TERMS: single occupancy £18.50, double £33–£37; half-price for children under 12; deposit: 1 night's charge CARDS: none DETAILS: children welcome; dogs by arrangement; no smoking; car park; garden

---

ST MARGARET'S AT CLIFFE   Kent   map 3

Merzenich Guest House

Station Road, St Margaret's at Cliffe CT15 6AY
TEL: (01304) 852260   FAX: (01304) 852167
off A258 Dover to Deal road, 2m NE of Dover

This modern guesthouse in a quiet coastal village offers clean and comfortable accommodation and friendly hosts. Rob Claringbould used to be a fireman and a collection of fire-engine cartoons decorates the staircase. Breakfast only is served in the dining-room, and in the conservatory in summer. One of the five bedrooms is in the attic. There are lovely clifftop walks with views to the French coast, and the house is only five to six minutes away from Dover and half an hour from the Channel Tunnel. There is a good selection of pubs locally for evening meals.

OWNERS: Dolly and Rob Claringbould OPEN: all year ROOMS: 3 double, 1 twin, 1 family; all rooms with bath/shower; TV in all bedrooms TERMS: single occupancy £22, twin/double £34; family room rates by arrangement; children under 5 free, half-price for ages 5 to 13; deposit: £5 per person CARDS: none DETAILS: children welcome; no dogs; car park; garden

---

ST MARTIN'S   Isles of Scilly   map 1

Glenmoor Cottage

St Martin's TR25 0QL
TEL: (01720) 422816

Glenmoor Cottage stands behind a stone wall in Higher Town and has lovely views over the pretty garden to the golden sandy beach and the islands beyond. It is an original island cottage that has been extended and modernised, and there is a gift shop in the adjacent building, also run by Barbara Clarke. The three bedrooms are quite small, but there is a large lounge/dining-room. Home-cooked evening meals can include vegetarian options by arrangement and guests are welcome to bring their own wine. The nearest beach is only a few minutes' walk away through bulbfields, and is a good centre for water-related activities such as scuba diving and sailing.

OWNER: Barbara Clarke OPEN: all year exc Christmas ROOMS: 1 single, 1 double, 1 family; all rooms with wash-basin; TV lounge TERMS: rates include dinner; single £28, double £56, family room £56 plus children's charge; half-price for children from 2 to 12; deposit: £20 CARDS: none DETAILS: no children under 2; dogs welcome; garden

Polreath

Higher Town, St Martin's TR25 0QL
TEL: (01720) 422046

This attractive granite Victorian house, built as the residence for a local farmer, is in the centre of the island and a few minutes from the quay. Geoff and Elaine Watt run it as a licensed guesthouse and tea-room, where a selection of home-made food is available for breakfast, lunch and dinner. The house is sparklingly clean, with fresh and bright décor; the bedrooms, some with good views, are small and neatly furnished. St Martin's is a sparsely populated island with unspoilt beaches, pretty farmland and fine coastal and country walks. Packed lunches can be provided.

OWNERS: Geoff and Elaine Watt OPEN: all year exc Christmas ROOMS: 1 single, with wash-basin; 3 double, 1 with bath/shower, 2 with wash-basin; 2 twin, 1 with bath/shower, 1 with wash-basin; TV lounge TERMS: rates inc dinner; single/single occupancy £23.50–£39.50, twin/double £47–£78.50; 25% reduction for children from 5 to 10; deposit: 20% CARDS: none DETAILS: no children under 5; no dogs; smoking in lounge only; garden

ST MARY'S   Isles of Scilly   map 1

The Boathouse

St Mary's TR21 0LN
TEL: (01720) 422688

With a gentle, relaxed atmosphere and stunning views of the islands, the Boathouse is a small guesthouse situated right on the seafront and close to the centre of town. Three of the five simply furnished bedrooms have sea views and the first-floor lounge leads out on to a small terrace. Home-cooked evening meals using fresh produce from the vegetable garden, and always with a vegetarian option, are served in the dining-room every day except Friday. St Mary's makes a good base for visiting all the other islands.

OWNER: Maureen Stuttaford OPEN: Easter to Oct ROOMS: 3 double, 2 twin; all rooms with wash-basin TERMS: single occupancy £20, twin/double £40; half-price for children over 6 sharing with parents; dinner £12.50; deposit: £50 CARDS: none DETAILS: no children under 6; dogs welcome; smoking in lounge only

Carn Warvel

Church Road, St Mary's TR21 0NA
TEL: (01720) 422111
halfway between Hugh Town and Old Town

This old granite house was originally two cottages and stands in a quiet country lane in a sunny spot protected from the prevailing winds. Carn Warvel is one of the first listed buildings in St Mary's and is set in three-quarters of an acre of gardens with lovely views to the Lower Moors and Old Town. The house has recently been converted to provide comfortable accommodation; two of the bedrooms are on the ground floor. The dining-room is licensed and the lounge has an open granite fireplace and doors out to the sun terrace.

OWNERS: Neil and Jenny Hedges OPEN: Mar to Nov ROOMS: 1 single, 2 double, 2 twin; all rooms with bath/shower; TV in all bedrooms TERMS: single/single occupancy £23, twin/double £46; dinner £11; deposit: 10% CARDS: none DETAILS: no children under 8; no dogs; no smoking in dining-room; car park; garden

ST MAWES   Cornwall   **map 1**

Braganza

St Mawes TR2 5BJ
TEL: (01326) 270281

This classically elegant Georgian house stands in a commanding position in the centre of St Mawes, with wonderful views over the picturesque fishing village and boats towards Falmouth on the other side of the water. Visitors to Braganza enjoy a feeling of space, tranquillity and old-fashioned hospitality in this typical English country house which has a period feel to it, with pre-war bathroom fittings, fresh flowers in the rooms and the beds turned down at night. There is a TV in the upstairs sitting-room, and breakfast is served at one table in the elegant dining-room. The house is surrounded by a large garden and is off a narrow steep lane, which leads down to the harbour.

OWNERS: the Moseley family OPEN: Easter to Nov ROOMS: 1 single, with wash-basin; 5 twin, 3 with bath/shower, 2 with wash-basin; TV lounge TERMS: single £20, single occupancy £25–£30, twin £42–£50; reductions for babies in cots; deposit: £20 CARDS: none DETAILS: children welcome; no dogs in public rooms; no smoking in dining-room; car park; garden

If we know a B&B has an alcohol licence, we say so.

We state at the end of an entry whether children are welcome. If we know of any restrictions on children, we give them.

SALCOMBE   Devon   map 1

Suncroft

Fortescue Road, Salcombe TQ8 8AP
TEL: (01548) 843975

This family home sits high above the entrance to the picturesque port of Salcombe on a very quiet 'unmade-up' residential road. All three guest rooms face the front and enjoy lovely coastal views. Breakfast is served in a large room which doubles as a sitting-room, and the bedrooms are bright and comfortably furnished. Guests may sit out on the pretty patio in summer. Suncroft is a family home in a lovely position halfway between the town and North Sands beach. Packed lunches can be provided.

OWNERS: Peter and Jenny Sherlock   OPEN: all year exc Christmas   ROOMS: 3 double, 2 with bath/shower, 1 with wash-basin; TV in all bedrooms   TERMS: single occupancy £25–£30, double £36–£50; reductions for children sharing with parents; deposit: £20–£50   CARDS: none   DETAILS: children welcome; no dogs; no smoking in bedrooms or at meals; car park; garden

Sunningdale

Main Road, Salcombe TQ8 8JW
TEL: (01548) 843513

Sunningdale has glorious views out to sea, to Bolt Head and the rolling Devon farmland. It is a substantial house dating from the 1930s and has a beautifully maintained garden, with a sunny patio where tables and chairs are set in summer. Two of the large, bright and comfortably furnished ground-floor bedrooms share a bathroom, and have the lovely sea view; the third *en suite* bedroom is upstairs. The dining-room, where breakfast only is served, has a bay window facing south-west; packed lunches can be provided by arrangement. The Poynters previously had a bed-and-breakfast establishment in London and have taken over Sunningdale since our last edition. They also have a self-catering flat for rental. The centre of town is only a ten-minute downhill walk.

OWNERS: Erica and Michael Poynter   OPEN: all year exc 15 to 28 Dec   ROOMS: 1 double, with wash-basin; 2 twin, 1 with bath/shower, 1 with wash-basin; TV in some bedrooms   TERMS: single occupancy £22.50, twin/double £45   CARDS: none   DETAILS: no children under 12; dogs by prior arrangement; no smoking; car park; garden

Please let us know if you think a B&B should be included in this Guide. Report forms are at the back of the book – or use your own stationery if you prefer (no stamps are needed within the UK).

Brooklands Luxury Lodge

208 Marsland Road, Sale M33 3NE
TEL: (0161) 973 3283
on A6144, 1m W of M63 junction 8

Built in 1851 in Austrian style, Brooklands is an attractive lodge set
back from the road in its own grounds and conveniently located two
minutes' walk from the tram line into the centre of Manchester.
Guests take self-service Continental breakfast in the large, well-
equipped bedrooms with breakfast bars, four of which are on the
ground floor. Cooked breakfasts can be provided by arrangement.
Dinner is served between 5.30 and 6.30pm, again in the bedrooms.
Facilities include a sunbed and a whirlpool bath, and there is a
laundry room. Long-term parking is available for guests using the
lodge as a stopover on the way to the airport.

OWNERS: Les and Ann Bowker   OPEN: all year   ROOMS: 5 single, 1 with bath/shower, 4
with wash-basin; 1 double, with bath/shower; 1 twin, with bath/shower; 1 four-poster,
with bath/shower; 1 family, with bath/shower; TV in all bedrooms   TERMS: single
£22–£30, single occupancy £28–£30, twin/double £38–£40, four-poster £40–£42,
family room £48–£50; free for children under 10 sharing with parents; dinner £8;
deposit: £20   CARDS: Access, Visa   DETAILS: children welcome; no dogs; no smoking in
some bedrooms; car park; garden

Cornerstones

230 Washway Road, Sale M33 4RA
TEL/FAX: (0161) 283 6909
on A56 between M63 and M56

Cornerstones was built in 1871 by Sir William Cunliff Brooks, the
lord of the manor, and was tastefully restored several years ago. The
house has retained its Victorian character and the rooms are
comfortable, spacious, tastefully decorated and furnished to a high
standard. Tea, coffee and cake can be served up at just about any time
in the sitting-room. Evening meals are also available and
Cornerstones is licensed, but there is also a variety of eating places
within walking distance. Dorothy and Tony Casey are an
accommodating couple who keep the house immaculate. The house is
in a convenient location 15 minutes' drive from Manchester city
centre and only a five-minute walk from the tram.

OWNERS: Anthony and Dorothy Casey   OPEN: all year exc Christmas   ROOMS: 3 single,
1 with bath/shower, 2 with wash-basin; 4 double, all with bath/shower; 2 twin, both with
bath/shower; TV in all bedrooms   TERMS: single £20–£26, single occupancy £20–£35,
twin/double £40–£47; £5 for children under 5; dinner £10–£11; deposit required
CARDS: Access, Visa   DETAILS: children welcome; no dogs; no smoking; car park;
garden

Farthings

9 Swaynes Close, Salisbury SP1 3AE
TEL: (01722) 330749

This Victorian town house stands in its own garden in a quiet position on the north side of town, about a ten-minute walk to the centre. Mrs Rodwell is a charming lady who goes out of her way to be helpful and informative. The bedrooms are tastefully decorated, and a collection of black-and-white photographs decorates the sitting-room and dining-room. There is a good choice for breakfast, and although evening meals are not served there are many nearby restaurants.

OWNER: Gill Rodwell OPEN: all year exc Christmas ROOMS: 2 single, both with wash-basin; 1 double, with bath/shower; 1 twin, with bath/shower; TV lounge TERMS: single £18–£20, single occupancy £27–£30, twin/double £36–£40; deposit: 33% CARDS: none DETAILS: no children; no dogs; no smoking; car park; garden

Glen Lyn House

6 Bellamy Lane, Milford Hill, Salisbury SP1 2SP
TEL: (01722) 327880

This red-brick Victorian house is in a quiet lane a ten minutes' uphill walk from the centre of Salisbury. It has a pleasant atmosphere and, at the back, an attractive mature garden. The nine bedrooms are simply furnished, and there is a residents' lounge. Home-made bread is served at breakfast and licensed dinners are available, by request, at 7pm. Notice is required for vegetarian meals.

OWNER: Brian Stuart OPEN: all year exc Christmas week ROOMS: 1 single, with wash-basin; 4 double, 1 with bath/shower, 3 with wash-basin; 3 twin, 2 with bath/shower, 1 with wash-basin; 1 family, with bath/shower; TV in all bedrooms and lounge TERMS: single £20–£22, single occupancy £26–£36, twin/double £36–£42, family room £57; dinner £9; deposit: 25% CARDS: none DETAILS: no children under 12; guide dogs only; no smoking; car park; garden

Hayburn Wyke

72 Castle Road, Salisbury SP1 3RL
TEL: (01722) 412627
on A345 Amesbury road, 1m N of Salisbury city centre

This turn-of-the-century guesthouse is named after the place in Scotland where its builder had his honeymoon. The accommodation is very clean and consists of six small, bright bedrooms which are all freshly decorated; two of the bedrooms are up a narrow staircase on the second floor. Breakfast only is served in the dining-room, but packed lunches can be provided.

OWNERS: Alan and Dawn Curnow   OPEN: all year   ROOMS: 3 double, 1 with bath/shower, 2 with wash-basin; 1 twin, with wash-basin; 2 family, 1 with bath/shower, 1 with wash-basin; TV in all bedrooms and lounge   TERMS: single occupancy £23–£36, twin/double £34–£40, family room from £40; children's reductions according to age   CARDS: none   DETAILS: children welcome; no dogs; no smoking in dining-room; car park; garden

Old Bakery

35 Bedwin Street, Salisbury SP1 3UT
TEL: (01722) 320100

This delightful establishment was a bakery until 1971, and is a sixteenth-century listed property built around a frame of ships' timbers. It is in the centre of Salisbury, and although the house is on a busy street the noise is minimal because of double glazing. Guests have use of a large, homely TV lounge/breakfast room and the three small and quite simple bedrooms are tucked away up narrow staircases and under low beams. Breakfast only is available. The owners minimise the fat used in cooked breakfasts and take an environment-friendly approach to running the establishment.

OWNERS: Peter and Evelyn Bunce   OPEN: all year exc Christmas   ROOMS: 1 single, with wash-basin; 1 double, with bath/shower; 1 twin, with bath/shower; TV in all bedrooms   TERMS: single £18, single occupancy £20–£30, twin/double £34–£42; deposit: £10–£20   CARDS: none   DETAILS: no children under 10; no dogs; no smoking in breakfast room; garden

Stratford Lodge

4 Park Lane, Castle Road, Salisbury SP1 3NP
TEL: (01722) 325177   FAX: (01722) 412699

This beautifully furnished, welcoming Victorian property is down a quiet lane overlooking Victoria Park, just off the Salisbury to Amesbury road. Jill Bayly is a cheerful lady who loves gardening and is also a gourmet cook; her food attracts return guests. Four-course dinners with lots of choice at each stage, including vegetarian dishes and daily specials, are served. Wine by the bottle or glass, as well as liqueurs, is sold separately. All the comfortably furnished bedrooms are *en suite*, and there is a lovely big sitting-room, music room, breakfast room and attractive dining-room. In addition to the garden, guests have use of an indoor swimming-pool. The centre of Salisbury can be reached by a pleasant 15-minute walk along the river.

OWNER: Jill Bayly OPEN: all year exc Christmas and New Year ROOMS: 2 single, 2 double, 2 twin, 2 family; all rooms with bath/shower; TV in all bedrooms TERMS: single £30, single occupancy £30–£35, twin/double £50–£56, family room £60; reductions for children over 8 sharing with parents; dinner £18; deposit: credit card details CARDS: Access, Amex, Delta, Switch, Visa DETAILS: no children under 8; no dogs; no smoking; car park; garden; swimming-pool

SANDFORD ORCAS Dorset   map 2

The Alders

Sandford Orcas, nr Sherborne DT9 4SB
TEL: (01963) 220666
from Sherborne take B3148 N, after 2½m turn right signposted Sandford Orcas; at village T-junction turn left

This attractive stone house is set in a lovely walled garden, and has been cleverly converted by its architect owner, who works from home. It is tucked away from the main road in the charming conservation village of Sandford Orcas. The house is tastefully furnished, with a real fire in the comfortable lounge, and the two smartly decorated bedrooms are equipped to a high standard. Breakfast only is served, but there is good food to be had in the village pub. The Alders overlooks a Tudor manor house, which is open to the public, and the medieval church. Sherborne is only three miles away.

OWNERS: John and Sue Ferdinando OPEN: all year ROOMS: 1 double, 1 twin; both rooms with bath/shower; TV in both bedrooms and lounge TERMS: single occupancy £23.50–£25, twin/double £37–£40; reductions for children under 14 sharing with parents CARDS: none DETAILS: children welcome; no dogs; no smoking; car park; garden

SCARBOROUGH North Yorkshire   map 9

Highbank Hotel

5 Givendale Road, Scarborough YO12 6LE
TEL: (01723) 365265

Highbank is a modern property set in a quiet, tree-lined area close to Peasholm Park, the sea and all attractions. The hotel is strictly non-smoking. The comfortable lounge has attractive cushioned wicker furniture and plenty of literature about the local area. Breakfast and excellent home-cooked evening meals are served in the adjacent dining-room, which has an interesting collection of hand-painted French porcelain moulds. There is a lawned front garden with a patio and garden furniture. The *en suite* bedrooms are fresh and bright with colourful duvets and matching fabrics.

OWNERS: Ted and Margaret Marsh OPEN: Mar to Oct ROOMS: 2 single, 3 double, 1 twin, 1 family; all rooms with bath/shower; TV in all bedrooms TERMS: single/single occupancy £17.50, twin/double £35, family room £53; half-price for children sharing with parents; dinner £6; deposit: £17.50 per person CARDS: none DETAILS: children welcome; dogs in bedrooms only; no smoking; car park; garden

Lyncris Manor

45 Northstead Manor Drive, Scarborough YO12 6AF
TEL: (01273) 361052

This attractive red-brick building with leaded-light windows overlooks a park and is just a five-minute walk from the beach. The immaculate *en suite* bedrooms are of a good size, with modern teak and mahogany furniture. Breakfast and good-value home-cooked dinners are served in the licensed dining-room on pretty china and lace tablecloths. Children's helpings and vegetarian choices may be requested in advance. There is also a very pleasant TV lounge. The ambience here is warm and friendly and guests find it easy to relax.

OWNERS: John and Patricia Cass OPEN: all year ROOMS: 2 double, 4 family; all rooms with bath/shower; TV in all bedrooms and lounge TERMS: double £32–£40, family room from £32; babies free, children's reductions by arrangement; dinner £5; deposit: £20 per person CARDS: none DETAILS: children welcome; no dogs; smoking in bar lounge only; car park; garden

SEDBERGH Cumbria map 8

Marshall House

Main Street, Sedbergh LA10 5BL
TEL: (01539) 621053 FAX: (01539) 620046

Standing in the town centre, this listed eighteenth-century house retains many of its original features, such as a grand staircase, coved ceilings and several old fireplaces. It is named after a former master at Sedbergh School and has plenty of historical associations: a sixteenth-century vaulted cellar under the house was reputed to have held slaves on their way to be sold; an old French cannon by the side of the house is thought to have been left by Bonnie Prince Charles. One of the two ground-floor bedrooms is suitable for wheelchair-users. Walkers who return after a wet day out are happy to have use of a drying-room, and an oak-panelled lounge with a log fire. Breakfast is served in the bright kitchen, and dinner – if pre-arranged – in the panelled dining-room. The house is unlicensed, but guests may bring their own wine to dinner. Packed lunches can be provided.

OWNERS: Mr and Mrs David Kerry OPEN: all year exc Christmas ROOMS: 1 double, 2 twin; all rooms with bath/shower; 1 room suitable for wheelchair-users; TV in all bedrooms TERMS: single occupancy £33 (out of season only), twin/double £42–£50; dinner £17.50; deposit: £5 per person per night CARDS: none DETAILS: no children under 12; no dogs; no smoking in one twin bedroom; car park; garden

Randall Hill

Sedbergh LA10 5HJ
TEL: (01539) 620633
on A583, ½m W of Sedbergh, or 4½m E of M6 junction 37

Set in three acres of grounds within the Yorkshire Dales National
Park, this turn-of-the-century house offers four comfortable ground-
floor bedrooms, furnished in mahogany and pine, and a TV lounge.
All the bedrooms are named after the trees they overlook. The Snows
treat their guests as friends, and offer a hot drink upon arrival; Peter
is a keen fisherman and is happy to advise on local fishing.
Breakfasts only are served, and include free-range eggs and home-
made breads and marmalades. Packed lunches can be provided. The
guesthouse is well placed for visiting 'Herriot country' and for walks
in the beautiful hills and valleys around Sedbergh.

OWNERS: Peter and Joan Snow   OPEN: all year   ROOMS: 2 double, 1 with wash-basin; 2
twin, both with wash-basin; TV lounge   TERMS: single occupancy £17, twin/double
£30–£34; deposit: £10   CARDS: none   DETAILS: children welcome; dogs welcome; no
smoking; car park; garden

SEDLESCOMBE   East Sussex   map 3

Platnix Farm

Harts Green, Sedlescombe, nr Battle TN33 0RT
TEL: (01424) 870214
*from A21 take B2244 towards Sedlescombe, then left towards Westfield for
1m and turn left to farm*

Platnix Farm stands in an isolated rural position with lovely views
over the surrounding farmland. Part of a small working sheep farm,
the building is a clever conversion of a former oast house. The
restored roundels make for three unusual round rooms: the dining-
and sitting-rooms and one of the bedrooms. Mrs Howard is a very
friendly and hospitable lady and keeps an immaculate and
comfortable house. The farm can be found down a series of narrow
lanes and is well situated for visiting Rye and Battle.

OWNER: Benedetta Howard   OPEN: all year   ROOMS: 2 double, 1 twin; all rooms with
bath/shower; TV in all bedrooms   TERMS: single occupancy £25–£35, twin/double
£40–£60; half-price for children; deposit: £20 per room   CARDS: none   DETAILS: children
welcome; dogs in kennel only; car park; garden

*Many B&Bs are in remote places, and although in many cases we provide
directions, it is always advisable to ask for clear instructions when
booking.*

SELLING   Kent   **map 3**

Owens Court Farm

Selling, nr Faversham ME13 9QN
TEL/FAX: (01227) 752247
*off A2 London to Dover road SE of Faversham, turn right at Shell Garage
signposted Selling*

This elegant Georgian farmhouse stands in quiet countryside, and is
part of a traditional hop and fruit farm. The house has many of its
original features and has well-proportioned rooms. The comfortable
bedrooms are pleasantly furnished and there is a first-floor lounge
with TV. Coffee/tea-making facilities and biscuits are available on the
landing, and breakfast only is served in the dining-room. The Higgses
are a friendly couple and keen gardeners. Owens Court Farm is
within easy reach of Canterbury and is a good place for country
walks. Evening meals can be taken at the nearby village pub.

OWNER: Mrs E. Higgs   OPEN: all year   ROOMS: 1 single, 1 twin, 1 family; all with wash-
basin; TV in all bedrooms and lounge   TERMS: single/single occupancy £17, twin £34,
family from £42.50; half-price for children; deposit: £10   CARDS: none   DETAILS:
children welcome; no dogs; no smoking in bedrooms; car park; garden

SELSIDE   Cumbria   **map 8**

Low Jock Scar

Selside, nr Kendal LA8 9LE
TEL: (01539) 823259   FAX: (01539) 823645
just off A6, 6m N of Kendal

This attractive, low-built property constructed of Lakeland stone
occupies an extremely rural, quiet riverside setting. Low Jock Scar is
sheltered by a screen of trees and surrounded by six acres of gardens
and woodland, including lovely walks all around. Five spacious
bedrooms are well appointed with traditional and pine furnishings;
three have *en suite* bathrooms and two are on the ground floor.
Breakfast, and dinner by arrangement, is taken in the licensed
conservatory/dining-room, which has creeper-covered slate walls.
Vegetarians can be catered for with notice. A handwritten weather
report for the next day is thoughtfully included on the reverse of the
menu.

OWNERS: Philip and Alison Midwinter   OPEN: Mar to Oct   ROOMS: 3 double, 2 with bath/
shower, 1 with wash-basin; 2 twin, 1 with bath/shower, 1 with wash-basin   TERMS:
single occupancy £27–£32, twin/double £40–£50; dinner £14.50; deposit: £20 per
person   CARDS: none   DETAILS: no children; no dogs in public rooms; no smoking; car
park; garden

SETLEY Hampshire   map 2

Setley Lodge

Setley, Brockenhurst SO42 7UG
TEL: (01590) 622146
off A337, 1m S of Brockenhurst, behind the Filly Inn

Surrounded by lush woodland and three acres of garden, this large
whitewashed building is in a quiet location at the edge of the New
Forest. Norman and Thea Gillett maintain high standards and
guests have a choice of a twin or double, both very comfortable and
both *en suite*. Breakfast is served in the kitchen. Two well-equipped
self-catering flats with their own entrances are available on a weekly
basis. Riding, sailing and fishing are on offer nearby. The
neighbouring Filly Inn is an old country pub offering good food.
Lymington is only four miles away.

OWNERS: Norman and Thea Gillett OPEN: all year exc Christmas ROOMS: 1 double, 1
twin; both rooms with bath/shower; TV in both bedrooms TERMS: single occupancy
£25, twin/double £34–£36; deposit: £10 CARDS: none DETAILS: no children; no dogs;
no smoking; car park; garden

SHALDON Devon   map 1

Virginia Cottage

Brook Lane, Shaldon, Teignmouth TQ14 0HL
TEL/FAX: (01626) 872634
off B3199, just S of Teignmouth

This attractive, whitewashed early seventeenth-century house
stands in a lovely, partly walled garden and is on a narrow, quiet lane
in a peaceful setting. The entrance to the cottage is through a heavy,
elaborately carved front door with decorated porch timbers which
came from South Africa. The three bedrooms are attractively
furnished and decorated, and guests have the use of a sitting-room
and a dining-room, where breakfast only is served. At the rear of the
cottage is a small heated swimming-pool. The River Teign is just a
five-minute walk away. Shaldon has several pubs and restaurants,
and Torquay and Exeter are within easy driving distance.

OWNERS: Jennifer and Michael Britton OPEN: Mar to Dec ROOMS: 2 twin, 1 family; all
rooms with bath/shower; TV lounge TERMS: single occupancy £26, twin/family room
£42; £14 for children over 12 sharing with parents in family room; deposit: £15 CARDS:
none DETAILS: no children under 12; no dogs; no smoking; car park; garden;
swimming-pool

---

*Entries in the Guide are listed under town or village. There are also two
indexes at the back of the book, one listing B&Bs by county, the other by
name.*

Orchard Cottage

2 Mill Road, Shalfleet, nr Newport PO30 4NE
TEL: (01983) 531589
4m from ferry at Yarmouth on A3054

Orchard Cottage is an attractive cream-painted cottage set in a
pretty two-acre garden with a stream. June Thompson loves cooking,
specialising in breakfasts, and also offers tea in the afternoon, either
in the garden room or in the garden itself. All the well-furnished
bedrooms are most attractive, and there is a comfortable sitting-
room, and a dining-room where breakfast is provided. The New Inn,
opposite, serves good food at both lunch and dinner, and is a very
popular place which gets very crowded at weekends. Visitors enjoy
the walk down to Shalfleet quay, and the area is very popular with
yachtsmen.

OWNER: June Thompson   OPEN: all year exc Christmas   ROOMS: 1 double, 1 twin; both
with wash-basin; 1 family, with bath/shower; TV in all bedrooms   TERMS: single
occupancy £20–£25, twin/double £34–£36, family room £36–£40; children's reductions
according to age   CARDS: none   DETAILS: children by arrangement; no dogs; no
smoking; garden

Shalfleet House

Shalfleet, nr Newport PO30 4NS
TEL/FAX: (01983) 531280
400yds W of the village

This substantial Victorian house stands in extensive gardens that
include a hard tennis court, and overlooks the Newtown Estuary
Nature Reserve and Bird Sanctuary. Lying just outside the village, it
was built as the vicarage and is sheltered from the road by trees. The
charming owners have being doing B&B for a number of years in
their comfortable family home. The bedrooms are large and well
furnished, and the ground-floor twin room with *en suite* shower and
WC has its own entrance. There is a sitting-room/kitchen above it,
and the suite can also be let separately as a self-catering unit. The
house has partial central heating. Breakfast only is served in the
dining-room, which has an attractive Victorian fireplace. Packed
lunches can be provided.

OWNERS: Lt Col and Mrs J.R.E. Laird   OPEN: all year exc Easter, Christmas and New
Year   ROOMS: 1 double, with wash-basin; 2 twin, 1 with shower, 1 with wash-basin
TERMS: single occupancy £20–£25; twin/double £36; children under 3 free, reductions
for older children; deposit   CARDS: none   DETAILS: children welcome; dogs in ground-
floor room only; no smoking; car park; tennis

Cavendish House

8 Eastmount Road, Shanklin PO37 6DN
TEL/FAX: (01983) 862460

This comfortable, welcoming house is in a quiet road, close to the centre of Shanklin, the cliff path and beach. It is a substantial Victorian house with a friendly owner. The three large, attractive bedrooms have bathrooms, TV, telephone and a dining area where English breakfast is served. Although there is no sitting-room for guests' use, a small conservatory is available, as is the large back garden with lawns and shrubs.

OWNERS: Peter and Lesley Cavaciuti OPEN: all year exc Christmas and 2 weeks Feb ROOMS: 3 double; all rooms with bath/shower; TV in all bedrooms TERMS: single occupancy £17.50–£23.50, double £32–£38; deposit: £10 per person CARDS: Access, Delta, Switch, Visa DETAILS: no children under 12; dogs by arrangement; car park; garden

Knaptoft House Farm / The Greenway

Bruntingthorpe Road, Shearsby, nr Lutterworth LE17 6PR
TEL/FAX: (0116) 2478388
leave A50 4m S of Leicester at Shearsby and continue 1m towards Bruntingthorpe

This traditional mixed farm is set in the rolling Leicester countryside, and includes a cobbled stableyard where horses are kept at livery. The farmhouse has recently been upgraded to add *en suite* facilities and TVs in some bedrooms. The sun lounge has superb views and catches the afternoon light and the TV lounge has a wood-burning stove. The Greenway is a modern bungalow in the old orchard; it has similar facilities and three ground-floor bedrooms. The medieval fish ponds in the grounds have been restored and restocked, and guests may fish by arrangement. Breakfast only is served in the dining-room. Guests are welcome to use the garden, which includes a barbecue.

OWNER: Mrs A.T. Hutchinson OPEN: all year exc Christmas ROOMS: 1 single, with wash-basin; 2 double, both with bath/shower; 2 twin, 1 with bath/shower, 1 with wash-basin; 1 family, with wash-basin; TV in some bedrooms and lounge TERMS: single £18, single occupancy £20, twin/double £35–£42, family room £45; children's reductions; deposit CARDS: none DETAILS: no children under 5; no dogs; no smoking in dining-room and some bedrooms; car park; garden

SHEEPWASH Devon	map 1

Half Moon Inn

Sheepwash, nr Beaworthy EX21 5NE
TEL: (01409) 231376   FAX: (01409) 231673
off A3072, 4m W of Hatherleigh

The Inniss family has owned the Half Moon since 1958, and it is very much a family-run establishment. It has been the village inn for over 200 years, and forms one side of the picturesque square in the centre of the village of Sheepwash. Whitewashed and built of cob, it is 400 years old and has a large garden. The bar, with its flagstone floor and large stone fireplace, is a popular meeting place for locals and visitors alike. Dinner is served in the attractive dining-room, and residents have use of a small lounge with TV. Three of the well-equipped bedrooms are on the ground floor. Fishermen are well looked after here: there is a large rod room, excellent drying facilities, and a small shop stocking the basic requirements for fishing; tuition and advice are all available if required. The inn has access to salmon and trout fishing on the River Torridge. For non-fishermen, the Half Moon is still a relaxing place to stay and is ideal as a base from which to explore Dartmoor, Exmoor and the north Devon and Cornish coastlines. Packed lunches can be provided.

OWNERS: Benjamin and Charles Inniss   OPEN: all year   ROOMS: 2 single, 4 double, 9 twin, 2 family; all rooms with bath/shower; TV in all bedrooms and lounge   TERMS: single £27.50–£35.50, single occupancy £32.50–£40.50, twin/double £50–£68; children's reductions by arrangement; dinner £18   CARDS: Access, Visa   DETAILS: children welcome; no dogs in public rooms; no smoking in dining-room; car park; games room; garden

SHEET Hampshire	map 2

Westmark House

Sheet, nr Petersfield GU31 5AT
TEL: (01730) 263863
on A272 N of Petersfield, turn right after Half Moon pub, follow signs to Midhurst, then approx ¾m farther (on a rather dangerous corner)

Westmark is a charming Georgian house set in two acres of gardens in a quiet position enjoying wonderful views. Mrs Pennefather is a delightful hostess and there is a relaxing and pleasant atmosphere. Beautiful furnishings are to be found in the sitting- and dining-rooms, and all three bedrooms have lovely views. Guests also have use of a conservatory, and the extensive garden which includes a hard tennis court and a heated swimming-pool. Evening meals can be provided by arrangement, and guests can bring their own wine to dinner as there is no licence. Westmark House is ideally placed for visiting Cowdray Park and Goodwood for racing, Portsmouth and Emsworth for sailing, and Chichester for the theatre.

OWNERS: Cdr and Mrs W. Pennefather OPEN: all year exc Christmas and New Year
ROOMS: 1 single, 1 double, 1 twin; all rooms with bath/shower; TV in all bedrooms
TERMS: single/single occupancy £24, twin/double £48; dinner £15 CARDS: none
DETAILS: no children under 8; no dogs; smoking in conservatory only; car park; garden; swimming-pool; tennis

SHEFFIELD   South Yorkshire   map 8

Holme Lane Farm

38 Halifax Road, Grenoside, Sheffield S30 3PB
TEL: (0114) 2468858
on A61, 5m N of Sheffield

Holme Farm is an unusual find situated not far from the M1 in a secluded and peaceful setting. Dating from the seventeenth century, the building was totally derelict and has been tastefully restored, providing an extremely high standard of accommodation with attractive décor and well-furnished bedrooms. Some of these are in the converted barn – which is ideal for those wanting extra privacy. Three bedrooms are on the ground floor. Breakfasts are served in the pleasant dining-room overlooking green fields with grazing horses. Self-catering is also available.

OWNERS: Keith and Sheila Hill OPEN: all year ROOMS: 4 single, 1 double, 2 twin; all rooms with bath/shower; 1 room suitable for wheelchair-users; TV in all bedrooms and lounge TERMS: single/single occupancy £26, twin/double £45; reductions for children under 8 sharing with parents; deposit: £10 CARDS: Access, Visa DETAILS: children welcome; no dogs; no smoking in dining-room or lounge; car park; games room; garden

SHEFFORD WOODLANDS   Berkshire   map 2

Fishers Farm

Shefford Woodlands, nr Hungerford RG17 7AB
TEL: (01488) 648466   FAX: (01488) 648706
from M4 junction 14 take A338 towards Wantage, then first left on B4000; farm is 400yds beyond Pheasant Inn on right

This traditional red-brick farmhouse sits in a large garden and is part of a 600-acre farm. The owners are a friendly and inviting couple who like visitors to make themselves at home and relax. If a quiet corner or a choice from the large classical CD collection doesn't suit, then the beautiful heated indoor swimming-pool or croquet on one of the lawns may tempt, but TV is not an option as the house has no sets. The well-appointed bedrooms are fresh and bright and the drawing-room has a log fire. Breakfast is served in the family kitchen and home-cooked evening meals can be provided by arrangement. The Wilsons usually join guests at dinner.

OWNER: Mary Wilson OPEN: all year ROOMS: 1 double, 1 twin, 1 family; all rooms with bath/shower TERMS: single occupancy £30, twin/double £40–£44, family room £50–£60; children's reductions by arrangement; dinner £15 CARDS: none DETAILS: children welcome; dogs by arrangement; smoking in sitting-room only; car park; garden; swimming-pool

SHENINGTON   Oxfordshire   map 5

Sugarswell Farm

Shenington OX15 6HW
TEL/FAX: (01295) 680512
leave A422 3m W of Banbury at sign for Shenington, continue through village, turn right at T-junction then right at crossroads

Rosemary Nunneley's cooking has become so popular that she has written a recipe book available to guests staying at this splendid modern brick farmhouse. It stands in a large garden and is surrounded by open countryside. Log fires glow in the large comfortable drawing-room on chilly days. The house has been furnished to a very high standard, with huge colour-matched bedrooms and bathrooms. Dinner is served by arrangement between 6.30 and 7.30pm; the house style is typified by pork in brandy and apple sauce followed by home-made chocolate soufflé. Vegetarians can be catered for with notice and guests are welcome to bring their own wine. All meals are served in the elegant dining-room, which has a fine display of paintings. This is also a lovely area for country walks.

OWNER: Rosemary Nunneley OPEN: all year ROOMS: 1 double, 2 twin; all rooms with bath/shower; TV in some bedrooms TERMS: single occupancy £30–£40, twin/double £50–£60; dinner £17; deposit: £25 CARDS: none DETAILS: no children under 12; no dogs; no smoking; car park; garden

SHEPHERDSWELL   Kent   map 3

Sunshine Cottage

The Green, Mill Lane, Shepherdswell, nr Dover CT15 7LQ
TEL: (01304) 831359
1m off A2 between Canterbury and Dover

This delightful listed cottage dates from 1635 and overlooks the village green in pretty Shepherdswell. The Popples also own the antique shop next door, and Sunshine Cottage retains a lot of its original features, including beams and an inglenook fireplace in the lounge. The dining-room, where dinner is served by arrangement, has antique pine furniture and stickback chairs. Although the house is unlicensed, guests are welcome to bring their own wine to dinner, and packed lunches can be provided. Two of the comfortable bedrooms are on the ground floor, and one of these will take wheelchairs; some of the bedrooms have antique bedsteads. Sunshine Cottage is on the North Downs Way.

OWNERS: Barry and Lyn Popple OPEN: all year ROOMS: 4 double, 2 with bath/shower, 2 with wash-basin; 1 twin, 1 family; both with wash-basin; 1 room suitable for wheelchair-users; TV lounge TERMS: single occupancy £20–£30; twin/double £38–£42; family room from £47; children's reductions by arrangement; dinner £14; deposit CARDS: none DETAILS: children welcome; no dogs; no smoking; car park; garden

SHERBOURNE   Warwickshire   map 5

Fulbrook Edge

Sherbourne Hill, nr Warwick CV35 8AG
TEL: (01926) 624242
off westbound carriageway of A46, just W of M40 junction 15

This long, low red-brick building stands on the rim of an escarpment overlooking the Avon Valley and the Cotswolds. Horses and pheasants may be found in the five-acre paddock which sweeps down towards the river. The two-and-a-half-acre garden includes a full-sized croquet lawn, which guests may use in return for a small contribution towards its upkeep. The lounge is well furnished and plenty of local information is available to peruse. The Lillywhites are knowledgeable about the area and will help to plan itineraries. The three very large ground-floor bedrooms are beautifully furnished and all have a sitting area. Two have countryside views and all are suitable for disabled guests. Breakfasts only are served, but menus for several local eating places are kept in the house.

OWNERS: Mr and Mrs R.B. Lillywhite OPEN: all year exc Christmas and New Year ROOMS: 1 double, 2 twin; all rooms with wash-basin; all rooms suitable for wheelchair-users; TV in all bedrooms and lounge TERMS: single occupancy £27–£31, twin/double £38–£44; deposit: £10 CARDS: none DETAILS: no children under 15; no dogs; no smoking in bedrooms or dining-room; car park; garden

SHERINGHAM   Norfolk   map 6

Fairlawns

26 Hooks Hill Road, Sheringham NR26 8NL
TEL: (01263) 824717

Impeccably maintained Fairlawns is a large, secluded Victorian house set in a beautiful garden (which includes a croquet lawn) a few minutes from the town centre. The bedrooms have been freshly decorated and all have *en suite* facilities. One visitor found the reception he received at Fairlawns 'excellent and polite' and his room 'classy'. There is a choice of traditional or Continental breakfasts (Sundays instead feature brunch starting with a glass of buck's fizz) and dinners are provided by arrangement. Vegetarian and special diets can be catered for with prior notice, and there is a small wine list. Packed lunches can be provided.

OWNER: Elizabeth A. McGill OPEN: March to November ROOMS: 2 double, 3 twin; all rooms with bath/shower; TV in all bedrooms TERMS: single occupancy £30, twin/ double £40; dinner £12.50; deposit: £20 CARDS: none DETAILS: no children under 12; guide dogs only; no smoking in bedrooms; car park; garden

Oak Lodge

2 Morris Street, Sheringham NR26 8JX
TEL: (01263) 823158

This Edwardian house is in the centre of Sheringham. The Halls are an easy-going couple who provide comfortable, good-value accommodation in their spotlessly clean and tastefully decorated home. The bedrooms are very large. Substantial breakfasts are served and several nearby establishments offer evening meals.

OWNERS: Charles and Mary Hall OPEN: Mar to Oct ROOMS: 2 double, 1 twin; all rooms with wash-basin; TV in all bedrooms TERMS: twin/double £35–£37; deposit: £10 CARDS: none DETAILS: no children; dogs welcome

SHINCLIFFE   Co Durham   map 10

Bracken View Guest House

Shincliffe, nr Durham DH1 2PD
TEL: (0191) 386 2966
just off A177, 2m SE of Durham

Bracken View is pleasantly situated in two acres of grounds in a conservation area, just two minutes' drive from Durham. Guests, however, would be well advised to walk into town or take the bus, which runs at ten-minute intervals. Seven bedrooms are decorated to a high standard, with some pine furniture and attractive quilts and drapes. There are four ground-floor rooms, one of which is suitable for disabled guests. Breakfast, lunch and pre-arranged evening meals are served in the licensed dining-room; children's helpings, vegetarian food and packed lunches can be provided. There is also a comfortable lounge with a small bar. Close by are some lovely walks, and red squirrels and deer are often to be seen. Owners Alan and Rhona Whitley are an accommodating couple, and Cassie their labrador is friendly.

OWNERS: Rhona and Alan Whitley OPEN: all year ROOMS: 1 single, 5 double, 1 twin, 1 family; all rooms with bath/shower; 1 room suitable for wheelchair-users; TV in all bedrooms and lounge   TERMS: single from £25, single occupancy £35, twin/double from £45, family room £60; dinner £12.50   CARDS: Access, Delta, Switch, Visa   DETAILS: children welcome; small dogs welcome; no smoking; car park; garden

SHIPTON BELLINGER   Hampshire   map 2

Parsonage Farm

Shipton Bellinger, nr Tidworth SP9 7UF
TEL: (01980) 842404
in High Street off A338, opposite the church

This brick and flint building is in the middle of a quiet village convenient for visitors to Stonehenge, Marlborough and Salisbury, and has direct access to Salisbury Plain. This is a wonderful area for walking and riding, and the owners keep horses. Parsonage Farm is very much a family home, where guests are treated like friends and have use of a large sitting-room and the lovely walled garden with tables and chairs for sitting out on warm days. The sixteenth-century dining-room, where breakfast is served, has a beamed ceiling and an enormous dining table. The village pub serves evening meals.

OWNERS: Col and Mrs J. Peecock   OPEN: all year exc Christmas and New Year   ROOMS: 2 twin, both with wash-basin; 1 family, with bath/shower; TV in all bedrooms and lounge   TERMS: single occupancy £18, twin £30, family room £45; deposit: £10   CARDS: none   DETAILS: no children under 10; no dogs; no smoking; car park; garden

SHOTTLE   Derbyshire   map 5

Dannah Farm

Bowmans Lane, Shottle, nr Belper DE5 2DR
TEL: (01773) 550273   FAX: (01773) 550590
from A517 2m W of Belper turn at sign for Shottle, go straight over crossroads then next right

This substantial Georgian farmhouse and the converted farm buildings are set in remote and beautiful countryside high above the Ecclesbourne Valley, with views over six counties. The working farm of 128 acres is home to a colourful collection of animals, including calves, ducks, hens, lambs and Vietnamese pot-bellied pigs. The house and bedrooms are sumptuously decorated and furnished with antiques and old pine. The romantic four-poster suite includes its own sitting-room and a lace-draped bed. Guests can socialise in the comfortable lounge and enjoy a drink from the bar. Wholesome meals are served in the licensed restaurant, including breakfasts with a huge choice of goodies. Vegetarians can be catered for.

OWNERS: Martin and Joan Slack   OPEN: all year exc Christmas   ROOMS: 1 single, 3 double, 2 twin, 1 four-poster, 1 family; all rooms with bath/shower; 1 room suitable for wheelchair-users; TV in all bedrooms   TERMS: single/single occupancy £35, twin/

double £54, four-poster £70, family room £70 plus children's charge; £12.50 for children sharing with parents; dinner £15; deposit: £20 per room or credit card details CARDS: Access, Visa DETAILS: children welcome; no dogs; no smoking in bedrooms or restaurant; car park; garden

Shottle Hall

Shottle, nr Belper DE56 2EB
TEL: (01773) 550203   FAX: (01773) 550276
off B5032, 200yds N of A517

Shottle Hall dates from the mid-nineteenth century and has a grandeur of scale, with two dining-rooms and ten spacious bedrooms. Two lounges provide alternative means of relaxation: one has a bar adjoining it and no TV, the other has games and TV, including a snooker table. The breakfast and dining-rooms have different countryside views. Dinner is served at 7.30pm every day except Sunday, when lunch is served instead. Vegetarian meals are provided if requested and wine is available. A suite of rooms on the ground floor is suitable for disabled guests. Items of interest displayed around the house include a collection of cheese dishes, an old spinning wheel and an early Singer sewing machine. The house is set in three acres of its own grounds in the picturesque Ecclesbourne Valley.

OWNERS: Philip and Phyllis Matthews   OPEN: all year exc Nov, Christmas and New Year   ROOMS: 1 single, with bath/shower; 7 double, 6 with bath/shower, 1 with wash-basin; 2 twin, 1 with bath/shower, 1 with wash-basin; 1 room suitable for wheelchair-users; TV in some bedrooms   TERMS: single/single occupancy £29–£35, twin/double £42–£60; children's reductions according to age; dinner £12.50   CARDS: none   DETAILS: children welcome; no dogs in public rooms; no smoking in bedrooms; car park; games room; garden

SHREWSBURY   **Shropshire**   **map 5**

Fieldside

38 London Road, Shrewsbury SY2 6NX
TEL: (01743) 353143   FAX: (01743) 358645

This large Victorian house dates from 1835 and stands in attractive, secluded gardens. A large statue of lions at the entrance makes it easy to locate. On display all around the house are a multitude of pictures, antiques and brass, copper and china items. The bedrooms are decorated in soft colours and some have half-tester beds. Breakfasts are generous, with a help-yourself buffet before the cooked breakfast, and are served in the elegant dining-room which opens out on to the patio and gardens. Fieldside is only a mile and a half from the town centre, and the neighbourhood offers many eating places.

OWNERS: Ian and Pat Fraser OPEN: all year exc 3 weeks in Nov ROOMS: 5 double, 1 twin; all rooms with bath/shower; TV in all bedrooms TERMS: single occupancy £28–£30, twin/double £40–£42; deposit: £10 CARDS: Access, Amex, Diners, Visa DETAILS: no children under 9; no dogs; no smoking; car park; garden

---

SIBLE HEDINGHAM Essex map 6

Comfrey Cottage

29–31 Queen Street, Sible Hedingham CO9 3RH
TEL: (01787) 460271
just off A1017, 3m NW of Halstead

Two Victorian cottages have been converted into one property, which is set back from the road in two acres of attractive gardens with seats for guests. The three bedrooms are modestly furnished but cosy; the family room has *en suite* facilities and all have views of the Colne Valley. Breakfast only is served, and includes preserves made with fruit from the garden. For other meals Barbara Rowney is happy to make local recommendations.

OWNERS: Stuart and Barbara Rowney OPEN: all year exc Christmas ROOMS: 1 single, with wash-basin; 1 twin, with wash-basin; 1 family, with bath/shower; TV in dining-room TERMS: single £15, single occupancy £20, twin £30, family room from £36; children's reductions according to age CARDS: none DETAILS: children welcome; no dogs; no smoking; car park; garden

---

SIDMOUTH Devon map 2

Old Farmhouse

Hillside Road, Sidmouth EX10 8JG
TEL: (01395) 512284

This sixteenth-century whitewashed thatched house is very pretty, and stands close to the centre of Sidmouth on a quiet lane. Many original features remain, and the furnishings are tasteful and comfortable. The beamed bedrooms are traditionally decorated; one is on the ground floor. A flower-filled garden and sheltered courtyard are pleasant for sitting out in, and the adjoining cottage, with further accommodation, once housed the local cider mill. The Old Farmhouse is licensed; the cosy Inglenook bar is open in the evenings. Three-course dinners are available by arrangement at 6.30pm; children's helpings and vegetarian dishes can be provided with notice, as can packed lunches.

OWNER: Susan Wiltshire OPEN: Feb to Nov ROOMS: 2 single, 1 with bath/shower, 1 with wash-basin; 5 double, 3 with bath/shower, 2 with wash-basin; 1 twin, with bath/shower; 1 family, with bath/shower; TV in some bedrooms and lounge TERMS: single/single occupancy £17–£23, twin/double £34–£46, family room price by arrangement;

reductions for children according to age; dinner £10; deposit: £20 per person CARDS: Access, Visa DETAILS: children welcome; dogs by arrangement; smoking in lounge only; car park; garden

SILVERDALE   Lancashire   map 8

Limes Village Guest House

23 Stankelt Road, Silverdale LA5 0TF
TEL/FAX: (01524) 701454

Ornate cornices and a sunken bathtub are among the original features retained in this well-converted, attractive Victorian house, set in half an acre of lovely landscaped gardens. The floral décor of the sizeable bedrooms is in keeping with the character of the house, and all rooms have either *en suite* facilities or a private bathroom, and are equipped with easy chairs. Two self-catering units are also available. Five-course evening meals can be pre-arranged; vegetarians are catered for, and although the Limes is unlicensed, guests may bring their own wine to dinner. Bird-watchers should note that the RSPB sanctuary at Leighton Moss is just two miles away.

OWNERS: Noel and Andree Livesey OPEN: all year ROOMS: 1 double, 1 twin, 1 family; all rooms with bath/shower; TV in all bedrooms TERMS: single occupancy £23–£24.50, twin/double £35.50–£39, family room from £44; half-price for children sharing with parents; dinner £12.50 CARDS: none DETAILS: children welcome; no dogs; no smoking; car park; garden

SINNINGTON   North Yorkshire   map 9

Riverside Farm

Sinnington, nr York YO6 6RY
TEL: (01751) 431764
off A170, 4m W of Pickering

This elegant Georgian house overlooks the River Seven and the village green, and is set in two acres of beautiful landscaped gardens. Owner Jane Baldwin runs the National Gardens Scheme in North Yorkshire, and the gardens here are open to the public once a year. The welcome is warm and the ambience friendly, with a good choice at breakfast, which is served family-style in the dining-room with its wood-burning stove. The bedrooms are comfortable, with antique and traditional furniture, and there is a well-furnished drawing-room with TV. A pub within walking distance serves evening meals. Guests can walk on the moors, or along the river bank to the next village.

OWNERS: William and Jane Baldwin OPEN: Apr to end Oct ROOMS: 1 single, with wash-basin; 1 double, 1 twin, both rooms with bath/shower; TV lounge TERMS: single £18–£20, single occupancy £20, twin/double £36–£40; children's reductions by arrangement; deposit: £10 per room CARDS: none DETAILS: no children under 7; no dogs; no smoking; car park; garden

SITTINGBOURNE   Kent   **map 3**

The Beaumont

74 London Road, Sittingbourne ME10 1NS
TEL: (01795) 472536   FAX: (01795) 425921

The main part of this former farmhouse dates from the seventeenth
century, and has a Victorian extension. It retains many of its original
features, such as oak beams, sloping floors and an inglenook
fireplace. The Beaumont is a warm and inviting place and is
attractively furnished and immaculately kept. Hand-painted murals
and door panels depicting climbing plants and flowers with
butterflies set a different decorative style for each room. The
bedrooms are very well equipped, and excellent breakfasts are served
in a large farmhouse-style dining-room/lounge. There is a charming
garden and off-road car parking. Packed lunches can be provided. The
Beaumont is on the main A2, and is conveniently placed for
motorways and the major ports.

OWNER: Marcia Brennand   OPEN: all year   ROOMS: 3 single, 2 with shower, 1 with wash-
basin; 4 double, 2 with shower; 1 twin, with shower; 1 family, with shower; TV in all
bedrooms and lounge   TERMS: single £22–£36, single occupancy £34–£40, twin/double
£42–£52, family room £48–£66; children's reductions according to age   CARDS:
Access, Delta, Switch, Visa   DETAILS: children welcome; dogs by arrangement;
smoking in smokers' lounge only; car park; garden

SKELTON   North Yorkshire   **map 9**

Grange Farmhouse

Skelton, nr York YO3 6YQ
TEL: (01904) 470780
on A19, 3m NW of York; turn at Blacksmith's Arms pub then second right

Conveniently situated for visiting York city centre, this creeper-
covered eighteenth-century farmhouse offers clean and comfortable
accommodation in quiet ground-floor bedrooms. These are the
cleverly converted former farm milking parlours to the rear of the
house, each with its own front door. The family room consists of two
adjacent bedrooms. The house has a pretty walled garden with seats.
Breakfast is served in the sunny dining-room, and dinner can be
bought at the village pub just two minutes away near the twelfth-
century church of St Giles.

OWNERS: David and Julie Appleton   OPEN: all year exc Christmas   ROOMS: 1 single, with
bath/shower; 3 double, all with bath/shower; 1 twin, with bath/shower; 1 family; 3
rooms suitable for wheelchair-users; TV in all bedrooms   TERMS: single/single
occupancy £30, twin/double £40, family room £50–£60; half-price for children under 10;
deposit: £15   CARDS: none   DETAILS: children welcome; small dogs welcome; no
smoking in bedroom; car park; garden

Low Skibeden Farmhouse

Skibeden Road, Skipton BD23 6AB
TEL: (01756) 793849
1m E of Skipton just by junction of A65 and A59

This modernised sixteenth-century farmhouse stands in a large
lawned garden bordered with shrubs, and is part of a smallholding
with sheep and Charolais cattle. Heather Simpson offers comfortable
farmhouse accommodation and guests are greeted on arrival with a
hot drink and home-made cakes, which can be enjoyed in the guests'
lounge. The spacious bedrooms have a mixture of modern and
traditional furniture. Breakfast only is served, but it is only a mile to
Skipton's large selection of pubs and restaurants. Laundry facilities
are available at a modest cost, which is good news for guests using the
farmhouse as a base for Dales walking.

OWNERS: William and Heather Simpson   OPEN: all year exc Christmas and New Year
ROOMS: 2 double, 1 with bath/shower, 1 with wash-basin; 1 twin, with wash-basin; 2
family, both with bath/shower; TV lounge   TERMS: single occupancy £20–£32, twin/
double £34, family room £36 plus children's charge; reductions for children from 10 to
14; deposit: 1 night's charge   CARDS: none   DETAILS: no children under 10; no dogs; no
smoking; car park; garden

Chessed

Slad, Stroud GL6 7QD
TEL: (01452) 812253   FAX: (01452) 813473
on B4070 Stroud to Birdlip road

Chessed is situated on the edge of the unspoilt village of Slad, and is a
blaze of colour in summer with lots of beautiful hanging baskets. It
was built in 1903 and retains many original features, including the
beautiful stained-glass windows in the hall. The lovely grounds
include a terraced garden with sitting area, and a swimming-pool for
guests' use. The bedrooms are furnished with antiques, and one has a
unique brass bed. Wendy Wood is a charming host who prepares
excellent evening meals on request, although there are several eating
establishments in the village; packed lunches can be provided. As the
house is elevated and has a number of steps, it is not suitable for
disabled guests.

OWNERS: Peter and Wendy Wood   OPEN: all year   ROOMS: 1 double, 1 four-poster, 1
family; all rooms with bath/shower; TV in all bedrooms   TERMS: single/single occupancy
£30, double £50, family room from £65; £15 for children under 14; deposit: £10   CARDS:
none   DETAILS: children welcome; no dogs; car park; garden; swimming-pool

ENGLAND

SLAIDBURN Lancashire   map 8

Pages Farm

Woodhouse Lane, Slaidburn, nr Clitheroe BB7 3AH
TEL: (01200) 446205
*off B6478; at Slaidburn go W past the Hark-to-Bounty inn, farm is ½m on
left*

The beautiful countryside near the Forest of Bowland in the Ribble
Valley – an officially designated Area of Outstanding Natural Beauty
– provides the backdrop for Pages Farm. Peter and Mary Cowking
greet new arrivals with a hot drink and home-made biscuits, and
make them feel at home. The bedrooms all have their own bathrooms.
Guests can relax in the TV lounge, which has an open fire on chilly
days. Breakfasts, and evening meals if pre-arranged, are available in
the separate dining-room, and guests may bring their own wine to
dinner. Alternatively, there is a pub half a mile away that serves
meals in the evening. Packed lunches can be provided.

OWNERS: Mary and Peter Cowking OPEN: all year exc Christmas ROOMS: 2 double, 1
twin; all rooms with bath/shower; TV lounge TERMS: single occupancy £16, twin/
double £32; children under 3 free, half-price for children from 3 to 11; dinner £10;
deposit CARDS: none DETAILS: children welcome; no dogs; no smoking in bedrooms;
car park; garden

SLINGSBY North Yorkshire   map 9

The Hall

Slingsby, nr York YO6 7AL
TEL: (01653) 628375
just off B1257, 6m W of Malton

The Hall, a creeper-covered Regency country house, stands in five
acres of grounds. It was built by Captain Ward, a midshipman who
was on the ship that brought Nelson's body back to England. The
spacious rooms are tastefully furnished, with several antiques, and
there is a comfortable and welcoming atmosphere. All the bedrooms
are *en suite* and have TV; the sitting-room has log fires and lots of
comfy chairs. Breakfasts, and dinner 6.30 to 7pm by arrangement,
are served in the licensed dining-room. Owners Peter and Cynthia
Fell are a most helpful and friendly couple. The large garden includes
a croquet lawn, bicycles are for hire, and Castle Howard is just up the
road. Packed lunches can be provided.

OWNERS: Peter and Cynthia Fell OPEN: Easter to Nov ROOMS: 3 double, 2 twin, 1
family; all rooms with bath/shower; TV in all bedrooms and lounge TERMS: single
occupancy £21–£23, twin/double £35–£39, family room from £39; children's reductions
according to age; dinner £9.50; deposit: £20 per person CARDS: none DETAILS:
children welcome; no dogs in lounge or dining-room, and must be on leads; no smoking
in lounge or dining-room; car park; garden

SMARDEN   Kent   **map 3**

Munk's Farm

Smarden, nr Ashford TN27 8PN
TEL: (01233) 770265
just off A274, at Headcorn follow road to Smarden for 2m

This early eighteenth-century listed building is set in one acre of
attractive gardens and has a solar-heated swimming-pool available
from June to August. The old village gaol, which has an interesting
history and is also a listed building, stands in the grounds. The
weatherboarded house is full of character and old-world charm, with
oak beams and inglenook fireplaces, and has a warm and cosy
atmosphere. The good-sized bedrooms are attractively decorated and
there is a pleasant and comfortable lounge. Breakfast is served in the
dining-room, and evening meals are available on Fridays and
Saturdays if booked in advance. Munk's Farm is very well situated
for visiting all parts of the county.

OWNERS: Mr and Mrs Ian B. Scott OPEN: all year exc Christmas ROOMS: 2 twin; both
rooms with bath/shower; TV in both bedrooms TERMS: single occupancy £25–£27,
twin £40–£44; deposit CARDS: none DETAILS: no children under 12; no dogs; no
smoking; car park; garden; swimming-pool

SOUTHBOROUGH   Kent   **map 3**

Number Ten

10 Modest Corner, Southborough TN4 0LS
TEL: (01892) 522450

This small brick-built terraced house seems miles from anywhere
with its peaceful woodland views to front and rear. In fact, the quiet
cul-de-sac it sits in is only half a mile from the main road. Apparently,
former owners played host to Queen Victoria's servants when she
visited Tunbridge Wells, which neighbours Southborough. Current
owner Anneke Leemhuis maintains the tradition of hospitality and
also runs a picture-framing studio on the ground floor. Guests are
treated as part of the family, and breakfast is taken at the kitchen
table or, on fine days, on the back patio. The two simply furnished
double rooms are on the ground floor and share a bathroom which has
a power shower. The family room is on the first floor and has the use
of another bathroom on the floor below. Evening meals are available
on request. Modest Corner is on the Wealdway walk.

OWNER: Anneke Leemhuis OPEN: all year ROOMS: 2 double, 1 family; TV in all
bedrooms TERMS: single occupancy £20, double £37, family room £50; reductions for
children under 4; dinner £8.50 to £10 CARDS: none DETAILS: children welcome; dogs
welcome; no smoking; car park; garden

SOUTHEND-ON-SEA   Essex   map 3

Pebbles Guest House

190 Eastern Esplanade, Thorpe Bay, Southend-on-Sea SS1 3AA
TEL: (01702) 582329

The front of this well-maintained Victorian house welcomes guests
with a joyful display of flowers in hanging baskets, pots and tubs.
Pebbles, in fact, is a winner of the Southend in Bloom contest. It also
has a rooftop garden which makes up for the lack of a lounge, with
fine views over the estuary and down the esplanade. The owners'
extremely high standards are evident indoors too, in the tastefully
decorated bedrooms, some with sea views, and in the home-cooked
evening meals, which are available by arrangement. Vegetarian and
special meals can be provided with advance notice.

OWNERS: Colin and Edna Christian   OPEN: all year   ROOMS: 1 single, 2 double, 2 twin; all
rooms with bath/shower; TV in all bedrooms   TERMS: single £25, single occupancy
£25–£40, twin/double £40; £10 for children under 6 sharing with parents; dinner
£12.50   CARDS: none   DETAILS: children welcome; no dogs; no smoking in public
rooms; garden

SOUTH KILVINGTON   North Yorkshire   map 9

Thornborough House Farm

South Kilvington, nr Thirsk YO7 2NP
TEL/FAX: (01845) 522103
*from Thirsk follow signs for Teeside, continue through South Kilvington,
cross roundabout and farm is 100yds ahead on left*

This is a good choice for families. The 200-year-old farmhouse is
situated on a large sheep and arable farm and its owners offer a
warm welcome and a homely atmosphere. Guests are welcome to pull
on some wellington boots and explore. David Williamson grew up
here and is very knowledgeable about the area; he has prepared a
comprehensive information pack for guests to browse through. The
bedrooms are prettily decorated and have sturdy old-fashioned
furniture. An open fire warms the guests' lounge, which also has an
interesting old dresser. Home-style evening meals are served at
6.30pm and a high chair is available for small children. Vegetarians
can be catered for with advance notice and guests may bring their
own wine to dinner.

OWNER: Tess Williamson   OPEN: all year   ROOMS: 1 double, with bath/shower; 1 twin,
with wash-basin; 1 family, with bath/shower; TV in all bedrooms and lounge   TERMS:
single occupancy £14–£18, twin/double £28–£36, family room £32–£36 plus children's
charge; children's reductions by arrangement; dinner £8.50; deposit: £5 per person
CARDS: Access, Visa   DETAILS: children welcome; dogs by arrangement; smoking in
lounge only; car park; garden

SOUTH MILTON   Devon   **map 1**

Old Granary

Upton Barton, South Milton, nr Kingsbridge TQ7 3JF
TEL: (01548) 560449
2m from Kingsbridge

This lovely family home is in a rural setting with lovely views over
the countryside to the sea at Thurlestone two miles away. Ann and
Geoff Hill have done a splendid job in converting this Victorian barn.
The original roof and beams have been retained and give both the
living rooms a feeling of space and character. The semi-circular end of
the dining-room was originally the old granary, and the original
cartwheels now hang on the sitting-room wall. The prettily decorated
bedrooms all have *en suite* facilities. Outside, there is an attractive
garden and patio with tables and chairs, beyond which is the small
indoor heated swimming-pool; there is also a self-catering unit. The
Old Granary makes an excellent base for exploring the beaches,
coastal walks and pretty villages of the South Hams.

OWNERS: Ann and Geoff Hill   OPEN: all year exc Christmas   ROOMS: 1 double, 1 twin, 1
four-poster; all rooms with bath/shower; TV in all bedrooms   TERMS: single occupancy
£22, twin/double £38, four-poster £40; 10% reductions for children over 10; deposit:
£10 per person   CARDS: none   DETAILS: no children under 10; dogs by arrangement; no
smoking; car park; garden; swimming-pool

SOUTHWOLD   Suffolk   **map 6**

Acton Lodge

18 South Green, Southwold IP18 6HB
TEL: (01502) 723217

The owners of this unique 1872 Italian/Gothic-style building are fully
committed to recreating the atmosphere and décor of a Victorian
family home. The house stands out from the surrounding Georgian
architecture and fishermen's cottages and inside retains its ten-foot
ceilings, marble fireplaces and a turret offering views around
Southwo'd, out to sea and across the marshes. It is decorated
exquisitely in plush Victorian-style and the bedrooms are beautifully
appointed, one with the original bath in its *en suite* bathroom. The
sitting-room has a well-stocked library and the house is full of
interesting pictures. Southwold has a strong reputation for its pubs
and eating places.

OWNER: Brenda Smith   OPEN: all year   ROOMS: 2 double, 1 twin, 1 family; all rooms with
bath/shower; TV in all bedrooms and lounge   TERMS: single occupancy £25–£40, twin/
double £50, family room £60–£70; £10 for children over 6 sharing with parents; deposit:
£25   DETAILS: no children under 6; no dogs; no smoking

SOWERBY BRIDGE   West Yorkshire   map 9

Park Villa Guesthouse

141 Park Villas, Bolton Brow, Sowerby Bridge, Halifax HX6 2BE
TEL: (01422) 832179

Marion Lane took over at Park Villa in November 1994 and since
then has been busy upgrading the property. The house retains many
of its original Victorian features, including a ceiling rose and stained-
glass windows. The bedrooms are colour co-ordinated in soft pastels
and are well equipped, offering hair-dryers and toiletries. There is a
separate dining-room and guest lounge. Several establishments
serving evening meals can be found nearby.

OWNERS: Mr and Mrs R.F. Lane   OPEN: all year   ROOMS: 2 single; 1 double, with wash-
basin; 1 twin, with wash-basin; 1 family, with wash-basin; TV in all bedrooms and
lounge   TERMS: single/single occupancy £15, twin/double £30, family room £40;
children's reductions according to age; deposit: 10%   CARDS: none   DETAILS: children
welcome; dogs welcome; no smoking; car park; garden

SPALDING   Lincolnshire   map 6

Bedford Court

10 London Road, Spalding PE11 2TA
TEL/FAX: (01775) 722377

This pale-blue-washed Georgian house occupies a peaceful location at
the end of a private drive close by the River Welland. Records of
Bedford Court date back to 1711, though it has seen various
extensions over the years. Several original features remain, such as
the bevelled glass in the dining-room and the coving, some of which
came from Hampton Court. The four large bedrooms are smartly
decorated in shades of blue and pink; all have TV, desk, armchairs
and *en suite* facilities. The house is impeccably maintained by owners
Russell and Pam Herd, who have installed new carpets. Breakfast
only (and afternoon tea in season) is served in the elegant dining-
room overlooking the garden. Evening meals are no longer available,
but the White Horse pub serves food and is just a two-minute walk
away.

OWNERS: Mr and Mrs W.R. Herd   OPEN: all year   ROOMS: 1 single, 1 double, 2 twin; all
rooms with bath/shower; TV in all bedrooms   TERMS: single/single occupancy from
£25, twin/double £40; deposit: £10   CARDS: none   DETAILS: no children; no dogs; no
smoking; car park; garden

---

*If a B&B offers off-street car parking, we note 'car park' in the details at the
end of the entry. If we are aware of particular car-parking difficulties, we
mention them.*

SPAXTON   Somerset   map 2

Gatesmoor

Hawkridge, Spaxton, nr Bridgwater TA5 1AL
TEL: (01278) 671353
2m S of A39 between Nether Stowey and Bridgwater

This attractive seventeenth-century cottage is set in a delightful
garden which borders a reservoir on the edge of the Quantock Hills.
The Harveys are a charming couple, who tend to their guests' every
need. The house is elegantly furnished and includes a sitting-room
with inglenook fireplace. Evening meals are available, by
arrangement, and are served in the beamed dining-room, while
breakfast is served in the sun room, with wonderful views up the
valley to the hills; packed lunches can also be provided. The two
upstairs bedrooms, one of which is very large, share a bathroom on
the ground floor. This is a wonderful area for walking, bird-watching
and riding.

OWNER: Mrs R.E. Harvey   OPEN: all year exc Christmas   ROOMS: 1 double, 1 twin; both
rooms with wash-basin; TV lounge   TERMS: single occupancy £22.50, twin/double £36;
deposit required   CARDS: none   DETAILS: no children; no dogs; no smoking; car park;
garden

SPORLE   Norfolk   map 6

Corfield House

Sporle, nr Swaffham PE32 2EA
TEL: (01760) 723636
½m N of A47, 3m E of Swaffham

Corfield House dates from 1852 and was further extended in the
1950s. This handsome red-brick house stands back from the road in a
quiet location. The five bedrooms, with sloping ceilings, are in the
original part of the house, and tastefully decorated with co-ordinated
Laura Ashley designs; all have pine furniture, TV and hair-dryer.
Just one bedroom is on the ground floor and this can accommodate
wheelchair-users. Both house and garden are well-maintained, and
in summer the lavender and rose bushes are lovely. There is a sunny
lounge and a licensed dining-room where breakfast and dinner are
served; vegetarian choices and children's helpings can be requested,
and there is a wine list. Packed lunches are also available. Martin
Hickey runs the local tourist office and can provide a comprehensive
fact-file on places to visit in the area. The well-known Peddars Way
skirts the village.

OWNERS: Linda and Martin Hickey   OPEN: end Mar to mid-Dec   ROOMS: 1 single, 2
double, 2 twin; all rooms with bath/shower; 1 room suitable for wheelchair-users; TV in
all bedrooms   TERMS: single £23, single occupancy £35, twin/double £37–£43;

children's reductions by arrangement; dinner £12; deposit: £10–£40 CARDS: Access, Visa DETAILS: children welcome; dogs in ground-floor bedroom only; no smoking; car park; garden

STAINDROP   Co Durham   map 10

Fawn Lea

10 Winston Road, Staindrop, nr Darlington DL2 3NN
TEL/FAX: (01833) 660536
just off A688, 5m NE of Barnard Castle

Fawn Lea is run by a friendly couple who provide good-value accommodation, not far from Darlington. The house is well maintained, clean and comfortable; the bedrooms (two of which are on the ground floor) and guest lounge are in a fairly recent extension. The rooms are small but pretty, with floral wallpapers, fitted wardrobes, pine desks and *en suite* facilities. Substantial breakfasts are served in the family kitchen, where there is a collection of horse brasses and ribbons won by Les Robson, who trains horses for harness-racing. The garden has a patio area with ample seating for warmer weather.

OWNER: Joy Robson   OPEN: all year   ROOMS: 2 double, 1 twin; all rooms with bath/shower; 2 rooms suitable for wheelchair-users; TV lounge   TERMS: single occupancy £15, twin/double £30; children under 3 free, half-price for older children   CARDS: none
DETAILS: children welcome; dogs by arrangement; smoking in lounge only; car park; garden

STAMFORD   Lincolnshire   map 6

Martins

20 St Martins, Stamford PE9 2LF
TEL: (01780) 52106   FAX: (01780) 482691

This Georgian listed house, elegantly sited next to St Martins church, is just five minutes' walk from the rail station. Inside, the atmosphere is informal and relaxed, and the owners extend the warmest hospitality to their guests. The bedrooms are spacious and furnished with antiques; most have a private bathroom or shower room. The family suite consists of two connecting twin bedrooms. Breakfasts and (optional) evening meals are served in the dining-room; dinners feature fresh vegetables and herbs from the kitchen garden, and vegetarian options can be arranged in advance. Children's portions are available, and guests are encouraged to bring their own wine to dinner. Packed lunches can be provided. Guests can relax in the downstairs drawing-room with its TV and video or, in summer, in the large walled garden with its croquet lawn. There is car parking in the street.

OWNER: Marie Martin OPEN: all year exc Christmas and New Year ROOMS: 3 double; 1 twin; 1 family, with bath/shower; TV lounge TERMS: single occupancy £30, twin/double £45, family room £85; 10% reduction for children; dinner £15; deposit: 10% DETAILS: children welcome; no dogs; no smoking in dining-room; garden

---

STAPLEHAY Somerset map 2

West Amberd Cottage

Amberd Lane, Staplehay, nr Taunton TA3 7AA
TEL: (01823) 270765
2½m S of Taunton on minor road off A38

West Amberd Cottage overlooks the Quantock Hills and is on a quiet road in the village of Staplehay surrounded by mature trees. It is a semi-detached cottage and was probably built as the gardener's cottage for West Amberd House in about 1912. Joan Oliver is a very friendly, welcoming lady, and with just one comfortable twin-bedded room guests can be assured of personal attention. Both the house and small, pretty garden are immaculate. There is a large sitting-room, and a garden room with armchairs at the back of the house, which is ideal to relax in on sunny days.

OWNER: Joan Oliver OPEN: all year exc Christmas ROOMS: 1 twin, with bath/shower; TV in bedroom and lounge TERMS: single occupancy £18.50, twin £33; children's reductions CARDS: none DETAILS: children welcome; no dogs; no smoking; car park; garden

---

STARCROSS Devon map 1

Old Vicarage

Starcross, Exeter EX6 8PX
TEL: (01626) 890206
on A379 at S end of village

This 300-year-old house began as a farmhouse, was a vicarage until 1975 and since 1991 has been a guesthouse. Built with thick cob walls, it stands in three acres of grounds overlooking the sea. The Hayeses are a welcoming couple and the house has an informal, comfortable atmosphere. It is simply furnished, and the lounge has a piano and games for guests to play. Breakfast only is served. The Exe Estuary is renowed for its bird life and the Dawlish Warren Reserve is only three miles away.

OWNER: Maggie Hayes OPEN: all year ROOMS: 2 double, 1 with bath/shower, 1 with wash-basin; 2 twin, 1 with bath/shower, 1 with wash-basin; 1 family, with bath/shower; TV lounge TERMS: single occupancy £18.50–£21, twin/double £29–£33, family room £37 plus children's charge; children under 2 free, reductions for older children according to age; deposit: 1 night's charge CARDS: none DETAILS: children welcome; no dogs; car park; garden

357

STAUNTON   Gloucestershire   map 5

Mayfield Cottage

Moat Lane, Staunton, nr Gloucester GL19 3QA
TEL: (01452) 840673
*from Gloucester take A417 Ledbury road; on approaching Staunton keep
left at mini-roundabout, then Moat Lane is first turning on right; or from
M50 junction 2 take A417 to Staunton in Gloucester direction*

This beamed seventeenth-century crofter's cottage is set in a
beautifully landscaped garden in a peaceful rural area. The delightful
house has been tastefully renovated, with most of the work being
done by Mr Clayton, and has retained its old-world charm. The
friendly owners make their guests feel very much at home and offer a
cup of tea or coffee on arrival. The three immaculate bedrooms are
prettily decorated with dainty fabrics and wallpapers. Breakfast and
dinner (by arrangement), featuring local produce and home-made
desserts, are served in the dining-room, which has a lovely sideboard
displaying blue willow-pattern china. Guests also have use of a
sitting-room in which a fire is lit on chilly days. Jennifer Clayton
belongs to the local rambling club and is happy to give information on
local walks.

OWNERS: John and Jennifer Clayton   OPEN: all year exc Christmas and New Year
ROOMS: 1 single, with wash-basin; 1 double, 1 twin, both with bath/shower; TV in all
bedrooms and lounge   TERMS: single £17, single occupancy £20, twin/double £34;
dinner £10; deposit: £10 per person   CARDS: none   DETAILS: no children; dogs by prior
arrangement; no smoking; car park; garden

STEEPLE BUMPSTEAD   Essex   map 6

Yew Tree House

15 Chapel Street, Steeple Bumpstead, nr Haverhill CB9 7DQ
TEL/FAX: (01440) 730364
on B1054, 3m S of Haverhill

Yew Tree is a red-brick Victorian house on the Essex/Suffolk border,
run by Mrs Stirling for a number of years. The bedrooms are
decorated along a floral theme; one has a marble antique dressing
table, the other an original fireplace. There is a comfortable lounge
with a real fire, lit on chilly days, a comprehensive selection of
information on the area and board games, including Scrabble.
Breakfast is served at a time to suit individuals, and modestly priced
evening meals are available, if pre-arranged. Children's helpings and
vegetarian dishes can be provided; guests may bring their own wine
as there is no alcohol licence. Packed lunches are also possible for
those exploring the area. Saffron Walden with its pargeted buildings
is only ten miles away; the Jacobean mansion Audley End is on its
outskirts.

OWNER: Mrs S.J. Stirling OPEN: all year exc Christmas and New Year ROOMS: 1 double, with shower; 1 twin, with wash-basin; TV lounge TERMS: single occupancy £17–£22, twin/double £29–£36; £5 for children over 2 in extra bed in parents' room; dinner £8.50; deposit: 25% DETAILS: no children under 2; no dogs; no smoking in bedrooms; car park

STOCKLAND Devon   map 2

Kings Arms Inn

Stockland, nr Honiton EX14 9BS
TEL: (01404) 881361   FAX: (01404) 881732
signposted from A30 Chard to Honiton road, or from A35 take Shute garage exit W of Axminster

Skittles, cribbage and a busy restaurant and bars are all part of the scene in this ancient thatched inn that offers three well-appointed bedrooms with *en suite* bathrooms. It is a lively place, and live music fills the pub on Sunday nights. Breakfast for residents is served between 9 and 10am in the Cotley Restaurant Bar, which, with its inglenook fireplace, also provides a pleasant meeting place evenings and at lunch-times. The Kings Arms attracts a large clientele for its food and real ales, and it is advisible for guests to book for meals. The selection of dishes is extensive, and includes vegetarian options and children's portions. Although the house is licensed, guests may bring their own wine if they choose; there is a corkage charge. Packed lunches can be provided.

OWNERS: Heinz Kiefer and Paul Diviani OPEN: all year exc Christmas Day ROOMS: 2 double, 1 twin; all rooms with bath; TV in all bedrooms and lounge TERMS: single occupancy £20, twin/double £60; reductions for children sharing with parents; dinner £16.50–£21; deposit: 1 night's charge CARDS: Access, Delta, Switch, Visa DETAILS: children welcome; dogs welcome; car park; games room; garden (*The Good Food Guide*)

STOCKSFIELD Northumberland   map 11

The Dene

11 Cade Hill Road, Stocksfield NE43 7PB
TEL: (01661) 842025
off A695, 1m W of village

This spacious Edwardian house stands peacefully in its beautiful garden surrounded by woodland, yet it is only a 15-minute drive from Newcastle-upon-Tyne. The charming owners enjoy sharing their house with guests and offer a taste of gracious living, with linen tablecloths, silver cutlery and quality home-made bread and preserves at breakfast. Antiques and artefacts collected from around the world furnish the house, which has three original fireplaces and an elegant drawing-room/library overlooking the garden.

OWNERS: Mr and Mrs P.A. Mitchell OPEN: all year exc Christmas ROOMS: 1 single, 2 twin; all rooms with bath/shower; TV in all bedrooms TERMS: single/single occupancy £20, twin £40; deposit: £10 CARDS: none DETAILS: no children; no dogs; no smoking in bedrooms; car park; garden

STOKE GABRIEL   Devon   map 1

Red Slipper

Stoke Gabriel, nr Totnes TQ9 6RU
TEL: (01803) 782315
off A385 Totnes to Paignton road, opposite post office in centre of village

The Red Slipper offers bed-and-breakfast accommodation, as well as meals in licensed tea-rooms. It is a very well-run establishment and the Wattses are a friendly and hospitable couple who go out of their way to take care of their guests' needs. The Red Slipper is in the centre of the picturesque village of Stoke Gabriel, which is beside the River Dart and surrounded by lovely countryside. The meals are varied and of a high standard, and both breakfast and dinner, by arrangement, are served in the dining-room. Cream teas and a tempting array of cakes are served in the pretty garden, and packed lunches can be provided. The bedrooms are attractively furnished and have every possible extra. There is an upstairs lounge and one on the ground floor. Stoke Gabriel is an excellent base for walking and sailing.

OWNERS: John and Elizabeth Watts OPEN: mid-Mar to end Oct ROOMS: 1 double, 2 twin, 1 family; all rooms with bath/shower; TV in all bedrooms and lounge TERMS: single occupancy £28, twin/double £44–£46, family room from £57.50; children under 2 free, older children's reductions according to age; dinner £13.50–£15.50; deposit: £10 CARDS: none DETAILS: children welcome; no dogs in restaurant; no smoking; car park; garden

STOKE-ON-TRENT   Staffordshire   map 5

Corrie Guest House

13 Newton Street, Basford, Stoke-on-Trent ST4 6JN
TEL: (01782) 614838
200 yards S of A53 / A500 junction

This pleasant Victorian house is in a quiet cul-de-sac not far from the centre of town. The owners live in the adjacent house, but are always available to assist guests. A cup of tea or coffee is offered on arrival. Reasonably priced evening meals are served, if ordered in advance, and vegetarians can be catered for; guests are welcome to bring their own wine as there is no licence. The small bedrooms are clean and prettily decorated, and three have *en suite* facilities. Guests are advised to leave their cars in the owners' large car park and take the bus into town. Packed lunches can be provided.

OWNERS: Rob and Averill Burton OPEN: all year ROOMS: 2 single, with wash-basin; 2 double, with bath/shower; 2 twin, with wash-basin; 2 family, 1 with bath/shower, 1 with wash-basin; TV in all bedrooms and lounge TERMS: single £19, single occupancy £19–£26, twin/double £34–£38, family room £41; half-price for children under 12; dinner £8; deposit: £5 per room CARDS: none DETAILS: children welcome; no dogs; smoking in guest lounge only; car park; garden

Westfield House

312 Princes Road, Penkhull, Stoke-on-Trent ST4 7JP
TEL: (01782) 44582

There is a homely atmosphere in this well-maintained Victorian house in a residential area about ten minutes' walk from the town centre, and Mrs White treats guests as her friends. The simple accommodation is comfortable, and visitors are welcome to relax in the TV lounge. Breakfast only is available, but there are plenty of places nearby for evening meals.

OWNER: Norma White OPEN: all year exc Christmas ROOMS: 1 twin; 1 family; TV lounge TERMS: single occupancy £16, twin £30, family room from £30; children's reductions according to age CARDS: none DETAILS: children welcome; no dogs; no smoking in bedrooms; car park

STOKE ST GREGORY Somerset map 2

Slough Court

Stoke St Gregory, nr Taunton TA3 6JQ
TEL/FAX: (01823) 490311
just S of A361, 8m E of Taunton

Slough Court is an unusual and lovely moated manor house dating from the fourteenth century. The house has been in Sally Gothard's family for generations and is part of a working farm run by Sally's husband. Through the farmyard is a stone archway leading to a lawn and an attractive terrace with an outdoor heated swimming-pool. The interior has oak beams, mullioned windows, open fires and relaxing sofas in the spacious sitting-room. The three *en suite* bedrooms are tastefully decorated. Breakfast only is served in the family dining-room. As well as the pool, guests have use of a grass tennis court, croquet lawn and bicycles for hire. This is a comfortable and friendly place to stay in peaceful countryside.

OWNER: Sally Gothard OPEN: Mar to end Nov ROOMS: 2 double, 1 twin; all rooms with bath/shower; TV in all bedrooms TERMS: single occupancy £24, twin/double £48; deposit: £10 CARDS: none DETAILS: no children under 12; no dogs; no smoking; car park; garden; swimming-pool; tennis

Old Post House

Stone in Oxney, nr Tenterden TN30 7JN
TEL: (01233) 758258
off B2082, 1¾m E of Wittersham and 5m NE of Rye

This white-painted wooden building, built in 1772, stands on the edge
of the expanses of Romney Marsh and the military canal built to keep
out Napoleon. Inside, what was once the post office is now an
attractive large lounge/dining-room lined with bookshelves. The
accommodation is light, bright and cheerful. A feature of breakfast –
which on fine days is served in the garden – is an array of home-made
jams. Packed lunches can be provided, and there are also a couple of
pubs offering food in the village. In addition, the towns of Rye and
Tenterden are just a ten-minute drive away.

OWNER: Mrs M.R. O'Connor   OPEN: all year   ROOMS: 2 double, 1 with bath/shower, 1
with wash-basin; 1 twin, with wash-basin; TV in all bedrooms and lounge   TERMS:
single occupancy £20, twin/double £36–£40; deposit: £20   CARDS: none   DETAILS: no
children under 8; no dogs; car park; garden

STOW-ON-THE-WOLD   Gloucestershire   map 5

Wyck Hill Lodge

Wyck Lodge, Stow-on-the-Wold GL54 1HT
TEL: (01451) 830141
on A424 Burford to Stow-on-the-Wold road

This impeccably maintained, listed early-Victorian lodge stands in its
own grounds overlooking the Vale of Bourton. The Aldertons are a
very hospitable couple and offer a warm welcome. A comfortable
lounge is available for guests' use. Of the three attractive *en suite*
bedrooms, two are on the ground floor with one having a brass bed
and the other leading out to the garden. The upstairs bedroom, which
has sloping ceilings, pine furniture and a large bathroom, is very
popular. Substantial breakfasts are served, and there are several
eating establishments in Stow for evening meals; packed lunches can
be provided.

OWNER: Mrs J.A. Alderton   OPEN: all year exc Christmas and owner's holiday   ROOMS: 2
double; 1 twin; TV in all bedrooms   TERMS: single occupancy £30–£40, twin/double
£40–£44; deposit   CARDS: none   DETAILS: children by prior arrangement; no dogs; no
smoking; car park; garden

---

*Please let us know if you need more report forms and we will send you a
fresh supply.*

Brook Lodge

192 Alcester Road, Stratford-upon-Avon CV37 9DR
TEL/FAX: (01789) 295988

Situated just around the corner from Anne Hathaway's cottage on the edge of open countryside, Brook Lodge is one mile from the city centre. The well-appointed bedrooms with their pretty wallpaper are tastefully decorated; most are *en suite* and all have their own showers. The house is spotlessly clean throughout, and there is a comfortable residents' lounge with TV. Yvonne and Robert Charlett are a local couple and are happy to assist guests with sightseeing itineraries.

OWNERS: Yvonne and Robert Charlett OPEN: all year exc Christmas and New Year
ROOMS: 3 double, 2 twin, 2 family, all with shower; TV in all bedrooms and lounge
TERMS: single occupancy £25–£35, twin/double £36–£44, family room £45–£55; half-price for children sharing with parents; deposit: 1 night's charge or credit card details
CARDS: Access, Amex, Delta, Visa DETAILS: children welcome; no dogs; no smoking; car park

Moonraker House

40 Alcester Road, Stratford-upon-Avon CV37 9DB
TEL: (01789) 267115/299346   FAX: (01789) 295504

Just five minutes' walk from the centre of town, Moonraker is an immaculate and elegant house adorned with hanging baskets. Some of the bedrooms are in a second building which has a large sun lounge with wicker furnishings. All the bedrooms are decorated to a high standard with tasteful matching fabrics. The two four-poster rooms have their own patios looking out on to the garden. One suite has its own sitting-room and entrance, and would be ideal for a family or a group of friends. Breakfast only is available, but the owners are prepared to help with the good things in life by arranging theatre tickets and even champagne and flowers for special occasions.

OWNERS: Michael and Mauveen Spencer OPEN: all year exc Christmas ROOMS: 5 double, 2 twin, 2 four-poster, 1 family; all rooms with bath/shower; TV in all bedrooms
TERMS: single occupancy £28, twin/double £39–£45, four-poster £59, family room £49; £10 for children; deposit: £30 CARDS: Access, Visa DETAILS: children welcome; dogs by arrangement; no smoking in some bedrooms and dining-room; car park

If a deposit is required for an advance booking, this is stated in the details at the end of the entry.

Victoria Spa Lodge

Bishopton Lane, Stratford-upon-Avon CV37 9QY
TEL: (01789) 267985   FAX: (01789) 204728
at intersection of A3400 and A46, 1½m S of Stratford-upon-Avon

Standing in one and a half acres of its own grounds and overlooking
the canal, this attractive nineteenth-century building was originally
built as a spa. Queen Victoria gave her name to the hotel – look for
her coat-of-arms built into the gables. Impeccably maintained, the
Lodge offers seven bedrooms, some retaining their original cornicing
and fireplaces and all with *en suite* bathrooms. The rooms are well
appointed and have comfortable armchairs. The attic rooms are
ideally suited for families or friends travelling together. Breakfast
only is served in the elegant dining-room.

OWNERS: Paul and Dreen Tozer   OPEN: all year   ROOMS: 3 double, 1 twin, 3 family; all
rooms with bath/shower; TV in all bedrooms   TERMS: single occupancy £35–£45, twin/
double £39–£50, family room terms by arrangement; children's reductions; deposit: 1
night's charge or credit card details   CARDS: Access, Visa   DETAILS: children welcome;
no dogs; no smoking; car park; garden

Woodstock

30 Grove Road, Stratford-upon-Avon CV37 6PB
TEL: (01789) 299881

Only a few minutes' walk from the town centre, this family-run
Edwardian guesthouse offers five attractive and well-appointed
bedrooms. Although the house is on a main road, double glazing helps
keep the traffic noise to a minimum. Pretty fabrics, lace coronets and
traditional furnishings feature in the good-sized, colour co-ordinated
rooms. The one ground-floor room has *en suite* facilities. Breakfast
only is served in the attractive dining-room with its tablecloths and
beautiful draped curtains.

OWNERS: Maisie and Roland Haufe   OPEN: all year exc 24 to 26 Dec   ROOMS: 1 single,
with wash-basin; 2 double, 1 twin, 1 family, all with bath/shower; TV in all bedrooms
TERMS: single £23, single occupancy £40–£46, twin/double £44–£48, family room £58;
half-price for children from 3 to 12; deposit: £20 or first night's charge for longer
bookings   CARDS: none   DETAILS: no children under 3; no dogs; no smoking; car park

---

*B&B rates specified in the details at the end of each entry are given (as
applicable) for a single room, for single occupancy of a double room, and
then per room in the case of two people sharing a double or twin-bedded
room, or for a family room.*

*No stamps are needed if you write to the Guide from within the UK. Report
forms are at the end of the book, or use your own stationery if you prefer.*

STREFFORD   Shropshire   map 5

Strefford Hall

Strefford, Craven Arms SY7 8DE
TEL: (01588) 672383
¼m off A49, 2m N of Craven Arms

This imposing stone-built Victorian house is surrounded by 360 acres
of working farmland which lies at the foot of Wenlock Edge. The
house has solid, old-fashioned furnishings, a Victorian pine stairway,
quarry tile entrance way, stripped pine doors and a grandfather
clock. There is a sense of spaciousness and of comfortable informality.
Both breakfast and dinner are served in the dining-room, which has a
piano that guests can play. Children's portions are available, and
although Strefford Hall is unlicensed, guests may bring their own
wine to dinner. Packed lunches can be provided. As we went to press,
plans were in progress to install central heating. Strefford is an ideal
location for walking – the Shropshire Way and Offa's Dyke Path are
not far – and for visiting a range of local attractions such as Stokesay
Castle and the Severn Valley Railway.

OWNERS: Mr and Mrs John Morgan   OPEN: all year exc Christmas and New Year
ROOMS: 2 double, 1 twin; all rooms with bath/shower; TV in all bedrooms and lounge
TERMS: single occupancy £20, twin/double £36–£38; children under 2 free, half-price for
ages 2 to 10, 25% reduction for ages 10 to 14; dinner £10; deposit required for longer
stays   CARDS: none   DETAILS: children welcome; no dogs; no smoking; car park;
garden

STURMINSTER NEWTON   Dorset   map 2

Stourcastle Lodge

Gough's Close, Sturminster Newton DT10 1BU
TEL: (01258) 472320   FAX: (01258) 473381
Gough's Close is a small lane running off the town square

This attractive long, whitewashed house stands in a quiet road right
in the centre of the pretty little town of Sturminster Newton. It was
originally a small thatched farmhouse but has been cleverly
extended, preserving its clean lines. Guests have the use of the
beautifully kept garden with a large lawn and a dovecote, and the
bedrooms are comfortable and well equipped. Jill prepares meals
using vegetables, herbs and flowers from the garden, and serves them
in the dining-room at separate tables.

OWNERS: Ken and Jill Hookham-Bassett   OPEN: all year   ROOMS: 2 double, both with
bath/shower; 2 twin, 1 with bath/shower; 1 family, with bath/shower; TV in some
bedrooms and lounge   TERMS: single occupancy £27–£40, twin/double £42–£68,
family room £68; half-price for children sharing with parents; dinner £16; deposit: £20
CARDS: Access, Visa   DETAILS: children welcome; no dogs; no smoking in dining-room
or bedrooms; car park; garden

STOURCASTLE LODGE, STURMINSTER NEWTON

STURTON BY STOW Lincolnshire

map 9

Gallows Dale Farm

Marton Road, Sturton by Stow, nr Lincoln LN1 2AH
TEL: (01427) 788387
on A1500, 1m W of Sturton by Stow

This listed brick building is part of a 33-acre arable farm lying midway between Lincoln and Gainsborough. Brenda Williams is a
congenial host who keeps her house spotlessly clean; she also makes
all the curtains and does most of the upholstering. The single room
has a cast-iron bed, and the four-poster has an *en suite* shower. An
extra bed for a child can be arranged in the double room and is
charged at £10 or less according to age. Guests can relax in the cosy
sitting-room with TV; substantial breakfasts are served in the
separate dining-room. Packed lunches can be provided. Guests
wanting an evening meal not too far afield might want to try one of
the two pubs in the village, about a mile away.

OWNER: Brenda Williams OPEN: all year ROOMS: 1 single; 1 double, with wash-basin; 1
twin; 1 four-poster, with bath/shower; TV lounge TERMS: single £17, single occupancy
£20, twin/double £30, four-poster £40; children's reductions according to age CARDS:
none DETAILS: children welcome; dogs by arrangement; no smoking; car park; garden

Clough House Farm

Summer Bridge, nr Harrogate HG3 4JR
TEL: (01423) 780823
leave A61 6m S of Ripon and follow B6165 towards Pateley Bridge for 6m

This seventeenth-century farmhouse in the heart of Nidderdale
includes a successful riding school, and guests can take lessons or
hire horses for trekking. Summer sees the house light up with
colourful flowers in hanging baskets and old stone troughs. Guests'
bedrooms and bathrooms are in old farm buildings converted to
sumptuous standards with colour co-ordinated décor. Traditional
home-cooked evening meals are served in the attractive dining-room
at any time that suits guests. Vegetarian options can be included and
wine is of the bring-your-own variety. The patio outside the lounge is
a good vantage point for the spectacular views. Self-catering cottages
are also available.

OWNERS: Kenneth and Brenda Walmsley   OPEN: all year   ROOMS: 3 double, 3 twin, 1
family; all rooms with bath/shower; TV lounge   TERMS: single occupancy £30, twin/
double £40, family room £45; dinner £10; deposit required   CARDS: none   DETAILS:
children welcome; no dogs; car park; garden

Mayfield Hotel

Sea Lane, Seaborn, Sunderland SR6 9EE
TEL: (0191) 529 3345

This bright and well-maintained turn-of-the-century house is close to
the sea and about a mile from the centre of Sunderland. The spotless
bedrooms are comfortable and well furnished, and some have sea
views; four are on the ground floor. Breakfasts are freshly cooked to
order and there are several venues for evening meals within walking
distance.

OWNER: Vincent Richardson   OPEN: all year exc Christmas and New Year   ROOMS: 1
single, with wash-basin; 5 double, all with bath/shower; 5 twin, all with bath/shower; 2
family, both with wash-basin; TV in all bedrooms   TERMS: single/single occupancy
£17.50–£28, twin/double £33–£38; £5 for children under 5; deposit: £10   CARDS: none
DETAILS: children welcome; dogs welcome; car park

*If a B&B caters for vegetarians, we note this in the entry. It is always best,
however, to check when booking and make it clear what your requirements
are, especially if you require a special diet.*

Dever View

17 Uppper Bullington, Sutton Scotney, nr Winchester SO21 3RB
TEL: (01962) 760566
leave A34 or A303 at Bullington Cross and follow signs to Bullington

Dever View is a large, tastefully modernised cottage in a very quiet
position surrounded by fields in the heart of the country. The
Somertons are welcoming and friendly people and the
accommodation is clean and well maintained. Guests have use of a
large sitting-room with TV, and breakfast is served in this room.
Dever View is within a five minutes' drive of the A303 and is a good
place for walking. Winchester is about ten minutes' drive away.

OWNERS: Daphne and Bob Somerton   OPEN: all year exc Christmas   ROOMS: 1 double,
with bath/shower; 2 twin; TV in some bedrooms and lounge   TERMS: single occupancy
£25, twin/double £35–£38; children's reductions according to age; deposit: £10 per
person   CARDS: none   DETAILS: children welcome; dogs welcome with own bedding; no
smoking; car park; garden

The Old Rectory

Swaffham Bulbeck, nr Cambridge CB5 0LX
TEL: (01223) 811986
off B1102 in village, behind old church

The Old Rectory is a late-Georgian residence in a secluded spot
approached up a private drive. It stands in three and a half acres of
gardens, with a stream and a heated swimming-pool available in
summer. It was once the home of the Rev Jenyns, the naturalist who
tutored Charles Darwin. Jenny and Ian Few-Mackay have been busy
upgrading recently, but have retained a friendly and informal
atmosphere as well as the many features of interest: a stone entance
way, casement shutters, a marble fireplace and antique furniture.
The bedrooms are of a good size, one having a cast-iron and brass bed.
The shared bathroom has soft pink wallpaper and curtains. The
sitting-room and dining-room, where breakfast only is served, are
both comfortable. Good evening meals are available at a pub within
easy walking distance.

OWNER: Jenny Few-Mackay   OPEN: all year exc Christmas   ROOMS: 2 double, both with
bath/shower; 1 twin, with wash-basin; TV in all bedrooms   TERMS: twin/double £38
CARDS: none   DETAILS: no children under 12; dogs welcome; no smoking; car park;
games room; garden; swimming-pool

SWARRATON   Hampshire   map 2

Severals House

Swarraton, nr Alresford SO24 9TQ
TEL: (01962) 734582
on B3046, 4m from Alresford, next to Northington Grange

This large, elegant Edwardian country house is set in extensive,
beautiful grounds in lovely, peaceful surroundings in the Candover
Valley. Mrs Peisley is a charming lady, interested in horses, and her
daughter teaches riding; both croquet and lawn tennis can be played
in the garden. The spacious bedrooms are beautifully furnished, and
breakfast only is served in the dining-room. Severals House is
convenient for visiting Winchester and makes an ideal base for
exploring the New Forest; the property has direct access to the
Wayfarers Walk.

OWNER: Diana Peisley   OPEN: all year exc Christmas   ROOMS: 2 twin; both rooms with
bath/shower; TV lounge   TERMS: single occupancy £25, twin £40; reductions for
children under 12; deposit: £20   CARDS: none   DETAILS: children welcome; dogs by
arrangement; no smoking in bedrooms; car park; garden; tennis

SWAY   Hampshire   map 2

Kingfishers

Coombe Lane, Sway SO41 6BP
TEL: (01590) 682414   FAX: (01590) 683460
off B3055, 3m SW of Brockenhurst

This modern house was designed by the Smiths and lies on the
outskirts of Sway, in a quiet position with lovely views on the edge of
the New Forest. Mrs Smith is a friendly person who welcomes her
guests with tea and cake. There is a conservatory overlooking the
pleasant lawned garden, and both bedrooms are of a good size.
Breakfast only is served, but packed lunches can be provided. Sway is
a small, peaceful village and is convenient for Lymington, with its
marinas, for the ferry to the Isle of Wight, and for riding.

OWNER: Lesley Smith   OPEN: all year exc Christmas   ROOMS: 2 double; both rooms with
bath/shower; TV lounge   TERMS: single occupancy £25, double £45   CARDS: none
DETAILS: children welcome; no dogs; no smoking; car park; garden

*It is always best to check prices, especially for single occupancy, when
booking.*

*If the establishment does not take credit cards, we say so in the details at
the end of the entry.*

Hoe Hill

Swinhope, nr Binbrook LN3 6HX
TEL: (01472) 398206
on B 1203, 1m N of Binbrook

Set in the rolling countryside of the Lincolnshire Wolds, this big,
comfortable white-and-black-trimmed farmhouse dates from around
1780. The house is impeccably maintained, with bright, fresh
bedrooms, one of which now has an *en suite* luxury bathroom. A log
fire burns in the spacious lounge, from where french doors lead out on
to the patio and lovely gardens, complete with croquet lawn. Erica
Curd is locally renowned as an excellent cook, and imaginative
evening meals by prior arrangement are served in the separate
dining-room (which also as an open fire). Vegetarians are catered for,
and children's portions are available; although the house is
unlicensed, guests are welcome to bring their own wine to dinner.
Breakfasts include yoghurts, muesli, home-baked bread and home-
made marmalade, as well as a variety of cooked fare. Packed lunches
can be provided.

OWNERS: Ian and Erica Curd   OPEN: all year exc owners' holidays   ROOMS: 2 double, 1
with bath/shower, 1 with wash-basin; 1 twin, with wash-basin; TV lounge   TERMS:
single occupancy £18–£25, twin/double £34–£50; children's reductions according to
age; dinner £12 (not available at Christmas and New Year); deposit required for 3
nights' stay or longer   CARDS: none   DETAILS: no children under 5; no dogs; smoking in
lounge only; car park; garden

Old Mill

Mill Lane, Tallington, nr Stamford PE9 4RR
TEL: (01780) 740815
just off A16, 4m E of Stamford

The Old Mill was built in 1682 although there are records of an
earlier version in the Domesday Book. Converted to provide unique
accommodation, the house retains many original features, such as
wood floors, oak beams, low ceilings, an inglenook fireplace and the
original mill workings in the dining-room. The luxuriously appointed
bedrooms, furnished with antiques, some with mill workings, all have
en suite bathrooms and TV. Sue and John Olver are an enthusiastic
couple who provide lunch, dinner and packed lunches if required.
Children's helpings and vegetarian options can be arranged and
guests can bring their own wine to table as there is no licence. There
are plans to renovate the ground floor for wheelchair-suitable
accommodation. Fishing is available on the Welland and a private
seven-acre stocked lake.

OWNERS: Sue and John Olver OPEN: all year ROOMS: 2 double, 2 twin, 1 family; all rooms with bath/shower; TV in all bedrooms TERMS: single occupancy £25, twin/double £40, family room £40; children under 10 free, £5 for ages 10 to 15 sharing with parents; dinner £7.50–£15 CARDS: none DETAILS: children welcome; dogs welcome; no smoking in bedrooms; car park; garden

TANSLEY Derbyshire   map 9

Packhorse Farm

Tansley, nr Matlock DE4 5LF
TEL/FAX: (01629) 580950
from A615 at Tansley turn at sign for Tansley Knoll and continue through village

Just two miles from Matlock, Packhorse Farm is a 200-year-old farmhouse, with more recent additions, set in a large garden on a working farm in Derbyshire's beautiful countryside, with views of hills and moors. The bedrooms are brightly decorated and Margaret Haynes takes care of her guests with substantial breakfasts served in the sunny dining-room. The beamed guests' lounge has an open fire and an attractive plate display. The garden includes a putting green and a small nature reserve.

OWNERS: Mr and Mrs B.L. Haynes OPEN: all year exc Christmas ROOMS: 1 double, 1 twin, 2 family; all rooms with wash-basin; TV in all bedrooms and lounge TERMS: single occupancy £18, twin/double £32, family room £36–£54; children's reductions according to age; deposit: £10 DETAILS: children welcome; no dogs; no smoking in some areas; car park; garden

TARVIN Cheshire   map 7

Grove House

Holme Street, Tarvin, nr Chester CH3 8EQ
TEL: (01829) 740893   FAX: (01829) 741769
on A54 near junction with A51

This impressive red-brick Victorian house stands in a walled garden of one acre which has several listed trees. The house is elegantly furnished with antiques and is tastefully decorated. The double bedroom has a king-sized bed. The spacious drawing-room has doors leading out to the garden. The Spiegelbergs are an interesting, well-travelled family who speak French, Italian and German. They also have musical talent and the youngest son is a percussionist with the National Children's Orchestra. Breakfasts only are available, but there are several eating establishments within two miles.

OWNER: Helen Spiegelberg OPEN: all year exc Christmas and New Year ROOMS: 1 single, with wash-basin; 1 double, with bath/shower; 1 twin, with wash-basin; TV in all bedrooms and lounge   TERMS: single £19, single occupancy £25–£35, twin/double £40–£50; deposit: £10 per person   DETAILS: no children under 12; no dogs; smoking in drawing-room only; car park; garden

TAUNTON   Somerset   map 2

Forde House

9 Upper High Street, Taunton TA1 3PX
TEL: (01823) 279042

Behind the plain green exterior and red door facing the main road lies an elegant and peaceful period house with spacious rooms. It has been carefully renovated and the lovely drawing-room has a grand piano, log fire and french windows leading to the large walled rear garden. A sheltered, wistaria-covered terrace with shuttered windows makes for a delightful place to sit on a summer day. The comfortable bedrooms all have TV and tasteful furnishings. A substantial breakfast is served in the cosy dining-room, which has an ancient slate floor, pine dresser, inglenook fireplace and beams, and which was probably the original kitchen. This is an ideal base for exploring the Quantock, Blackdown and Mendip hills.

OWNERS: Peter and Sheila Naylor   OPEN: all year exc Christmas and New Year   ROOMS: 1 single, 2 double, 2 twin; all rooms with bath/shower; TV in all bedrooms   TERMS: single £25, single occupancy £28, twin/double £48   CARDS: none   DETAILS: no children under 10; no dogs; car park; garden

Huntersmead

Hele, Taunton TA4 1AJ
TEL: (01823) 461315
from M5 junction 26 take A38 towards Taunton, then first left after Sheppy's cider, then first right; house is on right after 1m

Huntersmead is in a beautiful and peaceful spot, and offers a quiet retreat for those wanting to relax in the countryside. The property dates from different periods, the main house being a low whitewashed building, joined to a grey stone cottage, and standing in a lovely big garden. The Amors are friendly, welcoming people and the comfortable house is beautifully furnished and decorated. Hele is a tiny village surrounded by fields, and it is advisable to ask for directions as it does not appear on all maps.

OWNERS: Mr and Mrs Keith Amor   OPEN: all year exc Christmas   ROOMS: 1 double, 1 twin; both with wash-basin; TV in all bedrooms and lounge   TERMS: single occupancy £18–£20, twin/double/family room from £34–£36; children under 5 free if sharing with parents; £2 for breakfast for children over 5; dinner £12; deposit: £10   CARDS: none   DETAILS: children welcome; no dogs; car park; garden

TAVERHAM   Norfolk

map 6

Foxwood

Fakenham Road, Taverham, nr Norwich NR8 6HR
TEL: (01603) 868474
on A1067, 5m NW of Norwich

Foxwood, built in the 1930s, is set in 18 acres of well-maintained grounds and woodland inhabited by peacocks and two dogs, Pudding and Pie. In summer, barbecues are often organised. There are several sitting areas for guests' use, and the house is furnished with interesting pieces including a *chaise-longue* and carved chest in the entrance hall. The three bedrooms are of a good size and two have their own bathroom. Inexpensive evening meals are served by arrangement at 6.30pm in the licensed dining-room. Vegetarian options and children's helpings can be requested; packed lunches are also provided.

OWNER: Yvonne Todd   OPEN: all year exc Christmas   ROOMS: 1 double, with bath/ shower; 2 twin, 1 with bath/shower, 1 with wash-basin; TV lounge   TERMS: twin/double from £40; dinner £7; deposit: £10   DETAILS: children welcome; no dogs; no smoking; car park; games room; garden

TAVISTOCK   Devon

map 1

April Cottage

Mount Tavy Road, Tavistock PL19 9JB
TEL: (01822) 613280

This stone-built Victorian semi-detached cottage stands on the banks of the River Tavy in a small pretty garden. Although on the edge of Tavistock, five minutes' walk brings one right into town, and it is pleasant to stroll alongside the river. The house is cosy and warm and the Bacons are friendly and solicitous of their guests' needs. One of the bedrooms overlooks the river, and there are plans to upgrade all three rooms in 1996 to *en suite* status. A comfortable lounge/dining-room has individual tables where breakfast only is served. Packed lunches can, however, be made up. Tavistock is an interesting market town and Dartmoor is nearby.

OWNERS: Rose and Norman Bacon   OPEN: all year exc Christmas   ROOMS: 2 double, 1 with bath/shower; 1 with wash-basin; 1 twin, with wash-basin; TV in all bedrooms and lounge   TERMS: single occupancy £18–£22, twin/double £28–£36; half-price for children under 10; deposit: £5 per person   CARDS: none   DETAILS: children welcome; dogs by arrangement; no smoking; car park; garden

Use the maps and indexes at the back of the Guide to plan your trip.

TAYNTON   Oxfordshire   map 2

Coombe Brook Lodge

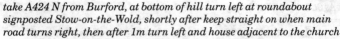

Taynton, nr Burford OX18 4UH
TEL: (01993) 823616
*take A424 N from Burford, at bottom of hill turn left at roundabout
signposted Stow-on-the-Wold, shortly after keep straight on when main
road turns right, then after 1m turn left and house adjacent to the church*

Coombe Brook Lodge is situated in a quiet corner of the pretty
Cotswold hamlet of Taynton, and stands in extensive gardens in the
Windrush valley. Michael and Janet Florey have converted this old
farm building cleverly, providing a high standard of accommodation.
The two *en suite* bedrooms are tastefully decorated with pretty pastel
wallpapers and matching fabrics. The double bedroom has a king-
sized bed and both rooms have countryside views. Substantial
breakfasts are served in the huge country kitchen, or on the patio
when the weather allows.

OWNER: Mrs J.M. Florey   OPEN: Mar to end Nov   ROOMS: 1 double, 1 twin; both rooms
with bath/shower; TV in all bedrooms and lounge   TERMS: single occupancy £25, twin/
double £50   CARDS: none   DETAILS: no children under 8; no dogs; car park; garden

TESTON   Kent   map 3

Court Lodge Farm House

The Street, Teston, nr Maidstone M18 5AQ
TEL: (01622) 812570   FAX: (01622) 814200
off A26, 4m W of Maidstone

This sixteenth-century, brick-faced country house stands in an
elevated position at one end of the small village of Teston next to the
church, with lovely views over the Medway Valley. It overlooks
Teston Country Park, and fruit and hop fields, and is a picture at
apple-blossom time. Court Lodge Farm was once a meeting place for
those campaigning for the abolition of slavery. Guests have use of a
large, comfortably furnished beamed sitting-room with leaded-light
windows, an open fireplace, and splendid views of the well-kept
garden. Breakfast is served at one large table in the dining-hall. Mr
Bannock has an excellent knowledge of local places of historic
interest, and can also help with tracing ancestry.

OWNER: Rosemarie Bannock   OPEN: all year exc Christmas and New Year   ROOMS: 1
double, with bath/shower; 2 twin, 1 with bath/shower, 1 with wash-basin; TV lounge
TERMS: single occupancy £27, twin/double £40   CARDS: Visa   DETAILS: no children
under 10; no dogs; no smoking; garden

THAXTED Essex

map 6

Folly House

Watling Lane, Thaxted CM6 2QY
TEL: (01371) 830618

This modern brick building is in a quiet location overlooking open
countryside in this unspoilt village which pre-dates the Domesday
Book. The well-appointed bedrooms are all a good size and
comfortably furnished and the lounge is large too. Jackie and Gerald
King have had many years' experience in the catering trade and
provide excellent breakfasts and, by arrangement, freshly prepared
evening meals. Vegetarians can be catered for and guests are
welcome to bring wine to the meal. Alternatively, Thaxted offers a
variety of eating establishments. Complimentary tea and coffee are
available at any time in the dining-room. Stansted is six miles away
and the Kings offer transport to and from the airport at a modest
charge.

OWNER: Jacqueline King OPEN: all year exc Christmas ROOMS: 2 double, both with
bath/shower; 1 twin, with wash-basin; TV in all bedrooms and lounge TERMS: single
occupancy £35, twin/double £40–£50; children's reductions; dinner £15 CARDS: none
DETAILS: children welcome; no dogs; no smoking; car park; garden

THELNETHAM Norfolk

map 6

Lodge Farm

High Street, Thelnetham, nr Diss IP22 1LJ
TEL/FAX: (01379) 898203
off A143 / B1113, 7m SW of Diss

No longer running a working farm, Nick and Christine Palmer are
concentrating on their bed-and-breakfast business in this
seventeenth-century thatched and timber-framed house. The
rambling, spacious interior has old beams, a quarry-tiled floor and
inglenook fireplace, and the well-appointed bedrooms have Laura
Ashley furnishings and private bathroom facilities. Guests may relax
in the sitting-room, which overlooks the walled garden and has
warming log fires in chilly weather. To the rear of the house is a lake
stocked with carp and trout where fishing can be arranged. Dinner is
available if booked in advance; there is an alcohol licence, and
vegetarians can be catered for with notice. Packed lunches can be
provided. There is also a pub within five minutes' walk that serves
evening meals. Nearby, the Bressingham Live Steam Museum and
Gardens includes a large collection of road and rail engines.

OWNER: Christine Palmer OPEN: all year exc Christmas and New Year ROOMS: 1
double, 2 twin, 1 family; all rooms with bath/shower; TV in some bedrooms TERMS:

single occupancy £25, twin/double £36–£40, family room £55; dinner £12.50; deposit: £20 CARDS: Diners DETAILS: no children under 10; no dogs; smoking in sitting-room only; car park; garden

---

THETFORD Norfolk
map 6

The Wilderness

Earls Street, Thetford IP24 2AF
TEL: (01842) 764646

Built on the site of an old priory, the remains of which are still visible in the beautiful landscaped garden, this is a mock-Tudor house which, despite its name, is just two minutes from the centre of town. High standards are maintained and Marian Pomorski is an excellent host who greets all her guests with a freshly brewed cup of tea or coffee. The house is furnished with antiques and the bedrooms are all comfortable. Breakfast only is served, but Thetford offers several eating establishments.

OWNERS: John and Marian Pomorski OPEN: all year ROOMS: 1 single, 2 double, 1 twin; all rooms with wash-basin; TV in all bedrooms and lounge TERMS: single £19, single occupancy £20, twin/double £34; 30% reduction for children over 8; deposit CARDS: none DETAILS: no children under 8; no dogs; no smoking; car park; garden

---

THIRLMERE Cumbria
map 10

Brackenrigg

Thirlmere, nr Keswick CA12 4TF
TEL: (01768) 772258
on A591, 3m S of Keswick

Guests continue to endorse the welcome and hospitality experienced at this beautiful Victorian house. Brackenrigg is set in two acres of gardens, which now boast a summer house and croquet lawn, and has beautiful views. The large, well-appointed bedrooms are named after local beauty spots; some rooms are in the converted barn. A log fire provides a welcome in the comfortable lounge, and breakfast and four-course dinners are served in the elegant dining-room with its beams and garden views. There is no licence, but guests may bring their own wine to dinner. Self-catering is also available and is suitable for guests with walking difficulties.

OWNERS: Roy and Anne Wilson OPEN: Mar to end Oct ROOMS: 1 single, with wash-basin; 4 double, all with bath/shower; 1 twin, with bath/shower; 1 family, with wash-basin; TV in all bedrooms TERMS: single £20–£23, single occupancy £32–£35, twin/double £44–£50; half-price for children from 5 to 12 sharing with parents; dinner £15; deposit: £20 per person CARDS: none DETAILS: no children under 5; no dogs; no smoking in dining-room; car park; garden

THIRSK   North Yorkshire   map 9

St James House

36 The Green, Thirsk YO7 1AQ
TEL: (01845) 524120

This eighteenth-century listed property faces the Green, a
conservation area in central Thirsk. The market-place is only a short
walk away, and the town has a good choice of eating establishments.
The beautifully furnished interior is full of antiques and is in
excellent decorative order. A large lounge has a grandfather clock,
and there is a dining-room where breakfasts only are served. The
bedrooms are colour co-ordinated, each room named after its décor;
one has an attractive old spindle bedstead. One bedroom is on the
ground floor. In summer the garden with its lily pond is full of colour,
and window boxes decorate the house. Castle Howard, Fountains
Abbey and many pretty villages are nearby.

OWNER: Elisabeth Ogleby   OPEN: mid-Mar to mid-Nov   ROOMS: 1 double, with wash-
basin; 1 twin, with wash-basin; 2 family, both with bath/shower; TV in all bedrooms
TERMS: single occupancy £25, twin/double from £32, family room from £32; deposit:
£15   CARDS: none   DETAILS: children welcome; no dogs; no smoking; garden

THOMPSON   Norfolk   map 6

Thatched House

Pockthorpe Corner, Thompson, nr Thetford IP24 1PJ
TEL: (01953) 483577
off A1075, 3m S of Watton

This pretty sixteenth-century whitewashed cottage is in a relaxingly
rural location. The three bedrooms have original beams and lots of
character. Two are on the ground floor: one has an old stable door
leading out to the garden, the other has french windows opening out
on to a patio. One of these bedrooms is suitable for wheelchair-users.
The upstairs room with its sloping ceiling is reached via a narrow,
steep staircase. Guests can share the TV lounge with the family, and
there is a dining-room where breakfast and modestly priced evening
meals are served. Vegetarian options (also packed lunches) can be
provided, and guests should bring their own wine to table as there is
no alcohol licence.

OWNER: Brenda Mills   OPEN: all year   ROOMS: 1 double, 2 twin; all rooms with bath/
shower; 1 room suitable for wheelchair-users; TV in all bedrooms and lounge   TERMS:
single occupancy £20, twin/double £38; dinner £7.50   CARDS: none   DETAILS: no
children under 7; dogs welcome; no smoking; car park; garden

THATCHED HOUSE, THOMPSON

THORALBY North Yorkshire   map 9

Low Green House

Thoralby, nr Leyburn DL8 3SZ
TEL: (01969) 663623
on minor road off A684, 1m S of Aysgarth

Built in 1850, Low Green House is a typical Dales stone house at the edge of the village with lovely views. Marilyn and Tony Philpott are a warm and friendly couple who pay great attention to their guests' comfort. The bedrooms are of a good size, two in the main house decorated in soft pastels, and two in the converted stable and hayloft, one of which is on the ground floor. The spacious dining-room/lounge has comfortable green furnishings, an attractive window-seat, beams, a log fire and an antique pine sideboard. Breakfasts include free-range eggs and dinners, by arrangement, are available every day except Thursdays. Vegetarians can be catered for and guests may bring their own wine. Close by is a friendly pub that serves bar meals. This is a popular area for walkers and footpaths criss-cross the village.

OWNERS: Tony and Marilyn Philpott OPEN: all year exc Christmas ROOMS: 3 double, 1 twin; all rooms with bath/shower; TV in all bedrooms TERMS: single occupancy £24, twin/double £40; £6 for children under 2; dinner £13; deposit: £10 per night CARDS: none DETAILS: children welcome; dogs in bedrooms only, with own bedding; no smoking; car park; garden

THORNBOROUGH   Buckinghamshire   map 5

Old Manor

Thornborough, nr Buckingham MK18 2DF
TEL: (01280) 812345   FAX: (01280) 824911
from A421 2m E of Buckingham follow signs to Thornborough

This stone-built Elizabethan manor house looks the part with its
grand chimneys and ancient walls, and was once the venue for
manorial courts; to complete the picture, it is reputed to be haunted.
It stands in five acres of stately park-like grounds, with a pond and a
hard tennis court. Inside are some enormous rooms, flagstones,
sloping floors, beams and panelling. The elegant drawing-room has
an inglenook fireplace. Pippa Deacon is a delightful host and a good
cook. Two- or three-course evening meals are available by
arrangement on most nights, and when she cannot cook Pippa points
guests in the direction of an excellent local pub. Vegetarians can be
catered for and everything is freshly prepared using home-grown
vegetables and herbs. The single rooms are not always available.

OWNERS: Pippa and Tim Deacon   OPEN: all year exc Christmas   ROOMS: 2 single; 2
twin, both with bath/shower; TV lounge   TERMS: single/single occupancy £25, twin
£40–£60; dinner £12.50–£16.50; deposit required in high season   CARDS: none
DETAILS: no children; no dogs; no smoking; car park; games room; garden; tennis

THRELKELD   Cumbria   map 10

Blease Farm

Blease Road, Threlkeld, nr Keswick CA12 4SF
TEL/FAX: (017687) 79087
turn off A66 4m E of Keswick into Threlkeld, then right into Blease Road

The spectacular setting for this 250-year-old farmhouse is 40 acres of
land on the southern-facing slopes of Blencathra. The stone building
is decorated in a warm, traditional style to a sumptuous standard,
something hospitable owners John and Ruth Knowles have worked
long and hard to achieve so successfully. The *en suite* bedrooms have
pine furniture, TV, hair-dryer and radio alarm. Dinners for four or
more people can be arranged, but three nearby pubs offer
alternatives. All meals are cooked on the Aga and are served in the
beamed dining-room on a massive refectory table. There is a
tremendous amount of information provided on walking and climbing
in the area.

OWNERS: John and Ruth Knowles   OPEN: all year   ROOMS: 2 double, 1 twin; all rooms
with bath/shower; TV in all bedrooms   TERMS: single occupancy £27, twin/double £48;
dinner £17.50; deposit: £50 or 1 night's charge   CARDS: none   DETAILS: no children
under 12; no dogs; no smoking; car park; garden

THROPTON   Northumberland   **map 11**

Thropton Demesne Farmhouse

Thropton, nr Morpeth NE65 7LT
TEL/FAX: (01669) 620196
off B6341 at W end of village

Quietly situated at the end of its own private lane, this Georgian
house was once the home of the fourth Lord Armstrong, who had it
modernised in the Victorian era. Much of the house is decorated with
William Morris wallpapers, and the bedrooms are in rich colours, one
purple, one lemon and one dusty pink. All have pristine white duvets
and two have original fireplaces. There is a separate dining-room and
a quiet lounge with a piano. Breakfasts feature home-made bread
and several nearby establishments offer evening meals. Guests are
welcome to relax in the walled garden and to walk down to the river
through the rolling farmland.

OWNERS: Tim and Alison Giles   OPEN: all year exc Christmas   ROOMS: 2 double, 1 twin;
all rooms with bath/shower; TV in all bedrooms   TERMS: single occupancy £25, twin/
double £38; children's reductions; deposit: £10   CARDS: none   DETAILS: children
welcome; no dogs; no smoking; car park; garden

THROWLEIGH   Devon   **map 1**

The Stables

Throwleigh, nr Okehampton EX20 2HS
TEL: (01647) 231497
leave A30 at Whiddon Down, 5m E of Okehampton, then follow signs for
Throwleigh

This old stone house is right in the centre of the tiny and lovely
Dartmoor village of Throwleigh with its old church and manor house.
As its names implies, it is a conversion from stables and stands in a
pleasant garden with lovely views to Dartmoor. Mrs Ford is a very
friendly lady who treats her guests as friends, and she is happy to
accept horses too. There are two simply furnished, small twin-bedded
rooms and a cosy lounge, with log fire, shared with the owner.
Breakfast only is served in the dining-room, where guests sit on two
old church pews.

OWNER: Freda Ford   OPEN: all year   ROOMS: 2 twin, both with bath/shower; TV lounge
TERMS: single occupancy £15, twin £30; deposit: £10   CARDS: Access, Visa   DETAILS:
no children under 8; dogs welcome (not on beds); no smoking in bedrooms; car park;
garden

Please let us know if an establishment has changed hands.

Well Farm

Throwleigh, nr Okehampton EX20 3JQ
TEL: (01647) 231291   FAX: (01647) 231561
off A30, 8m SE of Okehampton and 1½m outside Throwleigh; phone or write for map

Found down a succession of lanes on the edge of Dartmoor, this attractive one-time medieval longhouse with sixteenth- and seventeenth-century additions is part of a 200-acre family-run working dairy and pig farm. With its collection of peacocks, free-range poultry and resident cats and dogs, Well Farm is well suited to guests who are fond of animals and a country lifestyle. Sheelagh Knox treats her guests as family and encourages them to feel at home, and Bryan is a keen wildlife photographer. The main house has two bedrooms, both *en suite*, while an annexe at the rear has a ground-floor family unit consisting of two small bedrooms, a bathroom and a small sitting-room. There are two lounges with TV. Evening meals include local produce and cider, and vegetarians are catered for; guests may bring their own wine to dinner. Packed lunches can be provided. Guests without cars can arrange to be met at Exeter station.

OWNERS: Bryan and Sheelagh Knox   OPEN: all year exc Christmas   ROOMS: 1 double, 1 twin, 1 family, all with bath/shower; 2 rooms suitable for wheelchair-users; TV lounge   TERMS: single occupancy £18, twin/double £36, family room from approx £40; reductions for children under 12; dinner £12   CARDS: Amex   DETAILS: children welcome; dogs by arrangement; no smoking; car park; garden

---

THURSBY   Cumbria   **map 10**

How End Farm

Thursby, nr Carlisle CA5 6PX
TEL: (016973) 42487
on A595, 7m W of Carlisle

Guests continue to enjoy the warm hospitality found at this 250-year-old listed farmhouse with views over the Lakeland fells. The comfortable bedrooms have hair-dryers and tea-making facilities, and there are two bathrooms for the use of guests. The walking sticks on display in the house are the family's own work. Other furnishings are solid and old-fashioned, and the beams and staircase date back to 1764.

OWNER: Margaret Swainson   OPEN: all year   ROOMS: 1 twin, 1 family; TV lounge   TERMS: single occupancy £15, twin/family £30; children's reductions according to age   CARDS: none   DETAILS: children welcome; dogs welcome; smoking in lounge only; car park; garden

TILSTON   Cheshire   map 7

Tilston Lodge

Tilston, nr Malpas SY14 7DR
TEL/FAX: (01829) 250223
from Whitchurch take A41 N for 1½m, turn left at Horse and Jockey pub on to B5395, continue through Malpas and for further 3m, Tilston Lodge is on left

This attractive Victorian country house was originally a gentleman's hunting lodge, and stands in 16 acres of landscaped gardens and pasture. The Ritchies are charming and helpful, and breed sheep and poultry. Original features, such as fireplaces and a handsome mahogany galleried landing, have been retained, and antiques include a grandfather clock and *chaise-longue*. The *en suite* spacious bedrooms are elegantly decorated with a selection of fine prints. Two have four-posters and there is one ground-floor bedroom. An enormous drawing-room is available to guests, and excellent breakfasts are served in the separate dining-room. There is a pub serving food within walking distance. Visitors are welcome to wander through the gardens and see the rare-breed farm animals, and the nearby Bickerton Hills provide walkers with laid-out trails and tremendous views.

OWNERS: Kathie and Neil Ritchie   OPEN: all year   ROOMS: 1 twin, 2 four-poster; all rooms with bath/shower; TV in all bedrooms and lounge   TERMS: single occupancy £30–£40, twin £50, four-poster £60; half-price for children   CARDS: none   DETAILS: children welcome; no dogs; no smoking; car park; garden

TINTAGEL   Cornwall   map 1

Ye Olde Malthouse

Fore Street, Tintagel PL34 0DA
TEL: (01840) 770461
take B3263 off A39 Bude to Wadebridge road

Ye Olde Malthouse is principally a restaurant-with-rooms. It is a charmingly picturesque fourteenth-century building standing right in the centre of Tintagel, just a few yards from the track down to the castle. In season Tintagel is humming with tourists, and the restaurant is a popular venue for meals, both at lunch-time and in the evening; packed lunches can also be provided. The comfortable bedrooms are attractively decorated and vary in size and facilities; there is also a cosy guests' lounge. This is good value for money in one of Cornwall's most popular tourist towns.

OWNERS: Mr and Mrs E.J. Ridgewell   OPEN: Mar to Oct   ROOMS: 1 single, with wash-basin; 5 double, 3 with bath/shower, 2 with wash-basin; 2 twin, 1 with bath/shower, 1 with wash-basin; TV in all bedrooms TERMS: single £15, single occupancy £20, twin/double £29–£44; reductions for children from 2 to 11; dinner £9; deposit: 1 night's charge CARDS: Access, Visa DETAILS: no children under 2; no dogs; car park

---

TIVERTON Devon map 1

Hornhill

Exeter Hill, Tiverton EX16 4PL
TEL: (01884) 253352
from M5 junction 27 take A361 for 4½m; turn off at Gornhay Cross and follow signs for Grand Western Canal; at Canal Hill take first right into Exeter Hill

---

Hornhill was originally built as a coaching-inn in the eighteenth century and has been in the Pugsley family for over 100 years. Now a farmhouse with 75 acres of farmland, the house is a few minutes from Tiverton on top of a steep hill and set in an acre of its own gardens; there are wonderful views over the Exe Valley. The Pugsley family are friendly and hospitable, and guests enjoy the quiet, peaceful setting. Of the three bedrooms, one has a Victorian four-poster bed and one *en suite* ground-floor room is suitable for the partially disabled, though not for wheelchair-users. Two of the rooms, though not *en suite*, have their own bathrooms. Evening meals by arrangement, as well as breakfast, are served for both guests and family at one long table in the enormous dining-room; guests may bring their own wine to dinner as Hornhill is unlicensed. The comfortable drawing-room, which overlooks the garden, has an open fire and plenty of books. Although there is no central heating, the bedrooms have automatic electric fires and there are woodburners in the public rooms.

OWNERS: Peter and Barbara Pugsley OPEN: all year exc Christmas ROOMS: 1 double, 1 twin, 1 four-poster; all rooms with bath/shower; TV in all bedrooms TERMS: single occupancy £18.50–£20.50, twin/double/four-poster £36–£39; dinner £12; deposit: 33% of 1 night's charge CARDS: none DETAILS: no children under 12; no dogs; no smoking; car park; garden

---

TORMARTON Avon map 2

Chestnut Farm

Tormarton, nr Badminton GL9 1HS
TEL: (01454) 218563
just off M4 at junction 18, 3m SE of Chipping Sodbury

This modern stone-built house lies just off the M4 between Bath and Bristol, and is in an attractive village with an interesting church. Part of the accommodation is in the main house, and a further twin and double room with sitting-room, kitchenette and bathroom are in a separate cottage on the ground floor. The house has a relaxed atmosphere and the owners are friendly and chatty, and run a small farm. Breakfast is served in the conservatory. Competitively priced two- or three-course evening meals are available by arrangement, and children's helpings and vegetarian dishes may be requested; guests may bring their own wine. Packed lunches can be made up for those out exploring.

OWNERS: Mr and Mrs R. Cadei   OPEN: all year   ROOMS: 2 double, 3 twin; all rooms with bath/shower; TV in all bedrooms   TERMS: twin/double £40; reductions for children sharing with parents; dinner £9.50; deposit: summer only, by arrangement   CARDS: none   DETAILS: children welcome; dogs welcome; car park; garden

TORQUAY   Devon   map 1

Fairmount House Hotel

Herbert Road, Chelston, Torquay TQ2 6RW
TEL/FAX: (01803) 605446

Built in 1900 as a family residence, this Victorian house stands in a quiet residential area on a south-facing hillside. It has a small, pretty rear garden with views to Brixham and is just a mile from the harbour. Fairmount has a very friendly, welcoming atmosphere and is comfortably furnished. The TV lounge, with its sunny balcony, has a small library that includes maps and guidebooks, and the bar is in a small conservatory overlooking the garden. Each bedroom takes its name from the *Lord of the Rings* (appropriate given the owners name), and two of the rooms open out on to the garden; one of these has wheelchair access. Dinner is available, and bar lunches can be arranged; packed lunches can also be provided. Close by is the well-known beauty spot of Cockington village with its fourteenth-century thatched forge.

OWNERS: Mr and Mrs Noel Tolkien   OPEN: end Mar to end Oct   ROOMS: 2 single, 4 double, 2 family; all rooms with bath/shower; 2 rooms suitable for wheelchair-users; TV in all bedrooms and lounge   TERMS: single £25–£29, single occupancy £25–£45, twin/double £50–£58, family room £50–£75; reductions for children according to age; dinner £11.50; deposit: £10–£50   CARDS: Access, Amex, Visa   DETAILS: children welcome; dogs by arrangement; no smoking in dining-room and bedrooms; car park; garden

Walnut House

7 Walnut Road, Chelston, Torquay TQ2 6HP
TEL: (01803) 606854

This Victorian sandstone house stands just off a busy road close to the seafront and shops. Marie Landau is a delightful ex-teacher who has been running her bed-and-breakfast business since 1986. The house is comfortable and clean, and the bedrooms are very well equipped; one is on the ground floor. The front garden is a blaze of colour and there is a patio for sitting outside. Evening meals are only available by arrangement during the winter, but the pub next door serves good food. Walnut House offers excellent value in a warm and friendly atmosphere.

OWNER: Marie Landau OPEN: all year exc owner's holiday ROOMS: 1 single, 2 double, 1 twin; all rooms with bath/shower; TV in all bedrooms and lounge TERMS: single/single occupancy £14, twin/double £26–£28; children under 10 half-price in twin room; dinner £6; deposit: 1 night's charge per person CARDS: none DETAILS: children welcome; no dogs; no smoking; car park

---

TOTNES Devon   map 1

Old Forge

Seymour Place, Totnes TQ9 5AY
TEL: (01803) 862174   FAX: (01803) 865385

This 600-year-old stone-built forge was converted just over ten years ago into an attractive small hotel. Only a few minutes' walk from the town centre, the Old Forge offers comfortable, well-appointed accommodation along with a friendly atmosphere. The eight pleasantly furnished bedrooms are colour co-ordinated; several have *en suite* facilities, and two ground-floor rooms and a suite are suitable for the partially disabled. Breakfast only – including cooked vegetarian options – is served in the Tudor-style dining-room, where cream teas are also available during the summer. The Old Forge has a large walled garden that includes a patio where drinks are served in fine weather.

OWNER: Jeannie Allnutt OPEN: all year exc Christmas ROOMS: 1 single, with wash-basin; 3 double, 2 with bath/shower, 1 with wash-basin; 2 twin, both with bath/shower; 4 family, all with bath/shower; TV in all bedrooms and lounge TERMS: single £32, single occupancy £32–£44, twin/double £42–£64, family room £62–£94; reductions for children sharing with parents; deposit: 1 night's charge CARDS: Access, Delta, Visa DETAILS: children welcome; guide dogs only; no smoking except in undercover archway; car park; garden

---

TOY'S HILL Kent   map 3

Corner Cottage

Toy's Hill, nr Westerham TN16 1PY
TEL: (01732) 750362
take A25 to Brasted, turn left at King's Arms, then 3m to Puddledock Lane, turn right; first house on left

---

Corner Cottage is a picturesque fifteenth-century cottage set in a garden of terraces and lawns. The long, low building stands at the top of a hill and enjoys magnificent views over the Weald of Kent. It is full of beams and has an old green mangle in the entrance hall. Mrs

Olszowska is a charming host, and with only one guest bedroom is able to offer individual attention. The spacious bedroom, with brass bed, is above the garage block, giving complete privacy. Breakfast only is taken in the dining-room, which also enjoys the spectacular view.

OWNER: Kerstin Olszowska OPEN: all year ROOMS: 1 double/family, with bath/shower; TV in bedroom TERMS: single occupancy £25, double £37 or as family room from £55.50; half-price for children under 12; deposit: £10 CARDS: none DETAILS: children welcome; no dogs; no smoking in bedroom; car park; garden

---

TRESILLIAN Cornwall   map 1

Manor Cottage

Tresillian, nr Truro TR1 4BN
TEL: (01872) 520212
2½m from Truro on A39 towards St Austell

Carlton and Gillian took over this attractive 200-year-old building set back from the main road a couple of years ago and, having completed the renovations, are now working on improving the facilities. The small bedrooms currently share a couple of bathrooms, with plans to make some of the bedrooms *en suite* at a future date. Enthusiasm and a welcoming atmosphere prevail in this small restaurant-with-rooms (open to non-residents only on Friday and Saturday evenings). Carlton cooks imaginative meals which are served in a small conservatory-style room off the front of the house; vegetarian choices are always available, and packed lunches can be provided.

OWNERS: Gillian Jackson and Carlton Moyle OPEN: all year exc last week in Oct, 25 and 26 Dec ROOMS: 1 single, 2 double, 1 twin, 1 family; all rooms with wash-basin; TV in all bedrooms TERMS: single/single occupancy £17, twin/double £32–£34; family room from £44; reductions for children sharing with parents; dinner £17.50; deposit: 25% CARDS: Access, Visa DETAILS: children welcome; no dogs; smoking in bedrooms only; car park

---

Polsue Manor Farm

Tresillian, nr Truro TR1 4BP
TEL: (01872) 520234
up driveway N of A39 at W edge of Tresillian

This sixteenth-century farmhouse was extended to the front in the Victorian era, adding some large rooms with high ceilings. The overall effect is spacious and unpretentious. It stands above the main road into Truro up a long, well-maintained track and is part of a 190-acre mixed farm. It has lovely views and overlooks the tidal Tresillian River. The simply furnished and decorated bedrooms share a bathroom, shower room and WC, and the family room is on the ground-floor. The sitting-room has large, cosy armchairs and french windows and there is a pleasant dining-room where breakfast and evening meals are served.

OWNER: Geraldine Holliday OPEN: all year exc Christmas ROOMS: 2 double, 1 twin, 2 family; all with wash-basin; TV lounge TERMS: single occupancy £18–£25, twin/double £32–£34, family room £50–£58; half-price for children under 10 sharing with parents; dinner £8.50; deposit: 10% CARDS: none DETAILS: children welcome; dogs by arrangement; car park; garden

TROTTON   West Sussex
map 2

Trotton Farm

Trotton, Rogate, nr Petersfield GU31 5EN
TEL: (01730) 813618   FAX: (01730) 816093
on A272 between Midhurst and Petersfield

This farm is in the tiny hamlet of Trotton in pleasant countryside with views of fields and farmland. Guests are accommodated in an old converted barn adjoining the house. There is a new ground-floor twin-bedded room, and one of the first-floor twins has been made into a double. On the ground floor a large games room/lounge offers table tennis, TV and access to a patio through french windows. Breakfast is served in the farmhouse dining-room. Guests will find plenty of pubs nearby for evening meals.

OWNER: Mrs J.E. Baigent OPEN: all year ROOMS: 1 double, 2 twin; all rooms with bath/shower; TV lounge TERMS: single occupancy £25–£30, twin/double £35–£40 CARDS: none DETAILS: children welcome; well-behaved dogs only; no smoking; car park; games room; garden

TROUTBECK   Cumbria
map 8

Yew Grove

Troutbeck, nr Windermere LA23 1PG
TEL: (01539) 433304

Standing in the unspoilt village of Troutbeck on the old road from Windermere to Ullswater is Yew Grove, a seventeenth-century whitewashed house built in the traditional manner from Lakeland stone. Lake Windermere is two miles distant, and Kirkstone Pass four miles. The building was once upon a time the village post office and an office for a bank. The simply furnished bedrooms are clean and comfortable; most still have the original fireplaces, and the front rooms have lovely views. Guests may relax in the cosy lounge, which has lots of books, local information as well as a TV. Derek and Angela are very accommodating, and the atmosphere at Yew Grove is warm and friendly. Breakfast only is served; a pub that provides evening meals is about half a mile away. Packed lunches can be arranged.

OWNERS: Angela and Derek Pratt OPEN: all year exc Christmas ROOMS: 3 double, 1 with bath/shower, 2 with wash-basin; 1 twin, with wash-basin; TV lounge TERMS: single occupancy £19–£20, twin/double £33–£41; 30% reduction for children under 12 sharing with parents; deposit: £10 per room CARDS: none DETAILS: children welcome; no dogs; no smoking; car park; garden

TUNBRIDGE WELLS Kent   map 3

Danehurst House Hotel

41 Lower Green Road, Rusthall, Tunbridge Wells TN4 8TW
TEL: (01892) 527739   FAX: (01892) 514804
on A264, 1½m W of town centre

This large Victorian family home is clean, comfortable and professionally run, and has a reputation for good food. Dinner is served in the dining-room, which has yellow-striped wallpaper, richly swagged curtains and a mixture of Victorian and modern furniture. Breakfast, for which orders are taken the previous night, is served in the pretty conservatory. There is also a drawing-room and a bar. The bedrooms are very well equipped and decorated in pastel colours. Drinks from the bar can be enjoyed on the terrace in the mature garden.

OWNERS: Michael and Angela Godbold OPEN: all year exc last 2 weeks of Aug ROOMS: 1 single, with wash-basin; 4 twin/double, all with bath/shower; TV in all bedrooms and lounge TERMS: single £35–£45, single occupancy £45, twin/double £65; dinner £19–£26; deposit: credit card details CARDS: Access, Amex, Visa DETAILS: no children under 8; no dogs; no smoking; car park; garden

TWEEDMOUTH Northumberland   map 11

Old Vicarage

Church Road, Tweedmouth, Berwick-upon-Tweed TD15 2AN
TEL: (01289) 306909
on A1167 approaching Berwick-upon-Tweed, turn right at Queen's Head pub then first left

This unusual nineteenth-century stone-built house with intriguing windows stands in its own grounds conveniently situated just across the old bridge from the centre of Berwick-upon-Tweed. It has been refurbished to a very high standard while retaining all its original features. The large bedrooms with their own fireplaces are furnished with solid old-fashioned furniture. Attractive stencilling adorns the entry way and stairwell, and all the curtains are hand-made by Tina Richardson. The lounge contains a mine of information on where to go and what to eat locally, as well as a good supply of books, magazines and games. Traditional breakfasts include locally smoked kippers.

OWNER: Tina Richardson OPEN: all year exc Christmas and New Year ROOMS: 1 single, with wash-basin; 4 double, 2 with bath/shower, 2 with wash-basin; 1 twin, with bath/shower; 1 family, with bath/shower; TV in all bedrooms TERMS: single £14–£16, single occupancy £20–£35, twin/double £28–£46, family room £36–£50; half-price for children under 5; deposit: £10 CARDS: none DETAILS: children welcome; dogs welcome; no smoking in lounge or dining-room; car park; garden

TWYFORD Berkshire   map 3

The Hermitage

63 London Road, Twyford RG10 9EJ
TEL/FAX: (01734) 340004

This smart red-brick Georgian house with Victorian additions stands proudly in a secluded landscaped garden. It is a large, comfortable family home with a friendly and informal atmosphere which is genuinely relaxing. Four of the spacious and attractive bedrooms are in the house and two have recently been added in the converted stables. They are decorated in soft colours and have antique and stripped-pine furniture. Filling breakfasts are served in the enormous dining-room and excellent, home-cooked evening meals are available by arrangement; vegetarians can be catered for. Twyford also offers a number of eating places.

OWNER: Carel Barker OPEN: all year exc Christmas ROOMS: 3 double, 1 with bath/shower, 2 with wash-basin; 3 twin, 2 with bath/shower, 1 with wash-basin; TV in all bedrooms TERMS: single occupancy £25–£35, twin/double £35–£50; deposit: £10 CARDS: none DETAILS: no children; no dogs; no smoking; car park; garden

UGLEY GREEN Essex   map 3

Thatched Cottage

Snakes Lane, Ugley Green, nr Bishop's Stortford CM22 6HW
TEL: (01279) 812341
off B1383, 3m NE of Bishop's Stortford

Just three miles from Gatwick Airport is this charming Elizabethan black-and-white timbered thatched cottage set in nine acres of land with lovely gardens. There have been several recent improvements to the house, including an enlarged entry and new furniture. The ground-floor twin bedroom is particularly charming with its wealth of beams and sloping ceiling; all the bedrooms have matching bedspreads and curtains. The lounge has a TV as well as lots of books to read. Excellent breakfasts cooked on the Aga are served in the cosy kitchen.

OWNER: Mrs J.E. Hilton OPEN: all year exc Christmas and New Year ROOMS: 3 twin, 2 with wash-basin; TV lounge TERMS: single occupancy £20, twin £35; children's reductions if child sleeps on mattress in parents' room CARDS: none DETAILS: children welcome; dogs welcome; no smoking in dining-room; car park; garden

UPPER CLATFORD Hampshire   map 2

Malt Cottage

Upper Clatford, nr Andover SP11 7QL
TEL: (01264) 323469 FAX: (01264) 334100
off A303; take A3057 towards Stockbridge, then first right, first left, and right at T-junction opposite Crook & Shears pub, house at bottom of lane

This modernised old cottage stands in a picturesque position in a quiet Hampshire village surrounded by six acres of lovely gardens which lead down to a lake and stream. The spacious house is beautifully decorated and the hosts are welcoming and knowledgeable about the area. Richard Mason is a landscape gardener. Guests have use of a beamed sitting-room, which has a log-burning stove for chilly evenings. The single bedroom is *en suite*, while the other two have private bathrooms. Breakfast only is served, but evening meals can be obtained at a pub only 100 yards up the lane.

OWNERS: Richard and Patricia Mason OPEN: all year exc Christmas ROOMS: 1 single, 1 double, 1 twin; all rooms with bath/shower; TV in some bedrooms and lounge TERMS: single/single occupancy £25, twin/double £37–£44 CARDS: none DETAILS: children welcome; no dogs; smoking in sitting-room only; car park; garden

UPPER MINETY Wiltshire   map 2

Flisteridge Cottage

Flisteridge Road, Upper Minety, nr Malmesbury SN16 9PS
TEL: (01666) 860343
take A429 Cirencester to Malmesbury road, turn left at Crudwell by Plough Inn, signposted Oaksey and Minety, through Eastcourt and Flisteridge Woods, cottage is down gravel drive on right

Beautiful countryside and a pretty garden with pond and seats surround this small whitewashed cottage. The house is comfortably furnished and clean, with a log fire in the sitting-room in winter. Mrs Toop-Rose is welcoming, and can offer à la carte evening meals by arrangement. There is no alcohol licence, but guests may bring their own wine; vegetarians can be catered for with notice. Flisteridge Cottage makes a peaceful base for exploring the Cotswolds.

OWNER: Fay Toop-Rose OPEN: all year ROOMS: 1 single; 1 double, with bath/shower; 1 twin; TV lounge TERMS: single £15, single occupancy £17, twin/double £30–£36; dinner £8–£10 CARDS: none DETAILS: no children under 11; dogs by arrangement; no smoking in bedrooms and some public rooms; car park; garden

---

UPPER ODDINGTON   Gloucestershire   map 5

Orchard Cottage

Back Lane, Upper Oddington, nr Moreton-in-Marsh GL56 0XL
TEL: (01451) 830785
off A436, 2m E of Stow-on-the-Wold

This pretty eighteenth-century cottage with its charming garden is just a couple of miles from Stow-on-the-Wold, in the heart of the Cotswolds. The bedrooms might be on the small side, but are immaculate and have comfortable beds with lace bedspreads. Guests have use of a lounge with open fire and TV. With just two bedrooms, Jane Beynon is able to extend personal attention and is adept at helping to prepare itineraries. She is an excellent cook and provides imaginative two- and three-course dinners cooked on the Aga. Children's helpings and vegetarian dishes can be requested. There is no alcohol licence, so diners should bring their own wine. Breakfasts include home-made marmalades and preserves. The fourteenth-century village church is worth a visit.

OWNER: Jane Beynon OPEN: Mar to end Nov ROOMS: 1 double, 1 twin; both rooms with bath/shower; TV lounge TERMS: single occupancy £24, twin/double £37; half-price for children sharing with parents; dinner £12–£14; deposit: £10 CARDS: none DETAILS: no children under 5; dogs by arrangement; no smoking; car park; garden

---

UPPER QUINTON   Warwickshire   map 5

Winton House

The Green, Upper Quinton, nr Stratford-upon-Avon CV37 8SX
TEL: (01789) 720500
off B4632, 6m S of Stratford-upon-Avon

This attractive, creeper-covered Victorian farmhouse in a beautiful part of the Cotswolds offers three comfortable, spacious *en suite* bedrooms that feature antique beds, hand-made quilts, lavender pillows, old lace and embroidery. All the rooms have views over either the garden or Meon Hill, which is steeped in witchcraft and folklore. A guest lounge with a log fire and new furniture is reached down an old pine staircase. Breakfasts are varied and feature healthy and cooked vegetarian options, and home-made jams and fruits; the 'Winton House Special' changes daily. The village church is worth a visit as it has a rare Royal Arms board of Queen Elizabeth I. Bicycles are available for hire, and cyclists may wish to ride on a disused railway track that goes to Stratford.

OWNER: Mrs G. Lyon OPEN: all year exc Christmas and New Year ROOMS: 1 twin, 1 four-poster, 1 family; all rooms with bath/shower; TV lounge TERMS: single occupancy £32, twin £45, four-poster £45, family room £60; deposit: £10 CARDS: none DETAILS: children welcome; no dogs; no smoking; car park; garden

UPTON SNODSBURY   Hereford & Worcester   map 5

Upton House

Upton Snodsbury, nr Worcester WR7 4NR
TEL: (01905) 381226
just off A422, 6m E of Worcester

Upton House is a twelfth-century listed manor house behind the village church. The two beamed bedrooms are elegantly furnished, with *en suite* bathrooms, caddies filled with many types of tea, and trouser presses. Downstairs is beautifully furnished with antiques and items of interest. Breakfast and pre-booked suppers or dinners are served in the dining-room with its log fire and display of china. Upton House is not licensed, but guests may bring their own wine. Children's helpings, vegetarian dishes and packed lunches can be ordered in advance. Just about everything has been considered for visitors' comfort in this efficiently run place, which retains its cottage cosiness. Croquet is on offer in the old-fashioned garden.

OWNERS: Angela and Hugh Jefferson OPEN: all year exc Christmas and New Year ROOMS: 1 double, 1 twin; both rooms with bath/shower; TV in both bedrooms TERMS: single occupancy £32.50, twin/double £65; supper £13.50, dinner £23.50; deposit: £10 CARDS: none DETAILS: children welcome; dogs by arrangement in kennels; no smoking in bedrooms; car park; garden; swimming-pool

VERYAN   Cornwall   map 1

Broom Parc

Camels, Veryan, nr Truro TR2 5PJ
TEL: (01872) 510803   FAX: (01872) 501109
off A3078, 5m SE of Truro

This substantial whitewashed National Trust house stands in a fantastic position, high above the cliffs on the Roseland peninsula, with panoramic views of coast and sea. The attractive sloping garden is bordered with shrubs. The property was used as the Cornish location in the television series made from Mary Wesley's novel *The Camomile Lawn*. Two of the three bedrooms have *en suite* facilities. Evening meals are available by arrangement and, as there is no licence, guests are welcome to bring their own wine to dinner; packed lunches can also be provided.

OWNERS: Lindsay and Keith Righton   OPEN: all year exc Christmas   ROOMS: 3 twin, 2
with bath/shower; TV lounge   TERMS: twin £37–£50; dinner £11.50   CARDS: none
DETAILS: no children; dogs welcome; car park; garden

WALBERTON   West Sussex   map 3

Berrycroft

Tye Lane, Walberton, nr Arundel BN18 0LU
TEL/FAX: (01243) 551323
just off A27 between Arundel and Chichester

Berrycroft is set in its own grounds on the edge of the village of
Walberton. Breakfast only is served in the dining-room, and visitors
have the use of an attractively furnished sitting-room. Mrs Hayward
is an excellent host and, with only one bedroom, guests can be sure
that they will be looked after well. There is a swimming-pool in the
one-and-a-half acre garden.

OWNERS: Mr and Mrs G.L. Hayward   OPEN: all year exc Christmas   ROOMS: 1 twin, with
bath/shower; TV in bedroom and lounge   TERMS: single occupancy £25, twin £36–£40;
£6 for children sharing with parents; deposit: £5 per person for stays of more than 3
nights   CARDS: none   DETAILS: children welcome; no dogs; smoking in sitting-room
only; car park; garden; swimming-pool

WALDRIDGE   Co Durham   map 10

Waldridge Hall Farm

Waldridge, nr Chester-le-Street DH2 3SL
TEL: (0191) 388 4210
*from A1(M) take exit to Chester-le-Street, go straight across two
roundabouts then right at sign to Old Waldridge*

This seventeenth-century farmhouse set in pretty countryside has a
pleasant and informal atmosphere. It is within walking distance of
Waldridge Fell, the last remaining area of lowland heath in the
county. The large, high-ceilinged bedrooms are furnished with
antiques, including some particularly fine beds: a half-tester and a
nineteenth-century French single in the family room and a Queen
Anne in the top-floor room, which has pink décor. Guests have one
side of the house to themselves and the owners have private access
through a different door. Breakfast, featuring the speciality
preserves made and sold in the farmhouse, is served in the cosy
dining-room, which has an open fire and its original shutters. A cot
and high chair can be provided for small children.

OWNERS: Arthur and Joan Smith   OPEN: all year exc Christmas   ROOMS: 1 twin, with
wash-basin; 1 four-poster; 1 family, with wash-basin; TV in all bedrooms and lounge
TERMS: single occupancy £22–£25, twin £32–£33, four-poster/family room £35–£36; £8
for children under 12; deposit: £10 per room   CARDS: none   DETAILS: children welcome;
no dogs; smoking in lounge only; car park; garden

Stratton Farm

West Drove North, Walton Highway, nr Wisbech PE14 7DP
TEL: (01945) 880162
from B198 follow signs to Walton Highway; go through village, turn left
½m past Highwayman pub into West Drove North; farm is on left after ½m

---

This modern ranch-style bungalow set on a 22-acre working farm
continues to maintain its extremely high standards. Outside, visitors
have the use of a private fishing lake and, in summer, a heated
covered swimming-pool; they may also view the farm animals,
including a prize-winning herd of Shorthorn cattle. Inside, the
accommodation includes three large bedrooms, all with *en suite*
facilities and comfortable sitting areas with easy chairs. One room
has been specifically designed for disabled people. Breakfast,
described by one visitor as 'fab', includes home-produced good farm
fare. Packed lunches can be arranged. There are several pubs within
a five-minute drive that serve evening meals.

OWNERS: Mr and Mrs D.R. King   OPEN: all year   ROOMS: 2 double, 1 twin; all rooms with
bath/shower; 1 room suitable for wheelchair-users; TV in all bedrooms   TERMS: single
occupancy £23, twin/double £46; children £14.50   CARDS: none   DETAILS: no children
under 6; no dogs; no smoking; car park; garden; swimming-pool

Stoneacre

Elton Road, Wansford, nr Peterborough PE8 6JT
TEL: (01780) 783283
on A6118 (formerly B671) between Elton and Wansford

This luxurious modern country residence is set in an acre of secluded
grounds in a rural area, with views across the Nene Valley. It also
has its own five-hole pitch-and-putt golf course, which guests are
welcome to use. The charming owners have thought of just about
everything for their visitors. Most of the bedrooms are on the ground
floor and these all open out on to a patio. One luxury room is popular
with honeymooners. The guests' lounge on the first floor has a
balcony. A kitchen is provided for guests and the Wilkinsons keep the
fridge stocked with soft drinks at no extra charge. For those who
prefer to eat out, three pubs in Wansford, only 400 yards away, will
be happy to be of service. This is a wonderful place from which to visit
Burghley House and Sibson Airfield.

OWNERS: Peter and Ann Wilkinson   OPEN: all year   ROOMS: 3 double, 1 with bath/
shower, 2 with wash-basin; 1 twin, with bath/shower; 1 family, with bath/shower; TV in
all bedrooms and lounge   TERMS: single occupancy £22–£38, twin/double £28–£44,
family room £42–£48; deposit: £20   CARDS: none   DETAILS: children welcome; well-
behaved dogs welcome; smoking in lounge and summer house only; car park

WARGRAVE Berkshire
map 3

Windy Brow

204 Victoria Road, Wargrave RG10 8AJ
TEL: (01734) 403336

This 1880 red-brick building on the edge of the village is adorned with hanging baskets in summer. It is comfortable and traditionally furnished. The *en suite* ground-floor room has its own entrance and can adapt into a family room. The house is centrally heated and hot-water bottles and individual heaters are provided for really cold nights. Heather Carver is a friendly outgoing lady who began her B&B business ten years ago after taking in a rowing crew. Breakfast is cooked on the Aga and served in the conservatory in summer. Evening meals are not provided but there are three pubs and a riverside restaurant within walking distance.

OWNERS: Heather and Michael Carver   OPEN: all year   ROOMS: 1 single; 3 double/twin, 1 with bath/shower, 1 with wash-basin; 1 room suitable for wheelchair-users; TV in all bedrooms   TERMS: single £20–£30, single occupancy £25–£30, twin/double £36–£45, family room £50; children under 4 free, half-price for ages 4 to 12; deposit required   CARDS: none   DETAILS: children welcome; dogs by arrangement; no smoking; car park; garden

WARTON Lancashire
map 8

Cotestones Farm

Sand Lane, Warton LA5 9NH
TEL: (01524) 732418

Guests are treated like friends by the charming owner, Mrs Gill Close, in this immaculately modernised farmhouse offering good-value accommodation. It is a 120-acre dairy farm surrounded by peaceful countryside and is ideal for bird-watchers. The comfortable dining-room/lounge has TV, and excellent breakfasts are served. The three bedrooms have solid old-fashioned furniture with comfortable beds, and share two bathrooms between them.

OWNER: Gill Close   OPEN: all year exc Christmas   ROOMS: 1 double, 1 twin, 1 family; all rooms with wash-basin; TV lounge   TERMS: single occupancy £15, twin/double £28, family room from £42; babies free, children half-price in family room   CARDS: none   DETAILS: children welcome; dogs welcome; car park; garden

Breakfast at B&Bs tends to mean a cooked breakfast of bacon, eggs and so on. If you prefer a different style of breakfast, it is best to discuss this when you make a booking.

Recommendations for B&Bs for our next edition are very welcome.

Avon Guest House

7 Emscote Road, Warwick CV34 4PH
TEL/FAX: (01926) 491367

Just five minutes' walk from Warwick Castle, this Victorian brick-built house close to the centre of town offers simply furnished but clean and comfortable accommodation. All the bedrooms now have showers and TVs, and three are *en suite*. Lyn Bolton is a friendly, outgoing lady who enjoys providing modestly priced three-course evening meals (if pre-arranged). Children's portions are available, and vegetarians can be catered for with advance notice. The house is licensed, though guests are welcome to bring their own wine to dinner if they prefer. Packed lunches can be provided. Guests would be well advised to leave their cars here and walk into town.

OWNERS: Lyn and Nobby Bolton OPEN: all year ROOMS: 3 single, 2 double, 1 twin, 3 family; all rooms with shower; TV in all bedrooms TERMS: single £16–£17, single occupancy £20, twin/double £32–£34; family room from £40; half-price for children under 10; dinner £7 CARDS: none DETAILS: children welcome; no dogs; no smoking in dining-room and some bedrooms; car park; garden

Forth House

44 High Street, Warwick CV34 3AX
TEL: (01926) 401512

This beautifully kept old house with its Georgian façade is right in the town centre, though the two guest suites are quietly located at the back of the building. Each suite has a bedroom, a small sitting-room and full *en suite* facilities; the larger, ground-floor suite has its own door to the garden, and is particularly suitable for families. Both suites have zip-linked beds, providing either twin or double accommodation as required. Freshly cooked breakfasts are served in guests' rooms or – if desired and when weather permits – in the garden. Evening meals are available by prior arrangement, though not at weekends; the house is unlicensed but guests may bring their own wine to dinner. Long-stay guests may have use of a small kitchen if they wish to self-cater. Forth House is just a seven-minute walk downhill to the castle and very close to a number of restaurants.

OWNER: Elizabeth Draisey OPEN: all year ROOMS: 2 double/twin/family, both with bath/shower; 1 room suitable for wheelchair-users; TV in both bedrooms TERMS: single occupancy £35, twin/double £42–£50, family room £50–£70; dinner £12; deposit: £10 CARDS: none DETAILS: children welcome; dogs by arrangement; no smoking; car park; garden

Pageant Lodge

2 Castle Lane, Warwick CV34 4BU
TEL: (01926) 491244

Pageant Lodge is a listed building first recorded in the Warwick
Castle archives in 1482; most of the present building, which has
attracted architectural interest, dates from 1750. Sited right next to
the castle entrance and to the Dolls Museum at Oaken's House, the
guesthouse offers three freshly decorated bedrooms, all with private
facilities and with new curtains and attractive duvets. Breakfast only
is served, but many restaurants are within close walking distance. A
morning newspaper is all part of the service.

OWNERS: Mr and Mrs C. King OPEN: all year ROOMS: 1 single, 1 double, 1 twin; all
rooms with bath/shower; TV in all bedrooms TERMS: single/single occupancy £25–£30,
twin/double £40–£45; deposit: £10 CARDS: none DETAILS: no children; no dogs; no
smoking

WATERBEACH   **Cambridgeshire**   **map 6**

Berry House

High Street, Waterbeach, nr Cambridge CB5 9JU
TEL/FAX: (01223) 860702
just off A10, 5m NE of Cambridge

This lovely listed building dates from the eighteenth century and is
situated in a traditional village which has an ancient church and
green. The beautifully decorated house has a lounge with log fire, TV,
games and a fridge stocked with soft drinks. A red-brick wall behind
the fireplace has survived from the 1600s and is part of the original
'Berry' house, the medieval word for manor. Both the bedrooms, with
Georgian and Edwardian furniture, are to the rear in a converted
beamed hayloft; they are *en suite* with powerful Victorian-style
showers. The Blue Room is spacious enough to take an extra single
bed and thus become a twin or family room. Breakfasts feature wood-
smoked kippers and home-baked bread. Imaginative candlelit
dinners are served by Sally Peck, who joins guests to eat. Vegetarian
options and children's helpings are available and guests should bring
their own wine as there is no licence. Sally is also happy to
recommend local establishments for guests wishing to dine alone.
The pretty gardens complete with frog pond, two friendly dogs and a
croquet set are a bonus in summer.

OWNER: Sally Peck OPEN: all year ROOMS: 2 double; both rooms with bath/shower; TV
lounge TERMS: single occupancy £40, double £50–£65; dinner £18 CARDS: none
DETAILS: children welcome; dogs by arrangement; car park; garden

WATERMILLOCK Cumbria

map 10

Waterside House

Watermillock, Penrith CA11 0JH
TEL: (01768) 486038
on A592, 4m SW of Penrith

Sited in a secluded position at the edge of Lake Ullswater, this eighteenth-century listed building retains many interesting features, such as a carved dresser in the dining-room and an original marble fireplace. Guests may fish and windsurf on the lake, and have the use of a small boat. Wildlife too is an attraction here; bird-watchers especially will find this an ideal spot. The house is totally non-smoking, and one twin-bedded room located on the ground floor has been adapted for wheelchair-users. Suzi Jenner extends a warm welcome to guests, and is always pleased to give advice on local places of interest. Breakfast only is served, but guests will find a number of eating establishments in the area.

OWNER: Suzi Jenner OPEN: all year exc Christmas ROOMS: 5 double, 3 with bath/shower, 2 with wash-basin; 1 twin, with bath/shower; 1 family, with wash-basin; 1 room suitable for wheelchair-users; TV lounge TERMS: single occupancy £35, twin/double £50–£60, family room from £75; children under 2 free, half-price for ages 2 to 11; deposit: 1 night's charge CARDS: none DETAILS: children welcome; well-behaved dogs welcome, must have own bed; no smoking; car park

WATERROW Somerset

map 2

Manor Mill

Waterrow, nr Taunton TA4 2AY
TEL: (01984) 623317
take Waterrow turning off B3227 3m after Wiveliscombe (at Rock Inn), then a further ¼m to Manor Mill sign

Manor Mill is a seventeenth-century stone-built watermill which, together with its neighbouring barns, makes up an attractive complex bordered by a fast-flowing river. It is set in the depths of hilly, peaceful farmland and is a relaxing place to stay. The Mill is immaculately maintained and the spacious bedrooms are simply furnished in country style. One sitting-room is for guests' use, and breakfast is taken at one end of the owners' sitting-room. There is a pretty garden, and indoor heated swimming-pool, and also five self-catering flats and a cottage. Food is available in the pub just down the road.

OWNERS: Elizabeth and Eddie Genrey OPEN: all year exc Christmas and New Year ROOMS: 1 single, 1 double, 1 twin/family room; all rooms with bath/shower; TV lounge TERMS: single £20, single occupancy £25, twin/double £36, family room from £53; 20% reduction for children sharing with parents; deposit: 20% CARDS: none DETAILS: children welcome; no dogs; no smoking in bedrooms; car park; garden; swimming-pool

WEARE GIFFARD   Devon   map 1

Burnards

Weare Giffard, nr Bideford EX39 4QR
TEL: (01237) 473809
off A386, 2m NW of Torrington

This neat, whitewashed cottage with its pretty garden is 200 years
old and set in the picturesque village of Weare Giffard, on the edge of
the Torridge Valley between Bideford and Torrington. It is
everything one would expect from an old country cottage, with
rambling roses, views to the river and wooded hills and, inside, low
ceilings and a cosy atmosphere. One end of the cottage is for guests'
use, with a small, comfortable sitting-room and a dining-room
downstairs and two simple, pretty bedrooms with a shared bathroom
upstairs. Evening meals are available by arrangement, and although
there is no alcohol licence, guests are welcome to bring their own wine
to dinner.

OWNER: Julia Carter   OPEN: Mar to end Sept   ROOMS: 1 double, 1 twin; both rooms with
wash-basin; TV lounge   TERMS: single occupancy £15, twin/double £30; half-price for
children over 10; dinner £8.50   CARDS: none   DETAILS: no children under 10; no dogs;
smoking permitted downstairs only; car park; garden

WEAVERHAM   Cheshire   map 7

Beechwood House

206 Wallerscote Road, Weaverham, nr Northwich CW8 3LZ
TEL: (01606) 852123

This comfortable farmhouse is part of an 18-acre stock farm in a
peaceful position, with horses and cattle grazing in the fields and over
50 varieties of birdlife. The guests' quarters are in a separate wing of
the house, although the warm and friendly owners are very
accessible. The lounge has a piano which guests may play. One of the
single rooms is on the ground floor, with a bathroom close by. The
house is spotlessly clean and has a mixture of modern and traditional
furniture. For the energetic a stroll up the bank will be rewarded
with lovely views.

OWNER: Janet Kuypers   OPEN: all year exc Christmas   ROOMS: 2 single, both with wash-
basin; 1 twin, with shower; TV lounge   TERMS: single £15, single occupancy £17.50,
twin £34; deposit: £7   CARDS: none   DETAILS: no children; no dogs; no smoking; car
park; garden

*Many B&Bs, especially if they are unlicensed, allow guests to bring their
own wine to dinner. If this is the case, we say so in the entry.*

WELLS   Somerset   map 2

Infield House

36 Portway, Wells BA5 2BN
TEL: (01749) 670989   FAX: (01749) 679093

This Victorian house backs on to a wooded conservation area and is
only a five-minute walk from the centre of this historic town. The
Ingerfields are a friendly, welcoming couple; Julie comes from
California and Maurice is a local man. The house has spacious rooms
and is furnished with taste; the bedrooms feature their original
fireplaces. Breakfasts are served at separate tables in the attractive
dining-room and guests can relax in the elegant lounge.

OWNERS: Maurice and Julie Ingerfield   OPEN: all year exc Christmas   ROOMS: 2 double,
1 twin; all rooms with bath/shower; TV in all bedrooms   TERMS: single occupancy £31,
twin/double £42–£46; deposit: credit card details or 1 night's charge   CARDS: Access,
Visa   DETAILS: no children under 14; no dogs; no smoking; car park; garden

WELLS-NEXT-THE-SEA   Norfolk   map 6

Ilex House

Bases Lane, Wells-next-the-Sea NR23 1LD
TEL: (01328) 710556

Ilex House is a large, listed Georgian property with a classical porch,
situated in its own grounds, close to the centre of Wells. Nada
McJannet is a friendly, outgoing lady who offers special breaks for
bird-watchers. The four bedrooms are spacious, tastefully decorated
in green, blue, pink or cream, all with fitted wardrobes. Three of the
rooms have a shower unit *en suite*, one has a private bathroom, and
there is one shared bathroom and three shared WCs. Visitors have
the use of a TV lounge, and breakfast is served family-style. Evening
meals can be pre-arranged for two or more guests, and vegetarian
choices provided. The house is licensed but guests may also bring
their own wine, for which there is a corkage charge. The magnificent
Palladian-style Holkham Hall is just up the road, and there are many
pleasant walks across its parkland.

OWNERS: Nada and Tom McJannet   OPEN: all year exc Christmas   ROOMS: 1 single,
with shower; 1 double, with bath; 2 twin, with shower; TV lounge   TERMS: single £21,
single occupancy £38, twin/double £38; children's reductions by arrangement; dinner
£13; deposit: £10   DETAILS: small dogs welcome; no smoking; car park; garden

---

*The end details for each entry state whether dogs are allowed, but it is
always best to check when booking.*

ILEX HOUSE, WELLS-NEXT-THE-SEA

WEST BRIDGFORD   Nottinghamshire   **map 5**

Gallery Hotel

8–10 Radcliffe Road, West Bridgford, nr Nottingham NG2 5FW
TEL: (01159) 813651 and 811346   FAX: (01559) 813732

Don and Brenda Masson are a charming couple who extend a warm
welcome to their guests in their beautifully maintained licensed
guesthouse. The immaculate, tastefully decorated rooms are
comfortable; one two-bedroom ground-floor suite is especially
suitable for families or friends. Reasonably priced home-cooked
meals, including vegetarian choices, are served Monday through
Friday in the extended dining-room. Guests also have the use of a
lounge with satellite TV, a conservatory and a small bar that has a
pool table. Sports enthusiasts should note that the hotel is next to the
Trent Bridge Cricket Ground and one mile from the National Sports
Centre.

OWNERS: Don and Brenda Masson   OPEN: all year   ROOMS: 3 single, 4 double, all with
shower; 5 twin, 3 with bath/shower, 2 with wash-basin; 3 family, 1 with bath/shower, 2
with wash-basin; TV in all bedrooms and lounge   TERMS: single £25, single occupancy
£26, twin/double £34–£38, family room £34; children under 5 free, half-price for ages 5
to 10; dinner £7.50; deposit: £5 per person   CARDS: Access, Visa   DETAILS: children
welcome; no dogs; smoking in bar and some rooms only; car park; games room;
garden

WEST BUCKLAND   Devon   map 1

Huxtable Farm

West Buckland, nr Barnstaple EX32 0SR
TEL/FAX: (01598) 760254
*leave A361 5m E of Barnstaple at signs for West and East Buckland; farm
entrance is opposite school between the two villages*

This lovely farm originated in the fourteenth century and all the
stone buildings added over the years are now listed. The house itself
was built in 1520 and has many original features, such as oak beams,
screen panelling, open fireplaces with bread ovens, low doorways and
flagstone floors. The décor and furnishings are in keeping with the
style and age of the house. The lovely drawing-room has recently
been refurbished, and guests also have use of a small library, a sauna
and a games room with snooker, darts, bar billiards and table tennis.
Candelit dinners, beginning with a complimentary glass of home-
made wine, are served at 7.30pm in the attractive dining-room.
Guests are also welcome to bring their own wine, and vegetarians can
be catered for. The two family rooms are in the outbuildings and the
remaining bedrooms are in the house. The Paynes are a friendly
young couple with small children, and they welcome families.
Children are encouraged to feed the tame farmyard animals.
Huxtable Farm is in a secluded position, with open fields, woods and
a stream.

OWNERS: Antony and Jackie Payne   OPEN: all year exc Christmas   ROOMS: 2 double, 1
twin, 3 family; all rooms with bath/shower; TV in all bedrooms   TERMS: single
occupancy £26, twin/double £46, family room £46 plus children's charge; children £10;
dinner £13; deposit: 10%   CARDS: none   DETAILS: children welcome; no dogs; no
smoking in dining-room; car park; games room; garden; tennis

WEST CHILTINGTON   West Sussex   map 3

New House Farm

Broadford Bridge Road, West Chiltington, nr Pulborough RH20 2LA
TEL: (01798) 812215
*take B2133 from A29, after 2m turn right signposted West Chiltington and
Golf Course, farmhouse is on left*

New House Farm is right in the centre of the village of West
Chiltington. It is a delightful fifteenth-century farmhouse and
although Mr Steele has retired from farming, he still keeps a few
sheep on the 50 acres. The house has a pleasant atmosphere and is
decorated inside in white with black woodwork. It is immaculately
clean and the bedrooms are comfortably furnished. There is one very
large bedroom, and the tiny double room in the garden annexe is

particularly popular with those who cannot cope with stairs. Breakfast only is served in an attractive dining-room/sitting area with open fire, and there is a separate sitting-room for summer use.

OWNER: Alma Steele   OPEN: all year   ROOMS: 1 double, 2 twin; all rooms with bath/shower; TV in all bedrooms and lounge   TERMS: single occupancy £25–£35, twin/double £40–£50; deposit: 25%   CARDS: none   DETAILS: no children under 10; dogs by arrangement; no smoking in bedrooms; car park; garden

WEST CLANDON Surrey   map 3

Ways Cottage

Lime Grove, West Clandon, nr Guildford GU4 7UT
TEL: (01483) 222454
just off A247, 4m NE of Guildford

This 1930s detached brick house stands on a lovely, lime-tree-lined avenue and is a good location for those wishing to explore the Surrey countryside, or have a quiet place to stay within easy reach of London. The house is surrounded by a pleasant garden, and has a large, comfortable well-furnished sitting-room. The Hugheses are friendly and welcoming and will provide dinner if arranged in advance; a complimentary glass of wine is served, or guests may bring their own bottle of wine to table if they prefer. Children's helpings, vegetarian dishes and packed lunches, can all be requested. Continental-style breakfasts are served or, for an additional £2.50, cooked breakfasts can be arranged.

OWNERS: Mr and Mrs Christopher Hughes   OPEN: all year   ROOMS: 2 twin, 1 with bath/shower; TV in both bedrooms and lounge   TERMS: single occupancy £17–£19, twin £30–£33; babies free, half-price for children from 5 to 10; dinner £10   CARDS: none   DETAILS: children welcome; no dogs; no smoking; car park; garden

WESTCLIFF-ON-SEA Essex   map 3

Archery's Guest House

27 Grosvenor Road, Westcliff-on-Sea, Southend-on-Sea SS0 8EP
TEL: (01702) 353323

This large detached Victorian house is in a quiet street 100 yards from the sea. It was tastefully refurbished in 1993 and although there are no *en suite* facilities, two bathrooms and a WC are for guests' use only. Breakfast is served on a beautiful carved table from southern Africa. The dining-room/lounge combination is quite spacious and has the original ceiling rose and coving. There is a wide selection of eating places in town.

OWNER: Glen Archery   OPEN: all year   ROOMS: 1 single, 3 double, 2 twin; TV lounge
TERMS: single £16–£18, twin/double £32–£35; children's reductions according to age
CARDS: none   DETAILS: children welcome; dogs welcome; car park

WEST DEAN   East Sussex   map 3

Old Parsonage

West Dean BN25 4AL
TEL: (01323) 870432
off A259 Brighton to Hastings road, E of Seaford

This delightful house is reputed to be the oldest inhabited small
medieval house in England. Dating from 1280, it was built by monks
from Wilmington Priory from local flint, and an extension was added
in the Victorian era. The sitting-room, where breakfast only is served,
is in the original old part and above are two bedrooms, both of which
can be reached by very narrow spiral staircases. The spacious double
room is a favourite with honeymooners and the third bedroom is on
the ground floor; the bedrooms all have their own private bath/
shower rooms. The pretty rear garden backs on to Friston Forest and
the house is next to the twelfth-century church in the lovely
conservation area of West Dean. The Woodhamses are a delightful
couple and love being able to share their unique house with guests.
Both Seven Sisters and Beachy Head are within walking distance.

OWNERS: Raymond and Angela Woodhams   OPEN: all year exc Christmas and New
Year   ROOMS: 1 double, 1 twin, 1 four-poster; all rooms with bath/shower; TV lounge
TERMS: single occupancy £35–£42, twin/double £50–£60, four-poster £65   CARDS:
none   DETAILS: no children under 12; no dogs; no smoking; car park; garden

WEST GRAFTON   Wiltshire   map 2

Rosegarth

West Grafton, nr Marlborough SN8 3BY
TEL: (01672) 810288
just off A338, 7m S of Marlborough

Rosegarth was built in 1580 as a terrace of four servants' cottages
belonging to the Crown and was converted into one house about 40
years ago. Now it is an attractive thatched, whitewashed cottage
standing in three acres of garden with pleasant farmland views. The
guests' accommodation is at one end of the house and consists of a
large, comfortable sitting-room with TV and, up a narrow, steep
staircase, two bedrooms. The two private bathrooms are on the
ground floor, off the sitting-room. Breakfast is served in the dining-
room, and the owners can provide a taxi service to and from local

ROSEGARTH, WEST GRAFTON

pubs or restaurants. Packed lunches can be provided. Rosegarth is convenient for Stonehenge, Avebury, the Kennet and Avon Canal, and Lacock Abbey.

OWNERS: Rick and Anne Ruddock-Brown OPEN: all year ROOMS: 1 twin, 1 family; both rooms with bath/shower; TV lounge TERMS: single occupancy £21, twin £35, family room £46; deposit: £10 per room CARDS: none DETAILS: no children; no dogs; no smoking; car park; garden

---

WEST MALLING   Kent   map 3

Scott House

High Street, West Malling ME19 6QH
TEL: (01732) 841380   FAX: (01732) 870025
½m from M20 junction 4

This attractive listed town house can be found on the main street, just opposite the library. The Smiths also run an antique business, and the entrance to the property is through the shop. The house is beautifully furnished and has been decorated with simplicity and taste. The bedrooms are well appointed, and there is an enormous and very comfortable first-floor drawing-room. Breakfast is served in the large dining-room. A small paved courtyard with a grapevine is a pleasant place to sit in fine weather. West Malling is a small, istorically interesting town with an eleventh-century abbey, and has a good selection of restaurants and inns for evening meals. Packed lunches can be provided.

OWNER: Ernest G. Smith OPEN: all year exc Christmas ROOMS: 2 double, 1 twin; all rooms with shower; TV in all bedrooms TERMS: single occupancy £39, twin/double £49; deposit: credit card details CARDS: Access, Delta, Switch, Visa DETAILS: no children; no dogs; no smoking

WEST MEON   Hampshire

map 2

Home Paddocks

West Meon, nr Petersfield GU32 1NA
TEL: (01730) 829241   FAX: (01730) 829577
just off A32, 10m SW of Alton; from village take East Meon road for ½m

Home Paddocks was the one-time home of Thomas Lord (of cricketing fame), having begun life as cottages in the 1560s, with later additions. It benefits from a three-acre garden complete with croquet lawn and tennis court, on the outskirts of the village of West Meon. Inside, the house is attractively decorated and furnished with antiques; the two bedrooms have their own bathrooms. Breakfast is sometimes taken in the charming Victorian conservatory and there is also a drawing-room as well as a dining-room. Evening meals are served if booked in advance, when vegetarian dishes can be requested. There is no alcohol licence, but guests may bring their own wine to table.

OWNERS: the Ward family OPEN: all year exc Christmas and Easter ROOMS: 2 twin; both rooms with bath/shower; TV in one bedroom TERMS: single occupancy £30, twin £40–£44; dinner £12; deposit: £10 CARDS: none DETAILS: no children under 7; no dogs; smoking in drawing-room only; car park; garden; tennis

WEST PORLOCK   Somerset

map 1

Bales Mead

West Porlock, nr Minehead TA24 8NX
TEL: (01643) 862565
off A39 half-way between Porlock and Porlock Weir

This small country house has been exquisitely restored by owners Stephen Blue and Peter Clover. It lies in a lovely position on the edge of the hamlet of West Porlock with wonderful views across Porlock Bay to Hurlestone Point and beyond, and behind are the steep wooded hills of Exmoor National Park. Two of the beautifully furnished bedrooms have sea views and one overlooks the garden and hills. The elegant and comfortable sitting-room has a baby-grand piano, and breakfast only is served in the small dining-room with charming, individual tables. Bales Mead stands in a pretty garden and is within walking distance of the village and close to the harbour of Porlock Weir.

OWNERS: Stephen Blue and Peter Clover   OPEN: all year exc Christmas   ROOMS: 3 double, all with bath/shower; TV in all bedrooms   TERMS: single occupancy £30, double £46; deposit: £15 per person   CARDS: none   DETAILS: no children; no dogs; no smoking; car park; garden

West Porlock House

West Porlock, nr Minehead TA24 8NX
TEL: (01643) 862880
follow sign for Porlock Weir from A39 at Porlock, house is ¾m along road on left

This large stone-built house dating from the early part of the century was once the local manor. It is reached up a long drive and is in a quiet and peaceful position surrounded by a huge woodland garden with lovely views of the sea and countryside. The house is comfortable with a homely atmosphere and spacious rooms. The bedrooms are well furnished, the lounge is tastefully decorated and the dining-room overlooks the garden. There is also a sitting area in the hall and a bar. Dinner is served on weekend evenings at 7.30pm. West Porlock House is a short walk from the harbour and the beach. A gate in the grounds offers direct access to footpaths to the woods and Exmoor.

OWNERS: Mr and Mrs H. Dyer   OPEN: Feb to Nov   ROOMS: 2 double, both with bath/ shower; 2 twin, both with wash-basin; 1 family, with wash-basin; TV in all bedrooms and lounge   TERMS: single occupancy £27.50; twin/double £46–£50; half-price for children from 2 to 12; dinner £15.50   CARDS: none   DETAILS: children welcome; no dogs; smoking in one lounge only; car park; garden

---

WEST WITTON   North Yorkshire   **map 9**

Ivy Dene

West Witton, nr Leyburn DL8 4LP
TEL: (01969) 622785
on A684 in village

Well maintained and immaculate, this 300-year-old listed farmhouse is in one of Wensleydale's oldest villages, and is a good spot from which to tour the Dales National Park. Most rooms are *en suite*, and those on the top floor are especially attractive, with sloping ceilings and a chintzy décor; extra touches are provided by floral coronets and lace canopies. All rooms have good views. Guests may relax in the oak-beamed lounge with its open fire and grandfather clock, or enjoy a drink at the small bar in the hallway. Evening meals are served at 6.45pm in the dining-room, which has a decorative plaster ceiling; children's portions are available. Packed lunches can be provided.

OWNERS: Bob and June Dickinson OPEN: all year ROOMS: 1 double, 1 twin, 1 four-poster, 2 family; all rooms with bath/shower; TV in some bedrooms and lounge TERMS: single occupancy £30, twin/double £40–£44, four-poster £44, family room from £66; half-price for children from 5 to 12, second child under 10 free; dinner £12; deposit: £25 per person CARDS: none DETAILS: no children under 5; no dogs; no smoking; car park; garden

WETHERDEN   Suffolk   map 6

Brickwall Farmhouse

Wetherden, nr Stowmarket IP14 3JW
TEL: 0359 242732   FAX: 0359 242711
off A14, 4m NW of Stowmarket

Brickwall Farmhouse is a Grade II listed sixteenth-century timber-framed farmhouse situated half a mile from the village. It was in a very run-down condition when purchased in 1993, but has been beautifully restored with all modern comforts, yet retaining its old-world charm. Many original features have been retained, including exposed oak beams and an inglenook fireplace, and the rooms are traditionally decorated and furnished in old pine. There are fine views across open countryside. Dinner is by arrangement, and children's helpings and vegetarian dishes can be requested. There is no alcohol licence, but guests may bring their own wine. There is also a kitchen for residents' use. A good supply of information on the area and local walks is to hand, and for the business traveller a fax machine and copying facilities are provided. Pauline Newby is a charming host who enjoys welcoming people into her characterful house.

OWNER: Pauline Newby OPEN: all year exc Christmas ROOMS: 1 single, with wash-basin; 1 double, with bath/shower; 1 twin, with bath/shower; TV in all bedrooms and lounge TERMS: single £16–£18, twin/double £32–£36; children under 3 free, reductions for ages 3 to 12; dinner £10–£15; deposit: by arrangement CARDS: none DETAILS: children welcome; dogs welcome; no smoking; car park; garden

If there are reduced rates for children, this is mentioned in the details at the end of the entry. If no reductions are specified, assume you will have to pay full rates for children.

If there are any bedrooms with TV, we mention this in the details at the end of the entry.

WHEDDON CROSS Somerset

map 1

Raleigh Manor

Wheddon Cross, nr Dunster TA24 7BB
TEL: (01643) 841484
just off B3224, 5m E of Exford

Raleigh Manor is approached along a half-mile drive through parkland with grazing sheep and terrific views across Exmoor. It is a peaceful, secluded spot and the house stands in one and a half acres of woods and gardens. An attractive Victorian country house, it was built in 1889 by a local landowner as the manor house to the Cutcombe Estate. It is a relaxing place with log fires in the comfortable lounge, small library and dining-room and a good selection of books and magazines. Diners have wonderful views from the dining-room and there is also a conservatory. Almost all of the seven bedrooms benefit from the views and have recently been redecorated. One room, named the Squire's bedroom, has an antique half-tester bed. Raleigh Manor is a haven for walkers, and a footpath from the hotel grounds leads to Dunkery Beacon, the highest point on Exmoor. Dinner is a four-course affair, with wine available, and the owners are happy to cater for vegetarians and any other special requirements with advance notice.

OWNERS: Jenny and Chris Piper OPEN: Mar to Nov ROOMS: 1 single, 3 double, 2 twin, 1 four-poster; all rooms with bath/shower; TV in all bedrooms TERMS: single/single occupancy £25–£28, twin/double £50–£56, four-poster £62–£68; £15 for children over 5 sharing with parents; dinner £15; deposit: £20 per person CARDS: Access, Visa DETAILS: no children under 5; no dogs in public rooms; no smoking in lounge or restaurant; car park; garden

WHIMPLE Devon

map 2

Down House

Whimple, nr Exeter EX5 2QR
TEL: (01404) 822860
just off A30, between Exeter and Honiton

This Edwardian country house is set in five acres of gardens, paddocks and orchard, and is in a secluded position up a narrow lane about a mile from Whimple. It has lovely views over the village to hills and, on a clear day, to Dartmoor. Mike and Joanne Sanders took over the house in 1994 and have made a lot of improvements. The spacious lounge has an unusual fireplace and there is a second sitting area on the large landing. Afternoon tea and packed lunches are available by arrangement. Killerton House is nearby, and there are plenty of footpaths for walkers.

OWNERS: Mike and Joanne Sanders OPEN: all year exc Christmas ROOMS: 2 single, both with wash-basin; 3 double, 1 with bath/shower, 2 with wash-basin; 2 twin, 1 with bath/shower, 1 with wash-basin; 1 family, with bath/shower; 1 room suitable for wheelchair-users; TV in all bedrooms and lounge TERMS: single £18, single occupancy £25, twin/double £36–£40, family room £50; children's reductions by arrangement; deposit: 10% CARDS: none DETAILS: children welcome; dogs by arrangement; no smoking; car park; garden

WHITBY North Yorkshire map 9

Elford

10 Prospect Hill, Whitby YO21 1QE
TEL: (01947) 602135

Set back from the main road, this pleasant Victorian property stands in its own grounds. The pine stairway is a beautiful feature and the house also boasts a fine ceiling rose and an attractive frieze in the dining-room, plus pieces of needlepoint and embroidery which are Mrs Dixon's handiwork. The house is well maintained and has a spacious lounge with predominantly pink décor and an original tiled fireplace. There are no *en suite* facilities, but two bathrooms and an additional WC are exclusively for guests' use. Breakfast only is served, but Whitby has some excellent choices for eating out and the town centre is only a ten-minute walk away.

OWNER: Mrs M.D. Dixon OPEN: Easter to 1 Nov ROOMS: 2 double, 2 twin, 1 family; all rooms with wash-basin; TV lounge TERMS: twin/double £32–£34; half-price for children from 4 to 10 CARDS: none DETAILS: no children under 4; no dogs; no smoking; car park

Grove Hotel

36 Bagdale, Whitby YO21 1QL
TEL: (01947) 603551

This large four-storey house has a commanding view over Pannett Park and is near the spa, beach and town centre. It retains many original Victorian features including the coving and the pine staircase. The bedrooms are clean and comfortable, with floral patterned duvets, and the TV lounge is cosy. The house is licensed and provides home-cooked evening meals. It is set back from and above the main road, so traffic noise is not a problem.

OWNERS: Mr and Mrs Jackson OPEN: all year exc Christmas ROOMS: 5 double, 4 with bath/shower, 1 with wash-basin; 1 twin, with wash-basin; 2 family, both with bath/shower; TV in all bedrooms TERMS: single occupancy £16–£18.50, twin/double £32–£37, family room £37 plus children's charge; two-thirds reduction for children under 6, half-price for older children; dinner £8.50; deposit: £10 CARDS: none DETAILS: children welcome; no dogs; no smoking in dining-room; car park; garden

Lansbury Guest House

29 Hudson Street, Whitby YO21 3EP
TEL: (01947) 604821

This refurbished Victorian house is well placed just three minutes from the beach and a short walk from Whitby's famous East Side with its associations with Captain James Cook. The bright and spotlessly clean bedrooms are decorated in pale shades and are well equipped. Traditional home-cooked dinners ae served on smart Royal Doulton china in the dining-room and guests are invited to bring their own wine to dinner. Vegetarians can be catered for with advance notice. An abundance of tourist information is provided in the comfortable lounge.

OWNERS: Tom and Anne Wheeler OPEN: all year exc Christmas and New Year ROOMS: 2 single, both with wash-basin; 5 double, 3 with bath/shower, 2 with wash-basin; 1 twin, with bath/shower; 1 family, with wash-basin; TV in all bedrooms and lounge TERMS: single £15, single occupancy £25–£30, twin/double £30–£36, family room £35; children under 5 free, half-price for ages 5 to 12; dinner £8; deposit: £10 per person CARDS: none DETAILS: children welcome; dogs by arrangement; no smoking in dining-room

---

WHITSTABLE   Kent   **map 3**

Windyridge

Wraik Hill, Whitstable CT5 3BY
TEL: (01227) 263506
off A299 Thanet Way

A mixture of stone, bricks and archways makes this an interesting-looking building. Up a quiet lane in peaceful countryside and standing in a huge garden, Windyridge has lovely views across the estuary and the Isle of Sheppey. The new owners are welcoming and hospitable and have done a wonderful job of refurbishing the house, which has been furnished and decorated with flair and imagination. There is an enormous lounge, and every room has a wealth of exposed beams and a variety of stone and brickwork walls. Breakfasts and evening meals (by arrangement) are served in the dining-room. Whitstable is famous for its oysters, and good sailing is nearby.

OWNERS: Colin and Elizabeth Dyke OPEN: all year ROOMS: 3 single, all with wash-basin; 3 double, 2 twin, 2 family, all with bath/shower; 1 room suitable for wheelchair-users; TV in all bedrooms and lounge TERMS: single £20, single occupancy £25, twin/double £40, family room £50; dinner £12 CARDS: Access, Visa DETAILS: children welcome; dogs welcome; car park; garden

---

Bath / shower in the details under each entry means that the rooms have private facilities. The B&B may have other, shared bathroom facilities as well. We say if rooms have wash-basins.

WIDEGATES   Cornwall   map 1

Coombe Farm

Widegates, nr Looe PL13 1QN
TEL: (01503) 240223
on B3253 just S of Widegates village

Coombe Farm is set in several acres of gardens, woodland and fields, just outside the village of Widegates, and with glimpses of the sea. The property was originally part of a large estate and the house was built in the 1920s to the design of an Indian hill-station bungalow, with rooms added in the roof. Alexander and Sally Low are enthusiastic and professional hosts who are constantly seeking to improve the property. The lounge has a log fire and the dining-room extends into a glassed-in verandah overlooking the garden. Huge breakfasts and four-course dinners with vegetarian options are served, and the dining-room is licensed. Families are welcome, and several of the rooms are designed for three or more people. Five bedrooms are on the ground floor, three of them suitable for wheelchair-users. There is plenty to do at Coombe Farm, with a heated outdoor swimming-pool, a croquet lawn and a games room in one of the stone outhouses.

OWNERS: Alexander and Sally Low   OPEN: Mar to Oct   ROOMS: 3 double, 3 twin, 4 family; all rooms with bath/shower; 3 rooms suitable for wheelchair-users; TV in all bedrooms   TERMS: single occupancy £20–£25, twin/double £40–£50; 25% reduction for children 5 to 13; dinner £14; deposit: £15 per person   CARDS: none   DETAILS: no children under 5; no dogs; no smoking; car park; games room; garden; swimming-pool

WIGMORE   Hereford & Worcester   map 5

Queen's House

Wigmore HR6 9UN
TEL: (01568) 770451
on A4110, 7m NW of Leominster

In the centre of a quiet village, this 500-year-old property lives up to the promise of its age: flagstone floors, oak beams, thick stone walls and inglenook fireplaces are set off by lots of brass and copper. The renovation involved combining two cottages and the result is a rambling, characterful house. The large bedrooms are furnished with antiques and those at the back of the house overlook the countryside. The lounge includes a small bar. Breakfast is served in what was the hallway and home-cooked evening meals are eaten in the licensed restaurant. Vegetarians can be catered for.

OWNERS: Anne and Jack Webb   OPEN: all year   ROOMS: 1 single, 1 double, 1 twin, 1 family; TV lounge   TERMS: single £16, single occupancy £24, twin/double £32; half-price for children under 13; dinner £12   CARDS: none   DETAILS: children welcome; dogs welcome; car park; garden

WILLINGTON   Cheshire   **map 7**

Roughlow Farm

Chapel Lane, Willington, nr Tarporley CW6 0PG
TEL/FAX: (01829) 751199
leave A54 at Kelsall, head up Waste Lane then Chapel Lane to Willington Corner

With magnificent views across the Cheshire plains to Shropshire and Wales, this delightful late-eighteenth-century house offers an even greater sense of space than its flower-filled courtyard and four and a half acres of land would suggest. The house has a charm and elegance in no way compromised by the sensitive modernisation, and the galleried drawing-room with oak beams, double doors and brick fireplace evokes a particularly potent sense of a country house of the past. The three bedrooms are spacious, tastefully decorated and luxuriously furnished. Food is cooked on the Aga and dinners are available for parties of four or more if arranged in advance. Alternative eating places can be found within walking distance.

OWNER: Mrs S.L. Sutcliffe   OPEN: all year   ROOMS: 3 twin, all with bath/shower; TV lounge   TERMS: single occupancy £30–£35, twin £50–£60; dinner £15–£20; deposit: £20   DETAILS: no children under 6; no dogs; no smoking; car park; garden; tennis

WIMBORNE   Dorset   **map 2**

Acacia House

2 Oakley Road, Wimborne BH21 1QJ
TEL: (01202) 883958   FAX: (01202) 881943
on A31, 5m N of Poole

This lovely warm, inviting home is maintained to a very high standard. The solid red-brick 1930s house is set back a little from the main road on the edge of Wimborne. The pretty bedrooms are comfortably furnished and have colour TV. Guests may sit in the conservatory, and breakfast only is served in the dining-room. The Stimpsons welcome their guests with tea and home-made fruit cake and are more than happy to offer advice on what to see and do in the area. There is a pub almost next door serving evening meals. Kingston Lacy House is just nearby, and has a park and gardens. Packed lunches can be provided.

OWNER: Eveline Stimpson   OPEN: all year exc Christmas   ROOMS: 1 single, with wash-basin; 1 double, with bath/shower; 1 twin, with wash-basin; 1 family, with wash-basin; TV in all bedrooms   TERMS: single £16.50–£17, single occupancy £21–£25, twin/double £34–£39; family room £49–£54; children's reductions by arrangement; deposit: 10%   CARDS: none   DETAILS: children welcome; no dogs; no smoking; car park; garden

Ashton Lodge

10 Oakley Hill, Wimborne BH21 1QH
TEL: (01202) 883423   FAX: (01202) 886180
on A349 to Poole

This detached 1930s family home with bow windows is set back a
little from the main road. The rear garden is attractive and the four
bedrooms are all brightly decorated, each with a private or *en suite*
bathroom. A long hill leads to the town centre and Wimborne
Minster. Breakfast only is available, but the nearby pub serves food.

OWNER: Margaret Gregory   OPEN: all year   ROOMS: 1 single, with wash-basin; 1 double,
with bath/shower; 1 twin, with wash-basin; 1 family, with bath/shower; TV in all
bedrooms and lounge   TERMS: single £17.50, single occupancy £20, twin/double £37,
family room £37; reductions for children sharing with parents   CARDS: none   DETAILS:
children welcome; no dogs; no smoking; car park; garden

WINCHCOMBE   Gloucestershire   map 5

Gower House

16 North Street, Winchcombe GL54 5LH
TEL: (01242) 602616
just off B4632 Cheltenham to Broadway road

This listed seventeenth-century property stands in the centre of
Winchcombe in half an acre of beautiful gardens. Mick and Sally are
a delightful couple who keep the house immaculate. It has exposed
stone walls, oak beams, creaky floors and 'duck your head' doors. The
sitting-room has TV and there are three attractive bedrooms,
furnished with wicker, pine and antique furniture. Breakfast only is
served, but there are numberous pubs and restaurants for evening
meals within a short walk. Guests are encouraged to make use of the
secluded patio and gardens. This is an excellent base for touring the
Cotswolds, and the village of Winchcombe has a railway museum
which is worth a visit.

OWNERS: Mick and Sally Simmonds   OPEN: all year exc Christmas and New Year's Eve
ROOMS: 1 double, 2 twin; all rooms with wash-basin; TV lounge   TERMS: single
occupancy £20, twin/double £32   CARDS: none   DETAILS: children welcome; no dogs;
no smoking in dining-room; car park; garden

The Homestead

Footbridge, Broadway Road, Winchcombe GL54 5JG
TEL: (01242) 602536   FAX: (01242) 602127
just off B4632 at edge of village

Only a few yards from the Cotswold Way, this traditional cottage
built of local stone is in an ideal location for walkers. The unspoilt

village of Winchcombe is just a four-minute walk away across the footbridge, and the house shares its character, with flagstone floors, exposed beams and bare stone walls. The beautiful bedrooms have a more modern but equally relaxed feel, with colour co-ordinated chintz fabrics. The lounge is well stocked with up-to-date magazines.

}OWNERS: Allan and Maureen Brooker OPEN: all year exc Christmas ROOMS: 2 double, both with bath/shower; 1 twin, with wash-basin; TV in all bedrooms and lounge TERMS: single occupancy £25, twin/double £36–£39; dinner £12.50; deposit: £10 per room CARDS: none DETAILS: children welcome; dogs welcome; no smoking; car park; garden

WINCHELSEA   East Sussex   map 3

Cleveland House

Winchelsea TN46 6EE
TEL: (01797) 226256

Cleveland House is a beautiful listed eighteenth-century house in the centre of the historic Cinque Port town of Winchelsea. It has an immaculately kept one-and-a-half-acre walled garden which includes a heated swimming-pool. The house is stylishly furnished and breakfast only is served in the dining-room. The double bedroom has a sea view, and the twin-bedded room overlooks the rose garden. Cleveland House is a peaceful and comfortable place to stay in a delightful and unspoilt small town.

OWNERS: Sarah and Jonathan Jempson OPEN: all year exc Christmas and New Year ROOMS: 1 double, 1 twin; both rooms with bath/shower; TV in both bedrooms TERMS: single occupancy £37.50, twin/double £55; deposit: £25 CARDS: Access, Visa DETAILS: children welcome; small dogs by arrangement; no smoking; garden; swimming-pool

WINCHESTER   Hampshire   map 2

Camellias

24 Ranelagh Road, Winchester SO23 9TA
TEL: (01962) 878223

This small Victorian town house stands on a busy corner about 20 minutes' walk from the centre of town. The house has a warm and friendly atmosphere and is comfortably furnished, and the small garden is immaculately kept. One of the *en suite* bedrooms is tucked away and almost like an apartment. Breakfast only is served in the light breakfast room.

OWNER: Jan Lowe OPEN: all year ROOMS: 1 single, with wash-basin; 1 double, 1 family, both with bath/shower; TV in all bedrooms TERMS: single £15–£18, double £34–£38, family room £40; children's reductions by arrangement CARDS: none DETAILS: children welcome; no smoking; car park; garden

Dellbrook

Hubert Road, St Cross, Winchester SO23 9RG
TEL/FAX: (01962) 865093
1m S of city centre

This attractive Edwardian family home lies on the edge of
Winchester and has views out to the Hampshire countryside.
Christine Leonard is a warm, friendly and energetic host and the
house has a welcoming atmosphere. The spacious, bright bedrooms
are simply decorated and furnished. Tea, offered on arrival, can be
taken on the terrace, which overlooks the old church and St Cross
Hospital, and dinner is available on some days by arrangement.
Vegetarians can be catered for and meals are served in the dining
annexe of the large kitchen.

OWNERS: John and Christine Leonard OPEN: all year exc owners' holiday ROOMS: 1
twin, with wash-basin; 2 family, both with bath/shower; TV in all bedrooms and lounge
TERMS: single occupancy £25–£30, twin £36–£42, family room £53; children under 3
free, reductions for ages 4 to 9; dinner £12; deposit required CARDS: Visa DETAILS:
children welcome; dogs by arrangement; smoking in bedrooms only; car park; garden

East View

16 Clifton Hill, Winchester SO22 5BL
TEL/FAX: (01962) 862986

This large Victorian town house is in a fairly quiet, elevated position,
with views over the city to the surrounding hills. It is about a 20-
minute walk from the cathedral and city centre. East View has a very
welcoming atmosphere and there is an attractive sitting-room with
TV. Breakfast only is served in the conservatory overlooking the
garden. The three bedrooms all have private facilities, and one twin
can take an extra bed for a child.

OWNERS: Judy and John Parker OPEN: all year exc Christmas & New Year ROOMS: 1
double, 2 twin; all rooms with bath/shower; TV in all bedrooms TERMS: single
occupancy £35, twin/double £45; £10 per night for children sharing with parents;
deposit: £10 CARDS: Access, Visa DETAILS: no children under 5; no dogs; no smoking;
car park; garden

54 St Cross Road

54 St Cross Road, Winchester SO23 9PS
TEL/FAX: (01962) 852073

This large and elegant Victorian town house is set in a small garden
on a busy main road. It is a comfortable, tastefully decorated house,
with a welcoming atmosphere and friendly owner. The three
bedrooms share a bathroom. The cathedral is about a 12-minute walk

from the house. Breakfast only is served in the dining-room, and packed lunches can be provided by arrangement.

OWNER: Mrs R.A. Blockley OPEN: all year exc Christmas ROOMS: 1 single, 1 double, 1 twin; all rooms with wash-basin; TV in all bedrooms TERMS: single £18, single occupancy £22.50–£25, twin/double £34–£36; £5 reduction for children over 3 CARDS: none DETAILS: no children under 3; no dogs; no smoking; car park; garden

Florum House Hotel

47 St Cross Road, Winchester SO23 9PS
TEL/FAX: (01962) 840427

This small, neat Victorian brick house was built in 1887. The bedrooms are quite small too, but all are *en suite*; a few are in a modern extension. The pleasant sitting-room has an open fire in winter, and leads out to the patio and rear garden, where guests can sit on warmer days. Florum House has a small bar and simple, home-cooked evening meals are served in the pretty dining-room. The centre of town is easily accessible and there is a parking area in front of the house.

OWNERS: Joy and Frank Hollick OPEN: all year exc Christmas ROOMS: 2 single, 3 double, 3 twin, 1 family; all rooms with bath/shower; TV in all bedrooms TERMS: single £36, single occupancy £42, twin/double £52–£56, family room £60–£64; dinner £12 CARDS: Access, Visa DETAILS: children welcome; well-behaved dogs welcome; no smoking; car park; garden

10B Edgar Road

10B Edgar Road, Winchester SO23 9SJ
TEL: (01962) 852502

This Victorian cottage is set in a quiet side street above the cathedral and only a five-minute walk from the city centre. It is a cosy and immaculately maintained house with elegant furnishings and small front and back gardens. The two bedrooms share a bathroom with the owner and there is no lounge. A TV can be provided in either bedroom if requested.

OWNER: Mrs T.H. Robinson OPEN: all year exc Christmas ROOMS: 1 single; 1 twin TERMS: single £18, twin £33 CARDS: none DETAILS: children between 6 and 8 only; no dogs

We state at the end of an entry whether children are welcome. If we know of any restrictions on children, we give them.

Please let us know if an establishment has changed hands.

WINDERMERE   Cumbria

map 8

The Archway

13 College Road, Windermere LA23 1BU
TEL: (01539) 445613

One of the highlights of a stay at this small Victorian guesthouse
near the centre of Windermere is the food. Exceptional breakfasts
feature home-made muesli and yoghurt, home-baked bread and
freshly squeezed juices, as well as traditional cooked fare or
American-style pancakes. Dinners, served at 6.45pm, might include
'naturally reared' lamb along with organically grown vegetables and
home-made desserts. The Archway is licensed, so guests may enjoy a
glass of wine with their dinner. Furnishings match the character of
the building, and include Victorian bed covers, a Welsh pine dresser
and a high bed that belonged to Aurea Greenhalgh's grandmother.
Rooms at the front of the house have good mountain views. There is a
small car park at the back, or guests may park at the front of the
house on College Road. The Greenhalghs are always happy to give
advice on walks and to provide maps to walkers.

OWNERS: Anthony and Aurea Greenhalgh   OPEN: all year   ROOMS: 2 double, 2 twin; all
rooms with bath/shower; TV in all bedrooms   TERMS: twin/double £48–£52; dinner £12;
deposit: £20   CARDS: Access, Amex, Visa   DETAILS: no children under 10; no dogs; no
smoking; car park; garden

Kirkwood Guest House

Princes Road, Windermere LA23 2DD
TEL: (01539) 443907

Kirkwood is an attractive Lakeland stone house situated on a quiet
side street. The *en suite* bedrooms are of a good size; two have four-
poster beds and one has a corner bath. There is an antique *chaise-
longue* in the sitting-room and a grandfather clock in the hall.
Substantial cooked breakfasts are served, and packed lunches can be
provided. Transport to and from the railway station can be arranged
with prior notice.

OWNERS: Neil and Carol Cox   OPEN: all year exc 2 weeks for owners' holiday   ROOMS: 1
double, 2 twin, 3 four-poster, 1 family; all rooms with bath/shower; TV in all bedrooms
and lounge   TERMS: single occupancy £25–£30, twin/double £38–£42, four-poster
£40–£50; deposit: £15 per person   CARDS: Access, Visa   DETAILS: children welcome;
no dogs in dining-room or left unattended in bedrooms; no smoking in bedrooms; car
park; garden

If we know a B&B has an alcohol licence, we say so.

Villa Lodge

Cross Street, Windermere LA23 1AE
TEL/FAX: (01539) 443318

This nineteenth-century traditional Lakeland house, in a quiet cul-de-sac, is just a two-minute walk from the town centre. The house is tastefully decorated, and most of the bedrooms have attractive floral wallpapers. One room has a four-poster bed, four have *en suite* facilities and one has its own bathroom. Dried-flower arrangements dotted here and there add to the interest. Guests can relax in the comfortable lounge or in the sunny conservatory. Breakfast only is served in the separate dining-room. In summer, barbecues take place in the pretty, secluded garden, from which there is access to the centre of town. John and Liz Christopherson are happy to help arrange mini-coach tours, horse-riding and other activities for guests. Packed lunches can be provided. At Christmas, a special three-day D,B&B stay is available.

OWNERS: John and Liz Christopherson OPEN: all year ROOMS: 1 single, with wash-basin; 3 double, all with bath/shower; 1 twin, with wash-basin; 1 four-poster, with bath/shower; 1 family, with bath/shower; TV in all bedrooms TERMS: single/single occupancy £17, twin/double £36, four-poster £44, family from £30; half-price for children under 10 sharing with parents; deposit: 1 night's charge CARDS: Access, Visa DETAILS: children welcome; dogs welcome but not to be left unattended in bedrooms; no smoking in dining-room and main lounge; car park; games room; garden

WINDSOR Berkshire   map 3

Alma House

56 Alma Road, Windsor SL4 3HA
TEL: (01753) 862983   FAX: (01753) 855620

Two terraced Victorian houses have been combined to make this guesthouse. It is in a pleasant, quiet residential district, only five minutes' walk from the town centre and castle. The accommodation is clean and bright, with simple white blinds in the bedrooms. A good supply of tourist information is available. Breakfast only is served, but Windsor is not short of eating places.

OWNER: Sally Shipp OPEN: all year ROOMS: 1 single, with wash-basin; 2 double, both with bath/shower; 2 twin, both with wash-basin; 1 family, with wash-basin; TV in all bedrooms TERMS: single £26, single occupancy £30–£35, twin/double £38–£45, family room £50; children under 2 free; deposit: £10–£20 CARDS: none DETAILS: children welcome; dogs welcome; no smoking in breakfast room; car park; garden

---

No stamps are needed if you write to the Guide from within the UK. Report forms are at the end of the book, or use your own stationery if you prefer.

Langton House

46 Alma Road, Windsor SL4 3HA
TEL: (01753) 858299

Langton House is a substantial double-fronted Victorian house just a few minutes' walk from the town centre and castle. Marjorie Fogg extends a warm welcome to her guests, who are offered a cup of tea upon arrival. The bedrooms are large and in good decorative order. The house is well maintained and the atmosphere relaxed and friendly. Marjorie and Roy are a delightful, well-travelled couple, and Roy, who recently retired, enjoys assisting guests with planning itineraries. Heathrow Airport is a 15-minute drive away.

OWNER: Marjorie Fogg   OPEN: all year exc Christmas   ROOMS: 1 double, 1 twin; both rooms with wash-basin; TV in both bedrooms   TERMS: twin/double £35–£40; 10% reduction for children; deposit: 10%   CARDS: none   DETAILS: children welcome; no dogs; no smoking

---

WINEHAM   West Sussex   **map 3**

Frylands

Frylands Lane, Wineham, nr Henfield BN5 9BP
TEL: (01403) 710214   FAX: (01403) 711449
from A23 follow A272 1½m W, then left into Wineham Lane and right at red telephone box

Frylands has been the Fowler family's home almost continuously since 1622. It is a Tudor farmhouse dating from around 1570, constructed of brick and timber with a stone roof, and retains many of its original features, such as the leaded windows, oak beams, flagstone floors and thick stone walls. The house is set in an acre of landscaped garden, with a swimming-pool, which guests are welcome to use in the summer when it is heated. Dinner is available by arrangement, as is coarse fishing, and there is a self-catering cottage. Frylands is at the end of a quiet country lane, three miles north-east of Henfield.

OWNER: Sylvia Fowler   OPEN: all year exc Christmas week   ROOMS: 1 double, with bath/shower; 1 twin, with wash-basin; 1 family, with wash-basin; TV in all bedrooms   TERMS: single occupancy £18–£20, twin/double £36–£38; family room from £45; reductions for children sharing with parents   CARDS: none   DETAILS: children welcome; no dogs; car park; garden; swimming-pool

---

If a B&B offers off-street car parking, we note 'car park' in the details at the end of the entry. If we are aware of particular car-parking difficulties, we mention them.

WINFRITH NEWBURGH   Dorset   map 2

Manor House

Winfrith Newburgh, nr Dorchester DT2 8JR
TEL: (01305) 852988   FAX: (01305) 854988
¾m off A352, 3m SW of Wool

The Manor house sits just opposite the village church in the picturesque village of Winfrith Newburgh. It is a beautiful listed house dating from the sixteenth century, although it has a Georgian appearance as a result of work carried out in the eighteenth century. One couple found the house 'atmospheric – like a photograph from *Homes and Gardens* but 'friendly first'. Charles and Jennie Smith are welcoming people who enjoy working on the house and maintaining its large walled garden. Fresh flowers fill the rooms and excellent breakfasts featuring fresh fruit are served. This is a wonderful area for walks and for visiting the beaches along the Dorset coast; Lulworth Cove and Corfe Castle are nearby.

OWNERS: Charles and Jennie Smith   OPEN: all year exc Christmas   ROOMS: 1 double, 1 twin; both rooms with bath/shower; TV in both bedrooms   TERMS: single occupancy £25–£27, twin/double £40–£44; reductions for children by arrangement; deposit: £20   CARDS: none   DETAILS: children welcome; no dogs; no smoking; car park; garden

WINSLEY   Wiltshire   map 2

Burghope Manor

Winsley, Bradford-on-Avon BA15 2LA
TEL: (01225) 723557   FAX: (01225) 723113
2m W of Bradford-on-Avon

Dating from the thirteenth century, Burghope Manor is an excellent example of a medieval manor house, with strong links to Henry VIII. The house has been lovingly preserved and offers guests every possible modern comfort, while still retaining many historical features. These include an enormous fireplace in the Cranmer Room that takes up almost one side of the room and is engraved with Elizabethan writing. The bedrooms have been tastefully furnished, all have *en suite* facilities, and most can be used as family rooms. Elaborate dinner parties, which guests can join by arrangement, are held on a fairly regular basis. The beautiful gardens include a tennis court. Burghope Manor is only five miles from Bath, and a number of excellent restaurants and country pubs are nearby.

OWNERS: Elizabeth and John Denning   OPEN: all year   ROOMS: 2 double, 3 twin, 2 family; all rooms with bath/shower; TV in all bedrooms   TERMS: single/single occupancy £50, twin/double £65–£70, family room £90; dinner for groups by arrangement £25–£30   CARDS: Access, Amex, Visa   DETAILS: children welcome; no dogs; no smoking in bedrooms; car park; garden

WINSTER   Derbyshire   map 5

Dower House

Main Street, Winster DE4 2DH
TEL: (01629) 650213   FAX: (01629) 650894

This Grade II listed Elizabethan country house, adjacent to the
village church, offers three large, comfortable bedrooms beautifully
decorated in soft pinks, greys and greens. One room has *en suite*
facilities and the others each have their own private bathroom.
Guests also have the use of an elegant beamed sitting-room, which
has a log fire on chilly days. Breakfast features home-made
marmalade and jams and is served at one table in the dining-room.
Two cats, a friendly brown dog and a Dalmatian are now part of the
family. This is a wonderfully peaceful base from which to explore this
area, and Helen Bastin, a Blue Badge Guide, is happy to assist with
itineraries. Packed lunches can be provided.

OWNERS: Helen Bastin and Geoff Dalton   OPEN: Mar to Oct   ROOMS: 1 double, 2 twin; all
rooms with bath/shower; TV in all bedrooms   TERMS: single occupancy £23–£35, twin/
double £36–£55; deposit: £20   CARDS: none   DETAILS: no children under 10; no dogs;
no smoking; car park; garden

WINTERTON-ON-SEA   Norfolk   map 6

Tower Cottage

Black Street, Winterton-on-Sea, nr Great Yarmouth NR29 4AP
TEL: (01493) 394053

This 200-year-old brick-and-flint cottage stands in an unspoilt fishing
village just across from the old parish church. Tower Cottage has lots
of charm and a friendly atmosphere, with old beams and exposed flint
walls. The bedrooms in the main house are on the ground floor and
have pretty Laura Ashley décor; another room in the converted barn
attached to the cottage has its own sitting-room and *en suite*
bathroom. Breakfast – considered 'superb' by one reporter – is served
in the dining-room or attractive conservatory, and takes in home-
made bread and preserves. Dinner is not available, but packed
lunches are provided. The sheltered garden, overlooked by the
conservatory, has wooden benches and picnic tables and is a peaceful
place to sit. The larger resort of Great Yarmouth is eight miles away
and the Broads are close by.

OWNERS: Alan and Muriel Webster   OPEN: all year exc Christmas and New Year
ROOMS: 2 double, 1 with bath/shower, 1 with wash-basin; 1 twin, with wash-basin; TV in
all bedrooms   TERMS: single occupancy £25–£30, twin/double £32–£36; £12 for
children from 8 to 12   CARDS: none   DETAILS: no children under 8; dogs welcome in
barn accommodation; smoking in barn accommodation only; car park; garden

WITCHFORD   Cambridgeshire   map 6

Clare Farm House

Main Street, Witchford, nr Ely CB6 2HQ
TEL: (01353) 664135

This modern, spacious farmhouse in a peaceful village two miles from
Ely offers good-value accommodation. The house is impeccably
maintained and freshly decorated with new carpets. The beds are
comfortable and all bedrooms have a sitting area and views over open
farmland. The family room is very large and the single room is on the
ground floor. The large number of bird sanctuaries nearby make this
an ideal place for bird-watchers.

OWNERS: Peter and Rita Seymour   OPEN: all year   ROOMS: 1 single; 1 double, with bath/
shower; 1 twin; 1 family, with bath/shower; TV in all bedrooms   TERMS: single £14,
single occupancy £15–£20, twin/double £28–£36; family room £36 plus children's
charge; children's reductions according to age; deposit   CARDS: none   DETAILS:
children welcome; no dogs; car park; garden

WIVELISCOMBE   Somerset   map 2

Alpine House

10 West Road, Wiveliscombe, nr Taunton TA4 2TF
TEL: (01984) 623526
on B3227 at W edge of town

This Victorian house stands in the small town of Wiveliscombe
overlooking the cricket and rugby ground. One of the features of
Alpine House is its terraced garden, which has been lovingly
landscaped and stocked with some unusual plants by Nevill and
Indrani, both keen gardeners. They are caring, hospitable hosts, and
if there is sufficient demand Indrani will prepare Sri Lankan food.
Alpine House is very comfortable and well furnished and all rooms
have their original Victorian fireplaces. One bedroom is on the
ground floor. This is wonderful walking country, and the Brendon
and Blackdown hills can be seen from the garden.

OWNERS: Nevill and Indrani Hewitt   OPEN: all year   ROOMS: 3 double, 1 twin; all rooms
with bath/shower; TV in all bedrooms   TERMS: single occupancy £27.50, twin/double
£50; dinner £15; deposit: £10 per person   CARDS: Access, Visa   DETAILS: no children;
no dogs; no smoking; garden

---

*Where we know a B&B accepts credit cards, we list them in the details at
the end of an entry. There may be a surcharge if you pay by credit card. It is
always best to check whether the card you want to use is acceptable when
booking.*

423

New Farm House

Spinnel's Lane, Wix, nr Manningtree CO11 2UJ
TEL: (01255) 870365   FAX: (01255) 870837
from Wix crossroads take Bradfield Road under A120 to top of hill, then right and continue for 200yds

This modern house with a recent annexe and extension offers well-maintained and hospitable accommodation. It is surrounded by an attractive ornamental garden and 50 acres of its own working farmland, and also has a large play area for children. Improvements are ongoing and the house is in excellent decorative order; the bedrooms are large and have matching bedspreads and curtains. Six of them are on the ground floor and two of these are equipped for partially disabled people, with space for a wheelchair and rails fitted in the bathroom. The guest lounge includes a microwave oven and drink-making facilities in a small kitchenette. The dinner menu comes in seven languages and includes vegetarian options. New Farm is licensed. The river nearby is a lovely place for walking and it is not far to the Stours Wood bird reserve.

OWNERS: Pat and George Mitchell   OPEN: all year   ROOMS: 3 single, 1 with bath/shower, 2 with wash-basin; 1 double, with bath/shower; 3 twin, 2 with bath/shower, 1 with wash-basin; 5 family, 3 with bath/shower, 2 with wash-basin; 2 rooms suitable for wheelchair-users; TV in all bedrooms and lounge   TERMS: single/single occupancy £20–£25, twin/double £39–£44; children under 5 free, half-price for ages 5 to 12; dinner £12; deposit: 10% or credit card details   CARDS: Access, Amex, Visa   DETAILS: children welcome; dogs in annexe rooms only; smoking in 2 bedrooms and TV lounge only; car park; garden

Knap Hill Manor

Carthouse Lane, Woking GU21 4XT
TEL: (01276) 857962   FAX: (01276) 855503

This late-eighteenth-century house is in a very rural setting, standing in pleasant countryside in six acres of gardens. It is a brick-built, rambling house which has been added on to over the years. The large drawing-room has a wood-burning stove, and breakfast and dinner (by arrangement) are served in the pleasant family dining-room, which has views out over the garden to fields and woods beyond. The traditionally decorated *en suite* bedrooms are comfortable and also have garden views. There is a croquet lawn, a hard tennis court, a water lily pond with fountains, and a terrace with chairs for sitting out. Knap Hill Manor is a pleasant place to stay within easy reach of London.

OWNERS: Kevin and Teresa Leeper OPEN: all year exc Christmas and Easter ROOMS: 3 double; all rooms with bath/shower; TV in all bedrooms and lounge TERMS: single occupancy £40, double £60–£65; 30%-50% reduction for children over 8 CARDS: Access, Delta, Switch, Visa DETAILS: no children under 8; no dogs; some non-smoking rooms; car park; garden; tennis

WOLLASTON   Northamptonshire   map 6

Duckmire

1 Duck End, Wollaston, nr Wellingborough NN29 7SH
TEL: (01933) 664249
from Wellingborough take A509 to Wollaston, turn left at Cuckoo Pub, left again by church, follow lane to no-entry sign and then to last house on left

This 200-year-old country house built from local limestone sits in an acre of beautiful secluded gardens. With its creaky floors, slab-stone entrance way and old fireplaces, the house is full of character and charm – ask to see the non-square door surround on the first floor. There are just two bedrooms (both good-sized), so guests are assured of personal attention from the delightful owners, who are happy to help outline itineraries. Although neither room has *en suite* facilities, guests have a bathroom exclusively for their own use. Breakfast and (by arrangement) evening meals are served in the elegant dining-room at one table; the house is unlicensed, but guests may bring their own wine to dinner. Packed lunches can be provided.

OWNER: Mrs S.M. Woodrow OPEN: all year exc Christmas and New Year ROOMS: 1 single, 1 twin, both with wash-basin; TV in twin room and lounge TERMS: single £16.50, single occupancy £18, twin £30; reductions for children over 5 sharing with parents; dinner £10; deposit: £10 for early bookings CARDS: none DETAILS: no children under 5; no dogs; no smoking; car park; garden

WOODCHESTER   Gloucestershire   map 2

Southfield House

Woodchester, nr Stroud GL5 5PA
TEL: (01993) 830723
just off B4066, 3m S of Stroud

Southfield House is a charming old Cotswold mill-house situated in six acres of garden and paddock. The house dates from 1560 and is of great architectural and historical interest. There are flagstone floors, oak beams and an inglenook fireplace. Two of the bedrooms are *en suite* and the third has a private bathroom. Suzanne and Tony Richardson are extremely gracious hosts who have created a warm, informal ambience in their charming home. There are some lovely walks close by and three pubs serving food are within walking distance. Total, the family black labrador, is friendly. There is an unheated swimming-pool available in summer.

OWNERS: Suzanne and Tony Richardson OPEN: all year exc Christmas ROOMS: 1 single, 2 twin; all rooms with bath/shower; TV in some bedrooms TERMS: single £20–£22, single occupancy £25; twin £40; deposit: by arrangement CARDS: none DETAILS: no dogs; smoking in dining-room only; car park; garden; swimming-pool

WOODMANCOTE   West Sussex   map 3

Eaton Thorne House

Henfield Road, Woodmancote, nr Henfield BN5 9BH
TEL: (01273) 492591
on B2116, W of A23

This attractive fifteenth-century small house stands in open countryside near the South Downs and is set in lovely gardens and paddocks. The house has all the characteristics one would expect in a building of this period, with low-beamed ceilings and little nooks and crannies. It is a comfortable family home and has a relaxed, informal atmosphere. The Langhornes are a friendly couple and great animal lovers. They have a particular interest in horses and there is a stable block in the grounds. Their daughter is a qualified riding instructor and is happy to give lessons to guests. Breakfast is served in the attractive dining-room and there is a pub within walking distance serving evening meals. Transport from Gatwick Airport and local car hire can be arranged.

OWNER: Mrs K.A. Langhorne OPEN: all year exc Christmas ROOMS: 1 double, with wash-basin; 1 twin, with wash-basin; 1 family; TV in some bedrooms TERMS: single occupancy £20, twin/double £30–£35, family room £50; children under 5 free; deposit: 50% CARDS: none DETAILS: children welcome; no dogs; smoking in bedrooms only; car park; garden

Tithe Barn

Brighton Road, Woodmancote, nr Henfield BN5 9ST
TEL: (01273) 492267
on A281, 1½m from Henfield

Tithe Barn was converted from an old barn in the 1920s, and the alterations carried out since then have kept its old character. The large, pleasant sitting/dining-room is shared with the family, and has a wood-burning stove. The bedrooms are comfortably furnished and have splendid views across the garden to the South Downs. Breakfast only is served.

OWNERS: Michael and Mary Chick OPEN: all year exc Christmas ROOMS: 1 double, 2 twin; all rooms with bath/shower; TV in all bedrooms TERMS: single occupancy £22, twin/double £36–£40; reductions for children under 5 CARDS: none DETAILS: children welcome; no dogs; no smoking; car park; garden

WOODSTOCK   Oxfordshire   map 2

Pine Trees

44 Green Lane, Woodstock OX20 1JZ
TEL: (01993) 811587/812740   FAX: (01993) 813332
leave A34 in Woodstock just S of river and turn into Lower Brook Hill; Green Lane is on right

Pine Trees is an attractive house in a quiet residential area a few minutes' walk from the centre of Woodstock. Trees are not the only feature of the colourful garden, which also has flower-filled terraces, a low hedge trimmed into the shape of battlements bordering the lawn and large fish ponds stocked with carp and goldfish. Indoors, a spiral staircase leads to the good-sized bedrooms, with comfortable beds. The spacious beamed lounge has a log fire burning in winter. This is a friendly, informal house where guests may come and go as they please. Breakfast only is served but Woodstock has several eating places. Blenheim Palace is very near and a visit there is highly recommended.

OWNER: Malcolm Snell OPEN: all year ROOMS: 1 twin; 2 family, 1 with bath/shower; TV in all bedrooms and lounge TERMS: twin £30, family room from £30–£35; children's reductions according to age; deposit required CARDS: none DETAILS: children welcome; no dogs; smoking in lounge only; car park; garden

WOOL   Dorset   map 2

East Burton House

East Burton, Wool, nr Wareham BH20 6HE
TEL: (01929) 463857   FAX: (01929) 463026
from Wareham take A352 Wool road, turn right just before level crossing, ¾m on right

This lovely part-seventeenth-century, part-Victorian house is set in an acre of gardens, on the main village road yet in a quiet position. Sonia and Mike Francis are a charming couple who take great pride in giving the best possible attention and service to their guests. A cheerful TV lounge is shared with the family, and the three bedrooms with antique brass beds are attractively decorated. The only meal served is breakfast, but this is quite a feast, with home-made and locally produced ingredients. There is a selection of bicycles for visitors to borrow.

OWNERS: Sonia and Mike Francis OPEN: all year ROOMS: 2 double; 1 twin, with wash-basin; TV lounge TERMS: single occupancy £19–£30, twin/double £38–£42; children's reductions by arrangement CARDS: none DETAILS: children welcome; no dogs; no smoking; car park; garden

WOOTTON BRIDGE Isle of Wight   map 2

Bridge House

Kite Hill, Wootton Bridge, Ryde PO33 4LA
TEL: (01983) 884163
on A3054 next to bridge

This attractive listed Georgian house has lovely views, especially at high tide on a summer's evening, from the pretty front garden which leads down to the river. The bedrooms are clean and bright and simply furnished and the bathroom has an old-fashioned bath and WC. There is one table in the dining-room, where breakfast only is served, and the entrance hall has a small sitting area. Although the house stands next to the bridge on the main road into Ryde, double glazing helps to cut down traffic noise. There is a public slipway for boats next to Bridge House and a couple of large popular pubs within easy walking distance. The owners are happy to pick up visitors from the ferry.

OWNER: Mrs D. Blackman OPEN: all year exc Christmas ROOMS: 2 double, both with wash-basin; 1 twin with shower; TV in all bedrooms TERMS: twin/double £30–£36; deposit: £10 CARDS: none DETAILS: no children; dogs by arrangement; no smoking; car park

Oakenshore

New Road, Wootton Bridge, Ryde PO33 4HY
TEL: (01983) 884117

Oakenshore stands in a pleasant location overlooking a wide creek, where small boats pass by. The Minnses have very high standards, and they are helpful and informative on what to see and do on the island. The accommodation is very spacious and clean, and both bedrooms are on the ground floor. The double has an *en suite* shower room and the twin, which has *en suite* bath and shower, is big enough to accommodate two extra beds and a cot if required. The dining-room is in the owners' private area; guests also have use of their own kitchen, for cooking evening meals or preparing picnic lunches. In addition, packed lunches can be arranged. Adult guests are welcome to use the garden, though it is not suitable for young children to play in.

OWNER: Mrs P.A. Minns OPEN: all year ROOMS: 1 double, 1 twin/family; both rooms with bath/shower; TV in both bedrooms TERMS: single occupancy £20–£24, twin/

family room from £32–£36; children under 2 free, half-price for children over 2; deposit: 1 night's charge CARDS: none DETAILS: children welcome; dogs by arrangement; no smoking; car park; garden

WOOTTON FITZPAINE   Dorset   map 2

Rowan House

Wootton Fitzpaine, Charmouth DT6 6NE
TEL: (01297) 560514
just off A35 Axminster to Bridport road

Rowan House is a stone-built house in a peaceful location, with gorgeous country views on the outskirts of Wootton Fitzpaine. A footpath running from the back of the garden through fields to Charmouth makes a pleasant stroll of just over a mile. There is an attractive sitting-room, and breakfast and evening meals are served in the conservatory extension which overlooks the garden. There is no alcohol licence, but guests are welcome to bring their own wine to dinner. The small bedrooms are prettily decorated and furnished. The patio is a pleasant place to sit in summer and enjoy the rural views.

OWNER: Linda Dedman OPEN: all year exc Christmas ROOMS: 1 single, 3 double, 2 twin, 1 family; all rooms with bath/shower; TV lounge TERMS: single £19, single occupancy £24, twin/double £37–£38, family room £46–£49; half-price for children sharing with parents, 25% reduction in own room; dinner £10; deposit: 20% CARDS: none DETAILS: well-behaved children welcome; no dogs; no smoking; car park; garden

WORCESTER   Hereford & Worcester   map 5

Burgage House

4 College Precincts, Worcester WR1 2LG
TEL: (01905) 25396

This is a beautifully maintained listed Georgian house with a peaceful ambience in a cobbled street adjacent to the cathedral and ideally located for exploring Worcester and the surrounding countryside. It has an unusual curved stone staircase climbing the three floors of colour co-ordinated bedrooms, one of which has a reproduction Jacobean bed. The layout of the house makes it unsuitable for the less mobile. Breakfast only is served in the dining-room and guests can relax in the lounge or an additional sitting area with flagstone floors and an inglenook fireplace.

OWNER: Janette Ratcliffe OPEN: all year exc Christmas ROOMS: 1 single; 1 double, with bath/shower; 1 twin, with bath/shower; 1 family; TV in all bedrooms TERMS: single £24–£26, single occupancy £28–£30, twin/double £36–£46, family room £36–£40 plus children's charge; half-price for children sharing with parents in family room CARDS: none DETAILS: children welcome; no dogs; smoking in lounge only

40 Britannia Square

40 Britannia Square, Worcester WR1 3DN
TEL: (01905) 611920   FAX: (01905) 27152

This large Regency house is situated in a conservation area within walking distance of the town centre. It has been tastefully refurbished and is furnished in keeping with its character. Two rooms are in the basement, but they are bright and have pretty duvets and matching wall stencilling. A ground-floor room in the courtyard has twin beds and a sofa bed, making it ideal as a family room. Parking is available close to the house after 4.30pm and daytime spaces can be found not too far away.

OWNER: Val Lloyd   OPEN: all year exc Christmas   ROOMS: 1 double, 2 twin; all rooms with bath/shower; TV in all bedrooms   TERMS: single occupancy £40, twin/double £50, family room £65; deposit: £10   CARDS: none   DETAILS: children welcome; no dogs; garden

WORMSHILL   Kent   map 3

Saywell Farm House

Bedmonton, Wormshill, nr Sittingbourne ME9 0EH
TEL/FAX: (01622) 884444
off B2163 Hollingbourne to Sittingbourne road

The oldest part of this listed period former farmhouse dates from the thirteenth century, and the date 1611 is inscribed on the massive carved beam which crosses the large open fireplace in the dining-room. It is a most attractive whitewashed building standing in farmland at the end of a quiet lane on the North Downs. The house has been cleverly updated and tastefully renovated while retaining all the old features. The comfortable *en suite* bedrooms are attractively decorated, and evening meals and packed lunches are available if arranged in advance.

OWNER: Yvonne Carter   OPEN: all year exc Christmas   ROOMS: 2 double, 1 twin; all rooms with bath/shower; TV in all bedrooms   TERMS: single occupancy £25, twin/double £45; dinner £16.50; deposit: £15   CARDS: none   DETAILS: no children under 12; no dogs; no smoking; car park; garden

If a B&B offers off-street car parking, we note 'car park' in the details at the end of the entry. If we are aware of particular car-parking difficulties, we mention them.

Entries in the Guide are listed under town or village. There are also two indexes at the back of the book, one listing B&Bs by county, the other by name.

WORTHING   West Sussex   map 3

Delmar Hotel

1–2 New Parade, Worthing BN11 2BQ
TEL: (01903) 211834   FAX: (01903) 219052

This small, unpretentious and rather gaudy-looking hotel stands on
the sea front, with only the narrow, quiet road and grass separating it
from the beach. Jenny and Norman Elms are a cheerful, welcoming
couple, and nothing is too much trouble for them. The comfortable
bedrooms have fridges and some have balconies. There is a roof
garden, a bar and TV lounge, and both breakfast and evening meals
are available in the dining-room. The Delmar is about half a mile east
of the pier, and is next to the leisure centre.

OWNERS: Mr N. and Mrs J. Elms   OPEN: all year   ROOMS: 6 single, 2 double, 2 twin, 2
four-poster, 4 family; all rooms with bath/shower; 2 rooms suitable for wheelchair-
users; TV in all bedrooms and lounge   TERMS: single/single occupancy £27.50, twin/
double £50, four-poster £75; children under 3 free, half-price for ages 3 to 12; dinner
£15; deposit: £10 per person   CARDS: Access, Amex, Delta, Diners, Switch, Visa
DETAILS: children welcome; no dogs in public rooms; no smoking in bedrooms; car park;
garden

WROXHAM   Norfolk   map 6

Garden Cottage

The Limes, 96 Norwich Road, Wroxham, nr Norwich NR12 8RY
TEL: (01603) 784376
on A1151, 7m NE of Norwich

Exceptional standards at this delightful converted eighteenth-
century barn and stables make for a comfortable stay. Three smartly
decorated bedrooms are furnished in pine and have *en suite*
bathrooms. The one on the ground floor is suitable for wheelchair-
users. Bob Partridge amd Brian Cooper previously ran an art gallery
and they have displayed photographs and paintings throughout the
property. Guests are welcome to make use of the gardens and patio,
and snug sitting-room with wicker chairs. The owners live in an
adjacent cottage, but are very accessible should any help be needed.
Although breakfast only is served, there are several eating
establishments within walking distance. Wroxham is in the Norfolk
Broads National Park, and day boats can be hired from nearby.

OWNERS: Brian Cooper and Bob Partridge   OPEN: all year   ROOMS: 1 double, 2 twin; all
rooms with bath/shower; 1 room suitable for wheelchair-users; TV in all bedrooms
TERMS: single occupancy £30, twin/double £40   CARDS: Access, Amex, Diners, Visa
DETAILS: no children under 10; no dogs; smoking in sitting-room only; car park; garden

ENGLAND

YELVERTON Devon

map 1

Cider House

Buckland Abbey, Yelverton PL20 6EZ
TEL: (01822) 853285   FAX: (01822) 853626
off A386, 5m S of Tavistock; from Yelverton follow NT signs to Buckland Abbey, just before Abbey entrance at crossroads take Buckland turn, then first left signposted 'Abbey deliveries private'

This beautiful stone house with mullioned windows dates from the fourteenth century and was originally a refectory for Buckland Abbey, and in Elizabethan times a cider barn. It stands in 15 landscaped acres (open under the National Gardens Scheme) containing a hard tennis court and self-catering cottages. An informal atmosphere pervades, and the large rooms have interesting furnishings. There are both a breakfast and a dining-room; evening meals (and packed lunches) are by arrangement, with vegetarian dishes and children's helpings available. There is no alcohol licence but guests may bring their own wine.

OWNER: Mrs M.J. Stone   OPEN: all year exc Christmas and New Year   ROOMS: 1 double, with wash-basin; 1 twin; TV in one bedroom and lounge   TERMS: single occupancy £27, twin/double £45; half-price for children under 12; dinner £15   CARDS: none   DETAILS: children welcome; no dogs; no smoking; car park; garden; tennis

YEOVIL Somerset

map 2

Sunnymede

26 Lower Wraxhill Road, Yeovil BA20 2JU
TEL: (01935) 25786

This 1920s house is in a quiet position in a side street on the edge of Yeovil. It has leaded glass windows, is decorated in keeping with the period of the house and is spotlessly clean. Margaret Lock is a very friendly lady who enjoys meeting her guests. Breakfast is served in the dining-room/lounge, which also has a microwave for residents' use. Sunnymede stands in a large terraced garden and is about a 20-minute walk from the centre of town. Montacute House is nearby and T.S. Eliot is buried in East Coker church a mile away.

OWNER: Margaret Lock   OPEN: all year   ROOMS: 1 double, with wash-basin; 1 twin, with bath/shower; 1 family, with wash-basin; 1 room suitable for wheelchair-users; TV in all bedrooms and lounge   TERMS: single occupancy £18, twin/double £32–£34, family room £40–£42; children under 5 free, half-price for ages 5 to 15; deposit: 33% of charge   CARDS: none   DETAILS: children welcome; no dogs; no smoking in residents' lounge; car park; garden

YETMINSTER   Dorset

Manor Farmhouse

High Street, Yetminster, nr Sherborne DT9 6LF
TEL: (01935) 872247

This seventeenth-century farmhouse is in the centre of the historic
village of Yetminster, renowned for its attractive stone-built houses.
Although retaining many original features, it has been modernised to
a high standard with spacious and comfortable bedrooms. Ann
Partridge is a very friendly, welcoming lady and a mine of
information on local history and architecture. She also keeps an
extensive library of books and guidebooks in the sitting-room for
guests to consult. Evening meals, served by arrangement, feature
traditional home cooking using home-grown vegetables and meat
from the farm, which is set apart from the house.

OWNER: Ann Partridge   OPEN: all year   ROOMS: 1 single, 1 double, 2 twin; all rooms with
bath/shower; 3 rooms suitable for wheelchair-users; TV in all bedrooms   TERMS: single/
single occupancy £30, twin/double £50; dinner £15; deposit £25   CARDS: Access,
Delta, Visa   DETAILS: no children under 12; no dogs; no smoking; car park; garden

YORK   North Yorkshire
map 9

Abbeyfields Guesthouse

19 Bootham Terrace, York YO3 7DH
TEL: (01904) 636471

This early-Victorian house is on a quiet side street ten minutes' walk
from the city centre. It has recently been refurbished by Richard and
Gwen to a very high standard. The bedrooms have pine furniture and
matching dainty floral fabrics, and the attractive attic rooms have
sloping ceilings. The quiet lounge has a fine display of plants, a good
selection of books and a marble fireplace. Excellent breakfasts are
served in the bright dining-room and there are lots of eating
establishments within walking distance. A self-catering unit is
available.

OWNERS: Richard Martin and Gwen Derrett   OPEN: all year   ROOMS: 3 single, 5 double, 1
twin; all rooms with bath/shower; TV in all bedrooms   TERMS: single/single occupancy
£26, twin/double £40; deposit £20   CARDS: none   DETAILS: no children under 10; no
dogs; no smoking; car park

Use the maps and indexes at the back of the Guide to plan your trip.

*We state at the end of an entry whether children are welcome. If we know of
any restrictions on children, we give them.*

Curzon Lodge and Stable Cottages

23 Tadcaster Road, Dringhouses, York YO2 2QG
TEL: (01904) 703157

Standing in a lovely landscaped garden in a quiet location overlooking the Knavesmire racecourse is this beautifully restored seventeenth-century house and converted stables. The bedrooms, four of which are on the ground floor, are elegantly furnished with antique pine and some boast four-poster beds or Victorian brass bedsteads. All have armchairs in which to relax, but there is also a smart drawing-room with a tempting selection of coffee-table books to browse through, and this is where guests are welcomed with a complimentary glass of sherry. The beamed dining-room has a quarry-tiled floor and overlooks mature conifers and the garden.

OWNERS: Richard and Wendy Wood OPEN: all year exc Christmas and New Year ROOMS: 1 single, 3 double, 3 twin, 2 four-poster, 1 family; all rooms with bath/shower; TV in all bedrooms TERMS: single £30–£39, single occupancy £39–£49, twin/double £45–£58, four-poster £50–£65, family room £67.50; half-price for children over 7 sharing with parents; deposit: £20 per person or credit card details CARDS: Access, Visa DETAILS: no children under 7; no dogs; no smoking in dining-room; car park; garden

Dairy Guesthouse

3 Scarcroft Road, York YO2 1ND
TEL: (01904) 639367

This lovingly restored Victorian town house combines the best original features, such as stained-glass windows and wonderfully ornate ceiling roses and cornices, with modern pine furniture. It is set around a flower-filled courtyard, originally the centre of activity for a joinery business and then for a dairy. It is well known for excellent wholefood breakfasts, for which guests can choose a bright-and-early 8.15am sitting or a more leisurely 9.15am start to the day. Vegetarians and people with special diets are well catered for. The bedrooms are tastefully decorated and well equipped, including a tempting selection of herbal teas. Garaging is available for cars.

OWNER: Keith Jackman OPEN: Feb to Dec exc Christmas ROOMS: 1 single, with bath/shower; 3 double, 1 with bath/shower, 2 with wash-basin; 1 twin, with bath/shower; 1 four-poster, with wash-basin; 1 family, with bath/shower; TV in all bedrooms TERMS: single occupancy £25–£32, twin/double £32–£40, four-poster £36, family room £36 plus children's charge; half-price for children under 14 sharing with parents CARDS: none DETAILS: children welcome; no dogs; no smoking

We asked the proprietors to estimate their 1996 prices in the autumn of 1995, so the rates may have changed since publication.

Farthings

5 Nunthorpe Avenue, York YO2 1PF
TEL: (01904) 653545

Farthings is a straightforward large Victorian town house standing close to the centre of York, near Micklegate Bar, one of the medieval gateways in the city walls. Accommodation is comfortable and the house is immaculately maintained. Improvements are ongoing. Breakfast is served at separate tables and includes unlimited fresh filtered coffee. The lounge has TV and a small bar ideal for a nightcap drink, where Audrey Reid often joins her guests. There is a good supply of information leaflets. Parking space is available on the street.

OWNER: Audrey Reid OPEN: all year exc Christmas ROOMS: 1 single, with wash-basin; 5 double, 2 with bath/shower, 3 with wash-basin; 1 twin, with wash-basin; 2 family, 1 with bath/shower, 1 with wash-basin; TV in some bedrooms and lounge TERMS: single £20, single occupancy £25, twin/double £30–£44, family room £45–£55; £5 for children under 5, half-price for ages 5 to 12 sharing with parents; deposit: £20 CARDS: Access, Visa DETAILS: children welcome; no dogs; no smoking in dining-room

Holme Lea Manor

18 St Peters Grove, Clifton YO3 6AQ
TEL: (01904) 623529

Holme Lea is a large, red-brick Victorian residence situated in a quiet tree-lined cul-de-sac, only ten minutes' walk to the city centre. The spacious bedrooms are very attractively decorated; all have *en suite* facilities and six of the rooms have four-poster beds. The house is full of old-world charm and the drawing-room has comfortable chairs, a marble fireplace and a fine display of china and glass. Excellent breakfasts are served at separate tables in the elegant dining-room, which overlooks the secluded garden. Holme Lea is licensed, enabling guests to enjoy a glass of wine after a busy day of sightseeing.

OWNER: Lynn Pearson OPEN: all year exc Christmas ROOMS: 1 twin, 6 four-poster, 1 family; all rooms with bath/shower; TV in all bedrooms and lounge TERMS: single occupancy £25, twin £40–£44, four-poster £40–£48, family room from £40; reductions for children in family room; deposit: £20 CARDS: Access, Delta, Visa DETAILS: children welcome; no dogs; no smoking in dining-room; car park; garden

Holmwood House

114 Holgate Road, York YO2 4BB
TEL: (01904) 626183   FAX: (01904) 670899

A listed nineteenth-century building originally built as two private houses, Holmwood has been beautifully restored and retains the

435

pleasant ambience of a private home. The rooms are individually and tastefully decorated with quality fabrics and wallpapers. The spacious bedrooms, all with their own bathroom or shower room, are elegantly furnished with a predominantly white and cream palette; one has a spa bath, two have four-posters, and four of the bedrooms are on the ground floor. A large sitting-room has an open fire, magazines and information about York. Breakfasts only are served but include a wide number of choices. Packed lunches can be provided.

OWNERS: Christina and Roberto Gramellini OPEN: all year ROOMS: 8 double, 2 twin, 2 four-poster; all rooms with bath/shower; TV in all rooms TERMS: single occupancy £35–£50, twin/double £50–£70, four-poster £55–£75; reductions for children over 8 sharing with parents; deposit: credit card details CARDS: Access, Amex, Visa DETAILS: no children under 8; small dogs by arrangement; smoking in drawing-room only; car park; garden

YOXFORD Suffolk   map 6

Sans Souci

Main Road, Yoxford, nr Saxmundham IP17 3EX
TEL/FAX: (01728) 668268
near junction of A12 and B1122

Sans Souci is a listed Georgian residence standing in about two acres of walled gardens on the outskirts of the village on a main road. Double glazing keeps traffic noise to a minimum. The house was used as a prison during the Napoleonic Wars. The three comfortable bedrooms all have a sitting area, and one has a brass bed. This is a very popular spot for bird-watchers and horse trials take place in neighbouring Rookery Park. A pub within 100 yards serves evening meals.

OWNERS: Stuart and Mary Andrews OPEN: all year ROOMS: 2 double, 1 twin; all rooms with wash-basin; TV in all bedrooms TERMS: single occupancy £24–£28, twin/double £36; £4 for children sharing with parents; deposit: £10 CARDS: Access, Visa DETAILS: children welcome; dogs by prior arrangement; no smoking; car park; garden

ZEALS Wiltshire   map 2

Stag Cottage

Fantley Lane, Zeals, nr Mere BA12 6NX
TEL: (01747) 840458
on B3092, 5m NE of Wincanton

This long seventeenth-century thatched house was originally three tiny cottages in the centre of an old village now mercifully bypassed by the main A303. Inside, it fulfils dreams of old-world charm, with beamed ceilings and an inglenook fireplace, and the light, bright decorations make the small rooms feel cosy rather than cramped. Afternoon cream teas are served in the sitting-room or on the lawn opposite the house on fine summer afternoons. Scones and cakes are all home-made. Stourhead Gardens are within walking distance.

OWNERS: Marie and Peter Boxall OPEN: all year ROOMS: 1 single, 2 double, 1 twin, 1 four-poster; all rooms with wash-basin; TV lounge TERMS: single £15, single occupancy £10.50, twin/double £30, four-poster £30; babies in cot £1.50, half-price for children under 12 CARDS: none DETAILS: children welcome; dogs by arrangement; no smoking; car park; garden

ZENNOR   Cornwall   map 1

Carnelloe House

Zennor, nr St Ives TR26 3DB
TEL: (01736) 798946
driveway off B3306 St Ives to St Just road

This small, rugged cliff-top farmhouse is reached down a long driveway. It has sea and farmland views and access to the coast. The Hawkinses are charming people and take great care of their guests. Of the two bedrooms one is in the house itself, and the other in a converted stone outbuilding. The barn conversion is particularly popular and has a sitting area and small outside patio. Breakfast only is served at one table in the attractive, rustic dining-room; a nearby pub has an excellent reputation for evening meals. Carnelloe offers comfortable, unpretentious accommodation in a peaceful and remote spot.

OWNERS: Mr and Mrs John Hawkins OPEN: Mar to Dec ROOMS: 1 double, 1 twin; both rooms with bath/shower; TV in both bedrooms TERMS: twin/double £40–£44 CARDS: none DETAILS: no children; dogs welcome; no smoking in dining-room; car park; garden

Tregeraint House

Zennor, nr St Ives TR26 3DB
TEL/FAX: (01736) 797061
¼m SW of Zennor on B3306

Tregeraint House is a simply constructed granite farmhouse with many original features. It stands above the road on the outskirts of Zennor in a remote, wild location with views across fields to the sea, and has a pretty back and side garden. The house is warm and cosy and the sitting-room and dining-room, with large stone fireplaces, are shared with John and Sue Wilson, who also run a publishing business from the house. The whitewashed bedrooms are simply furnished and have wash-basins built into old wash-stands. The house is conveniently located for visiting Land's End and St Ives.

OWNER: Sue Wilson   OPEN: all year exc Christmas   ROOMS: 1 double, 1 twin, 1 family; all rooms with wash-basin; TV in some bedrooms   TERMS: single occupancy £18, twin/double £30; family room from £37.50; half-price for children under 14; deposit: £5
CARDS: none   DETAILS: children welcome; no dogs; no smoking; car park; garden

Scotland

ABERDEEN   Grampian   m

Aberdeen Springdale Guest House

404 Great Western Road, Aberdeen AB1 6NR
TEL: (01224) 316561   FAX: (01224) 210773

Large rooms and some ornate ceilings are a feature of this terraced
Victorian residence on one of the main roads into Aberdeen — a road
where almost every house offers accommodation. Some of the warm,
comfortable bedrooms have shower units, while others share a
bathroom on the first floor and a shower on the ground floor. There is
a comfortable lounge, and breakfast only is served in the dining-
room. Packed lunches can be provided.

OWNER: Mrs F. Stirling   OPEN: all year   ROOMS: 1 single, with wash-basin; 2 double, with
bath/shower; 1 twin, with wash-basin; 2 family, 1 with bath/shower, 1 with wash-basin;
TV in all bedrooms   TERMS: single £20, single occupancy £24–£28, twin/double
£32–£36, family room from £30; children's reductions according to age   CARDS: none
DETAILS: children welcome; dogs welcome; no smoking in dining-room; car park

ABERDOUR   Fife   map 11

Hawkcraig House

Hawkcraig Point, Aberdour KY3 0TZ
TEL: (01383) 860335

Hawkcraig House stands at the foot of some cliffs, right on the water's
edge, accessed via a large car park and an extremely steep track.
There are spectacular views across the Firth of Forth to Edinburgh
and round the bay to Aberdour. A 15-minute walk along a shoreline
footpath leads you to Aberdour Station, from where Edinburgh is a
30-minute train ride. Elma Barrie is known locally for her cooking,
and prepares dinner for both bed-and-breakfast guests and non-
residents. Pre-dinner drinks are served in the upstairs sitting-room,
which has its own fire and overlooks the sea, and a four-course meal
is then served in the small dining-room. Guests may bring their own
wine to dinner. In addition, there is a small sun lounge also
overlooking the water, where breakfast is taken. Two comfortable
bedrooms comprise the accommodation; both are *en suite* and one has
views.

OWNER: Elma Barrie   OPEN: mid-Mar to end Oct   ROOMS: 1 double, 1 twin; both rooms
with bath/shower; TV in both bedrooms   TERMS: single occupancy £26–£28, twin/
double £40–£48; reductions for children sharing with parents; dinner £19   CARDS:
none   DETAILS: no children under 8; no dogs; no smoking; car park; garden

---

*We asked the proprietors to estimate their 1996 prices in the autumn of
1995, so the rates may have changed since publication.*

ABERLEMNO   Tayside   map 11

Wood of Auldbar Farmhouse

Aberlemno, nr Brechin DD9 6SZ
TEL: (01307) 830218
*from Brechin take A90 south for ½m to B9134 (signposted Aberlemno);
follow B9134 for ¼m and turn left onto Pitkennedy road; drive for 3m,
farm is on right*

This Victorian stone house has a small front garden and orchard and
is surrounded by open countryside. It is part of a working mixed farm
of 187 acres, in a rural location. The accommodation is simple and
clean with a sitting-room and TV. Breakfast and dinner are served in
the sun-room, which has a lovely view. There is no licence but guests
can bring their own wine; children's helpings and packed lunches can
be provided. The Angus Glens, Balmoral and Glamis Castle are all
within reach. The village has a couple of standing stones which may
be of interest.

OWNER: Jean Stewart   OPEN: all year exc Christmas and New Year   ROOMS: 1 single, 1
twin, 1 family; TV lounge   TERMS: single from £15, single occupancy from £18, twin £29,
family room from £42; children's reductions by arrangement; dinner £9.50   CARDS:
none   DETAILS: children welcome; no dogs; no smoking; car park; garden

---

ABINGTON   Strathclyde   map 11

Craighead Farm

Crawfordjohn Road, Abington ML12 6SQ
TEL/FAX: (01864) 502356
leave M74 at junction 13 and follow signs for Crawfordjohn

Part of a 600-acre mixed farm, this stone-built, whitewashed
farmhouse dates from the fourteenth century and has lovely views of
the nearby river. Although set in a remote spot in peaceful, rolling
countryside, Craighead Farm is only one and a half miles from the
main Glasgow to Carlisle road. The simple accommodation consists of
two comfortable bedrooms on the first floor, one with *en suite*
facilities, and the other having the use of a large bathroom on the
ground floor. Packed lunches and evening meals are available by
arrangement (guests may bring their own wine to dinner), and
fishing can be organised.

OWNERS: George and Mary Hodge   OPEN: May to Oct   ROOMS: 1 double, with wash-
basin; 1 twin, with bath/shower; TV lounge   TERMS: twin/double £30; children under 5
free, 25% reduction for children over 5; dinner £7 to £9; deposit: £5   CARDS: none
DETAILS: children welcome; no dogs; car park; garden

Use the maps and indexes at the back of the Guide to plan your trip.

Hazlehurst Lodge

Ballater Road, Aboyne AB34 5HY
TEL: (01339) 886921   FAX: (01339) 886660
on A93, 10m E of Ballater

Hazlehurst stands in an attractive, wooded garden close to the centre
of town. This rose-granite house was built in 1880 as the coachman's
lodge to Aboyne Castle and was also home to Robert Milne,
photographer to Queen Victoria. The smartly furnished interior is
decorated in a variety of different contemporary styles; flowers and
paintings fill the rooms. A Belgian architect designed the lighting,
and the furniture was made by students at Glasgow's Mackintosh
School of Architecture. The Strachans are an artistic, interesting
family, and one of Anne's concerns is the attached licensed
restaurant, also open to non-residents. Bookings are necessary;
vegetarian choices and children's helpings can be provided. A small
dining-room is at the front of the house, with another at the back.
There are two comfortable sitting-rooms, and a new addition is the
art gallery/studio in the garden. The three bedrooms have king-sized
beds which can zip together to make a large double or twins. There is
also a family suite in the annexe. Salmon fishing on the River Dee
and other sporting activities can be arranged.

OWNER: Anne Strachan   OPEN: Feb to Dec   ROOMS: 3 super-king, all with bath/shower;
1 family, with bath/shower; TV lounge   TERMS: single occupancy £32–£64, super-king
£64–£80, family room £75–£90; dinner £24; deposit: credit card details   CARDS:
Access, Amex, Diners, Visa   DETAILS: children welcome; no dogs in public areas; no
smoking; car park; garden

Struan Hall

Ballater Road, Aboyne AB34 5HY
TEL/FAX: (01339) 887241
at junction of A93 / B9094, ½m from village green

This spacious granite-built house stands in two acres of grounds,
complete with croquet lawn, and is surrounded by coniferous
woodland. It was originally built about five miles east of Aboyne,
where it was known as Tillydrine House, and in 1904 was moved
stone by stone to its present site. The Inghams used to own a hotel in
a different part of Scotland, and moved here in 1990, taking much
care in renovating the house to its present standard of comfort. The
rooms are light and tastefully decorated, and every possible comfort
is at hand to greet the visitor, including a warm welcome.

STRUAN HALL, ABOYNE

OWNERS: Phyllis and Michael Ingham   OPEN: Mar to end Oct   ROOMS: 1 double, 2 twin; all rooms with bath/shower; TV in all bedrooms and lounge   TERMS: single occupancy £27, twin/double £44; deposit: £20 per person   CARDS: Visa   DETAILS: no children under 7; no dogs; smoking in lounge only; car park; garden

---

ANCRUM   Borders   map 11

Ancrum Craig Guest House

Ancrum, nr Jedburgh TD8 6UN
TEL: (01835) 830280
turn west off A68 3½m N of Jedburgh, on to B6400 to Ancrum; take first fork left (signposted Denholm), drive 1¾m, turn right (signposted Lilliesleaf), drive uphill ¾m, turn left

---

This attractive sandstone Victorian country house stands at the end of a long driveway about two miles from the small village of Ancrum, and has spectacular hill views. The Hensenses also run the village shop and post office, and keep horses. Ancrum Craig has many of its original features, and both the dining-room and drawing-room are elegant; in winter there is an open fire. Two of the three spacious and comfortable bedrooms are in the front of the house and enjoy the wonderful outlook. Guests have use of the games room, with table tennis and darts, and the well-maintained garden.

OWNER: Jill Hensens   OPEN: April to Oct   ROOMS: 2 double, 1 twin; all rooms with bath/shower; TV in all bedrooms   TERMS: single occupancy £28–£33, twin/double £38–£44; children's reductions by arrangement   CARDS: none   DETAILS: children welcome; dogs welcome; car park; games room; garden

ARBROATH   Tayside   map 11

Farmhouse Kitchen

Grange of Conon, Arbroath DD11 3SD
TEL: (01241) 860202   FAX: (01241) 860424
from Arbroath take A933 for 1m, turn left at Redford sign, after 2m take private signposted drive

This spacious and comfortable family home is surrounded by rolling farmland, with lovely views to the hills and a glimpse of the sea. The mixed arable farm extends to some 560 acres. A long private road leads to the farm, and the owner can provide a helpful map giving directions. Two of the bedrooms are on the first floor, one having lovely views, with a third on the ground floor. The sun lounge has TV and the enormous games room has a snooker table, a table-tennis table, exercise equipment and a sunbed. Breakfast is served in the kitchen and packed lunches can be provided.

OWNER: Sandra Caldwell   OPEN: all year exc Christmas   ROOMS: 3 twin, 1 with bath/shower, 2 with wash-basin; 1 room suitable for wheelchair-users; TV in all rooms and lounge   TERMS: single occupancy £37.50, twin £60–£80   CARDS: none   DETAILS: no children; no dogs; no smoking in bedrooms; car park; games room; garden

ARDINDREAN   Highland   map 11

Taigh Na Mara Vegetarian Guest House

The Shore, Ardindrean, Loch Broom, nr Ullapool IV23 2SE
TEL/FAX: (01854) 655282
off A835, 8m S of Ullapool

This small, whitewashed guesthouse in what the owners call 'the middle of nowhere' was once the village store and lies on a shingle beach on the west shore of Loch Broom. It is reached – once you park your car – by a 200-metre walk down a steep hillside across a sometimes muddy field. New arrivals after the hike may be treated to a 'wee dram' before being shown to one of three comfortable bedrooms. Two of the rooms are in the guest wing up a spiral staircase and have skylights and views out over the loch. The third, the 'honeymoon suite', is in the separate boatshed. The cosy 30ft lounge/dining-room has a wood-burning stove. There is a kitchen for guests' use which includes a stove, washing machine and drying facilities. Taigh Na Mara is renowned for its vegetarian and vegan food; guests are encouraged to bring their own wine. An early dinner is provided for children under 10 at 5.30pm. Boats, bikes and packed lunches can be arranged. One visitor summed up her stay here as 'very peaceful, good hosts, great food, lovely room – what more do you want in a B&B?'

OWNERS: Jackie Redding and Tony Weston OPEN: all year ROOMS: 2 double, 1 with bath/shower; 1 twin, with wash-basin; TV in some bedrooms and lounge TERMS: rates inc dinner; single occupancy £40; twin/double £66–£76; reductions for children sharing with parents; deposit: 20% CARDS: Access, Delta, Switch, Visa DETAILS: no children under 10 at main dinner; dogs welcome in scullery and boatshed only; no smoking; car park; garden

ARDNADAM   Strathclyde   map 11

Lochside

Fir Brae, Ardnadam, Sandbank PA23 8QD
TEL: (01369) 706327
on A815 between Dunoon and Sandbank village

This whitewashed Edwardian villa is about two miles from Dunoon and enjoys wonderful views over Holy Loch to the wooded slopes of Strone and Blairmore. The bright, fresh bedrooms are decorated with floral wallpaper and pleasant fabrics, and the pretty dining-room has one table in the window where breakfast only is served. Packed lunches can be provided.

OWNER: Rosemary Brooks OPEN: Jan to Nov ROOMS: 1 double, 1 twin, 1 family; all rooms with wash-basin; TV in all bedrooms TERMS: single occupancy £17; twin/double £28–£32; family room from £35; half-price for children under 12 sharing with parents; deposit: £10 CARDS: none DETAILS: children welcome; no dogs; no smoking in dining-room; car park; garden

ARDRISHAIG   Strathclyde   map 11

Allt-na-Craig

Tarbert Road, Ardrishaig PA30 8EP
TEL: (01546) 603245
just S of Lochgilphead on A83

This substantial Victorian mansion stands in an extensive garden, commanding wonderful views over Loch Fyne. It has spacious, comfortable bedrooms, all *en suite*, and the lounge has an open fire, piano, games and guide-books, and overlooks the loch. Allt-na-Craig has a reputation for its excellent breakfast; home-cooked evening meals are also available, and packed lunches can be provided. Reduced prices can be arranged for D,B&B packages for longer stays, and self-catering units are also available to rent.

OWNERS: Harvey and Margaret McKay OPEN: all year ROOMS: 1 single, 2 double, 2 twin, 1 family; all rooms with bath/shower; TV lounge TERMS: single £25–£30; twin/

double £50–£60; children under 2 free, half-price for ages 2 to 12; dinner £14; deposit: £20 per person CARDS: Access, Visa DETAILS: children welcome; dogs by arrangement; no smoking in dining-room; car park; garden

ARISAIG   Highland   map 11

Old Library Lodge

Arisaig PH39 4NH
TEL: (01687) 450651   FAX: (01687) 450219
on A830, 7m S of Mallaig

The Old Library Lodge is firstly a licenced restaurant, serving home-cooked food using local fish, meat and game, at lunch and dinner. On fine days, visitors can sit outside with an aperitif and a menu. This converted whitewashed barn lies in the middle of the small village of Arisaig, with far-reaching views over Loch Nan Ceall to the islands of the Inner Hebrides. Two of the *en suite* bedrooms are in the main house and enjoy sea views, four more are in an extension at the back of the house. These spacious and comfortable rooms have small patios for guests to sit outside overlooking the small garden. Boats run daily from the harbour to Rhum, Eigg and Muck. Packed lunches can be provided.

OWNERS: Alan and Angela Broadhurst OPEN: Easter to end Oct ROOMS: 5 double, 1 twin; all rooms with bath/shower; TV in all bedrooms TERMS: single occupancy £42, twin/double £62; dinner £21; deposit: £20 CARDS: Access, Amex, Delta, Switch, Visa DETAILS: children welcome; no dogs; car park; garden

ASCOG   Strathclyde   map 11

Ascog Farm

Ascog, nr Rothesay, Isle of Bute PA20 9LL
TEL: (01700) 503372
3½m S of Rothesay ferry

Ascog Farm lies just south of Rothesay, a short distance from the road, with glimpses of the sea from the upper floor. It is an old, whitewashed building built around a courtyard. Most of the land is let out, but the Watsons keep a small amount to themselves for sheep, ducks, peacocks and hens. The interior is unusually furnished and decorated, with an enormous sitting-room and double bedroom covering the top floor. The shared bathroom is on the ground floor. Mrs Watson is very welcoming to her guests.

OWNER: Irene Watson OPEN: all year exc Christmas ROOMS: 1 single, 2 double; TV in some bedrooms and lounge TERMS: single/single occupancy £15; twin/double £30; children under 5 free, half-price for ages 6 to 15; deposit: £5 per person CARDS: none DETAILS: children welcome; dogs welcome; no smoking in bedrooms or dining-room; car park; garden

map 11

Ardchoille Farm

Dunshalt, Auchtermuchty KY14 7EY
TEL/FAX: (01337) 828414
from Auchtermuchty take B936 S to Dunshalt, then over bridge, first right

Ardchoille Farm has been in Donald Steven's family since the
beginning of the century, and now both he and Isobel run it as a
comfortable and welcoming guesthouse. The three small, south-
facing bedrooms, all with *en suite* facilities and many extras (such as
a supply of Isobel's home-made shortbread), also have views to the
Lomond Hills. Although all three bedrooms are twins, bunks for
children can be arranged. Four-course dinners, preceded by a glass of
sherry, are served at one convivial table in the dining-room.
Vegetarian choices are always on offer, and packed lunches are
provided by prior arrangement. Ardchoille is only a couple of miles
from Falkland Palace, and close to the Scottish Deer Centre.

OWNERS: Donald and Isobel Steven   OPEN: all year exc Christmas and New Year
ROOMS: 3 twin, all with bath/shower; TV in all bedrooms and lounge   TERMS: single
occupancy £35–£40, twin £50–£70; dinner £15 to £20; deposit: £20   CARDS: Access,
Visa   DETAILS: children welcome; no dogs; no smoking; car park; garden

 map 11

Alvie Manse

Aviemore PH22 1QB
TEL: (01479) 810248
just off B9152, 3m S of Aviemore

Alvie Manse is an attractive listed building, with a turreted entrance;
the approach is via a winding driveway shared with the church, past
a loch and through the lovely gardens of the house. The spacious
property is a mix of eighteenth- and nineteenth-century construction,
and is furnished with antiques. Rooms at the back of the house
overlook Loch Alvie and the mountains. Guests occupy the three top-
floor rooms, all sharing one pretty bathroom. Both the dining-room
and drawing-room with open fires are comfortable and attractive.
One reporter was impressed by the 'warm welcome' and 'excellent'
dinner from Helen Gillies. There is no licence, so dining guests may
bring their own wine; children's helpings and packed lunches can be
provided.

OWNERS: Helen and Jim Gillies   OPEN: all year   ROOMS: 1 single; 1 double; 1 twin, with
wash-basin; TV in all bedrooms and lounge   TERMS: single £15, single occupancy £20,
twin/double £30; dinner £15   CARDS: none   DETAILS: children welcome; no dogs; no
smoking; car park; garden

AYR   Strathclyde

Windsor Hotel

6 Alloway Place, Ayr KA7 2AA
TEL: (01292) 264689

Occupying the end position of a terrace, this Victorian hotel is a few minutes' walk from the main shopping street, bus and rail stations. It is also just two minutes' walk from beaches, and enjoys sea views from the back bedrooms and particularly the first-floor lounge. The Hamiltons are gradually doing up the hotel and have completed most of the inside work. The dining-room, in which a full Scottish breakfast and dinner are served, has a splendid old ceiling and original fireplace, and the big, solid chairs come from an old passenger liner. Three bedrooms are on the ground floor. Golfers are especially welcome, as well as visitors who have come for the well-known horse races. Children's portions are available at dinner, as are vegetarian options with prior notice. Although the Windsor is unlicensed, guests may bring their own wine. Packed lunches can be provided.

OWNERS: Mike and Anne Hamilton   OPEN: all year exc Christmas and New Year
ROOMS: 2 single, both with wash-basin; 3 double, 1 twin, 4 family, all with bath/shower; 3 rooms suitable for wheelchair-users; TV in all bedrooms and lounge   TERMS: single £20, single occupancy £28, twin/double £44, family room from £44; children under 3 free, reductions for children over 3; dinner £9; deposit: £10 per adult   CARDS: Access, Switch, Visa   DETAILS: children welcome; dogs welcome; no smoking in dining-room

BADACHRO   Highland   map 11

Harbour View

Badachro, Gairloch IV21 2AA
TEL: (01445) 741316
off B8056, on S shore of Gair Loch, 6m from Gairloch village

Originally a fisherman's cottage, this small whitewashed house stands above a narrow road with lovely views over a small bay. Harbour View is a characterful house, filled with knick-knacks, and is 'cosy and friendly' in the view of one reporter, and 'excellent value for money' according to another. Three of the bedrooms are in the main house, and there is a popular *en suite* double-room chalet at the top of the garden, which enjoys even more beautiful views than the house itself. Guests have use of a comfortable sitting-room, a sun-room and outside patio. Dinners are four courses and always include a vegetarian main-course option; guests may bring their own wine. This is a great place for walking and fishing, and all kinds of boats are available for hire. Packed lunches can be provided.

OWNERS: Liza and Graham Willey OPEN: Mar to Oct ROOMS: 3 double; 1 family; all rooms with bath/shower; TV in all bedrooms and lounge TERMS: single occupancy £19, double £38, family room from £47.50; children under 3 free, half-price for children 4 to 12, reductions for older children sharing with parents; dinner £9; deposit: 15% CARDS: none DETAILS: children welcome; no dogs in public rooms and must be on a lead; no smoking; car park; garden

BALESHARE Western Isles   map 11

Clachan Uaine

Baleshare, North Uist HS6 5HG
TEL: (01876) 580688

Clachan Uaine is on the island of Baleshare, which is connected by a causeway to North Uist. The house overlooks a small loch and is not far from white sandy beaches where otters can be spotted. Originally built as a mission house in 1907, the building was converted to a guesthouse in 1980 with three small bedrooms and a compact lounge. Breakfast and home-cooked evening meals are served in the dining-room or in the sun porch, which is particularly popular with bird-watchers. The Rankins are a friendly, caring couple and very knowledgeable about the islands. There is no alcohol licence, but guests may bring their own wine to dinner.

OWNER: Katie Rankin OPEN: all year exc Christmas ROOMS: 2 double, 1 twin; TV lounge TERMS: single occupancy £15, twin/double £30; children's reductions according to age; dinner £7 CARDS: none DETAILS: children welcome; dogs welcome; smoking in sun lounge only; car park

BALLACHULISH Highland   map 11

Ballachulish Home Farm

Ballachulish PA39 4JX
TEL: (01855) 811792
on A82 on S shore of Loch Leven

Home Farm was built in 1992 and can be found up a long driveway off the main road close to the Ballachulish Bridge. It has lovely views of hills and water, and is part of a sheep and cattle farm. The rooms are exceptionally spacious and very comfortably furnished. There is a large lounge for guests, and a dining-room where breakfast only is served.

OWNERS: Joan and Ronnie McLauchlan OPEN: all year exc Christmas ROOMS: 2 double, 1 twin; all rooms with bath/shower; TV in all bedrooms TERMS: single occupancy £25–£30; twin/double £40–£50; deposit: 20% CARDS: none DETAILS: no children; no dogs; no smoking; car park; garden

Lyn-Leven Guesthouse

West Laroch, Ballachulish, nr Fort William PA39 4JP
TEL: (01855) 811392   FAX: (01855) 811600

This modern bungalow lies just off the main road facing Loch Leven.
It makes an excellent base for hill-walking, skiing and visiting
Glencoe. The monument to the Glencoe massacre of 1692 is just two
miles away. All the bedrooms are *en suite* with TV. Guests have use of
the garden with seats in summer, a lounge and a spacious, semi-
circular dining-room with fine views. Evening meals are served here
by arrangement; there is an alcohol licence, and children's helpings
and vegetarian choices can be requested.

OWNERS: John and Priscilla MacLeod   OPEN: all year exc Christmas   ROOMS: 4 double,
3 twin, 1 family; all rooms with bath/shower; TV in all bedrooms   TERMS: single
occupancy from £20, twin/double £34–£37, family room from £43; reductions for
children under 12; dinner £9; deposit: £20 per person   CARDS: Access, Visa   DETAILS:
children welcome; dogs in bedroom only; no smoking in dining-room; car park; garden

---

BALLINLUIG   Tayside   **map 11**

Tulliemet House

Ballinluig, by Pitlochry PH9 0PA
TEL: (01796) 482419   FAX: (01796) 482617
off A9 at A827 Aberfeldy exit, then first left, first right and 1½m up hill

Tulliemet House is approached up a very long driveway and stands in
an elevated position with spectacular views over the Tay Valley. It is
part of the Atholl Estate and was built in 1820 as a hunting lodge.
Very much a family home, it has a sense of spaciousness and a happy,
informal atmosphere. There are two guest rooms, one particularly
large and facing the front; both have their own private bathrooms.
Evening meals are available, if booked in advance, and guests may
bring their own wine as there is no licence. A comfortable drawing-
room is available for guests' use. Tulliemet House is about four miles
south of the Festival Theatre in Pitlochry, and makes a very good
touring base.

OWNERS: Mr and Mrs G.K. Huggins   OPEN: all year exc sometimes closed at Christmas
ROOMS: 2 twin, both rooms with bath/shower   TERMS: single occupancy £30–£40, twin
£60; reductions for stays of 5 days or longer; dinner £15 to £18; deposit: £20   CARDS:
none   DETAILS: no children under 12; dogs allowed outside or in bedroom with own
basket; no smoking; car park; garden

---

*Many B&Bs are in remote places, and although in many cases we provide
directions, it is always advisable to ask for clear instructions when
booking.*

BALLYGRANT Strathclyde

map 11

Kilmeny Farmhouse

Ballygrant, Isle of Islay PA45 7QW
TEL: (01496) 840668
just off A846, 4m W of Port Askaig

This whitewashed farmhouse stands a little way up the hillside and has 'beautiful views down the valley', according to one reporter. Kilmeny is a working 300-acre beef farm, and the Rozgas work in co-operation with Scottish Natural Heritage to ensure geese are not disturbed while feeding on their land. Many visitors return for the comfort, friendly ambience and the very imaginative food, based mostly on local produce. One lady was particularly impressed with her 'spacious and beautifully furnished' room. Two of the bedrooms are on the ground floor; all bathrooms are *en suite*. There is a pleasant sitting-room, and the dining-room has one large, old table. Dinner is served at 7pm, vegetarians can be catered for with notice, and although Kilmeny is unlicensed guests may bring their own wine.

OWNER: Margaret Rozga OPEN: all year exc Christmas and New Year ROOMS: 2 double, 1 twin; all rooms with bath/shower; TV lounge TERMS: rates include dinner; twin/double £92–£100; deposit: £10 per person CARDS: none DETAILS: no children under 8; dogs by arrangement; no smoking; car park; garden

BALQUHIDDER Central

map 11

Calea Sona

Balquhidder, nr Lochearnhead FK19 8NY
TEL/FAX: (01877) 384260
off A84, 4m SW of Lochearnhead

This attractive small house stands in the peaceful village of Balquhidder, burial place of the outlaw Rob Roy. Rod Blain constructed Calea Sona using the stones from the ruins of an old homestead. It lies in its own grounds and has wonderful views over the valley to the hills beyond. The quiet area is wonderful for walking. The interior of the house is comfortable, and simply decorated and furnished. Breakfast only is served at a table in the front window of the owners' high-ceilinged barn-shaped sitting-room. There is a double room on the ground floor with private bathroom, and upstairs a twin bedded *en suite* room and a large sitting area for guests. Visitors get a warm welcome from Rod and Lesley. Packed lunches are provided.

OWNERS: Rod and Lesley Blain OPEN: all year exc Christmas ROOMS: 1 double, 1 twin; both rooms with bath/shower; TV lounge TERMS: single occupancy £25, twin/double £40 CARDS: none DETAILS: no children; no dogs; no smoking in bedrooms; car park; garden

Monachyle Mhor

Balquhidder, Lochearnhead FK19 8PQ
TEL: (01877) 384622   FAX: (01877) 384305
off A84, 8m SW of Lochearnhead

This charming small hotel is reached down a long, winding, narrow road which follows the entire length of Loch Voil, and is four miles from the tiny village of Balquhidder. Antique furniture and old sporting prints and pictures decorate the walls of this attractive old farmhouse. A bar and a comfortable lounge are available for guests' use, and meals are served to residents and non-residents either in the intimate dining-room with its one old refectory table, or in the adjoining conservatory. There are five bedrooms in the main house and, across the courtyard in the old stable block, a mixture of attractively furnished *en suite* bedrooms and self-catering flats. The 2,000-acre estate includes Blackface sheep and cattle, and the farm provides salmon and trout fishing, stalking and shooting.

OWNERS: Jean and Rob Lewis   OPEN: all year   ROOMS: 8 double; 2 twin; all rooms with bath/shower; TV in some bedrooms and lounge   TERMS: single occupancy £37.50, twin/double £55–£70; dinner £18 to £21; deposit: £20 or credit card number   CARDS: Access, Visa   DETAILS: no children; no dogs; smoking in bar only; car park; garden (*The Good Food Guide*)

BANFF   Grampian   **map 11**

Eden House

by Banff AB45 3NT
TEL: (01261) 821282   FAX: (01261) 821283
off A947 Aberdeen to Banff road, take left turn 5m after Turriff signposted 'Scatterty and Dunlugas', then ½m to Eden House

This spacious house with well-proportioned rooms is approached up a long, wooded driveway with spectacular views over the Deveron Valley. Parts of the house date from 1725 and the classical front with porticoed entrance was added in 1825. When the Sharps moved here from south-east England in 1988 the house was a virtual ruin, but it has now been restored and decorated with taste to provide a comfortable and friendly atmosphere. Guests have use of a large drawing-room, which features hand-painted nineteenth-century wallpaper; a smaller, cosier sitting-room; a billiard room and a basement games room. The Sharps often join their guests for dinner in the elegant dining-room, to which visitors may bring their own wine as there is no alcohol licence. There are plenty of local attractions to visit, from Eden Castle nearby to little-known fishing villages, and a little further away the whisky distilleries.

OWNERS: Mr and Mrs D.A. Sharp   OPEN: all year exc Christmas and New Year   ROOMS: 1 single, 2 double, 2 twin; all with bath/shower; TV lounge   TERMS: single/single

occupancy £34, twin/double £68; dinner £20; deposit: £10 per person   CARDS: none
DETAILS: no children under 12; dogs welcome downstairs only; smoking in one room
only; car park; games room; garden; tennis

BLAIR ATHOLL   Tayside   map 11

Woodlands

St Andrews Crescent, Blair Atholl, nr Pitlochry PH18 5SX
TEL: (01796) 481403

This rather plain little house in its own garden is in a peaceful spot on
the edge of Blair Atholl, and has views of the hills. Dolina Maclennan
has put her own mark on the refurbishment of the interior, which is
charmingly and imaginatively decorated and furnished. She splits
her time between the bed-and-breakfast business and her television
acting career. Woodlands closes when Dolina has a filming
commitment. When at home she is also a keen cook, and guests can be
assured of excellent hospitality. Dinner begins with a sherry at 7pm,
vegetarian options and children's helpings are served, and guests can
bring their own wine as there is no licence. Packed lunches are also
provided.

OWNER: Dolina Maclennan   OPEN: variable depending on owner's commitments
ROOMS: 2 double, 1 with bath/shower, 1 with wash-basin; 1 twin, with wash-basin
TERMS: single occupancy £25, twin/double £40; dinner £12.50–£17.50; deposit: £10
CARDS: none   DETAILS: half-price for children under 12; dogs welcome; no smoking in
bedrooms; car park; garden

BOAT OF GARTEN   Highland   map 11

Heathbank

Boat of Garten PH24 3BD
TEL: (01479) 831234

Heathbank dates from the turn of the century and is set back from
the road on the edge of the village. The Burges have done up what one
happy visitor called their 'delightful' house with care and attention to
period detail; all rooms are decorated in an individual style and
several retain their original cast-iron fireplaces. Two rooms have
four-poster beds, one has a sunken bath and two attic-style rooms are
on the top floor. One bedroom is on the ground floor. Graham trained
as a chef, and he and Lindsay previously ran a traditional Scottish
restaurant. A licensed conservatory dining-room extension has been
added, which contains Rennie Mackintosh-inspired furniture. From
the house are views to the golf course, the Abernethy Forest RSPB
Reserve and the Cairngorms. Packed lunches are provided.

OWNERS: Lindsay and Graham Burge   OPEN: all year exc Nov to 25 Dec   ROOMS: 2 double, 2 twin, 2 four-poster, 1 family; all rooms with bath/shower; TV lounge   TERMS: single occupancy from £23, twin/double £46–£56, four-poster £54–£66, family room from £63; half-price for children over 5 sharing with parents; dinner £16 to £18; deposit: £20 per person   CARDS: none   DETAILS: no children under 5; guide dogs only; no smoking; car park; garden

Moorfield House

Deshar Road, Boat of Garten PH24 3BN
TEL: (01479) 831646

Moorfield House has a warm and welcoming atmosphere, and the owners are cheerful and friendly. It is a comfortable Victorian house in the main street of the village next to the church. The bedrooms are simply furnished with small *en suite* shower rooms. The lounge has a dining area off it with a small bar, and good home-cooked Scottish meals are served in the evening. Boat of Garten is close to an RSPB reserve and the Cairngorm mountains, and is a good place for bird-watching and walking. A self-catering chalet is also available. Although unlicensed, guests are welcome to bring their own wine to dinner, and packed lunches can be provided.

OWNERS: Ron and Elizabeth Gould   OPEN: all year exc Christmas Day   ROOMS: 1 double, 2 twin, 1 family; all rooms with bath/shower; TV in all bedrooms and lounge   TERMS: single/single occupancy £21, twin/double £36, family room £50; reductions for children sharing with parents; dinner £10; deposit: 1 night's charge   CARDS: none   DETAILS: children welcome; no dogs to be left alone in bedrooms; no smoking; car park; garden

Old Ferryman's House

Boat of Garten PH24 3BY
TEL: (01479) 831370

This old stone-built house was until recently called Gartenmore: the change of name undoubtedly has something to do with the fact that the house was once where the ferryman lived. It lies just outside Boat of Garten, on the opposite bank of the river, and offers an atmosphere that is relaxed and welcoming. The house is TV-free, and the cosy sitting-room has a small open fire, lots of books and Indian cane furniture. Newly arrived guests are treated to a tray of home-made flapjacks and tea or coffee. The bedrooms are simply but attractively furnished, and have single beds with mattresses which can be zipped together; they share a bathroom and a toilet. Home-cooked meals are taken at one table in the dining-room, which is shared with the owner's office. Children's portions are available, as are vegetarian options by arrangement, and guests may bring their own wine.

Most guests come to bird-watch, fish, canoe, walk or take part in some other form of outdoor activity. Additionally, there are mountain bikes for hire.

OWNER: Elizabeth Matthews   OPEN: all year exc owner's holidays   ROOMS: 2 single, 1 double, 1 twin   TERMS: single/single occupancy £17, twin/double £34; half-price for children 3 to 11, one-quarter reduction for ages 12 to 16; dinner £11; deposit: 1 night's charge   CARDS: none   DETAILS: children welcome; no dogs in dining-room; no smoking; car park; garden

BRAEMAR   Grampian

map 11

Clunie Lodge

Clunie Bank Road, Braemar AB35 5YP
TEL: (01339) 741330

This large stone house on the edge of Braemar was formerly the manse. It occupies an attractive position, set in its own established gardens up a short driveway, with excellent views of river, village and Clunie Glen. There is a friendly, relaxed atmosphere, and visitors have use of a comfortable TV lounge and pine-panelled, unlicensed dining-room where evening meals are served. Children's helpings are available, and guests can bring their own wine. There is also a drying room for clothes which some find useful. Most of the simply furnished, spacious bedrooms have their own bathrooms and lovely views. Clunie Lodge is close to a golf course and the Glenshee ski slopes.

OWNERS: Roma and Jock Brown   OPEN: all year exc 2 weeks Nov, Christmas, 2 weeks Mar   ROOMS: 4 double, 3 with bath/shower, 1 with wash-basin; 3 family, 2 with bath/shower, 1 with wash-basin; TV lounge   TERMS: double £32–£36, family room £45–£55; children's reductions by arrangement; dinner £11; deposit: £10 per room   CARDS: none   DETAILS: children welcome; dogs welcome by arrangement; no smoking; car park; garden

Schiehallion House

Glenshee Road, Braemar AB35 5YQ
TEL: (01339) 741679

Only a few minutes' walk from the village centre, this traditional stone-built house has a warm and friendly atmosphere. The bedrooms are well appointed, with three in an outside annexe, and the pleasant lounge has an open fire. Breakfast and good home-cooked dinners are served in the dining-room, and packed lunches can be provided. Braemar makes a good base for fishing, skiing, walking, climbing and pony-trekking, among other activities.

OWNERS: Julie and Steven Heyes   OPEN: Jan to end Oct   ROOMS: 1 single, with wash-basin; 3 double, all with bath/shower; 1 twin, 2 family, all with wash-basin; TV lounge

TERMS: single £17.50, single occupancy £26–£36, twin/double £33–£37, family room from £39; children's reductions according to age; dinner £12.50   CARDS: Access, Visa   DETAILS: children welcome; dogs by arrangement; smoking in lounge only; car park; garden

BREASCLETE   Western Isles   map 11

Eshcol Guest House

Breasclete, Isle of Lewis HS2 9ED
TEL: (01851) 621357
on W coast of Lewis off A858, 13m W of Stornoway

This modern-looking house, an extension of an old croft, is located in a quiet position in a small weaving village within walking distance of the Callanish stones. Eshcol overlooks Loch Roag, the beautiful island of Great Bernera and the hills of Uig and Harris, and offers very comfortable accommodation and a warm welcome. It also has a reputation for good home-cooked food, and full board is available on Sundays. Packed lunches can be arranged on other days, and guests may bring their own wine to dinner. This is an excellent spot for walking, bird-watching and angling.

OWNERS: Neil and Isobel MacArthur   OPEN: Mar to Oct   ROOMS: 1 double, 2 twin; all rooms with bath/shower; TV in all bedrooms   TERMS: rates inc dinner (B&B rates can also be arranged); single occupancy £39; twin/double £78; half-price for children from 10 to 15; deposit: £20 per person   CARDS: none   DETAILS: no children under 10; dogs welcome if owner provides bed; smoking allowed in 1 area only; car park; garden

BRODICK   Strathclyde   map 11

Glencloy Farmhouse

Brodick, Isle of Arran KA27 8DA
TEL: (01770) 302351

Glencloy is a 100-year-old sandstone farmhouse set in a pretty, peaceful glen about half-a-mile down a narrow road and track from Brodick. The house has spacious rooms which have been interestingly decorated, reflecting some of Vicki Padfield's interests, which include embroidery and making doll houses. Embroidery courses are held on occasion at the house. There is a large comfortable sitting-room, with an open fire and a good selection of local guides for guests' use, and an elegant dining-room where dinner is served. Mark is an excellent chef, and meals include home-grown vegetables, free-range eggs and home-baked bread. Although unlicensed, guests may bring their own wine to dinner. Packed lunches can be provided.

OWNERS: Mark and Vicki Padfield   OPEN: Mar to 7 Nov   ROOMS: 1 single, with wash-basin; 2 double, 1 with bath/shower, 1 with wash-basin; 2 twin, 1 with bath/shower, 1 with wash-basin; TV in all bedrooms   TERMS: single £21–£25, single occupancy £35, twin/double £42–£50; 25% reductions for children 3 to 11; dinner £12.50; deposit: £15 per person CARDS: none DETAILS: no children under 3; small dogs welcome; no smoking in dining-room; car park; garden; tennis

Gowanlea

Sannox, Brodick, Isle of Arran KA27 8JD
TEL: (01770) 810253

This small, charming old whitewashed house stands just off the road between Lochranza and Brodick on the seafront overlooking the Firth of Clyde. Both sitting-room and dining-room are cosy rooms in the front of the house. June loves to cook and provides home-cooked evening meals for her guests. The simple accommodation comprises three bedrooms sharing one bathroom and one toilet. Sannox is an ideal base for fishing, golfing, walking, bird-watching and climbing. Although unlicensed, guests may bring their own wine to dinner; packed lunches can be provided.

OWNERS: June and Christopher Warburton OPEN: all year exc Christmas ROOMS: 1 twin, 2 family; TV lounge TERMS: rates include dinner; twin/double £40, family from £40; children's reductions by arrangement CARDS: none DETAILS: children welcome; no smoking in bedrooms; car park; garden

Royal Hotel

Shore Road, Whiting Bay, Brodick, Isle of Arran KA27 8PZ
TEL/FAX: (01770) 700286

Built in 1895, this sandstone property stands in its own grounds in the middle of Whiting Bay, opposite the sea front. Brenda and Brian Wilson are a charming, hospitable couple who provide an excellent service including home-cooked evening meals. The hotel is unlicensed, but guests can bring their own wine. Both the lounge and large dining-room overlook the Firth of Clyde. One of the front-facing bedrooms has its own small sitting-room, and another has a four-poster bed. There is one ground-floor room with a private bathroom, suitable for wheelchair-users; the rest of the comfortable bedrooms are on the first floor, all *en suite* with showers. In addition, one public bathroom contains a whirlpool bath, for those who prefer to have a soak after a day on the hills or golf course.

OWNERS: Mr and Mrs Brian Wilson OPEN: Mar to Nov ROOMS: 1 single, 2 double, 1 twin, 1 four-poster, 1 family; all rooms with shower; 1 room suitable for wheelchair-users; TV in all bedrooms TERMS: single/single occupancy from £22, twin/double/four-poster/family room from £44; children's reductions by arrangement; dinner £12 CARDS: none DETAILS: children welcome; no dogs in public rooms; no smoking in dining-room; car park; garden

Lynwood

Golf Road, Brora KW9 6QS
TEL/FAX: (01408) 621226
*on A9 Inverness to Wick road; in Brora turn right from S, or left from N,
into Golf road, house 250 yards on left*

Guests are made to feel very at home in this comfortable Victorian
house with its pleasant lounge and four good-sized bedrooms. Meals
are served in the conservatory, which overlooks the garden, and
guests are welcome to bring their own wine to dinner. One bedroom is
on the ground-floor and reached through the garden; this room is
particularly popular with wheelchair-users. The house stands in a
very pretty large garden, and is convenient for the nearby golf course,
beaches and Dunrobin Castle.

OWNER: Mary Cooper OPEN: all year exc Dec ROOMS: 2 double, with bath/shower; 2
twin, 1 with bath/shower, 1 with wash-basin; 1 room suitable for wheelchair-users; TV in
all bedrooms TERMS: single/single occupancy £20–£24, twin/double £32–£40; children
under 3 free, half-price for ages 3 to 12; dinner £10 to £13; deposit: £20 to £30 CARDS:
Access, Visa DETAILS: children welcome; dogs by arrangement; no smoking in
bedrooms; car park; garden

Tigh Fada

Golf Road, Brora KW9 6QS
TEL/FAX: (01408) 621332
on A9 Inverness to Wick road

This detached house on the edge of town occupies a peaceful spot,
with uninterrupted views of hills and sea. The garden is given over to
a four-hole pitch and putt course and croquet green. Through the
garden gate is a path leading down to the golf course and the sandy
beach. Two bedrooms have a private bathroom, and one *en suite* room
has its own sitting area overlooking the golf course and sea. TV is
available on request. The comfortable lounge has a large bay window
and a peat fire in cool weather; a recent addition is the sun porch.
Breakfast only is served in the dining- room, and complimentary tea
and home-baked cakes are offered each night. Brora's world-famous
woollen mill is worth a visit.

OWNERS: John and Ishbel Clarkson OPEN: all year exc Christmas and New Year
ROOMS: 1 double, 2 twin; all rooms with bath/shower TERMS: single occupancy
£16.50–£19.50, twin/double £33–£39; 20% reduction for children; deposit: £10 per
person CARDS: none DETAILS: children welcome; dogs by arrangement; no smoking;
car park; garden

If we know a B&B has an alcohol licence, we say so.

BROUGHTY FERRY Tayside   map 11

Invermark Hotel

23 Monifieth Road, Broughty Ferry DD5 2RN
TEL/FAX: (01382) 739430

This large house stands in its own grounds, just off the main A930 road from Dundee to Carnoustie, and is surrounded by a well-kept garden. The four bedrooms are all *en suite*. Books and games are provided in the spacious lounge, and breakfast only is served in the dining-room. The Invermark is only a few minutes from the shops and beach, four miles from Dundee station and about ten miles from Carnoustie. Packed lunches can be provided.

OWNER: Muriel Metcalf OPEN: all year ROOMS: 3 twin, 1 family; all rooms with bath/shower; TV in all bedrooms TERMS: single occupancy £25–£30, twin £40, family room £45–£55; children's reductions; deposit: £10 per room CARDS: Visa DETAILS: children welcome; no dogs; no smoking; car park; garden

BRUICHLADDICH Strathclyde   map 11

Anchorage

Bruichladdich, Isle of Islay PA49 7UN
TEL: (01496) 850540
take A846 to Bridgend, then A847 to Bruichladdich

This 100-year old stone-built house is opposite a pleasant sandy beach, and belongs to a delightful young couple with two small children. Anchorage is a comfortable family home with three guest bedrooms, two of which have sea views. The sitting-room is attractively furnished, with lots of books and a TV, and breakfast only is served. Islay is renowned for its whisky distilleries, and offers excellent walking, cycling and fishing.

OWNERS: Anne Macdonald OPEN: Mar to Oct ROOMS: 2 double, 1 twin; TV lounge TERMS: single/single occupancy £14–£15, twin/double £28–£30; reductions for children over 5 CARDS: none DETAILS: no children under 5; no dogs; no smoking in bedrooms; car park; garden

B&B rates specified in the details at the end of each entry are given (as applicable) for a single room, for single occupancy of a double room, and then per room in the case of two people sharing a double or twin-bedded room, or for a family room.

We welcome your feedback about B&Bs you have stayed in. Please make use of the report forms at the end of the book.

CALGARY   Strathclyde   **map 11**

Calgary Farmhouse Hotel

Calgary, nr Tobermory, Isle of Mull PA75 6QW
TEL/FAX: (01688) 400256
14m W of Tobermory

This imaginative conversion of old stone farm buildings is situated in
a sheltered valley just above the lovely beach of Calgary, considered
to be one of Mull's finest beaches. What started as a small bed-and-
breakfast in 1988 has developed into nine comfortable bedrooms, plus
a charming restaurant in what was the old dovecote, and a gallery.
This displays works of local artists for sale, including some
interesting wooden pieces, which are the creation of the owner,
Matthew Reade. The Gallery also serves snacks and lunches, and the
licensed Dovecote Restaurant, featuring local meat and fish, is also
open to non-residents. B&B guests have use of a cosy lounge with
wood-burning stove and a small TV room. All the bedrooms have
private bathrooms; three are on the ground floor.

OWNERS: Matthew and Julia Reade   OPEN: Apr to Nov   ROOMS: 1 single, 7 double, 2
twin, 2 family; all rooms with bath/shower; TV in some bedrooms and lounge   TERMS:
single £33, single occupancy £37.50, twin/double £60, family room from £60; children
under 3 free (£5 cot charge), £7.50 for ages 3 to 10, £12.50 for ages over 10; dinner £15;
deposit: 1 night's charge   CARDS: Access, Switch, Visa   DETAILS: children welcome;
dogs welcome; no smoking in restaurant; car park; garden

CALLANDER   Central   **map 11**

Leny House

Leny Estate, Callander FK17 8HA
TEL/FAX: (01877) 331078
just off A84, 1m N of Callander

Leny House, the ancestral home of the Buchanan family for 1,000
years, is set in 20 acres of parkland with views to the Trossachs. The
building, which was originally a small fortress, has been enlarged
over the centuries to its present manor-house status. It played its role
in the Jacobite Rebellion when it was used for secret meetings and
arms storage. Leny House is a family home with a friendly
atmosphere, and large, comfortably furnished rooms, including a
drawing-room. It has partial central heating. Although breakfast
only is served, the Roebucks have recently acquired the Lade Inn,
which is within sight and walking distance of the house and does bar
and restaurant meals. Several well-equipped self-catering lodges are
also available. The river is close by, as is the wild Leny Glen, where
deer graze and guests can walk. There are many local opportunities
for seasonal shooting and fishing.

OWNERS: A.F. and F. Roebuck OPEN: Easter to end Sept ROOMS: 2 twin, 1 with bath/ shower; 2 family, 1 with bath/shower; TV lounge TERMS: twin £44–£48, family room from £48; reductions for children under 12; deposit: £10 CARDS: Access, Amex, Switch, Visa DETAILS: children welcome; dogs welcome; car park; garden

CAMPBELTOWN Strathclyde

map 11

Balegreggan Country House

Balegreggan Road, Campbeltown PA28 6NN
TEL/FAX: (01586) 552062
approaching Campbeltown from the north on the A83, take the second left after the 30mph signs

Balegreggan House was built in 1861 as the Estate house. It stands in a superb position with views of hills and sea, about a half-mile up a farm track on the outskirts of Campbeltown. Halfway up the stairs is an enormous Art Nouveau stained-glass window showing a peacock in a grove of trees. The rooms, which are painted in bright, lively colours, are well-proportioned, with the front rooms having lovely views. The four spacious bedrooms are clean and comfortable, with one on the ground floor. Evening meals are served in the dining-room, which is furnished in pine, and guests also have use of a comfortable lounge. Vegetarian choices and packed lunches can be provided.

OWNERS: Morag and Bruce Urquhart OPEN: all year ROOMS: 3 double; 1 twin; all rooms with bath/shower; TV in all bedrooms TERMS: single occupancy £40–£45, twin/double £70, family room £80; children's reductions sharing with parents; dinner £17.50; deposit: £20 CARDS: Access, Visa DETAILS: children welcome; dogs welcome; no smoking; car park; garden

Sandiway

Fort Argyll Road, Campbeltown PA28 6SN
TEL: (01586) 552280

This modern bungalow, surrounded by a pretty garden with lovely roses and a patio at the back for sitting outside, has just one comfortable guest bedroom, located on the ground floor. The house is in a quiet residential area on the edge of town, and close to the north side of Campbeltown Loch. The Bells are a musical family, and there is a piano in the lounge. Home-cooked evening meals are available by arrangement, and guests may bring their own wine.

OWNERS: Mr and Mrs G. Bell OPEN: all year exc Christmas ROOMS: 1 twin, with wash-basin and WC; TV in bedroom and lounge TERMS: single occupancy £19, twin £31–£33; dinner £9 CARDS: none DETAILS: no children; no dogs; no smoking; car park; garden

CARDROSS   Strathclyde

map 11

Kirkton House

Darleith Road, Cardross G82 5EZ
TEL: (01389) 841951   FAX: (01389) 841868

This late-eighteenth-century converted farm stands in a lovely
position just above Cardross, overlooking the Clyde. Subsequent
alterations to the building have given it a more modern appearance.
Built around a pretty courtyard, full of flowers in summer and with
garden furniture for guests' use, the house has been completely
redecorated and refurbished inside. Two of the bedrooms are on the
ground floor, and the two attic-type rooms on the second floor have
skylights. Home-cooked meals are served in the large dining-room/
lounge, which has stone walls and old fireplaces at each end. There is
a large garden and paddock, with pony rides for children. Packed
lunches can be provided.

OWNERS: Stewart and Gillian Macdonald   OPEN: all year exc Christmas and New Year
ROOMS: 2 twin, 4 family; all rooms with bath/shower; 1 room suitable for wheelchair-
users; TV in all bedrooms   TERMS: single occupancy £38, twin/double £52–£59, family
room from £62; children £10 in family room; dinner £18; deposit: £20 per adult   CARDS:
Access, Amex, Delta, Visa   DETAILS: children welcome; dogs welcome; car park;
garden

CARRADALE   Strathclyde

map 11

Dunvalanree Guest House

Port Righ Bay, Carradale PA28 6SE
TEL: (01583) 431226   FAX: (01583) 431339
off B842, 1½m E of Dippen

Built as a guesthouse in 1938, this substantial three-storey building
stands right at the end of the village of Carradale in a lovely position.
Kilbrannan Sound and the island of Arran are to the front, and
Carradale Bay is to the rear, giving most rooms a sea view. On fine
days guests may sit in the sheltered front garden. Dunvalanree has
stained-glass windows, a comfortable lounge with a log fire and a
dining-room where evening meals are served by arrangement; it is
licensed for guests, and vegetarian options are available. The Pryors
are friendly, hospitable hosts, and most of their business comes from
repeat visitors. Packed lunches can be provided. Nearby are a nature
reserve and a golf course, and the area is a good centre for walking,
pony trekking and sea and river fishing.

OWNERS: John and Sue Pryor   OPEN: end Mar to mid-Oct   ROOMS: 3 single, 4 double, 2
twin, 3 family; all rooms with wash-basin; TV lounge   TERMS: single/single occupancy
£18, twin/double £36, family room from £36; children under 2 free; half-price for ages 2
to 7; 25% reduction for ages 8 to 13; dinner £10; deposit: 10%   CARDS: none   DETAILS:
children welcome; no dogs in public areas; no smoking in dining-room; car park; garden

CARRBRIDGE   Highland
map 11

Féith Mho'r Country House

Station Road, Carrbridge PH23 3AP
TEL: (01479) 841621
1¼m from village centre

Set in 1½ acres of its own well-maintained gardens, this small
Victorian country house has views of mountains and hills in all
directions. The setting is peaceful, and guests may sit out in the
partially walled garden when the weather is fine. Breakfast and
dinner are served in the large dining-room, and pre-dinner drinks
may be enjoyed in the pleasant lounge, which in winter has a log fire.
Vegetarian options at dinner are readily provided with advance
notice. The six bedrooms, one of which is on the ground floor, are
comfortably appointed. Penny Rawson is an artist, and some of the
pictures displayed in the house are for sale. Carrbridge is a good
centre for walking, skiing, bird-watching and golf.

OWNERS: Peter and Penny Rawson   OPEN: all year exc 26 Dec to 1 Jan   ROOMS: 2
double, 3 twin, 1 family; all bedrooms with bath/shower; TV in all bedrooms   TERMS:
single occupancy £23, twin/double £46, family room from £61; reductions for children
over 10 sharing with parents; dinner £12   CARDS: none   DETAILS: no children under 10;
no dogs in public rooms; no smoking in dining-room or lounge; car park; garden

CASTLEBAY   Western Isles
map 11

Terra Nova

Nasg, Castlebay, Isle of Barra HS9 5XN
TEL: (01871) 810458

Convenient for the ferry from Oban, Terra Nova is a well-kept family
home on the shore just outside the village. The Galbraiths, who are a
friendly couple, were born in Barra and had the house built about
fifteen years ago. Two of the three ground-floor guest bedrooms
overlook the sea and the large, pleasant lounge/dining-room also has
views of the water. Breakfast only is served.

OWNERS: Mr and Mrs Galbraith   OPEN: April to end Oct   ROOMS: 1 double, 1 twin, 1
family; TV in some bedrooms and lounge   TERMS: single occupancy £17.50, twin/
double £35, family room from £43.50; half-price for children under 14   CARDS: none
DETAILS: children welcome; dogs welcome; car park; garden

*If there are reduced rates for children, this is mentioned in the details at
the end of the entry. If no reductions are specified, assume you will have to
pay full rates for children.*

Tigh-na-Mara

Castlebay, Isle of Barra H59 5XD
TEL: (01871) 810304
turn left from top of road at ferry terminal; house is across road on right

This attractive old stone building looks across the bay to an old castle, standing on a rock, which can be visited during the summer months. The comfortable house has a small lounge, and two of the five bedrooms face the front. Both breakfast and evening meals are available, and guests are welcome to bring their own wine to dinner; packed lunches can also be provided. Barra can be reached by ferry from Oban, or by air from Glasgow. Planes land on the beautiful expanses of Traigh Mhor, Barra's largest beach, at low tide.

OWNERS: Linda and Archie Maclean OPEN: Apr to Oct ROOMS: 2 single, 1 double, 2 twin; all with bath/shower; TV in all bedrooms and lounge TERMS: single £16, single occupancy £19, twin/double £32; half-price for children under 13 CARDS: none
DETAILS: children welcome; no dogs; no smoking in bedrooms; car park; garden

---

CLACHAN Strathclyde **map 11**

Clachan Beag

Clachan Bridge, nr Kilninver, Oban PA34 4RH
TEL/FAX: (01852) 300381
on B844, 4m SW of Kilninver, before Atlantic Bridge

This delightful small country house is set above the narrow road leading to the Isle of Seil and enjoys spectacular views down the Clachan Sound as far as the islands of Scarba and Jura. Clachan Beag is a comfortable family home built during the last World War, and set in a lovely garden. The Tindals are long-time hoteliers, so guests can be assured of hospitality. The house has been attractively furnished and decorated, two of the bedrooms have views, and the third is on the ground floor with its own door out to the garden. There are two sitting-rooms, one with TV, and an attractive licensed dining-room, where evening meals are served if arranged in advance. Jane Tindal is an enthusiastic cook who specialises in local sea food. Alternatively, just five minutes' walk across the bridge is the Tigh an Truish Inn, which serves bar food.

OWNERS: Colin and Jane Tindal OPEN: all year exc Christmas and New Year ROOMS: 1 double, with bath/shower; 2 twin, 1 with bath/shower, 1 with wash-basin; TV lounge
TERMS: single occupancy £28, twin/double £50; children's reductions according to age; dinner £18 CARDS: Access, Visa DETAILS: children welcome; no dogs; no smoking in bedrooms; car park; garden

CLADDACH KIRKIBOST   Western Isles   map 11

Sealladh Traigh

Claddach Kirkibost, North Uist HS6 5EP
TEL: (01876) 580248   FAX: (01876) 510257
off Clachan to Bayhead road, 2½m N of Clachan, close to Westford Inn

With lovely views to Kirkibost Island, this modern house is close to the wonderful sandy beaches of North Uist. The Quarms are friendly, local people always willing to give advice and helpful tips. They have undertaken a number of commitments on the island, including owning the next-door stone-built pub (a lively place on Saturday nights), and successfully running the Lochmaddy Hotel; they now run the Bayhead shop. The bedrooms are small and bright, and good home-cooked dinners are served at the dining-table in the pleasant lounge. As there is no licence, guests are welcome to bring their own wine to dinner; packed lunches can be provided.

OWNERS: Mr and Mrs W.J. Quarm   OPEN: all year   ROOMS: 2 single, 2 double, 1 twin; all with wash-basin; TV in all bedrooms and lounge   TERMS: single £17, twin/double £34; half-price for children under 14; dinner £10   CARDS: Access, Visa   DETAILS: children welcome; car park; garden

CONNEL   Strathclyde   map 11

Ronebhal Guest House

Connel, by Oban PA37 1PJ
TEL: (01631) 710310
on A85 Glasgow to Oban road

This well-kept Victorian house has a warm atmosphere, and the Strachans are a friendly couple offering excellent service to their guests. Ronebhal stands above the main road on the edge of Connel, overlooking the mouth of Loch Etive and the Morvern hills. The bedrooms are spacious and well furnished, and have their own bathrooms. The twin-bedded room is on the ground floor. Both the comfortable lounge and dining-room, with individual tables, enjoy the view, and good home-cooked evening meals are available by arrangement. There is no alcohol licence, but visitors are welcome to bring their own wine to dinner. The guesthouse is just five miles from Oban.

OWNERS: Robert and Shirley Strachan   OPEN: Mar to mid-Oct   ROOMS: 1 single, 3 double, 1 twin, 1 family; all rooms with bath/shower; TV in all bedrooms   TERMS: single £17–£22.50, single occupancy £20–£40, twin/double £35–£55, family room £45–£65; children's reductions by arrangement; dinner £11; deposit: £10 per booking   CARDS: Access, Visa   DETAILS: no children under 5; no dogs; no smoking; car park; garden

CORRIECRAVIE Strathclyde   map 11

Rosebank Farm

Corriecravie, nr Blackwaterfoot, Isle of Arran KA27 8PD
TEL: (01770) 870228
on A841, 3m SE of Blackwaterfoot

Rosebank stands above the road on the south-western part of the
island with good sea views. It is a small whitewashed building,
combining both a small petrol station and sheep farm. The
accommodation is simple, the welcome warm. There is a log fire in the
TV lounge, and breakfast only is taken in the long sun porch built on
to the front of the house, which enjoys views of the Kilbrannan Sound
and – on a fine day – the Antrim Hills of Northern Ireland.

OWNERS: Robert and Pat Adamson OPEN: all year exc Christmas ROOMS: 1 single,
with wash-basin; 2 double, 1 with bath/shower, 1 with wash-basin; 1 twin, with wash-
basin; TV lounge TERMS: single £15, single occupancy £17, twin/double £30–£34,
family room £35; children's reductions according to age CARDS: none DETAILS:
children welcome; no dogs in lounge or dining-room; car park; garden

CRAIGNURE Strathclyde   map 11

Inverlussa

by Craignure, Isle of Mull PA65 6BD
TEL/FAX: (01680) 812436
on A849, 6m S of Craignure ferry

The Wilsons built Inverlussa in 1989 both as a family home and for
bed-and-breakfast guests. It is an attractive house set beside a
stream in peaceful countryside. Helen Wilson is a most welcoming
and hospitable host, and the house has a warm and friendly
atmosphere. The comfortable rooms are simply decorated and an
excellent breakfast is served. Packed lunches can be provided.

OWNER: Helen Wilson OPEN: Apr to Oct ROOMS: 1 single; 2 double, 1 with bath/
shower; 2 twin; 1 family; TV lounge TERMS: single/single occupancy £16, twin/double
£32, family room £40; half-price for children under 10; deposit CARDS: none DETAILS:
children welcome; dogs welcome; car park; garden

CRAIL Fife   map 11

Selcraig House

47 Nethergate, Crail KY10 3TX
TEL: (01333) 450697

This 200-year-old stone house has a warm and relaxing atmosphere.
Margaret Carstairs has decorated it with an Edwardian theme, and
has continued to make improvements to the property. Dinner is

served in a pretty ground-floor dining-room, and although there is no licence, guests may bring their own wine. Two of the well-equipped bedrooms are on the first floor and are quite spacious, while the top-floor bedrooms are very small, with no central heating (just convector heaters), with two having a sea view. Although bedrooms do not have their own bathrooms, the shared ones are pleasant. One couple were very pleased with the four-poster room, and their 'excellent' breakfast (served in the conservatory). There is a sitting-room, and at the back of the house a small garden with an area for sitting out. Selcraig House stands right in the middle of Crail, close to the picturesque harbour and beaches.

OWNER: Margaret Carstairs OPEN: all year ROOMS: 1 double, 2 twin, 1 four-poster, 1 family; all rooms with wash-basin; TV in all bedrooms and lounge TERMS: single occupancy £21, twin/double £32–£36, four-poster £38, family room from £34; children under 2 free, half-price for children under 10 sharing with parents; dinner £12; deposit: £10 CARDS: none DETAILS: children welcome; dogs welcome exc in dining-room and lounge; no smoking; garden

---

CRIANLARICH Central   **map 11**

Ewich Farmhouse

Strathfillan, Crianlarich FK20 8RU
TEL: (01838) 300300

This rather austere stone-built building lies just off the main Crianlarich to Tyndrum road in an isolated position. It was originally an old farmhouse, with the living area in the middle and barns for the animals at each end. The Walkers bought Ewich in 1994, when Ian retired from the army, and completed the renovation work started by the previous owner. All the bedrooms are on the first floor and are simply decorated and furnished – one has a pleasant view of the hills. The small lounge has an open fire and meals are taken at one table in the dining-room. The West Highland Way runs along the opposite side of the road.

OWNERS: Ian and Jean Walker OPEN: all year ROOMS: 2 double, 3 twin; all rooms with bath/shower; TV in all bedrooms TERMS: single/single occupancy £20–£25, twin/double £40–£50; reductions for children under 5; dinner £12; deposit: 20% CARDS: Access, Delta, Visa DETAILS: children welcome; no dogs; smoking in guest lounge only; car park; garden

---

It is always best to book a room in advance, even in winter. B&Bs with few rooms may close at short notice for periods not specified in the details.

Bath / shower in the details under each entry means that the rooms have private facilities. The B&B may have other, shared bathroom facilities as well. We say if rooms have wash-basins.

Briardale House

17 Haugh Road, Dalbeattie DG5 4AR
TEL: (01556) 611468
on B794 on outskirts of Dalbeattie

This solid, granite-built Victorian house stands in its own garden on
the edge of town, with pleasant views of the countryside. Briardale is
a comfortable home retaining many period features, such as
decorative cornices, wooden doors and staircase, and tiled fireplaces.
The three spacious bedrooms are attractively furnished and equipped
with every possible requisite. Dinner by arrangement (vegetarian
and special diets can be catered for, and guests can bring their own
wine) and breakfast are served at individual tables in the dining-
room, off which is a large conservatory with comfortable chairs. There
is also a lounge with (in winter) an open fire, and a patio area outside.
Bicycles for guests' use are free of charge; packed lunches are
provided.

OWNER: Verna Woodworth   OPEN: Jan to end Oct   ROOMS: 2 double, 1 twin; all rooms
with bath/shower; TV in all rooms   TERMS: twin/double £38; half-price for children
sharing with parents; dinner £11; children's helpings on request; deposit: £20 per
person   CARDS: none   DETAILS: children welcome; no dogs in public rooms; smoking in
bedrooms only; car park; garden

DALMALLY   Strathclyde   map 11

Orchy Bank

Orchy Bank, Dalmally PA33 1AS
TEL: (01838) 200370
on B8077, just N of junction with A85

This attractive guesthouse lies beside an eighteenth-century stone
bridge on the banks of the River Orchy. It stands just off the quiet
Stronmilchan road, and its garden stretches down to the river. Inside,
the atmosphere is pleasantly informal. All bedrooms except one have
views of the river, and the very large, warm lounge has a wood-
burning stove, as well as a piano which guests may use. The
guesthouse is licensed, and evening meals, which include vegetarian
options, are served by arrangement in the dining-room. This is a good
base for bird-watching, hill walking and fishing. Packed lunches can
be provided. There is no central heating.

OWNERS: Jinty and John Burke   OPEN: all year exc Christmas and New Year   ROOMS: 2
single, 2 double, 2 twin, 2 family; all rooms with wash-basin; TV lounge   TERMS: single
£16–£18, single occupancy £24–£26, twin/double £32–£36, family room from £40;
half-price for children under 11; dinner £9 to £10; deposit: £10   CARDS: none   DETAILS:
children welcome; dogs welcome; no smoking in dining-room; car park; garden

Daviot Mains Farm

Daviot, nr Inverness IV1 2ER
TEL/FAX: (01463) 772215
just off A9, 5m S of Inverness; take B851 signposted Croy for ¾m

Dating from the nineteenth century, Daviot Mains Farm is built
around a courtyard, the house part occupying most of one side with
old farm buildings making up the rest. It is still a working farm,
taking in some 350 acres of sheep, cattle, goats and barley. The
homely bedrooms are reached up a steep, central stairway, and there
is a TV lounge and cosy dining-room, warmed by a wood-burning
stove. The bedrooms are heated by convector heaters, while the public
rooms have radiators. Dinners are served if arranged in advance, and
guests can bring their own wine as there is no licence. Children's
helpings and packed lunches are available. The farm is only a few
miles from Culloden Moor, site of the famous battle of 1746.

OWNERS: Alex and Margaret Hutcheson   OPEN: all year exc 24 and 25 Dec   ROOMS: 1
double, with bath/shower; 1 twin, with bath/shower; 1 family, with wash-basin; TV
lounge   TERMS: single occupancy £16–£28, twin/double £32–£44, family room from
£32; children's reductions sharing with parents; dinner £10–£12; deposit: 30% or credit
card number   CARDS: Access, Delta, Visa   DETAILS: children welcome; dogs by
arrangement; no smoking; car park; garden

Lochend Farm

Carronbridge, Denny FK6 5JJ
TEL: (01324) 822778
off B818, 5m W of Denny

This low, stone-built eighteenth-century house along with its farm
buildings forms a courtyard with a very colourful garden in its centre.
Lockend is a working sheep farm that sits on top of a small rise: there
are marvellous views in all directions over more than 700 acres of
grazing sheep to hills, moorland and across Loch Coulter. The two
comfortable first-floor bedrooms share a bathroom, and downstairs is
a pleasant TV lounge. Breakfast only is served.

OWNERS: Andrew and Jean Morton   OPEN: Easter to Oct, or by arrangement   ROOMS: 1
double, 1 twin, both with wash-basin; TV lounge   TERMS: single occupancy from
£16.50, twin/double from £33; deposit: £10   CARDS: none   DETAILS: no children under
3; no dogs; car park; garden

Recommendations for B&Bs for our next edition are very welcome.

The Topps

Topps Farm, Fintry Road, Denny FK6 5JF
TEL: (01324) 822471   FAX: (01324) 823099
on B818, 2m W of Denny

The Topps is a working farm specialising in sheep and cashmere goats, with spectacular views of open countryside. What started as a small house has gradually been extended, and there are now eight purpose-built, chalet- style bedrooms, all on the ground floor, with the Rowan room suitable for disabled visitors. The Steels are a welcoming couple, and create an informal, relaxed atmosphere. There is one large room that accommodates a comfortable sitting area at one end and, at the other, a licensed dining area. This part, which takes advantage of the views, is also open to non-residents. Jennifer uses locally- and home-grown food in her mostly Scottish menus; children's helpings, vegetarian and special diets can be catered for with notice. Fishing on the River Carron is possible from the farm.

OWNER: Jennifer Steel   OPEN: all year   ROOMS: 1 single, 3 double, 3 twin, 1 family, all with bath/shower exc 1 double (with wash-basin); 1 room suitable for wheelchair-users; TV in all bedrooms   TERMS: single/single occupancy from £25, twin/double from £38, family room from £50; dinner £12; deposit: £10 per person   CARDS: Access, Visa   DETAILS: children welcome; dogs by arrangement; no smoking; car park; garden

---

DERVAIG   Strathclyde   **map 11**

Ardrioch Farm Guest House

Dervaig, Isle of Mull PA75 6QR
TEL/FAX: (01688) 400264
1m W of Dervaig on Calgary road

This small farm a mile from Dervaig extends to 70 acres and supports a herd of cows, Cheviot sheep, a pony, collies and cats. The approach to this cedar bungalow gives no impression of the charm of the interior, which is warm and cosy (despite not having full central heating). The comfortable, wood-panelled sitting-room is well supplied with books, maps and games, and the five small bedrooms are furnished in pine. Apart from running the farm and guesthouse, the owners organise boat trips around smaller islands; their Shetland skiff and Orkney ketch are kept nearby at the natural harbour of Croig. Jeremy Matthew is also a folk musician, while Jenny Matthew is an imaginative cook who prepares home-cooked evening meals using local produce. Children's helpings are served and, as there is no licence, guests can bring their own wine.

OWNERS: Jenny and Jeremy Matthew   OPEN: Easter to mid-Oct   ROOMS: 1 single, with wash-basin; 2 double, 1 with bath/shower, 1 with wash-basin; 2 twin, 1 with bath/shower, 1 with wash-basin; TV lounge   TERMS: single £18, single occupancy £20.50, twin/double £36–£41; £4 reduction for children over 5; dinner £11.50; deposit: £10–£20   CARDS: none   DETAILS: no children under 5; no dogs; no smoking; car park; garden

DORNOCH Highland

map 11

Trevose Guest House

Cathedral Square, Dornoch IV25 3SD
TEL: (01862) 810269

The Trevose Guest House stands in the middle of Dornoch, almost next to the cathedral and overlooking the tree-lined village green. Built in 1830, this sandstone building is set in a colourful garden. The Mackenzies are a friendly, hospitable couple, and the house is warm and comfortable, with a pleasant lounge. The guesthouse is licensed and the cosy dining-room has a small bar in one corner.

OWNERS: Donald and Jean A. Mackenzie OPEN: Mar to mid-Oct ROOMS: 1 single, with wash-basin; 1 double, with wash-basin; 1 twin, with WC; 2 family, both with bath/ shower; TV in some bedrooms and lounge TERMS: single £15.50, single occupancy £21, twin/double £31–£35, family room from £37; children under 5 free, half-price for children sharing with parents; deposit: £15 per room CARDS: none DETAILS: children welcome; dogs welcome but must not be left unattended; smoking in lounge only; garden

DRUMNADROCHIT Highland

map 11

Glenkirk

Drumnadrochit, Loch Ness IV3 6TZ
TEL: (01456) 450802
off A82 Inverness to Fort William road, take the A831 (Cannick road) in Drumnadrochit

This attractive and unusual building is a cleverly converted old chapel and has been simply furnished, mostly in pine. The guests' lounge is on a half-landing and is a light, bright room that retains the original large chapel window. The small first-floor bedrooms all have skylights and share a bathroom and shower room between them. The breakfast room is located on the ground floor, and informative brochures of the area are laid out on an old pew in the hall for guests to browse through. Packed lunches can be provided.

OWNERS: Ross and Fiona Urquhart OPEN: all year exc 10 Jan to 20 Feb ROOMS: 2 double, 1 twin, 1 family; all rooms with wash-basins only; TV lounge TERMS: single occupancy £21, twin/double £30, family room £30–£50; children under 2 free, half-price for ages 3 to 10, £10 for ages 10 to 14 CARDS: none DETAILS: children welcome; no dogs; smoking in lounge only; car park; garden

If you intend to spend several days at a B&B, it is worth asking whether there are reduced rates, particularly if the period is midweek or off-season.

DRYMEN   Central   map 11

Dunleen

Milton of Buchanan, Drymen G63 0JE
TEL: (01360) 870274

This modern bungalow is in a very attractive setting beside a pretty
stream, only about a mile from Loch Lomond and a mile-and-a-half
from the West Highland Way. The large lounge incorporates the
breakfast room, where breakfast only is served, and has windows
overlooking the stream and fields of sheep. The bedrooms are
comfortably furnished and spotlessly clean.

OWNERS: Mr and Mrs D. Macfadyen   OPEN: May to Oct   ROOMS: 1 double; 1 twin; both
rooms with wash-basin; TV lounge   TERMS: single occupancy £20, twin/double
£32–£33; babies free, half-price for children sharing with parents; deposit: £5   CARDS:
none   DETAILS: children welcome; no dogs; smoking in lounge only; car park; garden

DUNSYRE   Strathclyde   map 11

Dunsyre Mains

Dunsyre, nr Carnwath ML11 8NQ
TEL: (01899) 810251
off A721 / A702, 6m E of Carnwath

Dunsyre Mains is an attractive eighteenth-century stone building
standing just above the tiny village of Dunsyre. All around is
beautiful countryside of rolling hills; guests can fish in the nearby
stream. The simple farmhouse has a friendly atmosphere, and offers
three large, comfortable bedrooms, a TV lounge and a dining-room.
Evening meals are served by arrangement, children's helpings are
provided, and although there is no licence guests may bring their own
wine. The house is part of a 400-acre beef and sheep farm with a
pretty farmyard and colourful flowers and plants. Edinburgh and the
Borders are within easy reach; packed lunches are provided.

OWNER: Mrs Armstrong   OPEN: all year   ROOMS: 1 double, 1 twin, 1 family; all rooms
with wash-basin; TV lounge   TERMS: single occupancy £16, twin/double £32, family
room from £32; children's reductions by arrangement; dinner £9   CARDS: none
DETAILS: children welcome; dogs welcome; smoking in sitting-room only; car park;
garden

*Please let us know if you think a B&B should be included in this Guide.
Report forms are at the back of the book – or use your own stationery if you
prefer (no stamps are needed within the UK).*

Balmoral Guest House

32 Pilrig Street, Edinburgh EH6 5AL
TEL: (0131) 554 1857

This small, terraced guesthouse has a friendly, pleasant atmosphere, and although the amenities are fairly basic the simply furnished bedrooms are immaculately clean. The MacKenzies are experts on what to see in Edinburgh, and are only too happy to make recommendations. Breakfast only is served in the attractive dining-room with its tartan carpet. The Balmoral is close to the City centre and on a main bus route. Although there is no car park, unrestricted street parking is nearby.

OWNERS: Alex and Margaret MacKenzie   OPEN: all year   ROOMS: 1 single, 1 double, 3 twin, 2 family; all with wash-basin; TV lounge   TERMS: single £17–£19, single occupancy £20–£22, twin/double £34–£38, family room £34–£38; children's reductions; deposit: £10   CARDS: none   DETAILS: children welcome; dogs welcome; no smoking in dining-room

Bonnington Guest House

202 Ferry Road, Edinburgh EH6 4NW
TEL: (0131) 554 7610

This listed Victorian house not far from the docks is set back a little from the main road on the north side of Edinburgh. The city centre can be reached in ten minutes by bus. Four of the six bedrooms are *en suite* and have been comfortably furnished. The guest lounge has a piano, and breakfast only is served. Packed lunches can be provided on request.

OWNERS: Eileen and David Watt   OPEN: all year exc Christmas   ROOMS: 3 double, 2 with bath/shower, 1 with wash-basin; 1 twin, with wash-basin; 2 family, both with bath/shower; TV in all bedrooms and lounge   TERMS: single occupancy £30–£40, twin/double £36–£52, family room £50–£65; children under 3 free, half-price for children over 3; deposit: 1 night's charge   CARDS: none   DETAILS: children welcome; small dogs welcome; smoking in lounge only; car park

Classic House

50 Mayfield Road, Edinburgh EH9 2NH
TEL: (0131) 667 5847   FAX: (0131) 662 1016

This comfortable and professionally run guesthouse lies on a main road and bus route, with easy access to the city centre. It is a small, terraced Victorian house offering a high standard of accommodation.

The attractive breakfast room has individual tables, and dinner can be provided on request. Packed lunches are also available.

OWNER: Margaret Ismail OPEN: all year ROOMS: 1 single, 2 double, 1 twin, 2 family; TV in all rooms and lounge TERMS: single £25, single occupancy £40, twin/double £56, family room £56; reductions for children under 12 sharing with parents CARDS: Access, Visa DETAILS: children welcome; no dogs; no smoking

Craigelachie Hotel

21 Murrayfield Avenue, Edinburgh EH12 6AU
TEL: (0131) 337 4076 and 2619

A spacious, terraced Victorian building, Craigelachie Hotel is in a quiet tree-lined residential street not far from the city centre. Max and Jean Cruickshank are friendly, welcoming people and keep an immaculately clean house. It is simply furnished, with various-sized bedrooms and a pleasant dining-room, where breakfast only is served. Guests have use of a first-floor lounge. Craigelachie has gardens both to the front and rear, and lies close to a bus route.

OWNERS: Max and Jean Cruickshank OPEN: all year exc Christmas ROOMS: 1 single, 1 double, 2 twin, 3 family; all with wash-basin; TV in all bedrooms TERMS: single £21–£25, twin/double £36–£45, family room from £46.50; £10.50 for children ages 5 to 9, £12 for ages 10 to 13; deposit: 1 night's charge CARDS: none DETAILS: no children under 5; dogs by arrangement; smoking in hall and lounge only; car park

Highland Park Guest House

16 Kilmaurs Terrace, Edinburgh EH16 5DR
TEL: (0131) 667 9204

Highland Park is an attractive terraced house, with a neatly kept small front garden, on a quiet side street about a mile from the centre of Edinburgh. It is well served by buses, and the Royal Commonwealth Pool is only five minutes' walk away. The large, well-proportioned bedrooms and the public areas have been tastefully decorated. There is a small sitting area at one end of the breakfast room.

OWNER: Catherine Kelly OPEN: all year exc Christmas ROOMS: 2 single, 2 twin, 2 family; all rooms with wash-basin; TV in all bedrooms TERMS: single £14–£20, twin £28–£40, family from £42 CARDS: none DETAILS: children welcome; no dogs; no smoking in public areas

Please let us know if an establishment has changed hands.

Hopetoun Guest House

15 Mayfield Road, Edinburgh EH9 2NG
TEL: (0131) 677 7691

Rhoda Mitchell runs a clean, bright guesthouse, and visitors can be assured of personal attention. Hopetoun is a small, terraced Victorian property on a main road and bus route in a pleasant residential area, with easy access to the centre of Edinburgh. The bedrooms are spacious and comfortable, with two on the first floor and one on the second; they share two bathrooms. The breakfast room is at the rear of the house.

OWNER: Rhoda Mitchell OPEN: all year exc Christmas ROOMS: 1 double, 2 family; all rooms with bath/shower; TV in all bedrooms and lounge TERMS: single occupancy £20–£25, double £32–£44, family room £50–£65; reductions for children under 12 CARDS: none DETAILS: children welcome; no dogs; no smoking; car park

17 Abercromby Place

17 Abercromby Place, Edinburgh EH3 6LB
TEL: (0131) 557 8036   FAX: (0131) 558 3453

The Smiths moved to this larger house from their former premises in Northumberland Street in 1994. Eirlys has once again created a charming and elegantly comfortable house. The property is a listed Georgian house which was formerly the home of a famous Edinburgh architect, William Playfair, and is located conveniently in the heart of the New Town district. The attractively decorated bedrooms have good-sized bathrooms and are mainly to be found on the lower level; two favourites, however, are on the upper floor of the old mews house at the back of the main house. Breakfast is served in a smart dining-room and there is also a cosy sitting-room. An added bonus is the off-street parking at the rear of the property.

OWNER: Eirlys Smith OPEN: all year exc Christmas ROOMS: 2 single, 2 double, 2 twin; all rooms with bath/shower; TV in all bedrooms TERMS: single £35, single occupancy £45–£60, twin/double £70; children's reductions when sharing with parents; deposit: 1 night's charge CARDS: Visa DETAILS: children welcome; no dogs; no smoking; car park

Sibbet House

26 Northumberland Street, Edinburgh EH3 6LS
TEL: (0131) 556 1078   FAX: (0131) 557 9445

This elegant Georgian terraced house, built in 1809, is in the heart of Edinburgh's New Town. The Sibbets are a characterful couple who continue to maintain a very high standard, and the house is beautifully decorated and furnished. The comfortable bedrooms are reached by a unique hanging staircase crowned by a cupola – and one

has a four-poster bed. There is a formal drawing-room, and breakf₁
is taken at one end of a large dining-room. A few streets away is a
spacious self-catering flat which is excellent value and ideal for four
or six people travelling together. Sibbet House is only a ten-minute
walk from Princes Street.

OWNER: Aurora Sibbet   OPEN: all year exc Christmas   ROOMS: 1 double, 1 twin, 1 four-
poster, 1 family; all rooms with bath/shower; TV in all bedrooms and lounge   TERMS:
single occupancy £45–£55, twin/double £60–£70, four poster £70, family room from
£70; £15 for children under 14 sharing with parents; deposit: 1 night's charge   CARDS:
Access, Visa   DETAILS: children welcome; no dogs; no smoking; car park (2 spaces
only)

Sonas Guest House

3 East Mayfield, Edinburgh EH9 1SD
TEL: (0131) 667 2781   FAX: (0131) 667 0454

Guests can be assured of a warm welcome at this small guesthouse in
a quiet residential street. Built in 1876 for a director of the railway,
the property is about a mile south of the city centre. The breakfast/
sitting-room is on the ground floor, and the small, bright, well-
equipped bedrooms all have *en suite* facilities. There is a small car
park where guests can leave their cars and take the bus into town.

OWNERS: Irene and Dennis Robins   OPEN: all year exc Christmas   ROOMS: 1 single, 3
double, 2 twin, 2 family; all rooms with bath/shower; TV in all bedrooms and lounge
TERMS: single/single occupancy £25–£30, twin/double £40–£60, family room from £50;
children under 2 free, half-price under 12; deposit: required if arriving after 5pm   CARDS:
none   DETAILS: children welcome; dogs welcome; car park

The Town House

65 Gilmore Place, Edinburgh EH3 9NU
TEL: (0131) 229 1985

The Town House was built in 1876 as the manse for the adjoining
church and is only a ten to fifteen minute walk to Princes Street. The
Virtues have lived here for several years and offer comfortable
accommodation in a house which has been attractively decorated and
retains several of its original architectural features. All the double
bedrooms have *en suite* facilities, while the single has sole use of the
adjacent Victorian bathroom. Breakfast only is served. Limited car
parking is available at the rear of the house and should be reserved in
advance.

OWNER: Susan Virtue   OPEN: all year exc Christmas   ROOMS: 1 single, 2 double, 2 twin;
all rooms with bath/shower; TV in all bedrooms and lounge   TERMS: single £22–£30,

5, twin/double £44–£60; reductions for children over 8; deposit: 1
S: none DETAILS: no children under 8; no dogs; no smoking; car

Turret Guest House

8 Kilmaurs Terrace, Edinburgh EH16 5DR
TEL: (0131) 667 6704   FAX: (0131) 668 1368

Visitors can be sure of a warm welcome from Mrs Cameron at this
comfortable and immaculately clean guesthouse. The mid-terrace
Victorian villa is in a quiet road near a bus stop and with easy access
to the city centre. The wide, wooden staircase leads to a minstrels'
gallery. Bedrooms come in a variety of sizes and are prettily
decorated. There is a pleasant lounge/dining room where superb
breakfasts are served, including haggis and clootie 'dumplin', with a
good choice of tea and coffee. Packed lunches can be provided.

OWNERS: Jackie and Ian Cameron OPEN: all year exc Christmas ROOMS: 1 single, with
wash-basin; 2 double, 1 with bath/shower, 1 with wash-basin; 1 twin, 1 four-poster, 1
family; all with bath shower; TV in all bedrooms TERMS: single £18–£21, twin/double
£36–£48, four-poster £38–£52, family room from £48; half-price for children 2 to 12
CARDS: Visa DETAILS: no children under 2; no dogs; no smoking in lounge/dining-room
and 2 bedrooms

Twenty London Street

20 London Street, Edinburgh EH3 6NA
TEL: (0131) 557 0216   FAX: (0131) 556 6445

Gloria Stuart moved from Stuart House in nearby East Claremont
Street to London Street in 1994. Number Twenty is a smaller, more
intimate place and she has done a superb job in renovating this
Georgian town house. Guests have the use of a very comfortable,
large sitting-room, where breakfast is served, and the three well-
equipped bedrooms, all with small *en suite* shower or bathroom,
overlook the modest back garden. Two rooms are on the ground floor
and the double rooms have king-sized beds. London Street is in
Edinburgh's New Town district, and is very well located for Princes
Street and the shops.

OWNERS: Gloria Stuart OPEN: all year exc Christmas ROOMS: 2 double, 1 twin; all
rooms with bath/shower; TV in all bedrooms TERMS: single occupancy £30–£50, twin/
double £50–£64; deposit CARDS: Access, Visa DETAILS: children welcome; no dogs;
no smoking; garden

*If a deposit is required for an advance booking, this is stated in the details
at the end of the entry.*

478

[handwritten: Between Minto & Dalkisch Rd   Ida]

South Side of town

FALA Lothian

map 11

Fala Hall Farmhouse

[handwritten: 2nd (right) Rt   D lochgaten   Lt Dulkisch]

Fala, nr Pathhead EH37 5SZ
TEL: (01875) 833249
just N of A68, 4m SE of Pathhead

Fala Hall is part of a 285-acre farm in pretty, peaceful countryside within easy reach of Edinburgh. The sixteenth-century stone farmhouse is approached down a half-mile rough track from the tiny hamlet of Fala. An attractive garden at the front of the house is partly walled, and contains chairs, table and parasol for fine weather. Fala Hall offers straightforward farmhouse accommodation, with two spacious bedrooms sharing a bathroom. Breakfast only is served in the TV lounge-cum-dining-room at the rear of the house, although packed lunches can be provided.

OWNER: Helen Lothian OPEN: all year exc Christmas ROOMS: 1 double, 1 family; TV lounge TERMS: single occupancy £18, double £28, family room from £35; half-price for children under 12 CARDS: none DETAILS: children welcome; dogs welcome; car park; garden

FIONNPHORT Strathclyde

map 11

Achaban House

Fionnphort PA66 6BL
TEL: (01681) 700205

Achaban House stands in its own grounds overlooking Loch Poit na h-l (locally known as Loch Pottie), only a mile from the ferry at Iona, and is also well placed for boat trips to Staffa (Fingal's Cave). The spacious house was built around 1840 and was originally an old manse. It has good-sized, simply decorated bedrooms with pine furniture, two of which are on the ground floor. There is no alcohol licence, but guests may bring their own wine to dinner. This is served at large wooden tables in the former kitchen, which still has an old-fashioned range. Packed lunches can be provided.

OWNERS: Camilla and Chris Baigent OPEN: all year exc Christmas ROOMS: 1 single, 2 double, 3 twin, all with wash-basin; 1 family, with bath/shower; TV lounge TERMS: single £17, single occupancy £25–£30, twin/double £34, family room £44; children's reductions; dinner £13; deposit; off-season D,B&B terms also available CARDS: none DETAILS: children welcome; dogs must stay with guests at all times; smoking in TV lounge only; car park; garden

---

If you are forced to turn up later than planned, please telephone to warn the proprietor.

FORD   Strathclyde   map 11

Tigh an Lodan

Ford, nr Lochgilphead PA31 8RH
TEL: (01546) 810287
at southern end of Loch Awe, just off B840

Tigh an Lodan lies just beyond the tiny village of Ford and is in a
peaceful glen at the foot of Loch Awe. This wooden, chalet-style
bungalow was built in the 1970s and has a large garden backing on to
woods. The three bedrooms are all *en suite* and are functionally
furnished and equipped. A sitting-room, with open fire and lots of
books, overlooks the loch. Evening meals featuring local produce are
available by arrangement in the dining area; vegetarians can be
catered for with notice, and guests can bring their own wine as there
is no alcohol licence. Tigh an Lodan, which means 'house of the wet
shoes', is well placed for hill-walking, bird-watching and especially
fishing.

OWNERS: Dr D.W. and Mrs S.W. Bannister   OPEN: April to end Oct   ROOMS: 1 double, 2
twin; all rooms with bath/shower; TV lounge   TERMS: single occupancy £20, twin/
double £20; dinner £12; deposit: £10 per person   CARDS: Access, Visa   DETAILS: no
children under 13; no dogs in public rooms; no smoking; car park; garden

FORT AUGUSTUS   Highland   map 11

Old Pier House

Fort Augustus PH32 4BX
TEL: (01320) 366418   FAX: (01320) 366770
on A82 Fort William to Inverness road at north end of village

Old Pier House stands on the shores of Loch Ness, down a long
driveway, only a few minutes' drive from Fort Augustus. The
property includes a farm with Highland cattle and a riding centre.
The long, low whitewashed house was built about a hundred years
ago, and has a turreted entrance way, with a large patio overlooking
the loch. The large, comfortable lounge has an open fireplace, and the
floors and furniture are pine. Evening meals are served, by
arrangement, in the combined kitchen/dining-room. Guests are
welcome to bring their own wine to dinner as the house is unlicensed;
packed lunches can be provided. The small, simple bedrooms are all
on the ground floor and have *en suite* facilities. Boats, canoes and
mountain bikes are also available for guests' use. Jenny MacKenzie is
an extremely friendly lady who teaches the harp and speaks several
languages.

OWNER: Jenny Mackenzie   OPEN: Apr to Oct   ROOMS: 2 double, 1 twin, 1 family; all
rooms with shower; TV lounge   TERMS: twin/double £40–£50, family room £30–£50;
dinner £12.50 to £15; deposit: 1 night's charge   CARDS: none   DETAILS: no children
under 5; no dogs; no smoking; car park; garden

Ashburn House

1 Achintore Road, Fort William PH33 6RQ
TEL/FAX: (01397) 706000

Ashburn House is a substantial white Victorian building located on
the edge of Fort William just off the main road, and standing in its
own gardens. Loch Linnhe is on the other side of the road, providing a
wonderful backdrop. The Hendersons provide a professional and
friendly service to their guests, and the property is beautifully
maintained. They have restored much of it to its original state,
including the painstaking work of stripping all the pine doors and
staircase. The rooms are spacious, high-ceilinged and comfortable,
and some enjoy loch views. The attractive breakfast room overlooks
the water to the Ardgour Hills, and there is a conservatory lounge
with books and games sharing the same view. Dinner is not served,
but the town centre is only a five-minute walk away.

OWNERS: Allan and Sandra Henderson OPEN: Feb to end Nov ROOMS: 2 single, 4
double, 1 twin; all rooms with bath/shower; TV in all bedrooms TERMS: single £30–£35,
twin/double £50–£70; reductions for children sharing with parents; deposit: £25
CARDS: Access, Visa DETAILS: children welcome; no dogs; no smoking; car park;
garden

Glenlochy Guest House

Nevis Bridge, Fort William PH33 6PF
TEL: (01397) 702909
on A81, ½m N of town centre

This immaculately kept and well-run guesthouse is in a convenient
position on the edge of town. Glenlochy was built as a whisky
distillery manager's residence in 1930 and is opposite the old
distillery itself, which has now been converted into accommodation.
The functional bedrooms are on the small side, and seven of them are
on the ground floor. The dining-room, where breakfast only is served,
has been extended and there is a comfortable lounge. Two self-
catering units are available, adjacent to the house, which are ideal for
families and sometimes are used as an overflow for the guesthouse.
Mr MacBeth is a keen fisherman and was formerly a gamekeeper.
Packed lunches can be provided.

OWNERS: Mr and Mrs Donnie MacBeth OPEN: all year exc Christmas ROOMS: 6 double,
5 with bath/shower, 1 with wash-basin; 4 twin, 3 with bath/shower, 1 with wash-basin; 2
family, both with bath/shower; TV in all bedrooms and lounge TERMS: single
occupancy £18–£42, twin/double £29–£44, family room £35–£65; half-price for children
sharing family rooms with parents; deposit: £10 per person CARDS: Access, Delta,
Visa DETAILS: children welcome; small dogs by arrangement only; smoking in lounge
only; car park; garden

The Grange

Grange Road, Fort William PH33 6JF
TEL: (01397) 705516

The Grange stands in a superb position, above and on the edge of town with magnificent views over Loch Linnhe and surrounding hills. This interesting, white-painted Victorian house is on a quiet residential road and has an attractive large garden. The Campbells have gradually restored the property, and offer luxury accommodation. The beautifully furnished and spacious bedrooms all have a private bathroom, and enjoy lovely views. The cream drawing-room has a carved wooden fireplace, which came from a hunting lodge, and comfortable chairs. Superb breakfasts are served in the dining-room at individual tables. The Campbells are friendly, cheerful people who greet visitors with a glass of sherry on arrival. One couple, reporting on their stay here, summed it up as 'a gem of a place'.

OWNERS: John and Joan Campbell   OPEN: Mar to Nov   ROOMS: 3 double, all rooms with bath/shower; TV in all bedrooms and lounge   TERMS: double £52–£66; deposit   CARDS: Visa   DETAILS: children welcome; no dogs; no smoking; car park; garden

---

FYVIE   Grampian   **map 11**

Meikle Camaloun

Fyvie, nr Turriff AB53 8JY
TEL: (01651) 891319
on A947, 2m N of Fyvie and 6m S of Turriff

This attractive, warm and well-kept stone house is approached up a long driveway from the main road. It stands in a neat garden with an old monkey puzzle tree, and enjoys views of open countryside. Meikle Camaloun is a farm which runs to some two hundred acres; the farm buildings are behind and separate from the house. The accommodation has been recently decorated and furnished; of the two bedrooms, one is *en suite* and the other has the use of a private bathroom. Breakfast only is served in the dining-room and there is a large lounge for guests' use.

OWNER: Mrs M. Wyness   OPEN: Mar to Nov   ROOMS: 1 double, 1 twin; both rooms with bath/shower; TV lounge   TERMS: single occupancy £23, twin/double £36–£40; half-price for children under 14   CARDS: none   DETAILS: children welcome; no dogs; no smoking; car park; garden

---

Use the maps and indexes at the back of the Guide to plan your trip.

GAIRLOCH   Highland   **map 11**

Strathgair House

Gairloch, Wester Ross IV21 2BT
TEL: (01445) 712118

Standing in its own grounds in a peaceful spot just above the village
of Gairloch with views over the loch, Strathgair House was once a
Church of Scotland manse. It was built in 1790, with an extra wing
added to it in 1823. Miss Wylie offers good, old-fashioned Highland
hospitality and enjoys conversing with her guests, who come from
many parts of the world. Cups of tea are offered in the drawing-room,
but there is no TV in the house. A collection of oriental rugs covers
every inch of the floors, and sometimes even the walls, of the large
and comfortable rooms. The four bedrooms have the use of a
bathroom and two showers.

OWNER: Miss I.M. Wylie   OPEN: Easter to end Sept   ROOMS: 1 single, 1 double, 2 twin;
all rooms with wash-basin   TERMS: single/single occupancy £16, twin/double £32
CARDS: none   DETAILS: no children; dogs welcome in bedrooms only; smoking in
bedrooms only; car park; garden

GARTOCHARN   Strathclyde   **map 11**

Ardoch Cottage

Gartocharn G83 8NE
TEL: (01389) 830452
on A811 between Drymen and Balloch south of Loch Lomond

A good base for visiting Glasgow or Edinburgh, this 200-year-old
whitewashed cottage is run by a very enthusiastic, cheerful young
couple. All three bedrooms are at the back of the house, one of them
on the ground floor. The comfortable sitting-room has TV, and a log
fire in winter. Packed lunches can be provided, and evening meals are
served in the dining-room with vegetarian choices available on
request. Although there is no alcohol licence, guests are free to bring
their own wine to dinner.

OWNERS: Mabel and Paul Lindsay   OPEN: all year   ROOMS: 2 double; 1 twin; all rooms
with bath/shower; TV lounge   TERMS: single occupancy £30, twin/double £38–£44;
children under 5 free, half-price for children 5 to 14 sharing with parents; dinner £13;
deposit: £10   CARDS: none   DETAILS: children welcome; dogs welcome; no smoking;
car park; garden

Many B&Bs offer tea / coffee-making facilities in the bedroom.

GEOCRAB   Western Isles   map 11

Croft House

12 Geocrab, Geocrab, Isle of Harris HS3 3HB
TEL: (01859) 530205
7m S of Tarbert

This old croft is an attractive whitewashed small house standing
above the road with lovely views of sea, rocks and hills. It is located
on the scenic east side of Harris in a quiet, peaceful spot. The
property has been in the same family since the 1700s, and now Mrs
Wingad lives in the main croft and makes one very pretty double
bedroom available for guests. Her daughter lives in the attached
studio, where she displays and sells her interesting collection of
pictures. Mrs Wingad has made this cosy house quite charming, and
it is imaginatively decorated. Breakfast only is served.

OWNER: Mrs Wingad   OPEN: Apr to end Sept   ROOMS: 1 double; TV in bedroom and
lounge   TERMS: double £30   CARDS: none   DETAILS: car park; garden

GIFFORD   Lothian   map 11

Eaglescairnie Mains

Gifford, nr Haddington EH41 4HN
TEL/FAX: (01620) 810491
from Haddington take B6368 (formerly A6137) south, signposted Humbie;
drive for 4m through Bolton, fork left signposted Eaglescairnie, house is
½m on left

This interesting, white-painted eighteenth-century farmhouse is set
in peaceful countryside about a mile from Gifford. It has a lovely
garden and is on a 350-acre mostly sheep and arable farm. The
Williamses are particularly concerned about wildlife and landscape
conservation, and have improved their rough shoot and planted new
woodland. The house has been beautifully decorated and has a large
drawing-room and three spacious, pretty bedrooms. Breakfast only is
served at one table in a small plant-filled conservatory off the
kitchen. Eaglescairnie is an excellent base for the Borders and
Edinburgh, and there is also a hard tennis court for guests' use.

OWNER: Barbara Williams   OPEN: all year exc Christmas and New Year   ROOMS: 2
double, both with bath/shower; 1 twin, with wash-basin; TV lounge   TERMS: single
occupancy £18–£25, twin/double £32–£40; children under 2 free, £12 for ages 2 to 10;
deposit: £10 per person   CARDS: none   DETAILS: children welcome; dogs welcome;
smoking in lounge only; car park; games room; garden; tennis

Kirklee Hotel

11 Kensington Gate, Glasgow G12 9LG
TEL: (0141) 334 5555   FAX: (0141) 339 3828

This red-sandstone hotel is in an attractive crescent terrace
overlooking private gardens, within one of the city's conservation
areas yet close to the centre. In summer, beautiful flowers are
displayed in the window boxes and garden, which has won awards in
the past. The Kirklee was built in 1904 for a shipping magnate, and
retains many period features such as the wood-panelled hall,
staircase and the original drawing-room. It is a comfortable hotel
with a relaxing atmosphere. Breakfast is always served in the
bedrooms, which have tables and chairs. All nine rooms are *en suite*
and have TV, telephone and trouser press; one room is on the ground
floor. The hotel has an alcohol licence, and drinks are served either in
the bedrooms or in the lounge. Although there is no private car park
there is unrestricted on-street parking.

OWNERS: Mr and Mrs Peter H. Steven OPEN: all year ROOMS: 4 double, 2 twin, 3 family;
all rooms with bath/shower; TV in all bedrooms TERMS: single occupancy £44–£49,
twin/double £56–£62, family room £69–£84; reductions for children sharing with
parents CARDS: Access, Visa DETAILS: children welcome; no dogs; garden

Scott's Guest House

417 North Woodside Road, Glasgow G20 6NN
TEL: (0141) 339 3750

On a quiet cul-de-sac just off the Great Western Road, Scott's
overlooks Kelvin Park, from where one can walk or bicycle all the way
to Loch Lomond. Four of the eight comfortable bedrooms are *en suite*
and two are on the ground floor. The recently refurbished dining-
room, where breakfast only is served at separate tables, is on the first
floor overlooking the park. The guesthouse is only ten minutes from
the university and Botanical Gardens.

OWNERS: Kay and Bob Scott OPEN: all year ROOMS: 1 single, 3 double, all with bath/
shower; 2 twin, both with wash-basin; 2 family, both with wash-basin; 2 rooms suitable
for wheelchair-users; TV in all bedrooms and lounge TERMS: single £17, single
occupancy £20, twin/double £30–£35, family room £45; children under 10 free; deposit:
1 night's charge CARDS: none DETAILS: children welcome; dogs welcome; garden

---

*If there are any bedrooms with TV, we mention this in the details at the
end of the entry.*

The Town House

4 Hughenden Terrace, Glasgow G12 9XR
TEL: (0141) 339 0862   FAX: (0141) 339 9605
on A82 turn at sign for Hyndland, then first right and right again at mini-roundabout

The Town House is a fine example of Glasgow's Victorian architecture, with spacious, well-proportioned rooms and lovely ceiling cornices. The house was built in 1882, and is located in a quiet terrace with a park in front and tennis courts behind – yet close to the main road and only 15 minutes from the shops, art galleries and restaurants in Byres Road. The large bedrooms are well appointed and decorated in soft colours. Lots of reading material can be found in the comfortable lounge, and good Scottish breakfasts and evening meals are served in the original dining-room. Packed lunches can be provided.

OWNERS: Bill and Charlotte Thow   OPEN: all year exc Christmas   ROOMS: 2 double, 6 twin, 2 family; all rooms with bath/shower; TV in all bedrooms   TERMS: single occupancy £52, twin/double £62, family room from £67; reductions for children sharing with parents; dinner £20; deposit £20 per room   CARDS: Access, Switch, Visa   DETAILS: children welcome; no dogs; no smoking in dining-room; garden

GOLSPIE   Highland   map 11

Deo Greine Farmhouse

Backies, Golspie KW10 6SE
TEL: (01408) 633106

This modest farmhouse with its sizable interior kept in immaculate order is in a quiet, peaceful location with lovely views. It is approached up a narrow lane from the A9, just outside Golspie, and is very close to Dunrobin Castle. Nelly Grant, who is originally from Belgium, is an excellent cook and bases her dinners on established Scottish dishes. Three of the four *en suite* bedrooms are on the ground floor. Guests can relax in the fairly new sun lounge, which leads to a patio, or in the main lounge with its easy chairs, sofas and a piano. There is no alcohol licence, but guests are welcome to bring their own wine to dinner, which is served in the dining-room. Packed lunches can be provided.

OWNER: Nelly Grant   OPEN: April to Oct   ROOMS: 1 double, 2 twin, 1 family; all rooms with bath/shower; TV lounge   TERMS: twin/double £36, family room from £53; dinner from £10; deposit: 20%   CARDS: none   DETAILS: children welcome; dogs welcome; smoking in 1 sitting-room only; car park; garden

Culdearn House

Woodlands Terrace, Grantown-on-Spey PH26 3JU
TEL: (01479) 872106   FAX: (01479) 873641

This substantial, granite-built Victorian house sits in its own garden
just on the edge of Grantown-on-Spey. The proprietors provide every
comfort, good service and attention to detail. Evening meals based on
good Scottish cooking are served at individual tables in the elegant-
dining room. The lounge is warm and relaxing, and the bedrooms are
well-equipped. Grantown-on-Spey is an excellent base for many
activities, such as bird-watching, visiting the malt whisky
distilleries, and of course golf and fishing. Packed lunches can be
provided.

OWNERS: Isobel and Alasdair Little OPEN: Mar to Oct ROOMS: 1 single, 5 double, 3
twin; all rooms with bath/shower; 1 room suitable for wheelchair-users; TV in all
bedrooms TERMS: rates include dinner; single/single occupancy £49.50, twin/double
£99; deposit: £50 per person CARDS: Access, Amex, Delta, Diners, Switch, Visa
DETAILS: no children under 10; no dogs; no smoking in dining-room; car park; garden

Kinross House

Woodside Avenue, Grantown-on-Spey PH26 3JR
TEL: (01479) 872042 FAX: (01479) 873504

This Victorian stone house is located in a quiet residential road just a
short walk from the centre of town. The bedrooms are bright and
spacious, and the ground floor room is suitable for ambulant disabled
guests. Traditional evening meals are served by David Elder, wearing
his McIntosh kilt. After dinner, coffee is set out by the log fire in the
sitting-room. A pot of tea with home-made shortbread can also be
ordered later. Packed lunches can be provided.

OWNERS: David and Katherine Elder OPEN: Apr to end Oct ROOMS: 2 single, 1 with
bath/shower, 1 with wash-basin; 1 double, with bath/shower; 2 twin, both with bath/
shower; 1 family, with bath/shower; TV in all bedrooms TERMS: single £20–£28, twin/
double £44–£50, family room from £53; half-price for children over 7 sharing with
parents; dinner £12; deposit: £20 per person CARDS: none DETAILS: no children under
7; no dogs; no smoking; car park; garden

*It is always best to check prices, especially for single occupancy, when
booking.*

*We state at the end of an entry whether children are welcome. If we know of
any restrictions on children, we give them.*

GREENOCK   Strathclyde   map 11

Lindores Guest House

61 Newark Street, Greenock PA16 7TE
TEL: (01475) 783075

Lindores is an impressive stone-built Victorian house standing in a
large garden, in an elegant residential street, above the town of
Greenock. The ornate entrance hall has pillars and a tiled floor, and
the main hallway, which is used as the breakfast-room, is panelled in
wood. The bedrooms are enormous, and the front-facing rooms have
lovely views over the Clyde. As we went to press there were plans to
increase the number of bedrooms, to make them all *en suite* and
possibly add a TV lounge.

OWNER: Veronica Nelis   OPEN: all year   ROOMS: 2 double, one with bath/shower; 1 twin,
with bath/shower; TV in all bedrooms   TERMS: single occupancy £22, twin/double £35;
children's reductions by arrangement   CARDS: Access, Visa   DETAILS: children
welcome; car park; garden

GRIMSAY   Western Isles   map 11

Glendale

7 Kallin, Grimsay, North Uist HS62 5HY
TEL: (01870) 602029
*15m S of Lochmaddy off main road leading to Benbecula, over causeway to
Grimsay then signposted*

Glendale stands in a garden right above the tiny, picturesque fishing
harbour of Kallin on the small island of Grimsay, with lovely views of
rocky inlets. Mrs MacLeod is a very friendly lady, and her husband
has his fishing boat in the harbour, bringing back catches of shrimp,
crab and lobsters, which are freshly cooked for the guests. The very
comfortable accommodation includes two ground-floor twin bedrooms
and a first-floor double *en suite* room overlooking the water; the
double has proved particularly popular and can also be used as a
family room. Packed lunches can be provided.

OWNER: Mrs C. Macleod   OPEN: all year   ROOMS: 1 double, 2 twin; all rooms with bath/
shower; TV lounge   TERMS: single occupancy £18, twin/double £36; children's
reductions; deposit: £10 per room   CARDS: none   DETAILS: children welcome; no dogs
in bedrooms; no smoking in bedrooms or dining-room; car park; garden

---

*If we know of any particular payment stipulations, we mention them in the
details at the end of the entry. However, it is always best to check when
booking.*

HADDINGTON   Lothian

Barney Mains Farmhouse

Barney Mains, Haddington EH41 3SA
TEL: (01620) 880310   FAX: (01620) 880639

Part of a working farm – look for the herd of cross-Hereford/Friesian
cattle – Barney Mains stands in an elevated position with lovely
views in every direction to the Lammermuir Hills, the Bass Rock and
Traprain Law. A section of the farmhouse itself dates back to the
early eighteenth century, but inside, the rooms are spacious and
comfortable, and share a bathroom and shower-room. Home-made
bread is served at breakfast.

OWNER: Katie Kerr   OPEN: Mar to Nov   ROOMS: 1 double, 2 twin; TV in all bedrooms
TERMS: single occupancy £17–£23, twin/double £30–£40; children under 2 free, half-
price for children under 11; deposit: £20   CARDS: none   DETAILS: children welcome; no
dogs; no smoking in bedrooms or bathroom; car park; garden

HOUGHARRY   Western Isles   map 11

Sgeir Ruadh

Hougharry, nr Lochmaddy, North Uist HS6 5DL
TEL: (01876) 510312
*17m from ferry; take A867 to Clachan, then turn right on to A865 and after
8m turn left to Houghharry (Hogha Gearraidh)*

This modern house stands just above a lovely beach and on the
Balranald Bird Reserve, where corncrakes can be seen in spring and
summer. The small bedrooms are all on the ground floor and have *en
suite* facilities. Kathy Simpson provides a very warm welcome, and
breakfast and evening meals are served in the large lounge/dining-
room which overlooks the beach. Sgeir Ruadh is not licensed, but
guests are welcome to bring their own wine to dinner. This is a
perfect spot for families and bird-watchers; packed lunches can be
provided.

OWNERS: Mr and Mrs Simpson   OPEN: all year   ROOMS: 1 single, 1 double, 1 twin; all
rooms with bath/shower; TV lounge   TERMS: single/single occupancy £14, twin/double
£28; reductions for children sharing with parents; dinner £11   CARDS: none   DETAILS:
children welcome; dogs in bedrooms only; smoking in bedrooms only; car park; garden

*If the establishment does not take credit cards, we say so in the details at
the end of the entry.*

*If there are reduced rates for children, this is mentioned in the details at
the end of the entry. If no reductions are specified, assume you will have to
pay full rates for children.*

HUNTLY   Grampian
map 11

Faich-Hill Farmhouse

Gartly, nr Huntly AB54 4RR
TEL: (01466) 720240
just off A97, 5m S of Huntly; find Gartly church (not in centre of village), take farm road behind cottage next to church

A long driveway right beside the church leads to Faich-Hill, which forms one side of an immaculately kept farmyard. This traditional granite farmhouse, with views of rolling hills and fields, is in an isolated location, and has been in the Grant family since 1884. The entrance is via the conservatory, which has lots of helpful brochures on what to do in the area. The three bedrooms have their own bathrooms and are comfortably furnished, and there is a cosy TV lounge. Evening meals are served by arrangement at 6.30pm in the traditional dining-room; there is no licence but guests can bring their own wine.

OWNERS: Margaret and Theo Grant   OPEN: Easter to Oct   ROOMS: 1 double, 1 twin, 1 family; all rooms with bath/shower; TV lounge   TERMS: single occupancy £22, twin/double £34, family room from £34; dinner £10; deposit: £15 per person   CARDS: none
DETAILS: no children under 5; no dogs; smoking in sun lounge only; car park; garden

INNERLEITHEN   Borders
map 11

Caddon View Guest House

14 Pirn Road, Innerleithen EH44 6HH
TEL: (01896) 830208

Once a doctor's surgery, this large stone Victorian house is set back a little from the main road on the edge of town and has views of the Tweed Valley and its hills. It is surrounded by a beautifully kept garden, including an extensive vegetable bed. Will and Audrey Wright are an extremely friendly couple and offer comfortable, good-sized rooms, which are nicely decorated and immaculately clean. Breakfast is served at separate tables in the pretty dining-room and includes different kinds of porridge and smoked haddock. Dinner is also available by arrangement and, although Caddon View is unlicensed, guests may bring their own wine to dinner. Packed lunches can be provided. The Wrights' son has recently started a small restaurant at the back of the main house which is open to residents and non-residents at the weekend.

OWNERS: Will and Audrey Wright   OPEN: all year exc last 2 weeks Jan   ROOMS: 1 single, with wash-basin; 1 double, with bath/shower; 2 twin, 1 with bath/shower; 1 family, with wash-basin; TV in all bedrooms   TERMS: single £17–£18, single occupancy £18–£19, twin/double £36–£38, family room from £45; children under 3 free, half-price for ages 3 to 11; dinner £10 to £11; deposit: £5 per person   CARDS: none   DETAILS: children welcome; well-behaved dogs by arrangement only; no smoking in public rooms; car park; garden

INVERALLIGIN   Highland   map 11

Grianan

Inveralligin, Torridon IV22 2HB
TEL: (01445) 791264
off A896, on N shore of Upper Loch Torridon

Reached by a beautifully scenic, narrow road from Torridon, Grianan is a small, neat modern bungalow lying at the end of the tiny hamlet of Inveralligin. The position is spectacular, with wonderful views over the loch to the mountains on the other side. The house is immaculately kept, and both bedrooms are on the ground floor; they share a shower room between them and one overlooks the water. Breakfast, as well as evening meals by arrangement, is served in the pleasant lounge, and there is a patio for sitting outside on warm days. Guests may bring their own wine to dinner, and packed lunches can be provided.

OWNER: Marie Macdonald   OPEN: Apr to Sept   ROOMS: 1 double, 1 twin; TV lounge   TERMS: single occupancy £21, twin/double £29; deposit   CARDS: none   DETAILS: children welcome; no dogs; no smoking in bedrooms; car park

INVERARAY   Strathclyde   map 11

Creagh Dhubh

Inveraray PA32 8XT
TEL: (01499) 302430

Creag Dhubh is an attractive 150-year old stone-built house standing above the main A83 road in a large garden, on the edge of Inverary. The MacLugashes are a friendly couple, and the accommodation is simple and comfortable. One double room has an *en suite* bathroom on the ground floor; the remaining spacious rooms are upstairs and share bathroom facilities, the two front ones having wonderful loch views. Breakfast only is served.

OWNERS: Richard and Janice MacLugash   OPEN: Mar to Nov   ROOMS: 2 double, 1 with bath/shower, 1 with wash-basin; 1 twin, with wash-basin; 1 family, with wash-basin; TV in all bedrooms and lounge   TERMS: single occupancy £18, twin/double £29–£36, family room from £30; children's reductions according to age   CARDS: none   DETAILS: children welcome; no dogs; smoking in lounge only; car park; garden

CREAGH DHUBH, INVERARAY

INVERASDALE   Highland   map 11

Knotts Landing

12 Coast, Inverasdale, by Achnasheen IV22 2LR
TEL: (01445) 781331
on B8057, 5m N of Poolewe

This small house with its pretty front garden stands close to the sea
and has wonderful mountain views. It is reached down a narrow road
along the west side of Loch Ewe. One of the three bedrooms faces the
front and can be used either as a twin or double. The house is
spotlessly clean and, as well as a TV lounge, has a small dining-room
where breakfast and dinner are served. Although there is no alcohol
licence, guests may bring their own wine to dinner.

OWNER: Sandra Maclean   OPEN: all year exc Christmas and New Year   ROOMS: 1 single;
1 double, with wash basin; 1 twin, with wash-basin; TV in all bedrooms and lounge
TERMS: single £13, single occupancy £15, twin/double £26; half-price for children under
12; dinner £7; deposit: £5   CARDS: none   DETAILS: children welcome; no dogs; no
smoking; car park; garden

---

*Most establishments have central heating. When we know this is not the
case, we mention this in the entry.*

map 11

Clisham House

43 Fairfeld Road, Inverness IV3 5QP
TEL: (01463) 239965   FAX: (01463) 239965

Standing in its own grounds surrounded by trees, this large stone house is in a quiet, residential road. The centre of town is within easy walking distance, as is the footpath which follows the Caledonian Canal. Clisham House was originally the home of the Bishop, and now provides large *en suite* bedrooms. There is a comfortable lounge, and breakfast only is served at individual tables in the dining-room. Rhoda Beaton is a welcoming hostess.

OWNER: Rhoda Beaton   OPEN: all year   ROOMS: 2 double, 2 family; all rooms with bath/ shower; TV in all bedrooms and lounge   TERMS: double £42, family room from £42 CARDS: none   DETAILS: children welcome; no dogs; no smoking in dining-room or lounge; car park

Craigside Lodge

4 Gordon Terrace, Inverness IV2 3HD
TEL: (01463) 231576   FAX: (01463) 713409

This attractive house has lovely views over the castle and river. It is a pleasant detached Victorian residence with friendly owners, and only a few minutes' walk from the city centre. The rooms have been done up since our last edition, and all the bedrooms are now *en suite*. The large lounge on the ground floor and the breakfast room on the lower ground floor both have good views. Packed lunches can be provided on request.

OWNERS: Janette and Wilf Skinner   OPEN: all year   ROOMS: 3 double; 3 twin; all rooms with bath/shower; TV in all bedrooms   TERMS: single occupancy £20, twin/double £36; half-price for children under 11   CARDS: Access, Delta, Visa   DETAILS: children welcome; no dogs; smoking in lounge only; car park; garden

Culduthel Lodge

14 Culduthel Road, Inverness IV2 4AG
TEL/FAX: (01463) 240089

Culduthel Lodge continues to maintain its very high standard. This listed Georgian house stands in lovely gardens with views of the River Ness, and is conveniently located for the city centre. It has a spacious country-house feel, with lots of fresh flowers everywhere. Four of the well-appointed, individually decorated and furnished bedrooms are on the ground floor and all bedrooms have private bathrooms. Pre-dinner drinks are served in the comfortable lounge, or on the terrace in fine weather. The elegant dining-room has attractively set tables, and Marion Bonsor has an excellent reputation for her cooking. Packed lunches can be provided.

OWNERS: David and Marion Bonsor OPEN: all year exc Christmas ROOMS: 1 single, 7 double, 2 twin, 1 four-poster, 1 family; all rooms with bath/shower; TV in all bedrooms TERMS: single/single occupancy £43, twin/double £70, four-poster £75, family room £75–£80; reductions for children sharing with parents; dinner £17 CARDS: Access, Visa DETAILS: children welcome; no smoking in some bedrooms and dining-room; car park; garden

Old Rectory

9 Southside Road, Inverness IV2 3BG
TEL: (01463) 220969

This small detached house is built of attractive stone and is surrounded by pretty gardens. Most of the property has recently been refurbished, and all four bedrooms are now *en suite*. There is a comfortable TV lounge, and a pleasant dining-room with a Victorian fireplace where breakfast only is served. Packed lunches can be requested. The Old Rectory is only a short walk from the town centre.

OWNERS: John and Neina Lister OPEN: all year exc Christmas ROOMS: 2 double, 2 twin; all rooms with bath/shower; TV in all bedrooms and lounge TERMS: single occupancy £18–£25, twin/double £36–£40; deposit CARDS: none DETAILS: no children under 5; no dogs; no smoking; car park; garden

Sealladh Sona

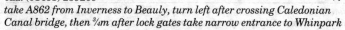

3 Whinpark, Muirtown, Inverness IV3 6NQ
TEL: (01463) 239209
take A862 from Inverness to Beauly, turn left after crossing Caledonian Canal bridge, then ¾m after lock gates take narrow entrance to Whinpark

Sealladh Sona stands in an idyllic location right beside the Caledonian Canal, with views over houses to open countryside, and is only about 15 minutes' walk into town. When the Cooks bought the cottage in 1992, it had been empty for 15 years. It has been renovated in character with its cottage origins, and been extended both at the back and the side. There are now three pretty *en suite* rooms, two on the first floor and a double on the ground floor. The entrance opens into the cosy sitting-room, and good Scottish home-cooking is available in the evening if arranged in advance. Although the B&B is unlicensed, guests may bring their own wine to dinner. Packed lunches can also be provided.

OWNER: Marjory Cook OPEN: all year ROOMS: 1 double; 2 twin; all rooms with bath/shower; TV in all bedrooms TERMS: single occupancy £20–£25; twin/double £34–£44; reductions for children sharing with parents CARDS: Access, Visa DETAILS: children welcome; no dogs; no smoking; car park

ISLE ORNSAY Highland map 11

Tawny Croft

Isle Ornsay, Sleat, Isle of Skye IV43 8QS
TEL/FAX: (01471) 833325
from A851 take A852, turn right for Camus Cross then 300yds on right

Roger and Pat Cottis have extended this whitewashed old croft that stands just outside and above the small village of Isle Ornsay. They have kept the old house for themselves, adding on a large lounge with conservatory for guests. The room has comfortable chairs, a wood-burning stove and lovely views complete with a telescope to watch the wildlife. The island where Gavin Maxwell, author of *Ring of Bright Water*, lived can be seen from here, and the Cottises can recommend interesting walks. The first floor of the extension houses two small, very comfortable *en suite* bedrooms, both looking out over the Sound, and equipped with binoculars. Evening meals are served in the dining-room; children's helpings and vegetarian choices can be catered for with notice, as can packed lunches. There is no licence but guests may bring their own wine. Bookings are taken for a minimum of two days' stay.

OWNERS: Roger and Pat Cottis OPEN: all year ROOMS: 2 family; both rooms with bath/shower; TV lounge TERMS: D,B&B £60–£68; B&B £40–£48; half-price for children 6 to 10; deposit: £10 CARDS: none DETAILS: no children under 6; no dogs; no smoking; car park; garden

JEDBURGH Borders map 11

Hundalee House

Jedburgh TD8 6PA
TEL/FAX: (01835) 863011
just off A68, 1m S of Jedburgh

This handsome Georgian house of grey stone stands in ten acres of established woodland and garden and enjoys views towards the Cheviot Hills. Mrs Whittaker maintains a first-class establishment with well-kept grounds and house, and offers a warm welcome to her guests. There is a small *en suite* bedroom on the ground floor through the kitchen and, among the upstairs rooms, a four-poster with its own private shower room. Visitors have use of a large, pleasant drawing-room and stylish dining-room where breakfast only is served at one big table.

OWNER: Sheila Whittaker OPEN: Mar to end Oct ROOMS: 1 double, with bath/shower; 2 twin, 1 with bath/shower, 1 with wash-basin; 1 four-poster, with bath/shower; 1 family room, with wash-basin; TV in all bedrooms TERMS: single occupancy £25–£35, twin/double £33–£40, four-poster £40, family room £40; children's reductions according to age; deposit CARDS: none DETAILS: children welcome; no dogs; no smoking; car park; garden

JOHNSHAVEN Grampian   map 11

The Retreat

South Street, Johnshaven, nr Montrose DD10 0HE
TEL: (01561) 362731   FAX: (01561) 362173
on A92 between Stonehaven and Montrose

This small modern bungalow in the tiny fishing village of Johnshaven is only a few minutes' walk to the harbour, and its compact garden opens straight on to the beach. Christine Hulton is a kindly, chatty lady who moved here from Lancashire with her husband in the mid-1980s. The two small bedrooms are both on the ground floor, one with a tiny *en suite* shower room. On the beach side of the house is a sun lounge, which is used as a sitting area with TV. Meals too can be taken there, or in the dining-room. Most guests choose to stay in for Christine's home-cooked evening meals, and may bring their own wine to dinner as the Retreat is unlicensed. Packed lunches can be provided.

OWNER: Christine Hulton OPEN: all year exc Jan ROOMS: 2 double, both with bath/shower; TV in both bedrooms and lounge TERMS: single/single occupancy £20–£22, double £34–£38; deposit: 10%, min £20 CARDS: none DETAILS: no children; no dogs; no smoking; car park; garden

KEITH Grampian   map 11

Haughs Farm Guest House

The Haughs, Keith AB55 3QN
TEL: (01542) 882238
just off A96 Aberdeen to Inverness road, ½m from Keith

Haughs Farm Guest House is a whitewashed building dating from 1614 and is part of a mixed 165-acre farm. Good views are enjoyed from the conservatory-style dining-room where breakfast and evening meals are served. Although Haughs Farm is unlicensed, guests are welcome to bring their own wine to dinner. Packed lunches can be provided. The four large bedrooms are either *en suite* or have private bathrooms. Although the main entrance to the house is up a steep flight of stairs, there is another, level entrance for those having difficulty with steps.

OWNERS: Peter and Jean Jackson OPEN: Apr to Oct ROOMS: 2 double; 2 twin; all rooms with bath/shower; TV in all bedrooms and lounge TERMS: single occupancy £22, twin/double £35; children's reductions if sharing with parents; dinner £10; deposit: £15 CARDS: none DETAILS: no children under 2; no dogs; no smoking in bedrooms; car park; garden

KELSO Borders   map 11

Bellevue House

Bowmont Street, Kelso TD5 7DZ
TEL: (01573) 224588

Bellevue House was built in the 1800s, and the well-known Kelso poet and angler Thomas Tod Stoddart lived here from 1860 until his death. The hotel has recently been taken over by Carole Orr, who has lived most of her life in Vancouver, and she has carried out a certain amount of refurbishment. All the bedrooms are *en suite*, except one double and the singles, which share a bathroom. Guests have the use of a large, comfortable lounge and evening meals are served by arrangement in the dining-room. Packed lunches can be provided. Bellevue House is within walking distance of all the local amenities, including Floors Castle.

OWNER: Carole Orr OPEN: all year ROOMS: 3 single, all with wash-basin; 3 double, 2 with bath/shower, 1 with wash-basin; 2 twin, 1 family; all with bath/shower; 1 room suitable for wheelchair-users; TV in some bedrooms and lounge TERMS: single £20–£23, single occupancy £25–£30, twin/double £45–£50, family room £56–£65; half-price for children under 12; dinner £15; deposit: £15 per room CARDS: Access, Switch, Visa DETAILS: children welcome; well-behaved dogs only; smoking in lounge only; car park; garden

KILLIN Central   map 11

Fairview Guest House

Main Street, Killin FK21 8UT
TEL: (01567) 820667

This stone building stands in the middle of the village of Killin; at the front are views of Ben Lawers and Loch Tay, and behind is the panoramic stretch of the Breadalbane Hills. Inside, the welcome is warm and the simple accommodation comfortable. The lounge is on the first floor, and evening meals are served in the dining-room, which has pine tables and chairs. Guests may bring their own wine to dinner, and packed lunches can be arranged.

OWNERS: Roger and Muriel Bedwell OPEN: all year exc Christmas ROOMS: 1 single, with wash-basin; 4 double, 2 with bath/shower, 2 with wash-basin; 2 twin, 1 with bath/shower, 1 with wash-basin; TV lounge TERMS: single £15, single occupancy £17, twin/double £30–£34; dinner £8; deposit: £20 per person for 3 nights or more CARDS: Access, Visa DETAILS: children welcome; dogs welcome; car park; garden

KILMUIR Highland

map 11

Kilmuir House

Kilmuir, by Uig, Isle of Skye IV51 9YN
TEL: (01470) 542262
on A855, 5m N of Uig

Formely a manse, this attractive whitewashed old house stands in its
own walled three-quarter-acre garden above the Staffin to Uig road,
overlooking Loch Snizort and the hills of the Outer Hebrides. Roy and
Sally Phelps bought the house in a derelict state about ten years ago
and have renovated it extensively to make it a comfortable family
home. The spacious rooms are furnished with antiques and the house
has a restful, relaxed atmosphere. Two bedrooms are on the first floor
and have lovely views, and there is a room suitable for families on the
ground floor. Fresh food, including home-grown vegetables and free-
range eggs, is in evidence at both breakfast and dinner (the latter
should be booked in advance). Vegetarians are catered for, and guests
are welcome to bring their own wine to dinner. Nearby are the Skye
Museum of Island Life, Flora MacDonald's grave, the site of Bonnie
Prince Charlie's first landing in Skye and the ruins of Duntulm
Castle.

OWNER: Sally Phelps OPEN: all year exc Christmas ROOMS: 2 double, 1 family; TV in
some bedrooms and lounge TERMS: single occupancy £21, double £29–£30, family
room £45; one-third reduction for children sharing with parents; dinner £9 to £10
CARDS: none DETAILS: children welcome; no dogs; no smoking; car park; garden

KINGARTH Strathclyde

map 11

New Farm Farmhouse

Mountstuart, nr Kingarth, Isle of Bute PA20 9NA
TEL: (01700) 831646
5m S of Rothesay

Kingarth is a small village in the south part of the Isle of Bute, and
this sheep-and-cattle farm of 1,000 acres sits above the road a mile or
so outside the village. The Howards moved here in 1994 and have
done a creative job decorating the four bedrooms. The rooms are
spacious and comfortable, share bathroom facilities, and one is on the
ground floor. There is also a pleasant lounge (no TV), where both
breakfast and evening meals are served. Lunches, or packed lunches,
are by arrangement, children's helpings are served, and guests may
bring their own wine as there is no licence. The farm is only a mile
from the very stunning Victorian mansion, Mountstuart, seat of the
Marquess of Bute and only recently open to the public.

OWNERS: Carole and Michael Howard OPEN: all year ROOMS: 1 single, 1 double, 1
twin, 1 family TERMS: single £15–£17.50, single occupancy £17.50, twin/double

£30–£35, family room £30–£35; children's reductions according to age; dinner £10.50–£12.50 CARDS: none DETAILS: children welcome; dogs welcome in attached kennels; no smoking in bedrooms; car park; garden

KINGUSSIE Highland   map 11

Osprey Hotel

Ruthven Road, Kingussie PH21 1EN
TEL/FAX: (01540) 661510
off the A9 Inverness to Perth road

Situated in a quiet area of the village in the heart of the Spey valley, this attractive granite-stone hotel overlooks the beautiful memorial gardens. It is a cheerful, comfortable place with enthusiastic, welcoming owners. Six of the nine small bedrooms have *en suite* facilities and one is on the ground floor. An osprey is depicted on the carpet which runs through the main part of the house. There are two lounges where drinks can be served, one leading to the dining-room with its plaid tablecloths and curtains. Four-course dinners are served, focusing mainly on Scottish dishes and making good use of home-made and local produce. Packed lunches can be provided on request.

OWNERS: Robert and Aileen Burrow OPEN: all year ROOMS: 2 single, 1 with bath/shower, 1 with wash-basin; 4 double, 3 with bath/shower, 1 with wash-basin; 3 twin, 2 with bath/shower, 1 with wash-basin; TV lounge TERMS: single £24–£34, single occupancy £34–£44, twin/double £48–£68; children's reductions according to age; dinner £20; deposit: £20 CARDS: Access, Amex, Diners, Visa DETAILS: children welcome; no dogs in public rooms; no smoking in most bedrooms and dining-room; car park; garden

KINLOCHBERVIE Highland   map 11

Old School Restaurant

Inshegra, Kinlochbervie IV27 4RH
TEL: (01971) 521383
off B801, on N shore of Loch Inchard halfway between Kinlochbervie and Rhiconich

This stone-built former schoolhouse dates from 1879 and has lovely views over the loch. The licensed restaurant draws in many visitors for lunch and dinner, and specialises in seafood. Vegetarians are also catered for and children's portions are available. Packed lunches, too, can be provided. The bedrooms, which are in a new annexe, all have a view of either mountains or sea, and there is a minute sitting-room.

OWNERS: Tom and Margaret Burt OPEN: all year exc Christmas and New Year ROOMS: 1 single, 1 double, 3 twin, 1 family; all rooms with bath/shower exc 2 twin (with wash-basins only); TV in all bedrooms TERMS: single £25, single occupancy £35, twin/double

£36–£52, family room from £62; £10 for children in family room; dinner £12 to £15
CARDS: Access, Visa DETAILS: children welcome; dogs welcome; no smoking in dining-room; car park; garden

KINLOCH RANNOCH Tayside   map 11

Cuilmore Cottage

Kinloch Rannoch PH16 5QB
TEL/FAX: (01882) 632218
first turning on left on southern loch road from Kinloch Rannoch

Set in a colourful garden, Cuilmore Cottage is a tiled and whitewashed crofter's cottage with vines covering the front porch. The house is warm and comfortable and has been simply decorated with taste and imagination. The first-floor bedrooms are surprisingly large and each has its own private bathroom, though one of these is on the ground floor. The cosy sitting-room has an open fire, and easy chairs and sofas. Dinner, which is one of the main reasons people come here, is served in the small, intimate dining-room with its old range, and is also open to non-residents. The mostly Scottish cuisine makes good use of home-grown organic fruit and vegetables; breakfasts include home-baked breads, pastries and free-range eggs. Guests are welcome to use the mountain bikes, canoe and sailing dinghy. Packed lunches can be provided.

OWNERS: Jens and Anita Steffen OPEN: Feb to Oct ROOMS: 1 double, 1 twin; both rooms with bath/shower TERMS: rates include dinner; twin/double £100; deposit: credit card details CARDS: Access, Visa DETAILS: no children; dogs welcome; no smoking; car park; garden (*The Good Food Guide*)

KIRKTON OF GLENISLA Tayside   map 11

Glenmarkie Farmhouse

Kirkton of Glenisla, nr Blairgowrie PH11 8QB
TEL/FAX: (01575) 582341
off B951, 8m N of Alyth

Glenmarkie is an ideal place for an away-from-it-all type of holiday. The farmhouse is reached down a rough three-mile track, with picturesque Forestry Commission land surrounding it. The attractive whitewashed building was originally servants' quarters for the lodge (now used for self-catering). The house is warm with an informal, relaxed atmosphere. The bedrooms are quite simple and small; two upstairs have dormer windows and share a bathroom, one ground-floor room is *en suite*. There is a cosy lounge, and both lunch and dinner are served in the dining-room. Simon, who trained in hotel management at the Savoy, takes care of the accommodation and cooks, while Sally runs the attached Riding Centre. She caters for all standards of riders for both hacking and trekking, and from one-hour to whole-day rides. Hill-walking and cross-country skiing are available on the doorstep, and there is downhill skiing at Glenshee. Salmon and trout fishing, stalking and shooting can also be arranged.

OWNERS: Simon and Sally Evans   OPEN: all year exc Christmas   ROOMS: 2 double, 1 with bath/shower, 1 with wash-basin; 1 twin, with wash-basin; TV lounge   TERMS: single occupancy £17.50, twin/double £35; half-price for children under 12; dinner £12.50   CARDS: none   DETAILS: children welcome; dogs welcome; smoking in lounge only; car park; garden

KIRKWALL   Orkney   map 11

Briar Lea

10 Dundas Crescent, Kirkwall KW15 1JQ
TEL: (01856) 872747

This Victorian stone house stands in its own garden very close to the town centre. It has a friendly, homely atmosphere and offers simple accommodation. There are two large twin bedrooms and two small singles, one of which is on the ground floor. This is the oldest part of the house and has flagstone floors. Breakfast only is served at one table in the dining-room, which also has a sitting area. Kirkwall's St Magnus Cathedral is worth visiting, and bird-watching and loch fishing are other local possibilities. Packed lunches can be provided.

OWNERS: Mr and Mrs Arthur Flett   OPEN: all year   ROOMS: 2 single, both with wash-basin; 2 twin; TV in some bedrooms and lounge   TERMS: single £16, single occupancy £16, twin £32; children's reductions by arrangement; deposit: £10   CARDS: none   DETAILS: children welcome; no dogs; no smoking; car park; garden

LARGS   Strathclyde   map 11

South Whittlieburn Farm

Brisbane Glen, Largs KA30 8SN
TEL: (01475) 675881
turn right off A78 ½m NE of Largs, signposted Brisbane Glen road; after 2m second farm on right

This whitewashed farmhouse is set in a sheltered position in a beautiful valley with hillside views. It is about two miles inland from Largs and the sea, and is part of a large sheep farm which also provides stabling for horses. The three bedrooms are clean, fresh and comfortable; one room has *en suite* facilities, and there are two additional bathrooms for guests' use. The lounge has a small organ, and there is also a sitting area in the breakfast room. Guests are welcome to look round the farm and help with feeding the lambs.

OWNER: Mary Watson   OPEN: all year exc Christmas   ROOMS: 1 double, with bath/
shower; 1 twin, 1 family, both rooms with wash-basin; TV in all bedrooms and lounge
TERMS: single occupancy £16.50, twin/double £32; reductions for children under 11
CARDS: none   DETAILS: children welcome; no dogs in house; smoking in lounge only; car
park; garden

LERWICK   Shetland   map 11

Whinrig

12 Burgh Road, Lerwick ZE1 0LB
TEL: (01595) 693554

Located in a quiet cul-de-sac only a few minutes from the shops and
museum, Whinrig is an immaculately kept, compact house. All the
small, comfortable bedrooms are on the ground floor. Breakfast only
is served in the dining-room. The attractive small garden has tables
and chairs for sitting outside and taking in the view. Packed lunches
can be provided.

OWNER: W.B. Gifford   OPEN: all year exc Christmas   ROOMS: 1 double, with wash-basin;
2 twin, 1 with bath/shower, 1 with wash-basin; TV in all bedrooms   TERMS: single
occupancy £18, twin/double £30–£36; deposit: 1 night's charge   CARDS: none
DETAILS: no dogs; no smoking; car park; garden

LEVERBURGH   Western Isles   map 11

St Kilda House

Leverburgh, Isle of Harris HS3 3UB
TEL: (01859) 520419

St Kilda was a virtual ruin when the owners moved here in 1992, and
they have spent the intervening time turning it into a comfortable
and very well-equipped small guesthouse. Originally this was the
schoolteacher's house, and plans are afoot to make the adjoining ruin,
once the school room, into a restaurant. Guests have two very
comfortable *en suite* bedrooms to choose from, one in the front with a
lovely sea view and the other at the back boasting a king-sized bed.
The lounge is comfortable and the tiny dining-room overlooks the sea.
Sue and Jim take particular pride in their cooking, making their own
bread and yoghurt, and providing what one reporter called 'huge'
breakfasts and evening meals. St Kilda is unlicensed, but guests can
bring their own wine to dinner. Packed lunches can also be provided.

OWNERS: Sue Massey and Jim Shaw   OPEN: all year   ROOMS: 1 double, 1 twin; both
rooms with bath/shower; TV in both bedrooms and lounge   TERMS: single occupancy
£35–£40, twin/double £50–£60; dinner £15 to £17.50; deposit   CARDS: none   DETAILS:
no children under 8; no dogs; no smoking

LOCHBOISDALE   Western Isles   map 11

Brae Lea House

Lasgair, Lochboisdale, South Uist HS8 5TH
TEL: (01878) 700497
½m along main road from ferry terminal, turn right at Lasgair Road

Brae Lea House stands in an elevated position on the edge of the town
of Lochboisdale almost at the end of a quiet side road. At low tide the
town centre and ferry can be reached by a short cut of a few minutes'
walk. Most of the rooms have good views down to the water and
towards the hills. The three ground-floor bedrooms are quite plain
and all are *en suite*. There is also a sauna. Evening meals are served
by arrangement, children's helpings provided, and guests can bring
their own wine as there is no licence. Mrs Murray is happy to provide
breakfast for guests catching early ferries.

OWNERS: Patricia and George Murray   OPEN: all year   ROOMS: 1 double, 1 twin, 1 family;
all rooms with bath/shower; TV lounge   TERMS: single occupancy £22, twin/double £40,
family room £60; babies free, half-price for children under 10; dinner £10   CARDS:
none   DETAILS: children welcome; dogs welcome; car park; garden

LOCHCARNAN   Western Isles   map 11

Orasay Inn

Lochcarnan, South Uist HS8 5PD
TEL: (01870) 610298   FAX: (01870) 610390
off A865, on NE coast of South Uist

Ideally placed for exploring the islands of North and South Uist and
Benbecula, the Orasay Inn is a low building offering simple
accommodation and a warm welcome. The dining-room has views
across the Minch to the mountains of South Uist, caters for both
residents and non-residents, and specialises in seafood. The
residents' cosy lounge/bar has a peat fire, and there is a separate bar
for non-residents. Windsurfers will be interested in visiting Loch Bee,
just four miles away; guests can also take advantage of the local
fishing, unspoilt beaches and archaeological sites. Packed lunches
can be provided.

OWNERS: Alan and Isobel Graham   OPEN: all year   ROOMS: 3 single, 2 double, 2 twin, 1
family; all rooms with bath/shower; TV in all bedrooms and lounge   TERMS: single
£26–£29, single occupancy £34–£37, twin/double £50–£58; family room from £50;
reductions for children sharing with parents; dinner from £12 to £20   CARDS: Access,
Visa   DETAILS: children welcome; dogs by arrangement; no smoking in dining-room; car
park; garden

LOCHCARRON   Highland
map 11

A'Chomraich

Lochcarron IV54 8YD
TEL: (01520) 722225
on A896, on N shore of Loch Carron

This attractive stone-built and partly whitewashed 100-year-old house is in the pretty village of Lochcarron, with wonderful views across the loch to the hills. The house is comfortably furnished, with a cosy lounge and two simple but pretty attic-type bedrooms which share a bathroom between them. Breakfast only is served at one table in the dining-room, which overlooks the sea.

OWNERS: Mr and Mrs A. Røre   OPEN: Easter to end Oct   ROOMS: 1 double, 1 twin; both rooms with wash-basin   TERMS: single occupancy £13–£15, twin/double £26–£30; children under 5 free, half-price for children under 12; deposit: required for longer stays   CARDS: none   DETAILS: children welcome; no dogs; no smoking in bedrooms; car park; garden

LOCHDONHEAD   Strathclyde
map 11

Old Mill Cottage

Lochdonhead, Craignure, Isle of Mull PA64 6AP
TEL: (01680) 812442
on A849, 3m S from ferry at Craignure

This attractive long, low whitewashed cottage stands just off the road in the village of Lochdonhead and was converted and added on to by Jim and Jenny Smith in 1994. Jim was the chef at the Craignure Inn for a number of years and the Old Mill Cottage already has quite a reputation locally for its food, which is served in the intimate restaurant. The two bedrooms are simply furnished, both with *en suite* bathrooms.

OWNERS: James and Jennifer Smith   OPEN: all year   ROOMS: 1 double, 1 twin; both rooms with bath/shower; both rooms suitable for wheelchair-users; TV in both bedrooms   TERMS: single occupancy £25, twin/double £42–£47; half-price for children; dinner à la carte from £10 to £20   CARDS: Access, Delta, Visa   DETAILS: children welcome; dogs welcome; no smoking in restaurant; car park; garden

If a B&B offers off-street car parking, we note 'car park' in the details at the end of the entry. If we are aware of particular car-parking difficulties, we mention them.

Many B&Bs are in remote places, and although in many cases we provide directions, it is always advisable to ask for clear instructions when booking.

LOCH ERIBOLL   Highland   map 11

Port-na-Con House

Loch Eriboll, by Altnaharra, Lairg IV27 4UN
TEL/FAX: (01971) 511367
just off A838, 7m SE of Durness

Originally a customs-house and harbour store, Port-na-Con has been
modernised and transformed into a small, comfortable whitewashed
guesthouse with its own little beach on the west side of Loch Eriboll.
All the small bedrooms are clean and comfortable, one now *en suite*
and another with a private bathroom, and all have loch views. There
is a first-floor lounge with a balcony, with plenty of local books and
maps provided by the Blacks, a very friendly English couple. There is
no television in the house because of the very poor reception. Evening
meals consisting of local produce, including prawns from Loch
Eriboll, are served in the dining-room, to both residents and non-
residents. Packed lunches can also be provided.

OWNERS: Ken and Lesley Black   OPEN: mid-Mar to mid-Oct   ROOMS: 2 double, 1 with
bath/shower, 1 with wash-basin; 1 twin with bath/shower; 1 family, with wash-basin
TERMS: single occupancy £22.50 to £24.50, twin/double £33–£37, family room from
£50; children's reductions by arrangement; dinner £11; deposit: £10 per room   CARDS:
Access, Visa   DETAILS: children welcome; no smoking; car park; garden

LOCHGILPHEAD   Strathclyde   map 11

Buidhe Lodge

Craobh Haven, by Lochgilphead PA31 8UA
TEL: (01852) 500291
on A816 to Oban, 17m N of Lochgilphead

This modern timber building sits by the water's edge in a sheltered
bay on the small island of Eilean Buidhe in Loch Shuna. Buidhe
Lodge and the adjacent Watersports Centre are linked to the
mainland village of Craobh Haven by a short causeway. All the small
bedrooms are on the ground floor and are simply furnished in pine
with *en suite* facilities. The large open-plan lounge has a dining area
at one end where Simone Twinn serves good home-cooked meals
using local produce. Running along this room is a balcony which gives
wonderful views of the loch and surrounding hills. A collection of
miniature sailing boats made by Nick Twinn is displayed in the
lounge. The property has its own slipway and mooring and is a
marvellous place for sailing; mountain bikes are available for hire.

OWNERS: Nick and Simone Twinn   OPEN: all year exc Christmas   ROOMS: 6 twin, all with
bath/shower; TV in all bedrooms and lounge   TERMS: twin £40–£50; dinner £13;
deposit: 33%   CARDS: Access, Visa   DETAILS: children welcome; dogs welcome with
own bedding; smoking in lounge only; car park; garden

The Albannach

Baddidarroch, Lochinver IV27 4LP
TEL/FAX: (01571) 844407
off A837, ½m W of Lochinver

All that is best in Highland hospitality can be found at The
Albannach which stands in a peaceful position just outside the fishing
village of Lochinver. The oldest part of the house dates back some two
hundred years, with the larger part added in the nineteenth century.
The 1990s addition to the house is the conservatory, where guests can
sit and have drinks while admiring the spectacular views across the
bay to the mountains of Assynt. The four bedrooms all have *en suite*
facilities and one has a four-poster bed. Four-course evening meals
are served in the wood-panelled candlelit dining-room, which is also
open to non-residents. Both proprietors are friendly and make sure
their guests are comfortable: Lesley cooks and Colin cuts a dashing
figure in a kilt.

OWNERS: Colin Craig and Lesley Crosfield OPEN: Mar to Christmas ROOMS: 1 double,
2 twin, 1 four-poster; all rooms with bath/shower; TV lounge TERMS: rates include
dinner; single occupancy £60–£66, twin/double £90–£100, four-poster £104; deposit: 1
night's charge CARDS: Access, Visa DETAILS: no children under 5; no dogs; no
smoking; car park; garden

Veyatie

66 Baddidarroch, Lochinver IV27 4LP
TEL: (01571) 844424
off A837, 1m NW of Lochinver

The house was built in the mid-1980s when the Garners returned
from Saudi Arabia. Veyatie is at the very end of the road in
Baddidarroch and has magnificent views over the village, port and
mountains. The terraced garden has a barbecue with tables and
chairs for guests' use. Of the three small bedrooms, two are *en suite*
and the third has a private bathroom. The large, light lounge
overlooks the garden and the panoramic view. Two steps lead up to
the dining area, where breakfast only is served at separate tables.
Various eating establishments are nearby in Lochinver, and fishing
trips can be arranged. Packed lunches are available by arrangement.

OWNERS: Ted and Margaret Garner OPEN: April to Nov ROOMS: 1 double, 2 twin; all
rooms with bath/shower; TV lounge TERMS: twin/double £40–£46; deposit: 10%
DETAILS: no children under 12; no dogs in lounge; no smoking in dining area or
bedrooms; car park; garden

LOCHRANZA   Strathclyde   **map 11**

Apple Lodge

Lochranza, Isle Of Arran KA27 8HJ
TEL/FAX: (01770) 830229

This whitewashed building standing on Lochranza's main road was originally the village manse. The Boyds have transformed the house into a place of elegance and comfort, with antique furniture in the sitting- and dining-rooms. The spacious bedrooms have been attractively decorated; two are *en suite* and the other has its own bathroom. One bedroom is on the ground floor. Evening meals are served at 7pm around one big table and make use of local produce and home-grown herbs. Guests can bring their own wine as there is no licence. The house is a mile from the ferry pier for Kintyre, and enjoys lovely views. One enthusiastic couple summed up their stay here as 'a memorable few days'.

OWNER: Mrs G.V. Boyd OPEN: all year exc Christmas ROOMS: 3 double, 1 twin; all rooms with bath/shower; TV in all bedrooms TERMS: single occupancy £40, twin/double £50; deposit £20 per person; dinner £14 CARDS: none DETAILS: no children; no dogs; smoking in lounge only; car park; garden

Butt Lodge Hotel

Lochranza, Isle of Arran KA27 8JF
TEL: (01770) 830240
take turning opposite outdoor field centre and follow signposts

Butt Lodge was built about 100 years ago as a shooting lodge, and is a pleasant whitewashed building standing in two acres of gardens. It lies just outside the village of Lochranza close to the ferry from Kintyre, and nestles under the hills in a quiet rural spot. The *en suite* bedrooms are fresh and clean, and the hotel has a cosy, friendly atmosphere. Evening meals are served in the licensed dining-room, and the comfortable sitting-room has a real fire. Next to the hotel is a golf course, and deer can often be seen grazing nearby.

OWNERS: Mr and Mrs P. Price OPEN: Apr to end Oct ROOMS: 4 double, 2 twin; all rooms with bath/shower; TV lounge TERMS: single occupancy £28–£31, twin/double £46–£52; dinner £12.50; deposit: £10–£30 CARDS: Access, Delta, Visa DETAILS: no children; no dogs; smoking in residents' lounge only; car park; garden

Bath / shower in the details under each entry means that the rooms have private facilities. The B&B may have other, shared bathroom facilities as well. We say if rooms have wash-basins.

LONGFORMACUS   Borders   **map 11**

Eildon Cottage

Longformacus, nr Duns TD11 3PB
TEL: (01361) 890230
off A6105/B6355, 6m W of Duns

This attractive grey house, with dormer windows and a pretty
garden, doubles as the post office in the tiny village of Longformacus.
The only visible sign is a desk in the postmistress's cosy sitting-room,
adjacent to the bed-and-breakfast accommodation. Eildon Cottage is
very comfortable, pleasantly decorated and furnished. One reporter
was 'most impressed' with the *en suite* accommodation, and along
with one other enjoyed 'an excellent tea, dinner and breakfast'. Meals
are served at a round table in the bay window of the sitting-room, and
although there is no licence, guests can bring their own wine. The
cottage is by the Southern Upland Way, and so is popular with
hikers; packed lunches are provided.

OWNER: Margaret Amos   OPEN: all year exc Christmas and New Year   ROOMS: 1 twin, 2
family; all rooms with bath/shower; TV in some bedrooms and lounge   TERMS: single
occupancy £16, twin £32, family room from £45; children under 2 free, £7 for ages 2 to
12; dinner £7 to £10; deposit: £2   CARDS: none   DETAILS: children welcome; dogs
welcome; car park; garden

LONGHOPE   Orkney   **map 11**

Burnhouse Farm

Longhope, South Walls KW16 3PA
TEL: (01856) 701263
*from Lyness ferry terminal follow directions for Longhope, take first road
on right, signposted*

Burnhouse stands just above Longhope village, with lovely views over
the bay to the hills of Hoy and over the South Isles and Scapa Flow to
Orkney mainland. This old farmhouse has a well-maintained garden
and a friendly atmosphere. There are two simple, pine-furnished
ground-floor bedrooms with books and games, and guests share the
large sitting/dining-room with the family. On sunny days meals can
be taken on the small sun porch. Dinner is at 6.30pm or by
arrangement; children's helpings and vegetarian choices can be
requested, and visitors can bring their own wine as there is no
licence. This is a wonderful location for walks, bird-watching and
enjoying the spectacular scenery, including the Old Man of Hoy.
Packed lunches are provided.

OWNER: Leslye Budge   OPEN: all year exc Christmas   ROOMS: 2 twin, both with wash-basin; TV in both bedrooms   TERMS: single occupancy £14–£16, twin £28–£32; children under 2 free; dinner £8; deposit: £5 per room per night   CARDS: none   DETAILS: children welcome; dogs by arrangement; smoking in sun porch only; car park; garden

LUNNING   Shetland
map 11

Skeo Green

Lunning, nr Vidlin, Shetland ZE2 9QB
TEL: (01806) 577302
16m N of Lerwick (ask for directions when booking)

Standing at the end of a very narrow road, Skeo Green is a large whitewashed house in an isolated and wild location close to the sea. The house accommodates an extended family and offers only one simple twin-bedded room, with meals being taken in the family dining-room. Although unlicensed, guests are welcome to bring their own wine to dinner, and packed lunches can be provided. There is an artist's studio and dark room available. The area is an excellent one for walking, fishing, bird-watching, and spotting otters and seals.

OWNER: Barbara Ford   OPEN: all year   ROOMS: 1 twin; TV lounge   TERMS: single occupancy £14, twin £28; children £7 to £10; dinner £6 to £9; deposit: 10%   CARDS: none   DETAILS: children welcome; no dogs in bedroom or dining area; car park; garden

LUSS   Strathclyde
map 11

Ardallie House

Luss, nr Alexandria G83 8NU
TEL: (01436) 860272

Ardallie House is a small, comfortable country house, up a drive off the Luss bypass, with wonderful views over trees to Loch Lomond and the hills beyond. Friendly owners and interesting furniture and pictures combine to provide a welcoming atmosphere. The three bedrooms are attractively decorated and share two bathrooms. The long, large sitting-room has a dining area at one end where evening meals are served if arranged in advance. Although Ardallie House is unlicensed, guests may bring their own wine to dinner.

OWNER: Diana Short   OPEN: Easter to Oct   ROOMS: 1 double, 2 twin; all rooms with wash-basin; TV lounge   TERMS: single occupancy £21–£23, twin/double £32–£36; children under 3 free; dinner £10 to £15; deposit: £5 per person   CARDS: none   DETAILS: children welcome; no dogs in public rooms; no smoking; car park; garden

Stoneyquoy Farm

Lyness, Hoy KW16 3NY
TEL: (01856) 791234

This comfortable, cosy family house is a traditional farmhouse with
low stone buildings and slate roofs, a sheltered garden and views over
Longhope Bay. The two simple, small bedrooms are in the extension
to the house and are now *en suite*. Guests share the new sun porch
and sitting-room with the family, enjoying the open peat fire on cooler
evenings as the house does not have full central heating. Louise
Budge, who is Dutch, produces good home-cooked dinners to which
guests are welcome to bring their own wine; packed lunches can also
be provided. Arthur Budge is always willing to take guests on a tour
of the 200-acre farm and will give advice on local walks and places to
visit.

OWNER: Louise Budge   OPEN: all year exc Christmas and New Year   ROOMS: 1 double,
1 twin; both rooms with bath/shower; TV lounge   TERMS: single occupancy £17, twin/
double £30; children half-price according to age; dinner £8; deposit: £2 per person
CARDS: none   DETAILS: children welcome; no dogs; no smoking; car park; garden

East Trodigal Cottage

Machrihanish PA28 6PT
TEL: (01586) 810305
take A83 from Tarbert to Campbeltown, then A843 towards Macrihanish

This pleasant whitewashed cottage stands on the road between
Campbeltown and Machrihanish. A stream runs round the garden
and back to a little ruined church and graveyard up the glen. The
house has been delightfully decorated and furnished, providing two
pretty bedrooms. Mrs Peacock is a particularly friendly lady.
Breakfast is served in the combined sitting-room and dining-room.
Machrihanish golf course is very close by, Glasgow airport is only
three miles away and Campbeltown about five miles. Packed lunches
can be provided.

OWNER: Mrs E. Peacock   OPEN: May to Oct   ROOMS: 1 double, 1 family; both rooms
with bath/shower; TV in both bedrooms   TERMS: single occupancy £18, double £32,
family room £32; children under 2 free, half-price for children from 2 to 12   CARDS:
none   DETAILS: children welcome; dogs welcome; no smoking; car park; garden

MELROSE Borders   map 11

Dunfermline House

Buccleuch Street, Melrose TD6 9LB
TEL/FAX: (01896) 822148

This small stone house stands right in the centre of Melrose about 50 yards from the abbey and close to the station. It is extremely well run and has a welcoming, friendly atmosphere. One couple reported that they were 'made to feel at home from the moment we arrived'. Dunfermline has been prettily decorated throughout and offers clean, comfortable accommodation. Apart from the single room, which has a private bathroom, all the bedrooms are *en suite*. There is a cosy lounge and an attractive dining-room, where breakfast only is served. Packed lunches can be provided. Arrivals should note that the property does not have its own car park.

OWNERS: Susan and Ian Graham OPEN: all year ROOMS: 1 single, 2 double, 2 twin; all rooms with bath/shower; TV in all bedrooms TERMS: single £21–£22, twin/double £42–£44; deposit: £10 CARDS: none DETAILS: children welcome; no dogs; no smoking

MELVICH Highland   map 11

The Sheiling

Melvich KW14 7YJ
TEL: (01641) 531256   FAX: (01641) 531356
on A836, 15m W of Thurso

Standing above the main road at the edge of the village, this unpretentious house enjoys panoramic views over the Atlantic and the River Halladale. The Campbells, who were born and brought up in the area, built The Sheiling as a family home. All three bedrooms are on the ground floor; two of them face the front, and the one at the back catches the afternoon sun. A visitor's stay was enhanced by Joan Campbell's 'personal service of a high quality'. Dinner is served at a single table, with guests eating together, in a dining-room that overlooks the river and beach. Food focuses on local produce, and vegetarian options are sometimes available. The house is unlicensed, but guests may bring their own wine to dinner. There are two lounges: one has TV and the other is for smokers. Across the road is a walkway down to the beach.

OWNERS: Joan and Hugh Campbell ROOMS: 2 double, 1 twin; all rooms with bath/shower; TV lounge TERMS: single occupancy £35, twin/double £46; reductions for children under 12; dinner £13; deposit: £10 CARDS: none DETAILS: children welcome; no dogs in dining-room and 1 lounge; smoking in 1 lounge only; car park; garden

---

MINNIGAFF **Dumfries & Galloway**   **map 11**

Auchenleck Farm

Minnigaff DG8 7AA
TEL: (01671) 402035
4m NE of Minnigaff

Auchenleck Farm is approached down a narrow lane five miles from
Newton Stewart, in an isolated position surrounded by farmland and
forests. It was built in 1863 by the Earl of Galloway as a shooting
lodge, and is a stone-built house with a circular staircase enclosed in
a turreted tower. The house is part of a working beef and sheep farm
and is set in a large garden. The rooms are freshly decorated, and
breakfast only is served in the dining-room. A TV lounge has books
and board games. The Glentrool National Park is good for forest
walking; packed lunches can be requested.

OWNER: Margaret Hewitson OPEN: Easter to end Oct ROOMS: 2 double, 1 twin; all
rooms with bath/shower; TV lounge TERMS: single occupancy £23.50, twin/double
£37; deposit: £10 per person CARDS: none DETAILS: children by arrangement; no
dogs; smoking in lounge only; car park; garden

MOFFAT **Dumfries & Galloway**   **map 11**

Alba House

20 Beechgrove, Moffat DG10 9RS
TEL: (01683) 220418

Alba House is a small, listed terraced house in a quiet street on the
outskirts of Moffat. It was built in 1731 and has views over fields and
the Annan valley. Birds and bird-watching are special interests of
Evelyn and Jake Lindsay, who are also avid collectors of pottery and
pictures. Their charming house – described by one couple as the 'best
of our journey' and 'masterfully decorated' – reflects their interests,
particularly the attractive dining-room (where breakfast only is
served) with its inglenook fireplace. The spacious, comfortable
bedrooms all have *en suite* bathrooms, and at the rear of the property
is a pretty terraced garden. Packed lunches can be provided. Moffat is
handy for golf, tennis, riding and fishing.

OWNERS: Evelyn and Jake Lindsay OPEN: all year exc Christmas ROOMS: 1 double, 1
twin, 1 family; all rooms with bath/shower; TV in all bedrooms and lounge TERMS:
single occupancy £18.50, twin/double £37, family room from around £50; children's
reductions by arrangement CARDS: none DETAILS: children welcome; no dogs; car
park; garden

---

*It is always best to check prices, especially for single occupancy, when
booking.*

Ericstane

Moffat DG10 9LT
TEL: (01638) 220127
at end of narrow road following River Annan, 4m N of Moffat

Ericstane is a rambling old farmhouse set in idyllic countryside some four miles outside Moffat. The house stands in a parklike valley setting, with views over the River Annan to the hills beyond. The Jacksons have considerably renovated the property, which has a warm atmosphere and is simply decorated. The two large, comfortably furnished bedrooms face the front. The original pine doors remain and there is a lovely collection of old paintings and prints. Mrs Jackson runs the 800-acre sheep and cattle farm, while Mr Jackson tends to the guests. Breakfast only is served at one end of the sitting/dining-room (packed lunches are provided). Moffat has a good selection of eating places.

OWNER: R.H. Jackson OPEN: all year ROOMS: 1 double, 1 twin; both rooms with bath/shower; TV in both bedrooms and lounge TERMS: single occupancy from £21, twin/double from £32 CARDS: none DETAILS: children welcome; dogs by arrangement; car park; garden

Fernhill

Grange Road, Moffat DG10 9HT
TEL: (01683) 220077

Fernhill has a warm and welcoming atmosphere and the Gourlays are very hospitable hosts. The house stands in an elevated position at the end of a short street enjoying views over the hills. It is very comfortably furnished and full of ornaments, pictures and trinkets. There is a large sitting-room, and breakfast only is served in the very pretty dining-room, which has another sitting area off it overlooking the colourful garden. The parking area is locked at night, though Fernhill is only a short walk to the centre of town. Packed lunches can be provided.

OWNERS: Mr and Mrs A.N. Gourlay OPEN: Apr to Sept ROOMS: 1 double, 2 twin; all with bath/shower; TV in all bedrooms and lounge TERMS: single occupancy £20, twin/double £33 CARDS: none DETAILS: no children under 10; no dogs; smoking in lounge only; car park; garden

Thai-Ville

3 Dundanion Place, Moffat DG10 9GD
TEL: (01683) 220922

Thai-Ville is a small modern bungalow standing in a quiet residential street, just a few minutes' walk from the town centre. The Batys are an older, kindly couple, very solicitous of their guests' needs, who have named their home after their many visits to Thailand. The house is very comfortable and full of ornaments and trinkets, and the *en suite* bedrooms are thoughtfully equipped. Guests have use of a TV lounge, garden and patio, and breakfast is taken at one table in the dining-room. Although dinner is not served, a complimentary supper tray is placed in guests' rooms during the evening.

OWNERS: John and Eileen Baty OPEN: mid-Mar to mid-Nov ROOMS: 2 twin; both rooms with bath/shower; TV in both bedrooms and lounge TERMS: twin £34 CARDS: none DETAILS: no children; no dogs in public rooms; no smoking; car park; garden

MUIR OF AIRD Western Isles map 11

Lennox Cottage

Muir of Aird, Isle of Benbecula PA88 5LA
TEL: (01870) 602965

Lennox Cottage belongs to a warm, friendly and hospitable local lady who was born in one of the island's oldest houses (it has associations with Bonnie Prince Charlie). The bedrooms are comfortably appointed, one having *en suite* facilities and the other two having the use of private bathrooms. The cosy lounge has an open fire, and good home-cooked meals are served in the kitchen. Although the cottage is unlicensed, guests may bring their own wine to dinner. Packed lunches can be provided. Muir of Aird is close to beaches and trout lochs and is an excellent location for exploring both South and North Uist.

OWNER: Emma Macdonald OPEN: all year ROOMS: 1 double, 2 twin; all with bath/shower; TV in all bedrooms and lounge TERMS: single occupancy £16, twin/double £34; dinner £8 CARDS: none DETAILS: children welcome; dogs welcome; no smoking in dining-room; car park; garden

NAIRN Highland map 11

Greenlawns

13 Seafield Street, Nairn IV12 4HG
TEL: (01667) 452738

This attractive Victorian house set in its own garden is only a few minutes' walk from the sea front and golf course. Three of the comfortable bedrooms are on the ground floor, and breakfast is the only meal served in the attractive breakfast room. A large gallery/lounge displays the works of local artists, and there is a separate upstairs lounge if guests wish to read there. The garden has chairs for sitting out on warm days. Packed lunches can be provided.

OWNERS: Bill and Isabel Caldwell   OPEN: all year exc Christmas   ROOMS: 2 double, with wash-basin; 3 twin, 1 four-poster; all with bath/shower; 2 rooms suitable for wheelchair-users; TV in all bedrooms and lounge   TERMS: single occupancy £30, twin/double £34–£42, four-poster £48; babies free, half-price for children   CARDS: Access, Visa
DETAILS: children welcome; no dogs in public rooms; car park; garden

NENTHORN   Borders   map 11

Whitehill Farm

Nenthorn, nr Kelso TD5 7RZ
TEL/FAX: (01573) 470203
take the A6089 out of Kelso towards Edinburgh, the farm is next right turn after passing through Nenthorn

This early Victorian farmhouse on a working farm is in a wonderful location, surrounded by trees and lawns, with marvellous views of the Cheviots hills. The comfortable house has been tastefully decorated, and most bedrooms have a view. The two single bedrooms are very spacious, and share a bathroom with one of the twin rooms; the other twin has *en suite* facilities. The large, pleasant sitting-room has an open fire on cooler nights. Evening meals are served by arrangement only in the front-facing dining-room; children's helpings are offered. There is no licence but guests can bring their own wine. Visitors are welcome to walk round the farm and there is access to tracks for walks. The area has an abundance of castles and old houses, including nearby Floors Castle.

OWNERS: Mr and Mrs David Smith   OPEN: all year exc Christmas, New Year and owners' holiday   ROOMS: 2 single, both with wash-basin; 2 twin, 1 with bath/shower, 1 with wash-basin; TV lounge   TERMS: single £16.50, single occupancy (not June to Sept) £25, twin/double £33–£35; reductions for children according to age; dinner £14; deposit
CARDS: none   DETAILS: children welcome; dogs welcome; no smoking in bedrooms; car park; garden

NEWTON STEWART   Dumfries & Galloway   map 11

Oakbank

Corsbie Road, Newton Stewart DG8 6JB
TEL: (01671) 402822   FAX: (01671) 403050

Set on a hill above the town, Oakbank enjoys lovely views of the hills. It is a Victorian stone-built property standing in a large garden, with spacious rooms. The house is attractively decorated and furnished with a nice collection of prints. The main rooms are unusually designed with slanting windows affording good views. There is a comfortable TV sitting-room, and dinner is available by arrangement, served at one table in the dining-room. Guests may bring their own wine as there is no licence. Packed lunches can be provided.

OWNER: Sheila Limbrey OPEN: all year exc Dec ROOMS: 2 double, 1 with bath/shower, 1 with wash-basin; 1 twin, with bath/shower; TV in some bedrooms and lounge TERMS: twin/double £32–£36; dinner £10 CARDS: none DETAILS: no children; dogs welcome; no smoking; car park; garden

NORTH ERRADALE   Highland

map 11

Little Lodge

North Erradale, Gairloch IV21 2DS
TEL: (01445) 771237
off B8021 Gairloch to Melvaig road, just after turning to North Erradale

Little Lodge, an expanded working croft house, is an attractive whitewashed building standing on its own on a wild moorland peninsula looking over the Minch to Skye and across to the Torridon Mountains. It is located about six miles from Gairloch down a narrow road. Di and Inge are welcoming, friendly and unobtrusive hosts, and guests immediately feel at home. The sitting-room, which is one of the old croft rooms, has an open fire, exposed stone walls, and the original panelled wood which has been painstakingly stripped. The sun room with windows all round is where good home-cooked meals are served at individual tables; guests are free to bring their own wine as there is no licence. The three bedrooms are very comfortable, all with *en suite* facilities; one is on the ground floor.

OWNERS: Di Johnson and Inge Ford OPEN: Apr to Oct ROOMS: 2 double, 1 twin; all rooms with bath/shower TERMS: rates include dinner; single occupancy £47.50–£52.50, twin/double £75–£85; deposit: 1 night's charge CARDS: none DETAILS: no children; no dogs; no smoking; car park; garden

OBAN   Strathclyde

map 11

Don-Muir

Pulpit Hill, Oban PA34 4LX
TEL: (01631) 564536   FAX: (01631) 563739

Don-Muir is a modern villa-style bungalow on a hill above Oban. It has a well-kept front garden and Mrs Robertson gives her guests a very friendly welcome. The five bedrooms are on the small side, but are comfortable and three are on the ground floor. There is a lounge for guests, and a small breakfast room where dinner is served by arrangement; visitors may bring their own wine to dinner. Packed lunches can be provided.

OWNERS: Peigi and Malcolm Robertson OPEN: Feb to Nov ROOMS: 1 single, with wash-basin; 3 double, all with bath/shower; 1 twin, with wash-basin; TV in all bedrooms TERMS: single £16–£17, single occupancy £25, twin/double £30–£34; dinner £11; deposit: £5 per person CARDS: none DETAILS: children welcome; no dogs in dining-room; no smoking in dining-room; car park; garden

Dungrainach

Pulpit Hill, Oban PA34 4LX
TEL: (0131) 562840

Dungrainach occupies one of the most spectacular positions in Oban. Set on Pulpit Hill in a large, mature and beautifully kept garden the views of the sea and islands are superb. This 100-year-old house has spacious rooms, which are attractively furnished and decorated and immaculately kept. Guests have use of a bright TV lounge, and breakfast only is served at one table in the dining-room. The Robertsons are a hard-working couple, very involved in local affairs.

OWNER: Elaine Robertson OPEN: Easter to Oct ROOMS: 1 double, 2 twin; all rooms with bath/shower; TV in all bedrooms and lounge TERMS: single occupancy £18.50, twin/double £37; deposit: £10–£20 CARDS: none DETAILS: children welcome; dogs welcome; car park; garden

Lorne View

Ardconnel Road, Oban PA34 5DW
TEL: (01631) 565500

This small terraced house in a quiet street only a few minutes' walk from the centre of town has lovely views over Oban Bay. The three bedrooms are small and attractively decorated; each has its own shower unit and TV. The two doubles (one of which has a wonderful view) are on the second floor and have an adjacent WC, and the twin is on the first floor beside the bathroom and WC. Evening meals are served by arrangement at 6.15pm in the small lounge/dining-room; guests may bring their own wine to dinner. Packed lunches are provided on request.

OWNER: Mrs E.M. Maclean OPEN: all year exc Christmas ROOMS: 2 double, 1 twin; all rooms with shower; TV in all bedrooms TERMS: single occupancy £30, twin/double £64; dinner £11; deposit: £20 CARDS: none DETAILS: children welcome; no dogs in dining-room; no smoking in dining-room

OLD DAILLY   Strathclyde   **map 11**

Hawkhill Farm

Old Dailly, nr Girvan KA26 9RD
TEL: (01465) 871232
just off B734 / B741, 3m E of Girvan

This working arable farm on the edge of the tiny village of Old Dailly originally started life as a coaching-inn. Mrs Kyle is a welcoming and friendly lady who fills the house with lovely flower arrangements. The comfortable and spacious rooms include an attractive first-floor sitting-room with TV and a log fire. Croquet can be played in the garden, which enjoys views of Killochan Castle. Culzean Castle and Galloway Forest Park are nearby, and golf, pony trekking and fishing can be arranged.

OWNERS: Isobel Kyle OPEN: Mar to Oct ROOMS: 2 double, 1 with bath/shower, 1 with wash-basin; 1 twin, with bath/shower; TV lounge TERMS: single occupancy from £20, twin/double from £36; children half-price sharing with parents; deposit: £10 per person CARDS: none DETAILS: children welcome; dogs welcome in bedrooms only (not on beds); car park; garden

---

OLDMELDRUM Grampian

map 11

Cromlet Hill

South Road, Oldmeldrum, nr Inverurie AB51 0AB
TEL: (01651) 872315   FAX: (01651) 872164

Cromlet Hill stands in the small historic town of Oldmeldrum, which makes an excellent base for visiting castles and distilleries. The listed Georgian house dates from around 1805, with an Italianate rear wing added in the Victorian era. Large, secluded gardens surround the property. Originally the house belonged to the Manson family; Sir Patrick Manson helped found the London School of Tropical Medicine. The bedrooms are spacious and very well appointed, and

CROMLET HILL, OLDMELDRUM

there is an elegant lounge. Four-course dinners are available by prior arrangement, and vegetarians can be catered for with notice. There is no licence, but guests may bring their own wine.

OWNERS: John and Isabel Page OPEN: all year exc Christmas ROOMS: 1 double, 1 twin, 1 family; all rooms with bath/shower; TV in all bedrooms and lounge TERMS: single occupancy £30, twin/double £50, family room £75; dinner £15; deposit 20% CARDS: none DETAILS: children welcome in family room only; no dogs; no smoking in bedrooms; car park; garden

PEEBLES Borders

map 11

Whitestone House

Innerleithen Road, Peebles EH45 8BD
TEL: (01721) 720337

This solid stone house is on the main A72 road, close to the centre of Peebles. It was built in 1892 as a manse and is set in a large, pretty garden with lovely views of the hills. The bedrooms, some with fine views, are of a good size and simply furnished. Overlooking the garden is a comfortable sitting/breakfast room which has an original black marble fireplace. Breakfast only is served at one table.

OWNER: Mrs M. Muir OPEN: all year exc Christmas ROOMS: 3 double, 1 twin, 1 family; all with wash-basin; TV lounge TERMS: single occupancy £20, twin/double £30–£32, family room from £32; children's reductions by arrangement; deposit: for late arrival times CARDS: none DETAILS: children welcome; no dogs; car park; garden

PERTH Tayside

map 11

Achnacarry Guest House

3 Pitcullen Crescent, Perth PH2 7HT
TEL: (01738) 621421   FAX: (01738) 444110
on A94 Perth to Forfar road

Achnacarry is one of a row of guesthouses in Pitcullen Crescent about ten minutes' walk from the centre of Perth. The house is warm and comfortable and the welcome friendly. All the compact bedrooms are *en suite* and the small lounge is a restul place in which to relax. Breakfast, as well as evening meals by previous arrangement, is available in the dining-room. Although Achnacarry is unlicensed, guests are welcome to bring their own wine to dinner.

OWNERS: Eileen and John Cowan OPEN: all year ROOMS: 1 double, 1 twin, 2 family; all rooms with bath/shower; TV in all bedrooms and lounge TERMS: single occupancy £21–£35, twin/double £37–£40, family room £50–£58; half-price for children over 2; dinner £9 to £10; deposit: one night's charge CARDS: Access, Amex, Delta, Visa DETAILS: children welcome; dogs welcome in bedrooms only; no smoking in dining-room; car park

Sunbank House Hotel

50 Dundee Road, Perth PH2 7BA
TEL: (01738) 624882   FAX: (01738) 442515
on A85, near junction with M85

This very comfortable and professionally run guesthouse dates from 1853. The extension to the building in 1992 was awarded a prize and contains five very well-appointed bedrooms with good-sized bathrooms, three of which are on the ground floor. There is a very attractive, light dining-room which overlooks the front garden and has fine views across the city to the hills beyond, and also a comfortable guests' lounge. Sunbank is fully licensed and dinner is available. Packed lunches can also be provided.

OWNERS: Gordon and Florence Laing   OPEN: all year   ROOMS: 1 single, with wash-basin; 5 double, 2 twin, 2 family, all with bath/shower; 1 room suitable for wheelchair-users; TV in all rooms   TERMS: single £28, single occupancy £38–£45, twin/double £56–£68, family room from £85; children half-price in family room; dinner £19; deposit: £10 per adult   CARDS: Access, Visa   DETAILS: children welcome; no dogs; smoking in lounge only; car park; garden

PITLOCHRY   Tayside   map 11

Arrandale House

Knochfarrie Road, Pitlochry PH16 5DN
TEL: (01796) 472987

Built in the 1860s as a manse for Pitlochry East Church, this attractive stone-built house lies on the edge of Pitlochry and commands splendid views over the valley to the hills. Inside, the rooms are spacious, some retaining their original ceilings. The atmosphere is relaxed and the Irvines are, in the words of a guest, 'genuinely helpful'. Another visitor found Arrandale 'very good – roomy and friendly.' There is no lounge, but the bedrooms have their own sitting areas. Breakfast only is served in the dining-room.

OWNERS: Atholl and Pat Irvine   OPEN: Mar to Nov   ROOMS: 1 single, with wash-basin; 2 double, 1 with bath/shower, 1 with wash-basin; 1 twin, with bath/shower; 2 family, both with bath/shower; TV in all bedrooms   TERMS: single £15–£20, single occupancy £30, twin/double £30–£40, family room £50; half-price for children sharing with parents; deposit: £10 per room   CARDS: none   DETAILS: children welcome; no dogs; no smoking; car park; garden

We state at the end of an entry whether children are welcome. If we know of any restrictions on children, we give them.

Any smoking restrictions that we know of are given in the details at the end of the entry.

PLOCKTON   Highland
map 11

The Shieling

Plockton IV52 8TL
TEL: (01599) 544282
on S side of Loch Carron 5m north of Kyle of Lochalsh

Occupying an enviable position in the picturesque conservation village of Plockton, The Shieling stands on a little peninsula just a couple of minutes' walk from the village centre along a footpath on top of a narrow causeway. The previous house on the site was constructed by Mr MacDonald's father at the end of World War II, and the present low, narrow house was built to resemble it as closely as possible. One side faces the village and the other the water, with wonderful views to the hills and Duncraig Castle across the bay. All three bedrooms are on the ground floor, and the two bedrooms without private bathroom have sea views. If children are to be accommodated, only two people are permitted in a bedroom, i.e. only one adult and one child per room. The large lounge has sliding doors out to the garden, and although there is a separate dining-room, by popular request meals usually end up being served in the light-filled lounge with its lovely views. The MacDonalds are cheerful, welcoming people and the house has a happy atmosphere. Packed lunches can be provided.

OWNERS: Mr and Mrs John MacDonald   OPEN: Apr to Oct   ROOMS: 2 double, 1 with bath/shower, 1 with wash-basin; 1 twin, with wash-basin; TV lounge   TERMS: twin/double £34–£40; deposit: £10   CARDS: none   DETAILS: children welcome; no dogs; smoking in lounge only; car park; garden

PORTPATRICK   Dumfries & Galloway
map 11

Carlton House

21 South Crescent, Portpatrick DG9 8JR
TEL: (01776) 810253

In the centre of town right on the sea front, this terraced nineteenth-century house is fresh and clean and all the bedrooms except two are *en suite*. Some of the bedrooms have excellent sea views, and the lounge benefits from large sunny windows looking out over the bay and harbour: on a fine day the distant hills of Ireland can be seen. Dinner and breakfast are served in the pretty dining-room on the ground floor, and this room is also used to serve afternoon cream teas. Carlton House is unlicensed, but guests may bring their own wine to dinner. Packed lunches can be provided. On-street parking is nearby. Walkers will be interested to know that the Southern Upland Way, which crosses the entire width of Scotland, starts nearby.

OWNERS: R. and E. Thorburn OPEN: all year ROOMS: 4 double, 2 twin, 1 family room; all rooms with bath/shower exc 1 twin (with wash-basin); 1 room suitable for wheelchair-users; TV in all bedrooms TERMS: single occupancy £25, twin/double £36, family room from £36; children under 5 free, reductions for children over 5 sharing with parents; dinner £8.50; deposit: £10 CARDS: none DETAILS: children welcome; no dogs

Melvin Lodge

Dunskey Street, South Crescent, Portpatrick DG9 8LE
TEL: (01776) 810238
6m SW of Stromness

Melvin Lodge stands in a superb position at one end of the small harbour of Portpatrick, commanding views over the town and sea to the Irish coast. It has the appearance of a Victorian villa, but started life as a simple two-room cottage which has now become the lounge. The house has a welcoming atmosphere and is freshly decorated. Some of the ten small bedrooms are *en suite*, with the majority having sea views. There is a pleasant lounge, and a dining-room where breakfast only is served. Packed lunches can be provided.

OWNERS: Michael and Eileen Pinder OPEN: all year exc Christmas week ROOMS: 2 single, with wash-basin; 3 double, 1 with bath/shower, 1 with wash-basin; 1 twin, with wash-basin; 4 family, 3 with bath/shower, 1 with wash-basin; TV in all bedrooms and lounge TERMS: single £17, single occupancy £17–£22, twin/double £34–£38, family room £34–£38; children under 3 free; £4 for ages 3 to 10; £6 for ages 10 to 14; deposit: £10 per person CARDS: none DETAILS: children welcome; well-behaved dogs welcome; smoking in bedrooms only; car park; garden

PORTREE Highland   map 11

Balloch

Viewfield Road, Portree, Isle of Skye IV51 9ES
TEL: (01478) 612093

This small, modern house just off the main road on the outskirts of Portree has views over the Sound from the garden, where guests can sit on fine days. The four bedrooms are simply but comfortably furnished, all having
en suite facilities. Breakfast only is available in the lounge/dining-room. The town centre is just five minutes' walk away.

OWNER: Ena Macphie OPEN: Mar to Nov ROOMS: 1 single, 2 double, 1 twin; all with bath/shower; TV lounge TERMS: single from £18, twin/double from £36; children's reductions CARDS: none DETAILS: children welcome; dogs welcome; car park; garden

The end details for each entry state whether dogs are allowed, but it is always best to check when booking.

CONUSG, PORTREE

Conusg

Coolin Hills Gardens, Portree, Isle of Skye IV51 9NB
TEL: (01478) 612426

This attractive old whitewashed house was built in the 1880s,
originally belonging to the hunting lodge, now the Cuillin Hills Hotel.
The coachman and gardener lived upstairs, and below were stables.
This is how the Murrays, who are local Skye inhabitants, found the
property when they bought it over 20 years ago. The accommodation
is very simple, the welcome warm, and there is a combined breakfast-
room and lounge. The house stands in an elevated position above and
on the edge of the town, in a very peaceful location with wonderful
views of the hills and bay.

OWNER: Catriona Murray OPEN: Mar to Oct ROOMS: 2 single, 1 double, 1 twin; all
rooms with wash-basin; TV lounge TERMS: single from £15, twin/double from £30
CARDS: none DETAILS: no children; no dogs in public rooms; no smoking in dining-
room; car park; garden

*Please let us know if you need more report forms and we will send you a
fresh supply.*

Alamein House Hotel

28 Battery Place, Rothesay, Isle of Bute PA20 9DU
TEL: (01700) 502395

This attractive, small whitewashed Victorian house on the sea front
has wonderful views across the bay. Hazel Maughan-Davie is
continually upgrading and renovating the house with loving care,
bringing it back to its Victorian past. Each room has been
meticulously furnished and decorated, with many trinkets and
ornaments. One bedroom is on the ground floor. Both breakfast and
evening meals are served in the attractive dining-room and the cosy
sitting-room is at the back of the house. Hazel provides excellent
meals and is constantly acquiring more culinary skills. Although
Alamein House is unlicensed, guests may bring their own wine to
dinner. Special aromatherapy and calligraphy breaks are offered.

OWNER: Hazel Maughan-Davie   OPEN: all year, exc 3 weeks Nov, Christmas and New
Year   ROOMS: 2 single, both with wash-basin; 3 double, 2 with bath/shower, 1 with
wash-basin; 2 twin, both with bath/shower; TV in all bedrooms   TERMS: single £19.50,
single occupancy £21.50, twin/double £37; children's reductions according to age;
dinner £9; deposit: £20 per person   DETAILS: children welcome; dogs welcome exc in
public rooms; no smoking in dining-room; car park

Commodore

12 Battery Place, Rothesay, Isle of Bute PA20 9DP
TEL: (01700) 502178

Standing on the sea front in the centre of Rothesay, this handsome
whitewashed guesthouse offers six fairly small bedrooms on the
second floor, all *en suite* and freshly decorated. The front-facing rooms
have marvellous sea views. There is a lounge-cum-breakfast room,
and guests are welcome to use the garden at the rear of the house,
which gets plenty of sun. A couple of self-catering cottages with good
facilities are also available.

OWNERS: Mike and Maggie Spear   OPEN: all year   ROOMS: 3 double, 2 twin, 1 family; all
rooms with bath/shower; TV in all bedrooms   TERMS: single from £20, single occupancy
from £20, twin/double from £36, family room from £36; children under 5 free, half-price
for ages 6 to 12; deposit: £10–£20   CARDS: none   DETAILS: children welcome; small
dogs by arrangement; no smoking in lounge and dining-room; garden

*No stamps are needed if you write to the Guide from within the UK. Report
forms are at the end of the book, or use your own stationery if you prefer.*

ROY BRIDGE   Highland

map 11

Station House

Roy Bridge, nr Inverness PH31 4AG
TEL: (01397) 712285

This immaculately kept property house was formerly the station-master's house. It stands in a quiet location and has a colourful front garden, and friendly and welcoming hosts. The three good-sized bedrooms share a bathroom and a shower room. The lounge also doubles as the dining-room, where breakfast and evening meals (if booked in advance) are served. Station House is unlicensed, but guests may bring their own wine to dinner. There is no television available for guests' use.

OWNER: Mrs F. Grieve   OPEN: Apr to Oct   ROOMS: 2 double, 1 twin, all with wash-basin
TERMS: single occupancy £28, twin/double £28; £8 for children under 12; dinner £10;
deposit: £10   CARDS: none   DETAILS: children welcome; dogs welcome; car park;
garden

ST ABBS   Borders

map 11

Castle Rock

Murrayfield, St Abbs, Eyemouth TD14 5PP
TEL: (01890) 771715   FAX: (01890) 771520
off B6438, 3m NW of Eyemouth

This whitewashed Victorian house with its upstairs Gothic-shaped windows stands on its own at the end of the pretty village of St Abbs, high on the cliffs overlooking the harbour. All the bedrooms have sea views, are *en suite* and equipped with telephones, hairdryers, clock radios and satellite TV. Castle Rock is fully licensed, and evening meals always include a vegetarian option. There are lovely walks along the cliffs, birdwatching at St Abbas head and a sandy beach at nearby Coldingham Bay.

OWNERS: Peter and Kathryn Lutas   OPEN: Easter to end Oct   ROOMS: 1 single, 1 twin, 1
four-poster, 1 family; all rooms with bath/shower; TV in all bedrooms and lounge
TERMS: single £22, twin/double £44, four-poster £44, family room £66; dinner £14;
deposit: £20 per person   CARDS: Access, Amex, Delta, Visa   DETAILS: no children; dogs
welcome by prior arrangement and in bedrooms only; no smoking in dining-room; car
park; garden

The end details for each entry state whether dogs are allowed, but it is always best to check when booking.

Cadzow Guest House

58 North Street, St Andrews KY16 9AH
TEL: (01334) 476933

Cadzow Guest House stands in one of St Andrews' main streets, minutes away from the shops and only a ten-minute walk to the Old Course. It is a cosy, comfortable house with simple accommodation providing eight small but bright bedrooms. Breakfast only is served in the large basement sitting-room/breakfast room which leads out to the beautifully kept back garden.

OWNERS: Alexander and Elizabeth Small OPEN: Feb to Nov ROOMS: 1 single, with bath/shower; 4 double, 2 with bath/shower, 2 with wash-basin; 2 twin, both with bath/shower; 1 family, with bath/shower; TV in all bedrooms and lounge TERMS: single £20–£23, single occupancy £25, twin/double £30–£42, family room £46–£54; reductions for children sharing with parents; deposit: £10 per person CARDS: none
DETAILS: children welcome; dogs welcome; no smoking in some bedrooms and dining-room; garden

Glenderran Guest House

9 Murray Park, St Andrews KY16 9AW
TEL: (01334) 477951   FAX: (01334) 477908

This late-Victorian terraced town house exudes an air of quiet elegance and comfort. It has been furnished and decorated with care and taste, has very well-equipped bedrooms and a comfortable lounge. The two single rooms have their own adjacent bathrooms and the other bedrooms are *en suite*. The house, which was built in 1870, stands on land once owned by a local writer, William Murray, after whom the street was named. Glenderran is in the middle of St Andrews, in a one-way street close to shops and golf courses. Packed lunches are available.

OWNERS: Brian Hitchcock and Derrick Armitage OPEN: all year ROOMS: 2 single, 2 double, 1 twin; all rooms with bath/shower; TV in all bedrooms TERMS: single £20–£26, single occupancy £35–£47, twin/double £40–£52; deposit: one night's charge CARDS: Access, Visa DETAILS: no children under 12; no dogs; no smoking

Riverview

Edenside, by St Andrews KY16 9SQ
TEL/FAX: (01334) 838009

This modern, motel-style guesthouse is on the main road just north of St Andrews, overlooking the Eden Estuary. Each spacious bedroom has its own front door and *en suite* good-sized shower. Three of the rooms are at ground level and have courtyard benches and tables, the others have balconies for sitting out on, and all bedrooms have estuary views. Breakfast only is served at individual tables in the cheerful breakfast room, but food is available in the nearby pub. With enough notice, the Gatherums can help golfers organise a game at St Andrews or other nearby courses.

OWNER: David Gatherum OPEN: all year exc Christmas and New Year ROOMS: 1 double, 3 twin, 3 family; all rooms with shower; TV in all bedrooms TERMS: single occupancy £25, twin/double £40, family room £60; half-price for children sharing with parents; deposit: 25% CARDS: none DETAILS: children welcome; no dogs; no smoking; car park; garden

ST CATHERINES Strathclyde   map 11

Thistle House

St Catherines, by Cairndow PA25 8AZ
TEL: (01499) 302209
off A815, on E shore of Loch Fyne

Thistle House is a substantial Victorian property that stands above the A815 in two acres of well-maintained gardens, and has wonderful views across Loch Fyne to Inverary and Inverary Castle. The house is immaculate and provides comfortable bedrooms and a pleasant TV lounge. The front rooms have lovely loch views and all the rooms are *en suite* or have private bathrooms.

OWNER: Sandra Cameron OPEN: Easter to end Oct ROOMS: 2 double, 1 twin, 1 family; all rooms with bath/shower TERMS: single occupancy £25, twin/double £40–£45, family room £52.50; children's reductions if sharing with parents CARDS: Access, Delta, Visa DETAILS: children welcome; dogs by arrangement; no smoking in dining-room; car park; garden

ST MARGARET'S HOPE Orkney   map 11

Bellevue Guest House

St Margaret's Hope, South Ronaldsay KW17 2TL
TEL: (01856) 831294

With beautiful views over the attractive fishing village of St Margaret's Hope, this stone-built house offers well-appointed and spacious accommodation. It was built by Mr Gunn's great-grandfather in 1886 and is a comfortable family home. The three sizable bedrooms share a large bathroom and a shower room. Good home-cooked evening meals as well as breakfast are served at one large table in the dining-room; guests are welcome to bring their own wine to dinner, as Bellevue is unlicensed. Packed lunches can be provided. This is a good area for walking, beaches and bird-watching.

OWNER: Evelyn Gunn OPEN: all year ROOMS: 1 double, 1 twin, 1 family; all rooms with wash-basin; TV in all bedrooms and lounge TERMS: single occupancy £15, twin/double £30, family room £45; children's reductions; dinner £8; deposit CARDS: none DETAILS: children welcome; no dogs; smoking in lounge only; car park; garden

Blanster House

St Margaret's Hope, South Ronaldsay KW17 2TG
TEL: (01856) 831549

On the outskirts of the village, this nineteenth-century stone farmhouse stands back from the road behind a long walled garden surrounded by trees. There is a children's swing, and a neat path leads up to the front door. The three upstairs bedrooms are spacious; one is *en suite* and the other two share a bathroom. Angela Brown is a relaxed hostess who serves breakfast only in the attractive dining-room, although she will also make up packed lunches on request. There is a TV sitting-room for guests' use.

OWNERS: Graeme and Angela Brown OPEN: all year ROOMS: 2 double, 1 with bath/shower, 1 with wash-basin; 1 twin, with wash-basin; TV in all bedrooms and lounge TERMS: single £13–£14, single occupancy £12–£14, twin/double £24–£28; children's reductions by arrangement CARDS: none DETAILS: children welcome; dogs welcome; no smoking in dining-room; car park; garden

The Creel

Front Road, St Margaret's Hope, South Ronaldsay KW17 2SL
TEL: (01856) 831311

This small restaurant-with-rooms lies on the quayside in the centre of the village. The food here enjoys an excellent reputation, and draws in diners from near and far. Of the three spacious and attractive bedrooms, one has an open fire and two have sea views. Guests have use of a small kitchen on the top floor and a tiny lounge. The restaurant, which is fully licensed, seats 38 people and bookings are recommended. Vegetarian options are available on request; packed lunches can be provided.

OWNERS: Joyce and Alan Craigie OPEN: all year exc Jan ROOMS: 1 double, 2 twin; all rooms with bath/shower; TV in all bedrooms TERMS: single occupancy £30–£35, twin/double £50; dinner £20 to £25; children's reductions; deposit CARDS: Access, Visa DETAILS: no children under 5; no dogs; no smoking in bedrooms, or in restaurant before 9pm; car park (*The Good Food Guide*)

SALEN   Strathclyde   map 11

The Craig

Salen, nr Aros, Isle of Mull PA72 6JG
TEL: (01680) 300347

The Craig is conveniently located on the main road in Salen, about
halfway between Craignure and Tobermory. It is a small, friendly
hotel overlooking the Sound of Mull and is an ideal location for
touring the island and for the ferries. The pretty garden has a sun-
trap area to the side of the house and extends to a small stream,
which borders the property. The bedrooms are small and simply
furnished, and the sitting-room has a piano, games, magazines and
books. Breakfast only is served in the pine-furnished dining-room,
but there is a restaurant nearby for meals.

OWNERS: Jim and Lorna Mcintyre   OPEN: Easter to Oct   ROOMS: 2 double, 3 twin; all
rooms with wash-basin; TV lounge   TERMS: single occupancy £18–£20, twin/double
£32–£36   CARDS: Access, Visa   DETAILS: children welcome; dogs welcome exc in
public rooms; no smoking in dining-room; car park; garden

SCOURIE   Highland   map 11

Minch View

Scouriemore, Scourie, Lairg IV27 4TG
TEL: (01971) 502010
off A894, 3rd road on right S of Scourie

Splendid views over water and hills are enjoyed by visitors to this
simple, whitewashed building on the outskirts of Scourie. Nearby lies
the old family croft with sheep grazing around it. The bedrooms are
small and plainly furnished, and two are on the ground floor. There is
a large sitting-room, and evening meals are available by
arrangement. Guests may bring their own wine to dinner; packed
lunches can be provided.

OWNER: Christine B. Macdonald   OPEN: Mar to Oct   ROOMS: 2 double, both with wash-
basin; 1 twin; TV lounge   TERMS: single occupancy £20, twin/double £30; children's
reductions by arrangement; dinner £10   CARDS: none   DETAILS: children welcome; no
dogs in public rooms; car park; garden

---

*If any bedrooms are suitable for wheelchair-users, we mention this in the
details at the end of the entry.*

*If you disagree with any assessment made in this guide, please write and
tell us why. Address your letter to The Good Bed and Breakfast Guide,
FREEPOST, 2 Marylebone Road, London NW1 1YN.*

SEAMILL   Strathclyde   map 11

Spottiswoode

Sandy Road, Seamill, West Kilbride KA23 9NN
TEL: (01294) 823131   FAX: (01294)823179
just off A78

This large Victorian house is on a narrow, private road in the middle
of the resort. It stands in a walled garden and has lovely views of the
sea and islands; a sandy beach is just 100 yards away, accessed by the
road. Christine and Jim Ondersma are an enthusiastic and friendly
couple, who have decorated Spottiswoode with flair. The lovely
dining-room, furnished with William Morris wallpaper, overlooks the
sea. Breakfast is an event: there is a different main course each day,
such as eggs florentine on toast, as well as porridge and home-baked
muffins. Dinner is served by arrangement at the time of booking.
There is no licence so guests may bring their own wine. The pretty
sitting-room has lots of reading matter, and the three beautifully
decorated bedrooms are either *en suite* or have a private bathroom.
This makes an ideal base for exploring the Ayrshire coast; packed
lunches are provided.

OWNERS: Christine and Jim Ondersma   OPEN: all year   ROOMS: 2 double, 1 twin; all
rooms with bath/shower; TV in all bedrooms   TERMS: single occupancy £34–£46, twin/
double £40–£54; dinner £18 to £22; deposit   CARDS: Access, Visa   DETAILS: no children
under 12 exc babies; no dogs; no smoking; garden

SKELLISTER   Shetland   map 11

The Knowes

Skellister, South Nesting ZE2 9PP
TEL: (01595) 890204
just off B9075, 13m N of Lerwick

This small family home offering very comfortable accommodation is
in a beautiful location overlooking South Nesting Bay. The Jenners
are a young English couple who give a warm welcome to their guests,
and Julie provides home-cooked evening meals. There is no licence
but visitors can bring their own wine; children's helpings, vegetarian
choices and packed lunches can be provided. Upstairs is a cheerful
lounge with TV, video, Ordnance Survey maps, books and tourist
information. The shared downstairs bathroom has a Jacuzzi bath and
a sauna room off it (for which there is an additional charge). All
bedrooms have telephone and TV; the single room is on the ground
floor.

OWNER: Julie Jenner   OPEN: all year   ROOMS: 1 single, 1 double, 1 family, all with wash-
basin; TV in all bedrooms   TERMS: single £15–£17.50, single occupancy £15–£22.50,
double £30–£35, family room £30–£35; half-price for children under 5; dinner £11–£13
CARDS: none   DETAILS: children welcome; no dogs; no smoking; car park; garden

Corriegour Lodge

Loch Lochy, nr Spean Bridge PH34 4EB
TEL: (01397) 712685   FAX: (01397) 712696
just off A82 midway between Spean Bridge and Invergarry

Placed well above Loch Lochy, this former Victorian hunting lodge
commands superb loch views from bedrooms and public rooms. The
licensed dining area is in a conservatory-style room overlooking the
water. This leads through to a cosy bar and a comfortable sitting-
room with log fire. The smartly decorated bedrooms are all large and
en suite. Six acres of private, mature woodland and gardens lead
down to a lochside beach with jetty; a boat and fishing reels can be
provided to keen fishermen. Mountain bikes can be hired locally.
Packed lunches are available on request.

OWNERS: Rod and Lorna Bunney   OPEN: Mar to end Oct   ROOMS: 2 single, 4 double, 3
twin; all rooms with bath/shower; TV in all bedrooms   TERMS: single £28–£35, twin/
double £56–£70; children's reductions according to age if sharing with parents; dinner
£18.50   CARDS: Access, Amex, Visa   DETAILS: no children under 8; no dogs; no
smoking in dining-room; car park; garden

Invergloy House

Spean Bridge PH34 4DY
TEL: (01397) 712681
*on A82, 5½m N of Spean Bridge; entrance on left at white fence and down
signposted drive*

Invergloy House was formerly the stables to the big house, which was
burnt down. It shares part of the driveway with Riverside (see entry,
below), and has the same winding approach through woodland. The
house stands in 50 acres of grounds and has splendid views,
particularly from the drawing room, which overlooks Loch Lochy. The
comfortable bedrooms are attractively decorated, and Mrs Cairns
plans to install new bathrooms. Evening meals are available on
request, and are served in the dining-room with its grand piano.
Guests can enjoy free fishing on the loch, and there are rowing boats
for hire and a hard tennis court.

OWNER: Margaret Cairns   OPEN: all year   ROOMS: 1 single, with wash-basin; 3 twin, all
with bath/shower; TV lounge   TERMS: single £17, single occupancy £24, twin from £34;
dinner £10; deposit: £3 per person per night   CARDS: none   DETAILS: no children under
8; no dogs; no smoking; car park; garden; tennis

Many B&Bs offer tea / coffee-making facilities in the bedroom.

Old Pines

Gairlochy Road, Spean Bridge PH34 4EG
TEL: (01397) 712324   FAX: (01397) 712433
on B8004, about 1m NW of Spean Bridge and junction A82 / A86

The Barbers are constantly seeking to maintain and improve this
very hospitable guesthouse/restaurant-with-rooms. The
Scandinavian-style house was built in the early 1980s and is a long,
low, mostly wooden building with some stone additions. It stands in
30 acres of grounds just 300 yards from the famous Commando
Memorial and has views across the Great Glen and Glen Spean to
Aonach Mor and Ben Nevis. Sukie Barber, assisted by Bill, provides
lunches and dinners and is a cheerful hostess. The food is one of the
highlights of a stay here, with the focus on local produce delivered
fresh daily. Vegetarian options and children's portions are always
available; children may have high tea in place of dinner. The dining-
room, which is also open to non-residents, and sitting area are in a
conservatory-style room, which is light and bright and has warming
log fires. The bedrooms are simply furnished in pine and there is
wheelchair access throughout most of the house. Although Old Pines
is not licensed, diners may bring their own wine to dinner. Packed
lunches can be provided.

OWNERS: Bill and Sukie Barber   OPEN: all year exc 2 weeks Nov   ROOMS: 2 single, 2
twin, 2 double, 2 family; all rooms with bath/shower; 4 rooms suitable for wheelchair-
users; TV lounge   TERMS: rates include dinner; single £50–£55, single occupancy
£50–£55, twin/double £100, family room from £100; reductions for longer stays;
children under 10 charged for meal only, reduced rates for ages 11 to 14; deposit £20
for 1 night, £50 for 3 or more nights   CARDS: Access, Delta, Switch, Visa   DETAILS:
children welcome; no dogs; no smoking; car park; play room; garden

Riverside

Invergloy, Spean Bridge PH34 4DY
TEL/FAX: (01397) 712684
*on A82, 5½m NE of Spean Bridge; entrance on left at white fence and down
signposted drive*

Riverside is approached down a long, winding drive through mature
trees on the east side of Loch Lochy. It shares the lane with Invergloy
House (see entry, above). Built in the 1960s, the bungalow stands
close to the loch and has an attractive garden and excellent views.
There are two large, comfortable bedrooms, one *en suite* and the other
with private bathroom. Guests have their own lounge, with an eating
area off it where breakfast only is served – although packed lunches
can be requested. There are no TVs in the house. Three self-catering
chalets are situated in the grounds.

OWNER: Joan C. Bennet OPEN: all year exc Christmas ROOMS: 1 double, 1 family; both rooms with bath/shower TERMS: single occupancy £22–£24, double £34–£36, family room £34–£51; half-price for children under 11; deposit: £5 CARDS: none DETAILS: children welcome; no dogs; no smoking in bedrooms; car park; garden

Tirindrish House

Spean Bridge PH34 4EU
TEL. (01397) 712520 FAX. (01397) 712398
on A86 ½m from Spean Bridge

Standing in 15 acres of grounds with its own hard tennis courts, Tirindrish House enjoys wonderful views of Ben Nevis and the surrounding mountains. The rear of the house dates from the fifteenth or sixteenth century, and is where two of the large guest bedrooms are located, each having its own staircase and bathroom. The third bedroom is at the front of the house and overlooks the mountains. Guests have use of a sitting-room, and breakfast and evening meals (by arrangement) are served in the attractive dining-room. Self-catering accommodation is also available. Although unlicensed, guests may bring their own wine to dinner and packed lunches can be provided.

OWNERS: Peter and Jean Wilson OPEN: Apr to Oct ROOMS: 1 double, 1 twin, 1 family; all rooms with bath/shower; TV in some bedrooms TERMS: single occupancy £25, twin/double £34, family room rate by arrangement; childrens reductions by arrangement; dinner £10; deposit CARDS: none DETAILS: children welcome; dogs welcome with own bedding; car park; garden; tennis

STAFFIN Highland   map 11

Glenview Inn

Culnacnoc, Staffin, Isle of Skye IV51 9JH
TEL: (01470) 562248
12m N of Portree, on A855 between the Old Man of Storr and the Quiraing

The Booths took over the Glenview Inn in 1994, after it had been empty for a year, and have run it as a restaurant and inn. The old public bar has been closed and the restaurant is open all day for meals. Paul Booth is an experienced chef and has an interesting menu featuring local produce. The bedrooms are simple but comfortable and the residents' lounge has an open fire in winter. Standing just off the road from Portree to Staffin on the Trotternish peninsula, the inn is in a Gaelic-speaking area, which also boasts some spectacular land formations, finds such as the Ichthyosaurus at Bearreraig Bay and the dinosaur footprint at Valtos.

OWNERS: Paul and Cathie Booth OPEN: all year exc 6 Jan to mid-March ROOMS: 1 double, 1 twin, 1 four-poster, 1 family; all rooms with bath/shower; TV lounge TERMS: twin/double £40–£60, four-poster £40–£60, family room £40–£60; children under 5 free,

half-price for children under 12 sharing with parents; dinner £12 to £20; deposit
CARDS: Amex, Visa DETAILS: children welcome; dogs welcome; no smoking in eating
areas; car park; garden

STANLEY Tayside   map 11

Newmill Farm

Stanley, nr Perth PH1 4QD
TEL/FAX: (01738) 828281
*from Perth take A9 driving north; ignore turn-off for Stanley, drive further
1½m up A9 and take Tullybelton turn-off*

This simple stone-built farmhouse offers a warm welcome and
comfortable bedrooms. Newmill Farm dates back four or five hundred
years, and is conveniently located, just off the A9. The comfortable
house has large rooms and simply decorated bedrooms, all *en suite*.
There are good hill views from upstairs windows; one of the bedrooms
is on the ground floor. The Guthries are a welcoming couple, who offer
home-baking in the evening. There is a TV lounge, and a dining-room
where evening meals are served. Children's helpings, vegetarian
choices and packed lunches can be provided, and as there is no licence
guests may bring their own wine.

OWNERS: Mr and Mrs A.D.C. Guthrie OPEN: 1 Mar to 1 Nov ROOMS: 1 double, 1 twin, 1
family; all rooms with bath/shower; TV in some bedrooms and lounge TERMS: single
occupancy £18–£20, twin/double £36–£38, family room £36–£45; children under 2 free,
£6 for ages 2 to 6, £8 for ages 6 to 12; dinner £12; deposit: £10 CARDS: none DETAILS:
children welcome; dogs welcome exc in dining-room; no smoking in bedrooms; car
park; garden

STIRLING Central   map 11

Castlecroft

Ballengeich Road, Stirling FK8 1TN
TEL: (01786) 474933

This modern house stands just below Stirling Castle and enjoys
wonderful views, particularly from the lounge, which has windows all
round. The castle can be reached by a series of footpaths, or by the
road into the centre of town. There is a garden and various patios
with seats and tables for sitting out. The bedrooms are all *en suite*,
some with newly enlarged showers, and the two on the ground floor
are particularly suited for the disabled. The accommodation is clean,
comfortable and practical, but the house has a rather business-like
atmosphere. Breakfast only is served.

OWNER: Bill Salmond OPEN: all year exc Christmas and New Year ROOMS: 3 double, 2
twin, 1 family, all rooms with bath/shower; 2 rooms suitable for wheelchair users; TV in

all bedrooms TERMS: single £22, twin/double £44; reductions for children sharing with parents; deposit: 10% CARDS: none DETAILS: children welcome; dogs welcome; no smoking in bedrooms or breakfast room; car park; garden

Forth Guest House

23 Forth Place, Riverside, Stirling FK8 1UD
TEL: (01786) 471020   FAX: (01786) 447220

Set in the middle of a Georgian terrace, Forth Guest House has a frontage of immaculately painted woodwork, with hanging flower baskets making it a riot of colour in an otherwise sombre street. The pretty dining-room has been completely refurbished, and overlooks the tiny front garden with a small sitting area at the back of the room. Breakfast is served here, as well as evening meals if arranged in advance. The bedrooms are small, well equipped, comfortable and attractively decorated. The two top-floor rooms can be connected to make a family suite. The guesthouse is only a five-minute walk to the town centre, bus and railway stations.

OWNERS: Sheena and Jim Loudon OPEN: all year exc Christmas and New Year ROOMS: 2 double, 2 twin, 2 family; all rooms with bath/shower; TV in all bedrooms TERMS: single occupancy £25–£35, twin/double £36–£40, family £36–£40; £3 for children under 2, £10 for children under 12; dinner £10; deposit: 25% CARDS: Access, Visa DETAILS: children welcome; no dogs in lounge or dining-room; smoking in some bedrooms only; car park

STORNOWAY   Western Isles   map 11

The Old House

4 Lewis Street, Stornoway, Isle of Lewis PA87 2QH
TEL: (0185) 704495

When the Macdonalds bought this house seven years ago it was not even weatherproof, and had virtually to be gutted to bring it up to its present standard. Now a comfortable, well-appointed home, it stands in a large garden in the centre of Stornoway and retains some of its old features, such as the winding staircase. Mrs Macdonald is a cheerful person who takes pride in running a professional guesthouse. The bedrooms are comfortable, with two on the ground floor, and there is a guest lounge. Breakfast only is served in the dining-room.

OWNER: Mrs M. Macdonald OPEN: all year ROOMS: 2 single, 2 double, all with bath/shower; 1 twin, with wash-basin; 1 family, with bath/shower; TV in all bedrooms TERMS: single £23, single occupancy £30, twin/double £46, family room from £58; half-price for children under 5 CARDS: none DETAILS: children welcome; no dogs; car park; garden

Kildrochet House

Kildrochet, Stranraer DG9 9BB
TEL: (01776) 820216
on A716, 3m S of Stranraer

An impressive whitewashed house standing in six acres of grounds
with views of the Rhins of Galloway. Kildrochet House was built as a
dower house in 1723 by William Adam, and is just south of Stranraer.
Mr and Mrs Whitworth offer a very warm welcome to their guests
and do everything to make their stay enjoyable. The house has
spacious and elegant rooms, including a large drawing-room, and is
attractively decorated. Two of the three private bathrooms are
en suite. Both dinner, by arrangement, and breakfast are served at
separate tables in the dining-room. Guests can bring their own wine.
There is a croquet set for garden use. This is an ideal base for the
Galloway beaches, walking, bird-watching and the ferry to Ireland.

OWNERS: Mr and Mrs P. Whitworth   OPEN: all year   ROOMS: 1 double, 2 twin; all rooms
with bath/shower; TV lounge   TERMS: single occupancy £26, twin/double £46; dinner
£13; deposit: 10%   CARDS: Access, Delta, Visa   DETAILS: children welcome; no dogs;
no smoking; car park; games room; garden

Millwell Farm

Chapelton, Strathaven ML10 6SJ
TEL: (013552) 43248
1m off A726 between East Kilbride and Strathaven

This old stone farmhouse is on a 96-acre working dairy farm and is
surrounded by farmland. The Taylors are delightful, welcoming
people and Fred Taylor both sings and makes excellent porridge. The
simple accommodation is immaculately clean, and includes a large
beamed sitting/dining-room with open fire where breakfast only is
served. The three simply furnished bedrooms are on the ground floor,
and are suitable for disabled guests.

OWNERS: Fred and Betty Taylor   OPEN: all year exc Christmas   ROOMS: 1 single, 1
double, 1 twin; 3 rooms suitable for wheelchair users; TV lounge   TERMS: single
occupancy from £12, twin/double from £24; children's reductions according to age;
deposit required   CARDS: none   DETAILS: children welcome; no dogs; car park; garden

*If the establishment does not take credit cards, we say so in the details at
the end of the entry.*

Craigvar

The Square, Strathpeffer IV14 9DL
TEL: (01997) 421622
off A834, 5m W of Dingwall

Craigvar overlooks the square in the charming Victorian spa village
of Strathpeffer and is a small, listed stone house, built in 1839, with a
well-kept front garden. Original Victorian fireplaces feature in the
good-sized rooms, which are attractively decorated. Two upstairs
bedrooms, one a four-poster and the other a twin (which has received
particular praise) with its own dressing room, have views over the
square. The smallest room is the downstairs double. An extensive
breakfast menu is served in the attractive dining-room, which has a
baby grand piano, and the lounge has an open fire for cooler days.
Packed lunches are provided on request. Many events take place in
Strathpeffer during the year, including a Victorian week in June and
the Strathpeffer Games in August. During the peak holiday season a
pipe band plays in the square every Saturday evening.

OWNER: Margaret Scott   OPEN: Easter to Oct   ROOMS: 1 double, 1 twin, 1 four-poster;
all rooms with bath/shower; TV in all bedrooms   TERMS: single occupancy £25, twin/
double/four-poster £44; deposit: £10   CARDS: Visa   DETAILS: children welcome; no
dogs; car park; garden

Inver Lodge

Strathpeffer IV14 9DL
TEL: (01997) 421392
off A834, 5m W of Dingwall

To find this compact Victorian house, once you are in Strathpeffer,
take the road by Spa Pavilion marked 'Bowling Green'; Inver Lodge is
the second house on the right. Although on a quiet road in the centre
of town, the guesthouse has lovely views of wooded hills. The
accommodation is simple but comfortable, with two guest bedrooms,
one of which can be used as either a double or a family room. Fresh
local produce, home-baked desserts and cakes feature at evening
meals, which are taken at a dining table in the sitting-room.
Although Inver Lodge is unlicensed, guests can bring their own wine.
Packed lunches can be provided and vegetarians catered for with
prior notice. Strathpeffer has its annual Games and a Victorian week,
and is an excellent centre for walking, fishing and golf.

OWNERS: Kate and Alan Derbyshire   OPEN: Mar to Dec   ROOMS: 1 twin, 1 family; both
rooms with wash-basin; TV in both bedrooms   TERMS: single occupancy £18–£21,
twin/double £30, family room £40–£47; children under 3 free, £11 for ages 3 to 10;
dinner £10.50; deposit £25 for weekly bookings   CARDS: Access, Visa   DETAILS:
children welcome; no dogs; no smoking; car park; garden

STRATHY   Highland   map 11

Catalina

Aultivullin, Strathy Point, Strathy KW14 7RY
TEL/FAX: (01641) 541279
off A836, 24m W of Thurso, guesthouse signposted in Strathy

Originally a small croft, Catalina stands at the very end of a long,
narrow road on a wild and desolate moorland headland that is
surrounded on three sides by the Atlantic ocean. Although the sea is
out of sight of the house, it is only a short walk to a marvellous
viewpoint and it is possible to walk along the cliffs right round the
head. The Salisburys have enlarged the house, giving guests a
complete wing to themselves consisting of a bedroom, small lounge,
dining-room and bathroom, all attractively and comfortably
furnished; a further bedroom is upstairs. Good home-cooked food is
served in the evening by arrangement and, although there is no
licence, guests may bring their own wine.

OWNERS: Jane and Peter Salisbury   OPEN: all year   ROOMS: 1 single; 1 twin; TV lounge
TERMS: single £13–£17, single occupancy £17, twin £26; children under 5 free, half-
price for children 5 to 13; dinner £7   CARDS: none   DETAILS: children welcome; well-
behaved dogs welcome; no smoking; car park; garden

STROMNESS   Orkney   map 11

Millburn

Sandwick, by Stromness, South Ronaldsay KW16 3JB
TEL: (01856) 841656
14m S of Kirkwall

This modern, one-storey, spacious house has lovely views over Loch
Harray, and stands in ten acres of grounds. There is a large, light
sitting-room, and a pretty dining-room with separate tables where
breakfast only is served. The three bedrooms all have the use of a
private bathroom. Loch Harray is famous for its wild brown trout,
and the Kirkpatricks have a small boat which guests may use.
Packed lunches can be provided.

OWNER: Mrs H. Kirkpatrick   OPEN: Feb to Nov   ROOMS: 1 double, 2 twin; all rooms with
bath/shower; TV lounge   TERMS: single occupancy £20–£23, twin/double £34–£36;
children's reductions by arrangement   CARDS: none   DETAILS: children welcome; no
dogs; no smoking; car park; garden

*No stamps are needed if you write to the Guide from within the UK. Report
forms are at the end of the book, or use your own stationery if you prefer.*

TARBERT   Western Isles   map 11

Allan Cottage

Tarbert, Isle of Harris HS3 3DJ
TEL: (01859) 502146
first house in village street above road to ferry

Allan Cottage is only a five minutes' walk from the ferry and the
Harris Hotel. Once the telephone exchange, this old stone-built house
has since been extended and modernised, while preserving some of its
original features. An open fire is lit in the small, cosy lounge on cold
days. The comfortably furnished bedrooms are equipped with every
possible amenity. The Reeds are a friendly couple, and Bill prides
himself on his cooking and likes to prepare evening meals for guests
at which a complimentary glass of wine is offered. Guests can also
bring their own wine if they prefer. Packed lunches can be provided.

OWNERS: Bill and Evelyn Reed   OPEN: Apr to Sept   ROOMS: 2 double, 1 twin; all rooms
with bath/shower; TV in all bedrooms and lounge   TERMS: single occupancy £25, twin/
double £50; reductions for children's meals; dinner £16; deposit: £20   CARDS: none
DETAILS: no children under 6; dogs with own bedding; smoking in lounge only

TARBET   Strathclyde   map 11

Tarbet House

Loch Lomond, Tarbet, by Arochar G83 7DE
TEL: (01301) 702349
on private road off A82, 200 metres NE of junction with A83

Standing in its own seven acres of mature gardens immediately
above the loch, Tarbet House has its own beach and launching area
for boats. Almost all the bedrooms as well as the large sitting/dining-
room have splendid views of the loch and hills. The interior of the
house has a 1960s look about it (the period in which the house was
built) and the rooms are spacious. John and Christine Harvey are
both experienced mountaineers and sailors, and the focus here is on
activity holidays for adults, including mountain-walking, scrambling,
orienteering and 'skippered' sailing in the Harveys' own boat. The
grounds include a tennis court.

OWNERS: Christine and John Harvey   OPEN: Apr to Sept; Jan to Mar and Oct by
arrangement   ROOMS: 1 single, with wash-basin; 2 double, 1 with bath/shower, 1 with
wash-basin; 2 twin, both with wash-basin; TV lounge   TERMS: single £20–£25, single
occupancy £20–£25, twin/double £32–£50; deposit: £10 per person   CARDS: Access,
Visa   DETAILS: no children; no dogs; no smoking; car park; garden; tennis

*Many B&Bs, especially if they are unlicensed, allow guests to bring their
own wine to dinner. If this is the case, we say so in the entry.*

THURSO   Highland

map 11

Ulbster Villa

South Toll, Thurso KW14 8RE
TEL: (01847) 893664

This unusual-looking villa stands just off the main road on the edge of Thurso. Built a hundred years ago, it is a small, compact stone house in a lovely well-tended garden. The first floor, which is where one of the two good-sized bedrooms is located, is reached by a narrow circular stairway; the other *en suite* bedroom is on the ground floor. Guests have use of a sitting-room, beyond which is a sun-lounge where breakfast only is served. Mrs McKenzie's mother did B&B here before her, and the house is comfortable.

OWNER: Mrs A. McKenzie OPEN: all year exc Dec ROOMS: 1 double, with bath/shower; 1 family, with wash-basin; TV lounge TERMS: single occupancy £15, twin/double £30, family room from £39; children's reductions by arrangement; deposit: £7 CARDS: none DETAILS: children welcome; no dogs; smoking in lounge only; car park; garden

TOBERMORY   Strathclyde

map 11

Fàilte Guest House

Main Street, Tobermory, Isle of Mull PA75 6NU
TEL: (01688) 302495

This attractive terraced building stands right in the centre of Tobermory overlooking the harbour and was originally a bank. As a guesthouse, Fàilte has been in the family for two generations; it has been continually updated and is now freshly decorated, with all rooms *en suite*. There is no lounge, but all the bedrooms are of a good size with TV, and breakfast is taken in an attractive dining-room facing the sea. Packed lunches can be provided, and there are several restaurants within walking distance.

OWNER: Mrs E.M Macintyre OPEN: Mar to Oct ROOMS: 3 double, 3 twin, 1 family; all rooms with bath/shower; TV in all bedrooms TERMS: single from £25, single occupancy from £25, twin/double £40–£50, family room from £50 CARDS: none DETAILS: children's reductions; dogs with own bedding only; no smoking in dining-room

Where we know a B&B accepts credit cards, we list them in the details at the end of an entry. There may be a surcharge if you pay by credit card. It is always best to check whether the card you want to use is acceptable when booking.

It is always best to book a room in advance, even in winter. B&Bs with few rooms may close at short notice for periods not specified in the details.

TORRIDON   Highland   **map 11**

Upper Diabaig Farm

by Torridon, Achnasheen IV22 2HE
TEL: (01445) 790227
from Torridon take Diabaig road for 8m, until reaching farm gate

Few bed-and-breakfasts are situated in such a remote and wildly
spectacular location. It is a daunting eight-mile drive from the village
of Torridon along a winding and, at times, steep narrow road to
Upper Diabaig, which stands between two freshwater lochs. Less
than a mile beyond the house the road drops down to the village of
Lower Diabaig, from where there are spectacular views across Loch
Torridon to the Applecross peninsula. Upper Diabiag is a modern
house built beside the ruins of an old croft, and is furnished simply
and comfortably. There is partial central heating, but all bedrooms,
one of which is on the ground floor, have their own heaters. The three
bedrooms share a bathroom, although there are plans to install one
en suite bathroom. Roy Peacock is a farmer and vet, and Brenda
prepares home-cooked food for her guests.

OWNER: Brenda Peacock OPEN: Apr to Sept ROOMS: 1 double, 2 twin; both with wash-
basin; TV lounge TERMS: single occupancy by arrangement, twin/double £28; dinner
£12; deposit CARDS: none DETAILS: no children; no dogs; no smoking; car park

ULLAPOOL   Highland   **map 11**

The Sheiling Guest House

Garve Road, Ullapool IV26 2SX
TEL: (01854) 612947

Built in 1989 on the site of the original family home, The Sheiling
stands in an acre of grounds just below the main road, on the edge of
town, and enjoys panoramic views over Loch Broom. Three of the
seven small, bright bedrooms are on the ground floor and some have
lovely views. Both the pleasant lounge and the dining-room overlook
the loch. Duncan MacKenzie, who is a very keen fisherman, recently
completed a separate building within the grounds which houses a rod
room, drying-room, sauna and shower, a secure motorcycle store and
a laundry room. Fishing is available exclusively for guests on a
variety of lochs over 25 square miles. Packed lunches can be provided.

OWNERS: Duncan and Mhairy MacKenzie OPEN: all year exc Christmas and New Year
ROOMS: 4 double, 3 twin; all rooms with bath/shower; TV lounge TERMS: single
occupancy £25, twin/double £40; half-price for children under 10; deposit: £20 CARDS:
none DETAILS: children welcome; no dogs; no smoking; car park

Walston Mansion Farmhouse

Walston, nr Carnwath ML11 8NF
TEL: (01899) 810338
off A721, 5m E of Carnwath

This attractive grey-stone house is reached via a narrow lane, and
stands in the middle of peaceful and unspoilt countryside. There are
views of hills all around, a pretty garden, and a children's swing.
Margaret Kirby offers comfortable accommodation and home-cooked
food; although there is no licence, guests may bring their own wine.
There is a TV lounge, and open fires burn in both the dining-room and
sitting-room.

OWNER: Margaret Kirby   OPEN: all year   ROOMS: 1 double, with wash-basin; 1 twin, with
wash-basin; 1 four-poster, with bath/shower; 1 family, with bath/shower; TV in all
bedrooms and lounge   TERMS: single occupancy £13–£15; twin/double £26–£30, four-
poster £30, family room from £30; children's reductions by arrangement; dinner £7
CARDS: none   DETAILS: children welcome; no dogs in dining-room or lounge; no
smoking in dining-room; car park; garden

Lismore

Waternish IV55 8GE
TEL: (01470) 592318
*take A850 towards Dunvegan, then turn right on to B886 for approx 2m,
second house on left*

Lismore must have one of the finest views in Skye. It stands high
above the cliffs on the Waternish peninsula, looking straight down
Loch Bay to the Western Isles. Sunsets are particularly memorable
here. To take advantage of the view, the Dames have built on a sun-
lounge at the front of the house, which is where breakfast, evening
meals and also teas for non-residents are served. The two simple
bedrooms are in the old part of the building; both are on the ground
floor. There is no alcohol licence, but guests may bring their own wine
to dinner. Vegetarian choices are available and packed lunches can be
provided.

OWNERS: Bill and Janet Dame   OPEN: Apr to Oct   ROOMS: 1 double, 1 family; both with
wash-basin; TV lounge   TERMS: double £29, family room from £43.50; half-price for
children sharing with parents; dinner £9 to £15   CARDS: none   DETAILS: children
welcome; no dogs; no smoking; car park; garden

Whitekirk Mains

Whitekirk EH42 1SX
TEL: (01620) 870245   FAX: (01620) 870330
from A1 from Edinburgh take A198 just after East Linton

This very attractive old farmhouse is in the centre of the small village, near the church. The middle of the house is the oldest, and could date back to the fifteenth century. The pretty front part is Georgian, enhanced by creepers and a lovely garden to the front and sides. Mrs Tuer is a keen gardener and golfer, and her husband looks after the quite sizable farm. The bedrooms are delightfully decorated and have every possible amenity. Guests have use of a comfortable sitting-room, and breakfast only is served. The Tuers' latest venture is a golf-course next door, which has a restaurant that guests can use.

OWNER: Mrs J. Tuer   OPEN: Mar to end Oct   ROOMS: 1 double, with wash-basin; 2 twin, both with bath/shower; TV in all bedrooms and lounge   TERMS: single occupancy £20, twin/double £36; babies free, £5 to £8 for children under 8 sharing with parents   CARDS: Access, Switch, Visa   DETAILS: children welcome; no dogs; smoking in lounge only; car park; garden

Bilbster House

Bilbster, nr Wick KW1 5TB
TEL: (01955) 621212
from Wick take A882 for 5½m, turn right at line of trees and signpost

This mid-eighteenth-century house was extensively renovated by the Stewarts when they bought it over 20 years ago. The five-acre grounds are a mixture of garden and woodland and are described by one reporter as 'palatial'. A stream runs along one side of the walled garden. More recently, the Stewarts have further updated Bilbster House, making two of the three bedrooms *en suite*. All the rooms are spacious and furnished in an old-fashioned way. The large, comfortable drawing-room has TV, and the attractive dining-room, where breakfast only is served, has small tables set with flowers, linen napkins and tablecloths and silver cutlery. Reporters have found the Stewarts 'endlessly gracious and helpful'.

OWNERS: A.D. and J.Y. Stewart   OPEN: Easter to end Sept   ROOMS: 2 double, 1 with bath/shower, 1 with wash-basin; 1 twin, with shower; TV lounge   TERMS: single occupancy £14–£15, twin/double £28; children under 5 free, £4 for ages 6 to 12   CARDS: none   DETAILS: children welcome; dogs welcome; smoking in lounge only; car park; garden

Wales

ABERHAFESP   Powys
map 4

Dyffryn Farm

Aberhafesp, nr Newtown SY16 3JD
TEL: (01686) 688817   FAX: (01686) 688324
just off B4568, 3m W of Newtown

Dyffryn Farm is a beautfully restored half-timbered barn standing in a lovely garden on the banks of a stream. It is part of a 100-acre beef and cattle farm, where guests and supervised children are welcome to wander. This is a wonderful place for families: outside there is a play area as well as a nature trail, while inside a cot, high chair and babysitting can be provided. Three luxurious bedrooms are furnished in country style and have *en suite* facilities and TV. Breakfast, and dinner if ordered in advance, is served in the beamed dining-room at a large oval table, and guests may bring their own wine as there is no licence. Vegetarian and special diets can be catered for with notice, and children's helpings provided. The very comfortable lounge overlooks the stream and adjoining farmyard. Owners Dave and Sue Jones, are experts at making guests feel at home and this is a delightful spot from which to explore the many nearby places of interest, including the upland lakes; packed lunches can be provided.

OWNERS: David and Sue Jones   OPEN: all year exc Christmas   ROOMS: 2 double, 1 twin; all rooms with bath/shower; TV in all bedrooms and lounge   TERMS: single occupancy £20, twin/double £38–£44; dinner £12; deposit: £20   CARDS: none   DETAILS: children welcome; no dogs; no smoking; car park; garden

ABERYSTWYTH   Dyfed
map 4

Glyn-Garth

South Road, Aberystwyth SY23 1JS
TEL: (01970) 615050

This attractive double-fronted Victorian house is in a conservation area within the walls of the old castle and only a minute's walk from the castle and the sea. Mike and Betty Evans have been maintaining their impeccable standards for 34 years and have recently refurbished several of the rooms with some style. Wallpapers are pastel-coloured and the fabrics co-ordinated. The guests' lounge is well furnished, and substantial breakfasts are served in the separate dining-room.

OWNERS: Mike and Betty Evans   OPEN: all year exc Christmas   ROOMS: 2 single; 6 double, 4 with bath/shower; 1 twin; 2 family, both with bath/shower; TV in all bedrooms and lounge   TERMS: single £17–£18, single occupancy £24–£34, twin/double £34–£46, family room £57; reductions for children over 7 sharing with parents; deposit: £10 per person   CARDS: none   DETAILS: no children under 7; no dogs; no smoking

Sinclair Guest House

43 Portland Street, Aberystwyth SY23 2DX
TEL/FAX: (01970) 615158

Sinclair Guest House is centrally situated in a tree-lined street, close to the sea-front and town centre. It is a late-Victorian terraced house that has been carefully refurbished, while retaining the leaded windows, tiled entrance and stripped-pine doors. The Wards have been in the hotel and catering industries for 12 years and serve tasty home-cooked evening meals with fresh vegetables from their allotment; guests may bring their own wine to dinner. The good-sized bedrooms have wicker and pine furniture and sitting areas, and there is also a guests' lounge.

OWNERS: Lester and Sarah Ward OPEN: all year exc Christmas ROOMS: 1 double, 2 twin; all rooms with bath/shower; TV in all bedrooms TERMS: single occupancy £27.50, twin/double £45; dinner £10; deposit: £10 CARDS: none DETAILS: no children under 14; no dogs; no smoking; car park

Yr Hafod

1 South Marine Terrace, Aberystwyth SY23 1JX
TEL: (01970) 617579

This immaculate guesthouse is on the sea-front between the castle and the harbour. The bedrooms, some with sea views, are colour co-ordinated and have pine furniture. The top-floor rooms are particularly attractive with their sloping ceilings. Excellent breakfasts are served in the bright, airy dining-room, and a wide range of pubs and restaurants offer evening meals. This is good-value accommodation in an excellent location.

OWNER: John Evans OPEN: all year exc Christmas and New Year ROOMS: 2 single, both with wash-basin; 2 double, 1 with bath/shower, 1 with wash-basin; 2 twin, 1 with bath/shower, 1 with wash-basin; 1 family, with wash-basin; TV in all bedrooms and lounge TERMS: single £16–£17, single occupancy £22–£35, twin/double £32–£40, family room £32–£34 plus children's charge CARDS: none DETAILS: children welcome; no dogs; no smoking

BALA   Gwynedd   map 7

Abercelyn

Llanycil, Bala LL23 7YF
TEL: (01678) 521109   FAX: (01678) 520556
on A494 on W shore of Bala Lake, 1m SW of Bala

This old rectory dates back to 1729 and stands in seven acres of landscaped grounds alongside Bala Lake in the Snowdonia National Park. Although tastefully modernised, the stone-built house retains

ABERCELYN, BALA

many original features such as a Georgian staircase, marble fireplaces, panelled doors and shuttered windows with seats. The three spacious bedrooms have a poppy wallpaper décor and are furnished with pine and antiques. Breakfasts feature home-baked bread from the Aga, fresh eggs and home-made preserves, and are served in the dining-room overlooking the garden and waterfall. The sitting-room has an open fire lit on cool evenings and a library which guests are welcome to browse through. This is a tranquil spot from which to explore the beautiful area; there are drying facilities for walking gear, and packed lunches can be requested.

OWNERS: Mr and Mrs B.E.R. Cunningham   OPEN: all year exc Christmas and New Year
ROOMS: 2 double, 1 twin; all rooms with bath/shower; TV lounge   TERMS: single occupancy £23, twin/double £37–£49; £10 for children under 12 sharing with parents; deposit   CARDS: none   DETAILS: children welcome; no dogs; no smoking; car park; garden

---

Entries in the Guide are listed under town or village. There are also two indexes at the back of the book, one listing B&Bs by county, the other by name.

Please let us know if you think a B&B should be included in this Guide. Report forms are at the back of the book – or use your own stationery if you prefer (no stamps are needed within the UK).

Bryn Melyn Hotel

Panorama Road, Barmouth LL42 1DQ
TEL: (01341) 280556 FAX: (01341) 280276
off A496, ½m E of town centre

This small hotel with a lovely terraced garden is in a quiet position above the town with excellent views over the estuary and across to Cader Idris. It is a 15-minute walk from the town centre. Guests can make use of the lounge, the well-stocked bar or the conservatory for relaxation, and the comfortable bedrooms are well furnished with floral wallpapers and co-ordinated fabrics. Traditional breakfasts and interesting dinners are served in the restaurant. Vegetarian choices are always available.

OWNERS: David and Carol Clay OPEN: Mar to mid-Nov ROOMS: 5 double, 3 twin, 1 family; all rooms with bath/shower; TV in all bedrooms TERMS: single occupancy £35, twin/double £48–£56, family room £65; half-price for children; dinner £14.50; deposit: £20 per person CARDS: Access, Amex, Diners, Visa DETAILS: children welcome; dogs in bedrooms only; car park; garden

The Sandpiper

7 Marine Parade, Barmouth LL42 1NA
TEL: (01341) 280318

The Sandpiper is on the sea-front overlooking Barmouth Sands and Cardigan Bay. It is a well-maintained guesthouse and the bedrooms have been freshly decorated. The quiet lounge on the top floor is a good place in which to relax and read. The bedrooms are furnished and decorated to a high standard and the front ones have magnificent views; one is on the ground floor with its own bathroom. Breakfast only is served, but Barmouth offers a range of eating places.

OWNERS: Susan and John Palmer OPEN: Mar to Oct ROOMS: 2 single, both with wash-basin; 5 double, 3 with bath/shower, 2 with wash-basin; 4 family, 3 with bath/shower, 1 with wash-basin; 1 room suitable for wheelchair-users; TV in all bedrooms TERMS: single £14–£15.50, twin/double £25–£35, family room from £37.50; half-price for children; deposit: 1 night's charge CARDS: none DETAILS: children welcome; no dogs; no smoking in breakfast room; garden

If a B&B caters for vegetarians, we note this in the entry. It is always best, however, to check when booking and make it clear what your requirements are, especially if you require a special diet.

We state at the end of an entry whether children are welcome. If we know of any restrictions on children, we give them.

BENLLECH   Gwynedd   **map 7**

Belvoir

8 Lon Fferam, Benllech, Anglesey LL74 8RL
TEL: (01248) 852907
off A5025, 7m N of Britannia Bridge

This modern bungalow with its friendly home-from-home atmosphere
is situated on a quiet residential street, just seven minutes' walk from
the sandy beach. The two immaculate bedrooms, one of which is on
the ground floor, are well furnished and have comfortable beds. There
is a sitting-room and an adjacent conservatory, where excellent
breakfasts are served; potato fritters, home-made marmalades and
Anglesey honey are a feature. There are several pubs and restaurants
serving evening meals within walking distance.

OWNER: Valerie Evans   OPEN: Mar to end Oct   ROOMS: 1 double, 1 twin; both rooms
with bath/shower; TV in both bedrooms   TERMS: single occupancy £29, twin/double
£33; deposit: by arrangement   CARDS: none   DETAILS: no children; no dogs; no
smoking; car park

BETWS-Y-COED   Gwynedd   **map 7**

Fron Heulog

Pont-y-Pair, Betws-y-Coed LL24 0BL
TEL: (01690) 710736
*turn off A5 in town over stone bridge on to B5106, then take first left along
river bank for 100yds*

This large Victorian stone-built house is in a quiet location just out of
the village, with south-facing views from a furnished verandah over a
wooded valley. The owners bought the property a decade ago when it
was derelict and restored it with the help of local craftsmen. The
Victorian charm has been retained, as has the rare opportunity to
choose between three lounges in which to relax. The bedrooms are
well equipped. Breakfasts offer the chance to really fill up, with a
help-yourself buffet followed by a cooked breakfast. Evening meals
are available by arrangement and the menu is tailored to the tastes of
the guests. There is also a wide choice of eating places in the village.
This is an ideal base for walkers and tourists, and clothes-drying
facilities are provided.

OWNERS: Jean and Peter Whittingham   OPEN: all year   ROOMS: 1 single, 2 double, 2
twin; all rooms with bath/shower; TV in 2 lounges   TERMS: single £16–£30, single
occupancy £24–£40, twin/double £32–£50; dinner £15; deposit: £20 per person
CARDS: none   DETAILS: children welcome by arrangement; no dogs; no smoking; car
park; garden

BONTDDU   Gwynedd
map 7

Farchynys Cottage Garden

Farchynys, Bontddu, nr Barmouth LL42 1TM
TEL: (01341) 430245
on A496, 4m W of Dolgellau

The Townshends are developing a really beautiful garden in the four acres belonging to what was formerly an estate gardener's cottage and they have already won prizes for it. The cottage has views over the Mawddach Estuary to Cader Idris and the furnished terrace is the ideal place to relax and enjoy the magnificent scenery. A forest walk beyond the top of the garden provides a more active alternative. The bedrooms are medium-sized except for one huge room, and all are decorated in soft colours. Meals are served in the cosy dining-room which has an antique Welsh dresser and a grandfather clock. Dinner is available by arrangement at 6.30pm; guests may bring their own wine.

OWNERS: Mr and Mrs J.I. Townshend   OPEN: Apr to Oct   ROOMS: 1 single, 2 double, 1 family; all rooms with wash-basin; TV lounge   TERMS: single £12.50, double £25, family room £25 plus children's charge; children's reductions according to age; dinner £7.50; deposit: £10 per person   CARDS: none   DETAILS: children welcome; no dogs; no smoking; car park; garden

BORTH   Dyfed
map 4

Hafan Wen

Borth SY24 5JA
TEL: (01970) 871739
on B4353, 6m N of Aberystwyth

This simple guesthouse is a white-painted terraced building on the sea-front in a quiet area of the town. The bedrooms are clean and bright; one double is on the ground floor with an adjacent bathroom. The first-floor sitting-room has sea views from the large picture window. Guests are greeted with a hot drink upon arrival. Breakfast only is served, but there are several eating places within walking distance. Keen golfers have the choice of two courses within a few yards of the house.

OWNERS: Christine and David Cox   OPEN: all year exc Christmas   ROOMS: 2 double, 1 family; TV lounge   TERMS: single occupancy £15, double £30, family room £30 plus children's charge; reductions for children over 8 according to age; deposit: £5   CARDS: none   DETAILS: no children under 8; dogs on ground floor only; smoking in lounge only

Many B&Bs, especially if they are unlicensed, allow guests to bring their own wine to dinner. If this is the case, we say so in the entry.

BUILTH WELLS   Powys

map 4

Querida

43 Garth Road, Builth Wells LD2 3AR
TEL: (01982) 553642

This modest guesthouse is within easy walking distance of all the amenities in this attractive market town. The smallish bedrooms are immaculately clean and there are two bathrooms for guests' use. The comfortable lounge is decorated in autumnal colours. The large traditional breakfast is enough to set you up for the day, and on baking days guests are greeted with Welsh teacakes and a hot drink.

OWNER: Mrs C.M. Hammond   OPEN: all year   ROOMS: 2 double, 1 twin; all rooms with wash-basin; TV lounge   TERMS: single occupancy £13–£14, twin/double £26–£28; reductions for children sharing with parents; deposit   CARDS: none   DETAILS: children welcome; no dogs in dining-room; no smoking; car park; garden

CAERNARFON   Gwynedd

map 7

Isfryn

11 Church Street, Caernarfon LL55 1SW
TEL/FAX: (01286) 675628

This spacious Victorian property is within the old town walls close to the castle. It is maintained in spotless condition and is bright and airy. The lounge has cosy sofas, and a gas fire in the original fireplace. A collection of Wedgwood china is displayed in a glass-fronted cabinet. Dinner is served at 6.30pm, vegetarians can be catered for and guests may bring their own wine. Packed lunches can be requested.

OWNERS: Graham and Jenny Bailey   OPEN: Mar to end Oct   ROOMS: 1 single, with wash-basin; 2 double, 2 twin, 2 family, all with bath/shower; TV in all bedrooms and lounge   TERMS: single £17.50, twin/double £39–£40, family room from £48; £9 for children under 12; dinner £15   CARDS: none   DETAILS: children welcome; small dogs by arrangement; no smoking in dining-room and some bedrooms

CAPEL DEWI   Dyfed

map 4

Capel Dewi Uchaf Farm

Capel Dewi, nr Carmarthen SA32 8AD
TEL: (01267) 290799   FAX: (01267) 290003
off B4300, 4m E of Carmarthen

This friendly farm with 34 acres of land supports a breeding herd of deer. It dates back over 500 years and old coins were found when Fredena Burns renovated the property and created the garden. She has cleverly combined the best of modern comforts and the old-world charm of the medieval door, inglenook fireplace and exposed stone walls. The bedrooms have fireplaces and are well decorated with antique furniture; the beds have cotton sheets and embroidered white bedspreads. The spacious sitting-room has a pine floor and large comfortable armchairs. Wholesome breakfasts are served in the separate dining-room decorated in the style of a baronial hall. Evening meals are served at 8pm by arrangement, and vegetarians can be catered for. A short, well-chosen wine list is offered. The farm has its own fishing rights on the Towy River.

OWNER: Fredena Burns OPEN: all year exc Christmas and New Year ROOMS: 2 double, 1 twin; all rooms with bath/shower; TV in all bedrooms and lounge TERMS: single occupancy £30, twin/double £40; reductions for children sharing with parents; dinner £21; deposit: 20% CARDS: none DETAILS: children welcome; no dogs; no smoking; car park; garden

CARDIFF South Glamorgan   map 4

Marlborough Guest House

98 Newport Road, Roath, Cardiff CF2 1DG
TEL/FAX: (01222) 492385

This cosy and impeccably maintained Victorian guesthouse is just an easy five-minute stroll from the city centre. Although it has nine rooms and a small bar, the house retains the ambience of a family home. The bedrooms are of a good size and are tastefully decorated with pretty quilts. Annette Howard is friendly and efficient and guests are assured of good service. A hot drink and complimentary sandwiches are offered upon arrival, and for guests who do not take breakfast a bar meal of comparable value may be substituted. Breakfasts are very large, enough to set the heartiest eater up for the day. The lounge-bar has satellite TV and a laundry service can be provided.

OWNERS: Paul and Annette Howard OPEN: all year ROOMS: 2 single, 1 with bath/shower, 1 with wash-basin; 2 double, 1 with bath/shower, 1 with wash-basin; 3 twin, 2 with bath/shower, 1 with wash-basin; 2 family, both with bath/shower; TV in all bedrooms and lounge TERMS: single/single occupancy £22–£32, twin/double £35–£45, family room £50–£75; reductions for children under 6; dinner £8–£12 CARDS: none DETAILS: children welcome; no dogs; smoking in guests' lounge only; car park; garden

B&B rates specified in the details at the end of each entry are given (as applicable) for a single room, for single occupancy of a double room, and then per room in the case of two people sharing a double or twin-bedded room, or for a family room.

CAREW Dyfed

map 4

Old Stable Cottage

Carew, nr Tenby SA70 8SL
TEL: (01646) 651889
turn off A477 6m W of Kilgetty on to A4075; cottage is close to entrance to Carew Castle

This cottage is a lovely conversion of the stables and cart house originally belonging to neighbouring Carew Castle. The huge, mellow lounge with comfortable sofas and teak beams from a local shipyard opens on to the bright conservatory/dining-room with glass ceiling and terracotta tiles, beyond which is the walled garden. Exposed brickwork, the original stone walls and old pine furniture lend a warm feel to this stylishly decorated country home. Polished boards are scattered with hand-woven rugs, and low cottage windows and latched doors add to the charm. A cast-iron spiral staircase leads up to the pretty bedrooms. Excellent, wholesome breakfasts and evening meals are cooked on the Aga, and vegetarians can be catered for. Packed lunches, too, can be provided.

OWNERS: Lionel and Joyce Fielder OPEN: Apr to end Nov ROOMS: 1 double, 1 twin, 1 family; all rooms with bath/shower; TV in all bedrooms TERMS: single occupancy £35, twin/double £45, family room £65; dinner £17.50 CARDS: none DETAILS: no children under 10; no dogs; no smoking; car park; games room; garden

CEFN-DDWYSARN Gwynedd

map 7

Cwm Hwylfod

Cefn-ddwysarn, Bala LL23 7LN
TEL: (01678) 530310
heading NE from Bala on A494, after 3m turn right at phone box in Cefn-ddwysarn, take fourth small turning on left, pass farmhouse and go through 2 gates

This 400-year-old farmhouse is in an elevated and beautiful setting in a remote area. The friendly owners and homely atmosphere make this a popular destination for families, and children enjoy accompanying Edward Best on his rounds of the sheep farm. Wellington boots are provided in all sizes for exploring the farm. Other family-oriented facilities include those for washing and drying, and a selection of toys and board games. There are two bathrooms exclusively for guests' use and a small dining-room/lounge. Free-range eggs are served at breakfast, and dinner is available by arrangement except during lambing season (mid-March to April); vegetarians can be catered for and guests may bring their own wine.

OWNERS: Edward and Joan Best OPEN: all year exc 25 Dec ROOMS: 2 twin, 1 family; all rooms with wash-basin; TV lounge TERMS: single occupancy £14–£16, twin £28–£32, family room £28–£32 plus children's charge; reductions for children under 11; dinner £9.50 CARDS: none DETAILS: children welcome; no dogs; no smoking; car park; garden

CHURCH STOKE   Powys
map 4

Greystones

Brompton, Church Stoke, nr Montgomery SY15 6SP
TEL: (01588) 620393
from Montgomery drive S on B4385 for 2m, turn left on to A489, house is 1m before Church Stoke village

Greystones is a 250-year-old farmhouse, situated on the border of England and Wales. Seventeen acres surround the property, taking in a lake with trout and coarse fishing. There are no fancy frills here, just good old-fashioned Welsh hospitality at modest prices. Three comfortable bedrooms have a blue décor, and the family room has *en suite* facilities. There is a pleasant lounge on the first floor. Breakfast and pre-arranged home-cooked dinners are served in the dining-room with its inglenook fireplace. Children's helpings, vegetarian choices and packed lunches can all be requested, and guests may bring their own wine as there is no alcohol licence. Montgomery, Welshpool and Powis Castle with its formal garden are nearby and worth a visit.

OWNER: June Ferguson OPEN: all year exc Christmas ROOMS: 1 double, 1 twin, both with wash-basin; 1 family, with bath/shower; TV in all bedrooms TERMS: single occupancy £14, twin/double £28, family room £34; children under 2 free, £8 for ages 2 to 12; dinner £8; deposit: £10 per room CARDS: none DETAILS: children welcome; no dogs; no smoking; car park; garden

COLWYN BAY   Clwyd
map 7

Holcombe Hotel

9 Grosvenor Road, Colwyn Bay LL29 7YF
TEL/FAX: (01492) 530423

This turn-of-the-century property is situated in a quiet residential street close to the town centre and all amenities. The bedrooms are of a good size and are clean and comfortable; all have *en suite* facilities and TV. There are two ground-floor rooms. Residents can relax in the sitting-room and there is a separate small bar. Evening meals are available at 6pm, vegetarians can be catered for with advance notice, and children's helpings are provided. Although the Holcombe Hotel is licensed, guests are also welcome to bring their own wine to table. Packed lunches can be requested.

OWNER: Mrs E.W. Wellings OPEN: all year exc Christmas ROOMS: 2 single, 5 double, 2 twin, 1 family; all rooms with bath/shower; TV in all bedrooms and lounge TERMS:

single £17–£19, twin/double £34–£38, family room £50; children under 4 free, half-price for older children; dinner £7; deposit: 15% CARDS: none DETAILS: well-behaved children welcome; no dogs; no smoking in dining-room; car park; garden

CONWY Gwynedd   map 7

Town House

18 Rosehill Street, Conwy LL32 8LD
TEL: (01492) 596454
opposite castle car park

This 150-year-old local-stone house overlooks the castle and is only two minutes from the visitors' entrance. Elaine Priestley offers a warm welcome and a homely atmosphere. The cosy rooms are spotless and prettily decorated with patterned wallpapers. Breakfasts are served in the bright and sunny dining-room at separate pine tables.

OWNER: Elaine Priestley OPEN: all year exc Christmas and owner's annual holiday ROOMS: 1 single, with wash-basin; 4 double, 2 with bath/shower, 2 with wash-basin; 1 twin, with bath/shower; TV in all bedrooms TERMS: single £15, twin/double £26–£32; small bed for children £6 CARDS: Access, Delta, Visa DETAILS: children welcome; small dogs welcome; car park

CRICCIETH Gwynedd   map 7

Trefaes

Y Maes, Criccieth LL52 0AE
TEL: (01766) 523204   FAX: (01766) 523013
on B4411 Caernarfon road

This spacious double-fronted Edwardian house was originally a builder's residence, based on the house he constructed for Lloyd George. It now stands in mature gardens and has been tastefully modernised, retaining the lovely stained-glass front door and original pine internal doors. A *chaise-longue* adorns the hallway and there are other interesting antiques. The guests' sitting-room is small and cosy and the bedrooms are individually decorated in pink, green and gold. Pat Clayton is an excellent cook and provides an extensive and innovative menu for vegetarians, plus chicken and fish dishes. Guests are welcome to bring their own wine to dinner.

OWNER: Pat Clayton OPEN: all year exc Christmas ROOMS: 2 double, 1 twin; all rooms with bath/shower; TV in all bedrooms TERMS: single occupancy £24, twin/double £40; 33% reduction for children from 12 to 15; dinner £13.50; deposit: £10 per person CARDS: none DETAILS: no children under 12; dogs welcome; no smoking in dining-room; car park; garden

map 7

Fron Goch Farmhouse

Cynwyd, nr Corwen LL21 0NA
TEL: (01490) 440418
on B4401, 4m SW of Corwen

Sheltered by the Berwyn Mountains, this charming stone farmhouse overlooks riverside meadows and sheep-dotted hillsides. It stands in its own gardens with a cobbled patio and an arbour where Sarah Stille grows 55 different varieties of rose. Tame ewes and their lambs graze in the paddock alongside the free-range hens. The spacious bedrooms are well decorated, and some are in converted farm buildings, one of which has wide doorways and a roll-in shower for wheelchair-users. Sarah Stille serves delicious dinners every night except Tuesdays; Fron Goch is licensed and vegetarian dishes are offered. Cream teas and light snacks are available in the garden in summer months. Breakfast is served in the main house. Sarah is a qualified walks guide and can arrange conducted tours or simply advise on good walks in the area. Drying facilities are available, as are packed lunches.

OWNER: Sarah Stille OPEN: all year ROOMS: 2 single, 1 with bath/shower, 1 with wash-basin; 3 double, 2 with bath/shower, 1 with wash-basin; 2 twin, 1 with bath/shower, 1 with wash-basin; 1 room suitable for wheelchair-users; TV in all bedrooms TERMS: single £19, single occupancy £22, twin/double £38–£50; £2 for babies, reductions for children sharing with parents; dinner £14.50; deposit: 1 night's charge CARDS: none DETAILS: children welcome; no dogs in public rooms, £2 per dog; no smoking in dining-room; car park; garden

 map 4

Point Farm

Dale, nr Haverfordwest SA62 3RD
TEL: (01646) 636254
take B4327 from Haverforwest to Dale, then continue up minor road towards Dale Point

Point Farm is a beautiful period farmhouse in a spectacular position overlooking the sea and approached up a narrow leafy lane. It is in the Pembrokeshire National Park right on the coastal path. The house retains several original features, including a stone-floored entrance hall, beams and old doors. It is furnished with antiques and the bedrooms are very comfortable, with extra touches such as coronets and fabric headboards. The eight acres surrounding the house are populated by horses, guinea-fowl, peacocks and the chickens that produce the free-range eggs for breakfast. Evening meals can be provided by arrangement, but the unspoilt village of Dale with its sheltered harbour is also a good place for evening meals. Sailing, windsurfing and even flying can be arranged.

OWNERS: John and Elizabeth Webber OPEN: all year exc Christmas ROOMS: 1 single, 2 double, 1 twin; all rooms with bath/shower; TV in all bedrooms TERMS: single £15, single occupancy £15–£17.50, twin/double £35–£40; dinner £15; deposit: 33% CARDS: none DETAILS: children welcome; no dogs in bedrooms; car park; garden

---

DINGESTOW Gwent   map 2

Cider Mill

Lower Pen-y-Clawdd Farm, Dingestow, nr Monmouth NP5 4BG
TEL: (01600) 740223/740667
6m SW of Monmouth leave A40 at Granada services and cross cattle-grid into farm drive

---

With a free-and-easy atmosphere and offering good-value accommodation, this 100-acre cattle and sheep farm is a good place for families. The Cider Mill is a 200-year-old building adjacent to the owners' seventeenth-century farmhouse. Guests and their children (under supervision) are welcome to wander around the farmyard, where they will come across ducks, chickens, white peacocks and dogs. The spacious bedrooms have brass and mahogany antique beds. There are several antique pieces of furniture, including a *chaise-longue*, an oakwood coal-scuttle and a beautiful dresser. Breakfasts only are served, but several pubs which serve evening meals are within easy driving distance.

OWNER: Averil Bayliss OPEN: all year ROOMS: 1 double, 1 twin, 1 family; all rooms with wash-basin; TV lounge TERMS: single occupancy £16–£20, twin/double £30–£32, family room £40–£45; half-price for children sharing with parents; deposit: £15 CARDS: none DETAILS: children welcome; dogs welcome; no smoking; car park; garden

---

DOLGELLAU Gwynedd   map 7

Ivy House

Finsbury Square, Dolgellau LL40 1RF
TEL: (01341) 422535 FAX: (01341) 422689

This imposing granite building in the centre of town combines efficient management with a friendly atmosphere. The restaurant is open to the general public, but guests have plenty of space to themselves and the owners live in a neighbouring property. The bedrooms are decorated to a high standard and there is a comfortable lounge. The dinner menu is wide-ranging, from simple homely food to four-course meals, and is served from 5 to 9pm. Drinks are available in the dining-room and the cosy cellar bar. Dolgellau is in the Snowdonia National Park and an ideal base for walking or pony trekking.

OWNERS: James and Margaret Bamford OPEN: all year ROOMS: 3 double, 2 with bath/shower, 1 with wash-basin; 2 twin, 1 with bath/shower, 1 with wash-basin; TV in all

bedrooms and lounge TERMS: single occupancy £20–£27, twin/double £36–£48;
children's reductions according to age; dinner from £11; deposit: £10 per person
CARDS: Access, Amex, Delta, Switch, Visa DETAILS: children welcome; dogs welcome;
no smoking in main dining-room; garden

Llety Nêst

Brithdir, Dolgellau LL40 2RY
TEL: (01341) 450326
off B4416 to Bont Newydd, 3m NE of Dolgellau

This modern stone-built bungalow is part of a 120-acre farm in a
remote location with magnificent views of the Obeth Mountains. The
accommodation is of a high standard, with well-decorated rooms all
on the ground floor. Colours are bold, with patchwork quilts (made by
owner Mary Price) on the beds and strong reds and blues in the
Queen Anne-style sitting-room. This room is extremely comfortable,
with polished copper kettles and brass candlesticks adorning the
stone fireplace. Around Brithdir is ideal walking country, with an
abundance of wildlife and a river running close to the house.
Breakfasts are traditional, as are the evening meals served from 6.30
to 8pm. Vegetarians can be catered for and guests may bring their
own wine. Llety Nêst is quite tricky to find, so guests should ask for
directions when booking.

OWNER: Mary Price OPEN: Mar to Nov ROOMS: 1 double, 1 family; both rooms with
bath/shower; TV lounge TERMS: single occupancy £25, twin/double £30, family room
£45; reductions for children under 12; dinner £7; deposit CARDS: none DETAILS:
children welcome; dogs welcome; no smoking; car park; garden

DOLWYDDELAN Gwynedd   map 7

Bryn Tirion Farm

Dolwyddelan LL25 0JD
TEL: (01690) 750366
off A470, 5m SW of Betws-y-Coed

This farmhouse is not only in a magnificent setting overlooking the
Lledr Valley but also has within its grounds the 900-year-old
Dolwyddelan Castle. The owners are cheerful and energetic people.
The three bedrooms all have firm mattresses, and the front room has
the best view. Breakfast is served in the dining-room/lounge and
there is a tea-shop adjacent to the property which sells home-made
cakes and snacks, as well as tickets to view the castle.

OWNERS: Caroline and Robert Price OPEN: all year exc Christmas and New Year
ROOMS: 1 double, 1 twin, 1 family; all rooms with wash-basin; TV lounge TERMS: twin/
double £30, family room from £45; children's reductions according to age; deposit
CARDS: none DETAILS: children welcome; no dogs; no smoking; car park

DYFFRYN ARDUDWY Gwynedd **map 7**

Cors-y-Gedol Hall

Dyffryn Ardudwy LL44 2RJ
TEL: (01341) 247230
1m off A496 Barmouth to Harlech road; drive opposite Llanddwywe
church

Readers have commented on the excellent value Janet Bailey offers
for such a grand night's stay. A long drive flanked by lime trees leads
through an arched gateway with an Inigo Jones-designed clock tower
to this listed Elizabethan and Jacobean mansion. The Hall is part of a
large sheep and cattle farm and the owners may be out at work on the
farm when guests arrive; a car horn will attract attention. The
showcase feature of this fascinating old house is the panelled
drawing-room with oak beams taken from the Spanish Armada and a
vast stone fireplace with a coat of arms and Latin inscription. The
bedrooms are spacious and comfortable. Breakfast only is served, but
plenty of eating places can be found nearby.

OWNER: Janet Bailey OPEN: all year exc Christmas and New Year ROOMS: 2 double, 1
twin; all rooms with bath/shower; TV lounge TERMS: single occupancy £17.50, twin/
double £30; half-price for children under 10 CARDS: none DETAILS: children welcome;
no dogs; car park; games room; garden

GELLILYDAN Gwynedd **map 7**

Tyddyn Du

Gellilydan, nr Blaenau Ffestiniog LL41 4RB
TEL/FAX: (01766) 590281
off A470 near junction with A487, ½m from Gellilydan village

This delighful seventeenth-century farmhouse in the Snowdonia
National Park makes a charming guesthouse. It is part of a working
farm with plenty of friendly animals, which guests can help to feed.
They can collect their own fresh breakfast eggs too if they wish.
Tyddyn Du has been tastefully restored, retaining exposed stone
walls, an inglenook fireplace and Welsh slate walls in the dining-
room. The bedrooms have exposed beams and antique German pine
furniture. The two-bedroom cottage suite is ideal for a family. Guests
can relax in the luxurious sitting-room with its rich Sanderson
furnishings. Candlelit dinners are served by arrangement and
vegetarian choices can be provided; guests may bring their own wine
to dinner.

OWNERS: Paula and Meredydd Williams OPEN: all year exc Christmas ROOMS: 1 single;
2 double, both with bath/shower; 1 twin, with wash-basin; 1 four-poster, 1 family, both
with bath/shower; 1 room suitable for wheelchair-users; TV in all bedrooms TERMS:
single/single occupancy £20, twin/double £32–£35, four-poster £40, family room £38

plus children's charge; children's reductions according to age; dinner £10; deposit: 20% CARDS: none DETAILS: well-behaved children welcome; dogs welcome; no smoking; car park; garden

HAY-ON-WYE   Powys   map 5

Brookfield Guest House

Brook Street, Hay-on-Wye, nr Hereford HR3 5BQ
TEL: (01497) 820518

Guests continue to find this architecturally splendid listed sixteenth-century residence a charming and delightful place to stay. The character of the house has been retained, with sloping ceilings, exposed beams, some horse-hair and plaster walls and some exposed stone. The lighting fixtures were produced by a local craftsman to match the originals. The bedrooms are well decorated and have delicate white bedspreads. The lounge is comfortable. Breakfast only is served, but several places in the town offer evening meals. This is a good area for walking, and gentler exercise can be taken by exploring the many craft and book shops for which Hay-on-Wye is renowned.

OWNER: Cheryl Price OPEN: all year exc Christmas ROOMS: 3 double, 2 twin, all with wash-basin; 2 family, 1 with bath/shower, 1 with wash-basin; TV in some bedrooms and lounge TERMS: single occupancy £18, twin/double £30, family room from £45; deposit: £10 CARDS: none DETAILS: no children under 5; no dogs; smoking downstairs only; car park

HOLYHEAD   Gwynedd   map 7

Roselea

26 Holborn Road, Holyhead LL65 2AT
TEL: (01407) 764391

This cosy guesthouse is close to the ferry terminal and Mrs Foxley will stay up for visitors arriving on the late ferry, provided advance notice is given. In summer the outside of the house is a riot of colour with floral displays and, inside, guests can admire the collection of plates hanging on the walls. Roselea is spotlessly clean and the well-appointed bedrooms have orthopaedic beds. Breakfasts only are provided, as well as packed lunches if requested.

OWNER: Mrs S. Foxley OPEN: all year exc Christmas ROOMS: 1 double, 1 twin, 1 family; all rooms with wash-basin; TV in all bedrooms and lounge TERMS: single occupancy £18, twin/double £28, family room £24–£28 plus children's charge; reductions for children sharing with parents; deposit CARDS: none DETAILS: children welcome; no dogs; smoking in lounge only; garden

LITTLE HAVEN   Dyfed   map 4

Whitegates

Little Haven, nr Haverfordwest SA62 3LA
TEL/FAX: (01437) 781552
off B4341, 7m W of Haverfordwest

This handsome 150-year-old house stands in an elevated position
with views over St Bride's Bay and the village of Little Haven. There
are still three ostriches, two cats and a friendly springer spaniel
named Skeet. An unusual ash staircase leads to the large bedrooms,
three of which now have *en suite* facilities. Guests have the use of a
sitting-room with TV, and, in summer, an outside terrace and a
heated swimming-pool. Freshly prepared breakfasts and dinners are
served at individual tables, vegetarian choices can be arranged and,
as there is no alcohol licence, guests may bring their own wine to
dinner. Richard Llewellin is very knowledgeable about the area and
happy to help with itineraries.

OWNERS: Richard and Marion Llewellin   OPEN: all year   ROOMS: 3 double, 2 with bath/
shower, 1 with wash-basin; 1 family, with bath/shower; TV lounge   TERMS: single
occupancy £25, double £36–£44, family room £55; children's reductions by
arrangement; dinner £14.50; deposit   CARDS: Access, Visa   DETAILS: children welcome;
dogs by prior arrangement; car park; garden; swimming-pool

LITTLE MILL   Gwent   map 2

Pentwyn Farm

Little Mill, nr Pontypool NP4 0HQ
TEL/FAX: (01495) 785249
on A472, 3m W of Usk

This pink-washed sixteenth-century longhouse is situated in the
hamlet of Little Mill, and looks out across fields and valleys to the
Gwent hills. It is a stock farm of 120 acres, with ten acres of woodland
where adults can take advantage of rough shooting. Inside, the house
is comfortable, and a large, beamed sitting-room has a piano, log fire
and lots of books and games. There is an outdoor swimming-pool, and
table tennis in the barn. The individually decorated bedrooms are
well furnished. Ann Bradley is an enthusiastic cook and three-course
dinners are served at 7.30pm at one large table in the beamed dining-
room which has Laura Ashley décor and several antiques, including a
grandfather clock. Pentwyn Farm is licensed, vegetarians can be
catered for with notice, and children's helpings served. The stables
have been converted into two self-catering cottages with french
windows opening out on to the garden.

OWNERS: Ann and Stuart Bradley   OPEN: all year exc Christmas and New Year   ROOMS:
2 double, 1 with bath/shower, 1 with wash-basin; 1 family, with bath/shower; TV
lounge   TERMS: single occupancy £20–£24, double £30–£38, family room from £37.50;

half-price for children from 4 to 10; dinner £11   CARDS: none   DETAILS: no children under 4; no dogs; no smoking in dining-room; car park; games room; garden; swimming-pool

LLANANO   Powys   map 4

Bwlch Farm

Llananno, nr Llandrindod Wells LD1 6TT
TEL: (01597) 840366
from Llandrindod Wells take A483 towards Newtown, turn left towards Bwlch-y-sarnau 1½m N of Llanbister, then first left

Bwlch Farm stands in eight acres and is set in the hills of mid-Wales overlooking the Ithon Valley. It was originally a cruck-framed hall dating from the fifteenth century and, although it has modern comforts, it retains its flagstone floors, beams and a recently exposed beautiful carved beam over the fireplace in the dining-room. The house is furnished with a mixture of traditional and antique furniture. There is also a sitting-room with a log fire. Dinner is at a time to suit guests, and vegetarians can be catered for with advance notice. Guests may bring their own wine to dinner.

OWNERS: Roy and Dorothy Taylor   OPEN: Apr to Oct   ROOMS: 2 double, 1 twin; all rooms with bath/shower; TV lounge   TERMS: single occupancy £19, twin/double £35; children under 3 free, half-price for ages 4 to 12 except bank holidays and high season; dinner £9.50; deposit: £10   CARDS: none   DETAILS: children welcome; well-behaved dogs welcome; no smoking in bedrooms; car park; garden

LLANBEDR   Gwynedd   map 7

Plas y Bryn Hall

Llanbedr, nr Harlech LL45 2DX
TEL: (01341) 241520   FAX: (01341) 241214
off A496, 3m S of Harlech

This large Edwardian stone house with a black-and-white Tudor-style front stands in an acre of beautiful landscaped gardens, with views of Cardigan Bay and the mountains. Owners Janis and Alan Redshaw are a charming couple who purchased the property in a run-down condition and have carefully restored it. Original features include an attractive ceiling rose and cornices. Only two couples at a time are catered for; guests are made to feel at home, are free to come and go as they please, and are encouraged to ask for recommendations for walks and drives nearby. The two bedrooms are well appointed; one has a comfortable antique iron bed and its own bathroom. A sitting-room is available exclusively for guests' use. Shell Island beach is a mile away, Harlech is three miles and Barmouth seven.

OWNERS: Janis and Alan Redshaw OPEN: all year ROOMS: 2 double; 1 with bath/
shower, 1 with wash-basin; TV in both bedrooms TERMS: double £34–£40; deposit: by
arrangement CARDS: none DETAILS: no children; no dogs; no smoking; car park;
garden

LLANDECWYN   Gwynedd   map 7

Tegfan

Llandecwyn, Talsarnau, nr Harlech LL47 6YG
TEL: (01766) 771354
on A496, 4m N of Harlech

This attractive house is run by a charming couple who are dedicated
to their guests' comfort. All the rooms have views overlooking hills
where sheep graze and on to the distant sea. The attic room is
exceptionally spacious, with roof windows and armchairs in which to
relax and absorb the magnificent views. The separate annexe room
has its own bathroom and sitting-room and would be ideal for a
family or anyone wanting a little extra privacy. There is also a
separate guest lounge. Breakfast only is served, on attractive
Portmerion china, and Roy and Dawn King are happy to recommend
local restaurants for evening meals.

OWNERS: Roy and Dawn King OPEN: all year exc Christmas ROOMS: 3 double, 1 with
bath/shower, 2 with wash-basin; 1 twin, with wash-basin; TV lounge TERMS: single
occupancy £16, twin/double £28–£32 CARDS: none DETAILS: no children; no dogs; no
smoking; car park; garden

LLANDRINDOD WELLS   Powys   map 4

Charis

Pentrosfa, Llandrindod Wells LD1 5AL
TEL: (01597) 824732
off A483, S of town centre

This large Edwardian house is bright with hanging baskets in
summer and has an intriguing turret-style entrance. It is on a quiet
residential road and has a colourful garden to the rear which guests
are welcome to use. Warm Welsh hospitality is on the menu, along
with delicious breakfasts served in the dining-room. The spacious
bedrooms are spotless and well-lit with tall elegant windows. The
décor is in soft colours and all the beds have firm mattresses. The
guests' lounge has a one-handed grandfather clock.

OWNER: Pat Gimson OPEN: all year exc Christmas ROOMS: 2 double, 1 twin, 1 family;
all rooms with bath/shower; TV in all bedrooms and lounge TERMS: single occupancy
£18, twin/double £32, family room £46; children under 5 free, half-price for ages 5 to 10;
deposit CARDS: none DETAILS: children welcome; dogs welcome; no smoking; car
park; garden

LLANDUDNO   Gwynedd

map 7

Amber Court

West Parade, West Shore, Llandudno LL30 2BD
TEL: (01492) 874521

Ann Pickup is a keen interior designer and has used her expertise to
good effect in this detached Victorian house in a quiet area of town
with panoramic sea views. The bedrooms are beautifully decorated in
soft greens, pinks, beige and peach, and are well furnished too. Each
room has its own wash-basin and WC, and the main bathroom is
exclusively for guests' use. The front rooms have the sea views. The
lounge is shared with Ann, who is a charming host. It has a lovely
marble fireplace and the hall has an antique carved sideboard.
Breakfast only is served.

OWNER: Ann Pickup   OPEN: Mar to Nov   ROOMS: 2 double, 2 twin; all rooms with wash-
basin; TV in all bedrooms and lounge   TERMS: single occupancy £18–£25, twin/double
£32–£40; children's reductions according to age   CARDS: none   DETAILS: no children
under 7; no dogs; no smoking

Beach Cove

8 Church Walks, Llandudno LL30 2HD
TEL: (01492) 879638

A friendly welcome awaits guests at this Victorian property, well
situated for the beaches and town centre. It is in excellent decorative
order, warm and comfortable. The bedrooms are bright and airy and
the lounge has a rich red carpet and a grandfather clock. Bob Carroll
has a good sense of humour and enjoys a chat with his guests; Karen
is an excellent cook and serves up good-value traditional dinners with
plenty of vegetables at 5.30pm. Vegetarians can be catered for. A two-
bedroomed self-catering cottage with panoramic sea views is also
available.

OWNERS: Bob and Karen Carroll   OPEN: all year exc Christmas   ROOMS: 2 single, both
with wash-basin; 6 double, 5 with bath/shower, 1 with wash-basin; 1 four-poster, with
bath/shower; 1 family; TV in all bedrooms and lounge   TERMS: single/single occupancy
£17, double £34, four-poster £38, family room £54; £8–£10 for children; dinner £9;
deposit: £30   CARDS: none   DETAILS: children welcome; no dogs; no smoking in lounge
or dining-room

*If there are any bedrooms with TV, we mention this in the details at the
end of the entry.*

*Bath / shower in the details under each entry means that the rooms have
private facilities. The B&B may have other, shared bathroom facilities as
well. We say if rooms have wash-basins.*

The Lighthouse

Marine Drive, Great Ormes Head, Llandudno LL30 2XD
TEL/FAX: (01492) 876819
from sea-front in Llandudno follow signs for Great Orme Scenic Route

The Lighthouse is a listed building situated at the head of the Great
Orme, a spectacular headland rising to 656ft. It is a magical place
and on clear days the views stretch to the Isle of Man. The Lighthouse
was in continuous operation until 1985, and in 1988 John Callin took
on the challenge of converting it into a high-class B&B. The entrance
hall is one of the most interesting rooms, with its 19-foot pitch-pine
panelling and gallery. The Lighthouse is furnished with antiques and
the bedrooms are individually decorated, with glorious sunrise views
from the east-facing room. The Lamp Suite features a sitting-room
with panoramic views in the original glass-walled lamp room.
Breakfast only is served in the dining-room overlooking a 360-foot
sheer drop to the sea. The lounge has a large stone fireplace where log
fires burn on cool evenings.

OWNER: John Callin OPEN: all year ROOMS: 2 double, 1 family; all rooms with bath/
shower; 1 room suitable for wheelchair-users; TV in all bedrooms and lounge TERMS:
single occupancy £37.50, double £70, family room £70 plus children's charge; children
under 3 free, half-price for ages 3 to 12 sharing with parents; deposit: 1 night's charge
CARDS: Access, Visa DETAILS: children welcome; no dogs; no smoking; car park;
garden

LLANFAIR CAEREINION Powys map 4

Bryn Penarth

Llanfair Caereinion, nr Welshpool SY21 0BZ
TEL: (01938) 810535
just off B4389, 1m S of Llanfair Caereinion

Bryn Penarth is a large, red-brick 250-year old farmhouse that has
been so restored on the outside as to look like new. It stands in an
acre of well-kept gardens and 37 acres of farmland, in an elevated
position with outstanding views of the countryside and the Berwyn
Mountains. The interior is beautifully maintained and traditionally
furnished; the attractive bedrooms are decorated in Victorian style
and all but one have their own bathroom. A sitting-room has an open
fire and TV, and a sun room, where breakfast is sometimes served,
overlooks the garden. There is a separate beamed dining-room where
breakfast and pre-arranged home-cooked dinners are taken around
one table; vegetarian choices and children's helpings can be provided
if requested in advance, and guests may bring their own wine. Ivernia
Watkin is an enthusiastic lady who has created a warm and
welcoming ambience. Llanfair Caereinion is a quiet little market
town with riverside walks.

OWNERS: Glyn and Ivernia Watkin OPEN: all year exc Christmas ROOMS: 2 single, 1 with bath/shower, 1 with wash-basin; 2 double, 1 twin, all with bath/shower; TV in some bedrooms and lounge TERMS: single £15–£18, single occupancy £18–£20, twin/double £32–£36; half-price for children under 16; dinner £8 CARDS: none DETAILS: children welcome; no dogs in dining-room and sitting-room; no smoking in bedrooms; car park; garden

Cwmllwynog

Llanfair Caereinion, nr Welshpool SY21 0HF
TEL: (01938) 810791
leave A458 at Llanfair Caereinion and continue W on B4385, take second left

This traditional Welsh farmhouse dates from the seventeenth century and is part of a working dairy farm. Joyce Cornes is a keen gardener: she tends a lovely garden which leads down to a stream, and has surrounded the house with tubs and hanging baskets full of flowers. The large bedrooms have traditional furnishings and the double has designer fabrics and wallpaper. There are sturdy beams throughout and the lounge has a huge stone fireplace with a wood-burning stove and a splendid Welsh dresser, on which a fine collection of Portmerion china is displayed. The home-cooked meals use produce from the garden, and bread and puddings are home-made too. Vegetarians can be catered for and guests may bring their own wine to dinner.

OWNER: Joyce Cornes OPEN: all year ROOMS: 1 double, with bath/shower; 1 twin, with wash-basin; 1 family; TV in all bedrooms and lounge TERMS: single occupancy £18, twin/double £32, family room price by arrangement; children's reductions by arrangement; dinner £8–£10 CARDS: none DETAILS: children welcome; dogs by arrangement; no smoking in bedroom; car park; garden

LLANFIHANGEL GLYN MYFYR   Clwyd   map 7

Old Rectory

Llanfihangel Glyn Myfyr, nr Corwen LL21 9UN
TEL: (01490) 420568   FAX: (01490) 420773
just off B5105 Cerrigydrudion to Ruthin road beside River Alwen

The grey-stone exterior of this building is set off beautifully by colourful flower borders and climbers. It is tucked away in a peaceful valley rich with wildlife, including some rare birds. The house is furnished to a high standard with three individually decorated bedrooms, all with lovely countryside views. The main guests' bathroom has the luxury of a whirlpool bath and is fitted out in Victorian style. Jenny and Elwyn Hughes enjoy sharing their home and treat visitors as friends. Breakfast is cooked on the Aga and served in the large kitchen, where jugs, china and other interesting items hang from the ceiling beams. The garden includes a children's play area.

OWNERS: Elwyn and Jenny Hughes OPEN: all year exc Christmas ROOMS: 1 double, 2 family; all rooms with wash-basin; TV lounge TERMS: single occupancy £20, double £40; family room from £50; babies free, half-price for children under 14; deposit: 10% CARDS: none DETAILS: well-behaved children welcome; dogs welcome in kennel; no smoking in bedrooms; car park; garden

LLANGEITHO Dyfed   map 4

Glanrhyd Isaf

Stags Head, Llangeitho, nr Tregaron SY25 6QU
TEL: (01974) 298762
on B4342 between Tregaron and Llangeitho

This simple bungalow with a charming garden stands above the road and enjoys lovely views. The 22 steps up to the front door make it unsuitable for disabled people. It is maintained in spotless condition and the two ground-floor rooms have pretty wallpaper. The lounge has french windows leading out to the garden, which includes an orchard and a wild- flower area. The substantial breakfasts set you up for the day, which could profitably be spent bird-watching in this area. For evening meals, the village pub and a restaurant are only a mile away.

OWNER: Winifred Owen OPEN: all year ROOMS: 1 double, with shower; 1 twin; TV in both bedrooms TERMS: single occupancy £15, twin/double £29; babies under 2 free, half-price for children from 3 to 12; deposit: 10% CARDS: none DETAILS: children welcome; well-behaved dogs welcome exc in lounge; no smoking in lounge; car park; garden

LLANGOLLEN Clwyd   map 7

Adanhurst

Abbey Road, Llangollen LL20 8SS
TEL: (01978) 860562

Adanhurst is an attractive modern bungalow in a superb position, backing on to the River Dee and the steam railway line. Annie and Mike Pearce are a friendly couple and keen gardeners. They are also railway buffs and the conservatory and sitting-room, shared with the owners, are full of railway memorabilia. Breakfast only is served, but there are several eating establishments a ten-minute walk away in town.

OWNER: Annie Pearce   OPEN: all year   ROOMS: 1 double; 1 twin; TV in one bedroom
TERMS: single occupancy £25, twin/double £30; children's reductions by arrangement;
deposit: £5 per person   CARDS: none   DETAILS: children by arrangement; no dogs; no
smoking; car park; garden

LLANIGON   Powys

map 4

Old Post Office

Llanigon, nr Hay-on-Wye HR3 5QA
TEL: (01497) 820008
*from Hay-on-Wye take B4350 Brecon road, after ½m turn left signposted
Llanigon, after 1½m turn left just before school, house on right*

This cosy, whitewashed seventeenth-century house of great character
is in the Brecon Beacons National Park, close to Offa's Dyke. It is
furnished in period style and retains a winding oak staircase, thick
stone walls, heavy beams and sloping floors. Two of the three
bedrooms are *en suite*, and all have rich floral matching fabrics and
original polished board floors. There is a relaxing ambience and
guests are free to come and go as they please. Breakfast only is served
at one table in the dining-room which has an old fireplace and Welsh
dresser full of china. An extensive breakfast menu is entirely
vegetarian, and home-made preserves feature. This is wonderful
walking country, and maps are provided showing local pubs and
places of interest. Packed lunches can be requested.

OWNERS: Linda Webb and Edmund Moore   OPEN: all year exc Jan   ROOMS: 2 double, 1
with bath/shower, 1 with wash-basin; 1 twin, with bath/shower; TV lounge   TERMS:
single occupancy £17–£25, twin/double £28–£38; children's reductions according to
age; deposit: 1 night's charge   CARDS: none   DETAILS: children welcome; dogs
welcome; no smoking; car park

LLANRHAEADR-YM-MOCHNANT   Clwyd

map 7

Bron Heulog

Waterfall Road, Llanrhaeadr-ym-Mochnant, nr Oswestry SY10 0JX
TEL: (01691) 780521
on B4580, 10m W of Oswestry

Ken and Karon Raines took over Bron Heulog in early 1995 and
improvements have been ongoing since then. It is a spacious
Victorian house and the large bedrooms have all been refurbished
with pretty pastel wallpapers and Victorian-style bathrooms. One of
the beds is a four-poster made by the owners. Dinner is served by
arrangement, and vegetarians can be catered for with advance notice.
A licence has been applied for, but guests are welcome to bring their
own wine. Pony trekking and fishing can be arranged, and Ken
Raines is a qualified paragliding instructor.

OWNERS: Ken and Karon Raines OPEN: all year ROOMS: 1 twin, 1 four-poster, 1 family; all rooms with bath/shower; TV in all bedrooms and lounge TERMS: single occupancy £20, twin £36, four-poster £40, family room £50–£65; children under 2 free, £12 for ages 3 to 16 sharing with parents; dinner £10; deposit: £10 per person CARDS: none DETAILS: children welcome; no dogs; no smoking; car park; garden

Llys Morgan

Llanrhaeadr-ym-Mochnant, nr Oswestry SY10 0JZ
TEL: (01691) 780345
on B4580, 10m W of Oswestry

This charming house dating from the sixteenth century is 200 yards from the village and stands in an acre of lovely gardens with a fish pond. It was formerly the vicarage, and the Bible was translated into Welsh here in 1588; the dining-room has seven Bibles set into the fireplace. The spacious bedrooms are comfortable and there are two lounges, one with a fire that is lit on chilly evenings. On pleasant days guests can enjoy the garden and walled patio. The Morgans are a relaxed and friendly couple who provide home-cooked evening meals if ordered in advance; vegetarians can be catered for. Guests may bring their own wine to dinner. The Pistyll Rhaeadr waterfall is four miles away.

OWNER: Mrs J. Morgan OPEN: all year exc Christmas ROOMS: 3 double, 1 with bath/shower, 2 with wash-basin; 1 twin, with bath/shower; 1 family, with bath/shower; TV lounge TERMS: single occupancy £15–£16.50, twin/double £30–£33, family room from £45; half-price for children under 12; dinner £7 CARDS: none DETAILS: children welcome; dogs by arrangement; car park; games room; garden

LLANRUG   Gwynedd   map 7

Lakeside

Llanrug, nr Caernarfon LL55 4ED
TEL: (01286) 870065
from Llanrug follow signs to Bryn Bras Castle, go under arch of castle and up hill for 600yds

This delightful Welsh-stone house dates from the seventeenth century and was originally the gamekeeper's cottage of nearby Bryn Bras Castle. Six acres of woods and a landscaped garden surround the cottage and are inhabited by dogs, peacocks, geese, chickens, quail and Vietnamese pot-bellied pigs. The property includes a private lake, and a two-seater canoe and a rowing boat are available for interested guests. This is a friendly, welcoming place and the lounge has a hearty log fire on colder days. Dinner is available by arrangement and guests may bring their own wine.

OWNER: Lyn Kane OPEN: all year ROOMS: 2 double, 1 with bath/shower, 1 with wash-basin; 1 twin, 1 family, both with wash-basin; TV in all bedrooms and lounge TERMS: single occupancy £24–£27, twin/double £36, family room from £45; half-price for children sharing with parents; dinner £12.50 CARDS: none DETAILS: children welcome; dogs welcome; no smoking; car park; garden

---

LLANRWST   Gwynedd

map 7

White Cottage

Maenan, Llanrwst LL26 0UL
TEL: (01492) 640346
just off A470, 2m N of Llanrwst and 15m S of Llandudno

This delightful Welsh stone cottage stands in a pretty garden in the large grounds of Maenan Hall. Kathleen Isherwood is a cheerful lady who runs her house in a home-from-home fashion, and offers good-value accommodation. There is a lounge/dining-room with TV where breakfast only is served. The comfortable bedrooms are simply furnished, and share a bathroom and separate WC.

OWNER: Kathleen Isherwood OPEN: all year exc Christmas ROOMS: 2 double, 1 twin; all rooms with wash-basin; TV lounge TERMS: single occupancy £16, twin/double £30; children's reductions according to age; deposit: £10 per room CARDS: none DETAILS: children welcome; no dogs; car park; garden

---

MAMHILAD   Gwent

map 2

Ty-Cooke Farm

Mamhilad, nr Pontypool NP4 8QZ
TEL: (01873) 880382
on minor road heading NW from A4042, 2m N of Pontypool

This eighteenth-century farmhouse with a cobbled yard is close to the Monmouthshire and Brecon Canal and is well placed for visiting the Brecon Beacons National Park. It is part of a working mixed farm, which guests are welcome to explore. The owners have a good sense of humour and enjoy sharing their home with their guests, who are greeted with a hot drink upon arrival. The spacious lounge has a beautiful carved fireplace from nearby Maindiff Court. The Welsh collie is friendly and has been known to jump into guests' cars. Evening meals are not available, but there is a pub that serves good food within walking distance.

OWNER: Marion Price OPEN: all year exc Christmas ROOMS: 1 double, 1 twin, 1 family; all rooms with wash-basin; TV lounge TERMS: single occupancy £18, twin/double £32, family room from £40; half-price for children under 12 CARDS: none DETAILS: children welcome; no dogs; no smoking; car park; garden

MONTGOMERY   Powys

map 7

Beeches

New Road, Montgomery SY15 6UJ
TEL/FAX: (01686) 668663
off B4388, just N of town

This tastefully designed modern house is well placed on the edge of
town with views of the castle and the Severn Valley. It has a
charming conservatory and a large landscaped garden, but the views
are best enjoyed from the lounge with its balcony. Guests are
welcome to use the full-sized snooker table and anyone who
challenges the owner faces a formidable opponent. The atmosphere is
friendly and hospitable. The bedrooms are beautifully decorated with
colour co-ordinated fabrics and wallpapers, and one is on the ground
floor with a shower room opposite. Traditional breakfasts are served
in the elegant dining-room, and evening meals are available by prior
arrangement. Vegetarians can be catered for and guests may bring
their own wine. There are also several eating places in town, which is
within walking distance.

OWNERS: Basil and Hilary Thomas   OPEN: all year   ROOMS: 1 double, 1 twin, 1 family; all
rooms with bath/shower; TV in all bedrooms and lounge   TERMS: single occupancy £20,
twin/double £36, family room from £42; £10 for children under 5; dinner £10; deposit:
£10 per person   CARDS: none   DETAILS: children welcome; no dogs; no smoking; car
park; garden

MOYLGROVE   Dyfed

map 4

Old Vicarage

Moylgrove, nr Cardigan SA43 3BN
TEL: (01239) 881231
*head W from A487 3m S of Cardigan on B4582; then take minor road on
right to Moylgrove*

The Old Vicarage is a spacious Edwardian house in an acre of
paddocks and gardens, with views down to the coastal village of
Moylgrove and on out to sea. The elegantly decorated home is owned
by a charming couple who really enjoy running the business. The
large bedrooms have co-ordinated fabrics and friezes set against
pastel walls. One is a suite leading out to a patio. The dining-room
and lounge have log fires for winter time and both have views of the
valley and Cardigan Bay. Interesting and varied four-course dinners
are served by arrangement. Vegetarians can be catered for and wine
is available.

OWNERS: Anthony and Peggy Govey   OPEN: all year   ROOMS: 1 single, with wash-basin;
2 double, 1 twin, all with bath/shower; TV lounge   TERMS: single £20, single occupancy

£22.50, twin/double £45; half-price for children from 3 to 12; dinner £13.50; deposit: £10 per person CARDS: none DETAILS: no children under 3; no dogs; smokers' lounge available; car park; garden

NEATH   West Glamorgan   map 4

Cwmbach Cottages

Cadoxton-juxta-Neath, Neath SA10 8AH
TEL: (01639) 639825 and 641436
exit M4 at junction 43 on to A465, after 3m at Aberdulais roundabout take first left signposted Cadoxton, after ½m turn right opposite church, follow for ½m

This tasteful conversion of six miners' cottages stands in an elevated position overlooking the valley, 200 yards from a golf course. The bedrooms are individually decorated in pastel colours, have good-sized bathrooms and Sky TV. One ground-floor bedroom is suitable for disabled visitors, with direct access from the car park and a ramp for wheelchairs. There is a large, well-furnished lounge and a separate dining-room which leads out on to the patio – a pleasant spot to relax on warm days. North of here, along the wooded Neath Gorge, is a riverside path taking in a spectacular series of waterfalls. The Brecon Beacons National Park, a magnet for walkers, is within reach. Packed lunches can be provided.

OWNER: Lynda Morgan OPEN: all year ROOMS: 3 double, 1 twin, 1 family; all rooms with bath/shower; 1 room suitable for wheelchair-users; TV in all bedrooms and lounge
TERMS: single occupancy £24, twin/double £42, family room £42–£58; reductions for children by arrangement; deposit: £10 per room CARDS: none DETAILS: children welcome; no dogs; no smoking in bedrooms or dining-room; car park; garden

NEWPORT   Dyfed   map 4

Llysmeddyg

East Street, Newport SA42 0SY
TEL: (01239) 820008
on A487 between Fishguard and Cardigan

Not to be confused with Newport in Gwent, this is a small town on the Pembrokeshire coast. LLysmeddyg is a spacious listed Georgian house, impeccably maintained by the Rosses, who are very knowledgeable about the area. The large bedrooms include armchairs to relax in, or guests can choose the lounge with original casement shutters and a log fire. A fire also burns in the dining-room, where three-course candlelit dinners are served at 7.45pm. Vegetarian choices can be provided and there is an extensive wine list (a glass is included in the price of dinner). For smaller appetites, light meals are also available. Breakfast time is when guests choose, and kippers and home-made preserves are on the menu. The house is not far from the iron bridge over the Nyfer Estuary. Spanish is spoken.

OWNERS: Ian and Penny Ross OPEN: all year exc Christmas ROOMS: 2 single, both with wash-basin; 2 double, 1 with shower, 1 with bath/shower, 1 with wash-basin; TV lounge TERMS: single/single occupancy £18.50, double £37–£42; dinner £15.50; deposit CARDS: none DETAILS: children by arrangement; no dogs; smoking in sitting-room only; car park; games room; garden

NEWPORT   Gwent   map 2

Kepe Lodge

46A Caerau Road, Newport NP9 4HH
TEL: (01633) 262351

Kepe Lodge is maintaining its high standards and Ken and Peggy Long are as friendly and charming as ever. The house is tucked away in a quiet position just off the main road, surrounded by lovely gardens with roses around the lawn and a furnished patio leading out from the dining-room. The tastefully decorated bedrooms have comfortable beds, plus chairs and writing desks. Excellent breakfasts include a buffet selection of cereals and juices. The Longs are happy to share their knowledge of places and events in the area.

OWNERS: Peggy and Ken Long OPEN: all year exc Christmas ROOMS: 5 single, all with wash-basin; 1 double, 2 twin, all with shower; TV in all bedrooms TERMS: single £19, single occupancy £22, twin/double £34; deposit CARDS: none DETAILS: no children; no dogs; no smoking in public rooms; car park; garden

PENCELLI   Powys   map 4

Cambrian Cruisers Marina

Ty Newydd, Pencelli, nr Brecon LD3 7LJ
TEL/FAX: (01874) 665315
on B4558, 4m SE of Brecon

This unusual set-up offers a unique combination holiday for those unable to make up their minds: a stay in a farmhouse overlooking the marina, or a few days afloat on a canal narrow boat, or both. The restored eighteenth-century house is of whitewashed stone, and lies beneath Pen-y-Fan, the highest peak of the Brecon Beacons. The four bedrooms are attractively furnished with new and antique pine; all have *en suite* facilities, chairs or sofas and TV. Guests have their own entrance to the accommodation, and there is a conservatory for their use. Breakfast only is served, but packed lunches can be provided and there are several eating places within a short drive. The comfortable, well-equipped narrow boats cruise 33 miles on the Monmouthshire and Brecon Canal; booking is through the one telephone number.

OWNERS: Peter and Ruth Griffiths OPEN: Mar to end Oct ROOMS: 2 double, 1 twin, 1 family; all rooms with bath/shower; TV in all bedrooms TERMS: single occupancy £19, twin/double £35, family room from £40; children's reductions by arrangement; deposit: £20 CARDS: none DETAILS: children welcome; no dogs; no smoking; car park; garden

---

PENMARK   South Glamorgan   map 4

The Cottage

Penmark, nr Barry CF62 3BP
TEL: (01446) 710327
off A4226, 3m W of Barry

This pretty whitewashed cottage stands in a large landscaped garden, opposite the village church, and next to the Six Bells pub. Inside, it is beautifully maintained and a delightful place to stay, with low beamed ceilings, two inglenook fireplaces, antiques, a conservatory and sitting-room. Three charming bedrooms share a bathroom with a power shower and two additional WCs. Guests are welcome to use the garden on pleasant days. Evening meals are not served, but can be had in the local pub; however, there is a microwave and cooker in the conservatory for guests' use.

OWNERS: Richard and Jennifer Kidwell OPEN: all year ROOMS: 1 double, 1 twin, both with wash-basin; 1 family; TV in all bedrooms and lounge TERMS: single occupancy

THE COTTAGE, PENMARK

from £18, twin/double from £36, family room from £40; children's reductions by arrangement; deposit: by arrangement CARDS: none DETAILS: children welcome; no dogs; no smoking upstairs; car park; garden

PENTRE HALKYN   Clwyd   map 7

The Hall

Lygan-y-Wern, Pentre Halkyn, nr Holywell CH8 8BD
TEL: (01352) 780215   FAX: (01352) 780187
leave A55 2m SE of Holywell, follow signs to Bagillt for ¼m to large house on left

This sixteenth-century hall stands in 13 acres and overlooks the Dee Estuary. Bantams, ducks and hens will be encountered on a walk through the grounds. The well-maintained house combines modern comforts with many original features, such as flagstone floors, a listed dovecote and seventeenth-century outdoor privvies, which are to be viewed rather than used. The bedrooms are enormous and brightly decorated with pine furnishings. Breakfasts are served in the lounge/dining-room. Davinia Vernon is a warm and friendly lady who greets guests with a hot drink upon arrival.

OWNER: Davinia Vernon OPEN: all year ROOMS: 1 single, with wash-basin; 1 double, with bath/shower; 2 twin, 1 family, all with wash-basin; TV lounge TERMS: single £15, single occupancy £16–£25, twin/double £30, family room £30 plus children's charge; children's reductions according to age CARDS: Access, Visa DETAILS: children welcome; no dogs; smoking in lounge only; car park; garden

PENYBONTFAWR   Powys   map 7

Glyndwr

Penybontfawr, nr Oswestry SY10 0NT
TEL: (01691) 860430
just off B4396 in centre of village

Penybontfawr is in the heart of the Tanat Valley in the Berwyn Mountains, and Glyndwr is easily found on its main street next to the stone river bridge. It is a whitewashed seventeenth-century stone cottage with hanging baskets adorning the outside walls. Enid Henderson keeps it sparkling clean inside and warms it with an open fire in the traditionally beamed sitting-room. In fine weather the patio and quiet garden may tempt guests outdoors. Evening meals prepared with fresh local ingredients are served at 7pm; vegetarian choices can be cooked by arrangement. Guests may bring their own wine to dinner. Glyndwr has no central heating, but there are storage and panel heaters. A self-catering unit is available, which is sometimes used as an overflow for the B&B.

OWNER: Enid Henderson OPEN: all year exc Christmas and New Year ROOMS: 2
double, 1 twin; all rooms with bath/shower; TV lounge TERMS: single occupancy
£17–£19, twin/double £30–£34; half-price for children under 12; dinner £9.50; deposit
CARDS: none DETAILS: children welcome; no dogs; no smoking in bedrooms; car park;
garden

PRESTATYN Clwyd

map 7

Traeth Ganol

41 Beach Road West, Prestatyn LL19 7LL
TEL: (01745) 853594   FAX: (01745) 886687
follow brown tourist signs to Nova Centre and Beaches

Traeth Ganol is well placed for holidaymakers, right on the sea-front
in a quiet cul-de-sac with a leisure complex and the town centre
nearby. Chris and Jo Groves welcome their guests warmly and the
house has a pleasant, relaxed feel. The bedrooms are well appointed
and tastefully decorated in soft colours with matching curtains and
bedspreads. Three of them are on the ground floor and are suitable for
wheelchair-users. The ground-floor rooms have access to a south-
facing patio. The lounge has comfortable sofas and armchairs in co-
ordinated colours. Chris Groves has a background in catering and
prepares excellent traditional dishes and offers an à la carte menu
from Wednesday to Saturday. Vegetarians can be catered for with
advance notice. Traeth Ganol is licensed.

OWNERS: Chris and Jo Groves OPEN: all year ROOMS: 1 single, 1 double, 1 twin, 6
family; all rooms with bath/shower; 3 rooms suitable for wheelchair-users; TV in all
bedrooms TERMS: single £30, single occupancy £39, twin/double £45, family room
£64–£79; babies under 1 free; dinner £8 to £10; deposit: £25 CARDS: Access, Visa
DETAILS: children welcome; no dogs; smoking in bar only; car park; garden

RHAYADER Powys

map 4

Glyn Gwy

Rhayader LD6 5LE
TEL: (01597) 810441
on A470, 3½m N of Rhayader

A tree-lined drive off the main road leads to Glyn Gwy, which is
surrounded by 14 acres of romantic parkland on the banks of the
River Wye. Stunning views open up across the valley and a (fairly
lengthy) walk over the hill opposite leads to the Elan Valley reservoir
complex, with its magnificent scenery, lovely walks and wildlife. Two
of the spacious bedrooms overlook the river and all are furnished in
keeping with the house's Victorian character. There are two lounges,
one with TV and the other a quiet place in which to relax round a log
fire. The house is furnished with all sorts of interesting items.

Breakfast and evening meals are served in the panelled dining-room; Glyn Gwy is licensed and vegetarians can be catered for. Salmon and trout fishing can be arranged.

OWNER: Anne Moorsom OPEN: Easter to end Oct ROOMS: 2 double, both with wash-basin; 1 twin, with bath/shower; TV lounge TERMS: twin/double £38; half-price for children under 7; dinner £10.50 CARDS: none DETAILS: children welcome; no dogs; smoking in sitting-room only; car park; garden

Raveloe

Doldowlod, Rhayader LD1 6NN
TEL/FAX: (01597) 810851
on A470, 3m S of Rhayader

In a quiet location overlooking lovely countryside and hills, this is a welcoming ranch-style bungalow. Rob and Julia Wilson are happy to share their home with guests, who are usually greeted with a hot drink upon arrival. The lounge is equipped with satellite TV and a CD player which guests may use. The bedrooms are sparklingly clean and all are on the ground floor. Breakfasts and modestly priced home-cooked evening meals are served. A cot is available for babies.

OWNER: Julia Wilson OPEN: all year exc Christmas ROOMS: 2 double, 1 with wash-basin; 1 twin, with wash-basin; TV lounge TERMS: single occupancy £20, twin/double £28; babies free, £4.50 for children under 5, £9 for ages 6 to 12; dinner £6–£8 CARDS: none DETAILS: children welcome; dogs to be kept on leads at all times; no smoking; car park; garden

RHYL Clwyd map 7

Romsley Guesthouse

8 Butterton Road, Rhyl LL18 1RF
TEL: (01745) 330300

This immaculate property undergoes regular refurbishment, and is conveniently sited close to Rhyl's promenade and beach. The tastefully decorated bedrooms are colour co-ordinated; one has a four-poster bed and all have TV. A comfortable lounge has a marble chess set and TV; Charles Bill has made a video of places to visit in the area which may be of interest. Freshly cooked breakfasts, and modestly priced dinners by arrangement, are served in the licensed dining-room. Children's helpings and vegetarian dishes can be requested. The house does not yet have full central heating, but each room has individual heaters and there are plans to install radiators in all rooms in the future.

OWNERS: Charles and Sheila Bill OPEN: all year exc Christmas ROOMS: 1 single, 1 double, 1 four-poster, 4 family; all rooms with wash-basin; TV in all bedrooms and lounge TERMS: single/single occupancy £13, double £26, four-poster £30, family room

£26 plus children's charge; children under 3 free, half-price for ages 3 to 10; dinner £6; deposit: 1 night's charge CARDS: none DETAILS: children welcome; no dogs; no smoking in dining-room

---

RUTHIN   Clwyd   map 7

Gorphwysfa

8A Castle Street, Ruthin LL15 1DP
TEL: (01824) 702748

This intriguing fifteenth-century house retains some extraordinary original features, including wattle-and-daub walls, carved ship's timbers in the hallway and an inglenook fireplace. The galleried hall with its open-plan floor is most unusual and the whole house is full of paintings, china and objects of interest. It is exquisitely furnished and the bedrooms are very spacious; the family room is enormous. The drawing-room has window-seats and casement shutters and there is also a small reading room. This is a friendly house and Ben the golden labrador welcomes guests too. There are several eating places within walking distance. Limited parking is available after 6pm and there are parking spaces in the town square, a short distance away.

OWNERS: Walter and Eleanor Jones OPEN: all year ROOMS: 1 double, 1 twin, both with wash-basin; 1 family, with bath/shower; TV lounge TERMS: single occupancy £16.50, twin/double £33, family room from £41.50; half-price for children under 11 CARDS: none DETAILS: children welcome; dogs welcome

---

ST BRIDE'S MAJOR   Mid Glamorgan   map 4

Hillcrest

Penylan Road, St Bride's Major, nr Bridgend CF32 0SB
TEL: (01656) 880787
on B4265, 3m S of Bridgend

This welcoming house offers good-value accommodation and a friendly atmosphere. It is in a beautiful position with views to the Bristol Channel. The bedrooms are comfortable and maintained in spotless condition. A collection of brass is on display in the hall and guests can relax in the separate lounge. A good selection is offered at breakfast and although evening meals are not available, there are a couple of local pubs which serve food.

OWNES: Mrs G.M. Lewis OPEN: all year exc Christmas ROOMS: 1 double, 1 family; TV in both bedrooms TERMS: twin/double £33, family room from £49.50; half-price for children under 12 CARDS: none DETAILS: children welcome; no dogs; no smoking; car park; garden

West Usk Lighthouse

Lighthouse Road, St Bride's Wentloog, nr Newport NP1 9SF
TEL: (01633) 810126/815860   FAX: (01633) 815582
leave M4 at junction 28, follow B4239 for 2m, then turn left at B&B sign

This really is an old lighthouse, a circular construction with wedge-shaped rooms and a spiral stone staircase in the centre, renovated from derelict condition by Frank and Danielle Sheahan. The peculiar but beautiful architecture of the 1821 building is matched by the unusual furnishings, such as a waterbed, a four-poster and an old red telephone box converted into a shower. The atmosphere is peaceful and facilities include a flotation tank which guests can relax in and then enjoy a massage. The rooms are filled with paintings, old pictures, plants and modern sculptures. A terrace with a roof garden has stunning circular views. Evening meals, including choices for vegetarians, are available by arrangement, and guests may bring their own wine.

OWNERS: Frank and Danielle Sheahan OPEN: all year ROOMS: 1 double, 1 twin, 1 four-poster; all rooms with bath/shower; TV in all bedrooms and lounge TERMS: single occupancy £35–£40, twin/double £50–£65, four-poster £60, family room £55; children's reductions according to age; dinner £15; deposit: 50% CARDS: Access, Amex, Delta, Switch, Visa DETAILS: children welcome; dogs by arrangement; no smoking; car park; garden

Craig-y-Mor

Whitesands, St David's, nr Haverfordwest SA62 6PT
TEL: (01437) 720431
take A487 from Haverfordwest to St David's, then continue on B4583 to Whitesands Beach and turn left at golf course

Craig-y-Mor means 'rock by the sea', and the house is located on the coastal path directly opposite the golf course and overlooking the bay and Carn Llidi mountain. The atmosphere is relaxed and informal and guests can use the kitchen for making hot drinks whenever they wish. The bedrooms are of a good size and all are on the ground floor. Each has its own sitting area with a view of the bay and the magnificent sunsets; two have TV. This is a popular spot for walkers and bird-lovers, who can visit Ramsey Island Nature Reserve. Breakfast only is served, but there is a good selection of eating establishments in St David's.

OWNER: Muriel Elaine Barton OPEN: all year ROOMS: 1 double, 1 twin, 1 family; all rooms with bath/shower; TV in some bedrooms TERMS: single occupancy £16.50, twin/double £33, family room from £49.50; free for children under 5 sharing with parents; deposit: 1 night's charge CARDS: none DETAILS: children welcome; no dogs; no smoking; car park

SAUNDERSFOOT Dyfed

map 4

Primrose Cottage

Stammers Road, Saundersfoot SA69 9HH
TEL: (01834) 811080
three houses up from Saundersfoot post office

This unassuming Victorian cottage stands behind neat railings in the centre of Saundersfoot, close to the harbour and beaches. The small bedrooms are kept immaculately clean and have comfortable beds. The double has an *en suite* bathroom and the twin can be adapted for use as a family room. The guests' lounge has lots of books and slides of the area. The Quinns are a friendly and informal couple, and Malcolm is willing to take guests on a guided tour in his car for a small fee. Evening meals are served by arrangement, vegetarians can be catered for and guests may bring their own wine.

OWNERS: Malcolm and Jennifer Quinn OPEN: all year exc Christmas ROOMS: 1 double, with bath/shower; 1 twin; TV lounge TERMS: single occupancy £15, twin/double £30–£32; children under 3 free, half-price for ages 3 to 10; dinner £6.50 CARDS: none DETAILS: children welcome; well-behaved dogs welcome; smoking in lounge only; garden

Sandyhill Guest House

Tenby Road, Saundersfoot SA69 9DR
TEL: (01834) 813165
on A478, 3m S of junction with A477, opposite nursery

The core of Sandyhill is a seventeenth-century farmhouse, which has been added to over the years. The bedrooms, one on the ground floor, are warm and comfortable and have double glazing to minimise traffic noise. Peggy and David Edwards are a friendly, welcoming couple who offer a high standard of accommodation in their immaculate house. The beautiful garden includes a swimming-pool which guests may use. Evening meals are served at 6pm and can include vegetarian options. There is a small bar/lounge in addition to the guests' lounge. Saundersfoot village and beach and Tenby beach are not far away.

OWNERS: Peggy and David Edwards OPEN: Mar to end Oct ROOMS: 3 double, 2 with bath/shower; 2 family, 1 with bath/shower; TV in all bedrooms TERMS: single occupancy £18–£21, double £30–£36, family room from £45; half-price for children over 3 sharing with parents; dinner £8; deposit: 10% CARDS: none DETAILS: no children under 3; no dogs in public rooms; no smoking in bedrooms or dining-room; car park; garden; swimming-pool

SOLVA Dyfed   **map 4**

Min Yr Afon

11 Y Gribin, Solva, Haverfordwest SA62 6UY
TEL: (01437) 721752
*take A487 NW from Haverfordwest for 10m, then turn down hill into Solva
and left before bridge*

The small, cosy whitewashed cottage is 200 years old, but ablaze with
fresh floral blooms every summer. The delightful bedrooms have
sloping ceilings and are decorated in chintzy style; one has a brass
bed. Tasty breakfasts are served in the beamed dining-room, where
lots of craft items are displayed, including dried-flower
arrangements, patchwork pillows and tapestry. Min Yr Afon is
popular with walkers and is only 150 yards from the coastal path.

OWNERS: David and Julia Hann OPEN: all year exc Christmas ROOMS: 1 double, 1 twin,
both with shower; 1 family, with wash-basin; TV in some bedrooms and lounge TERMS:
single occupancy £20, twin/double £30, family room from £34; £7 for children from 5 to
11; deposit: £10 CARDS: none DETAILS: no children under 5; no dogs; car park; garden

---

SWANSEA West Glamorgan   **map 4**

Alexandra House

366 Mumbles Road, Swansea SA3 5TN
TEL: (01792) 406406   FAX: (01792) 405605

This beautifully maintained house with a well-tended garden faces
the sea and a sandy beach. The spotless bedrooms are tastefully
decorated with co-ordinated fabrics and have cane or pine furniture.
The front rooms have sea views. The house has a friendly ambience,
and Christine Llewellyn extends a warm welcome to all guests. The
guests' lounge is comfortable and excellent breakfasts are served in
the bright basement dining-room. The bus into the city centre stops
right outside.

OWNER: Christine Llewellyn OPEN: all year exc Christmas ROOMS: 3 double, 1 twin, 1
family; all rooms with bath/shower; TV in all bedrooms TERMS: single occupancy £20,
twin/double £36, family room from £41; £5 for children over 5; deposit CARDS: none
DETAILS: no children under 5; no dogs; smoking in lounge only; garden

---

The Bays

97 Mumbles Road, Norton, Mumbles, Swansea SA3 5TW
TEL: (01792) 404775

This late-Victorian house is right by the promenade and the beach,
which can be reached through the back gate. It is in a quiet part of
Mumbles and has a relaxing, friendly atmosphere. The furnishings

583

and décor are Victorian in character and a nineteenth-century fireplace has recently been installed in the lounge to add to the original feel of the house. Breakfast only is served in the conservatory/dining-room, which opens out on to the patio and mature garden. There are plenty of places for evening meals nearby.

OWNER: Judy Burrell OPEN: all year exc Christmas ROOMS: 2 double, 1 twin; all rooms with bath/shower; TV in some bedrooms and lounge TERMS: single occupancy £30–£35, twin/double £40–£45; deposit: £15 per person CARDS: none DETAILS: no children; no dogs; no smoking; car park; garden

Uplands Court

134 Eaton Crescent, Uplands, Swansea SA1 4QR
TEL: (01792) 473046

This large cream-painted Edwardian house is in a quiet crescent half a mile out of Swansea. Susan and Allan Gray have owned Uplands Court since 1987, and every year since then have been awarded the Swansea Silver Seal in recognition of high standards of hygiene. The eight bedrooms are simply decorated and functional; all have TV. A licensed bar is in the guest lounge, and breakfast only is served in the dining-room. There is a good choice of local restaurants for other meals, although packed lunches can be requested. There is no private car park, but parking on the road is not a problem.

UPLANDS COURT, SWANSEA

OWNERS: Mr and Mrs A.G. Gray OPEN: all year ROOMS: 4 single, 2 with bath/shower, 2 with wash-basin; 2 double, 1 with bath/shower, 1 with wash-basin; 2 family, both with bath/shower; TV in all bedrooms TERMS: single £17–£20, single occupancy £20, double £35–£40, family room price by arrangement; children's reductions by arrangement; deposit: £10 per person CARDS: Access, Amex, Visa DETAILS: children welcome; no dogs; no smoking in dining-room

---

TENBY Dyfed   **map 4**

High Seas

8 The Norton, Tenby SA70 8AA
TEL/FAX: (01834) 843611

High Seas is a Georgian terraced house in a quiet spot facing the sea. It is spacious, comfortable and well maintained, and the atmosphere is welcoming and relaxed. Most of the bedrooms have views over the North Beach and all are tastefully decorated with interesting furnishings, including an antique brass bed in one room and a half-tester in another. The lounge retains the original elegant cornices and coving and has an antique couch and a baby-grand piano. Breakfasts are served in the pleasant dining-room, which has an original fireplace and casement shutters. Evening meals are not available but there are plenty of eating places in Tenby.

OWNERS: Mr and Mrs J. Macdonald OPEN: Apr to Oct ROOMS: 4 double, 3 with bath/shower, 1 with wash-basin; 1 twin, with wash-basin; 1 family, with bath/shower; TV in all bedrooms TERMS: single occupancy £18–£20, twin/double £36–£40, family room £40–£45; children under 5 free CARDS: none DETAILS: children welcome; no dogs; no smoking in dining-room

---

Tall Ships Hotel

34 Victoria Street, Tenby SA70 7DY
TEL: (01834) 842055

Very close to the South Beach, this family-run hotel is a friendly place. The well-appointed bedrooms are fresh and clean and all have armchairs in which to relax. Guests will also find plenty to read in the pleasant lounge. The cellar bar is decorated on a nautical theme, with a section of a ship's mast as a support beam and all sorts of interesting items in the cosy nooks. Modestly priced and good-quality dinners are served in the licensed dining-room at 6.30pm and vegetarians can be catered for with advance notice.

OWNERS: Marianne and Dilwyn Richards OPEN: Mar to Oct ROOMS: 1 single, 2 double, 2 twin, 2 family; all rooms with bath/shower; TV in all bedrooms and lounge TERMS: single £16–£21, single occupancy £18.50–£23.50, twin/double £33–£39, family room £33–£39 plus children's charge; £3 for children under 3, half-price for ages 3 to 13; dinner £8 CARDS: Access, Visa DETAILS: children welcome; no dogs; no smoking in dining-room

TINTERN Gwent

map 2

Old Rectory

Tintern, nr Chepstow NP6 6SG
TEL: 01291 689519
on A466 between Chepstow and Monmouth

This lovely old house dates from about 1725, and is in a beautiful elevated position overlooking the River Wye and its valley. Tintern is famous for its Cistercian Abbey ruins, and the nearby forests provide many attractive walks (packed lunches can be requested). The Old Rectory has been extended over the years, and offers five bedrooms, several of which have mahogany beds made by a local craftsman. A fine display of original line drawings of British pubs decorates the sitting-room, where the wood-burning stove is lit on chilly days. Maureen Newman is an enthusiastic cook whose dinner menus include home-grown vegetables and local trout and salmon in season. Children's helpings and vegetarian dishes can be requested, and guests may bring their own wine to dinner as there is no alcohol licence. The house has its own supply of spring water, which comes straight from the hillside and is used for most of the year.

OWNER: Maureen Newman OPEN: all year ROOMS: 1 single, 2 double, 2 twin; all rooms with wash-basin exc 1 twin; TV lounge TERMS: single £14.50, single occupancy £22.50, twin/double £29; children under 2 free, £8.50 for ages 2 to 12; dinner £9; deposit: £5 per person CARDS: none DETAILS: children welcome; dogs by arrangement; smoking in lounge only; car park

TRETOWER Powys

map 4

The Firs

Tretower, nr Crickhowell NP8 1RF
TEL: (01874) 730780
off A479, 3m NW of Crickhowell

This charming country house brims with old-world charm and is a near neighbour to the medieval Tretower Court and Castle. The Firs itself is 300 years old and has wooden beams and the original stone spiral staircase up to the spotless bedrooms. Most of the rooms have views of either the castle tower or the Black Mountains. Antique furniture includes a beautiful sideboard made in 1689, a dark wood dresser on which the fine bone china is displayed, and a lovely grandfather clock. Guests can relax in the spacious beamed lounge. Evening meals are not available, but the Nantyffin Cider Mill Inn is less than a mile away.

OWNER: Mary Eckley OPEN: all year ROOMS: 4 double, 2 with bath/shower, 2 with wash-basin; 1 twin; TV in some bedrooms and lounge TERMS: twin/double from £36; reductions for children sharing with parents CARDS: none DETAILS: children welcome; dogs welcome; no smoking in bedrooms; car park; garden

Gungrog House

Rhallt Lane, Rhallt, Welshpool SY21 9HS
TEL: (01938) 553381   FAX: (01938) 556224
off A483, 1½m NE of Welshpool

This spacious sixteenth-century farmhouse with roses round the door
is set in a lovely garden with magnificent views over the Severn
Valley. It is part of a 21-acre smallholding just out of Welshpool, and
there are horses in the paddock. The house is well maintained, and
the blue and cream lounge is elegantly furnished and very
comfortable. The two bedrooms are traditionally furnished and have
their own bathrooms and oak floors. Breakfast is taken in the large,
beamed dining-room. Mrs Jones does not as a rule provide evening
meals for guests any longer, although will do so occasionally by
special request. Packed lunches can be made up.

OWNERS: Mr and Mrs Stan Jones   OPEN: Apr to Oct   ROOMS: 1 double, 1 family; both
rooms with bath/shower; TV lounge   TERMS: single occupancy £21, double £38, family
room £57; half-price for children under 12   CARDS: none   DETAILS: children welcome;
no dogs; no smoking; car park; garden

Montgomery House

43 Salop Road, Welshpool SY21 7DX
TEL: (01938) 552693

This impeccably maintained house is conveniently located within
easy walking distance of the shops and restaurants of Welshpool. The
bedrooms are all on the second floor. They are average in size and
decorated with Laura Ashley wallpapers. Good breakfasts are served
in the cosy dining-room. The Welshpool and Llanfair Light Railway
terminus is nearby and it is a couple of miles to Powis Castle.

OWNER: Angela Kaye   OPEN: all year exc Christmas   ROOMS: 1 twin, 3 family; all rooms
with wash-basin; TV in all bedrooms   TERMS: single occupancy £16.50, twin £29, family
room from £38; £9 for children sharing with parents   CARDS: none   DETAILS: children
welcome; no dogs; no smoking in dining-room; car park

Tynllwyn Farm

Welshpool SY21 9BW
TEL: (01938) 553175/553054
*from Welshpool take Broad Street to roundabout, take A490 Llanfyllin
road till B&B sign on left*

This large family-run farm with an emphasis on a warm welcome and
home cooking is about a mile from Welshpool, and has wonderful

views of the Severn Valley and Long Mountain. Tynllwyn is mainly a dairy farm, but there are chickens, peacocks, pheasants, ducks, geese, calves and a goat; a pond and fountain are in the garden. The farmhouse dates from 1861, and has spacious, well-furnished bedrooms that are decorated to a high standard. A comfortable lounge contains an interesting plate collection. Farmhouse-style dinners (6.30pm) are served in the pleasant dining-room, and feature home-produced honey and eggs and home-made puddings. Children's helpings, vegetarian meals and packed lunches can be provided.

OWNER: Freda Emberton OPEN: all year ROOMS: 2 double, 2 twin, 2 family; all rooms with wash-basin; TV in all bedrooms and lounge TERMS: single occupancy £15, twin/double £30, family room from £45; children's reductions by arrangement; dinner £8.50 CARDS: none DETAILS: children welcome; dogs by arrangement; car park; garden

Isle of Man

Ballacain House

Little Mill Road, Onchan IM4 5BE
TEL: (01624) 621387   FAX: (01624) 675920

Only three miles from the Pier at Douglas is this charming country
house set in award-winning gardens full of trees and shrubs. There is
a guest lounge with original ham hooks still hanging from the ceiling,
and a collection of brass and jugs. The house has a licensed bar and
there is a full-sized snooker table for guests' use. The bedrooms in the
adjacent extension are a little on the small side, but are well
decorated and have *en suite* facilities. Breakfast and home-cooked
evening meals are available; vegetarian choices and packed lunches
can be provided with advance notice. Kerrowdhoo and Clypse
reservoirs and Molly Quirk's Glen are all within walking distance.

OWNERS: Mr and Mrs Peter Kennaugh   OPEN: all year exc Christmas   ROOMS: 2 single,
2 double, 2 twin, 2 family; all rooms with bath/shower; TV lounge   TERMS: single/single
occupancy £21, twin/double £42, family room from £42; children under 4 free; half-
price for ages 4 to 16; dinner £6.50; deposit: £20   CARDS: none   DETAILS: children
welcome; no dogs; car park; games room; garden

Hillberry Manor

Little Mill, Onchan IM4 5BD
TEL/FAX: (01624) 661660

This comfortable Victorian country house on the south-east of the
island is set in extensive grounds with spectacular views, and is
easily accessible by air and sea. The house has an old-fashioned
ambience and is elegantly furnished. The charming sitting-room
leads out to the terrace and walled garden. Of the three well-
appointed bedrooms, all with their own bathrooms, one is on the
ground floor with access to the garden. A traditional English
breakfast is served in the dining-room, and dinner is available (with
advance notice) using local and home-grown produce; packed lunches
can be provided by arrangement. Pony trekking, clay-pigeon shooting
and sea fishing can be organised.

OWNERS: Richard and Penny Leventhorpe   OPEN: all year exc Nov and Feb   ROOMS: 1
double, 2 twin; all rooms with bath/shower; TV in all bedrooms and lounge   TERMS:
single occupancy £25, twin/double £44; dinner £10.50; deposit: £25   CARDS: none
DETAILS: no children under 10; dogs by arrangement; no smoking in bedrooms, smoking
in public rooms only by agreement; car park; garden

Channel Islands

COBO BAY Guernsey map 1

Whispering Sands

Carteret Road, Cobo Bay GY5 7UT
TEL: (01481) 52944

For 11 years Bob and Sheila Holt have been running a successful business in Cobo Bay, which is renowned for its beautiful sunsets. The *en suite* bedrooms are well appointed and have comfortable beds; all have satellite TV, and tea-making facilities are available on request. The lounge has an open fire and lots of books. Substantial breakfasts are served at separate tables in the attractive dining-room, where fresh flowers add colour whenever possible. Numerous pubs and restaurants for evening meals are within walking distance. A railway line in front of the house was built during World War II to transport German troops between watchtowers. The Holts are happy to arrange bicycle hire, and taxis to and from the airport.

OWNERS: Bob and Sheila Holt OPEN: May to Sept ROOMS: 3 double, 1 twin; all rooms with bath/shower; TV in all bedrooms and lounge TERMS: single occupancy £35, twin/double £35; deposit: £25 per person CARDS: none DETAILS: no children under 8; no dogs; car park

---

FOREST Guernsey map 1

Tudor Lodge Deer Farm

Forest Road, Forest GY8 0AG
TEL: (01481) 37849 FAX: (01481) 35662

Tudor Lodge is a splendid 180-year-old residence situated in a unique position above Petit Bot Bay, with woods and meadows inhabited by approximately 20 red deer, pheasants, ducks, geese and the chickens which provide free-range eggs for breakfast. The well-appointed bedrooms are comfortably and attractively furnished. The lounge and dining-room both have open fires. The large conservatory is filled with plants and fruit trees, and Karen Gallienne, the owners' daughter, runs a tea-shop here that provides light meals, morning coffee and afternoon teas. Guests are served a full Guernsey breakfast with lots of fruit and yoghurt, and dinners are available if arranged in advance. This is a wonderfully peaceful place in which to stay, yet within walking distance of shops and restaurants.

OWNERS: John and Jackie Gallienne OPEN: mid-Jan to Nov ROOMS: 1 double, 2 twin, 2 family; all rooms with bath/shower; TV in all bedrooms TERMS: single occupancy £25–£32, twin/double £40–£55, family room £65; half-price for children over 12; dinner £10.50; deposit: £50 CARDS: none DETAILS: no children under 12; no dogs; no smoking in dining-room; car park; garden

ROZEL BAY Jersey

map 1

La Petite Chaire

Rozel Bay, St Martin JE3 6AN
TEL: (01534) 862682   FAX: (01534) 865005

This converted coach house is situated in the heart of the village, just 100 yards from a beautifully sheltered beach. Six of the bedrooms are on the ground floor. Breakfasts and modestly priced home-cooked dinners are served in the spacious dining-room, and guests can unwind in the small bar or on the sun terrace in summer. This is a popular venue with people returning regularly to enjoy the warm welcome and excellent hospitality. Visitors planning to visit St Helier should make use of the bus service.

OWNERS: Sergio and Maureen Michieli OPEN: Easter to Oct ROOMS: 1 single, 7 double, 2 twin, 2 family; all rooms with bath/shower; TV in some bedrooms and lounge TERMS: single from £20, single occupancy £35, twin/double from £40, family room from £50; half-price for children under 5, 33% reduction for ages 6 to 10; dinner £6; deposit: £30 per person CARDS: Access, Delta, Switch, Visa DETAILS: children welcome; dogs by arrangement; car park; garden

ST HELIER Jersey

map 1

La Bonne Vie

Roseville Street, St Helier JE2 4PL
TEL: (01534) 35955   FAX: (01534) 33357

La Bonne Vie is a blaze of colour in the summer with its hanging baskets and window boxes, which have won awards three years running. The house is beautifully maintained and decorated. The matching soft furnishings are made by Carol Hetherington, who has a real flair for décor. One of the bedrooms has an antique brass bed and two have four-posters. Breakfast only is served in the elegant dining-room, which has linen tablecloths and napkins. The Adam-style fireplace in the guests' lounge is lit on cooler evenings.

OWNERS: Mr and Mrs R. Hetherington OPEN: all year ROOMS: 2 single, 6 double, 1 twin, 2 four-poster; all rooms with bath/shower; TV in all bedrooms and lounge TERMS: single £16.50–£23, single occupancy £33–£46, twin/double £33–£46, four-poster £51; 25% reduction for children from 8 to 12; deposit: £25 per person per week CARDS: Access, Visa DETAILS: no children under 8; no dogs; smoking in sitting-room only; garden

The end details for each entry state whether dogs are allowed, but it is always best to check when booking.

If a deposit is required for an advance booking, this is stated in the details at the end of the entry.

Kaieteur Guest House

4 Raleigh Avenue, St Helier JE2 3ZG
TEL: (01534) 37004   FAX: (01534) 67423

Kaieteur was named after a favourite spot in New Zealand by a fisherman who owned the house at one time. It is an elegant Victorian town house on a quiet avenue within easy walking distance of the beach and most amenities. The house is immaculately kept and the bedrooms are furnished and decorated to a high standard. The well-furnished lounge is stocked with information and books on the area, and guests can sit in the small well-tended patio garden on pleasant days. Excellent breakfasts are served in the separate dining-room and include fresh fruit in season, a wide choice of cereals and traditional cooked food.

OWNERS: Peter and Anne Mauger   OPEN: all year   ROOMS: 1 single, with wash-basin; 4 double, 4 twin, 1 family, all with bath/shower; TV in all bedrooms and lounge   TERMS: single £16–£24.50, twin/double £32–£49, family room £32–£49 plus children's charge; children under 2 free, half-price for ages 2 to 12; deposit: £20 per person   CARDS: Access, Amex, Delta, Visa   DETAILS: children welcome; no dogs; no smoking in dining-room or lounge; car park; garden

La Sirene

23 Clarendon Road, St Helier JE2 3YS
TEL: (01534) 23364   FAX: (01534) 509727

The friendly couple who run La Sirene are proud winners of the Jersey Courtesy Award. Sandy Hitchmough is a cabaret singer who performs at Fort Regent, for which guests can obtain half-price tickets when she is on the bill. The house is situated in a quiet residential road and is maintained in immaculate condition with a high standard of décor and furnishings. The bedrooms are decorated in nautical blue and white, while the exterior has jaunty pink shutters. Guests have access to the house at all times, and there is a pleasant lounge and a licensed dining-room where evening meals are served. Vegetarians can be catered for.

OWNERS: Laurence and Sandy Hitchmough   OPEN: all year   ROOMS: 2 single, 4 double, 2 twin, 1 family; all rooms with bath/shower; TV in all bedrooms and lounge   TERMS: single occupancy £13–£19, twin/double £26–£38, family room from £26; free for children from 5 to 10 sharing with parents, half-price for older children; dinner £5; deposit: £25 per person per week   CARDS: none   DETAILS: no children under 5; no dogs; no smoking in dining-room

---

Breakfast at B&Bs tends to mean a cooked breakfast of bacon, eggs and so on. If you prefer a different style of breakfast, it is best to discuss this when you make a booking.

ST MARTIN Guernsey   map 1

Santi Villa Guest House

La Rue Maze, St Martin GY4 6LJ
TEL: (01481) 37332   FAX: (01481) 36764

Marie Finch has been running her bed and breakfast for the past nine
years. It is a pleasant Victorian house with a large garden and is in
an excellent location for visiting places of interest on the island. Four
of the six bedrooms have *en suite* facilities, and the other two share a
bathroom. The beamed lounge has TV, and computer facilities are
available. Breakfast only is served in the separate dining-room;
vegetarian and special diets can be catered for with advance notice.

OWNERS: Ken and Marie Finch OPEN: all year ROOMS: 2 double, both with wash-basin;
1 twin, 3 family, all with bath/shower; TV in some bedrooms TERMS: single occupancy
£17–£23, twin/double £24–£36, family room from £36; half-price for children under 12
sharing with parents, 25% reduction for older children sharing with parents; deposit:
£20 per person per week CARDS: none DETAILS: children welcome; no dogs; smoking
in bedrooms only; car park; garden

Woodlands

La Route de Blanches, St Martin GY4 6AG
TEL: (01481) 37481   FAX: (01481) 39286

This attractive house set in a large garden with a patio is situated on
Guernsey's beautiful south coast, which is a walkers' and bird-
watchers' paradise. Anita Carr was formerly in the hotel business
and has brought her expertise to her B&B. The bedrooms, three of
which are on the ground floor, are well furnished and comfortable.
The lounge has antique furniture, including a 1747 grandfather clock
and a stone-clad fireplace. Breakfasts only are served at separate
tables in the bright beamed dining-room, but Anita has prepared a
portfolio of local restaurants for evening-meal suggestions. Light
laundry facilities are available. There is a shuttle bus to the nearby
beaches and St Peter Port.

OWNER: Anita Carr OPEN: Mar to Oct ROOMS: 1 single, 2 double, 3 twin; all rooms with
bath/shower; TV in all bedrooms TERMS: single/single occupancy £18.50, twin/double
£31; 25% reduction for children; deposit: £7 per person per day CARDS: Access, Visa
DETAILS: no children under 5; small dogs welcome; no smoking in dining-room; car park;
garden

*If you disagree with any assessment made in this guide, please write and
tell us why. Address your letter to The Good Bed and Breakfast Guide,
FREEPOST, 2 Marylebone Road, London NW1 1YN.*

ST MARTIN Jersey   map 1

Le Relais de St Martin

St Martins House, St Martin JE3 6UG
TEL: (01534) 853271   FAX: (01534) 855241

This impeccably maintained house is an ideal place from which to
visit the beaches and the famous Gerald Durrell Zoo. Said to be one of
the oldest houses on the island, it stands in almost three acres of
grounds, with a swimming-pool and boules pitch. The bedrooms are
pleasant and have duvets. The beamed dining-room and bar have
granite fireplaces, and guests can play bar billiards. Good-value
home-cooked meals, served from 6.30 to 7pm, use fresh local
ingredients and home-grown fruit. Vegetarians can be catered for by
arrangement. Ten self-catering units are also available.

OWNERS: Mr and Mrs J. Gicquel OPEN: Mar to Oct ROOMS: 3 single, 4 double, 4 family;
all rooms with bath/shower; TV in all bedrooms and lounge TERMS: single £19–£25,
double £38–£50, family room £38–£50 plus children's charge; babies free, half-price for
children from 3 to 7, 25% reduction for ages 8 to 10; dinner £9; deposit CARDS:
Access, Delta, Visa DETAILS: children welcome; no dogs; no smoking in dining-room;
car park; garden; swimming-pool

ST OUEN Jersey   map 1

Lecq Farm Guest House

Leoville, St Ouen JE3 2BU
TEL: (01534) 481745

This Jersey longhouse dates from the 1700s and is set in peaceful
countryside, with a large landscaped garden full of mature trees,
shrubs and flowers. The comfortable bedrooms are of a good size. Mrs
Renouf has been running her B&B for 35 years and has established a
steady stream of regular guests, so early reservations are
recommended. Both the dining-room and lounge have a fireplace of
Jersey granite. Breakfast only is served, but there are several pubs
within a few minutes' drive, or guests can use the frequent bus
service into town for evening restaurant meals.

OWNERS: Mr and Mrs D.C. Renouf OPEN: Easter to Oct ROOMS: 1 double, with wash-
basin; 1 twin, with bath/shower; TV lounge TERMS: twin/double £30; half-price for
children under 6; 33% reduction for ages 6 to 12; deposit: £10 per person CARDS:
none DETAILS: children welcome; dogs welcome; car park; garden

*If there are reduced rates for children, this is mentioned in the details at
the end of the entry. If no reductions are specified, assume you will have to
pay full rates for children.*

ST PETER PORT   Guernsey   map 1

Kenwood House

Allez Street, St Peter Port GY1 1NG
TEL: (01481) 726146   FAX: (01481) 725632

This early-Victorian town house is conveniently situated in the old
quarter of St Peter Port. The house is well maintained and the
bedrooms, two of which are on the ground floor, are clean and
comfortable, some with their original fireplace. Generous breakfasts are
served in the dining-room overlooking the garden, which has patio
chairs and sun loungers. Afternoon tea and evening hot drinks are also
offered. A public car park is available close by.

OWNERS: Val and Andy Rout   OPEN: all year exc Christmas and New Year   ROOMS: 4
double, 2 twin; all rooms with bath/shower; TV in all bedrooms   TERMS: single occupancy
£26, twin/double £37; deposit: £3 per person per day   CARDS: Access, Visa   DETAILS: no
children; no dogs; no smoking in dining-room; garden

Marine Hotel

Well Road, St Peter Port GY1 1WS
TEL: (01481) 724978   FAX: (01481) 711729

Guests continue to enjoy this well-maintained family-run hotel just 30
yards from the sea-front and the marina. Also very near are St Peter
Port's picturesque shopping centre and the starting point for island bus
tours. Most of the public rooms and the well-appointed bedrooms have
sea views. TVs can be provided in the bedrooms for a modest charge, but
there is also a TV lounge with a large, well-stocked bookcase providing
alternatives. Guests can also relax on the furnished sun patio. Excellent
breakfasts include kippers, a selection of cheeses and yoghurts as well
as traditional cooked fare.

OWNERS: Margaret and Arthur Clegg   OPEN: all year   ROOMS: 1 single, 4 double, 3 twin, 3
family; all rooms with bath/shower; TV lounge   TERMS: single £20–£24.50, single
occupancy £22–£30, twin/double £37–£46, family room from £46; half-price for children
under 5, 25% reduction for ages 5 to 10 sharing with parents; deposit: £30 per person
CARDS: Access, Visa   DETAILS: children welcome; no dogs; no smoking in dining-room or
lounge; garden

---

*Any smoking restrictions that we know of are given in the details at the end of
the entry.*

*Where we know a B&B accepts credit cards, we list them in the details at the
end of an entry. There may be a surcharge if you pay by credit card. It is
always best to check whether the card you want to use is acceptable when
booking.*

map 1

Bordeaux Guesthouse

Roques Barrees Road, Bordeaux, nr St Sampson GY3 5LX
TEL: (01481) 47461   FAX: (01481) 43669
at north end of island 50 metres inland from Bordeaux Bay

This 200-year-old building, formerly a farmhouse, has all modern
comforts and is situated in the peaceful and attractive harbour of
Bordeaux, within walking distance of St Sampson. The guests' lounge
with a small bar has a honey-coloured stone fireplace and a huge
oriental rug. Three of the bedrooms have four-poster beds, one has an
enormous brass bed, and three are on the ground floor. Generous home-
cooked dinners are served by arrangement in the dining-room, which
retains its Victorian fireplace. Vegetarians can be catered for.
Arrangements can be made to meet guests at the airport or the harbour.

OWNERS: Roy and Helen Ackrill OPEN: all year exc Christmas and New Year ROOMS: 4
double, 4 twin, 3 four-poster, 4 family; all rooms with bath/shower; TV in all bedrooms and
lounge TERMS: single occupancy £23, twin/double/four-poster £36, family room £36 plus
children's charge; children under 5 free, half-price for older children sharing with parents;
dinner £7.50; deposit: £20 per person CARDS: none DETAILS: children welcome; dogs by
arrangement; no smoking in dining-room; car park; garden

 map 1

Hivernage Guesthouse

Sark GY9 0SA
TEL: (01481) 832000   FAX: (01481) 832472
at W edge of island

This guesthouse has been in Marilyn Carré's family since 1914. She is a
very congenial host who provides excellent home-cooked evening meals
using fresh local produce and meat; vegetarian options and alcohol are
available. The bedrooms are comfortable and spotlessly clean, and
guests can relax in the lounge or conservatory, or make use of the
peaceful garden with views to Guernsey, Herm and Jethou, and the
Pilcher Monument. Visitors to Sark arrive by boat and there are no
motorised vehicles other than a farm tractor to take them to their
destination. Bicycles are for hire and the island is so small that all parts
are within walking distance.

OWNER: Marilyn Carré OPEN: Easter to Sept ROOMS: 2 single, 1 with bath/shower, 1 with
wash-basin; 2 double, 1 with bath/shower, 1 with wash-basin; 1 twin, with wash-basin; 2
family, both with wash-basin TERMS: single £16.50–£18, single occupancy £21.50–£23,
twin/double £33–£36, family room from £45.50; 25% reduction for children; dinner £10;
deposit: £15 per person CARDS: none DETAILS: children welcome; no dogs; garden

Le Petit Coin

Le Petit Coin de la Tour, Sark GY9 0SF
TEL: (01481) 832077   FAX: (01481) 832603

Le Petit Coin is a bungalow situated at the north end of the island in a
peaceful location at the end of Rue du Fort. Ann and Tom Long are a
charming, hospitable couple who have created a warm home-from-home
atmosphere. The cosy lounge is an ideal place in which to read and
relax. All the ground-floor bedrooms have sea views and there is a
bathroom exclusively for guests' use. Tom is an excellent cook and
dinners are provided by arrangement; vegetarians can be catered for
and guests may bring wine. Marty the black labrador is a friendly dog,
and five cats also share the house.

OWNER: Ann Long   OPEN: all year   ROOMS: 1 single, 1 double, both with wash-basin; 2
twin, 1 with bath/shower, 1 with wash-basin; TV lounge   TERMS: rates include dinner;
single/single occupancy £28, twin/double £56; half-price for children under 11; deposit: £5
per person per night   CARDS: none   DETAILS: children welcome; no dogs in dining-room;
no smoking in bedrooms; garden

Les Quatre Vents

Sark GY9 0SE
TEL: (01481) 832247   FAX: (01481) 832332

This friendly family-run guesthouse stands in its own grounds close to
the harbour, shops and beaches. The bedrooms, two of which are on the
ground floor, have sea views and are fresh and clean with pretty duvets.
The quiet lounge is a good place to relax in at the end of the day, and
there is a dining-room where breakfast and evening meals are served at
separate tables. Seats are provided in the garden for pleasant days.
Sylvia Godwin's daughter runs a horse-and-carriage business, and
guests can watch the horses being groomed in the grounds. Laundry
facilities can be provided at a modest charge. Visitors to Sark arrive by
boat and there are no paved roads or cars, but bicycles are for hire and it
is easy to walk everywhere.

OWNER: Sylvia Godwin   OPEN: all year exc Christmas   ROOMS: 1 single, 1 double, 2 family;
all rooms with bath/shower; TV in all bedrooms and lounge   TERMS: single/single
occupancy £22, twin/double £44, family room from £44; children's reductions by
arrangement; dinner £15; deposit: 10%   CARDS: none   DETAILS: children welcome; no
dogs; no smoking in bedrooms and dining-room; garden

---

*We welcome your feedback about B&Bs you have stayed in. Please make use
of the report forms at the end of the book.*

*It is always best to book a room in advance, even in winter. B&Bs with few
rooms may close at short notice for periods not specified in the details.*

Note on changes to counties

During the life of this *Guide* a number of organisational and name changes affecting counties and regions will take place in England, Scotland and Wales. Some county names will disappear for good – Avon, for example – while others will remain unchanged. Some counties, particularly in Scotland and Wales, will revert to what they were in the early 1970s. Because the changes are being implemented in stages (finishing in early 1997), we have retained the pre-April 1996 county names in the entries and maps of this edition in order to avoid confusion.

To help you while travelling around the country, we have set out below some of the new names that you are likely to encounter. This is not meant to be a comprehensive list, but will give some idea of the changes that are taking place. The new county (or unitary authority) names are listed under the old county name for that area.

England

Avon
Bath and North East Somerset
City of Bristol
North Somerset
South Gloucestershire

Cleveland
Hartlepool
Redcar and Cleveland
Middlesbrough
Stockton

Humberside
East Riding of Yorkshire
North Lincolnshire
North East Lincolnshire
City of Kingston upon Hull

Leicestershire
City of Leicester
Leicestershire
Rutland

Scotland

Central
Clackmannan
Falkirk
Stirling

Grampian
City of Aberdeen
Aberdeenshire
Moray

Lothian
East Lothian
City of Edinburgh
Midlothian
West Lothian

Strathclyde
Argyll and Bute
East Dunbartonshire
Dumbarton and Clydebank
South Lanarkshire
North Lanarkshire

East Ayrshire
North Ayrshire
East Renfrewshire
City of Glasgow
Inverclyde
South Ayrshire
Renfrewshire

Tayside
Angus
City of Dundee
Perthshire and Kinross

Wales

Clwyd
Denbighshire
Flintshire
Wrexham

Dyfed
Cardiganshire
Carmarthenshire
Pembrokeshire

Gwent
Blaenau Gwent
Caerphilly
Monmouthshire
Newport
Torfaen

Gwynedd
Anglesey
Aberconwy and Colwyn
Caernarfonshire and
 Merionethshire

Mid Glamorgan
Bridgend
Merthyr Tydfil
Rhondda Cynon Taff

South Glamorgan
Cardiff
Vale of Glamorgan

West Glamorgan
Neath and Port Talbot
Swansea

Indexes

Index 1

Towns and villages by county

ESSEX

BARDFIELD END GREEN *Wellcroft* 43

BRAN END *Elmcroft Guest House* 73

BRIGHTLINGSEA *Birch House* 78

CHELMSFORD *Aarandale Guest House* 106

COLCHESTER *14 Roman Road* 121
Four Sevens Guesthouse 121
Old Manse 122

DEDHAM *May's Barn Farm* 142

FINCHINGFIELD *Finchingfield House* 166

FORDHAM *Kings Vineyard* 169

FRINTON-ON-SEA *Uplands Guesthouse* 175

GREAT DUNMOW *Homelye Farm* 185

HARWICH *Reids of Harwich* 197

HATFIELD PEVEREL *The Wick* 199

MARGARET RODING *Greys* 263

NEWNEY GREEN *Moor Hall* 282

SIBLE HEDINGHAM *Comfrey Cottage* 346

SOUTHEND-ON-SEA *Pebbles Guest House* 352

STEEPLE BUMPSTEAD *Yew Tree House* 358

THAXTED *Folly House* 375

UGLEY GREEN *Thatched Cottage* 389

WESTCLIFF-ON-SEA *Archery's Guest House* 403

WIX *New Farm House* 424

GLOUCESTERSHIRE

BOURTON-ON-THE-WATER *Larch House* 67
Windrush Farm 67

BROOKTHORPE *Gilbert's* 82

CHELTENHAM *Hannaford's* 106
Parkview 107

CHIPPING CAMPDEN *Rosary Cottage* 113
Sparlings 113

CIRENCESTER *26 Victoria Road* 116
Wimborne House 116

EBRINGTON *Holly House* 155

GLOUCESTER *Lulworth Guest House* 178
Notley House 178

HAZLETON *Windrush House* 204

HIGHNAM *Linton Farm* 211

KEMPLEY *Lower House Farm* 222

MEYSEY HAMPTON *Old Rectory* 269

MINCHINHAMPTON *Hunters Lodge* 271

MITCHELDEAN *Gunn Mill House* 272

NORTHLEACH *Market House* 285

ST BRIAVELS *Cinderhill House* 322

SLAD *Chessed* 349

STAUNTON *Mayfield Cottage* 358

STOW-ON-THE-WOLD *Wyck Hill Lodge* 362

UPPER ODDINGTON *Orchard Cottage* 391

WINCHCOMBE *Gower House* 414
The Homestead 414

WOODCHESTER *Southfield House* 425

GREATER MANCHESTER

ALTRINCHAM *Marron Guest House* 33

SALE *Brooklands Luxury Lodge* 329
Cornerstones 329

HAMPSHIRE

ANDOVER *Lotties* 35

BASHLEY *Yew Tree Farm* 44

BROCKENHURST *Caters Cottage* 81
The Cottage Hotel 82

BURLEY *Brandon Thatch* 89
Holmans 90

CADNAM *Walnut Cottage* 95

EAST MEON *Coombe Cross House* 153
Drayton Cottage 153

FLEET *8 Chinnock Close* 167

HAYLING ISLAND *Cockle Warren Cottage* 203

LYMINGTON *Wheatsheaf* 257

MILFORD ON SEA *Seawinds* 270

ODIHAM *Poland Mill* 289

PICKET HILL *Picket Hill House* 301

PORTSMOUTH *Fortitude Cottage* 304

RINGWOOD *Little Forest Lodge* 310
Moortown Lodge 310

ROCKBOURNE *Shearings* 312

SETLEY *Setley Lodge* 336

SHEET *Westmark House* 339

Index 2

B&Bs

Maps

For an explanation of changes to some county names that will be occurring during the life of this edition of the *Guide*, see page 603.